I Pledge Allegiance To the Flag!

READINGS
and Lecture Notes
IN
AMERICAN GOVERNMENT

ORAL ROBERTS UNIVERSITY

Sonny Branham

Oral Roberts University

 **Custom Publishing**

Boston Burr Ridge, IL Dubuque, IA Madison, WI New York
San Francisco St. Louis Bangkok Bogotá Caracas Kuala Lumpur
Lisbon London Madrid Mexico City Milan Montreal New Delhi
Santiago Seoul Singapore Sydney Taipei Toronto

I Pledge Allegiance to the Flag
Readings and Lecture Notes in American Government
Oral Roberts University

1 2 3 4 5 6 7 8 9 0   QSR QSR   0 9 8 7 6 5 4

ISBN 0-07-304243-9

Editor: Nada Mraovic
Production Editor: Patricia Dausener
Printer/Binder: Quebecor World

Star Spangled Banner

Oh, say, can you see, by the dawn's early light,
What so proudly we hailed at the twilight's last gleaming?
Whose broad stripes and bright stars, thro' the perilous fight'
O'er the ramparts we watched, were so gallantly streaming.
And the rockets red glare, the bombs bursting in air,
Gave proof through the night that our flag was still there.
Oh, say, does that star-spangled banner yet wave
O'er the land of the free and the home of the brave?

On the shore dimly seen, thro' the mists of the deep,
Where the foe's haughty host in dread silence reposes,
What is that which the breeze, o'er the towering steep,
As it fitfully blows, half conceals, half discloses?
Now it catches the gleam of the morning's first beam,
In full glory reflected, now shines on the stream;
'Tis the star-spangled banner: oh, long may it wave
O'er the land of the free and the home of the brave.

And where is that band who so vauntingly swore
That the havoc of war and the battle's confusion
A home and a country should leave us no more?
Their blood has wash'd out their foul footstep's pollution.
No refuge could save the hireling and slave
From the terror of flight or the gloom of the grave,
And the star-spangled banner in triumph doth wave
O'er the land of the free and the home of the brave.

Oh, thus be it ever when free men shall stand,
Between their loved homes and the war's desolation;
Blest with vict'ry and peace, may the heav'n-rescued land
Praise the Power that has made and preserved us as a nation.
Then conquer we must, when our cause is just,
And this be our motto: "In God is our trust";
And the star-spangled banner in triumph shall wave
O'er the land of the free and the home of the brave.

Tune: Anacreon in Heaven

Written by Francis Scott Key on September 14th, 1814.

Preface

I Pledge Allegiance to the Flag of the United States of America.

Even with all of its current challenges, our nation is still, by the grace of God, the greatest nation upon the face of the Earth. It was not established by accident, but rather by Divine design. In *Readings in American Government*, we will explore the key historical documents that form the essential building blocks of that design

With the September 11, 2001, terrorist strike on America, our nation responded with courage, conviction, and steadfast commitment. Attacks against us deepened our resolve and strengthened our character. The events awakened, at least partially, the nation to the radical expressions of vengeance and hatred in much of the world for the values of freedom and our way of life. Our peace and security had been attacked, and Americans sought ways to "stand up and be counted." Patriotism blossomed and we waved the flag with zeal. If necessary, we indicated the willingness to give our lives before allowing freedom to perish. Faith, courage, sacrifice, and honor were the words on the lips of the nation, calling out to God in prayer for the ability to face the challenges ahead.

But that suddenly aroused zeal has already begun to fade – at our own peril. The complacency of a materialistic culture, political division and gridlock in high levels of government, and cynicism and apathy among the populace threaten to weaken the patriotic commitment of many Americans, particularly young people. It is essential that our young people, who embody the future of this nation, have a strong foundational understanding of what makes this country great. If our foundation erodes, our nation is ultimately doomed.

With this backdrop, Oral Roberts University students of American Government and Politics are presented with *Readings in American Government*, a collection of historical documents, speeches, Supreme Court decisions, treaties, and other writings from the public domain which chronicle the development of governance and nation-building in our land since its settling nearly 400 years ago. The theme for the collection is "The Pledge of Allegiance to the American Flag," presently quite a controversial issue in its own right. Each phrase of The Pledge is represented in a series of related documents.

An Introduction relating to the history of the American flag and the patriotism it has inspired begins the *Readings*. In the first section, "I Pledge Allegiance to the Flag," various documents highlight the importance of agreement, covenant, and contractual obligation. For "of the United States of America" the selections relate to the importance of the Union, with both the national government and individual states sharing responsibility for protections of freedom in a system of federalism. "And to the Republic for Which It Stands" holds documents in that section relating to a structure for government based on law rather than the opinions of its citizens that could change daily.

The chapter headed "One Nation, under God" contains documents that reflect the nation's belief, though often challenged, of the importance of a Divine Being who rules in the affairs of His Creation. "Indivisible" highlights historical documents emerging in different periods in United States history where war, scandal, economic downturns, and racial and social tensions have attempted to tear apart the nation. The concluding section, "With Liberty and Justice for All," sets out documents that particularly relate to the challenge of preserving individual liberty in conjunction and coordination with threats to national security.

During class sessions integrating assignments from *Readings* into discussion and instruction, students will answer questions such as:

+What type of document is this and when was it produced?
+Who created the document, what are its issues, and how does it relate to me?
+What does the existence of this document say about whoever created it?
+What does the existence of it say about American government and politics in the given era?

For example, a student may be asked to deliver a selected speech to the class, presenting a dynamic reading of the document. Discussion would follow. Or, an instructor may select a document that relates to a person, place, or event that is currently in the news and make a writing assignment for the class to complete. Another scenario would be to assign a document to read and then have the classes consider "what if" that document never existed; students would then share their observations in discussion sessions. Document analysis will relate to material from the textbook and lectures of the instructor.

In conclusion, America's Founding Fathers believed the source of liberty and freedom is from God above. It is not a grant from government or a right derived from citizenship, but an endowment from the Creator. Government serves to protect those God-given rights. "Divine Providence," as the founders called it, has been a guiding force in our nation's history. But what about the present and especially the future? To whom much is given, much is required. Oral Roberts University students should be at the forefront in assuming responsibility for preserving the great privileges in the United States by participating intelligently in the political process, whether their callings are in the religious or secular world. Principle-based decisions, not ones formed on personality or political party, can lead our nation away from decay, division, and destruction. Liberty is priceless, and *Readings in American Government* serves as a worthy source of historical documents reflecting those Godly ideals and values of the flag and to the republic for which it stands.

Our hope and prayer is that students enrolled in the teaching and learning of American Government and Politics at ORU will be willing to pursue the vision expressed by John F. Kennedy in his 1961 inaugural address to "pay any price, bear any burden, meet any hardship, support any friend, oppose any foe to assure the survival and success of liberty."

Sonny Branham, instructor
Department of History, Humanities, and Government
Oral Roberts University, Tulsa, Oklahoma

Table of Contents

Introduction

History of the American Flag

For more than 200 years, the American flag has been the symbol of our nation's strength and unity. It's been a source of pride and inspiration for millions of citizens. And it has been a prominent icon in our national history. Here are the highlights of its unique past.

On January 1, 1776, the Continental Army was reorganized in accordance with a Congressional resolution which placed American forces under George Washington's control. On that New Year's Day the Continental Army was laying siege to Boston which had been taken over by the British Army. Washington ordered the Grand Union flag hoisted above his base at Prospect Hill. It had 13 alternate red and white stripes and the British Union Jack in the upper left-hand corner (the canton).

In May of 1776, Betsy Ross reported that she sewed the first American flag. On June 14, 1777, in order to establish an official flag for the new nation, the Continental Congress passed the first Flag Act: "Resolved, That the flag of the United States be made of thirteen stripes, alternate red and white; that the union be thirteen stars, white in a blue field, representing a new Constellation."

Between 1777 and 1960, Congress passed several acts that changed the shape, design and arrangement of the flag and allowed for additional stars and stripes to be added to reflect the admission of each new state.

- Act of January 13, 1794 - provided for 15 stripes and 15 stars after May 1795.
- Act of April 4, 1818 - provided for 13 stripes and one star for each state, to be added to the flag on the 4th of July following the admission of each new state, signed by President Monroe.
- Executive Order of President Taft dated June 24, 1912 - established proportions of the flag and provided for arrangement of the stars in six horizontal rows of eight each, a single point of each star to be upward.
- Executive Order of President Eisenhower dated January 3, 1959 - provided for the arrangement of the stars in seven rows of seven stars each, staggered horizontally and vertically.
- Executive Order of President Eisenhower dated August 21, 1959 - provided for the arrangement of the stars in nine rows of stars staggered horizontally and eleven rows of stars staggered vertically.

Today the flag consists of thirteen horizontal stripes, seven red alternating with 6 white. The stripes represent the original 13 colonies, the stars represent the 50 states of the Union. The colors of the flag are symbolic as well: Red symbolizes Hardiness and Valor, White symbolizes Purity and Innocence, and Blue represents Vigilance, Perseverance and Justice.

American Flag Etiquette

Federal law stipulates many aspects of flag etiquette. The section of law dealing with American Flag etiquette is generally referred to as the Flag Code. Some general guidelines from the Flag Code answer many of the most common questions:

- The flag should be lighted at all times, either by sunlight or by an appropriate light source.

- The flag should be flown in fair weather, unless the flag is designed for inclement weather use.

- The flag should never be dipped to any person or thing. It is flown upside down only as a distress signal.

- The flag should not be used for any decoration in general. Bunting of blue, white and red stripes is available for these purposes. The blue stripe of the bunting should be on the top.

- The flag should never be used for any advertising purpose. It should not be embroidered, printed or otherwise impressed on such articles as cushions, handkerchiefs, napkins, boxes, or anything intended to be discarded after temporary use. Advertising signs should not be attached to the staff or halyard.

- The flag should not be used as part of a costume or athletic uniform, except that a flag patch may be used on the uniform of military personnel, fireman, policeman and members of patriotic organizations.

- The flag should never have any mark, insignia, letter, word, number, figure, or drawing of any kind placed on it, or attached to it.

- The flag should never be used for receiving, holding, carrying, or delivering anything.

- When the flag is lowered, no part of it should touch the ground or any other object; it should be received by waiting hands and arms. To store the flag it should be folded neatly and ceremoniously.

- The flag should be cleaned and mended when necessary.

- When a flag is so worn it is no longer fit to serve as a symbol of our country, it should be destroyed by burning in a dignified manner.

Flag Folding Ceremony

The flag folding ceremony described by the Uniformed Services is a dramatic and uplifting way to honor the flag on special days, like Memorial Day or Veterans Day, and is sometimes used at retirement ceremonies.

Here is a typical sequence of the reading:

(Begin reading as Honor Guard or Flag Detail is coming forward).
The flag folding ceremony represents the same religious principles on which our country was originally founded. The portion of the flag denoting honor is the canton of blue containing the stars representing the states our veterans served in uniform. The canton field of blue dresses from left to right and is inverted when draped as a pall on a casket of a veteran who has served our country in uniform.

In the Armed Forces of the United States, at the ceremony of retreat the flag is lowered, folded in a triangle fold and kept under watch throughout the night as a tribute to our nation's honored dead. The next morning it is brought out and, at the ceremony of reveille, run aloft as a symbol of our belief in the resurrection of the body.

(Wait for the Honor Guard or Flag Detail to unravel and fold the flag into a quarter fold--resume reading when Honor Guard is standing ready.)

- The first fold of our flag is a symbol of life.

- The second fold is a symbol of our belief in the eternal life.

- The third fold is made in honor and remembrance of the veteran departing our ranks who gave a portion of life for the defense of our country to attain a peace throughout the world.

- The fourth fold represents our weaker nature, for as American citizens trusting in God, it is to Him we turn in times of peace as well as in times of war for His divine guidance.

- The fifth fold is a tribute to our country, for in the words of Stephen Decatur, "Our country, in dealing with other countries, may she always be right; but it is still our country, right or wrong."

- The sixth fold is for where our hearts lie. It is with our heart that we pledge allegiance to the flag of the United States of America, and to the republic for which it stands, one nation, under God, indivisible, with liberty and justice for all.

- The seventh fold is a tribute to our Armed Forces, for it is through the Armed Forces that we protect our country and our flag against all her enemies, whether they be found within or without the boundaries of our republic.

- The eighth fold is a tribute to the one who entered in to the valley of the shadow of death, that we might see the light of day, and to honor mother, for whom it flies on mother's day.

- The ninth fold is a tribute to womanhood; for it has been through their faith, love, loyalty and devotion that the character of the men and women who have made this country great have been molded.

- The tenth fold is a tribute to father, for he, too, has given his sons and daughters for the defense of our country since they were first born.

- The eleventh fold, in the eyes of a Hebrew citizen, represents the lower portion of the seal of King David and King Solomon, and glorifies, in their eyes, the God of Abraham, Isaac, and Jacob.

- The twelfth fold, in the eyes of a Christian citizen, represents an emblem of eternity and glorifies, in their eyes, God the Father, the Son, and Holy Ghost.

When the flag is completely folded, the stars are uppermost, reminding us of our national motto, "In God We Trust."

(Wait for the Honor Guard or Flag Detail to inspect the flag--after the inspection, resume reading.)

After the flag is completely folded and tucked in, it takes on the appearance of a cocked hat, ever reminding us of the soldiers who served under General George Washington and the sailors and marines who served under Captain John Paul Jones who were followed by their comrades and shipmates in the Armed Forces of the United States, preserving for us the rights, privileges, and freedoms we enjoy today.

The Flag Folding Ceremony above is from the US Air Force Academy

The Story of the Pledge of Allegiance

The Pledge of Allegiance to the Flag of the United States, according to James A. Moss, an authority on the flag and its history, was first given national publicity through the official program of the National Public School Celebration of Columbus Day in October 1892. The Pledge had been published in the Youth's Companion for September 8, 1892, and at the same time sent out in leaflet form throughout the country. During the Celebration it was repeated by more than 12,000,000 public school pupils in every state in the Union.

Mr. Francis Bellamy of Rome, New York, and Mr. James Upham of Malden, Massachusetts were both members of the staff of the Youth's Companion when the Pledge was published. The family of each man has contended that his was the authorship and both hold evidence to substantiate their claims.

To determine, in the interest of historical accuracy, the actual authorship, the United States Flag Association (formerly in Washington, D.C., but now disbanded), in 1939, appointed a committee consisting of Charles C. Tansill, Professor of American History; W. Reed West, Professor of Political Science; and Bernard Mayo, Professor of American History, to carefully weigh the evidence of the two contending families. Unanimously, the committee decided in favor of Francis Bellamy, and on May 18, 1939, the decision was accepted by the American Flag Committee. Mr. Bellamy had been chairman of the executive committee which formulated the program for the National Public School Celebration and furnished the publicity when he was on the staff of the Youth's Companion.

In the material which he nationally circulated, he wrote, "Let the flag float over every school-house in the land and the exercise be such as shall impress upon our youth the patriotic duty of citizenship." He also included the original 23 words of the Pledge which he had developed. * 'to' added in October, 1892.

I pledge allegiance to my Flag,
and (to*) the Republic for which it stands:
one Nation indivisible,
With Liberty and Justice for all.

Thus it was that on Columbus Day in October 1892, the Pledge of Allegiance was repeated by more than 12 million public school children in every state in the union.

The wording of the Pledge has been modified three times.

On June 14, 1923, at the First National Flag Conference held in Washington, D.C., under the leadership of the American Legion and the Daughters of the American Revolution, changed the Pledge's words. The latter words were added on the ground that some foreign-born children and adults when giving the Pledge might have in mind the flag of their native land. In 1923, the words "the flag of the United States" were substituted for "my flag."

I pledge allegiance to the Flag of the United States,
and to the Republic for which it stands:
one Nation indivisible,
With Liberty and Justice for all.

In 1924, "of America" was added.

> I pledge allegiance to the Flag
> of the United States of America,
> and to the Republic for which it stands:
> one Nation indivisible,
> With Liberty and Justice for all.

On Flag Day, June 14, 1954, the words "under God" were added

The last change in the Pledge of Allegiance occurred on June 14 (Flag Day), 1954, when President Dwight D. Eisenhower approved adding the words "under God". As he authorized this change he said: "In this way we are reaffirming the transcendence of religious faith in America's heritage and future; in this way we shall constantly strengthen those spiritual weapons which forever will be our country's most powerful resource in peace and war."

This was the last change made to the Pledge of Allegiance. The 23 words what had been initially penned for a Columbus Day celebration now comprised a Thirty-one profession of loyalty and devotion to not only a flag, but to a way of life . . . the American ideal. Those words now read:

> "I pledge allegiance to the Flag
> of the United States of America
> and to the Republic for which it stands,
> one nation under God, indivisible,
> with liberty and justice for all."

The Pledge of Allegiance continued to be recited daily by children in schools across America, and gained heightened popularity among adults during the patriotic fervor created by World War II. It still was an "unofficial" pledge until June 22, 1942 when the United States Congress included the Pledge to the Flag in the United States Flag Code (Title 36). In 1945 the Pledge to the Flag received its official title as: The Pledge of Allegiance

When the Pledge is being given, all should stand with the right hand over the heart, fingers together and horizontal with the arm at as near a right angle as possible. After the words "justice to all," the arm should drop to the side. While giving the Pledge of Allegiance all should face the flag.

According to Colonel Moss, no disrespect is displayed by giving the Pledge with a gloved hand over the heart, but he calls our attention to the fact that an Army Officer or an enlisted man always removes his right glove upon taking his oath as a witness. The Daughters of the American Revolution follow the custom of having the right hand ungloved.

Flag Day and National Flag Week 2002

A Proclamation from the President of the United States

The American flag is a beacon of hope, a symbol of enduring freedom, and an emblem of unity. Many have given their lives in its defense, and countless men and women have worked to ensure that Old Glory continues to stand for the ideals of freedom, justice, and equal opportunity for all. Our flag symbolizes the purpose and resolve of our Nation, first expressed by our Founders who triumphed against great odds to establish this country.

Today, as we face the challenges of a new era, our flag reminds us that freedom will prevail over oppression and that good will overcome evil. Following the attacks of September 11, Americans embraced a renewed sense of the meaning and purpose of our flag. The unforgettable images of our Nation's colors flying defiantly over the debris of the World Trade Center inspired our country with a healing hope, uniting our people in purpose and consoling those who had suffered great loss. At the Pentagon, an American flag was hung from the building's damaged walls, expressing our collective resolve to rebuild and move forward. And earlier this year, during the Opening Ceremonies of the Winter Olympic Games in Salt Lake City, Americans, joined by peace-loving people from around the world, paid tribute to the tattered flag that had been recovered from the ruins of the World Trade Center.

As we reflect on what our flag represents, we recall the words of President Woodrow Wilson, who said just weeks before the onset of World War I: "My dream is that, as the years go on and the world knows more and more of America, it . . . will turn to America for those moral inspirations which lie at the basis of all freedom . . . that America will come into the full light of the day when all shall know that she puts human rights above all other rights, and that her flag is the flag, not only of America, but of humanity."

The flag that inspired Francis Scott Key to write our National Anthem 188 years ago still energizes and inspires the American spirit. Since September 11, we have seen our Nation's flag appear everywhere -- on cars and clothing, houses and hard hats -- showing our country's commitment to always remember those who lost their lives and to remain unremitting in the pursuit of justice.

Today, in Afghanistan and around the world, brave men and women are serving under our flag, fighting to preserve freedom and win the war against terrorism. All Americans are profoundly grateful for their service and their sacrifice. We also recognize and commend the contributions of our veterans who have bravely defended our Nation's founding principles throughout our history. The image of six marines raising the flag on the top of Mount Suribachi at Iwo Jima will always remind us that the struggle for liberty is a story of courage, sacrifice, and commitment to the unshakeable belief in freedom's promise.

On Flag Day, we remember the struggles and successes for which our flag stands. And we look to the flag as an everlasting symbol of our commitment to a world of peace, a Nation of principle, and a people of unity.

To commemorate the adoption of our flag, the Congress, by joint resolution approved August 3, 1949, as amended (63 Stat. 492), designated June 14 of each year as "Flag Day" and requested that the President issue an annual proclamation calling for its observance and for the display of the Flag of the United States on all Federal Government buildings. The Congress also requested, by joint resolution approved June 9, 1966, as amended (80 Stat. 194), that the President annually issue a proclamation designating the week in which June 14 occurs as "National Flag Week" and calling upon all citizens of the United States to display the flag during that week.

NOW, THEREFORE, I, GEORGE W. BUSH, President of the United States of America, by virtue of the authority vested in me by the Constitution and laws of the United States, do hereby proclaim June 14, 2002, as Flag Day and the week beginning June 9, 2002, as National Flag Week. I direct the appropriate officials to display the flag on all Federal Government buildings during that week, and I urge all Americans to observe Flag Day and National Flag Week by flying the Stars and Stripes from their homes and other suitable places. I also call upon the people of the United States to observe with pride and all due ceremony those days from Flag Day through Independence Day, also set aside by the Congress (89 Stat. 211), as a time to honor America, to celebrate our heritage in public gatherings and activities, and to publicly recite the Pledge of Allegiance to the Flag of the United States of America.

IN WITNESS WHEREOF, I have hereunto set my hand this seventh day of June, in the year of our Lord two thousand two, and of the Independence of the United States of America the two hundred and twenty-sixth.

George W. Bush

Newdow v. Congress

MICHAEL A. NEWDOW, Plaintiff-Appellant, v. **US CONGRESS; UNITED STATES OF AMERICA; WILLIAM JEFFERSON CLINTON**, President of the United States; **STATE CALIFORNIA; ELK GROVE UNIFIED SCHOOL DISTRICT; DAVID W. GORDON**, Superintendent **EGUSD; SACRAMENTO CITY UNIFIED SCHOOL DISTRICT; JIM SWEENEY**, Superintendent SCUSD, Defendants-Appellees.

No. 00-16423

UNITED STATES COURT OF APPEALS FOR THE NINTH CIRCUIT

March 14, 2002, Argued and Submitted, San Francisco, California

June 26, 2002, Filed

Appeal from the United States District Court for the Eastern District of California. D.C. No. CV-00-00495-MLS/PAN. Edward J. Schwartz, Senior Judge, Presiding.

Michael Newdow, Pro se, Sacramento, California, the plaintiff-appellant.

Kristin S. Door, Assistant United States Attorney, Sacramento, California, Lowell V. Sturgill, Jr., Department of Justice, Washington, D. C., for federal government defendants-appellees; A. Irving Scott, Terence J. Cassidy, Porter, Scott, Weiberg & Delehant, Sacramento, California, for school district defendants-appellees.

Before: Alfred T. Goodwin, Stephen Reinhardt and Ferdinand F. Fernandez, Circuit Judges. Opinion by Judge Goodwin, Partial Concurrence and Partial Dissent by Judge Fernandez.

Alfred T. Goodwin

GOODWIN, Circuit Judge:

✠ Michael Newdow appeals a judgment dismissing his challenge to the constitutionality of the words "under God" in the Pledge of Allegiance to the Flag. Newdow argues that the addition of these words by a 1954 federal statute to the previous version of the Pledge of Allegiance (which made no reference to God) and the daily recitation in the classroom of the Pledge of Allegiance, with the added words included, by his daughter's public school teacher are violations of the Establishment Clause of the First Amendment to the United States Constitution.

FACTUAL AND PROCEDURAL BACKGROUND

Newdow is an atheist whose daughter attends public elementary school in the Elk Grove Unified School District ("EGUSD") in California. In accordance with state law and a school district rule, EGUSD teachers begin each school day by leading their students in a recitation of the Pledge of Allegiance ("the Pledge"). The California Education Code requires that public schools begin each school day with "appropriate patriotic exercises" and that "the giving of the Pledge of Allegiance to the Flag of the United States of America shall satisfy" this requirement. Cal. Educ. Code § 52720 (1989) (hereinafter "California statute"). n1 To implement the California statute, the school district that Newdow's daughter attends has promulgated a policy that states, in pertinent part: "Each elementary school class [shall] recite the pledge of allegiance to the flag once each day." n2

The classmates of Newdow's daughter in the EGUSD are led by their teacher in reciting the Pledge codified in federal law. On June 22, 1942, Congress first codified the Pledge as "I pledge allegiance to the flag of the United States of America and to the Republic for which it stands, one Nation indivisible, with liberty and justice for all." Pub. L. No. 623, Ch. 435, § 7, 56 Stat. 380 (1942) (codified at 36 U.S.C. § 1972). On June 14, 1954, Congress amended Section 1972 to add the words "under God" after the word "Nation." Pub. L. No. 396, Ch. 297, 68 Stat. 249 (1954) ("1954 Act"). The Pledge is currently codified as "I pledge allegiance to the Flag of the United

States of America, and to the Republic for which it stands, one nation under God, indivisible, with liberty and justice for all." 4 U.S.C. § 4 (1998) (Title 36 was revised and recodified by Pub. L. No. 105-225, § 2(a), 112 Stat. 1494 (1998). Section 172 was abolished, and the Pledge is now found in Title 4.)

Newdow does not allege that his daughter's teacher or school district requires his daughter to participate in reciting the Pledge. n3 Rather, he claims that his daughter is injured when she is compelled to "watch and listen as her state-employed teacher in her state-run school leads her classmates in a ritual proclaiming that there is a God, and that our's [sic] is 'one nation under God.'"

Newdow's complaint in the district court challenged the constitutionality, under the First Amendment, of the 1954 Act, the California statute, and the school district's policy requiring teachers to lead willing students in recitation of the Pledge. He sought declaratory and injunctive relief, but did not seek damages.

The school districts and their superintendents (collectively, "school district defendants") filed a Federal Rule of Civil Procedure 12(b)(6) motion to dismiss for failure to state a claim. Magistrate Judge Peter A. Nowinski held a hearing at which the school district defendants requested that the court rule only on the constitutionality of the Pledge, and defer any ruling on sovereign immunity. The United States Congress, the United States, and the President of the United States (collectively, "the federal defendants") joined in the motion to dismiss filed by the school district defendants. The magistrate judge reported findings and a recommendation; District Judge Edward J. Schwartz approved the recommendation and entered a judgment of dismissal. This appeal followed.

DISCUSSION

A.   Jurisdiction

Newdow asks the district court to order the President of the United States ("the President") to "alter, modify or repeal" the Pledge by removing the words "under God"; and to order the United States Congress ("Congress") "immediately to act to remove the words 'under God' from the Pledge." The President, however, is not an appropriate defendant in an action challenging the constitutionality of a federal statute. *See Franklin v. Massachusetts*, 505 U.S. 788, 802-03, 120 L. Ed. 2d 636, 112 S. Ct. 2767 (1992) (plurality) (observing that a court of the United States "'has no jurisdiction of a bill to enjoin the President in the performance of his official duties'") (quoting *Mississippi v. Johnson*, 71 U.S. 475, 501, 18 L. Ed. 437 (1866)).

Similarly, in light of the Speech and Debate Clause of the Constitution, Art. I, § 6, cl. 1, the federal courts lack jurisdiction to issue orders directing Congress to enact or amend legislation. *See Eastland v. United States Servicemen's Fund*, 421 U.S. 491, 503, 44 L. Ed. 2d 324, 95 S. Ct. 1813 (1975). Because the words that amended the Pledge were enacted into law by statute, the district court may not direct Congress to delete those words any more than it may order the President to take such action. All this, of course, is aside from the fact that the President has no authority to amend a statute or declare a law unconstitutional, those functions being reserved to Congress and the federal judiciary respectively.

Newdow nevertheless argues that because the 1954 Act violates the Establishment Clause, Congress should not be protected by the Speech and Debate Clause. This argument misses the jurisdictional, or separation of powers, point. As the Court held in *Eastland*, in determining whether or not the acts of members of Congress are protected by the Speech and Debate Clause, the court looks solely to whether or not the acts fall within the legitimate legislative sphere; if they do, Congress is protected by the absolute prohibition of the Clause against being "questioned in any other Place." *Id*. at 501. "If the mere allegation that a valid legislative act was undertaken for an unworthy purpose would lift the protection of the Clause, then the Clause simply would not provide the protection historically under-girding it." *Id*. at 508-09 . Although the district court lacks jurisdiction over the President and the Congress, the question of the constitutionality of the 1954 Act remains before us. While the court correctly dismissed the claim against those parties, it survives against others.

B.   The State of California as a Defendant

The State of California did not join in the motion to dismiss or otherwise participate in the district court proceedings. It did, however, *sub silentio*, receive the benefit of the district court's ruling dismissing the complaint. Accordingly, a reversal of the order would result in the reinstatement of the complaint against the state. With respect to the validity of the California statute, however, unlike in the case of the Congressional enactment and the school district policy, no arguments, legal or otherwise, were advanced by the parties either below or here. Thus, we do not address separately the validity of the California statute.

C.   Standing

Article III standing is a jurisdictional issue. *See United States v. Viltrakis*, 108 F.3d 1159, 1160 (9th Cir. 1997). Accordingly, it "may be raised at any stage of the proceedings, including for the first time on appeal." *See A-Z Intern. v. Phillips*, 179 F.3d 1187, 1190-91 (9th Cir. 1999). To satisfy standing requirements, a plaintiff must prove that "(1) it has suffered an 'injury in fact' that is (a) concrete and particularized and (b) actual or imminent, not conjectural or hypothetical; (2) the injury is fairly traceable to the challenged action of the defendant; and (3) it is likely, as opposed to merely speculative, that the injury will be redressed by a favorable decision." *Friends of the Earth, Inc. v. Laidlaw Envtl. Servs. (TOC), Inc.*, 528 U.S. 167, 180-81, 145 L. Ed. 2d 610, 120 S. Ct. 693 (2000) (citing *Lujan v. Defenders of Wildlife*, 504 U.S. 555, 560-561, 119 L. Ed. 2d 351, 112 S. Ct. 2130 (1992)).

Newdow has standing as a parent to challenge a practice that interferes with his right to direct the religious education of his daughter. "Parents have a right to direct the religious upbringing of their children and, on that basis, have standing to protect their right." *Doe v. Madison Sch. Dist. No. 321*, 177 F.3d 789, 795 (9th Cir. 1999) (en banc); *see also Grove v. Mead Sch. Dist. No. 354*, 753 F.2d 1528, 1532 (9th Cir. 1985) ("Appellants have standing to challenge alleged violations of the establishment clause of the First Amendment if they are directly affected by use of [the challenged book] in the English curriculum. [Appellant] has standing as a parent whose right to direct the religious training of her child is allegedly affected.") (citation omitted).

Newdow has standing to challenge the EGUSD's policy and practice regarding the recitation of the Pledge because his daughter is currently enrolled in elementary school in the EGUSD. However, Newdow has no standing to challenge the SCUSD's policy and practice because his daughter is not currently a student there. The SCUSD and its superintendent have not caused Newdow or his daughter an "injury in fact" that is "actual or imminent, not conjectural or hypothetical." *Laidlaw*, 528 U.S. at 180 (citing *Lujan*, 504 U.S. at 560-561).

The final question of standing relates to the 1954 Act. Specifically, has Newdow suffered an "injury in fact" that is "fairly traceable" to the enactment of the 1954 Act? *Id*.

We begin our inquiry by noting the general rule that the standing requirements for an action brought under the Establishment Clause are the same as for any other action. *Valley Forge Christian Coll. v. Americans United for Separation of Church and State, Inc.*, 454 U.S. 464, 488-90, 70 L. Ed. 2d 700, 102 S. Ct. 752 (1982). "The requirement of standing focuses on the party seeking to get his complaint before a federal court and not on the issues he wishes to have adjudicated. Moreover, we know of no principled basis on which to create a hierarchy of constitutional values or a complementary 'sliding scale' of standing which might permit respondents to invoke the judicial power of the United States." *Id*. at 484 (citation and internal quotation marks omitted). In *Valley Forge*, an organization dedicated to the separation of church and state brought suit challenging the federal government's grant of surplus federal property to a church-related college. The suit alleged that this grant of real property, without any financial payment by the college, was a violation of the Establishment Clause. The Supreme Court found that the plaintiff had standing neither as a taxpayer, *see id*. at 479-80, nor as a party personally injured as a consequence of the alleged unconstitutional action, *see id* . at 484-86. The "psychological consequence presumably produced by observation of conduct with which one disagrees . . . is not an injury sufficient to confer standing under Art. III, even though the disagreement is phrased in constitutional terms." *Id*. at 485-86 . The Court emphasized that "'the assumption that if respondents have no standing to sue, no one would have standing, is not a reason to find standing.'" *Id*. at 489 (quoting *Schlesinger v. Reservists Comm. to Stop the War*, 418 U.S. 208, 227, 41 L. Ed. 2d 706, 94 S. Ct. 2925 (1974)).

While *Valley Forge* remains good law, the Supreme Court in more recent opinions has indirectly broadened the notion of Establishment Clause standing in public education cases by holding that the mere enactment of a statute may constitute an Establishment Clause violation. In *Wallace v. Jaffree*, 472 U.S. 38, 86 L. Ed. 2d 29, 105 S. Ct. 2479 (1985), the Court considered an Establishment Clause challenge to an Alabama statute that originally had authorized a one-minute period of silence in public schools "for meditation," but was later amended to authorize a period of silence "for meditation or voluntary prayer." *Id*. at 40-42 . Although the previous form of the statute specifically allowed students to use the moment of silence for "meditation," silent prayer was always an option. "It is undisputed that at the time of the enactment of [the amended statute] there was no governmental practice impeding students from silently praying for one minute at the beginning of each schoolday." *Id.* at 57 n. 45. Nor were students, under the amended form of the statute, compelled to use the allotted time for prayer. In sum, the amendment to the Alabama statute had no discernible effect on public school students other than to inform them that the state was encouraging them to engage in prayer during their daily moment of silence. Because the Supreme Court has repeatedly held that standing is a jurisdictional requirement, the existence of which each federal court must determine for itself, *see Lujan*, 504 U.S. at 559-561; *FW/PBS, Inc. v. City of Dallas*, 493 U.S. 215, 230-31, 107 L. Ed. 2d 603, 110 S. Ct. 596 (1990), we may presume that in *Wallace* the Court examined the standing question before deciding the merits, and that the Court determined that the schoolchildren's parents had standing to challenge the amended Alabama statute.

Our reading of *Wallace* is supported by *Santa Fe Independent School District v. Doe*, 530 U.S. 290, 147 L. Ed. 2d 295, 120 S. Ct. 2266 (2000), where the Court upheld a facial challenge to a school district's policy of permitting, but not requiring, prayer initiated and led by a student at high school football games. Noting that "the Constitution also requires that we keep in mind 'the myriad, subtle ways in which the Establishment Clause values can be eroded,'" *id.* at 314 (quoting *Lynch v. Donnelly*, 465 U.S. 668, 694, 79 L. Ed. 2d 604, 104 S. Ct. 1355 (1984) (O'Connor, J., concurring)), the Court held that the "mere passage by the District of a policy that has the purpose and perception of government establishment of religion," *id.*, violated the Establishment Clause. "The *simple enactment* of this policy, with the purpose and perception of school endorsement of student prayer, was a constitutional violation." *Id.* at 316 (emphasis added).

In *Wallace* and *Santa Fe*, the Court looked at the language of each statute, the context in which the statute was enacted, and its legislative history to determine that the challenged statute caused an injury in violation of the Establishment Clause. "We refuse to turn a blind eye to the context in which this policy arose, and that context quells any doubt that this policy was implemented with the purpose of endorsing school prayer." *Id.* at 315. Justice O'Connor's concurrence in *Wallace* noted that whether a statute actually conveys a message of endorsement of religion is "not entirely a question of fact .... The relevant issue is whether an objective observer, acquainted with the text, legislative history, and implementation of the statute, would perceive it as state endorsement of prayer in public schools." 472 U.S. at 76 (O'Connor, J., concurring in judgment). In *Santa Fe*, "the text and history of this policy ... reinforce our objective student's perception that the prayer is, in actuality, encouraged by the school." 530 U.S. at 308. In evaluating the purpose of the school district policy, the Court found "most striking ... the evolution of the current policy." *Id.* at 309. In *Wallace*, a review of the legislative history led the Court to conclude that enactment of the amended statute "was not motivated by any clearly secular purpose - indeed, the statute had *no* secular purpose." 472 U.S. at 56; *see also id.* at 57-60.

Operating within the above-described legal landscape, we now turn to the question initially posed, namely, does Newdow have standing to challenge the 1954 Act? Initially, we note that the 1954 statute challenged by Newdow is similar to the Alabama statute struck down in *Wallace*. Neither statute works the traditional type of "injury in fact" that is implicated when a statute compels or prohibits certain activity, nor do the amendments brought about by these statutes lend themselves to "as-applied" constitutional review. Nevertheless, the Court in *Wallace*, at least implicitly, determined that the schoolchildren's parents had standing to attack the challenged statute. Moreover, the legislative history of the 1954 Act shows that the "under God" language was not meant to sit passively in the federal code unbeknownst to the public; rather, the sponsors of the amendment knew about and capitalized on the state laws and school district rules that mandate recitation of the Pledge. The legislation's House sponsor, Representative Louis C. Rabaut, testified at the Congressional hearing that "the children of our land, in the daily recitation of the pledge in school, will be daily impressed with a true understanding of our way of life and its origins," and this statement was incorporated into the report of the House Judiciary Committee. H.R. Rep. No. 83-1693, at 3 (1954), *reprinted in* 1954 U.S.C.C.A.N. 2339, 2341. Taken within its context, the 1954 addendum was designed to result in the recitation of the words "under God" in school classrooms throughout the land on a daily basis, and therefore constituted as much of an injury-in-fact as the policies considered in *Wallace* and *Santa Fe*. As discussed earlier, Newdow has standing as a parent to challenge a practice that interferes with his right to direct the religious education of his daughter. The mere enactment of the 1954 Act in its particular context constitutes a religious recitation policy that interferes with Newdow's right to direct the religious education of his daughter. Accordingly, we hold that Newdow has standing to challenge the 1954 Act.

D.   Establishment Clause

The Establishment Clause of the First Amendment states that "Congress shall make no law respecting an establishment of religion," U.S. Const. amend. I, a provision that "the Fourteenth Amendment makes applicable with full force to the States and their school districts." *Lee v. Weisman*, 505 U.S. 577, 580, 120 L. Ed. 2d 467, 112 S. Ct. 2649 (1992). Over the last three decades, the Supreme Court has used three interrelated tests to analyze alleged violations of the Establishment Clause in the realm of public education: the three-prong test set forth in *Lemon v. Kurtzman*, 403 U.S. 602, 612-13, 29 L. Ed. 2d 745, 91 S. Ct. 2105 (1971); the "endorsement" test, first articulated by Justice O'Connor in her concurring opinion in *Lynch*, and later adopted by a majority of the Court in *County of Allegheny v. ACLU*, 492 U.S. 573, 106 L. Ed. 2d 472, 109 S. Ct. 3086 (1989); and the "coercion" test first used by the Court in *Lee*.

In 1971, in the context of unconstitutional state aid to non-public schools, the Supreme Court in *Lemon* set forth the following test for evaluating alleged Establishment Clause violations. To survive the "*Lemon* test," the government conduct in question (1) must have a secular purpose, (2) must have a principal or primary effect that neither advances nor inhibits religion, and (3) must not foster an excessive government entanglement with religion. *Lemon*, 403 U.S. at 612-13 . The Supreme Court applied the *Lemon* test to every Establishment case it decided between 1971 and 1984, with the exception of *Marsh v. Chambers*, 463 U.S. 783, 77 L. Ed. 2d 1019, 103 S. Ct. 3330 (1983), the case upholding legislative prayer. n4 *See Wallace*, 472 U.S. at 63 (Powell, J., concurring).

In the 1984 *Lynch* case, which upheld the inclusion of a nativity scene in a city's Christmas display, Justice O'Connor wrote a concurring opinion in order to suggest a "clarification" of Establishment Clause jurisprudence. 465 U.S. at 687 (O'Connor, J., concurring). Justice O'Connor's "endorsement" test effectively collapsed the first two prongs of the *Lemon* test:

> The Establishment Clause prohibits government from making adherence to a religion relevant in any way to a person's standing in the political community. Government can run afoul of that prohibition in two principal ways. One is excessive entanglement with religious institutions .... The second and more direct infringement is government endorsement or disapproval of religion. Endorsement sends a message to non-adherents that they are outsiders, not full members of the political community, and an accompanying message to adherents that they are insiders, favored members of the political community.

p>*Id.* at 687-88 (O'Connor, J., concurring).

The Court formulated the "coercion test" when it held unconstitutional the practice of including invocations and benedictions in the form of "nonsectarian" prayers at public school graduation ceremonies. *Lee*, 505 U.S. at 599. Declining to reconsider the validity of the *Lemon* test, the Court in *Lee* found it unnecessary to apply the *Lemon* test to find the challenged practices unconstitutional. *Id.* at 587. Rather, it relied on the principle that "at a minimum, the Constitution guarantees that government may not coerce anyone to support or participate in religion or its exercise, or otherwise to act in a way which establishes a state religion or religious faith, or tends to do so." *Id.* (citations and internal quotation marks omitted). n5 The Court first examined the degree of school involvement in the prayer, and found that "the graduation prayers bore the imprint of the State and thus put school-age children who objected in an untenable position." *Id.* at 590. The next issue the Court considered was "the position of the students, both those who desired the prayer and she who did not." *Id.* Noting that "there are heightened concerns with protecting freedom of conscience from subtle coercive pressure in the elementary and secondary public schools," *id.* at 592, the Court held that the school district's supervision and control of the graduation ceremony put impermissible pressure on students to participate in, or at least show respect during, the prayer, *id.* at 593. The Court concluded that primary and secondary school children may not be placed in the dilemma of either participating in a religious ceremony or protesting. *Id.* at 594.

Finally, in its most recent school prayer case, the Supreme Court applied the *Lemon* test, the endorsement test, and the coercion test to strike down a school district's policy of permitting student-led "invocations" before high school football games. *See Santa Fe*, 530 U.S. at 310-16 . Citing *Lee*, the Court held that "the delivery of a pregame prayer has the improper effect of coercing those present to participate in an act of religious worship." *Id.* at 312. Applying the *Lemon* test, the Court found that the school district policy was facially unconstitutional because it did not have a secular purpose. *Id.* at 314-16 . The Court also used language associated with the endorsement test. *Id.* at 315 ("This policy was implemented with the purpose of endorsing school prayer."); *id.* at 317

("Government efforts to endorse religion cannot evade constitutional reproach based solely on the remote possibility that those attempts may fail.").

We are free to apply any or all of the three tests, and to invalidate any measure that fails any one of them. The Supreme Court has not repudiated *Lemon*; in *Santa Fe*, it found that the application of each of the three tests provided an independent ground for invalidating the statute at issue in that case; and in *Lee*, the Court invalidated the policy solely on the basis of the coercion test. Although this court has typically applied the *Lemon* test to alleged Establishment Clause violations, *see, e.g., Am. Family Ass'n, Inc. v. City and County of San Francisco*, 277 F.3d 1114, 1120-21 (9th Cir. 2002), we are not required to apply it if a practice fails one of the other tests. Nevertheless, for purposes of completeness, we will analyze the school district policy and the 1954 Act under all three tests.

We first consider whether the 1954 Act and the EGUSD's policy of teacher-led Pledge recitation survive the endorsement test. The magistrate judge found that "the ceremonial reference to God in the pledge does not convey endorsement of particular religious beliefs." Supreme Court precedent does not support that conclusion.

In the context of the Pledge, the statement that the United States is a nation "under God" is an endorsement of religion. It is a profession of a religious belief, namely, a belief in monotheism. The recitation that ours is a nation "under God" is not a mere acknowledgment that many Americans believe in a deity. Nor is it merely descriptive of the undeniable historical significance of religion in the founding of the Republic. Rather, the phrase "one nation under God" in the context of the Pledge is normative. To recite the Pledge is not to describe the United States; instead, it is to swear allegiance to the values for which the flag stands: unity, indivisibility, liberty, justice, and - since 1954 - monotheism. The text of the official Pledge, codified in federal law, impermissibly takes a position with respect to the purely religious question of the existence and identity of God. A profession that we are a nation "under God" is identical, for Establishment Clause purposes, to a profession that we are a nation "under Jesus," a nation "under Vishnu," a nation "under Zeus," or a nation "under no god," because none of these professions can be neutral with respect to religion. "The government must pursue a course of complete neutrality toward religion." *Wallace*, 472 U.S. at 60. Furthermore, the school district's practice of teacher-led recitation of the Pledge aims to inculcate in students a respect for the ideals set forth in the Pledge, and thus amounts to state endorsement of these ideals. Although students cannot be forced to participate in recitation of the Pledge, the school district is nonetheless conveying a message of state endorsement of a religious belief when it requires public school teachers to recite, and lead the recitation of, the current form of the Pledge.

The Supreme Court recognized the normative and ideological nature of the Pledge in *Barnette*, 319 U.S. 624. There, the Court held unconstitutional a school district's wartime policy of punishing students who refused to recite the Pledge and salute the flag. *Id*. at 642. The Court noted that the school district was compelling the students "to declare a belief," *id*. at 631, and "requiring the individual to communicate by word and sign his acceptance of the political ideas [the flag] ... bespeaks," *id*. at 633. "The compulsory flag

17

salute and pledge requires affirmation of a belief and an attitude of mind." *Id*. The Court emphasized that the political concepts articulated in the Pledge n6 were idealistic, not descriptive: "'Liberty and justice for all,' if it must be accepted as descriptive of the present order rather than an ideal, might to some seem an overstatement." *Id*. at 634 n. 14. The Court concluded that: "If there is any fixed star in our constitutional constellation, it is that no official, high or petty, can prescribe what shall be orthodox in politics, nationalism, religion, or other matters of opinion or force citizens to confess by word or act their faith therein." *Id*. at 642.

The Pledge, as currently codified, is an impermissible government endorsement of religion because it sends a message to unbelievers "that they are outsiders, not full members of the political community, and an accompanying message to adherents that they are insiders, favored members of the political community." *Lynch*, 465 U.S. at 688 (O'Connor, J., concurring). Justice Kennedy, in his dissent in *Allegheny*, agreed:

> By statute, the Pledge of Allegiance to the Flag describes the United States as 'one nation under God.' To be sure, no one is obligated to recite this phrase, . . . but it borders on sophistry to suggest that the reasonable atheist would not feel less than a full member of the political community every time his fellow Americans recited, as part of their expression of patriotism and love for country, a phrase he believed to be false.

Allegheny, 492 U.S. at 672 (Kennedy, J., dissenting) (citations and internal quotation marks omitted). n7 Consequently, the policy and the Act fail the endorsement test. Similarly, the policy and the Act fail the coercion test. Just as in *Lee*, the policy and the Act place students in the untenable position of choosing between participating in an exercise with religious content or protesting. As the Court observed with respect to the graduation prayer in that case: "What to most believers may seem nothing more than a reasonable request that the nonbeliever respect their religious practices, in a school context may appear to the nonbeliever or dissenter to be an attempt to employ the machinery of the State to enforce a religious orthodoxy." *Lee*, 505 U.S. at 592. Although the defendants argue that the religious content of "one nation under God" is minimal, to an atheist or a believer in certain non-Judeo-Christian religions or philosophies, it may reasonably appear to be an attempt to enforce a "religious orthodoxy" of monotheism, and is therefore impermissible. The coercive effect of this policy is particularly pronounced in the school setting given the age and impressionability of schoolchildren, and their understanding that they are required to adhere to the norms set by their school, their teacher and their fellow students. n8 Furthermore, under *Lee*, the fact that students are not required to participate is no basis for distinguishing *Barnette* from the case at bar because, even without a recitation requirement for each child, the mere fact that a pupil is required to listen every day to the statement "one nation under God" has a coercive effect. n9 The coercive effect of the Act is apparent from its context and legislative history, which indicate that the Act was designed to result in the daily recitation of the words "under God" in school classrooms. President Eisenhower, during the Act's signing ceremony, stated: "From this day forward, the millions of our school children will daily proclaim in every city and town, every village and rural schoolhouse, the dedication of our Nation and our people to the Almighty." 100 Cong. Rec. 8618 (1954) (statement of

Sen. Ferguson incorporating signing statement of President Eisenhower). Therefore, the policy and the Act fail the coercion test. n10

Finally we turn to the *Lemon* test, the first prong of which asks if the challenged policy has a secular purpose. Historically, the primary purpose of the 1954 Act was to advance religion, in conflict with the first prong of the *Lemon* test. The federal defendants "do not dispute that the words 'under God' were intended" "to recognize a Supreme Being," at a time when the government was publicly inveighing against atheistic communism. Nonetheless, the federal defendants argue that the Pledge must be considered as a whole when assessing whether it has a secular purpose. They claim that the Pledge has the secular purpose of "solemnizing public occasions, expressing confidence in the future, and encouraging the recognition of what is worthy of appreciation in society." *Lynch*, 465 U.S. at 693.

The flaw in defendants' argument is that it looks at the text of the Pledge "as a whole," and glosses over the 1954 Act. The problem with this approach is apparent when one considers the Court's analysis in *Wallace*. There, the Court struck down Alabama's statute mandating a moment of silence for "meditation or voluntary prayer" not because the final version "as a whole" lacked a primary secular purpose, but because the state legislature had amended the statute specifically and solely to add the words "or voluntary prayer." 472 U.S. at 59-60.

By analogy to *Wallace*, we apply the purpose prong of the *Lemon* test to the amendment that added the words "under God" to the Pledge, not to the Pledge in its final version. As was the case with the amendment to the Alabama statute in *Wallace*, the legislative history of the 1954 Act reveals that the Act's *sole* purpose was to advance religion, in order to differentiate the United States from nations under communist rule. "The First Amendment requires that a statute must be invalidated if it is entirely motivated by a purpose to advance religion." *Id.* at 56 (citations omitted) (applying the *Lemon* test). As the legislative history of the 1954 Act sets forth:

> At this moment of our history the principles underlying our American Government and the American way of life are under attack by a system whose philosophy is at direct odds with our own. Our American Government is founded on the concept of the individuality and the dignity of the human being. Underlying this concept is the belief that the human person is important because he was created by God and endowed by Him with certain inalienable rights which no civil authority may usurp. The inclusion of God in our pledge therefore would further acknowledge the dependence of our people and our Government upon the moral directions of the Creator. At the same time it would serve to deny the atheistic and materialistic concepts of communism with its attendant subservience of the individual.

H.R. Rep. No. 83-1693 , at 1-2 (1954), *reprinted in* 1954 U.S.C.C.A.N. 2339, 2340. This language reveals that the purpose of the 1954 Act was to take a position on the question of theism, namely, to support the existence and moral authority of God, while "denying ...

atheistic and materialistic concepts." *Id.* Such a purpose runs counter to the Establishment Clause, which prohibits the government's endorsement or advancement not only of one particular religion at the expense of other religions, but also of religion at the expense of atheism.

> The Court has unambiguously concluded that the individual freedom of conscience protected by the First Amendment embraces the right to select any religious faith or none at all. This conclusion derives support not only from the interest in respecting the individual's freedom of conscience, but also from the conviction that religious beliefs worthy of respect are the product of a free and voluntary choice by the faithful, and from recognition of the fact that the political interest in forestalling intolerance extends beyond intolerance among Christian sects - or even intolerance among "religions" - to encompass intolerance of the disbeliever and the uncertain.

Wallace, 472 U.S. at 52-54.

In language that attempts to prevent future constitutional challenges, the sponsors of the 1954 Act expressly disclaimed a religious purpose. "This is not an act establishing a religion .... A distinction must be made between the existence of a religion as an institution and a belief in the sovereignty of God. The phrase 'under God' recognizes only the guidance of God in our national affairs." H.R. Rep. No. 83-1693, at 3 (1954), *reprinted in* 1954 U.S.C.C.A.N. 2339, 2341-42. This alleged distinction is irrelevant for constitutional purposes. The Act's affirmation of "a belief in the sovereignty of God" and its recognition of "the guidance of God" are endorsements by the government of religious beliefs. The Establishment Clause is not limited to "religion as an institution"; this is clear from cases such as *Santa Fe*, where the Court struck down student-initiated and student-led prayer at high school football games. 530 U.S. 310-16. The Establishment Clause guards not only against the establishment of "religion as an institution," but also against the endorsement of religious ideology by the government. Because the Act fails the purpose prong of *Lemon*, we need not examine the other prongs. *Lemon*, 403 U.S. at 612-14.

Similarly, the school district policy also fails the *Lemon* test. Although it survives the first prong of *Lemon* because, as even Newdow concedes, the school district had the secular purpose of fostering patriotism in enacting the policy, the policy fails the second prong. As explained by this court in *Kreisner v. City of San Diego*, 1 F.3d 775, 782 (9th Cir. 1993), and by the Supreme Court in *School District of Grand Rapids v. Ball*, 473 U.S. 373, 390, 87 L. Ed. 2d 267, 105 S. Ct. 3216 (1985), the second *Lemon* prong asks whether the challenged government action is sufficiently likely to be perceived by adherents of the controlling denominations as an endorsement, and by the nonadherents as a disapproval, of their individual religious choices." n11 *Ball*, 473 U.S. at 390. Given the age and impressionability of schoolchildren, as discussed above, particularly within the confined environment of the classroom, the policy is highly likely to convey an impermissible message of endorsement to some and disapproval to others of their beliefs regarding the existence of a monotheistic God. Therefore the policy fails the effects prong of *Lemon,* and fails the *Lemon* test. In sum, both the policy and the Act fail the *Lemon* test as well as the endorsement and coercion tests. n12

In conclusion, we hold that (1) the 1954 Act adding the words "under God" to the Pledge, and (2) EGUSD's policy and practice of teacher-led recitation of the Pledge, with the added words included, violate the Establishment Clause. The judgment of dismissal is vacated with respect to these two claims, and the cause is remanded for further proceedings consistent with our holding. Plaintiff is to recover costs on this appeal.

REVERSED AND REMANDED

Texas v. Johnson

No. 88-155

SUPREME COURT OF THE UNITED STATES

491 U.S. 397

Argued March 21, 1989

Decided June 21, 1989

Syllabus

✤　　During the 1984 Republican National Convention in Dallas, Texas, respondent Johnson participated in a political demonstration to protest the policies of the Reagan administration and some Dallas-based corporations. After a march through the city streets, Johnson burned an American flag while protesters chanted. No one was physically injured or threatened with injury, although several witnesses were seriously offended by the flag burning. Johnson was convicted of desecration of a venerated object in violation of a Texas statute, and a State Court of Appeals affirmed. However, the Texas Court of Criminal Appeals reversed, holding that the State, consistent with the First Amendment, could not punish Johnson for burning the flag in these circumstances. The court first found that Johnson's burning of the flag was expressive conduct protected by the First Amendment. The court concluded that the State could not criminally sanction flag desecration in order to preserve the flag as a symbol of national unity. It also held that the statute did not meet the State's goal of preventing breaches of the peace, since it was not drawn narrowly enough to encompass only those flag burnings that would likely result in a serious disturbance, and since the flag burning in this case did not threaten such a reaction. Further, it stressed that another Texas statute prohibited breaches of the peace and could be used to prevent disturbances without punishing this flag desecration.

✤ Held: Johnson's conviction for flag desecration is inconsistent with the First Amendment. Pp. 402-420.

(a) Under the circumstances, Johnson's burning of the flag constituted expressive conduct, permitting him to invoke the First Amendment. The State conceded that the conduct was expressive. Occurring as it did at the end of a demonstration coinciding with the Republican National Convention, the expressive, overtly political nature of the conduct was both intentional and overwhelmingly apparent. Pp. 402-406.

(b) Texas has not asserted an interest in support of Johnson's conviction that is unrelated to the suppression of expression and would therefore permit application of the test set forth in *United States v. O'Brien,* 391 U.S. 367, whereby an important governmental interest in regulating non-speech can justify incidental limitations on First Amendment freedoms when speech and non-speech elements are combined in the same course of conduct. An interest in preventing breaches of the peace is not implicated on this record. Expression may not be prohibited [398] on the basis that an audience that takes serious offense to the expression may disturb the peace, since the government cannot assume that every expression of a provocative idea will incite a riot but must look to the actual circumstances surrounding the expression. Johnson's expression of dissatisfaction with the Federal Government's policies also does not fall within the class of "fighting words" likely to be seen as a direct personal insult or an invitation to exchange fisticuffs. This Court's holding does not forbid a State to prevent "imminent lawless action" and, in fact, Texas has a law specifically prohibiting breaches of the peace. Texas' interest in preserving the flag as a symbol of nationhood and national unity is related to expression in this case and, thus, falls outside the *O'Brien* test. Pp. 406-410.

(c) The latter interest does not justify Johnson's conviction. The restriction on Johnson's political expression is content based, since the Texas statute is not aimed at protecting the physical integrity of the flag in all circumstances, but is designed to protect it from intentional and knowing abuse that causes serious offense to others. It is therefore subject to "the most exacting scrutiny." *Boos v. Barry,* 485 U.S. 312. The government may not prohibit the verbal or nonverbal expression of an idea merely because society finds the idea offensive or disagreeable, even where our flag is involved. Nor may a State foster its own view of the flag by prohibiting expressive conduct relating to it, since the government may not permit designated symbols to be used to communicate a limited set of messages. Moreover, this Court will not create an exception to these principles protected by the First Amendment for the American flag alone. Pp. 410-422.

755 S. W. 2d 92, AFFIRMED.

JUDGES: Brennan, J., delivered the opinion of the Court, in which Marshall, Blackmun, Scalia, and Kennedy, JJ., joined. Kennedy, J., filed a concurring opinion, *post,* p. 420. Rehnquist, C. J., filed a dissenting opinion, in which White and O'Connor, JJ., joined, *post,* p. 421. Stevens, J., filed a dissenting opinion, *post,* p. 436. [399]

JUSTICE BRENNAN delivered the opinion of the Court.

After publicly burning an American flag as a means of political protest, Gregory Lee Johnson was convicted of desecrating a flag in violation of Texas law. This case presents the question whether his conviction is consistent with the First Amendment. We hold that it is not.

I.

While the Republican National Convention was taking place in Dallas in 1984, respondent Johnson participated in a political demonstration dubbed the "Republican War Chest Tour." As explained in literature distributed by the demonstrators and in speeches made by them, the purpose of this event was to protest the policies of the Reagan administration and of certain Dallas-based corporations. The demonstrators marched through the Dallas streets, chanting political slogans and stopping at several corporate locations to stage "die-ins" intended to dramatize the consequences of nuclear war. On several occasions they spray-painted the walls of buildings and overturned potted plants, but Johnson himself took no part in such activities. He did, however, accept an American flag handed to him by a fellow protestor who had taken it from a flagpole outside one of the targeted buildings.

The demonstration ended in front of Dallas City Hall, where Johnson unfurled the American flag, doused it with kerosene, and set it on fire. While the flag burned, the protestors chanted: "America, the red, white, and blue, we spit on you." After the demonstrators dispersed, a witness to the flag burning collected the flag's remains and buried them in his backyard. No one was physically injured or threatened with injury, though several witnesses testified that they had been seriously offended by the flag burning. [400]

Of the approximately 100 demonstrators, Johnson alone was charged with a crime. The only criminal offense with which he was charged was the desecration of a venerated object in violation of Tex. Penal Code Ann. § 42.09(a)(3) (1989). [note 1] After a trial, he was convicted, sentenced to one year in prison, and fined $2,000. The Court of Appeals for the Fifth District of Texas at Dallas affirmed Johnson's conviction, 706 S. W. 2d 120 (1986), but the Texas Court of Criminal Appeals reversed, 755 S. W. 2d 92 (1988), holding that the State could not, consistent with the First Amendment, punish Johnson for burning the flag in these circumstances.

The Court of Criminal Appeals began by recognizing that Johnson's conduct was symbolic speech protected by the First Amendment: "Given the context of an organized demonstration, speeches, slogans, and the distribution of literature, anyone who observed appellant's act would have understood the message that appellant intended to convey. The act for which appellant was convicted was clearly 'speech' contemplated by the First Amendment." *Id.,* at 95. To justify Johnson's conviction for engaging in symbolic speech, the State asserted two interests: preserving the flag as a symbol of national unity and preventing breaches of the peace. The Court of Criminal Appeals held that neither interest supported his conviction. [401]

Acknowledging that this Court had not yet decided whether the Government may criminally sanction flag desecration in order to preserve the flag's symbolic value, the Texas court nevertheless concluded that our decision in *West Virginia Board of Education v. Barnette,* 319 U.S. 624 (1943), suggested that furthering this interest by curtailing speech was impermissible. "Recognizing that the right to differ is the centerpiece of our First Amendment freedoms," the court explained, "a government cannot mandate by fiat a feeling of unity in its citizens. Therefore, that very same government cannot carve out a symbol of unity and prescribe a set of approved messages to be associated with that symbol when it cannot mandate the status or feeling the symbol purports to represent." 755 S. W. 2d, at 97. Noting that the State had not shown that the flag was in "grave and immediate danger," *Barnette, supra,* at 639, of being stripped of its symbolic value, the Texas court also decided that the flag's special status was not endangered by Johnson's conduct. 755 S. W. 2d, at 97.

As to the State's goal of preventing breaches of the peace, the court concluded that the flag-desecration statute was not drawn narrowly enough to encompass only those flag burnings that were likely to result in a serious disturbance of the peace. And in fact, the court emphasized, the flag burning in this particular case did not threaten such a reaction. "'Serious offense' occurred," the court admitted, "but there was no breach of peace nor does the record reflect that the situation was potentially explosive. One cannot equate 'serious offense' with incitement to breach the peace." *Id.,* at 96. The court also stressed that another Texas statute, Tex. Penal Code Ann. § 42.01 (1989), prohibited breaches of the peace. Citing *Boos v. Barry,* 485 U.S. 312 (1988), the court decided that § 42.01 demonstrated Texas' ability to prevent disturbances of the peace without punishing this flag desecration. 755 S. W. 2d, at 96. [402]

Because it reversed Johnson's conviction on the ground that § 42.09 was unconstitutional as applied to him, the state court did not address Johnson's argument that the statute was, on its face, unconstitutionally vague and overbroad. We granted certiorari, 488 U.S. 907 (1988), and now affirm.

II.

Johnson was convicted of flag desecration for burning the flag rather than for uttering insulting words. [note 2] This fact [403] somewhat complicates our consideration of his conviction under the First Amendment. We must first determine whether Johnson's burning of the flag constituted expressive conduct, permitting him to invoke the First Amendment in challenging his conviction. See, e.g., *Spence v. Washington,* 418 U.S. 405, 409-411 (1974). If his conduct was expressive, we next decide whether the State's regulation is related to the suppression of free expression. See, e.g., *United States v. O'Brien,* 391 U.S. 367, 377 (1968); *Spence, supra,* at 414, n. 8. If the State's regulation is not related to expression, then the less stringent standard we announced in *United States v. O'Brien* for regulations of noncommunicative conduct controls. See *O'Brien, supra,* at 377. If it is, then we are outside of *O'Brien's* test, and we must ask whether this interest justifies Johnson's conviction under a more demanding standard. [note 3] See *Spence, supra,* at 411. A [404] third possibility is that the State's asserted interest is simply not implicated on these facts, and in that event the interest drops out of the picture. See 418 U.S., at 414, n. 8.

The First Amendment literally forbids the abridgment only of "speech," but we have long recognized that its protection does not end at the spoken or written word. While we have rejected "the view that an apparently limitless variety of conduct can be labeled 'speech' whenever the person engaging in the conduct intends thereby to express an idea," *United States v. O'Brien, supra,* at 376, we have acknowledged that conduct may be "sufficiently imbued with elements of communication to fall within the scope of the First and Fourteenth Amendments," *Spence, supra,* at 409.

In deciding whether particular conduct possesses sufficient communicative elements to bring the First Amendment into play, we have asked whether "[a]n intent to convey a particularized message was present, and [whether] the likelihood was great that the message would be understood by those who viewed it." 418 U.S., at 410-411. Hence, we have recognized the expressive nature of students' wearing of black armbands to protest American military involvement in Vietnam, *Tinker v. Des Moines Independent Community School Dist.,* 393 U.S. 503, 505 (1969); of a sit-in by blacks in a "whites only" area to protest segregation, *Brown v. Louisiana,* 383 U.S. 131, 141-142 (1966); of the wearing of American military uniforms in a dramatic presentation criticizing American involvement in Vietnam, *Schacht v. United States,* 398 U.S. 58 (1970); and of picketing about a wide variety of causes, see, e.g., *Food Employees v. Logan Valley Plaza, Inc.,* 391 U.S. 308, 313-314 (1968); *United States v. Grace,* 461 U.S. 171, 176 (1983).

Especially pertinent to this case are our decisions recognizing the communicative nature of conduct relating to flags. Attaching a peace sign to the flag, *Spence, supra,* at 409-410; refusing to salute the flag, *Barnette,* 319 U.S., at 632; and displaying a red flag, *Stromberg v. California,* 283 U.S. 359, 368-369 [405] (1931), we have held, all may find shelter under the First Amendment. See also *Smith v. Goguen,* 415 U.S. 566, 588 (1974) (White, J., concurring in judgment) (treating flag "contemptuously" by wearing pants with small flag sewn into their seat is expressive conduct). That we have had little difficulty identifying an expressive element in conduct relating to flags should not be surprising. The very purpose of a national flag is to serve as a symbol of our country; it is, one might say, "the one visible manifestation of two hundred years of nationhood." *Id.,* at 603 (Rehnquist, J., dissenting). Thus, we have observed:

> [T]he flag salute is a form of utterance. Symbolism is a primitive but effective way of communicating ideas. The use of an emblem or flag to symbolize some system, idea, institution, or personality, is a short cut from mind to mind. Causes and nations, political parties, lodges and ecclesiastical groups seek to knit the loyalty of their followings to a flag or banner, a color or design. *Barnette, supra,* at 632.

Pregnant with expressive content, the flag as readily signifies this Nation as does the combination of letters found in "America."

We have not automatically concluded, however, that any action taken with respect to our flag is expressive. Instead, in characterizing such action for First Amendment purposes, we have considered the context in which it occurred. In *Spence,* for example, we emphasized that Spence's taping of a peace sign to his flag was "roughly simultaneous with and concededly triggered by the Cambodian incursion and the Kent State tragedy." 418 U.S., at 410. The State of Washington had conceded, in fact, that Spence's conduct was a form of communication, and we stated that "the State's concession is inevitable on this record." *Id.,* at 409.

The State of Texas conceded for purposes of its oral argument in this case that Johnson's conduct was expressive conduct, Tr. of Oral Arg. 4, and this concession seems to us as [406] prudent as was Washington's in *Spence.* Johnson burned an American flag as part--indeed, as the culmination--of a political demonstration that coincided with the convening of the Republican Party and its re-nomination of Ronald Reagan for President. The expressive, overtly political nature of this conduct was both intentional and overwhelmingly apparent. At his trial, Johnson explained his reasons for burning the flag as follows: "The American Flag was burned as Ronald Reagan was being re-nominated as President. And a more powerful statement of symbolic speech, whether you agree with it or not, couldn't have been made at that time. It's quite a just position [juxtaposition]. We had new patriotism and no patriotism." 5 Record 656. In these circumstances, Johnson's burning of the flag was conduct "sufficiently imbued with elements of communication," *Spence,* 418 U.S., at 409, to implicate the First Amendment.

III.

The government generally has a freer hand in restricting expressive conduct than it has in restricting the written or spoken word. See *O'Brien,* 391 U.S. at 376-377; *Clark v. Community for Creative Non-Violence,* 468 U.S. 288, 293 (1984); *Dallas v. Stanglin,* 490 U.S. 19, 25 (1989). It may not, however, proscribe particular conduct because it has expressive elements. "[W]hat might be termed the more generalized guarantee of freedom of expression makes the communicative nature of conduct an inadequate basis for singling out that conduct for proscription. A law directed at the communicative nature of conduct must, like a law directed at speech itself, be justified by the substantial showing of need that the First Amendment requires." *Community for Creative Non-Violence v. Watt,* 227 U. S. App. D. C. 19, 55-56, 703 F. 2d 586, 622-623 (1983) (Scalia, J., dissenting) (emphasis in original), rev'd sub nom. *Clark v. Community for Creative Non-Violence, supra.* It is, in short, not simply the verbal or nonverbal nature of the expression, but the governmental [407] interest at stake, that helps to determine whether a restriction on that expression is valid.

Thus, although we have recognized that where "'speech' and 'nonspeech' elements are combined in the same course of conduct, a sufficiently important governmental interest in regulating the nonspeech element can justify incidental limitations on First Amendment freedoms," *O'Brien, supra,* at 376, we have limited the applicability of *O'Brien's* relatively lenient standard to those cases in which "the governmental interest is unrelated to the suppression of free expression." *Id.,* at 377; see also *Spence, supra,* at 414, n. 8. In stating, moreover, that *O'Brien's* test "in the last analysis is little, if any, different from the standard applied to time, place, or manner restrictions," *Clark, supra,* at 298, we have highlighted the requirement that the governmental interest in question be unconnected to expression in order to come under *O'Brien's* less demanding rule.

In order to decide whether *O'Brien's* test applies here, therefore, we must decide whether Texas has asserted an interest in support of Johnson's conviction that is unrelated to the suppression of expression. If we find that an interest asserted by the State is simply not implicated on the facts before us, we need not ask whether *O'Brien's* test applies. See *Spence, supra,* at 414, n. 8. The State offers two separate interests to justify this conviction: preventing breaches of the peace and preserving the flag as a symbol of nationhood and national unity. We hold that the first interest is not implicated on this record and that the second is related to the suppression of expression.

26

A.

Texas claims that its interest in preventing breaches of the peace justifies Johnson's conviction for flag desecration. [note 4] [408] However, no disturbance of the peace actually occurred or threatened to occur because of Johnson's burning of the flag. Although the State stresses the disruptive behavior of the protestors during their march toward City Hall, Brief for Petitioner 34-36, it admits that "no actual breach of the peace occurred at the time of the flagburning or in response to the flagburning." *Id.,* at 34. The State's emphasis on the protestors' disorderly actions prior to arriving at City Hall is not only somewhat surprising given that no charges were brought on the basis of this conduct, but it also fails to show that a disturbance of the peace was a likely reaction to Johnson's conduct. The only evidence offered by the State at trial to show the reaction to Johnson's actions was the testimony of several persons who had been seriously offended by the flag burning. *Id.,* at 6-7.

The State's position, therefore, amounts to a claim that an audience that takes serious offense at particular expression is necessarily likely to disturb the peace and that the expression may be prohibited on this basis. [note 5] Our precedents do not countenance such a presumption. On the contrary, they recognize that a principal "function of free speech under our system of government is to invite dispute. It may indeed best serve its high purpose when it induces a condition of unrest, creates dissatisfaction with conditions as they are, or [409] even stirs people to anger." *Terminiello v. Chicago,* 337 U.S. 1, 4 (1949). See also *Cox v. Louisiana,* 379 U.S. 536, 551 (1965); *Tinker v. Des Moines Independent Community School Dist.,* 393 U.S., at 508-509; *Coates v. Cincinnati,* 402 U.S. 611, 615 (1971); *Hustler Magazine, Inc. v. Falwell,* 485 U.S. 46, 55-56 (1988). It would be odd indeed to conclude both that "if it is the speaker's opinion that gives offense, that consequence is a reason for according it constitutional protection," *FCC v. Pacifica Foundation,* 438 U.S. 726, 745 (1978) (opinion of Stevens, J.), and that the government may ban the expression of certain disagreeable ideas on the unsupported presumption that their very disagreeableness will provoke violence.

Thus, we have not permitted the government to assume that every expression of a provocative idea will incite a riot, but have instead required careful consideration of the actual circumstances surrounding such expression, asking whether the expression "is directed to inciting or producing imminent lawless action and is likely to incite or produce such action." *Brandenburg v. Ohio,* 395 U.S. 444, 447 (1969) (reviewing circumstances surrounding rally and speeches by Ku Klux Klan). To accept Texas' arguments that it need only demonstrate "the potential for a breach of the peace," Brief for Petitioner 37, and that every flag burning necessarily possesses that potential, would be to eviscerate our holding in Brandenburg. This we decline to do.

Nor does Johnson's expressive conduct fall within that small class of "fighting words" that are "likely to provoke the average person to retaliation, and thereby cause a breach of the peace." *Chaplinsky v. New Hampshire,* 315 U.S. 568, 574 (1942). No reasonable onlooker would have regarded Johnson's generalized expression of dissatisfaction with the policies of the Federal Government as a direct personal insult or an invitation to exchange fisticuffs. See *id.,* at 572-573; *Cantwell v. Connecticut,* 310 U.S. 296, 309 (1940); *FCC v. Pacifica Foundation, supra,* at 745 (opinion of Stevens, J.). [410]

We thus conclude that the State's interest in maintaining order is not implicated on these facts. The State need not worry that our holding will disable it from preserving the peace. We do not suggest that the First Amendment forbids a State to prevent "imminent lawless action." Brandenburg, *supra,* at 447. And, in fact, Texas already has a statute specifically prohibiting breaches of the peace, Tex. Penal Code Ann. § 42.01 (1989), which tends to confirm that Texas need not punish this flag desecration in order to keep the peace. See *Boos v. Barry,* 485 U.S., at 327-329.

B.

The State also asserts an interest in preserving the flag as a symbol of nationhood and national unity. In *Spence,* we acknowledged that the government's interest in preserving the flag's special symbolic value "is directly related to expression in the context of activity" such as affixing a peace symbol to a flag. 418 U.S., at 414, n. 8. We are equally persuaded that this interest is related to expression in the case of Johnson's burning of the flag. The State, apparently, is concerned that such conduct will lead people to believe either that the flag does not stand for nationhood and national unity, but instead reflects other, less positive concepts, or that the concepts reflected in the flag do not in fact exist, that is, that we do not enjoy unity as a Nation. These concerns blossom only when a person's treatment of the flag communicates some message, and thus are related "to the suppression of free expression" within the meaning of *O'Brien.* We are thus outside of *O'Brien's* test altogether.

IV.

It remains to consider whether the State's interest in preserving the flag as a symbol of nationhood and national unity justifies Johnson's conviction.

As in *Spence,* "[w]e are confronted with a case of prosecution for the expression of an idea through activity," and "[a]ccordingly, we must examine with particular care the interests [411] advanced by [petitioner] to support its prosecution." 418 U.S., at 411. Johnson was not, we add, prosecuted for the expression of just any idea; he was prosecuted for his expression of dissatisfaction with the policies of this country, expression situated at the core of our First Amendment values. See, e.g., *Boos v. Barry, supra,* at 318; *Frisby v. Schultz,* 487 U.S. 474, 479 (1988).

Moreover, Johnson was prosecuted because he knew that his politically charged expression would cause "serious offense." If he had burned the flag as a means of disposing of it because it was dirty or torn, he would not have been convicted of flag desecration under this Texas law: federal law designates burning as the preferred means of disposing of a flag "when it is in such condition that it is no longer a fitting emblem for display," 36 U. S. C. § 176(k), and Texas has no quarrel with this means of disposal. Brief for Petitioner 45. The Texas law is thus not aimed at protecting the physical integrity of the flag in all circumstances, but is designed instead to protect it only against impairments that would cause serious offense to others. [note 6] Texas concedes as much: "Section 42.09(b) reaches only those severe acts of physical abuse of the flag carried out in a way likely to be offensive. The statute mandates intentional or knowing abuse, that is, the kind of mistreatment that is not innocent, but rather is intentionally designed to seriously offend other individuals." *Id.,* at 44.

28

Whether Johnson's treatment of the flag violated Texas law thus depended on the likely communicative impact of his expressive conduct. [note 7] Our decision in *Boos v. Barry, supra,* [412] tells us that this restriction on Johnson's expression is content based. In Boos, we considered the constitutionality of a law prohibiting "the display of any sign within 500 feet of a foreign embassy if that sign tends to bring that foreign government into 'public odium' or 'public disrepute.'" *Id.,* at 315. Rejecting the argument that the law was content neutral because it was justified by "our international law obligation to shield diplomats from speech that offends their dignity," *id.,* at 320, we held that "[t]he emotive impact of speech on its audience is not a 'secondary effect'" unrelated to the content of the expression itself. *Id.,* at 321 (plurality opinion); see also *id.,* at 334 (Brennan, J., concurring in part and concurring in judgment).

According to the principles announced in Boos, Johnson's political expression was restricted because of the content of the message he conveyed. We must therefore subject the State's asserted interest in preserving the special symbolic character of the flag to "the most exacting scrutiny." *Boos v. Barry, supra,* at 321. [note 8] [413]

Texas argues that its interest in preserving the flag as a symbol of nationhood and national unity survives this close analysis. Quoting extensively from the writings of this Court chronicling the flag's historic and symbolic role in our society, the State emphasizes the "'special place'" reserved for the flag in our Nation. Brief for Petitioner 22, quoting *Smith v. Goguen,* 415 U.S., at 601 (Rehnquist, J., dissenting). The State's argument is not that it has an interest simply in maintaining the flag as a symbol of something, no matter what it symbolizes; indeed, if that were the State's position, it would be difficult to see how that interest is endangered by highly symbolic conduct such as Johnson's. Rather, the State's claim is that it has an interest in preserving the flag as a symbol of *nationhood* and *national unity,* a symbol with a determinate range of meanings. Brief for Petitioner 20-24. According to Texas, if one physically treats the flag in a way that would tend to cast doubt on either the idea that nationhood and national unity are the flag's referents or that national unity actually exists, the message conveyed thereby is a harmful one and therefore may be prohibited. [note 9] [414]

If there is a bedrock principle underlying the First Amendment, it is that the government may not prohibit the expression of an idea simply because society finds the idea itself offensive or disagreeable. See, e.g., *Hustler Magazine, Inc. v. Falwell,* 485 U.S., at 55-56; *City Council of Los Angeles v. Taxpayers for Vincent,* 466 U.S. 789, 804 (1984); *Bolger v. Youngs Drug Products Corp.,* 463 U.S. 60, 65, 72 (1983); *Carey v. Brown,* 447 U.S. 455, 462-463 (1980); *FCC v. Pacifica Foundation,* 438 U.S., at 745-746; *Young v. American Mini Theatres, Inc.,* 427 U.S. 50, 63-65, 67-68 (1976) (plurality opinion); *Buckley v. Valeo,* 424 U.S. 1, 16-17 (1976); *Grayned v. Rockford,* 408 U.S. 104, 115 (1972); *Police Dept. of Chicago v. Mosley,* 408 U.S. 92, 95 (1972); *Bachellar v. Maryland,* 397 U.S. 564, 567 (1970); *O'Brien,* 391 U.S., at 382; *Brown v. Louisiana,* 383 U.S., at 142-143; *Stromberg v. California,* 283 U.S., at 368-369.

We have not recognized an exception to this principle even where our flag has been involved. In *Street v. New York,* 394 U.S. 576 (1969), we held that a State may not criminally punish a person for uttering words critical of the flag. Rejecting the argument that the conviction could be sustained on the ground that Street had "failed to show the respect for our national symbol which may properly be demanded of every citizen," we concluded that "the constitutionally guaranteed 'freedom to be intellectually . . . diverse or even contrary,' and the 'right to differ as to things that touch the heart of the existing order,' encompass the freedom to express publicly one's opinions about our flag, including those opinions which are defiant or contemptuous." *Id.,* at 593, quoting *Barnette,* 319 U.S., at 642. Nor may the government, we have held, compel conduct that would evince respect for the flag. "To sustain the compulsory flag salute we are required to say that a Bill of Rights which guards the individual's right to speak his own mind, left it open to public authorities to compel him to utter what is not in his mind." *Id.,* at 634. [415]

In holding in *Barnette* that the Constitution did not leave this course open to the government, Justice Jackson described one of our society's defining principles in words deserving of their frequent repetition: "If there is any fixed star in our constitutional constellation, it is that no official, high or petty, can prescribe what shall be orthodox in politics, nationalism, religion, or other matters of opinion or force citizens to confess by word or act their faith therein." *Id.,* at 642. In *Spence,* we held that the same interest asserted by Texas here was insufficient to support a criminal conviction under a flag-misuse statute for the taping of a peace sign to an American flag. "Given the protected character of [Spence's] expression and in light of the fact that no interest the State may have in preserving the physical integrity of a privately owned flag was significantly impaired on these facts," we held, "the conviction must be invalidated." 418 U.S., at 415. See also *Goguen, supra,* at 588 (White, J., concurring in judgment) (to convict person who had sewn a flag onto the seat of his pants for "contemptuous" treatment of the flag would be "[t]o convict not to protect the physical integrity or to protect against acts interfering with the proper use of the flag, but to punish for communicating ideas unacceptable to the controlling majority in the legislature").

In short, nothing in our precedents suggests that a State may foster its own view of the flag by prohibiting expressive conduct relating to it. [note 10] To bring its argument outside our [416] precedents, Texas attempts to convince us that even if its interest in preserving the flag's symbolic role does not allow it to prohibit words or some expressive conduct critical of the flag, it does permit it to forbid the outright destruction of the flag. The State's argument cannot depend here on the distinction between written or spoken words and nonverbal conduct. That distinction, we have shown, is of no moment where the nonverbal conduct is expressive, as it is here, and where the regulation of that conduct is related to expression, as it is here. See *supra,* at 402-403. In addition, both *Barnette* and *Spence* involved expressive conduct, not only verbal communication, and both found that conduct protected.

Texas' focus on the precise nature of Johnson's expression, moreover, misses the point of our prior decisions: their enduring lesson, that the government may not prohibit expression simply because it disagrees with its message, is not dependent on the particular mode in which one chooses to express an idea. [note 11] If we were to hold that a State may forbid flag burning wherever it is likely to endanger the flag's symbolic role, but allow it wherever burning a flag promotes that role--as where, for example, a person ceremoniously burns a dirty flag--we would be saying that when it comes to impairing the flag's physical integrity, the flag itself may be used as [417] a symbol--as a substitute for the written or spoken word or a "short cut from mind to mind"--only in one direction. We would be permitting a State to "prescribe what shall be orthodox" by saying that one may burn the flag to convey one's attitude toward it and its referents only if one does not endanger the flag's representation of nationhood and national unity.

We never before have held that the Government may ensure that a symbol be used to express only one view of that symbol or its referents. Indeed, in *Schacht v. United States,* we invalidated a federal statute permitting an actor portraying a member of one of our Armed Forces to "'wear the uniform of that armed force if the portrayal does not tend to discredit that armed force.'" 398 U.S., at 60, quoting 10 U. S. C. § 772(f). This proviso, we held, "which leaves Americans free to praise the war in Vietnam but can send persons like Schacht to prison for opposing it, cannot survive in a country which has the First Amendment." *Id.,* at 63.

We perceive no basis on which to hold that the principle underlying our decision in *Schacht* does not apply to this case. To conclude that the government may permit designated symbols to be used to communicate only a limited set of messages would be to enter territory having no discernible or defensible boundaries. Could the government, on this theory, prohibit the burning of state flags? Of copies of the Presidential seal? Of the Constitution? In evaluating these choices under the First Amendment, how would we decide which symbols were sufficiently special to warrant this unique status? To do so, we would be forced to consult our own political preferences, and impose them on the citizenry, in the very way that the First Amendment forbids us to do. See *Carey v. Brown,* 447 U.S., at 466-467.

There is, moreover, no indication--either in the text of the Constitution or in our cases interpreting it--that a separate juridical category exists for the American flag alone. Indeed, we would not be surprised to learn that the persons [418] who framed our Constitution and wrote the Amendment that we now construe were not known for their reverence for the Union Jack. The First Amendment does not guarantee that other concepts virtually sacred to our Nation as a whole--such as the principle that discrimination on the basis of race is odious and destructive-- will go unquestioned in the market-place of ideas. See *Brandenburg v. Ohio,* 395 U.S. 444 (1969). We decline, therefore, to create for the flag an exception to the joust of principles protected by the First Amendment.

It is not the State's ends, but its means, to which we object. It cannot be gainsaid that there is a special place reserved for the flag in this Nation, and thus we do not doubt that the government has a legitimate interest in making efforts to "preserv[e] the national flag as an unalloyed symbol of our country." *Spence,* 418 U.S., at 412. We reject the suggestion, urged at oral argument by counsel for Johnson, that the government lacks "any state interest whatsoever" in regulating the manner in which the flag may be displayed. Tr. of Oral Arg. 38. Congress has, for example, enacted precatory regulations describing the proper treatment of the flag, see 36 U. S. C. §§ 173-177, and we cast no doubt on the legitimacy of its interest in making such recommendations. To say that the government has an interest in encouraging proper treatment of the flag, however, is not to say that it may criminally punish a person for burning a flag as a means of political protest. "National unity as an end which officials may foster by persuasion and example is not in question. The problem is whether under our Constitution compulsion as here employed is a permissible means for its achievement." *Barnette,* 319 U.S., at 640.

We are fortified in today's conclusion by our conviction that forbidding criminal punishment for conduct such as Johnson's will not endanger the special role played by our flag or the feelings it inspires. To paraphrase Justice Holmes, we submit that nobody can suppose that this one gesture of an unknown [419] man will change our Nation's attitude towards its flag. See *Abrams v. United States,* 250 U.S. 616, 628 (1919) (Holmes, J., dissenting). Indeed, Texas' argument that the burning of an American flag "'is an act having a high likelihood to cause a breach of the peace,'" Brief for Petitioner 31, quoting *Sutherland v. DeWulf,* 323 F. Supp. 740, 745 (SD Ill. 1971) (citation omitted), and its statute's implicit assumption that physical mistreatment of the flag will lead to "serious offense," tend to confirm that the flag's special role is not in danger; if it were, no one would riot or take offense because a flag had been burned.

We are tempted to say, in fact, that the flag's deservedly cherished place in our community will be strengthened, not weakened, by our holding today. Our decision is a reaffirmation of the principles of freedom and inclusiveness that the flag best reflects, and of the conviction that our toleration of criticism such as Johnson's is a sign and source of our strength. Indeed, one of the proudest images of our flag, the one immortalized in our own national anthem, is of the bombardment it survived at Fort McHenry. It is the Nation's resilience, not its rigidity, that Texas sees reflected in the flag--and it is that resilience that we reassert today.

The way to preserve the flag's special role is not to punish those who feel differently about these matters. It is to persuade them that they are wrong. "To courageous, self-reliant men, with confidence in the power of free and fearless reasoning applied through the processes of popular government, no danger flowing from speech can be deemed clear and present, unless the incidence of the evil apprehended is so imminent that it may befall before there is opportunity for full discussion. If there be time to expose through discussion the falsehood and fallacies, to avert the evil by the processes of education, the remedy to be applied is more speech, not enforced silence." *Whitney v. California,* 274 U.S. 357, 377 (1927) (Brandeis, J., concurring). And, precisely because it is our flag that is involved, one's response to the flag [420] burner may exploit the uniquely persuasive power of the flag itself. We can imagine no more appropriate response to burning a flag than waving one's own, no better way to counter a flag burner's message than by saluting the flag that burns, no surer means of preserving the dignity even of the flag that burned than by--as one witness here did--according its remains a respectful burial. We do not consecrate the flag by punishing its desecration, for in doing so we dilute the freedom that this cherished emblem represents.

V.

Johnson was convicted for engaging in expressive conduct. The State's interest in preventing breaches of the peace does not support his conviction because Johnson's conduct did not threaten to disturb the peace. Nor does the State's interest in preserving the flag as a symbol of nationhood and national unity justify his criminal conviction for engaging in political expression. The judgment of the Texas Court of Criminal Appeals is therefore

AFFIRMED.

JUSTICE KENNEDY, concurring.

I write not to qualify the words Justice Brennan chooses so well, for he says with power all that is necessary to explain our ruling. I join his opinion without reservation, but with a keen sense that this case, like others before us from time to time, exacts its personal toll. This prompts me to add to our pages these few remarks.

The case before us illustrates better than most that the judicial power is often difficult in its exercise. We cannot here ask another Branch to share responsibility, as when the argument is made that a statute is flawed or incomplete. For we are presented with a clear and simple statute to be judged against a pure command of the Constitution. The outcome can be laid at no door but ours.

The hard fact is that sometimes we must make decisions we do not like. We make them because they are right, right [421] in the sense that the law and the Constitution, as we see them, compel the result. And so great is our commitment to the process that, except in the rare case, we do not pause to express distaste for the result, perhaps for fear of undermining a valued principle that dictates the decision. This is one of those rare cases.

Our colleagues in dissent advance powerful arguments why respondent may be convicted for his expression, reminding us that among those who will be dismayed by our holding will be some who have had the singular honor of carrying the flag in battle. And I agree that the flag holds a lonely place of honor in an age when absolutes are distrusted and simple truths are burdened by unneeded apologetics.

With all respect to those views, I do not believe the Constitution gives us the right to rule as the dissenting Members of the Court urge, however painful this judgment is to announce. Though symbols often are what we ourselves make of them, the flag is constant in expressing beliefs Americans share, beliefs in law and peace and that freedom which sustains the human spirit. The case here today forces recognition of the costs to which those beliefs commit us. It is poignant but fundamental that the flag protects those who hold it in contempt.

For all the record shows, this respondent was not a philosopher and perhaps did not even possess the ability to comprehend how repellent his statements must be to the Republic itself. But whether or not he could appreciate the enormity of the offense he gave, the fact remains that his acts were speech, in both the technical and the fundamental meaning of the Constitution. So I agree with the Court that he must go free.

CHIEF JUSTICE REHNQUIST, with whom JUSTICE WHITE and JUSTICE O'CONNOR join, dissenting.

In holding this Texas statute unconstitutional, the Court ignores Justice Holmes' familiar aphorism that "a page of history is worth a volume of logic." *New York Trust Co. v.* [422] *Eisner,* 256 U.S. 345, 349 (1921). For more than 200 years, the American flag has occupied a unique position as the symbol of our Nation, a uniqueness that justifies a governmental prohibition against flag burning in the way respondent Johnson did here.

At the time of the American Revolution, the flag served to unify the Thirteen Colonies at home, while obtaining recognition of national sovereignty abroad. Ralph Waldo Emerson's "Concord Hymn" describes the first skirmishes of the Revolutionary War in these lines:

"By the rude bridge that arched the flood
Their flag to April's breeze unfurled,
Here once the embattled farmers stood
And fired the shot heard round the world."

During that time, there were many colonial and regimental flags, adorned with such symbols as pine trees, beavers, anchors, and rattlesnakes, bearing slogans such as "Liberty or Death," "Hope," "An Appeal to Heaven," and "Don't Tread on Me." The first distinctive flag of the Colonies was the "Grand Union Flag"--with 13 stripes and a British flag in the left corner--which was flown for the first time on January 2, 1776, by troops of the Continental Army around Boston. By June 14, 1777, after we declared our independence from England, the Continental Congress resolved:

"That the flag of the thirteen United States be thirteen stripes, alternate red and white: that the union be thirteen stars, white in a blue field, representing a new constellation." 8 Journal of the Continental Congress 1774-1789, p. 464 (W. Ford ed. 1907).

One immediate result of the flag's adoption was that American vessels harassing British shipping sailed under an authorized national flag. Without such a flag, the British could treat captured seamen as pirates and hang them summarily; with a national flag, such seamen were treated as prisoners of war. [423]

During the War of 1812, British naval forces sailed up Chesapeake Bay and marched overland to sack and burn the city of Washington. They then sailed up the Patapsco River to invest the city of Baltimore, but to do so it was first necessary to reduce Fort McHenry in Baltimore Harbor. Francis Scott Key, a Washington lawyer, had been granted permission by the British to board one of their warships to negotiate the release of an American who had been taken prisoner. That night, waiting anxiously on the British ship, Key watched the British fleet firing on Fort McHenry. Finally, at daybreak, he saw the fort's American flag still flying; the British attack had failed. Intensely moved, he began to scribble on the back of an envelope the poem that became our national anthem:

"O say can you see by the dawn's early light
What so proudly we hail'd at the twilight's last gleaming,
Whose broad stripes & bright stars through the perilous fight
O'er the ramparts we watch'd, were so gallantly streaming?
And the rocket's red glare, the bomb bursting in air,
Gave proof through the night that our flag was still there,
O say does that star-spangled banner yet wave
O'er the land of the free & the home of the brave?"

The American flag played a central role in our Nation's most tragic conflict, when the North fought against the South. The lowering of the American flag at Fort Sumter was viewed as the start of the war. G. Preble, History of the Flag of the United States of America 453 (1880). The Southern States, to formalize their separation from the Union, adopted the "Stars and Bars" of the Confederacy. The Union troops marched to the sound of "Yes We'll Rally Round The Flag

Boys, We'll Rally Once Again." President Abraham Lincoln refused proposals to remove from the [424] American flag the stars representing the rebel States, because he considered the conflict not a war between two nations but an attack by 11 States against the National Government. *Id.,* at 411. By war's end, the American flag again flew over "an indestructible union, composed of indestructible states." *Texas v. White,* 7 Wall.
700, 725 (1869).

One of the great stories of the Civil War is told in John Greenleaf Whittier's poem, "Barbara Frietchie":

 ## Barbara Frietchie

"Up from the meadows rich with corn,
Clear in the cool September morn,

The clustered spires of Frederick stand
Green-walled by the hills of Maryland.

Round about them orchards sweep,
Apple- and peach-tree fruited deep,

Fair as a garden of the Lord
To the eyes of the famished rebel horde,

On that pleasant morn of the early fall
When Lee marched over the mountain wall;

Over the mountains winding down,
Horse and foot, into Frederick town.

Forty flags with their silver stars,
Forty flags with their crimson bars,

Flapped in the morning wind: the sun
Of noon looked down, and saw not one.

Up rose old Barbara Frietchie then,
Bowed with her fourscore years and ten;

Bravest of all in Frederick town,
She took up the flag the men hauled down;

In her attic-window the staff she set,
To show that one heart was loyal yet.

Up the street came the rebel tread,
Stonewall Jackson riding ahead.

Under his slouched hat left and right
He glanced: the old flag met his sight.

'Halt!'--the dust-brown ranks stood fast.
'Fire!'--out blazed the rifle-blast.

It shivered the window, pane and sash;
It rent the banner with seam and gash.

Quick, as it fell, from the broken staff
Dame Barbara snatched the silken scarf.

She leaned far out on the window-sill,
And shook it forth with a royal will.

'Shoot, if you must, this old gray head,
But spare your country's flag,' she said.

A shade of sadness, a blush of shame,
Over the face of the leader came;

The nobler nature within him stirred
To life at that woman's deed and word;

'Who touches a hair of yon gray head
Dies like a dog! March on!' he said.

All day long through Frederick street
Sounded the tread of marching feet:

All day long that free flag tost
Over the heads of the rebel host.

Ever its torn folds rose and fell
On the loyal winds that loved it well;

And through the hill-gaps sunset light
Shone over it with a warm good-night.

Barbara Frietchie's work is o'er,
And the Rebel rides on his raids no more.

Honor to her! and let a tear
Fall, for her sake, on Stonewall's bier.

Over Barbara Frietchie's grave,
Flag of Freedom and Union, wave!

Peace and order and beauty draw
Round thy symbol of light and law;

And ever the stars above look down
On thy stars below in Frederick town.

In the First and Second World Wars, thousands of our countrymen died on foreign soil fighting for the American cause. At Iwo Jima in the Second World War, United States Marines fought hand to hand against thousands of [426] Japanese. By the time the Marines reached the top of Mount Suribachi, they raised a piece of pipe upright and from one end fluttered a flag. That ascent had cost nearly 6,000 American lives. The Iwo Jima Memorial in Arlington National Cemetery memorializes that event. President Franklin Roosevelt authorized the use of the flag on labels, packages, cartons, and containers intended for export as lend-lease aid, in order to inform people in other countries of the United States' assistance. Presidential Proclamation No. 2605, 58 Stat. 1126.

During the Korean war, the successful amphibious landing of American troops at Inchon was marked by the raising of an American flag within an hour of the event. Impetus for the enactment of the Federal Flag Desecration Statute in 1967 came from the impact of flag burnings in the United States on troop morale in Vietnam. Representative L. Mendel Rivers, then Chairman of the House Armed Services Committee, testified that "[t]he burning of the flag . . . has caused my mail to increase 100 percent from the boys in Vietnam, writing me and asking me what is going on in America." Desecration of the Flag, Hearings on H. R. 271 before Subcommittee No. 4 of the House Committee on the Judiciary, 90th Cong., 1st Sess., 189 (1967). Representative Charles Wiggins stated: "The public act of desecration of our flag tends to undermine the morale of American troops. That this finding is true can be attested by many Members who have received correspondence from servicemen expressing their shock and disgust of such conduct." 113 Cong. Rec. 16459 (1967).

The flag symbolizes the Nation in peace as well as in war. It signifies our national presence on battleships, airplanes, military installations, and public buildings from the United States Capitol to the thousands of county courthouses and city halls throughout the country. Two flags are prominently placed in our courtroom. Countless flags are placed by the graves of loved ones each year on what was first called [427] Decoration Day, and is now called Memorial Day. The flag is traditionally placed on the casket of deceased members of the Armed Forces, and it is later given to the deceased's family. 10 U. S. C. §§ 1481, 1482. Congress has provided that the flag be flown at half-staff upon the death of the President, Vice President, and other government officials "as a mark of respect to their memory." 36 U. S. C. § 175(m). The flag identifies United States merchant ships, 22 U. S. C. § 454, and "[t]he laws of the Union protect our commerce wherever the flag of the country may float." *United States v. Guthrie,* 17 How. 284, 309 (1855).

No other American symbol has been as universally honored as the flag. In 1931, Congress declared "The Star-Spangled Banner" to be our national anthem. 36 U. S. C. § 170. In 1949, Congress declared June 14th to be Flag Day. § 157. In 1987, John Philip Sousa's "The Stars and Stripes Forever" was designated as the national march. Pub. L. 101-186, 101 Stat. 1286. Congress has also established "The Pledge of Allegiance to the Flag" and the manner of its deliverance. 36 U. S. C. § 172. The flag has appeared as the principal symbol on approximately 33 United States postal stamps and in the design of at least 43 more, more times than any other symbol. United States Postal Service, Definitive Mint Set 15 (1988).

Both Congress and the States have enacted numerous laws regulating misuse of the American flag. Until 1967, Congress left the regulation of misuse of the flag up to the States. Now, however, 18 U. S. C. § 700(a) provides that:

"Whoever knowingly casts contempt upon any flag of the United States by publicly mutilating, defacing, defiling, burning, or trampling upon it shall be fined not more than $1,000 or imprisoned for not more than one year, or both."

Congress has also prescribed, *inter alia,* detailed rules for the design of the flag, 4 U. S. C. § 1, the time and occasion of flag's display, 36 U. S. C. § 174, the position and manner of [428] its display, § 175, respect for the flag, § 176, and conduct during hoisting, lowering, and passing of the flag, § 177. With the exception of Alaska and Wyoming, all of the States now have statutes prohibiting the burning of the flag. [note 1] Most of the state statutes are patterned after the Uniform Flag Act of 1917, which in § 3 provides: "No person shall publicly mutilate, deface, defile, defy, trample upon, or by word or act cast contempt upon any such flag, standard, color, ensign or shield." Proceedings of National Conference of Commissioners on Uniform State Laws 323-324 (1917). Most were passed by the States at about the time of World War I. Rosenblatt, Flag Desecration Statutes: History and Analysis, 1972 Wash. U. L. Q. 193, 197. [429]

The American flag, then, throughout more than 200 years of our history, has come to be the visible symbol embodying our Nation. It does not represent the views of any particular political party, and it does not represent any particular political philosophy. The flag is not simply another "idea" or "point of view" competing for recognition in the marketplace of ideas. Millions and millions of Americans regard it with an almost mystical reverence regardless of what sort of social, political, or philosophical beliefs they may have. I cannot agree that the First Amendment invalidates the Act of Congress, and the laws of 48 of the 50 States, which make criminal the public burning of the flag.

More than 80 years ago in *Halter v. Nebraska,* 205 U.S. 34 (1907), this Court upheld the constitutionality of a Nebraska statute that forbade the use of representations of the American flag for advertising purposes upon articles of merchandise. The Court there said:

> "For that flag every true American has not simply an appreciation but a deep affection. . . . Hence, it has often occurred that insults to a flag have been the cause of war, and indignities put upon it, in the presence of those who revere it, have often been resented and sometimes punished on the spot." *Id.,* at 41.

Only two Terms ago, in *San Francisco Arts & Athletics, Inc. v. United States Olympic Committee,* 483 U.S. 522 (1987), the Court held that Congress could grant exclusive use of the word "Olympic" to the United States Olympic Committee. The Court thought that this "restrictio[n] on expressive speech properly [was] characterized as incidental to the primary congressional purpose of encouraging and rewarding the USOC's activities." *Id.,* at 536. As the Court stated, "when a word [or symbol] acquires value 'as the result of organization and the expenditure of labor, skill, and money' by an entity, that entity constitutionally may obtain a limited property right in the word [or symbol]." *Id.,* at 532, quoting *International News Service v. Associated Press,* 248 U.S. 215, 239 [430] (1918). Surely Congress or the States may recognize a similar interest in the flag.

But the Court insists that the Texas statute prohibiting the public burning of the American flag infringes on respondent Johnson's freedom of expression. Such freedom, of course, is not absolute. See *Schenck v. United States,* 249 U.S. 47 (1919). In *Chaplinsky v. New Hampshire,* 315 U.S. 568 (1942), a unanimous Court said:

> "Allowing the broadest scope to the language and purpose of the Fourteenth Amendment, it is well understood that the right of free speech is not absolute at all times and under all circumstances. There are certain well-defined and narrowly limited classes of speech, the prevention and punishment of which have never been thought to raise any Constitutional problem. These include the lewd and obscene, the profane, the libelous, and the insulting or 'fighting' words--those which by their very utterance inflict injury or tend to incite an immediate breach of the peace. It has been well observed that such utterances are no essential part of any exposition of ideas, and are of such slight social value as a step to truth that any benefit that may be derived from them is clearly outweighed by the social interest in order and morality." *Id.,* at 571-572 (footnotes omitted).

The Court upheld Chaplinsky's conviction under a state statute that made it unlawful to "address any offensive, derisive or annoying word to any person who is lawfully in any street or other public place." *Id.,* at 569. Chaplinsky had told a local marshal, """You are a God damned racketeer" and a "damned Fascist and the whole government of Rochester are Fascists or agents of Fascists.""" *Ibid.*

Here it may equally well be said that the public burning of the American flag by Johnson was no essential part of any exposition of ideas, and at the same time it had a tendency to incite a breach of the peace. Johnson was free to make any verbal denunciation of the flag that he wished; indeed, he was [431] free to burn the flag in private. He could publicly burn other symbols of the Government or effigies of political leaders. He did lead a march through the streets of Dallas, and conducted a rally in front of the Dallas City Hall. He engaged in a "die-in" to protest nuclear weapons. He shouted out various slogans during the march, including: "Reagan, Mondale which will it be? Either one means World War III"; "Ronald Reagan, killer of the hour, Perfect example of U. S. power"; and "red, white and blue, we spit on you, you stand for plunder, you will go under." Brief for Respondent 3. For none of these acts was he arrested or prosecuted; it was only when he proceeded to burn publicly an American flag stolen from its rightful owner that he violated the Texas statute.

The Court could not, and did not, say that Chaplinsky's utterances were not expressive phrases-- they clearly and succinctly conveyed an extremely low opinion of the addressee. The same may be said of Johnson's public burning of the flag in this case; it obviously did convey Johnson's bitter dislike of his country. But his act, like Chaplinsky's provocative words, conveyed nothing that could not have been conveyed and was not conveyed just as forcefully in a dozen different ways. As with "fighting words," so with flag burning, for purposes of the First Amendment: It is "no essential part of any exposition of ideas, and [is] of such slight social value as a step to truth that any benefit that may be derived from [it] is clearly outweighed" by the public interest in avoiding a probable breach of the peace. The highest courts of several States have upheld state statutes prohibiting the public burning of the flag on the grounds that it is so inherently inflammatory that it may cause a breach of public order. See, e.g., *State v. Royal,* 113 N. H. 224, 229, 305 A. 2d 676, 680 (1973); *State v. Waterman,* 190 N. W. 2d 809, 811-812 (Iowa 1971); see also *State v. Mitchell,* 32 Ohio App. 2d 16, 30, 288 N. E. 2d 216, 226 (1972). [432]

The result of the Texas statute is obviously to deny one in Johnson's frame of mind one of many means of "symbolic speech." Far from being a case of "one picture being worth a thousand words," flag burning is the equivalent of an inarticulate grunt or roar that, it seems fair to say, is most likely to be indulged in not to express any particular idea, but to antagonize others. Only five years ago we said in *City Council of Los Angeles v. Taxpayers for Vincent,* 466 U.S. 789, 812 (1984), that "the First Amendment does not guarantee the right to employ every conceivable method of communication at all times and in all places." The Texas statute deprived Johnson of only one rather inarticulate symbolic form of protest--a form of protest that was profoundly offensive to many--and left him with a full panoply of other symbols and every conceivable form of verbal expression to express his deep disapproval of national policy. Thus, in no way can it be said that Texas is punishing him because his hearers--or any other group of people--were profoundly opposed to the message that he sought to convey. Such opposition is no proper basis for restricting speech or expression under the First Amendment. It was Johnson's use of this particular symbol, and not the idea that he sought to convey by it or by his many other expressions, for which he was punished.

Our prior cases dealing with flag desecration statutes have left open the question that the Court resolves today. In *Street v. New York,* 394 U.S. 576, 579 (1969), the defendant burned a flag in the street, shouting "We don't need no damned flag" and "[i]f they let that happen to Meredith we don't need an American flag." The Court ruled that since the defendant might have been convicted solely on the basis of his words, the conviction could not stand, but it expressly reserved the question whether a defendant could constitutionally be convicted for burning the flag. *Id.,* at 581.

Chief Justice Warren, in dissent, stated: "I believe that the States and Federal Government do have the power to protect the flag from acts of desecration and disgrace. . . . [I]t is difficult [433] for me to imagine that, had the Court faced this issue, it would have concluded otherwise." *Id.,* at 605. Justices Black and Fortas also expressed their personal view that a prohibition on flag burning did not violate the Constitution. See *id.,* at 610 (Black, J., dissenting) ("It passes my belief that anything in the Federal Constitution bars a State from making the deliberate burning of the American Flag an offense"); *id.,* at 615-617 (Fortas, J., dissenting) ("[T]he States and the Federal Government have the power to protect the flag from acts of desecration committed in public. . . . [T]he flag is a special kind of personality. Its use is traditionally and universally subject to special rules and regulation. . . . A person may 'own' a flag, but ownership is subject to special burdens and responsibilities. A flag may be property, in a sense; but it is property burdened with peculiar obligations and restrictions. Certainly . . . these special conditions are not per se arbitrary or beyond governmental power under our Constitution").

In *Spence v. Washington,* 418 U.S. 405 (1974), the Court reversed the conviction of a college student who displayed the flag with a peace symbol affixed to it by means of removable black tape from the window of his apartment. Unlike the instant case, there was no risk of a breach of the peace, no one other than the arresting officers saw the flag, and the defendant owned the flag in question. The Court concluded that the student's conduct was protected under the First Amendment, because "no interest the State may have in preserving the physical integrity of a privately owned flag was significantly impaired on these facts." *Id.,* at 415. The Court was careful to note, however, that the defendant "was not charged under the desecration statute, nor did he permanently disfigure the flag or destroy it." *Ibid.*

In another related case, *Smith v. Goguen,* 415 U.S. 566 (1974), the appellee, who wore a small flag on the seat of his trousers, was convicted under a Massachusetts flag-misuse statute that subjected to criminal liability anyone who [434] "publicly . . . treats contemptuously the flag of the United States." *Id.,* at 568-569. The Court affirmed the lower court's reversal of appellee's conviction, because the phrase "treats contemptuously" was unconstitutionally broad and vague. *Id.,* at 576. The Court was again careful to point out that "[c]ertainly nothing prevents a legislature from defining with substantial specificity what constitutes forbidden treatment of United States flags." *Id.,* at 581-582. See also *id.,* at 587 (White, J., concurring in judgment) ("The flag is a national property, and the Nation may regulate those who would make, imitate, sell, possess, or use it. I would not question those statutes which proscribe mutilation, defacement, or burning of the flag or which otherwise protect its physical integrity, without regard to whether such conduct might provoke violence. . . . There would seem to be little question about the power of Congress to forbid the mutilation of the Lincoln Memorial. . . . The flag is itself a monument, subject to similar protection"); *id.,* at 591 (Blackmun, J., dissenting) ("Goguen's punishment was constitutionally permissible for harming the physical integrity of the flag by wearing it affixed to the seat of his pants").

But the Court today will have none of this. The uniquely deep awe and respect for our flag felt by virtually all of us are bundled off under the rubric of "designated symbols," *ante,* at 417, that the First Amendment prohibits the government from "establishing." But the government has not "established" this feeling; 200 years of history have done that. The government is simply recognizing as a fact the profound regard for the American flag created by that history when it enacts statutes prohibiting the disrespectful public burning of the flag.

The Court concludes its opinion with a regrettably patronizing civics lecture, presumably addressed to the Members of both Houses of Congress, the members of the 48 state legislatures that enacted prohibitions against flag burning, and the troops fighting under that flag in Vietnam who objected to its [435] being burned: "The way to preserve the flag's special role is not to punish those who feel differently about these matters. It is to persuade them that they are wrong." *Ante,* at 419. The Court's role as the final expositor of the Constitution is well established, but its role as a Platonic guardian admonishing those responsible to public opinion as if they were truant schoolchildren has no similar place in our system of government. The cry of "no taxation without representation" animated those who revolted against the English Crown to found our Nation--the idea that those who submitted to government should have some say as to what kind of laws would be passed. Surely one of the high purposes of a democratic society is to legislate against conduct that is regarded as evil and profoundly offensive to the majority of people--whether it be murder, embezzlement, pollution, or flag burning.

Our Constitution wisely places limits on powers of legislative majorities to act, but the declaration of such limits by this Court "is, at all times, a question of much delicacy, which ought seldom, if ever, to be decided in the affirmative, in a doubtful case." *Fletcher v. Peck,* 6 Cranch 87, 128 (1810) (Marshall, C. J.). Uncritical extension of constitutional protection to the burning of the flag risks the frustration of the very purpose for which organized governments are instituted. The Court decides that the American flag is just another symbol, about which not only must opinions pro and con be tolerated, but for which the most minimal public respect may not be enjoined. The government may conscript men into the Armed Forces where they must fight and perhaps die for the flag, but the government may not prohibit the public burning of the banner under which they fight. I would uphold the Texas statute as applied in this case. [note 2] [436]

JUSTICE STEVENS, dissenting.

As the Court analyzes this case, it presents the question whether the State of Texas, or indeed the Federal Government, has the power to prohibit the public desecration of the American flag. The question is unique. In my judgment rules that apply to a host of other symbols, such as state flags, armbands, or various privately promoted emblems of political or commercial identity, are not necessarily controlling. Even if flag burning could be considered just another species of symbolic speech under the logical application of the rules that the Court has developed in its interpretation of the First Amendment in other contexts, this case has an intangible dimension that makes those rules inapplicable.

A country's flag is a symbol of more than "nationhood and national unity." *Ante,* at 407, 410, 413, and n. 9, 417, 420. It also signifies the ideas that characterize the society that has chosen that emblem as well as the special history that has animated the growth and power of those ideas. The fleurs-de-lis and the tricolor both symbolized "nationhood and national unity," but they had vastly different meanings. The message conveyed by some flags--the swastika, for example-- may survive long after it has outlived its usefulness as a symbol of regimented unity in a particular nation. [437]

So it is with the American flag. It is more than a proud symbol of the courage, the determination, and the gifts of nature that transformed 13 fledgling Colonies into a world power. It is a symbol of freedom, of equal opportunity, of religious tolerance, and of good will for other peoples who share our aspirations. The symbol carries its message to dissidents both at home and abroad who may have no interest at all in our national unity or survival.

The value of the flag as a symbol cannot be measured. Even so, I have no doubt that the interest in preserving that value for the future is both significant and legitimate. Conceivably that value will be enhanced by the Court's conclusion that our national commitment to free expression is so strong that even the United States as ultimate guarantor of that freedom is without power to prohibit the desecration of its unique symbol. But I am unpersuaded. The creation of a federal right to post bulletin boards and graffiti on the Washington Monument might enlarge the market for free expression, but at a cost I would not pay. Similarly, in my considered judgment, sanctioning the public desecration of the flag will tarnish its value--both for those who cherish the ideas for which it waves and for those who desire to don the robes of martyrdom by burning it. That tarnish is not justified by the trivial burden on free expression occasioned by requiring that an available, alternative mode of expression--including uttering words critical of the flag, see *Street v. New York,* 394 U.S. 576 (1969)--be employed.

It is appropriate to emphasize certain propositions that are not implicated by this case. The statutory prohibition of flag desecration does not "prescribe what shall be orthodox in politics, nationalism, religion, or other matters of opinion or force citizens to confess by word or act their faith therein." *West Virginia Board of Education v. Barnette,* 319 U.S. 624, 642 (1943). The statute does not compel any conduct or any profession of respect for any idea or any symbol[438]

41

Nor does the statute violate "the government's paramount obligation of neutrality in its regulation of protected communication." *Young v. American Mini Theatres, Inc.,* 427 U.S. 50, 70 (1976) (plurality opinion). The content of respondent's message has no relevance whatsoever to the case. The concept of "desecration" does not turn on the substance of the message the actor intends to convey, but rather on whether those who view the act will take serious offense. Accordingly, one intending to convey a message of respect for the flag by burning it in a public square might nonetheless be guilty of desecration if he knows that others--perhaps simply because they misperceive the intended message--will be seriously offended. Indeed, even if the actor knows that all possible witnesses will understand that he intends to send a message of respect, he might still be guilty of desecration if he also knows that this understanding does not lessen the offense taken by some of those witnesses. Thus, this is not a case in which the fact that "it is the speaker's opinion that gives offense" provides a special "reason for according it constitutional protection," *FCC v. Pacifica Foundation,* 438 U.S. 726, 745 (1978) (plurality opinion). The case has nothing to do with "disagreeable ideas," see *ante,* at 409. It involves disagreeable conduct that, in my opinion, diminishes the value of an important national asset.

The Court is therefore quite wrong in blandly asserting that respondent "was prosecuted for his expression of dissatisfaction with the policies of this country, expression situated at the core of our First Amendment values." *Ante,* at 411. Respondent was prosecuted because of the method he chose to express his dissatisfaction with those policies. Had he chosen to spray-paint--or perhaps convey with a motion picture projector--his message of dissatisfaction on the facade of the Lincoln Memorial, there would be no question about the power of the Government to prohibit his means of expression. The prohibition would be supported by the legitimate interest in preserving the quality of an important [439] national asset. Though the asset at stake in this case is intangible, given its unique value, the same interest supports a prohibition on the desecration of the American flag. [note *]

The ideas of liberty and equality have been an irresistible force in motivating leaders like Patrick Henry, Susan B. Anthony, and Abraham Lincoln, schoolteachers like Nathan Hale and Booker T. Washington, the Philippine Scouts who fought at Bataan, and the soldiers who scaled the bluff at Omaha Beach. If those ideas are worth fighting for--and our history demonstrates that they are-- it cannot be true that the flag that uniquely symbolizes their power is not itself worthy of protection from unnecessary desecration.

I respectfully dissent.

United States v. Eichman, 496 U.S. 310 (1990)

SUPREME COURT OF THE UNITED STATES

496 U.S. 310

1990

Syllabus

✚ After this Court held, in *Texas v. Johnson,* 491 U.S. 397, that a Texas statute criminalizing desecration of the United States flag in a way that the actor knew would seriously offend onlookers was unconstitutional as applied to an individual who had burned a flag during a political protest, Congress passed the Flag Protection Act of 1989. The Act criminalizes the conduct of anyone who "knowingly mutilates, defaces, physically defiles, burns, maintains on the floor or ground, or tramples upon" a United States flag, except conduct related to the disposal of a "worn or soiled" flag. Subsequently, appellees were prosecuted in the District Courts for violating the Act: some for knowingly burning several flags while protesting various aspects of the Government's policies and others, in a separate incident, for knowingly burning a flag while protesting the Act's passage. In each case, appellees moved to dismiss the charges on the ground that the Act violates the First Amendment. Both District Courts, following *Johnson, supra,* held the Act unconstitutional as applied, and dismissed the charges.

✚ *Held:* Appellees' prosecution for burning a flag in violation of the Act is inconsistent with the First Amendment. The Government concedes, as it must, that appellees' flag-burning constituted expressive conduct, and this Court declines to reconsider its rejection in *Johnson* of the claim that flag-burning as a mode of expression does not enjoy the First Amendment's full protection. It is true that this Act, unlike the Texas law, contains no explicit content-based limitation on the scope of prohibited conduct. Nevertheless, it is clear that the Government's asserted interest in protecting the "physical integrity" of a privately owned flag in order to preserve the flag's status as a symbol of the Nation and certain national ideals is related to the suppression, and concerned with the content, of free expression. The mere destruction or disfigurement of a symbol's physical manifestation does not diminish or otherwise affect the symbol itself. The Government's interest is implicated only when a person's treatment of the flag communicates a message to others that is inconsistent with the identified ideals. The precise language of the Act's [p*311] prohibitions confirms Congress' interest in the communicative impact of flag destruction, since each of the specified terms -- with the possible exception of "burns" -- unmistakably connotes disrespectful treatment of the flag and suggests a focus on those acts likely to damage the flag's symbolic value, and since the explicit exemption for disposal of "worn or soiled" flags protects certain acts traditionally associated with patriotic respect for the flag. Thus, the Act suffers from the same fundamental flaw as the Texas law, and its restriction on expression cannot "'be justified without reference to the content of the regulated speech,'" *Boos v. Barry,* 485 U.S. 312 ,

320 . It must therefore be subjected to "the most exacting scrutiny," *id.* at 321 , and, for the reasons stated in *Johnson, supra,* at 413-415, the Government's interest cannot justify its infringement on First Amendment rights. This conclusion will not be reassessed in light of Congress' recent recognition of a purported "national consensus" favoring a prohibition on flag-burning, since any suggestion that the Government's interest in suppressing speech becomes more weighty as popular opposition to that speech grows is foreign to the First Amendment. While flag desecration -- like virulent ethnic and religious epithets, vulgar repudiations of the draft, and scurrilous caricatures -- is deeply offensive to many, the Government may not prohibit the expression of an idea simply because society finds the idea itself offensive or disagreeable. Pp. 313-319 .

No. 89-1433, 731 F.Supp. 1123 (DDC 1990); No. 89-1434, 731 F.Supp. 415, AFFIRMED.

BRENNAN, J., delivered the opinion of the Court, in which MARSHALL, BLACKMUN, SCALIA, and KENNEDY, JJ., joined. STEVENS, J., filed a dissenting opinion, in which REHNQUIST, C.J., and WHITE and O'CONNOR, JJ., joined, *post,* p. 319 . [p*312]

BRENNAN, J., Opinion of the Court

Justice BRENNAN delivered the opinion of the Court.

✚ In these consolidated appeals, we consider whether appellees' prosecution for burning a United States flag in violation of the Flag Protection Act of 1989 is consistent with the First Amendment. Applying our recent decision in *Texas v. Johnson,* 491 U.S. 397 (1989), the District Courts held that the Act cannot constitutionally be applied to appellees. We affirm.

I.

In No. 89-1433, the United States prosecuted certain appellees for violating the Flag Protection Act of 1989, 103 Stat. 777, 18 U.S.C.A. § 700 (Supp.1990), by knowingly setting fire to several United States flags on the steps of the United States Capitol while protesting various aspects of the Government's domestic and foreign policy. In No. 89-1434, the United States prosecuted other appellees for violating the Act by knowingly setting fire to a United States flag while protesting the Act's passage. In each case, the respective appellees moved to dismiss the flag-burning charge on the ground that the Act, both on its face and as applied, violates the First Amendment. Both the [p*313] United States District Court for the Western District of Washington, 731 F.Supp. 415 (1990), and the United States District Court for the District of Columbia, 731 F.Supp. 1123 (1990), following *Johnson, supra,* held the Act unconstitutional as applied to appellees and dismissed the charges. [n1] The United States appealed both decisions directly to this Court pursuant to 18 U.S.C.A. § 700(d) (Supp.1990). [n2] We noted probable jurisdiction and consolidated the two cases. 494 U.S. 1063 (1990).

II.

Last Term, in *Johnson,* we held that a Texas statute criminalizing the desecration of venerated objects, including the United States flag, was unconstitutional as applied to an individual who had set such a flag on fire during a political demonstration. The Texas statute provided that "[a] person commits an offense if he intentionally or knowingly desecrates . . . [a] national flag," where "desecrate" meant to "deface, damage, or otherwise physically mistreat in a way that the actor knows will seriously offend one or more persons likely to observe or discover his action." Tex. Penal Code Ann. § 42.09 (1989). We first held that Johnson's flag-burning was "conduct `sufficiently imbued with elements of communication' to implicate the First Amendment.'" 491 U.S. at 406 (citation omitted). We next considered and rejected the State's contention that, under *United States v. O'Brien,* [p*314] 391 U.S. 367 (1968), we ought to apply the deferential standard with which we have reviewed Government regulations of conduct containing both speech and non-speech elements where "the governmental interest is unrelated to the suppression of free expression." *Id.* at 377 . We reasoned that the State's asserted interest "in preserving the flag as a symbol of nationhood and national unity" was an interest "related `to the suppression of free expression' within the meaning of *O'Brien*" because the State's concern with protecting the flag's symbolic meaning is implicated "only when a person's treatment of the flag communicates some message." *Johnson, supra,* at 410 . We therefore subjected the statute to "`the most exacting scrutiny,'" *id.* at 412 , quoting *Boos v. Barry,* 485 U.S. 312 , 321 (1988), and we concluded that the State's asserted interests could not justify the infringement on the demonstrator's First Amendment rights.

After our decision in Johnson, Congress passed the Flag Protection Act of 1989. [n3] The Act provides in relevant part:

(a)   (1) Whoever knowingly mutilates, defaces, physically defiles, burns, maintains on the floor or ground, or tramples upon any flag of the United States shall be fined under this title or imprisoned for not more than one year, or both.

   (2) This subsection does not prohibit any conduct consisting of the disposal of a flag when it has become worn or soiled.

(b) As used in this section, the term "flag of the United States" means any flag of the United States, or any part thereof, made of any substance, of any size, in a form that is commonly displayed.

18 U.S.C.A. § 700 (1988 ed., Supp. I). [p*315]

The Government concedes in this case, as it must, that appellees' flag-burning constituted expressive conduct, Brief for United States 28; *see Johnson, supra,* at 405-406, but invites us to reconsider our rejection in *Johnson* of the claim that flag-burning as a mode of expression, like obscenity or "fighting words," does not enjoy the full protection of the First Amendment. *Cf. Chaplinsky v. New Hampshire,* 315 U.S. 568 , 572 (1942). This we decline to do. [n4] The only remaining question is whether the Flag Protection Act is sufficiently distinct from the Texas statute that it may constitutionally be applied to proscribe appellees' expressive conduct.

Proposed Constitutional Amendment
to Prohibit Flag Burning

A one-line change to the Constitution has been proposed - "The Congress shall have power to prohibit the physical desecration of the flag of the United States."

The Michael Christian Story

Condensed from a speech by Colonel Leo K. Thorsness, USAF (Retired) and a recipient of the Medal of Honor

You've probably seen the bumper sticker somewhere along the road. It depicts an American Flag, accompanied by the words "These colors don't run." I'm always glad to see this, because it reminds me of an incident from my confinement in North Vietnam at the Hao Lo POW Camp, or the Hanoi Hilton, as it became known. Then a major in the U.S. Air Force, I had been captured and imprisoned from 1967-73. Our treatment had been frequently brutal. After three years, however, the beatings and torture became less frequent.

During the last year, we were allowed outside most days for a couple of minutes to bathe. We showered by drawing water from a concrete tank with a homemade bucket. One day as we all stood by the tank stripped of our clothes, a young naval aviator named Mike Christian found the remnants of a handkerchief in a gutter that ran under the prison wall. Mike managed to sneak the grimy rag into our cell and began fashioning it into a flag.

Over time we all loaned him a little soap, and he spent days cleaning the material. We helped by scrounging and stealing bits and pieces of anything he could use. At night, under his mosquito netting, Mike worked on the flag. He made red and blue from ground roof tiles and tiny amounts of ink and painted the colors onto the cloth with watery rice glue. Using thread from his own blanket and a homemade bamboo needle, he sewed on stars.

Early in the morning a few days later, when the guards were not alert, he whispered loudly from the back of our cell, "Hey gang, look here." He proudly held up this tattered piece of cloth, waving it as if in a breeze. If you used your imagination, you could tell it was supposed to be an American Flag. When he raised that smudgy fabric, we automatically stood straight and saluted, our chests puffed out, and more than a few eyes had tears.

About once a week, the guards would strip us, run us outside and go through our clothing. During one of those shakedowns, they found Mike's flag. We all knew what would happen. That night they came for him.

Night interrogations were always the worst. They opened the cell door and pulled Mike out. We could hear the beginning of the torture before they even had him in the torture cell. They beat him most of the night.

About daylight they pushed what was left of him back through the cell door. He was badly broken; even his voice was gone. Within two weeks, despite the danger, Mike scrounged another piece of cloth and began another flag. The Stars and Stripes, our national symbol, was worth the sacrifice to him. Now whenever I see the flag, I think of Mike and the morning he first waved that tattered emblem of a nation. It was then, thousands of miles from home in a lonely prison cell, that he showed us what it is to be truly free.

Additional campaign co-sponsor comments on LCDR Christian

"It was three years (after he was shot down) before Charlotte received the first short, heavily censured letter. Our little grapevine got the good news which was spread to everyone immediately. Mike was at least alive. It was then our thoughts shifted to how he was being treated. We all cared a great deal for Mike; but part of his charm, and perhaps at times his Achilles heel, was his stubborn hardheadedness. We all knew he would be an SOB if he was caged. Unfortunately, our worst fears were realized as Mike became one of the most severely beaten prisoners over the longest period of time in the history of the United States Military."

- LCDR Clint D. Sadler, USN (ret) in Hall of Fame nominating letter by the Purdue classmate and friend of Michael Christian.

"His patriotism and resilience helped us keep alive our hope and our pride in difficult circumstances. I think of Mike often. We each have our own memories of him. One of my fondest recollections is stirred every time I hear our Pledge of Allegiance. For it was with Mike, standing before a tiny flag he had covertly made for us to pledge our allegiance to our country from a distant prison cell, that our love for America's blessings was so vividly reaffirmed."

- Senator John McCain (R-AZ) in a letter for the Michael Christian Purdue ROTC Hall of Fame induction ceremony.

Commentary on the Pledge of Allegiance
by Red Skelton

As a schoolboy, one of Red Skelton's teachers explained the words and meaning of the Pledge of Allegiance to his class. Skelton later wrote down, and eventually recorded, his recollection of this lecture. It is followed by his observation .

I - - Me; an individual; a committee of one.

Pledge - - Dedicate all of my worldly goods to give without self-pity.

Allegiance - - My love and my devotion.

To the Flag - - Our standard; *Old Glory* ; a symbol of Freedom; wherever she waves there is respect, because your loyalty has given her a dignity that shouts, Freedom is everybody's job.

United - - That means that we have all come together.

States - - Individual communities that have united into forty-eight great states. Forty-eight individual communities with pride and dignity and purpose. All divided with imaginary boundaries, yet united to a common purpose, and that is love for country.

And to the Republic - - Republic--a state in which sovereign power is invested in representatives chosen by the people to govern. And government is the people; and it's from the people to the leaders, not from the leaders to the people.

For which it stands

One Nation - - One Nation--meaning, so blessed by God.

Indivisible - - Incapable of being divided.

With Liberty - - Which is Freedom; the right of power to live one's own life, without threats, fear, or some sort of retaliation.

And Justice - - The principle, or qualities, of dealing fairly with others.

For All - - For All--which means, boys and girls, it's as much your country as it is mine. And now, boys and girls, let me hear you recite the Pledge of Allegiance:

I pledge allegiance to the Flag of the United States of America, and to the Republic, for which it stands; one nation, indivisible, with liberty and justice for all.

Since I was a small boy, two states have been added to our country, and two words have been added to the Pledge of Allegiance: **Under God**. Wouldn't it be a pity if someone said, "That is a prayer," and that would be eliminated from schools, too?

Patriot Day

A Proclamation from the President of the United States

By a joint resolution approved December 18, 2001 (Public Law 107-89), the Congress has authorized and requested the President to designate September 11 of each year as "Patriot Day."

NOW, THEREFORE, I, GEORGE W. BUSH, President of the United States of America, do hereby proclaim September 11, 2002, as Patriot Day. I call upon the people of the United States to observe this day with appropriate ceremonies and activities, including remembrance services and candlelight vigils. I also call upon the Governors of the United States and the Commonwealth of Puerto Rico, as well as appropriate officials of all units of government, to direct that the flag be flown at half-staff on Patriot Day. Further, I encourage all Americans to display the flag at half-staff from their homes on that day and to observe a moment of silence beginning at 8:46 a.m. eastern daylight time, or another appropriate commemorative time, to honor the innocent victims who lost their lives as a result of the terrorist attacks of September 11, 2001.

IN WITNESS WHEREOF, I have hereunto set my hand this fourth day of September, in the year of our Lord two thousand two, and of the Independence of the United States of America the two hundred and twenty-seventh.

GEORGE W. BUSH
President United States of America

Chapter 1
"I Pledge Allegiance to the Flag"

The Mayflower Compact
1620

In the name of God, Amen. We, whose names are underwritten, the Loyal Subjects of our dread Sovereign Lord, King James, by the Grace of God, of England, France and Ireland, King, Defender of the Faith, e&.

Having undertaken for the Glory of God, and Advancement of the Christian Faith, and the Honour of our King and Country, a voyage to plant the first colony in the northern parts of Virginia; do by these presents, solemnly and mutually in the Presence of God and one of another, covenant and combine ourselves together into a civil Body Politick, for our better Ordering and Preservation, and Furtherance of the Ends aforesaid; And by Virtue hereof to enact, constitute, and frame, such just and equal Laws, Ordinances, Acts, Constitutions and Offices, from time to time, as shall be thought most meet and convenient for the General good of the Colony; unto which we promise all due submission and obedience.

In Witness whereof we have hereunto subscribed our names at Cape Cod the eleventh of November, in the Reign of our Sovereign Lord, King James of England, France and Ireland, the eighteenth, and of Scotland the fifty-fourth. Anno Domini, 1620.

Plymouth Oath of Allegiance and Fidelity
1625

FORM OF OAT FOR ALL INHABITANTS:

You shall sweare by the name of the great God . . . & earth & in his holy fear, & presence that you shall no speake, or doe, devise, or advise, anything or things, acte or acts, directly, or indirectly, By land, or water, that doth , shall, or may, tend to the destruction or overthrowe of this present plantation, Colonie, or Corporation of this towne Plimoth in New England.

Neither shall you suffer the same to be spoken, or done, but shall hinder & opposse the same, by all due means you can.

You shall not enter into any league, treaty, Confederace or combination, with any, withink the dsaid Colonie or without the same that shall plote, or contrive any thing to the hurte & ruine of the growth, and good of the said plantation.

You shall not consente to any such confederatin, nor conceale any known unto you certainly, or by conje but shall forthwith manifest & make knowne by same, to the Governours of this said towne for the time being.

And this you promise & swear, simply & truly, & faithfully to performe as a true Christian [you hope for help from God, the God of truth & punisher of falsehoode].
FORM OF THE OATH GIVEN THE GOVERNOR AND COUNCIL AT EVERY ELECTION:

You shall swear, according to that wisdom, and measure of discerning given unto you; faithfully, equally & indifrently without respect of persons; to administer Justice, in all cause coming before you. And shall labor, to advance, & furder the good of this Colony, & plantation, to the utmost of your power, and oppose any thing that may hinder the same. So help you God.

Providence Agreement
August 20, 1637

We whose names are hereunder, desirous to inhabit in the town of Providence, do promise to subject ourselves in active an passive obedience to all such orders or agreements as shall be made for the public good of the body in an orderly way, by the major consent of present inhabitants, masters of families, incorporated together in a Towne fellowship, and others whom they shall admit unto them only in civil things.

The Fundamental Orders of Connecticut
January 14, 1639

For as much as it hath pleased Almighty God by the wise disposition of his divine providence so to order and dispose of things that we the Inhabitants and Residents of Windsor, Hartford and Wethersfield are now cohabiting and dwelling in and upon the River of Connectecotte and the lands thereunto adjoining; and well knowing where a people are gathered together the word of God requires that to maintain the peace and union of such a people there should be an orderly and decent Government established according to God, to order and dispose of the affairs of the people at all seasons as occasion shall require; do therefore associate and conjoin ourselves to be as one Public State or Commonwealth; and do for ourselves and our successors and such as shall be adjoined to us at any time hereafter, enter into Combination and Confederation together, to maintain and preserve the liberty and purity of the Gospel of our Lord Jesus which we now profess, as also, the discipline of the Churches, which according to the truth of the said Gospel is now practiced amongst us; as also in our civil affairs to be guided and governed according to such Laws, Rules, Orders and Decrees as shall be made, ordered, and decreed as followeth:

1. It is Ordered, sentenced, and decreed, that there shall be yearly two General Assemblies or Courts, the one the second Thursday in April, the other the second Thursday in September following; the first shall be called the Court of Election, wherein shall be yearly chosen from time to time, so many Magistrates and other public Officers as shall be found requisite:

Whereof one to be chosen Governor for the year ensuing and until another be chosen, and no other Magistrate to be chosen for more than one year: provided always there be six chosen besides the Governor, which being chosen and sworn according to an Oath recorded for that purpose, shall have the power to administer justice according to the Laws here established, and for want thereof, according to the Rule of the Word of God; which choice shall be made by all that are admitted freemen and have taken the Oath of Fidelity, and do cohabit within this Jurisdiction having been admitted Inhabitants by the major part of the Town wherein they live or the major part of such as shall be then present.

2. It is Ordered, sentenced, and decreed, that the election of the aforesaid Magistrates shall be in this manner: every person present and qualified for choice shall bring in (to the person deputed to receive them) one single paper with the name of him written in it whom he desires to have Governor, and that he that hath the greatest number of papers shall be Governor for that year. And the rest of the Magistrates or public officers to be chosen in this manner: the Secretary for the time being shall first read the names of all that are to be put to choice and then shall severally nominate them distinctly, and every one that would have the person nominated to be chosen shall bring in one single paper written upon, and he that would not have him chosen shall bring in a blank; and every one that hath more written papers than blanks shall be a Magistrate for that year; which papers shall be received and told by one or more that shall be then chosen by the court and sworn to be faithful therein; but in case there should not be six chosen as aforesaid, besides the Governor, out of those which are nominated, than he or they which have the most written papers shall be a Magistrate or Magistrates for the ensuing year, to make up the aforesaid number.

3. It is Ordered, sentenced, and decreed, that the Secretary shall not nominate any person, nor shall any person be chosen newly into the Magistracy which was not propounded in some General Court before, to be nominated the next election; and to that end it shall be lawful for each of the Towns aforesaid by their deputies to nominate any two whom they conceive fit to be put to election; and the Court may add so many more as they judge requisite.

4. It is Ordered, sentenced, and decreed, that no person be chosen Governor above once in two years, and that the Governor be always a member of some approved Congregation, and formerly of the Magistracy within this Jurisdiction; and that all the Magistrates, Freemen of this Commonwealth; and that no Magistrate or other public officer shall execute any part of his or their office before they are severally sworn, which shall be done in the face of the court if they be present, and in case of absence by some deputed for that purpose.

5. It is Ordered, sentenced, and decreed, that to the aforesaid Court of Election the several Towns shall send their deputies, and when the Elections are ended they may proceed in any public service as at other Courts. Also the other General Court in September shall be for making of laws, and any other public occasion, which concerns the good of the Commonwealth.

6. It is Ordered, sentenced, and decreed, that the Governor shall, either by himself or by the Secretary, send out summons to the Constables of every Town for the calling of these two standing Courts one month at least before their several times: And also if the Governor and the greatest part of the Magistrates see cause upon any special occasion to call a General

Court, they may give order to the Secretary so to do within fourteen days' warning: And if urgent necessity so required, upon a shorter notice, giving sufficient grounds for it to the deputies when they meet, or else be questioned for the same; And if the Governor and major part of Magistrates shall either neglect or refuse to call the two General standing Courts or either of them, as also at other times when the occasions of the Commonwealth require, the Freemen thereof, or the major part of them, shall petition to them so to do; if then it be either denied or neglected, the said Freemen, or the major part of them, shall have the power to give order to the Constables of the several Towns to do the same, and so may meet together, and choose to themselves a Moderator, and may proceed to do any act of power which any other General Courts may.

7. It is Ordered, sentenced, and decreed, that after there are warrants given out for any of the said General Courts, the Constable or Constables of each Town, shall forthwith give notice distinctly to the inhabitants of the same, in some public assembly or by going or sending from house to house, that at a place and time by him or them limited and set, they meet and assemble themselves together to elect and choose certain deputies to be at the General Court then following to agitate the affairs of the Commonwealth; which said deputies shall be chosen by all that are admitted Inhabitants in the several Towns and have taken the oath of fidelity; provided that none be chosen a Deputy for any General Court which is not a Freeman of this Commonwealth.

The aforesaid deputies shall be chosen in manner following: every person that is present and qualified as before expressed, shall bring the names of such, written in several papers, as they desire to have chosen for that employment, and these three or four, more or less, being the number agreed on to be chosen for that time, that have the greatest number of papers written for them shall be deputies for that Court; whose names shall be endorsed on the back side of the warrant and returned into the Court, with the Constable or Constables' hand unto the same.

8. It is Ordered, sentenced, and decreed, that Windsor, Hartford, and Wethersfield shall have power, each Town, to send four of their Freemen as their deputies to every General Court; and Whatsoever other Town shall be hereafter added to this Jurisdiction, they shall send so many deputies as the Court shall judge meet, a reasonable proportion to the number of Freemen that are in the said Towns being to be attended therein; which deputies shall have the power of the whole Town to give their votes and allowance to all such laws and orders as may be for the public good, and unto which the said Towns are to be bound.

9. It is Ordered, sentenced, and decreed, that the deputies thus chosen shall have power and liberty to appoint a time and a place of meeting together before any General Court, to advise and consult of all such things as may concern the good of the public, as also to examine their own Elections, whether according to the order, and if they or the greatest part of them find any election to be illegal they may seclude such for present from their meeting, and return the same and their reasons to the Court; and if it be proved true, the Court may fine the party or parties so intruding, and the Town, if they see cause, and give out a warrant to go to a new election in a legal way, either in part or in whole. Also the said deputies shall have power to fine any that shall be disorderly at their meetings, or for not coming in due time or place according to appointment; and they may return the said fines into the Court if it be refused to

be paid, and the Treasurer to take notice of it, and to escheat or levy the same as he does other fines.

10. It is Ordered, sentenced, and decreed, that every General Court, except such as through neglect of the Governor and the greatest part of the Magistrates the Freemen themselves do call, shall consist of the Governor, or some one chosen to moderate the Court, and four other Magistrates at least, with the major part of the deputies of the several Towns legally chosen; and in case the Freemen, or major part of them, through neglect or refusal of the Governor and major part of the Magistrates, shall call a Court, it shall consist of the major part of Freemen that are present or their deputies, with a Moderator chosen by them: In which said General Courts shall consist the supreme power of the Commonwealth, and they only shall have power to make laws or repeal them, to grant levies, to admit of Freemen, dispose of lands undisposed of, to several Towns or persons, and also shall have power to call either Court or Magistrate or any other person whatsoever into question for any misdemeanor, and may for just causes displace or deal otherwise according to the nature of the offense; and also may deal in any other matter that concerns the good of this Commonwealth, except election of Magistrates, which shall be done by the whole body of Freemen.

In which Court the Governor or Moderator shall have power to order the Court, to give liberty of speech, and silence unseasonable and disorderly speakings, to put all things to vote, and in case the vote be equal to have the casting voice. But none of these Courts shall be adjourned or dissolved without the consent of the major part of the Court.

11. It is Ordered, sentenced, and decreed, that when any General Court upon the occasions of the Commonwealth have agreed upon any sum, or sums of money to be levied upon the several Towns within this Jurisdiction, that a committee be chosen to set out and appoint what shall be the proportion of every Town to pay of the said levy, provided the committee be made up of an equal number out of each Town.

14th January 1639 the 11 Orders above said are voted.

The Articles of Confederation
November 15, 1777

To all to whom these Presents shall come, we the undersigned Delegates of the States affixed to our Names send greeting.

Articles of Confederation and perpetual Union between the states of New Hampshire, Massachusetts-bay Rhode Island and Providence Plantations, Connecticut, New York, New Jersey, Pennsylvania, Delaware, Maryland, Virginia, North Carolina, South Carolina and Georgia.

I.   The Stile of this Confederacy shall be "The United States of America."

II.   Each state retains its sovereignty, freedom, and independence, and every power, jurisdiction, and right, which is not by this Confederation expressly delegated to the United States, in Congress assembled.

III.   The said States hereby severally enter into a firm league of friendship with each other, for their common defense, the security of their liberties, and their mutual and general welfare, binding themselves to assist each other, against all force offered to, or attacks made upon them, or any of them, on account of religion, sovereignty, trade, or any other pretense whatever.

IV.   The better to secure and perpetuate mutual friendship and intercourse among the people of the different States in this Union, the free inhabitants of each of these States, paupers, vagabonds, and fugitives from justice excepted, shall be entitled to all privileges and immunities of free citizens in the several States; and the people of each State shall free ingress and regress to and from any other State, and shall enjoy therein all the privileges of trade and commerce, subject to the same duties, impositions, and restrictions as the inhabitants thereof respectively, provided that such restrictions shall not extend so far as to prevent the removal of property imported into any State, to any other State, of which the owner is an inhabitant; provided also that no imposition, duties or restriction shall be laid by any State, on the property of the United States, or either of them.

If any person guilty of, or charged with, treason, felony, or other high misdemeanor in any State, shall flee from justice, and be found in any of the United States, he shall, upon demand of the Governor or executive power of the State from which he fled, be delivered up and removed to the State having jurisdiction of his offense.

Full faith and credit shall be given in each of these States to the records, acts, and judicial proceedings of the courts and magistrates of every other State.

V.   For the most convenient management of the general interests of the United States, delegates shall be annually appointed in such manner as the legislatures of each State shall direct, to meet in Congress on the first Monday in November, in every year, with a powerreserved to each State to recall its delegates, or any of them, at any time within the year, and to send others in their stead for the remainder of the year.

No State shall be represented in Congress by less than two, nor more than seven members; and no person shall be capable of being a delegate for more than three years in any term of six years; nor shall any person, being a delegate, be capable of holding any office under the United States, for which he, or another for his benefit, receives any salary, fees or emolument of any kind.

Each State shall maintain its own delegates in a meeting of the States, and while they act as members of the committee of the States.

In determining questions in the United States in Congress assembled, each State shall have one vote.

Freedom of speech and debate in Congress shall not be impeached or questioned in any court or place out of Congress, and the members of Congress shall be protected in their persons from arrests or imprisonments, during the time of their going to and from, and attendence on Congress, except for treason, felony, or breach of the peace.

VI.   No State, without the consent of the United States in Congress assembled, shall send any embassy to, or receive any embassy from, or enter into any conference, agreement, alliance or treaty with any King, Prince or State; nor shall any person holding any office of profit or trust under the United States, or any of them, accept any present, emolument, office or title of any kind whatever from any King, Prince or foreign State; nor shall the United States in Congress assembled, or any of them, grant any title of nobility.

No two or more States shall enter into any treaty, confederation or alliance whatever between them, without the consent of the United States in Congress assembled, specifying accurately the purposes for which the same is to be entered into, and how long it shall continue.

No State shall lay any imposts or duties, which may interfere with any stipulations in treaties, entered into by the United States in Congress assembled, with any King, Prince or State, in pursuance of any treaties already proposed by Congress, to the courts of France and Spain.

No vessel of war shall be kept up in time of peace by any State, except such number only, as shall be deemed necessary by the United States in Congress assembled, for the defense of such State, or its trade; nor shall any body of forces be kept up by any State in time of peace, except such number only, as in the judgement of the United States in Congress assembled, shall be deemed requisite to garrison the forts necessary for the defense of such State; but every State shall always keep up a well-regulated and disciplined militia, sufficiently armed and accoutered, and shall provide and constantly have ready for use, in public stores, a due number of filed pieces and tents, and a proper quantity of arms, ammunition and camp equipage.

No State shall engage in any war without the consent of the United States in Congress assembled, unless such State be actually invaded by enemies, or shall have received certain advice of a resolution being formed by some nation of Indians to invade such State, and the danger is so imminent as not to admit of a delay till the United States in Congress assembled can be consulted; nor shall any State grant commissions to any ships or vessels of war, nor letters of marque or reprisal, except it be after a declaration of war by the United States in Congress assembled, and then only against the Kingdom or State and the subjects thereof, against which war has been so declared, and under such regulations as shall be established by the United States in Congress assembled, unless such State be infested by pirates, in which case vessels of war may be fitted out for that occasion, and kept so long as the danger shall continue, or until the United States in Congress assembled shall determine otherwise.

VII. When land forces are raised by any State for the common defense, all officers of or under the rank of colonel, shall be appointed by the legislature of each State respectively, by whom such forces shall be raised, or in such manner as such State shall direct, and all vacancies shall be filled up by the State which first made the appointment.

VIII. All charges of war, and all other expenses that shall be incurred for the common defense or general welfare, and allowed by the United States in Congress assembled, shall be defrayed out of a common treasury, which shall be supplied by the several States in proportion to the value of all land within each State, granted or surveyed for any person, as such land and the buildings and improvements thereon shall be estimated according to such mode as the United States in Congress assembled, shall from time to time direct and appoint.

The taxes for paying that proportion shall be laid and levied by the authority and direction of the legislatures of the several States within the time agreed upon by the United States in Congress assembled.

IX. The United States in Congress assembled, shall have the sole and exclusive right and power of determining on peace and war, except in the cases mentioned in the sixth article -- of sending and receiving ambassadors -- entering into treaties and alliances, provided that no treaty of commerce shall be made whereby the legislative power of the respective States shall be restrained from imposing such imposts and duties on foreigners, as their own people are subjected to, or from prohibiting the exportation or importation of any species of goods or commodities whatsoever -- of establishing rules for deciding in all cases, what captures on land or water shall be legal, and in what manner prizes taken by land or naval forces in the service of the United States shall be divided or appropriated -- of granting letters of marque and reprisal in times of peace -- appointing courts for the trial of piracies and felonies commited on the high seas and establishing courts for receiving and determining finally appeals in all cases of captures, provided that no member of Congress shall be appointed a judge of any of the said courts.

The United States in Congress assembled shall also be the last resort on appeal in all disputes and differences now subsisting or that hereafter may arise between two or more States concerning boundary, jurisdiction or any other causes whatever; which authority shall always be exercised in the manner following. Whenever the legislative or executive authority or lawful agent of any State in controversy with another shall present a petition to Congress stating the matter in question and praying for a hearing, notice thereof shall be given by order of Congress to the legislative or executive authority of the other State in controversy, and a day assigned for the appearance of the parties by their lawful agents, who shall then be directed to appoint by joint consent, commissioners or judges to constitute a court for hearing and determining the matter in question: but if they cannot agree, Congress shall name three persons out of each of the United States, and from the list of such persons each party shall alternately strike out one, the petitioners beginning, until the number shall be reduced to thirteen; and from that number not less than seven, nor more than nine names as Congress shall direct, shall in the presence of Congress be drawn out by lot, and the persons whose names shall be so drawn or any five of them, shall be commissioners or judges, to hear and finally determine the controversy, so always as a major part of the judges who shall hear the cause shall agree in the determination: and if either party shall neglect to attend at the day appointed, without showing reasons, which Congress shall judge sufficient, or being present shall refuse to strike, the Congress shall proceed to nominate three persons out of each State, and the secretary of Congress shall strike in behalf of such party absent or refusing; and the judgement and sentence of the court to be appointed, in the manner before prescribed, shall be final and conclusive; and if any of the parties shall refuse to submit to the authority of such court, or to appear or defend their claim or cause, the court shall nevertheless proceed to pronounce sentence, or judgement, which shall in like manner be final and decisive, the judgement or sentence and other proceedings being in either case transmitted to Congress, and lodged among the acts of Congress for the security of the parties concerned: provided that every commissioner, before he sits in judgement, shall take an oath to be administered by one of the judges of the supreme or superior court of the State, where the cause shall be tried, 'well and truly to hear and determine the matter in question, according to the best of his judgement, without favor, affection or hope of reward': provided also, that no State shall be deprived of territory for the benefit of the United States.

All controversies concerning the private right of soil claimed under different grants of two or more States, whose jurisdictions as they may respect such lands, and the States which passed such grants are adjusted, the said grants or either of them being at the same time claimed to have originated antecedent to such settlement of jurisdiction, shall on the petition of either party to the Congress of the United States, be finally determined as near as may be in the same manner as is before presecribed for deciding disputes respecting territorial jurisdiction between different States.

The United States in Congress assembled shall also have the sole and exclusive right and power of regulating the alloy and value of coin struck by their own authority, or by that of the respective States -- fixing the standards of weights and measures throughout the United States -- regulating the trade and managing all affairs with the Indians, not members of any of the States, provided that the legislative right of any State within its own limits be not infringed or violated -- establishing or regulating post offices from one State to another, throughout all the United States, and exacting such postage on the papers passing through the same as may be requisite to defray the expenses of the said office -- appointing all officers of the land forces, in the service of the United States, excepting regimental officers -- appointing all the officers of the naval forces, and commissioning all officers whatever in the service of the United States -- making rules for the government and regulation of the said land and naval forces, and directing their operations.

The United States in Congress assembled shall have authority to appoint a committee, to sit in the recess of Congress, to be denominated 'A Committee of the States', and to consist of one delegate from each State; and to appoint such other committees and civil officers as may be necessary for managing the general affairs of the United States under their direction

-- to appoint one of their members to preside, provided that no person be allowed to serve in the office of president more than one year in any term of three years; to ascertain the necessary sums of money to be raised for the service of the United States, and to appropriate and apply the same for defraying the public expenses -- to borrow money, or emit bills on the credit of the United States, transmitting every half-year to the respective States an account of the sums of money so borrowed or emitted

-- to build and equip a navy -- to agree upon the number of land forces, and to make requisitions from each State for its quota, in proportion to the number of white inhabitants in such State; which requisition shall be binding, and thereupon the legislature of each State shall appoint the regimental officers, raise the men and cloath, arm and equip them in a solid-like manner, at the expense of the United States; and the officers and men so cloathed, armed and equipped shall march to the place appointed, and within the time agreed on by the United States in Congress assembled. But if the United States in Congress assembled shall, on consideration of circumstances judge proper that any State should not raise men, or should raise a smaller number of men than the quota thereof, such extra number shall be raised, officered, cloathed, armed and equipped in the same manner as the quota of each State, unless the legislature of such State shall judge that such extra number cannot be safely spread out in the same, in which case they shall raise, officer, cloath, arm and equip as many of such extra number as they judeg can be safely spared. And the officers and men so cloathed, armed, and equipped, shall march to the place appointed, and within the time agreed on by the United States in Congress assembled.

The United States in Congress assembled shall never engage in a war, nor grant letters of marque or reprisal in time of peace, nor enter into any treaties or alliances, nor coin money, nor regulate the value thereof, nor ascertain the sums and expenses necessary for the defense and welfare of the United States, or any of them, nor emit bills, nor borrow money on the credit of the United States, nor appropriate money, nor agree upon the number of vessels of war, to be built or purchased, or the number of land or sea forces to be raised, nor appoint a commander in chief of the army or navy, unless nine States assent to the same: nor shall a question on any other point, except for adjourning from day to day be determined, unless by the votes of the majority of the United States in Congress assembled.

The Congress of the United States shall have power to adjourn to any time within the year, and to any place within the United States, so that no period of adjournment be for a longer duration than the space of six months, and shall publish the journal of their proceedings monthly, except such parts thereof relating to treaties, alliances or military operations, as in their judgement require secrecy; and the yeas and nays of the delegates of each State on any question shall be entered on the journal, when it is desired by any delegates of a State, or any of them, at his or their request shall be furnished with a transcript of the said journal, except such parts as are above excepted, to lay before the legislatures of the several States.

X.   The Committee of the States, or any nine of them, shall be authorized to execute, in the recess of Congress, such of the powers of Congress as the United States in Congress assembled, by the consent of the nine States, shall from time to time think expedient to vest them with; provided that no power be delegated to the said Committee, for the exercise of which, by the Articles of Confederation, the voice of nine States in the Congress of the United States assembled be requisite.

XI.   Canada acceding to this confederation, and adjoining in the measures of the United States, shall be admitted into, and entitled to all the advantages of this Union; but no other colony shall be admitted into the same, unless such admission be agreed to by nine States.

XII. All bills of credit emitted, monies borrowed, and debts contracted by, or under the authority of Congress, before the assembling of the United States, in pursuance of the present confederation, shall be deemed and considered as a charge against the United States, for payment and satisfaction whereof the said United States, and the public faith are hereby solemnly pledged.

XIII. Every State shall abide by the determination of the United States in Congress assembled, on all questions which by this confederation are submitted to them. And the Articles of this Confederation shall be inviolably observed by every State, and the Union shall be perpetual; nor shall any alteration at any time hereafter be made in any of them; unless such alteration be agreed to in a Congress of the United States, and be afterwards confirmed by the legislatures of every State.

And Whereas it hath pleased the Great Governor of the World to incline the hearts of the legislatures we respectively represent in Congress, to approve of, and to authorize us to ratify the said Articles of Confederation and perpetual Union. Know Ye that we the undersigned delegates, by virtue of the power and authority to us given for that purpose, do by these presents, in the name and in behalf of our respective constituents, fully and entirely ratify and confirm each and every of the said Articles of Confederation and perpetual Union, and all and singular the matters and things therein contained: And we do further solemnly plight and engage the faith of our respective constituents, that they shall abide by the determinations of the United States in Congress assembled, on all questions, which by the said Confederation are submitted to them. And that the Articles thereof shall be inviolably observed by the States we respectively represent, and that the Union shall be perpetual.

In Witness whereof we have hereunto set our hands in Congress. Done at Philadelphia in the State of Pennsylvania the ninth day of July in the Year of our Lord One Thousand Seven Hundred and Seventy-Eight, and in the Third Year of the independence of America.

Agreed to by Congress 15 November 1777

In force after ratification by Maryland, 1 March 1781

The Paris Peace Treaty of 1783

In the name of the most holy and undivided Trinity.

It having pleased the Divine Providence to dispose the hearts of the most serene and most potent Prince George the Third, by the grace of God, king of Great Britain, France, and Ireland, defender of the faith, duke of Brunswick and Lunebourg, arch- treasurer and prince elector of the Holy Roman Empire etc., and of the United States of America, to forget all past misunderstandings and differences that have unhappily interrupted the good correspondence and friendship which they mutually wish to restore, and to establish such a beneficial and satisfactory intercourse , between the two countries upon the ground of reciprocal advantages and mutual convenience as may promote and secure to both perpetual peace and harmony; and having for this desirable end already laid the foundation of peace and reconciliation by the Provisional Articles signed at Paris on the 30th of November 1782, by the commissioners empowered on each part, which articles were agreed to be inserted in and constitute the Treaty of Peace proposed to be concluded between the Crown of Great Britain and the said United States, but which treaty was not to be concluded until terms of peace should be agreed upon between Great Britain and France and his Britannic Majesty should be ready to conclude such treaty accordingly; and the treaty between Great Britain and France having since been concluded, his Britannic Majesty and the United States of America, in order to carry into full effect the Provisional Articles above mentioned, according to the tenor thereof, have constituted and appointed, that is to say his Britannic Majesty on his part, David Hartley, Esqr., member of the Parliament of Great Britain, and the said United States on their part, John Adams, Esqr., late a commissioner of the United States of America at the court of Versailles, late delegate in Congress from the state of Massachusetts, and chief justice of the said state, and minister plenipotentiary of the said United States to their high mightinesses the States General of the United Netherlands; Benjamin Franklin, Esqr., late delegate in Congress from the state of Pennsylvania, president of the convention of the said state, and minister plenipotentiary from the United States of America at the court of Versailles; John Jay, Esqr., late president of Congress and chief justice of the state of New York, and minister plenipotentiary from the said United States at the court of Madrid; to be plenipotentiaries for the concluding and signing the present definitive treaty; who after having reciprocally communicated their respective full powers have agreed upon and confirmed the following articles.

Article 1

His Brittanic Majesty acknowledges the said United States, viz., New Hampshire, Massachusetts Bay, Rhode Island and Providence Plantations, Connecticut, New York, New Jersey, Pennsylvania, Maryland, Virginia, North Carolina, South Carolina and Georgia, to be free sovereign and independent states, that he treats with them as such, and for himself, his heirs, and successors, relinquishes all claims to the government, propriety, and territorial rights of the same and every part thereof.

Article 2

And that all disputes which might arise in future on the subject of the boundaries of the said United States may be prevented, it is hereby agreed and declared, that the following are and shall be their boundaries, viz.; from the northwest angle of Nova Scotia, viz., that nagle which is formed by a line drawn due north from the source of St. Croix River to the highlands; along the said highlands which divide those rivers that empty themselves into the river St. Lawrence, from those which fall into the Atlantic Ocean, to the northwesternmost head of Connecticut River; thence down along the middle of that river to the forty-fifth degree of north latitude; from thence by a line due west on said latitude until it strikes the river Iroquois or Cataraquy; thence along the middle of said river into Lake Ontario; through the middle of said lake until it strikes the communication by water between that lake and Lake Erie; thence along the middle of said communication into Lake Erie, through the middle of said lake until it arrives at the water communication between that lake and Lake Huron; thence along the middle of said water communication into Lake Huron, thence through the middle of said lake to the water communication between that lake and Lake Superior; thence through Lake Superior northward of the Isles Royal and Phelipeaux to the Long Lake; thence through the middle of said Long Lake and the water communication between it and the Lake of the Woods, to the said Lake of the Woods; thence through the said lake to the most northwesternmost point thereof, and from thence on a due west course to the river Mississippi; thence by a line to be drawn along the middle of the said river Mississippi until it shall intersect the northernmost part of the thirty-first degree of north latitude, South, by a line to be drawn due east from the determination of the line last mentioned in the latitude of thirty-one degrees of the equator, to the middle of the river Apalachicola or Catahouche; thence along the middle thereof to its junction with the Flint River, thence straight to the head of Saint Mary's River; and thence down along the middle of Saint Mary's River to the Atlantic Ocean; east, by a line to be drawn along the middle of the river Saint Croix, from its mouth in the Bay of Fundy to its source, and from its source directly north to the aforesaid highlands which divide the rivers that fall into the Atlantic Ocean from those which fall into the river Saint Lawrence; comprehending all islands within twenty leagues of any part of the shores of the United States, and lying between lines to be drawn due east from the points where the aforesaid boundaries between Nova Scotia on the one part and East Florida on the other shall, respectively, touch the Bay of Fundy and the Atlantic Ocean, excepting such islands as now are or heretofore have been within the limits of the said province of Nova Scotia.

Article 3

It is agreed that the people of the United States shall continue to enjoy unmolested the right to take fish of every kind on the Grand Bank and on all the other banks of Newfoundland, also in the Gulf of Saint Lawrence and at all other places in the sea, where the inhabitants of both countries used at any time heretofore to fish. And also that the inhabitants of the United States shall have liberty to take fish of every kind on such part of the coast of Newfoundland as British fishermen shall use, (but not to dry or cure the same on that island) and also on the coasts, bays and creeks of all other of his Brittanic Majesty's dominions in America; and that the American fishermen shall have liberty to dry and cure fish in any of the unsettled bays, harbors, and creeks of Nova Scotia, Magdalen Islands, and Labrador, so long as the same shall remain unsettled, but so soon as the same or either of them shall be settled, it shall not be lawful for the said fishermen to dry or cure fish at such settlement without a previous agreement for that purpose with the inhabitants, proprietors, or possessors of the ground.

Article 4

It is agreed that creditors on either side shall meet with no lawful impediment to the recovery of the full value in sterling money of all bona fide debts heretofore contracted.

Article 5

It is agreed that Congress shall earnestly recommend it to the legislatures of the respective states to provide for the restitution of all estates, rights, and properties, which have been confiscated belonging to real British subjects; and also of the estates, rights, and properties of persons resident in districts in the possession on his Majesty's arms and who have not borne arms against the said United States. And that persons of any other description shall have free liberty to go to any part or parts of any of the thirteen United States and therein to remain twelve months unmolested in their endeavors to obtain the restitution of such of their estates, rights, and properties as may have been confiscated; and that Congress shall also earnestly recommend to the several states a reconsideration and revision of all acts or laws regarding the premises, so as to render the said laws or acts perfectly consistent not only with justice and equity but with that spirit of conciliation which on the return of the blessings of peace should universally prevail. And that Congress shall also earnestly recommend to the several states that the estates, rights, and properties, of such last mentioned persons shall be restored to them, they refunding to any persons who may be now in possession the bona fide price (where any has been given) which such persons may have paid on purchasing any of the said lands, rights, or properties since the confiscation. And it is agreed that all persons who have any interest in confiscated lands, either by debts, marriage settlements, or otherwise, shall meet with no lawful impediment in the prosecution of their just rights.

Article 6

That there shall be no future confiscations made nor any prosecutions commenced against any person or persons for, or by reason of, the part which he or they may have taken in the present war, and that no person shall on that account suffer any future loss or damage, either in his person, liberty, or property; and that those who may be in confinement on such charges at the time of the ratification of the treaty in America shall be immediately set at liberty, and the prosecutions so commenced be discontinued.

Article 7

There shall be a firm and perpetual peace between his Brittanic Majesty and the said states, and between the subjects of the one and the citizens of the other, wherefore all hostilities both by sea and land shall from henceforth cease. All prisoners on both sides shall be set at liberty, and his Brittanic Majesty shall with all convenient speed, and without causing any destruction, or carrying away any Negroes or other property of the American inhabitants, withdraw all his armies, garrisons, and fleets from the said United States, and from every post, place, and harbor within the same; leaving in all fortifications, the American artilery that may be therein; and shall also order and cause all archives, records, deeds, and papers belonging to any of the said states, or their citizens, which in the course of the war may have fallen into the hands of his officers, to be forthwith restored and delivered to the proper states and persons to whom they belong.

Article 8

The navigation of the river Mississippi, from its source to the ocean, shall forever remain free and open to the subjects of Great Britain and the citizens of the United States.

Article 9

In case it should so happen that any place or territory belonging to Great Britain or to the United States should have been conquered by the arms of either from the other before the arrival of the said Provisional Articles in America, it is agreed that the same shall be restored without difficulty and without requiring any compensation.

Article 10

The solemn ratifications of the present treaty expedited in good and due form shall be exchanged between the contracting parties in the space of six months or sooner, if possible, to be computed from the day of the signatures of the present treaty. In witness whereof we the undersigned, their ministers plenipotentiary, have in their name and in virtue of our full powers, signed with our hands the present definitive treaty and caused the seals of our arms to be affixed thereto.

Done at Paris, this third day of September in the year of our Lord, one thousand seven hundred and eighty-three.

D.HARTLEY.(SEAL)
JOHN ADAMS.(SEAL)
B.FRANKLIN.(SEAL)
JOHN JAY.(SEAL)

The United States Constitution

We the people of the United States, in order to form a more perfect union, establish justice, insure domestic tranquility, provide for the common defense, promote the general welfare, and secure the blessings of liberty to ourselves and our posterity, do ordain and establish this Constitution for the United States of America.

Article I

Section 1. All legislative powers herein granted shall be vested in a Congress of the United States, which shall consist of a Senate and House of Representatives.

Section 2. The House of Representatives shall be composed of members chosen every second year by the people of the several states, and the electors in each state shall have the qualifications requisite for electors of the most numerous branch of the state legislature.

No person shall be a Representative who shall not have attained to the age of twenty five years, and been seven years a citizen of the United States, and who shall not, when elected, be an inhabitant of that state in which he shall be chosen.

Representatives and direct taxes shall be apportioned among the several states which may be included within this union, according to their respective numbers, which shall be determined by adding to the whole number of free persons, including those bound to service for a term of years, and excluding Indians not taxed, three fifths of all other Persons. The actual Enumeration shall be made within three years after the first meeting of the Congress of the United States, and within every subsequent term of ten years, in such manner as they shall by law direct. The number of Representatives shall not exceed one for every thirty thousand, but each state shall have at least one Representative; and until such enumeration shall be made, the state of New Hampshire shall be entitled to chuse three, Massachusetts eight, Rhode Island and Providence Plantations one, Connecticut five, New York six, New Jersey four, Pennsylvania eight, Delaware one, Maryland six, Virginia ten, North Carolina five, South Carolina five, and Georgia three.

When vacancies happen in the Representation from any state, the executive authority thereof shall issue writs of election to fill such vacancies.

The House of Representatives shall choose their speaker and other officers; and shall have the sole power of impeachment.

Section 3. The Senate of the United States shall be composed of two Senators from each state, chosen by the legislature thereof, for six years; and each Senator shall have one vote.

Immediately after they shall be assembled in consequence of the first election, they shall be divided as equally as may be into three classes. The seats of the Senators of the first class shall be vacated at the expiration of the second year, of the second class at the expiration of the fourth year, and the third class at the expiration of the sixth year, so that one third may be chosen every second year; and if vacancies happen by resignation, or otherwise, during the recess of the legislature of any state, the executive thereof may make temporary appointments until the next meeting of the legislature, which shall then fill such vacancies.

No person shall be a Senator who shall not have attained to the age of thirty years, and been nine years a citizen of the United States and who shall not, when elected, be an inhabitant of that state for which he shall be chosen.

The Vice President of the United States shall be President of the Senate, but shall have no vote, unless they be equally divided.

The Senate shall choose their other officers, and also a President pro tempore, in the absence of the Vice President, or when he shall exercise the office of President of the United States.

The Senate shall have the sole power to try all impeachments. When sitting for that purpose, they shall be on oath or affirmation. When the President of the United States is tried, the Chief Justice shall preside: And no person shall be convicted without the concurrence of two thirds of the members present.

Judgment in cases of impeachment shall not extend further than to removal from office, and disqualification to hold and enjoy any office of honor, trust or profit under the United States: but the party convicted shall nevertheless be liable and subject to indictment, trial, judgment and punishment, according to law.

Section 4. The times, places and manner of holding elections for Senators and Representatives, shall be prescribed in each state by the legislature thereof; but the Congress may at any time by law make or alter such regulations, except as to the places of choosing Senators.

The Congress shall assemble at least once in every year, and such meeting shall be on the first Monday in December, unless they shall by law appoint a different day.

Section 5. Each House shall be the judge of the elections, returns and qualifications of its own members, and a majority of each shall constitute a quorum to do business; but a smaller number may adjourn from day to day, and may be authorized to compel the attendance of absent members, in such manner, and under such penalties as each House may provide.

Each House may determine the rules of its proceedings, punish its members for disorderly behavior, and, with the concurrence of two thirds, expel a member.

Each House shall keep a journal of its proceedings, and from time to time publish the same, excepting such parts as may in their judgment require secrecy; and the yeas and nays of the members of either House on any question shall, at the desire of one fifth of those present, be entered on the journal.

Neither House, during the session of Congress, shall, without the consent of the other, adjourn for more than three days, nor to any other place than that in which the two Houses shall be sitting.

Section 6. The Senators and Representatives shall receive a compensation for their services, to be ascertained by law, and paid out of the treasury of the United States. They shall in all cases, except treason, felony and breach of the peace, be privileged from arrest during their attendance at the session of their respective Houses, and in going to and returning from the same; and for any speech or debate in either House, they shall not be questioned in any other place.

No Senator or Representative shall, during the time for which he was elected, be appointed to any civil office under the authority of the United States, which shall have been created, or the emoluments whereof shall have been increased during such time: and no person holding any office under the United States, shall be a member of either House during his continuance in office.

Section 7.   All bills for raising revenue shall originate in the House of Representatives; but the Senate may propose or concur with amendments as on other Bills.

Every bill which shall have passed the House of Representatives and the Senate, shall, before it become a law, be presented to the President of the United States; if he approve he shall sign it, but if not he shall return it, with his objections to that House in which it shall have originated, who shall enter the objections at large on their journal, and proceed to reconsider it. If after such reconsideration two thirds of that House shall agree to pass the bill, it shall be sent, together with the objections, to the other House, by which it shall likewise be reconsidered, and if approved by two thirds of that House, it shall become a law. But in all such cases the votes of both Houses shall be determined by yeas and nays, and the names of the persons voting for and against the bill shall be entered on the journal of each House respectively. If any bill shall not be returned by the President within ten days (Sundays excepted) after it shall have been presented to him, the same shall be a law, in like manner as if he had signed it, unless the Congress by their adjournment prevent its return, in which case it shall not be a law.

Every order, resolution, or vote to which the concurrence of the Senate and House of Representatives may be necessary (except on a question of adjournment) shall be presented to the President of the United States; and before the same shall take effect, shall be approved by him, or being disapproved by him, shall be repassed by two thirds of the Senate and House of Representatives, according to the rules and limitations prescribed in the case of a bill.

Section 8.   The Congress shall have power to lay and collect taxes, duties, imposts and excises, to pay the debts and provide for the common defense and general welfare of the United States; but all duties, imposts and excises shall be uniform throughout the United States;

To borrow money on the credit of the United States;

To regulate commerce with foreign nations, and among the several states, and with the Indian tribes;

To establish a uniform rule of naturalization, and uniform laws on the subject of bankruptcies throughout the United States;

To coin money, regulate the value thereof, and of foreign coin, and fix the standard of weights and measures;

To provide for the punishment of counterfeiting the securities and current coin of the United States;

To establish post offices and post roads;

To promote the progress of science and useful arts, by securing for limited times to authors and inventors the exclusive right to their respective writings and discoveries;

To constitute tribunals inferior to the Supreme Court;

To define and punish piracies and felonies committed on the high seas, and offenses against the law of nations;

To declare war, grant letters of marque and reprisal, and make rules concerning captures on land and water;

To raise and support armies, but no appropriation of money to that use shall be for a longer term than two years;

To provide and maintain a navy;

To make rules for the government and regulation of the land and naval forces;

To provide for calling forth the militia to execute the laws of the union, suppress insurrections and repel invasions;

To provide for organizing, arming, and disciplining, the militia, and for governing such part of them as may be employed in the service of the United States, reserving to the states respectively, the appointment of the officers, and the authority of training the militia according to the discipline prescribed by Congress;

To exercise exclusive legislation in all cases whatsoever, over such District (not exceeding ten miles square) as may, by cession of particular states, and the acceptance of Congress, become the seat of the government of the United States, and to exercise like authority over all places purchased by the consent of the legislature of the state in which the same shall be, for the erection of forts, magazines, arsenals, dockyards, and other needful buildings;--And

To make all laws which shall be necessary and proper for carrying into execution the foregoing powers, and all other powers vested by this Constitution in the government of the United States, or in any department or officer thereof.

Section 9.   The migration or importation of such persons as any of the states now existing shall think proper to admit, shall not be prohibited by the Congress prior to the year one thousand eight hundred and eight, but a tax or duty may be imposed on such importation, not exceeding ten dollars for each person.

The privilege of the writ of habeas corpus shall not be suspended, unless when in cases of rebellion or invasion the public safety may require it.

No bill of attainder or ex post facto Law shall be passed.

No capitation, or other direct, tax shall be laid, unless in proportion to the census or enumeration herein before directed to be taken.

No tax or duty shall be laid on articles exported from any state.

No preference shall be given by any regulation of commerce or revenue to the ports of one state over those of another: nor shall vessels bound to, or from, one state, be obliged to enter, clear or pay duties in another.

No money shall be drawn from the treasury, but in consequence of appropriations made by law; and a regular statement and account of receipts and expenditures of all public money shall be published from time to time.

No title of nobility shall be granted by the United States: and no person holding any office of profit or trust under them, shall, without the consent of the Congress, accept of any present, emolument, office, or title, of any kind whatever, from any king, prince, or foreign state.

Section 10. No state shall enter into any treaty, alliance, or confederation; grant letters of marque and reprisal; coin money; emit bills of credit; make anything but gold and silver coin a tender in payment of debts; pass any bill of attainder, ex post facto law, or law impairing the obligation of contracts, or grant any title of nobility.

No state shall, without the consent of the Congress, lay any imposts or duties on imports or exports, except what may be absolutely necessary for executing its inspection laws: and the net produce of all duties and imposts, laid by any state on imports or exports, shall be for the use of the treasury of the United States; and all such laws shall be subject to the revision and control of the Congress.

No state shall, without the consent of Congress, lay any duty of tonnage, keep troops, or ships of war in time of peace, enter into any agreement or compact with another state, or with a foreign power, or engage in war, unless actually invaded, or in such imminent danger as will not admit of delay.

Article II

Section 1. The executive power shall be vested in a President of the United States of America. He shall hold his office during the term of four years, and, together with the Vice President, chosen for the same term, be elected, as follows:

Each state shall appoint, in such manner as the Legislature thereof may direct, a number of electors, equal to the whole number of Senators and Representatives to which the State may be entitled in the Congress: but no Senator or Representative, or person holding an office of trust or profit under the United States, shall be appointed an elector.

The electors shall meet in their respective states, and vote by ballot for two persons, of whom one at least shall not be an inhabitant of the same state with themselves. And they shall make a list of all the persons voted for, and of the number of votes for each; which list they shall sign and certify, and transmit sealed to the seat of the government of the United States, directed to the President of the Senate. The President of the Senate shall, in the presence of the Senate and House of Representatives, open all the certificates, and the votes shall then be counted. The person having the greatest number of votes shall be the President, if such number be a majority of the whole number of electors appointed; and if there be more than one who have such majority, and have an equal number of votes, then the House of Representatives shall immediately choose by ballot one of them for President; and if no person have a majority, then from the five highest on the list the said House shall in like manner choose the President. But in choosing the President, the votes shall be taken by States, the representation from each state having one vote; A quorum for this purpose shall consist of a member or members from two thirds of the states, and a majority of all the states shall be necessary to a choice. In every case, after the choice of the President, the person having the greatest number of votes of the electors shall be the Vice President. But if there should remain two or more who have equal votes, the Senate shall choose from them by ballot the Vice President.

The Congress may determine the time of choosing the electors, and the day on which they shall give their votes; which day shall be the same throughout the United States.

No person except a natural born citizen, or a citizen of the United States, at the time of the adoption of this Constitution, shall be eligible to the office of President; neither shall any person be eligible to that office who shall not have attained to the age of thirty five years, and been fourteen Years a resident within the United States.

In case of the removal of the President from office, or of his death, resignation, or inability to discharge the powers and duties of the said office, the same shall devolve on the Vice President, and the Congress may by law provide for the case of removal, death, resignation or inability, both of the President and Vice President, declaring what officer shall then act as President, and such officer shall act accordingly, until the disability be removed, or a President shall be elected.

The President shall, at stated times, receive for his services, a compensation, which shall neither be increased nor diminished during the period for which he shall have been elected, and he shall not receive within that period any other emolument from the United States, or any of them.

Before he enter on the execution of his office, he shall take the following oath or affirmation:--"I do solemnly swear (or affirm) that I will faithfully execute the office of President of the United States, and will to the best of my ability, preserve, protect and defend the Constitution of the United States."

Section 2.   The President shall be commander in chief of the Army and Navy of the United States, and of the militia of the several states, when called into the actual service of the United States; he may require the opinion, in writing, of the principal officer in each of the executive departments, upon any subject relating to the duties of their respective offices, and he shall have power to grant reprieves and pardons for offenses against the United States, except in cases of impeachment.

He shall have power, by and with the advice and consent of the Senate, to make treaties, provided two thirds of the Senators present concur; and he shall nominate, and by and with the advice and consent of the Senate, shall appoint ambassadors, other public ministers and consuls, judges of the Supreme Court, and all other officers of the United States, whose appointments are not herein otherwise provided for, and which shall be established by law: but the Congress may by law vest the appointment of such inferior officers, as they think proper, in the President alone, in the courts of law, or in the heads of departments.

The President shall have power to fill up all vacancies that may happen during the recess of the Senate, by granting commissions which shall expire at the end of their next session.

Section 3.   He shall from time to time give to the Congress information of the state of the union, and recommend to their consideration such measures as he shall judge necessary and expedient; he may, on extraordinary occasions, convene both Houses, or either of them, and in case of disagreement between them, with respect to the time of adjournment, he may adjourn them to such time as he shall think proper; he shall receive ambassadors and other public ministers; he shall take care that the laws be faithfully executed, and shall commission all the officers of the United States.

Section 4.   The President, Vice President and all civil officers of the United States, shall be removed from office on impeachment for, and conviction of, treason, bribery, or other high crimes and misdemeanors.

Article III

Section 1.   The judicial power of the United States, shall be vested in one Supreme Court, and in such inferior courts as the Congress may from time to time ordain and establish. The judges, both of the supreme and inferior courts, shall hold their offices during good behaviour, and shall, at stated times, receive for their services, a compensation, which shall not be diminished during their continuance in office.

Section 2.   The judicial power shall extend to all cases, in law and equity, arising under this Constitution, the laws of the United States, and treaties made, or which shall be made, under their authority;--to all cases affecting ambassadors, other public ministers and consuls;
--to all cases of admiralty and maritime jurisdiction;--to controversies to which the United States shall be a party;--to controversies between two or more states;--between a state and citizens of another state;-- between citizens of different states;--between citizens of the same state claiming lands under grants of different states, and between a state, or the citizens thereof, and foreign states, citizens or subjects.

In all cases affecting ambassadors, other public ministers and consuls, and those in which a state shall be party, the Supreme Court shall have original jurisdiction. In all the other cases before mentioned, the Supreme Court shall have appellate jurisdiction, both as to law and fact, with such exceptions, and under such regulations as the Congress shall make.

The trial of all crimes, except in cases of impeachment, shall be by jury; and such trial shall be held in the state where the said crimes shall have been committed; but when not committed within any state, the trial shall be at such place or places as the Congress may by law have directed.

Section 3. Treason against the United States, shall consist only in levying war against them, or in adhering to their enemies, giving them aid and comfort. No person shall be convicted of treason unless on the testimony of two witnesses to the same overt act, or on confession in open court.

The Congress shall have power to declare the punishment of treason, but no attainder of treason shall work corruption of blood, or forfeiture except during the life of the person attainted.

Article IV

Section 1. Full faith and credit shall be given in each state to the public acts, records, and judicial proceedings of every other state. And the Congress may by general laws prescribe the manner in which such acts, records, and proceedings shall be proved, and the effect thereof.

Section 2. The citizens of each state shall be entitled to all privileges and immunities of citizens in the several states.

A person charged in any state with treason, felony, or other crime, who shall flee from justice, and be found in another state, shall on demand of the executive authority of the state from which he fled, be delivered up, to be removed to the state having jurisdiction of the crime.

No person held to service or labor in one state, under the laws thereof, escaping into another, shall, in consequence of any law or regulation therein, be discharged from such service or labor, but shall be delivered up on claim of the party to whom such service or labor may be due.

Section 3. New states may be admitted by the Congress into this union; but no new states shall be formed or erected within the jurisdiction of any other state; nor any state be formed by the junction of two or more states, or parts of states, without the consent of the legislatures of the states concerned as well as of the Congress.

The Congress shall have power to dispose of and make all needful rules and regulations respecting the territory or other property belonging to the United States; and nothing in this Constitution shall be so construed as to prejudice any claims of the United States, or of any particular state.

Section 4. The United States shall guarantee to every state in this union a republican form of government, and shall protect each of them against invasion; and on application of the legislature, or of the executive (when the legislature cannot be convened) against domestic violence.

Article V

The Congress, whenever two thirds of both houses shall deem it necessary, shall propose amendments to this Constitution, or, on the application of the legislatures of two thirds of the several states, shall call a convention for proposing amendments, which, in either case, shall be valid to all intents and purposes, as part of this Constitution, when ratified by the legislatures of three fourths of the several states, or by conventions in three fourths thereof, as the one or the other mode of ratification may be proposed by the Congress; provided that no amendment which may be made prior to the year one thousand eight hundred and eight shall in any manner affect the first and fourth clauses in the ninth section of the first article; and that no state, without its consent, shall be deprived of its equal suffrage in the Senate.

Article VI

All debts contracted and engagements entered into, before the adoption of this Constitution, shall be as valid against the United States under this Constitution, as under the Confederation.

This Constitution, and the laws of the United States which shall be made in pursuance thereof; and all treaties made, or which shall be made, under the authority of the United States, shall be the supreme law of the land; and the judges in every state shall be bound thereby, anything in the Constitution or laws of any State to the contrary notwithstanding.

The Senators and Representatives before mentioned, and the members of the several state legislatures, and all executive and judicial officers, both of the United States and of the several states, shall be bound by oath or affirmation, to support this Constitution; but no religious test shall ever be required as a qualification to any office or public trust under the United States.

Article VII

The ratification of the conventions of nine states, shall be sufficient for the establishment of this Constitution between the states so ratifying the same.

Done in convention by the unanimous consent of the states present the seventeenth day of September in the year of our Lord one thousand seven hundred and eighty seven and of the independence of the United States of America the twelfth. In witness whereof We have hereunto subscribed our Names,

G. WASHINGTON-PRESIDENT, AND DEPUTY FROM VIRGINIA
NEW HAMPSHIRE: JOHN LANGDON, NICHOLAS GILMAN
MASSACHUSETTS: NATHANIEL GORHAM, RUFUS KING
CONNECTICUT: WM: SAMUEL JOHNSON, ROGER SHERMAN
NEW YORK: ALEXANDER HAMILTON
NEW JERSEY: WIL: LIVINGSTON, DAVID BREARLY, WM. PATERSON, JONA: DAYTON
PENNSYLVANIA: B. FRANKLIN, THOMAS MIFFLIN, ROBT. MORRIS, GEO. CLYMER,
        THOS. FITZSIMONS, JARED INGERSOLL, JAMES WILSON, GOUV MORRIS
DELAWARE: GEO: READ, GUNNING BEDFORD JUN, JOHN DICKINSON, RICHARD BASSETT,
        JACO: BROOM
MARYLAND: JAMES MCHENRY, DAN OF ST THOS. JENIFER, DANL CARROLL
VIRGINIA: JOHN BLAIR--, JAMES MADISON JR.
NORTH CAROLINA: WM. BLOUNT, RICHD. DOBBS SPAIGHT, HU WILLIAMSON
SOUTH CAROLINA: J. RUTLEDGE, CHARLES COTESWORTH PINCKNEY, CHARLES PINCKNEY,
        PIERCE BUTLER
GEORGIA: WILLIAM FEW, ABRAHAM BALDWIN

Amendments to the Constitution of the United States of America

---

Articles in addition to, and amendment of, the Constitution of the United States of America, proposed by Congress, and ratified by the several states, pursuant to the Fifth Article of the original Constitution.

Amendment I

Congress shall make no law respecting an establishment of religion, or prohibiting the free exercise thereof; or abridging the freedom of speech, or of the press; or the right of the people peaceably to assemble, and to petition the Government for a redress of grievances.

Amendment II

A well regulated Militia, being necessary to the security of a free State, the right of the people to keep and bear Arms, shall not be infringed.

Amendment III

No Soldier shall, in time of peace be quartered in any house, without the consent of the Owner, nor in time of war, but in a manner to be prescribed by law.

Amendment IV

The right of the people to be secure in their persons, houses, papers, and effects, against unreasonable searches and seizures, shall not be violated, and no Warrants shall issue, but upon probable cause, supported by Oath or affirmation, and particularly describing the place to be searched, and the persons or things to be seized.

Amendment V

No person shall be held to answer for a capital, or otherwise infamous crime, unless on a presentment or indictment of a Grand Jury, except in cases arising in the land or naval forces, or in the Militia, when in actual service in time of War or public danger; nor shall any person be subject for the same offence to be twice put in jeopardy of life or limb; nor shall be compelled in any criminal case to be a witness against himself, nor be deprived of life, liberty, or property, without due process of law; nor shall private property be taken for public use, without just compensation.

Amendment VI

In all criminal prosecutions, the accused shall enjoy the right to a speedy and public trial, by an impartial jury of the State and district wherein the crime shall have been committed, which district shall have been previously ascertained by law, and to be informed of the nature and cause of the accusation; to be confronted with the witnesses against him; to have compulsory process for obtaining witnesses in his favor, and to have the Assistance of Counsel for his defence.

Amendment VII

In Suits at common law, where the value in controversy shall exceed twenty dollars, the right of trial by jury shall be preserved, and no fact tried by a jury, shall be otherwise re-examined in any Court of the United States, than according to the rules of the common law.

Amendment VIII

Excessive bail shall not be required, nor excessive fines imposed, nor cruel and unusual punishments inflicted.

Amendment IX

The enumeration in the Constitution, of certain rights, shall not be construed to deny or disparage others retained by the people.

Amendment X

The powers not delegated to the United States by the Constitution, nor prohibited by it to the States, are reserved to the States respectively, or to the people.

Amendment XI

The Judicial power of the United States shall not be construed to extend to any suit in law or equity, commenced or prosecuted against one of the United States by Citizens of another State, or by Citizens or Subjects of any Foreign State.

Amendment XII

The Electors shall meet in their respective states and vote by ballot for President and Vice-President, one of whom, at least, shall not be an inhabitant of the same state with themselves; they shall name in their ballots the person voted for as President, and in distinct ballots the person voted for as Vice- President, and they shall make distinct lists of all persons voted for as President, and of all persons voted for as Vice-President, and of the number of votes for each, which lists they shall sign and certify, and transmit sealed to the seat of the government of the United States, directed to the President of the Senate;--The President of the Senate shall, in the presence of the Senate and House of Representatives, open all the certificates and the votes shall then be counted;--The person having the greatest Number of votes for President, shall be the President, if such number be a majority of the whole number of Electors appointed; and if no person have such majority, then from the persons having the highest numbers not exceeding three on the list of those voted for as President, the House of Representatives shall choose immediately, by ballot, the President. But in choosing the President, the votes shall be taken by states, the representation from each state having one vote; a quorum for this purpose shall consist of a member or members from two-thirds of the states, and a majority of all the states shall be necessary to a choice. And if the House of Representatives shall not choose a President whenever the right of choice shall devolve upon them, before the fourth day of March next following, then the Vice- President shall act as President, as in the case of the death or other constitutional disability of the President--The person having the greatest number of votes as Vice-President, shall be the Vice-President, if such number be a majority of the whole number of Electors appointed, and if no person have a majority, then from the two highest numbers on the list, the Senate shall choose the Vice-President; a quorum for the purpose shall consist of two-thirds of the whole number of Senators, and a majority of the whole number shall be necessary to a choice. But no person constitutionally ineligible to the office of President shall be eligible to that of Vice-President of the United States.

Amendment XIII

Section 1. Neither slavery nor involuntary servitude, except as a punishment for crime whereof the party shall have been duly convicted, shall exist within the United States, or any place subject to their jurisdiction.

Section 2. Congress shall have power to enforce this article by appropriate legislation.

Amendment XIV

Section 1. All persons born or naturalized in the United States and subject to the jurisdiction thereof, are citizens of the United States and of the State wherein they reside. No State shall make or enforce any law which shall abridge the privileges or immunities of citizens of the United States; nor shall any State deprive any person of life, liberty, or property, without due process of law; nor deny to any person within its jurisdiction the equal protection of the laws.

Section 2. Representatives shall be apportioned among the several States according to their respective numbers, counting the whole number of persons in each State, excluding Indians not taxed. But when the right to vote at any election for the choice of electors for President and Vice President of the United States, Representatives in Congress, the Executive and Judicial officers of a State, or the members of the Legislature thereof, is denied to any of the male inhabitants of such State, being twenty-one years of age, and citizens of the United States, or in any way abridged, except for participation in rebellion, or other crime, the basis of representation therein shall be reduced in the proportion which the number of such male citizens shall bear to the whole number of male citizens twenty-one years of age in such State.

Section 3. No person shall be a Senator or Representative in Congress, or elector of President and Vice President, or hold any office, civil or military, under the United States, or under any State, who, having previously taken an oath, as a member of Congress, or as an officer of the United States, or as a member of any State legislature, or as an executive or judicial officer of any State, to support the Constitution of the United States, shall have engaged in insurrection or rebellion against the same, or given aid or comfort to the enemies thereof. But Congress may by a vote of two-thirds of each House, remove such disability.

Section 4. The validity of the public debt of the United States, authorized by law, including debts incurred for payment of pensions and bounties for services in suppressing insurrection or rebellion, shall not be questioned. But neither the United States nor any State shall assume or pay any debt or obligation incurred in aid of insurrection or rebellion against the United States, or any claim for the loss or emancipation of any slave; but all such debts, obligations and claims shall be held illegal and void.

Section 5. The Congress shall have power to enforce, by appropriate legislation, the provisions of this article.

Amendment XV

Section 1. The right of citizens of the United States to vote shall not be denied or abridged by the United States or by any State on account of race, color, or previous condition of servitude.

Section 2. The Congress shall have power to enforce this article by appropriate legislation.

Amendment XVI

The Congress shall have power to lay and collect taxes on incomes, from whatever source derived, without apportionment among the several States, and without regard to any census or enumeration.

Amendment XVII

The Senate of the United States shall be composed of two Senators from each State, elected by the people thereof, for six years; and each Senator shall have one vote. The electors in each State shall have the qualifications requisite for electors of the most numerous branch of the State legislatures.

When vacancies happen in the representation of any State in the Senate, the executive authority of such State shall issue writs of election to fill such vacancies: Provided, That the legislature of any State may empower the executive thereof to make temporary appointments until the people fill the vacancies by election as the legislature may direct.

This amendment shall not be so construed as to affect the election or term of any Senator chosen before it becomes valid as part of the Constitution.

Amendment XVIII

Section 1. After one year from the ratification of this article the manufacture, sale, or transportation of intoxicating liquors within, the importation thereof into, or the exportation thereof from the United States and all territory subject to the jurisdiction thereof for beverage purposes is hereby prohibited.

Section 2. The Congress and the several States shall have concurrent power to enforce this article by appropriate legislation.

Section 3. This article shall be inoperative unless it shall have been ratified as an amendment to the Constitution by the legislatures of the several States, as provided in the Constitution, within seven years from the date of the submission hereof to the States by the Congress.

Amendment XIX

The right of citizens of the United States to vote shall not be denied or abridged by the United States or by any State on account of sex. Congress shall have power to enforce this article by appropriate legislation.

Amendment XX

Section 1. The terms of the President and Vice President shall end at noon on the 20th day of January, and the terms of Senators and Representatives at noon on the 3d day of January, of the years in which such terms would have ended if this article had not been ratified; and the terms of their successors shall then begin.

Section 2. The Congress shall assemble at least once in every year, and such meeting shall begin at noon on the 3d day of January, unless they shall by law appoint a different day.

Section 3. If, at the time fixed for the beginning of the term of the President, the President elect shall have died, the Vice President elect shall become President. If a President shall not have been chosen before the time fixed for the beginning of his term, or if the President elect shall have failed to qualify, then the Vice President elect shall act as President until a President shall have qualified; and the Congress may by law provide for the case wherein neither a President elect nor a Vice President elect shall have qualified, declaring who shall then act as President, or the manner in which one who is to act shall be selected, and such person shall act accordingly until a President or Vice President shall have qualified.

Section 4. The Congress may by law provide for the case of the death of any of the persons from whom the House of Representatives may choose a President whenever the right of choice shall have devolved upon them, and for the case of the death of any of the persons from whom the Senate may choose a Vice President whenever the right of choice shall have devolved upon them.

Section 5. Sections 1 and 2 shall take effect on the 15th day of October following the ratification of this article.

Section 6. This article shall be inoperative unless it shall have been ratified as an amendment to the Constitution by the legislatures of three-fourths of the several States within seven years from the date of its submission.

Amendment XXI

Section 1. The eighteenth article of amendment to the Constitution of the United States is hereby repealed.

Section 2. The transportation or importation into any State, Territory, or possession of the United States for delivery or use therein of intoxicating liquors, in violation of the laws thereof, is hereby prohibited.

Section 3. This article shall be inoperative unless it shall have been ratified as an amendment to the Constitution by conventions in the several States, as provided in the Constitution, within seven years from the date of the submission hereof to the States by the Congress.

Amendment XXII

Section 1. No person shall be elected to the office of the President more than twice, and no person who has held the office of President, or acted as President, for more than two years of a term to which some other person was elected President shall be elected to the office of the President more than once. But this Article shall not apply to any person holding the office of President, when this Article was proposed by the Congress, and shall not prevent any person who may be holding the office of President, or acting as President, during the term within which this Article becomes operative from holding the office of President or acting as President during the remainder of such term.

Section 2. This article shall be inoperative unless it shall have been ratified as an amendment to the Constitution by the legislatures of three-fourths of the several States within seven years from the date of its submission to the States by the Congress.

Amendment XXIII

Section 1. The District constituting the seat of Government of the United States shall appoint in such manner as the Congress may direct: A number of electors of President and Vice President equal to the whole number of Senators and Representatives in Congress to which the District would be entitled if it were a State, but in no event more than the least populous State; they shall be in addition to those appointed by the States, but they shall be considered, for the purposes of the election of President and Vice President, to be electors appointed by a State; and they shall meet in the District and perform such duties as provided by the twelfth article of amendment.

Section 2. The Congress shall have power to enforce this article by appropriate legislation.

Amendment XXIV

Section 1. The right of citizens of the United States to vote in any primary or other election for President or Vice President, for electors for President or Vice President, or for Senator or Representative in Congress, shall not be denied or abridged by the United States or any State by reason of failure to pay any poll tax or other tax.

Section 2. The Congress shall have power to enforce this article by appropriate legislation.

Amendment XXV

Section 1. In case of the removal of the President from office or of his death or resignation, the Vice President shall become President.

Section 2. Whenever there is a vacancy in the office of the Vice President, the President shall nominate a Vice President who shall take office upon confirmation by a majority vote of both Houses of Congress.

Section 3. Whenever the President transmits to the President pro tempore of the Senate and the Speaker of the House of Representatives has written declaration that he is unable to discharge the powers and duties of his office, and until he transmits to them a written declaration to the contrary, such powers and duties shall be discharged by the Vice President as Acting President.

Section 4. Whenever the Vice President and a majority of either the principal officers of the executive departments or of such other body as Congress may by law provide, transmit to the President pro tempore of the Senate and the Speaker of the House of Representatives their written declaration that the President is unable to discharge the powers and duties of his office, the Vice President shall immediately assume the powers and duties of the office as Acting President.

Thereafter, when the President transmits to the President pro tempore of the Senate and the Speaker of the House of Representatives has written declaration that no inability exists, he shall resume the powers and duties of his office unless the Vice President and a majority of either the principal officers of the executive department or of such other body as Congress may by law provide, transmit within four days to the President pro tempore of the Senate and the Speaker of the House of Representatives their written declaration that the President is unable to discharge the powers and duties of his office. Thereupon Congress shall decide the issue, assembling within forty-eight hours for that purpose if not in session. If the Congress, within twenty-one days after receipt of the latter written declaration, or, if Congress is not in session, within twenty-one days after Congress is required to assemble, determines by two-thirds vote of both Houses that the President is unable to discharge the powers and duties of his office, the Vice President shall continue to discharge the same as Acting President; otherwise, the President shall resume the powers and duties of his office.

Amendment XXVI

Section 1. The right of citizens of the United States, who are eighteen years of age or older, to vote shall not be denied or abridged by the United States or by any State on account of age.

Section 2. The Congress shall have power to enforce this article by appropriate legislation.

Amendment XXVII

No law varying the compensation for the services of the Senators and Representatives shall take effect, until an election of Representatives shall have intervened.

This document is sponsored by the United States Senate on the United States Government Printing Office web site.

Preamble to the
Charter of the United Nations
June 26, 1945

WE THE PEOPLES OF THE UNITED NATIONS DETERMINED to save succeeding generations from the scourge of war, which twice in our lifetime has brought untold sorrow to mankind, and to reaffirm faith in fundamental human rights, in the dignity and worth of the human person, in the equal rights of men and women and of nations large and small, and to establish conditions under which justice and respect for the obligations arising from treaties and other sources of international law can be maintained, and to promote social progress and better standards of life in larger freedom, AND FOR THESE ENDS to practice tolerance and live together in peace with one another as good neighbours, and to unite our strength to maintain international peace and security, and to ensure, by the acceptance of principles and the institution of methods, that armed force shall not be used, save in the common interest, and to employ international machinery for the promotion of the economic and social advancement of all peoples, HAVE RESOLED TO COMBINE OUR EFFORTS TO ACCOMPLISH THESE AIMS Accordingly, our respective Governments, through representatives assembled in the city of San Francisco, who have exhibited their full powers found to be in good and due form, have agreed to the present Charter of the United Nations and do hereby establish an international organization to be known as the United Nations.

CHAPTER I

PURPOSES AND PRINCIPLES

Article I

The Purposes of the United Nations are:

1.   To maintain international peace and security, and to that end: to take effective collective measures for the prevention and removal of threats to the peace, and for the suppression of acts of aggression or other breaches of the peace, and to bring about by peaceful means, and in conformity with the principles of justice and international law, adjustment or settlement of international disputes or situations which might lead to a breach of the peace;

2. To develop friendly relations among nations based on respect for the principle of equal rights and self-determination of peoples, and to take other appropriate measures to strengthen universal peace;

To achieve international co-operation in solving international problems of an economic, social, cultural, or humanitarian character, and in promoting and encouraging respect for human rights and for fundamental freedoms for all without distinction as to race, sex, language, or religion; and

3. To be a centre for harmonizing the actions of nations in the attainment of these common ends.

North Atlantic Treaty
April 4, 1949

Washington D.C.

The Parties to this Treaty reaffirm their faith in the purposes and principles of the Charter of the United Nations and their desire to live in peace with all peoples and all governments.

They are determined to safeguard the freedom, common heritage and civilisation of their peoples, founded on the principles of democracy, individual liberty and the rule of law.

They seek to promote stability and well-being in the North Atlantic area.

They are resolved to unite their efforts for collective defence and for the preservation of peace and security.

They therefore agree to this North Atlantic Treaty:

Article I

The Parties undertake, as set forth in the Charter of the United Nations, to settle any international dispute in which they may be involved by peaceful means in such a manner that international peace and security and justice are not endangered, and to refrain in their international relations from the threat or use of force in any manner inconsistent with the purposes of the United Nations.

Article II

The Parties will contribute toward the further development of peaceful and friendly international relations by strengthening their free institutions, by bringing about a better understanding of the principles upon which these institutions are founded, and by promoting conditions of stability and well-being. They will seek to eliminate conflict in their international economic policies and will encourage economic collaboration between any or all of them.

Article III

In order more effectively to achieve the objectives of this Treaty, the Parties, separately and jointly, by means of continuous and effective self-help and mutual aid, will maintain and develop their individual and collective capacity to resist armed attack.

Article IV

The Parties will consult together whenever, in the opinion of any of them, the territorial integrity, political independence or security of any of the Parties is threatened.

Article V

The Parties agree that an armed attack against one or more of them in Europe or North America shall be considered an attack against them all, and consequently they agree that, if such an armed attack occurs, each of them, in exercise of the right of individual or collective self defence recognised by Article 51 of the Charter of the United Nations, will assist the Party or Parties so attacked by taking forthwith, individually, and in concert with the other Parties, such action as it deems necessary, including the use of armed force, to restore and maintain the security of the North Atlantic area.

Any such armed attack and all measures taken as a result thereof shall immediately be reported to the Security Council. Such measures shall be terminated when the Security Council has taken the measures necessary to restore and maintain international peace and security.

Article VI

For the purpose of Article 5, an armed attack on one or more of the Parties is deemed to include an armed attack:

- on the territory of any of the Parties in Europe or North America, on the Algerian Departments of France, on the territory of Turkey or on the islands under the jurisdiction of any of the Parties in the North Atlantic area north of the Tropic of Cancer;

- on the forces, vessels, or aircraft of any of the Parties, when in or over these territories or any area in Europe in which occupation forces of any of the Parties were stationed on the date when the Treaty entered into force or the Mediterranean Sea or the North Atlantic area north of the Tropic of Cancer.

Article VII

The Treaty does not effect, and shall not be interpreted as affecting, in any way the rights and obligations under the Charter of the Parties which are members of the United Nations, or the primary responsibility of the Security Council for the maintenance of international peace and security.

Article VIII

Each Party declares that none of the international engagements now in force between it and any other of the Parties or any third State is in conflict with the provisions of this Treaty, and undertakes not to enter into any international engagement in conflict with this Treaty.

Article IX

The Parties hereby establish a Council, on which each of them shall be represented to consider matters concerning the implementation of this Treaty. The Council shall be so organised as to be able to meet promptly at any time. The Council shall set up such subsidiary bodies as may be necessary; in particular it shall establish immediately a defence committee which shall recommend measures for the implementation of Articles 3 and 5.

Article X

The Parties may, by unanimous agreement, invite any other European State in a position to further the principles of this Treaty and to contribute to the security of the North Atlantic area to accede to this Treaty. Any State so invited may become a party to the Treaty by depositing its instrument of accession with the Government of the United States of America. The Government of the United States of America will inform each of the Parties of the deposit of each such instrument of accession.

Article XI

This Treaty shall be ratified and its provisions carried out by the Parties in accordance with their respective constitutional processes. The instruments of ratification shall be deposited as soon as possible with the Government of the United States of America, which will notify all the other signatories of each deposit. The Treaty shall enter into force between the States which have ratified it as soon as the ratification of the majority of the signatories, including the ratifications of Belgium, Canada, France, Luxembourg, the Netherlands, the United Kingdom and the United States, have been deposited and shall come into effect with respect to other States on the date of the deposit of their ratifications.

Article XII

After the Treaty has been in force for ten years, or at any time thereafter, the Parties shall, if any of them so requests, consult together for the purpose of reviewing the Treaty, having regard for the factors then affecting peace and security in the North Atlantic area including the development of universal as well as regional arrangements under the Charter of the United Nations for the maintenance of international peace and security.

After the Treaty has been in force for twenty years, any Party may cease to be a Party one year after its notice of denunciation has been given to the Government of the United States of America, which will inform the Governments of the other Parties of the deposit of each notice of denunciation.

Article XIV

This Treaty, of which the English and French texts are equally authentic, shall be deposited in the archives of the Government of the United States of America. Duly certified copies will be transmitted by that government to the governments of the other signatories.

Contract With America
1994

As Republican Members of the House of Representatives and as citizens seeking to join that body, we propose not just to change its policies, but even more important, to restore the bonds of trust between the people and their elected representatives.

That is why, in this era of official evasion and posturing, we offer instead a detailed agenda for national renewal, a written commitment with no fine print.

This year's election offers the chance, after four decades of one-party control, to bring to the House a new majority that will transform the way Congress works. That historic change would be the end of government that is too big, too intrusive, and too easy with the public's money. It can be the beginning of a Congress that respects the values and shares the faith of the American family.

Like Lincoln, our first Republican president, we intend to act "with firmness in the right, as God gives us to see the right." To restore accountability to Congress. To end its cycle of scandal and disgrace. To make us all proud again of the way free people govern themselves.

On the first day of the 104th Congress, the new Republican majority will immediately pass the following major reforms, aimed at restoring the faith and trust of the American people in their government:

FIRST, require all laws that apply to the rest of the country also apply equally to the Congress;

SECOND, select a major, independent auditing firm to conduct a comprehensive audit of Congress for waste, fraud or abuse;

THIRD, cut the number of House committees, and cut committee staff by one-third;

FOURTH, limit the terms of all committee chairs;

FIFTH, ban the casting of proxy votes in committee;

SIXTH, require committee meetings to be open to the public;

SEVENTH, require a three-fifths majority vote to pass a tax increase;

EIGHTH, guarantee an honest accounting of our Federal Budget by implementing zero base-line budgeting.

Thereafter, within the first 100 days of the 104th Congress, we shall bring to the House Floor the following bills, each to be given full and open debate, each to be given a clear and fair vote and each to be immediately available this day for public inspection and scrutiny.

1.   THE FISCAL RESPONSIBILITY ACT

A balanced budget/tax limitation amendment and a legislative line-item veto to restore fiscal responsibility to an out-of-control Congress, requiring them to live under the same budget constraints as families and businesses.

2.   THE TAKING BACK OUR STREETS ACT

An anti-crime package including stronger truth-in-sentencing, "good faith" exclusionary rule exemptions, effective death penalty provisions, and cuts in social spending from this summer's "crime" bill to fund prison construction and additional law enforcement to keep people secure in their neighborhoods and kids safe in their schools.

3.   THE PERSONAL RESPONSIBILITY ACT

Discourage illegitimacy and teen pregnancy by prohibiting welfare to minor mothers and denying increased AFDC for additional children while on welfare, cut spending for welfare programs, and enact a tough two-years-and-out provision with work requirements to promote individual responsibility.

4.   THE FAMILY REINFORCEMENT ACT

Child support enforcement, tax incentives for adoption, strengthening rights of parents in their children's education, stronger child pornography laws, and an elderly dependent care tax credit to reinforce the central role of families in American society.

5.   THE AMERICAN DREAM RESTORATION ACT

A $500 per child tax credit, begin repeal of the marriage tax penalty, and creation of American Dream Savings Accounts to provide middle class tax relief.

6. THE NATIONAL SECURITY RESTORATION ACT

No U.S. troops under U.N. command and restoration of the essential parts of our national security funding to strengthen our national defense and maintain our credibility around the world.

7. THE SENIOR CITIZENS FAIRNESS ACT

Raise the Social Security earnings limit which currently forces seniors out of the work force, repeal the 1993 tax hikes on Social Security benefits and provide tax incentives for private long-term care insurance to let Older Americans keep more of what they have earned over the years.

8. THE JOB CREATION AND WAGE ENHANCEMENT ACT

Small business incentives, capital gains cut and indexation, neutral cost recovery, risk assessment/cost-benefit analysis, strengthening the Regulatory Flexibility Act and unfunded mandate reform to create jobs and raise worker wages.

9. THE COMMON SENSE LEGAL REFORM ACT

"Loser pays" laws, reasonable limits on punitive damages and reform of product liability laws to stem the endless tide of litigation.

10. THE CITIZEN LEGISLATURE ACT

A first-ever vote on term limits to replace career politicians with citizen legislators.

Further, we will instruct the House Budget Committee to report to the floor and we will work to enact additional budget savings, beyond the budget cuts specifically included in the legislation described above, to ensure that the Federal budget deficit will be less than it would have been without the enactment of these bills.

Respecting the judgment of our fellow citizens as we seek their mandate for reform, we hereby pledge our names to this Contract with America.

Oaths of Office

President of the United States (Executive Branch)

According to the 20th Amendment to the Constitution, a President's term of office begins at 12:00 p.m. (noon) on January 20th of the year following an election. In order to assume his/her duties, the President-elect must recite the Oath of Office. The Oath is administered by the Chief

Justice of the Supreme Court. The President-elect places his hand on the Bible, raises his right hand, and takes the Oath as directed by the Chief Justice. The Oath, as stated in Article II, Section I, Clause 8 of the U.S. Constitution, is as follows:

> "I do solemnly swear (or affirm) that I will faithfully execute the office of President of the United States, and will to the best of my ability, preserve, protect and defend the Constitution of the United States."

Vice President of the United States (Executive Branch)

The Vice President also takes an oath of office. Until 1933, the Vice President took the oath of office in the Senate. Today, both the President and Vice President are inaugurated in the same ceremony. The Vice President's oath is administered immediately before the President's. The Vice President's oath may be administered by the retiring vice president, by a member of Congress, or by some other government official, such as a justice of the Supreme Court. The Vice President's oath is as follows:

> "I do solemnly swear that I will support and defend the Constitution of the United States against all enemies, foreign and domestic, that I will bear true faith and allegiance to the same: that I take this obligation freely, without any mental reservation or purpose of evasion, and I will well and faithfully discharge the duties of the office on which I am about to enter. So help me God."

Members of Congress (Legislative Branch)

At the start of each new Congress, in January of every odd-numbered year, the entire House of Representatives and one-third of the Senate takes an oath of office. The Speaker of the House will direct the Members to rise and the oath is administered. The original oath was as follows: "I do solemnly swear (or affirm) that I will support the Constitution of the United States."

The oath was revised during the Civil War, when members of Congress were concerned about traitors. The current oath is as follows:

> "I do solemnly swear (or affirm) that I will support and defend the Constitution of the United States against all enemies, foreign and domestic; that I will bear true faith and allegiance to the same; that I take this obligation freely, without any mental reservation or purpose of evasion; and that I will well and faithfully discharge the duties of the office on which I am about to enter: So help me God."

Supreme Court Justices (Judicial Branch)

According to Title 28, Chapter I, Part 453 of the United States Code, each Supreme Court Justice takes the following oath:

> "I, [NAME], do solemnly swear (or affirm) that I will administer justice without respect to persons, and do equal right to the poor and to the rich, and that I will faithfully and impartially discharge and perform all the duties incumbent upon me as [TITLE] under the Constitution and laws of the United States. So help me God."

The Military Oath

The following oath is taken by all personnel inducted into the armed forces of the United States, as found in the US Code, Section 502.

I, _____, do solemnly swear (or affirm) that I will support and defend the Constitution of the United States against all enemies, foreign and domestic; that I will bear true faith and allegiance to the same; and that I will obey the orders of the President of the United States and the orders of the officers appointed over me, according to regulations and the Uniform Code of Military Justice. So help me God.

"Of the United States of America"

Federalist No. 1

General Introduction
For the *Independent Journal*

HAMILTON

To the People of the State of New York:

AFTER an unequivocal experience of the inefficiency of the subsisting federal government, you are called upon to deliberate on a new Constitution for the United States of America. The subject speaks its own importance; comprehending in its consequences nothing less than the existence of the UNION, the safety and welfare of the parts of which it is composed, the fate of an empire in many respects the most interesting in the world. It has been frequently remarked that it seems to have been reserved to the people of this country, by their conduct and example, to decide the important question, whether societies of men are really capable or not of establishing good government from reflection and choice, or whether they are forever destined to depend for their political constitutions on accident and force. If there be any truth in the remark, the crisis at which we are arrived may with propriety be regarded as the era in which that decision is to be made; and a wrong election of the part we shall act may, in this view, deserve to be considered as the general misfortune of mankind.

This idea will add the inducements of philanthropy to those of patriotism, to heighten the solicitude which all considerate and good men must feel for the event. Happy will it be if our choice should be directed by a judicious estimate of our true interests, unperplexed and unbiased by considerations not connected with the public good. But this is a thing more ardently to be wished than seriously to be expected. The plan offered to our deliberations affects too many particular interests, innovates upon too many local institutions, not to involve in its discussion a variety of objects foreign to its merits, and of views, passions and prejudices little favorable to the discovery of truth.

Among the most formidable of the obstacles which the new Constitution will have to encounter may readily be distinguished the obvious interest of a certain class of men in every State to resist all changes which may hazard a diminution of the power, emolument, and consequence of the offices they hold under the State establishments; and the perverted ambition of another class of men, who will either hope to aggrandize themselves by the confusions of their country, or will flatter themselves with fairer prospects of elevation from the subdivision of the empire into several partial confederacies than from its union under one government.

It is not, however, my design to dwell upon observations of this nature. I am well aware that it would be disingenuous to resolve indiscriminately the opposition of any set of men (merely because their situations might subject them to suspicion) into interested or ambitious views. Candor will oblige us to admit that even such men may be actuated by upright intentions; and it cannot be doubted that much of the opposition which has made its appearance, or may hereafter make its appearance, will spring from sources, blameless at least, if not respectable--the honest errors of minds led astray by preconceived jealousies and fears. So numerous indeed and so powerful are the causes which serve to give a false bias to the judgment, that we, upon many occasions, see wise and good men on the wrong as well as on the right side of questions of the first magnitude to society. This circumstance, if duly attended to, would furnish a lesson of moderation to those who are ever so much persuaded of their being in the right in any controversy. And a further reason for caution, in this respect, might be drawn from the reflection that we are not always sure that those who advocate the truth are influenced by purer principles than their antagonists. Ambition, avarice, personal animosity, party opposition, and many other motives not more laudable than these, are apt to operate as well upon those who support as those who oppose the right side of a question. Were there not even these inducements to moderation, nothing could be more ill-judged than that intolerant spirit which has, at all times, characterized political parties. For in politics, as in religion, it is equally absurd to aim at making proselytes by fire and sword. Heresies in either can rarely be cured by persecution.

And yet, however just these sentiments will be allowed to be, we have already sufficient indications that it will happen in this as in all former cases of great national discussion. A torrent of angry and malignant passions will be let loose. To judge from the conduct of the opposite parties, we shall be led to conclude that they will mutually hope to evince the justness of their opinions, and to increase the number of their converts by the loudness of their declamations and the bitterness of their invectives. An enlightened zeal for the energy and efficiency of government will be stigmatized as the offspring of a temper fond of despotic power and hostile to the principles of liberty. An over-scrupulous jealousy of danger to the rights of the people, which is more commonly the fault of the head than of the heart, will be represented as mere pretense and artifice, the stale bait for popularity at the expense of the public good. It will be forgotten, on the one hand, that jealousy is the usual concomitant of love, and that the noble enthusiasm of liberty is apt to be infected with a spirit of narrow and illiberal distrust. On the other hand, it will be equally forgotten that the vigor of government is essential to the security of liberty; that, in the contemplation of a sound and well-informed judgment, their interest can never be separated; and that a dangerous ambition more often lurks behind the specious mask of zeal for the rights of the people than under the forbidden appearance of zeal for the firmness and efficiency of government. History will teach us that the former has been found a much more certain road to the introduction of despotism than the latter, and that of those men who have overturned the liberties of republics, the greatest number have begun their career by paying an obsequious court to the people; commencing demagogues, and ending tyrants.

In the course of the preceding observations, I have had an eye, my fellow-citizens, to putting you upon your guard against all attempts, from whatever quarter, to influence your decision in a matter of the utmost moment to your welfare, by any impressions other than those which may result from the evidence of truth. You will, no doubt, at the same time, have collected from the general scope of them, that they proceed from a source not unfriendly to the new Constitution. Yes, my countrymen, I own to you that, after having given it an attentive consideration, I am clearly of opinion it is your interest to adopt it. I am convinced that this is the safest course for your liberty, your dignity, and your happiness. I affect not reserves which I do not feel. I will not amuse you with an appearance of deliberation when I have decided. I frankly acknowledge to you my convictions, and I will freely lay before you the reasons on which they are founded. The consciousness of good intentions disdains ambiguity. I shall not, however, multiply professions on this head. My motives must remain in the depository of my own breast. My arguments will be open to all, and may be judged of by all. They shall at least be offered in a spirit which will not disgrace the cause of truth.

I propose, in a series of papers, to discuss the following interesting particulars:

- THE UTILITY OF THE UNION TO YOUR POLITICAL PROSPERITY
- THE INSUFFICIENCY OF THE PRESENT CONFEDERATION TO PRESERVE THAT UNION
- THE NECESSITY OF A GOVERNMENT AT LEAST EQUALLY ENERGETIC WITH THE ONE PROPOSED, TO THE ATTAINMENT OF THIS OBJECT THE CONFORMITY OF THE PROPOSED CONSTITUTION TO THE TRUE PRINCIPLES OF REPUBLICAN GOVERNMENT
- ITS ANALOGY TO YOUR OWN STATE CONSTITUTION
- and lastly, THE ADDITIONAL SECURITY WHICH ITS ADOPTION WILL AFFORD TO THE PRESERVATION OF THAT SPECIES OF GOVERNMENT, TO LIBERTY, AND TO PROPERTY.

In the progress of this discussion I shall endeavor to give a satisfactory answer to all the objections which shall have made their appearance, that may seem to have any claim to your attention.

It may perhaps be thought superfluous to offer arguments to prove the utility of the UNION, a point, no doubt, deeply engraved on the hearts of the great body of the people in every State, and one, which it may be imagined, has no adversaries. But the fact is, that we already hear it whispered in the private circles of those who oppose the new Constitution, that the thirteen States are of too great extent for any general system, and that we must of necessity resort to separate confederacies of distinct portions of the whole.[1] This doctrine will, in all probability, be gradually propagated, till it has votaries enough to countenance an open avowal of it. For nothing can be more evident, to those who are able to take an enlarged view of the subject, than the alternative of an adoption of the new Constitution or a dismemberment of the Union. It will therefore be of use to begin by examining the advantages of that Union, the certain evils, and the probable dangers, to which every State will be exposed from its dissolution. This shall accordingly constitute the subject of my next address.

PUBLIUS

Federalist No. 9

The Union as a Safeguard Against Domestic Faction and Insurrection
For the *Independent Journal*

HAMILTON

To the People of the State of New York:

A FIRM Union will be of the utmost moment to the peace and liberty of the States, as a barrier against domestic faction and insurrection. It is impossible to read the history of the petty republics of Greece and Italy without feeling sensations of horror and disgust at the distractions with which they were continually agitated, and at the rapid succession of revolutions by which they were kept in a state of perpetual vibration between the extremes of tyranny and anarchy. If they exhibit occasional calms, these only serve as short-lived contrast to the furious storms that are to succeed. If now and then intervals of felicity open to view, we behold them with a mixture of regret, arising from the reflection that the pleasing scenes before us are soon to be overwhelmed by the tempestuous waves of sedition and party rage. If momentary rays of glory break forth from the gloom, while they dazzle us with a transient and fleeting brilliancy, they at the same time admonish us to lament that the vices of government should pervert the direction and tarnish the lustre of those bright talents and exalted endowments for which the favored soils that produced them have been so justly celebrated.

From the disorders that disfigure the annals of those republics the advocates of despotism have drawn arguments, not only against the forms of republican government, but against the very principles of civil liberty. They have decried all free government as inconsistent with the order of society, and have indulged themselves in malicious exultation over its friends and partisans. Happily for mankind, stupendous fabrics reared on the basis of liberty, which have flourished for ages, have, in a few glorious instances, refuted their gloomy sophisms. And, I trust, America will be the broad and solid foundation of other edifices, not less magnificent, which will be equally permanent monuments of their errors.

But it is not to be denied that the portraits they have sketched of republican government were too just copies of the originals from which they were taken. If it had been found impracticable to have devised models of a more perfect structure, the enlightened friends to liberty would have been obliged to abandon the cause of that species of government as indefensible. The science of politics, however, like most other sciences, has received great improvement. The efficacy of various principles is now well understood, which were either not known at all, or imperfectly known to the ancients. The regular distribution of power into distinct departments; the introduction of legislative balances and checks; the institution of courts composed of judges holding their offices during good behavior; the representation of the people in the legislature by deputies of their own election: these are wholly new discoveries, or have made their principal progress towards perfection in modern times. They are means, and powerful means, by which the excellences of republican government may be retained and its imperfections lessened or avoided. To this catalogue of circumstances that tend to the amelioration of popular systems of civil government, I shall venture, however novel it may appear to some, to add one more, on a principle which has been made the foundation of an objection to the new Constitution; I mean the ENLARGEMENT of the ORBIT within which such systems are to revolve, either in respect to the dimensions of a single State or to the consolidation of several smaller States into one great Confederacy. The latter is that which immediately concerns the object under consideration. It will, however, be of use to examine the principle in its application to a single State, which shall be attended to in another place.

The utility of a Confederacy, as well to suppress faction and to guard the internal tranquillity of States, as to increase their external force and security, is in reality not a new idea. It has been practiced upon in different countries and ages, and has received the sanction of the most approved writers on the subject of politics. The opponents of the plan proposed have, with great assiduity, cited and circulated the observations of Montesquieu on the necessity of a contracted territory for a republican government. But they seem not to have been apprised of the sentiments of that great man expressed in another part of his work, nor to have adverted to the consequences of the principle to which they subscribe with such ready acquiescence.

When Montesquieu recommends a small extent for republics, the standards he had in view were of dimensions far short of the limits of almost every one of these States. Neither Virginia, Massachusetts, Pennsylvania, New York, North Carolina, nor Georgia can by any means be compared with the models from which he reasoned and to which the terms of his description apply. If we therefore take his ideas on this point as the criterion of truth, we shall be driven to the alternative either of taking refuge at once in the arms of monarchy, or of splitting ourselves into an infinity of little, jealous, clashing, tumultuous commonwealths, the wretched nurseries of unceasing discord, and the miserable objects of universal pity or contempt. Some of the writers who have come forward on the other side of the question seem to have been aware of the dilemma; and have even been bold enough to hint at the division of the larger States as a desirable thing. Such an infatuated policy, such a desperate expedient, might, by the multiplication of petty offices, answer the views of men who possess not qualifications to extend their influence beyond the narrow circles of personal intrigue, but it could never promote the greatness or happiness of the people of America.

Referring the examination of the principle itself to another place, as has been already mentioned, it will be sufficient to remark here that, in the sense of the author who has been most emphatically quoted upon the occasion, it would only dictate a reduction of the SIZE of the more considerable MEMBERS of the Union, but would not militate against their being all comprehended in one confederate government. And this is the true question, in the discussion of which we are at present interested.

So far are the suggestions of Montesquieu from standing in opposition to a general Union of the States, that he explicitly treats of a CONFEDERATE REPUBLIC as the expedient for extending the sphere of popular government, and reconciling the advantages of monarchy with those of republicanism.

"It is very probable," (says he1) "that mankind would have been obliged at length to live constantly under the government of a single person, had they not contrived a kind of constitution that has all the internal advantages of a republican, together with the external force of a monarchical government. I mean a CONFEDERATE REPUBLIC.

"This form of government is a convention by which several smaller STATES agree to become members of a larger ONE, which they intend to form. It is a kind of assemblage of societies that constitute a new one, capable of increasing, by means of new associations, till they arrive to such a degree of power as to be able to provide for the security of the united body.

"A republic of this kind, able to withstand an external force, may support itself without any internal corruptions. The form of this society prevents all manner of inconveniences.

"If a single member should attempt to usurp the supreme authority, he could not be supposed to have an equal authority and credit in all the confederate states. Were he to have too great influence over one, this would alarm the rest. Were he to subdue a part, that which would still remain free might oppose him with forces independent of those which he had usurped and overpower him before he could be settled in his usurpation.

"Should a popular insurrection happen in one of the confederate states the others are able to quell it. Should abuses creep into one part, they are reformed by those that remain sound. The state may be destroyed on one side, and not on the other; the confederacy may be dissolved, and the confederates preserve their sovereignty. "As this government is composed of small republics, it enjoys the internal happiness of each; and with respect to its external situation, it is possessed, by means of the association, of all the advantages of large monarchies."

I have thought it proper to quote at length these interesting passages, because they contain a luminous abridgment of the principal arguments in favor of the Union, and must effectually remove the false impressions which a misapplication of other parts of the work was calculated to make. They have, at the same time, an intimate connection with the more immediate design of this paper; which is, to illustrate the tendency of the Union to repress domestic faction and insurrection.

A distinction, more subtle than accurate, has been raised between a CONFEDERACY and a CONSOLIDATION of the States. The essential characteristic of the first is said to be, the restriction of its authority to the members in their collective capacities, without reaching to the individuals of whom they are composed. It is contended that the national council ought to have no concern with any object of internal administration. An exact equality of suffrage between the members has also been insisted upon as a leading feature of a confederate government. These positions are, in the main, arbitrary; they are supported neither by principle nor precedent. It has indeed happened, that governments of this kind have generally operated in the manner which the distinction taken notice of, supposes to be inherent in their nature; but there have been in most of them extensive exceptions to the practice, which serve to prove, as far as example will go, that there is no absolute rule on the subject. And it will be clearly shown in the course of this investigation that as far as the principle contended for has prevailed, it has been the cause of incurable disorder and imbecility in the government.

The definition of a CONFEDERATE REPUBLIC seems simply to be "an assemblage of societies," or an association of two or more states into one state. The extent, modifications, and objects of the federal authority are mere matters of discretion. So long as the separate organization of the members be not abolished; so long as it exists, by a constitutional necessity, for local purposes; though it should be in perfect subordination to the general authority of the union, it would still be, in fact and in theory, an association of states, or a confederacy. The proposed Constitution, so far from implying an abolition of the State governments, makes them constituent parts of the national sovereignty, by allowing them a direct representation in the Senate, and leaves in their possession certain exclusive and very important portions of sovereign power. This fully corresponds, in every rational import of the terms, with the idea of a federal government.

In the Lycian confederacy, which consisted of twenty-three CITIES or republics, the largest were entitled to THREE votes in the COMMON COUNCIL, those of the middle class to TWO, and the smallest to ONE. The COMMON COUNCIL had the appointment of all the judges and magistrates of the respective CITIES. This was certainly the most, delicate species of interference in their internal administration; for if there be any thing that seems exclusively appropriated to the local jurisdictions, it is the appointment of their own officers. Yet Montesquieu, speaking of this association, says: "Were I to give a model of an excellent Confederate Republic, it would be that of Lycia." Thus we perceive that the distinctions insisted upon were not within the contemplation of this enlightened civilian; and we shall be led to conclude, that they are the novel refinements of an erroneous theory.

PUBLIUS

The Anti-Federalist Papers: Essay V

Taken from "Brutus" fifth essay, The New-York Journal of December 13, 1787.

This constitution considers the people of the several states as one body corporate, and is intended as an original compact; it will therefore dissolve all contracts which may be inconsistent with it. This not only results from its nature, but is expressly declared in the 6th article of it. The design of the constitution is expressed in the preamble, to be, "in order to form a more perfect union, to establish justice, insure domestic tranquility, provide for the common defense, promote the general welfare, and secure the blessings of liberty to ourselves and posterity." These are the ends this government is to accomplish, and for which it is invested with certain powers; among these is the power "to make all laws which are necessary and proper for carrying into execution the foregoing powers and all other powers vested by this constitution in the government of the United States, or in any department or officer thereof." It is a rule in construing a law to consider the objects the legislature had in view in passing it, and to give it such an explanation as to promote their intention. The same rule will apply in explaining a constitution. The great objects then are declared in this preamble in general and indefinite terms to be to provide for the common welfare, and an express power being vested in the legislature to make all laws which shall be necessary and proper for carrying into execution all the powers vested in the general government. The inference is natural that the legislature will have an authority to make all laws which they shall judge necessary for the common safety, and to promote the general welfare. This amounts to a power to make laws at discretion. No terms can be found more indefinite than these, and it is obvious, that the legislature alone must judge what laws are proper and necessary for the purpose. It may be said, that this way of explaining the constitution, is torturing and making it speak what it never intended. This is far from my intention, and I shall not even insist upon this implied power, but join issue with those who say we are to collect the idea of the powers given from the express words of the clauses granting them; and it will not be difficult to show that the same authority is expressly given which is supposed to be implied in the foregoing paragraphs.

In the lst article, 8th section, it is declared, "that Congress shall have power to lay and collect taxes, duties, imposts, and excises, to pay the debts, and provide for the common defense, and general welfare of the United States." In the preamble, the intent of the constitution, among other things, is declared to be to provide for the common defense, and promote the general welfare, and in this clause the power is in express words given to Congress "to provide for the common defense, and general welfare." And in the last paragraph of the same section there is an express authority to make all laws which shall be necessary and proper for carrying into execution this power. It is therefore evident, that the legislature under this constitution may pass any law which they may think proper. It is true the 9th section restrains their power with respect to certain subjects. But these restrictions are very limited, some of them improper, some unimportant, and others not easily understood, as I shall hereafter show. It has been urged that the meaning I give to this part of the constitution is not the true one, that the intent of it is to confer on the legislature the power to lay and collect taxes, etc., in order to provide for the common defense and general welfare. To this I would reply, that the meaning and intent of the constitution is to be collected from the words of it, and I submit to the public, whether the construction I have given it is not the most natural and easy. But admitting the contrary opinion to prevail, I shall nevertheless, be able to show, that the same powers are substantially vested in the general government, by several other articles in the constitution. It invests the legislature with authority to lay and collect taxes, duties, imposts and excises, in order to provide for the common defense, and promote the general welfare, and to pass all laws which may be necessary and proper for carrying this power into effect. To comprehend the extent of this authority, it will be requisite to examine

1st. What is included in this power to lay and collect taxes, duties, imposts and excises.

2nd. What is implied in the authority, to pass all laws which shall be necessary and proper for carrying this power into execution.

3rd. What limitation, if any, is set to the exercise of this power by the constitution.

First. To detail the particulars comprehended in the general terms, taxes, duties, imposts and excises, would require a volume, instead of a single piece in a newspaper. Indeed it would be a task far beyond my ability, and to which no one can be competent, unless possessed of a mind capable of comprehending every possible source of revenue; for they extend to every possible way of raising money, whether by direct or indirect taxation. Under this clause may be imposed a poll tax, a land tax, a tax on houses and buildings, on windows and fireplaces, on cattle and on all kinds of personal property. It extends to duties on all kinds of goods to any amount, to tonnage and poundage on vessels, to duties on written instruments, newspapers, almanacks, and books. It comprehends an excise on all kinds of liquors, spirits, wines, cider, beer, etc., and indeed takes in duty or excise on every necessary or conveniency of life, whether of foreign or home growth or manufactory. In short, we can have no conception of any way in which a government can raise money from the people, but what is included in one or other of these general terms. We may say then that this clause commits to the hands of the general legislature every conceivable source of revenue within the United States, Not only are these terms very comprehensive, and extend to a vast number of objects, but the power to lay and collect has great latitude; it will lead to the passing a vast number of laws, which may affect the personal rights of the citizens of the states, expose their property to fines and confiscation, and put their lives in jeopardy. It opens a door to the appointment of a swarm of revenue and excise collectors to prey upon the honest and industrious part of the community, [and] eat up their substance. . . .

Second. We will next inquire into what is implied in the authority to pass all laws which shall be necessary and proper to carry this power into execution.

It is, perhaps, utterly impossible fully to define this power. The authority granted in the first clause can only be understood in its full extent, by descending to all the particular cases in which a revenue can be raised; the number and variety of these cases are so endless, and as it were infinite, that no man living has, as yet, been able to reckon them up. The greatest geniuses in the world have been for ages employed in the research, and when mankind had supposed that the subject was exhausted they have been astonished with the refined improvements that have been made in modern times ' and especially in the English nation on the subject. If then the objects of this power cannot be comprehended, how is it possible to understand the extent of that power which can pass all laws which shall be necessary and proper for carrying it into executions It is truly incomprehensible. A case cannot be conceived of, which is not included in this power. It is well known that the subject of revenue is the most difficult and extensive in the science of government. It requires the greatest talents of a statesman, and the most numerous and exact provisions of the legislature. The command of the revenues 'Of a state gives the command of every thing in it. He that has the purse will have the sword, and they that have both, have everything; so that the legislature having every source from which money can be drawn under their direction, with a right to make all laws necessary and proper for drawing forth all the resource of the country, would have, in fact, all power.

Were I to enter into the detail, it would be easy to show how this power in its operation, would totally destroy all the powers of the individual states. But this is not necessary for those who will think for themselves, and it will be useless to such as take things upon trust; nothing will awaken them to reflection, until the iron hand of oppression compel them to it.

I shall only remark, that this power, given to the federal legislature, directly annihilates all the powers of the state legislatures. There cannot be a greater solecism in politics than to talk of power in a government, without the command of any revenue. It is as absurd as to talk of an animal without blood, or the subsistence of one without food. Now the general government having in their control every possible source of revenue, and authority to pass any law they may deem necessary to draw them forth, or to facilitate their collection, no source of revenue is therefore left in the hands 'Of any state. Should any state attempt to raise money by law, the general government may repeal or arrest it in the execution, for all their laws will be the supreme law of the land. If then any one can be weak enough to believe that a government can exist without having the authority to raise money to pay a door-keeper to their assembly, he may believe that the state government can exist, should this new constitution take place.

It is agreed by most of the advocates of this new system, that the government which is proper for the United States should be a confederated one; that the respective states ought to retain a portion of their sovereignty, and that they should preserve not only the forms of their legislatures, but also the power to conduct certain internal concerns. How far the powers to be retained by the states are to extend, is the question; we need not spend much time on this subject, as it respects this constitution, for a government without power to raise money is one only in name. It is clear that the legislatures of the respective states must be altogether dependent on the will of the general legislature, for the means of supporting their government. The legislature of the United States will have a right to exhaust every source of revenue in every state, and to annul all laws of the states which may stand in the way of effecting it; unless therefore we can suppose the state governments can exist without money to support the officers who execute them, we must conclude they will exist no longer than the general legislatures choose they should. Indeed the idea of any government existing, in any respect, as an independent one, without any means of support in their own hands, is an absurdity. If therefore, this constitution has in view, what many of its framers and advocates say it has, to secure and guarantee to the separate states the exercise of certain powers of government, it certainly ought to have left in their hands some sources of revenue. It should have marked the line in which the general government should have raised money, and set bounds over which they should not pass, leaving to the separate states other means to raise supplies for the support of their governments, and to discharge their respective debts. To this it is objected, that the general government ought to have power competent to the purposes of the union; they are to provide for the common defense, to pay the debts of the United States, support foreign ministers, and the civil establishment of the union, and to do these they ought to have authority to raise money adequate to the purpose. On this I observe, that the state governments have also contracted debts; they require money to support their civil officers; . . . if they give to the general government a power to raise money in every way in which it can possibly be raised, with . . . a control over the state legislatures as to prohibit them, whenever the general legislature may think proper, from raising any money, (the states will fail]. It is again objected that it is very difficult, if not impossible, to draw the line of distinction between the powers of the general and state governments on this subject. The first, it is said, must have the power to raise the money necessary for the purposes of the union; if they are limited to certain objects the revenue may fall short of a sufficiency for the public exigencies; they must therefore have discretionary power. The line may be easily and accurately drawn between the powers of the two governments on this head. The distinction between external and internal taxes, is not a novel one in this country. It is a plain one, and easily understood. The first includes impost duties on all imported goods; this species of taxes it is proper should be laid by the general government; many reasons might be urged to show that no danger is to be apprehended from their exercise of it. They may be collected in few places, and from few hands with certainty and expedition. But few officers are necessary to be employed in collecting them, and there is no danger of oppression in laying them, because if they are laid higher than trade will bear, the merchants will cease importing, or smuggle their goods. We have therefore sufficient security, arising from the nature of the thing, against burdensome, and intolerable impositions from this kind of tax. The case is far otherwise with regard to direct taxes; these include poll taxes, land taxes, excises, duties on written instruments, on everything we eat, drink, or wear; they take hold of every species of property, and come home to every man's house and pocket. These are often so oppressive, as to grind the face of the poor, and render the lives of the common people a burden to them. The great and only security the people can have against oppression from this kind of taxes, must rest in their representatives. If they are sufficiently numerous to be well informed of the circumstances, . . . and have a proper regard for the people, they will be secure. The general legislature, as I have shown in a former paper, will not be thus qualified,' and therefore, on this account, ought not to exercise the power of direct taxation. If the power of laying imposts will not be sufficient, some other specific mode of raising a revenue should have been assigned the general government; many may be suggested in which their power may be accurately defined and limited, and it would be much better to give them authority to lay and collect a duty on exports, not to exceed a certain rate per cent, than to have surrendered every kind of resource that the country has, to the complete abolition of the state governments, and which will introduce such an infinite number of laws and ordinances, fines and penalties, courts, and judges, collectors, and excise men, that when a man can number them, he may enumerate the stars of Heaven.

BRUTUS

A powerful rebuttal of Hamilton, the logic of Brutus can be found in a Supreme Court decision of 1819, McCulloch v. Maryland.

Jefferson's 1st Inaugural Address
March 4, 1801

Friends and Fellow-Citizens:

Called upon to undertake the duties of the first executive office of our country, I avail myself of the presence of that portion of my fellow-citizens which is here assembled to express my grateful thanks for the favor with which they have been pleased to look toward me, to declare a sincere consciousness that the task is above my talents, and that I approach it with those anxious and awful presentiments which the greatness of the charge and the weakness of my powers so justly inspire. A rising nation, spread over a wide and fruitful land, traversing all the seas with the rich productions of their industry, engaged in commerce with nations who feel power and forget right, advancing rapidly to destinies beyond the reach of mortal eye--when I contemplate these transcendent objects, and see the honor, the happiness, and the hopes of this beloved country committed to the issue, and the auspices of this day, I shrink from the contemplation, and humble myself before the magnitude of the undertaking. Utterly, indeed, should I despair did not the presence of many whom I here see remind me that in the other high authorities provided by our Constitution I shall find resources of wisdom, of virtue, and of zeal on which to rely under all difficulties. To you, then, gentlemen, who are charged with the sovereign functions of legislation, and to those associated with you, I look with encouragement for that guidance and support which may enable us to steer with safety the vessel in which we are all embarked amidst the conflicting elements of a troubled world.

During the contest of opinion through which we have passed the animation of discussions and of exertions has sometimes worn an aspect which might impose on strangers unused to think freely and to speak and to write what they think; but this being now decided by the voice of the nation, announced according to the rules of the Constitution, all will, of course, arrange themselves under the will of the law, and unite in common efforts for the common good. All, too, will bear in mind this sacred principle, that though the will of the majority is in all cases to prevail, that will to be rightful must be reasonable; that the minority possess their equal rights, which equal law must protect, and to violate would be oppression. Let us, then, fellow-citizens, unite with one heart and one mind. Let us restore to social intercourse that harmony and affection without which liberty and even life itself are but dreary things. And let us reflect that, having banished from our land that religious intolerance under which mankind so long bled and suffered, we have yet gained little if we countenance a political intolerance as despotic, as wicked, and capable of as bitter and bloody persecutions. During the throes and convulsions of the ancient world, during the agonizing spasms of infuriated man, seeking through blood and slaughter his long-lost liberty, it was not wonderful that the agitation of the billows should reach even this distant and peaceful shore; that this should be more felt and feared by some and less by others, and should divide opinions as to measures of safety. But every difference of opinion is not a difference of principle. We have called by different names brethren of the same principle. We are all Republicans, we are all Federalists. If there be any among us who would wish to dissolve this Union or to change its republican form, let them stand undisturbed as monuments of the safety with which error of opinion may be tolerated where reason is left free to combat it. I know, indeed, that some honest men fear that a republican government can not be strong, that this Government is not strong enough; but would the honest patriot, in the full tide of successful experiment, abandon a government which has so far kept us free and firm on the theoretic and visionary fear that this Government, the world's best hope, may by possibility want energy to preserve itself? I trust not. I believe this, on the contrary, the strongest Government on earth. I believe it the only one where every man, at the call of the law, would fly to the standard of the law, and would meet invasions of the public order as his own personal concern. Sometimes it is said that man can not be trusted with the government of himself. Can he, then, be trusted with the government of others? Or have we found angels in the forms of kings to govern him? Let history answer this question.

Let us, then, with courage and confidence pursue our own Federal and Republican principles, our attachment to union and representative government. Kindly separated by nature and a wide ocean from the exterminating havoc of one quarter of the globe; too high-minded to endure the degradations of the others; possessing a chosen country, with room enough for our descendants to the thousandth and thousandth generation; entertaining a due sense of our equal right to the use of our own faculties, to the acquisitions of our own industry, to honor and confidence from our fellow-citizens, resulting not from birth, but from our actions and their sense of them; enlightened by a benign religion, professed, indeed, and practiced in various forms, yet all of them inculcating honesty, truth, temperance, gratitude, and the love of man; acknowledging and adoring an overruling Providence, which by all its dispensations proves that it delights in the happiness of man here and his greater happiness hereafter--with all these blessings, what more is necessary to make us a happy and a prosperous people? Still one thing more, fellow-citizens--a wise and frugal Government, which shall restrain men from injuring one another, shall leave them otherwise free to regulate their own pursuits of industry and improvement, and shall not take from the mouth of labor the bread it has earned. This is the sum of good government, and this is necessary to close the circle of our felicities.

About to enter, fellow-citizens, on the exercise of duties which comprehend everything dear and valuable to you, it is proper you should understand what I deem the essential principles of our Government, and consequently those which ought to shape its Administration. I will compress them within the narrowest compass they will bear, stating the general principle, but not all its limitations. Equal and exact justice to all men, of whatever state or persuasion, religious or political; peace, commerce, and honest friendship with all nations, entangling alliances with none; the support of the State governments in all their rights, as the most competent administrations for our domestic concerns and the surest bulwarks against anti-republican tendencies; the preservation of the General Government in its whole constitutional vigor, as the sheet anchor of our peace at home and safety abroad; a jealous care of the right of election by the people--a mild and safe corrective of abuses which are lopped by the sword of revolution where peaceable remedies are unprovided; absolute acquiescence in the decisions of the majority, the vital principle of republics, from which is no appeal but to force, the vital principle and immediate parent of despotism; a well disciplined militia, our best reliance in peace and for the first moments of war, till regulars may relieve them; the supremacy of the civil over the military authority; economy in the public expense, that labor may be lightly burdened; the honest payment of our debts and sacred preservation of the public faith; encouragement of agriculture, and of commerce as its handmaid; the diffusion of information and arraignment of all abuses at the bar of the public reason; freedom of religion; freedom of the press, and freedom of person under the protection of the habeas corpus, and trial by juries impartially selected. These principles form the bright constellation which has gone before us and guided our steps through an age of revolution and reformation. The wisdom of our sages and blood of our heroes have been devoted to their attainment. They should be the creed of our political faith, the text of civic instruction, the touchstone by which to try the services of those we trust; and should we wander from them in moments of error or of alarm, let us hasten to retrace our steps and to regain the road which alone leads to peace, liberty, and safety.

I repair, then, fellow-citizens, to the post you have assigned me. With experience enough in subordinate offices to have seen the difficulties of this the greatest of all, I have learnt to expect that it will rarely fall to the lot of imperfect man to retire from this station with the reputation and the favor which bring him into it. Without pretensions to that high confidence you reposed in our first and greatest revolutionary character, whose preeminent services had entitled him to the first place in his country's love and destined for him the fairest page in the volume of faithful history, I ask so much confidence only as may give firmness and effect to the legal administration of your affairs. I shall often go wrong through defect of judgment. When right, I shall often be thought wrong by those whose positions will not command a view of the whole ground. I ask your indulgence for my own errors, which will never be intentional, and your support against the errors of others, who may condemn what they would not if seen in all its parts. The approbation implied by your suffrage is a great consolation to me for the past, and my future solicitude will be to retain the good opinion of those who have bestowed it in advance, to conciliate that of others by doing them all the good in my power, and to be instrumental to the happiness and freedom of all.

Relying, then, on the patronage of your good will, I advance with obedience to the work, ready to retire from it whenever you become sensible how much better choice it is in your power to make. And may that Infinite Power which rules the destinies of the universe lead our councils to what is best, and give them a favorable issue for your peace and prosperity.

McCulloch v. Maryland, 17 U.S. 316 (1819)

MARSHALL, Chief Justice, delivered the opinion of the Court.

The first question made in the cause is -- has Congress power to incorporate a bank? The power now contested was exercised by the first Congress elected under the present Constitution. The bill for incorporating the Bank of the United States did not steal upon an unsuspecting legislature and pass unobserved. Its principle was completely understood, and was opposed with equal zeal and ability. . . . In discussing this question, the counsel for the State of Maryland have deemed it of some importance, in the construction of the Constitution, to consider that instrument not as emanating from the people, but as the act of sovereign and independent States. The powers of the General Government, it has been said, are delegated by the States, who alone are truly sovereign, and must be exercised in subordination to the States, who alone possess supreme dominion. . . . No political dreamer was ever wild enough to think of breaking down the lines which separate the States, and of compounding the American people into one common mass. Of consequence, when they act, they act in their States. But the measures they adopt do not, on that account, cease to be the measures of the people themselves, or become the measures of the State governments.

From these conventions the Constitution derives its whole authority. The government proceeds directly from the people; is "ordained and established" in the name of the people, and is declared to be ordained, "in order to form a more perfect union, establish justice, insure domestic tranquillity, and secure the blessings of liberty to themselves and to their posterity." The assent of the States in their sovereign capacity is implied in calling a convention, and thus submitting that instrument to the people. But the people were at perfect liberty to accept or reject it, and their act was final. It required not the affirmance, and could not be negatived, by the State Governments. The Constitution, when thus adopted, was of complete obligation, and bound the State sovereignties.

. . . The Government of the Union then (whatever may be the influence of this fact on the case) is, emphatically and truly, a Government of the people. In form and in substance, it emanates from them. Its powers are granted by them, and are to be exercised directly on them, and for their benefit.

This Government is acknowledged by all to be one of enumerated powers. The principle that it can exercise only the powers granted to it would seem too apparent to have required to be enforced by all those arguments which its enlightened friends, while it was depending before the people, found it necessary to urge; that principle is now universally admitted. But the question respecting the extent of the powers actually granted is perpetually arising, and will probably continue to arise so long as our system shall exist.

In discussing these questions, the conflicting powers of the General and State Governments must be brought into view, and the supremacy of their respective laws, when they are in opposition, must be settled.

If any one proposition could command the universal assent of mankind, we might expect it would be this -- that the Government of the Union, though limited in its powers, is supreme within its sphere of action. This would seem to result necessarily from its nature. It is the Government of all; its powers are delegated by all; it represents all, and acts for all. Though any one State may be willing to control its operations, no State is willing to allow others to control them. The nation, on those subjects on which it can act, must necessarily bind its component parts. But this question is not left to mere reason; the people have, in express terms, decided it by saying, "this Constitution, and the laws of the United States, which shall be made in pursuance thereof," "shall be the supreme law of the land," and by requiring that the members of the State legislatures and the officers of the executive and judicial departments of the States shall take the oath of fidelity to it. The Government of the United States, then, though limited in its powers, is supreme, and its laws, when made in pursuance of the Constitution, form the supreme law of the land," anything in the Constitution or laws of any State to the contrary notwithstanding."

* * *

A Constitution, to contain an accurate detail of all the subdivisions of which its great powers will admit, and of all the means by which they may be carried into execution, would partake of the prolixity of a legal code, and could scarcely be embraced by the human mind. It would probably never be understood by the public. Its nature, therefore, requires that only its great outlines should be marked, its important objects designated, and the minor ingredients which compose those objects be deduced from the nature of the objects themselves. That this idea was entertained by the framers of the American Constitution is not only to be inferred from the nature of the instrument, but from the language. Why else were some of the limitations found in the 9th section of the 1st article introduced? It is also in some degree warranted by their having omitted to use any restrictive term which might prevent its receiving a fair and just interpretation. In considering this question, then, we must never forget that it is a Constitution we are expounding.

Although, among the enumerated powers of Government, we do not find the word "bank" or "incorporation," we find the great powers, to lay and collect taxes; to borrow money; to regulate commerce; to declare and conduct a war; and to raise and support armies and navies. The sword and the purse, all the external relations, and no inconsiderable portion of the industry of the nation are intrusted to its Government. It can never be pretended that these vast powers draw after them others of inferior importance merely because they are inferior. Such an idea can never be advanced. But it may with great reason be contended that a Government in trusted with such ample powers, on the due execution of which the happiness and prosperity of the Nation so vitally depends, must also be in trusted with ample means for their execution. The power being given, it is the interest of the Nation to facilitate its execution. It can never be their interest, and cannot be presumed to have been their intention, to clog and embarrass its execution by withholding the most appropriate means. . . . It is, then, the subject of fair inquiry how far such means may be employed.

The Government which has a right to do an act and has imposed on it the duty of performing that act must, according to the dictates of reason, be allowed to select the means.

* * *

But the Constitution of the United States has not left the right of Congress to employ the necessary means for the execution of the powers conferred on the Government to general reasoning. To its enumeration of powers is added that of making all laws which shall be necessary and proper for carrying into execution the foregoing powers, and all other powers vested by this Constitution in the Government of the United States or in any department thereof."

The counsel for the State of Maryland have urged various arguments to prove that this clause, though in terms a grant of power, is not so in effect, but is really restrictive of the general right which might otherwise be implied of selecting means for executing the enumerated powers.

. . . [Maryland argues that] Congress is not empowered by it to make all laws which may have relation to the powers conferred on the Government, but such only as may be "necessary and proper" for carrying them into execution. The word "necessary" is considered as controlling the whole sentence, and as limiting the right to pass laws for the execution of the granted powers to such as are indispensable, and without which the power would be nugatory. That it excludes the choice of means, and leaves to Congress in each case that only which is most direct and simple.

Is it true that this is the sense in which the word "necessary" is always used? . . . We think it does not. If reference be had to its use in the common affairs of the world or in approved authors, we find that it frequently imports no more than that one thing is convenient, or useful, or essential to another. To employ the means necessary to an end is generally understood as employing any means calculated to produce the end, and not as being confined to those single means without which the end would be entirely unattainable.

. . . Let this be done in the case under consideration. The subject is the execution of those great powers on which the welfare of a Nation essentially depends. It must have been the intention of those who gave these powers to insure, so far as human prudence could insure, their beneficial execution. This could not be done by confiding the choice of means to such narrow limits as not to leave it in the power of Congress to adopt any which might be appropriate, and which were conducive to the end. This provision is made in a Constitution intended to endure for ages to come, and consequently to be adapted to the various crises of human affairs. To have prescribed the means by which Government should, in all future time, execute its powers would have been to change entirely the character of the instrument and give it the properties of a legal code. It would have been an unwise attempt to provide by immutable rules for exigencies which, if foreseen at all, must have been seen dimly, and which can be best provided for as they occur. To have declared that the best means shall not be used, but those alone without which the power given would be nugatory, would have been to deprive the legislature of the capacity to avail itself of experience, to exercise its reason, and to accommodate its legislation to circumstances. If we apply this principle of construction to any of the powers of the Government, we shall find it so pernicious in its operation that we shall be compelled to discard it.

* * *

We admit, as all must admit, that the powers of the Government are limited, and that its limits are not to be transcended. But we think the sound construction of the Constitution must allow to the national legislature that discretion with respect to the means by which the powers it confers are to be carried into execution which will enable that body to perform the high duties assigned to it in the manner most beneficial to the people. Let the end be legitimate, let it be within the scope of the Constitution, and all means which are appropriate, which are plainly adapted to that end, which are not prohibited, but consist with the letter and spirit of the Constitution, are Constitutional.

*   *   *

It being the opinion of the Court that the act incorporating the bank is constitutional, and that the power of establishing a branch in the State of Maryland might be properly exercised by the bank itself, we proceed to inquire: Whether the State of Maryland may, without violating the Constitution, tax that branch?

That the power of taxation is one of vital importance; that it is retained by the States; that it is not abridged by the grant of a similar power to the Government of the Union; that it is to be concurrently exercised by the two Governments -- are truths which have never been denied. But such is the paramount character of the Constitution that its capacity to withdraw any subject from the action of even this power is admitted. The States are expressly forbidden to lay any duties on imports or exports except what may be absolutely necessary for executing their inspection laws. If the obligation of this prohibition must be conceded -- if it may restrain a State from the exercise of its taxing power on imports and exports -- the same paramount character would seem to restrain, as it certainly may restrain, a State from such other exercise of this power as is in its nature incompatible with, and repugnant to, the constitutional laws of the Union. A law absolutely repugnant to another as entirely repeals that other as if express terms of repeal were used.

*   *   *

This great principle is that the Constitution and the laws made in pursuance thereof are supreme; that they control the Constitution and laws of the respective States, and cannot be controlled by them. From this, which may be almost termed an axiom, other propositions are deduced as corollaries, on the truth or error of which, and on their application to this case, the cause has been supposed to depend. These are, 1st. That a power to create implies a power to preserve; 2d. That a power to destroy, if wielded by a different hand, is hostile to, and incompatible with these powers to create and to preserve; 3d. That, where this repugnancy exists, that authority which is supreme must control, not yield to that over which it is supreme.

. . . [T]axation is said to be an absolute power which acknowledges no other limits than those expressly prescribed in the Constitution, and, like sovereign power of every other description, is intrusted to the discretion of those who use it. But the very terms of this argument admit that the sovereignty of the State, in the article of taxation itself, is subordinate to, and may be controlled by, the Constitution of the United States. How far it has been controlled by that instrument must be a question of construction. In making this construction, no principle, not declared, can be admissible which would defeat the legitimate operations of a supreme Government.

*   *   *

All subjects over which the sovereign power of a State extends are objects of taxation, but those over which it does not extend are, upon the soundest principles, exempt from taxation. This proposition may almost be pronounced self-evident. The sovereignty of a State extends to everything which exists by its own authority or is introduced by its permission, but does it extend to those means which are employed by Congress to carry into execution powers conferred on that body by the people of the United States? We think it demonstrable that it does not. Those powers are not given by the people of a single State. They are given by the people of the United

States, to a Government whose laws, made in pursuance of the Constitution, are declared to be supreme. Consequently, the people of a single State cannot confer a sovereignty which will extend over them. . . . If we apply the principle for which the State of Maryland contends, to the Constitution generally, we shall find it capable of changing totally the character of that instrument. We shall find it capable of arresting all the measures of the Government, and of prostrating it at the foot of the States. The American people have declared their Constitution and the laws made in pursuance thereof to be supreme, but this principle would transfer the supremacy, in fact, to the States. . . . If the controlling power of the States be established, if their supremacy as to taxation be acknowledged, what is to restrain their exercising control in any shape they may please to give it? Their sovereignty is not confined to taxation; that is not the only mode in which it might be displayed. The question is, in truth, a question of supremacy, and if the right of the States to tax the means employed by the General Government be conceded, the declaration that the Constitution and the laws made in pursuance thereof shall be the supreme law of the land is empty and unmeaning declamation.

* * *

We are unanimously of opinion that the law passed by the Legislature of Maryland, imposing a tax on the Bank of the United States is unconstitutional and void. This opinion does not deprive the States of any resources which they originally possessed. It does not extend to a tax paid by the real property of the bank, in common with the other real property within the State, nor to a tax imposed on the interest which the citizens of Maryland may hold in this institution, in common with other property of the same description throughout the State. But this is a tax on the operations of the bank, and is, consequently, a tax on the operation of an instrument employed by the Government of the Union to carry its powers into execution. Such a tax must be unconstitutional.

First Inaugural Address of Ronald Reagan
Tuesday, January 20, 1981

Senator Hatfield, Mr. Chief Justice, Mr. President, Vice President Bush, Vice President Mondale, Senator Baker, Speaker O'Neill, Reverend Moomaw, and my fellow citizens: To a few of us here today, this is a solemn and most momentous occasion; and yet, in the history of our Nation, it is a commonplace occurrence. The orderly transfer of authority as called for in the Constitution routinely takes place as it has for almost two centuries and few of us stop to think how unique we really are. In the eyes of many in the world, this every-4-year ceremony we accept as normal is nothing less than a miracle.

Mr. President, I want our fellow citizens to know how much you did to carry on this tradition. By your gracious cooperation in the transition process, you have shown a watching world that we are a united people pledged to maintaining a political system which guarantees individual liberty to a greater degree than any other, and I thank you and your people for all your help in maintaining the continuity which is the bulwark of our Republic.

The business of our nation goes forward. These United States are confronted with an economic affliction of great proportions. We suffer from the longest and one of the worst sustained inflations in our national history. It distorts our economic decisions, penalizes thrift, and crushes the struggling young and the fixed- income elderly alike. It threatens to shatter the lives of millions of our people.

Idle industries have cast workers into unemployment, causing human misery and personal indignity. Those who do work are denied a fair return for their labor by a tax system which penalizes successful achievement and keeps us from maintaining full productivity.

But great as our tax burden is, it has not kept pace with public spending. For decades, we have piled deficit upon deficit, mortgaging our future and our children's future for the temporary convenience of the present. To continue this long trend is to guarantee tremendous social, cultural, political, and economic upheavals.

You and I, as individuals, can, by borrowing, live beyond our means, but for only a limited period of time. Why, then, should we think that collectively, as a nation, we are not bound by that same limitation?

We must act today in order to preserve tomorrow. And let there be no misunderstanding--we are going to begin to act, beginning today.

The economic ills we suffer have come upon us over several decades. They will not go away in days, weeks, or months, but they will go away. They will go away because we, as Americans, have the capacity now, as we have had in the past, to do whatever needs to be done to preserve this last and greatest bastion of freedom.

In this present crisis, government is not the solution to our problem.

From time to time, we have been tempted to believe that society has become too complex to be managed by self-rule, that government by an elite group is superior to government for, by, and of the people. But if no one among us is capable of governing himself, then who among us has the capacity to govern someone else? All of us together, in and out of government, must bear the burden. The solutions we seek must be equitable, with no one group singled out to pay a higher price.

We hear much of special interest groups. Our concern must be for a special interest group that has been too long neglected. It knows no sectional boundaries or ethnic and racial divisions, and it crosses political party lines. It is made up of men and women who raise our food, patrol our streets, man our mines and our factories, teach our children, keep our homes, and heal us when we are sick--professionals, industrialists, shopkeepers, clerks, cabbies, and truck drivers. They are, in short, "We the people," this breed called Americans.

Well, this administration's objective will be a healthy, vigorous, growing economy that provides equal opportunity for all Americans, with no barriers born of bigotry or discrimination. Putting America back to work means putting all Americans back to work. Ending inflation means freeing all Americans from the terror of runaway living costs. All must share in the productive work of this "new beginning" and all must share in the bounty of a revived economy. With the idealism and fair play which are the core of our system and our strength, we can have a strong and prosperous America at peace with itself and the world.

So, as we begin, let us take inventory. We are a nation that has a government--not the other way around. And this makes us special among the nations of the Earth. Our Government has no power except that granted it by the people. It is time to check and reverse the growth of government which shows signs of having grown beyond the consent of the governed.

It is my intention to curb the size and influence of the Federal establishment and to demand recognition of the distinction between the powers granted to the Federal Government and those reserved to the States or to the people. All of us need to be reminded that the Federal Government did not create the States; the States created the Federal Government.

Now, so there will be no misunderstanding, it is not my intention to do away with government. It is, rather, to make it work-work with us, not over us; to stand by our side, not ride on our back. Government can and must provide opportunity, not smother it; foster productivity, not stifle it.

If we look to the answer as to why, for so many years, we achieved so much, prospered as no other people on Earth, it was because here, in this land, we unleashed the energy and individual genius of man to a greater extent than has ever been done before. Freedom and the dignity of the individual have been more available and assured here than in any other place on Earth. The price for this freedom at times has been high, but we have never been unwilling to pay that price.

It is no coincidence that our present troubles parallel and are proportionate to the intervention and intrusion in our lives that result from unnecessary and excessive growth of government. It is time for us to realize that we are too great a nation to limit ourselves to small dreams. We are not, as some would have us believe, loomed to an inevitable decline. I do not believe in a fate that will all on us no matter what we do. I do believe in a fate that will fall on us if we do nothing. So, with all the creative energy at our command, let us begin an era of national renewal. Let us renew our determination, our courage, and our strength. And let us renew; our faith and our hope.

We have every right to dream heroic dreams. Those who say that we are in a time when there are no heroes just don't know where to look. You can see heroes every day going in and out of factory gates. Others, a handful in number, produce enough food to feed all of us and then the world beyond. You meet heroes across a counter--and they are on both sides of that counter. There are entrepreneurs with faith in themselves and faith in an idea who create new jobs, new wealth and opportunity. They are individuals and families whose taxes support the Government and whose voluntary gifts support church, charity, culture, art, and education. Their patriotism is quiet but deep. Their values sustain our national life.

I have used the words "they" and "their" in speaking of these heroes. I could say "you" and "your" because I am addressing the heroes of whom I speak--you, the citizens of this blessed land. Your dreams, your hopes, your goals are going to be the dreams, the hopes, and the goals of this administration, so help me God.

We shall reflect the compassion that is so much a part of your makeup. How can we love our country and not love our countrymen, and loving them, reach out a hand when they fall, heal them when they are sick, and provide opportunities to make them self- sufficient so they will be equal in fact and not just in theory?

Can we solve the problems confronting us? Well, the answer is an unequivocal and emphatic "yes." To paraphrase Winston Churchill, I did not take the oath I have just taken with the intention of presiding over the dissolution of the world's strongest economy.

In the days ahead I will propose removing the roadblocks that have slowed our economy and reduced productivity. Steps will be taken aimed at restoring the balance between the various levels of government. Progress may be slow--measured in inches and feet, not miles--but we will progress. Is it time to reawaken this industrial giant, to get government back within its means, and to lighten our punitive tax burden. And these will be our first priorities, and on these principles, there will be no compromise.

On the eve of our struggle for independence a man who might have been one of the greatest among the Founding Fathers, Dr. Joseph Warren, President of the Massachusetts Congress, said to his fellow Americans, "Our country is in danger, but not to be despaired of.... On you depend the fortunes of America. You are to decide the important questions upon which rests the happiness and the liberty of millions yet unborn. Act worthy of yourselves."

Well, I believe we, the Americans of today, are ready to act worthy of ourselves, ready to do what must be done to ensure happiness and liberty for ourselves, our children and our children's children.

And as we renew ourselves here in our own land, we will be seen as having greater strength throughout the world. We will again be the exemplar of freedom and a beacon of hope for those who do not now have freedom.

To those neighbors and allies who share our freedom, we will strengthen our historic ties and assure them of our support and firm commitment. We will match loyalty with loyalty. We will strive for mutually beneficial relations. We will not use our friendship to impose on their sovereignty, for or own sovereignty is not for sale.

As for the enemies of freedom, those who are potential adversaries, they will be reminded that peace is the highest aspiration of the American people. We will negotiate for it, sacrifice for it; we will not surrender for it--now or ever.

Our forbearance should never be misunderstood. Our reluctance for conflict should not be misjudged as a failure of will. When action is required to preserve our national security, we will act. We will maintain sufficient strength to prevail if need be, knowing that if we do so we have the best chance of never having to use that strength.

Above all, we must realize that no arsenal, or no weapon in the arsenals of the world, is so formidable as the will and moral courage of free men and women. It is a weapon our adversaries in today's world do not have. It is a weapon that we as Americans do have. Let that be understood by those who practice terrorism and prey upon their neighbors.

I am told that tens of thousands of prayer meetings are being held on this day, and for that I am deeply grateful. We are a nation under God, and I believe God intended for us to be free. It would be fitting and good, I think, if on each Inauguration Day in future years it should be declared a day of prayer.

This is the first time in history that this ceremony has been held, as you have been told, on this West Front of the Capitol. Standing here, one faces a magnificent vista, opening up on this city's special beauty and history. At the end of this open mall are those shrines to the giants on whose shoulders we stand.

Directly in front of me, the monument to a monumental man: George Washington, Father of our country. A man of humility who came to greatness reluctantly. He led America out of revolutionary victory into infant nationhood. Off to one side, the stately memorial to Thomas Jefferson. The Declaration of Independence flames with his eloquence.

And then beyond the Reflecting Pool the dignified columns of the Lincoln Memorial. Whoever would understand in his heart the meaning of America will find it in the life of Abraham Lincoln.

Beyond those monuments to heroism is the Potomac River, and on the far shore the sloping hills of Arlington National Cemetery with its row on row of simple white markers bearing crosses or Stars of David. They add up to only a tiny fraction of the price that has been paid for our freedom.

Each one of those markers is a monument to the kinds of hero I spoke of earlier. Their lives ended in places called Belleau Wood, The Argonne, Omaha Beach, Salerno and halfway around the world on Guadalcanal, Tarawa, Pork Chop Hill, the Chosin Reservoir, and in a hundred rice paddies and jungles of a place called Vietnam.
Under one such marker lies a young man--Martin Treptow--who left his job in a small town barber shop in 1917 to go to France with the famed Rainbow Division. There, on the western front, he was killed trying to carry a message between battalions under heavy artillery fire.

We are told that on his body was found a diary. On the flyleaf under the heading, "My Pledge," he had written these words: "America must win this war. Therefore, I will work, I will save, I will sacrifice, I will endure, I will fight cheerfully and do my utmost, as if the issue of the whole struggle depended on me alone."

The crisis we are facing today does not require of us the kind of sacrifice that Martin Treptow and so many thousands of others were called upon to make. It does require, however, our best effort, and our willingness to believe in ourselves and to believe in our capacity to perform great deeds; to believe that together, with God's help, we can and will resolve the problems which now confront us.

And, after all, why shouldn't we believe that? We are Americans. God bless you, and thank you.

Presidential Executive Order 12612
October 26, 1987

(NOTE: President Reagan's effort to re-establish the proper role of the federal government through this Executive Order on Federalism was revoked in 1998 by President Bill Clinton's new EO 13083, which largely re-justified the expanded role the federal government has assumed since the time of Franklin Roosevelt.)

FEDERALISM

By the authority vested in me as President by the Constitution and laws of the United States of America, and in order to restore the division of governmental responsibilities between the national government and the States that was intended by the Framers of the Constitution and to ensure that the principles of federalism established by the Framers guide the Executive departments and agencies in the formulation and implementation of policies, it is hereby ordered as follows:

Section 1. Definitions. For purposes of this Order:

(a) "Policies that have federalism implications" refers to regulations, legislative comments or proposed legislation, and other policy statements or actions that have substantial direct effects on the States, on the relationship between the national government and the States, or on the distribution of power and responsibilities among the various levels of government.

(b) "State" or "States" refer to the States of the United States or America, individually or collectively, and, where relevant, to State governments, including units of local government and other political subdivisions established by the States.

Section 2. Fundamental Federalism Principles. In formulating and implementing policies that have federalism implications, Executive departments and agencies shall be guided by the following fundamental federalism principles:

(a) Federalism is rooted in the knowledge that our political liberties are best assured by limiting the size and scope of the national government.

(b) The people of the States created the national government when they delegated to it those enumerated governmental powers relating to matters beyond the competence of the individual States.

All other sovereign powers, save those expressly prohibited the States by the Constitution, are reserved to the States or to the people.

(c) The constitutional relationship among sovereign governments, State and national, is formalized in and protected by the Tenth Amendment to the Constitution.

(d) The people of the States are free, subject only to restrictions in the Constitution itself or in constitutionally authorized Acts of Congress, to define the moral, political, and legal character of their lives.

(e) In most areas of governmental concern, the States uniquely possess the constitutional authority, the resources, and the competence to discern the sentiments of the people and to govern accordingly. In Thomas Jefferson's words, the States are "the most competent administrations for our domestic concerns and the surest bulwarks against anti-republican tendencies."

(f) The nature of our constitutional system encourages a healthy diversity in the public policies adopted by the people of the several States according to their own conditions, needs, and desires. In the search for enlightened public policy, individual States and communities are free to experiment with a variety of approaches to public issues.

(g) Acts of the national government--whether legislative, executive, or judicial in nature--that exceed the enumerated powers of that government under the Constitution violate the principle of federalism established by the Framers.

(h) Policies of the national government should recognize the responsibility of--and should encourage opportunities for--individuals, families, neighborhoods, local governments, and private associations to achieve their personal, social, and economic objectives through cooperative effort.

(i) In the absence of clear constitutional or statutory authority, the presumption of sovereignty should rest with the individual States. Uncertainties regarding the legitimate authority of the national government should be resolved against regulation at the national level.

Section 3. Federalism Policymaking Criteria. In addition to the fundamental federalism principles set forth in section 2, Executive departments and agencies shall adhere, to the extent permitted by law, to the following criteria when formulating and implementing policies that have federalism implications:

(a) There should be strict adherence to constitutional principles. Executive departments and agencies should closely examine the constitutional and statutory authority supporting any Federal action that would limit the policymaking discretion of the States, and should carefully assess the necessity for such action. To the extent practicable, the States should be consulted before any such action is implemented. Executive Order No. 12372 ("Intergovernmental Review of Federal Programs") remains in effect for the programs and activities to which it is applicable.

(b) Federal action limiting the policymaking discretion of the States should be taken only where constitutional authority for the action is clear and certain and the national activity is necessitated by the presence of a problem of national scope. For the purposes of this Order:

(1) It is important to recognize the distinction between problems of national scope (which may justify Federal action) and problems that are merely common to the States (which

will not justify Federal action because individual States, acting individually or together, can effectively deal with them).

(2) Constitutional authority for Federal action is clear and certain only when authority for the action may be found in a specific provision of the Constitution, there is no provision in the Constitution prohibiting Federal action, and the action does not encroach upon authority reserved to the States.

(c) With respect to national policies administered by the States, the national government should grant the States the maximum administrative discretion possible. Intrusive, Federal oversight of State administration is neither necessary nor desirable.

(d) When undertaking to formulate and implement policies that have federalism implications, Executive departments and agencies shall:

(1) Encourage States to develop their own policies to achieve program objectives and to work with appropriate officials in other States.

(2) Refrain, to the maximum extent possible, from establishing uniform, national standards for programs and, when possible, defer to the States to establish standards.

(3) When national standards are required, consult with appropriate officials and organizations representing the States in developing those standards.

Section 4. Special Requirements for Preemption.

(a) To the extent permitted by law, Executive departments and agencies shall construe, in regulations and otherwise, a Federal statute to preempt State law only when the statute contains an express preemption provision or there is some other firm and palpable evidence compelling the conclusion that the Congress intended preemption of State law, or when the exercise of State authority directly conflicts with the exercise of Federal authority under the Federal statute.

(b) Where a Federal statute does not preempt State law (as addressed in subsection (a) of this section), Executive departments and agencies shall construe any authorization in the statute for the issuance of regulations as authorizing preemption of State law by rule-making only when the statute expressly authorizes issuance of preemptive regulations or there is some other firm and palpable evidence compelling the conclusion that the Congress intended to delegate to the department or agency the authority to issue regulations preempting State law.

(c) Any regulatory preemption of State law shall be restricted to the minimum level necessary to achieve the objectives of the statute pursuant to which the regulations are promulgated.

(d) As soon as an Executive department or agency foresees the possibility of a conflict between State law and Federally protected interests within its area of regulatory responsibility, the department or agency shall consult, to the extent practicable, with appropriate officials and organizations representing the States in an effort to avoid such a conflict.

(e) When an Executive department or agency proposes to act through adjudication or rule-making to preempt State law, the department or agency shall provide all affected States notice and an opportunity for appropriate participation in the proceedings.

Section 5. Special Requirements for Legislative Proposals. Executive departments and agencies shall not submit to the Congress legislation that would:

(a) Directly regulate the States in ways that would interfere with functions essential to the States' separate and independent existence or operate to directly displace the States' freedom to structure integral operations in areas of traditional governmental functions;

(b) Attach to Federal grants conditions that are not directly related to the purpose of the grant; or

(c) Preempt State law, unless preemption is consistent with the fundamental federalism principles set forth in section 2, and unless a clearly legitimate national purpose, consistent with the federalism policymaking criteria set forth in section 3, cannot otherwise be met.

Section 6. Agency Implementation.

(a) The head of each Executive department and agency shall designate an official to be responsible for ensuring the implementation of this Order.

(b) In addition to whatever other actions the designated official may take to ensure implementation of this Order, the designated official shall determine which proposed policies have sufficient federalism implications to warrant the preparation of a Federalism Assessment. With respect to each such policy for which an affirmative determination is made, a Federalism Assessment, as described in subsection

(c) of this section, shall be prepared. The department or agency head shall consider any such Assessment in all decisions involved in promulgating and implementing the policy.

(d) Each Federalism Assessment shall accompany any submission concerning the policy that is made to the Office of Management and Budget pursuant to Executive Order No. 12291 or OMB Circular No. A-19, and shall:

> (1) Contain the designated official's certification that the policy has been assessed in light of the principles, criteria, and requirements stated in sections 2 through 5 of this Order;

> (2) Identify any provision or element of the policy that is inconsistent with the principles, criteria, and requirements stated in sections 2 through 5 of this Order;

> (3) Identify the extent to which the policy imposes additional costs or burdens on the States, including the likely source of funding for the States and the ability of the States to fulfill the purposes of the policy; and

> (4) Identify the extent to which the policy would affect the States' ability to discharge traditional State governmental functions, or other aspects of State sovereignty.

Section 7. Government-wide Federalism Coordination and Review. (a) In implementing Executive Order Nos. 12291 and 12498 and OMB Circular No. A-19, the Office of Management and Budget, to the extent permitted by law and consistent with the provisions of those authorities, shall take action to ensure that the policies of the Executive departments and agencies are consistent with the principles, criteria, and requirements stated in sections 2 through 5 of this Order.

(b) In submissions to the Office of Management and Budget pursuant to Executive Order No. 12291 and OMB Circular No. A-19, Executive departments and agencies shall identify proposed regulatory and statutory provisions that have significant federalism implications and shall address any substantial federalism concerns. Where the departments or agencies deem it appropriate, substantial federalism concerns should also be addressed in notices of proposed rule-making and messages transmitting legislative proposals to the Congress.

Section 8. Judicial Review. This Order is intended only to improve the internal management of the Executive branch, and is not intended to create any right or benefit, substantive or procedural, enforceable at law by a party against the United States, its agencies, its officers, or any person.

RONALD REAGAN

THE WHITE HOUSE

October 26, 1987.

Exec. Order No. 12612, 52 FR 41685, 1987 WL 181433 (Pres.)

Presidential Executive Order 13083

FEDERALISM

For Immediate Release May 14, 1998

By the authority vested in me as President by the Constitution and the laws of the United States of America, and in order to guarantee the division of governmental responsibilities, embodied in the Constitution, between the Federal Government and the States that was intended by the Framers and application of those principles by the Executive departments and agencies in the formulation and implementation of policies, it is hereby ordered as follows:

Section 1. Definitions. For purposes of this order:

(a) "State" or "States" refer to the States of the United States of America, individually or collectively, and, where relevant, to State governments, including units of local government and other political subdivisions established by the States.

(b) "Policies that have federalism implications" refers to Federal regulations, proposed legislation, and other policy statements or actions that have substantial direct effects on the States or on the relationship, or the distribution of power and responsibilities, between the Federal Government and the States.

(c) "Agency" means any authority of the United States that is an "agency" under 44 U.S.C. 3502(1), other than those considered to be independent regulatory agencies, as defined in 44 U.S.C. 3502(5).

Section 2. Fundamental Federalism Principles. In formulating and implementing policies that have federalism implications, agencies shall be guided by the following fundamental federalism principles:

(a) The structure of government established by the Constitution is premised upon a system of checks and balances.

(b) The Constitution created a Federal Government of supreme, but limited, powers. The sovereign powers not granted to the Federal Government are reserved to the people or to the States, unless prohibited to the States by the Constitution.

(c) Federalism reflects the principle that dividing power between the Federal Government and the States serves to protect individual liberty. Preserving State authority provides an essential balance to the power of the Federal Government, while preserving the supremacy of Federal law provides an essential balance to the power of the States.

(d) The people of the States are at liberty, subject only to the limitations in the Constitution itself or in Federal law, to define the moral, political, and legal character of their lives.

(e) Our constitutional system encourages a healthy diversity in the public policies adopted by the people of the several States according to their own conditions, needs, and desires. States and local governments are often uniquely situated to discern the sentiments of the people and to govern accordingly.

(f) Effective public policy is often achieved when there is competition among the several States in the fashioning of different approaches to public policy issues. The search for enlightened public policy is often furthered when individual States and local governments are free to experiment with a variety of approaches to public issues. Uniform, national approaches to public policy problems can inhibit the creation of effective solutions to those problems.

(g) Policies of the Federal Government should recognize the responsibility of -- and should encourage opportunities for -- States, local governments, private associations, neighborhoods, families, and individuals to achieve personal, social, environmental, and economic objectives through cooperative effort.

Section 3. Federalism Policymaking Criteria. In addition to adhering to the fundamental federalism principles set forth in section 2 of this order, agencies shall adhere, to the extent permitted by law, to the following criteria when formulating and implementing policies that have federalism implications:

(a) There should be strict adherence to constitutional principles. Agencies should closely examine the constitutional and statutory authority supporting any Federal action that would limit the policymaking discretion of States and local governments, and should carefully assess the necessity for such action.

(b) Agencies may limit the policymaking discretion of States and local governments only after determining that there is constitutional and legal authority for the action.

(c) With respect to Federal statutes and regulations administered by States and local governments, the Federal Government should grant States and local governments the maximum administrative discretion possible. Any Federal oversight of such State and local administration should not unnecessarily intrude on State and local discretion.

(d) It is important to recognize the distinction between matters of national or multi-state scope (which may justify Federal action) and matters that are merely common to the States (which may not justify Federal action because individual States, acting individually or together, may effectively deal with them). Matters of national or multi-state scope that justify Federal action may arise in a variety of circumstances, including:

(1) When the matter to be addressed by Federal action occurs interstate as opposed to being contained within one State's boundaries.

(2) When the source of the matter to be addressed occurs in a State different from the State (or States) where a significant amount of the harm occurs.

(3) When there is a need for uniform national standards.

(4) When decentralization increases the costs of government thus imposing additional burdens on the taxpayer.

(5) When States have not adequately protected individual rights and liberties.

(6) When States would be reluctant to impose necessary regulations because of fears that regulated business activity will relocate to other States.

(7) When placing regulatory authority at the State or local level would undermine regulatory goals because high costs or demands for specialized expertise will effectively place the regulatory matter beyond the resources of State authorities.

(8) When the matter relates to Federally owned or managed property or natural resources, trust obligations, or international obligations.

(9) When the matter to be regulated significantly or uniquely affects Indian tribal governments.

Section 4. Consultation.

(a) Each agency shall have an effective process to permit elected officials and other representatives of State and local governments to provide meaningful and timely input in the development of regulatory policies that have federalism implications.

(b) To the extent practicable and permitted by law, no agency shall promulgate any regulation that is not required by statute, that has federalism implications, and that imposes substantial direct compliance costs on States and local governments, unless:

(1) funds necessary to pay the direct costs incurred by the State or local government in complying with the regulation are provided by the Federal Government; or

(2) the agency, prior to the formal promulgation of the regulation,

(A) in a separately identified portion of the preamble to the regulation as it is to be issued in the Federal Register, provides to the Director of the Office of Management and Budget a description of the extent of the agency's prior consultation with representatives of affected States and local governments, a summary of the nature of their concerns, and the agency's position supporting the need to issue the regulation; and

(B) makes available to the Director of the Office of Management and Budget any written communications submitted to the agency by States or local governments.

Section 5. Increasing Flexibility for State and Local Waivers.

(a) Agencies shall review the processes under which States and local governments apply for waivers of statutory and regulatory requirements and take appropriate steps to streamline those processes.

(b) Each agency shall, to the extent practicable and permitted by law, consider any application by a State or local government for a waiver of statutory or regulatory requirements in connection with any program administered by that agency with a general view toward increasing opportunities for utilizing flexible policy approaches at the State or local level in cases in which the proposed waiver is consistent with applicable Federal policy objectives and is otherwise appropriate.

(c) Each agency shall, to the extent practicable and permitted by law, render a decision upon a complete application for a waiver within 120 days of receipt of such application by the agency. If the application for a waiver is not granted, the agency shall provide the applicant with timely written notice of the decision and the reasons therefore.

(d) This section applies only to statutory or regulatory requirements that are discretionary and subject to waiver by the agency.

Section 6. Independent Agencies. Independent regulatory agencies are encouraged to comply with the provisions of this order.

Section 7. General Provisions.

(a) This order is intended only to improve the internal management of the executive branch and is not intended to, and does not, create any right or benefit, substantive or procedural, enforceable at law or equity by a party against the United States, its agencies or instrumentalities, its officers or employees, or any other person.

(b) This order shall supplement but not supersede the requirements contained in Executive Order 12866 ("Regulatory Planning and Review"), Executive Order 12988 ("Civil Justice Reform"), and OMB Circular A-19.

(c) Executive Order 12612 of October 26, 1987, and Executive Order 12875 of October 26, 1993, are revoked.

(d) The consultation and waiver provisions in sections 4 and 5 of this order shall complement the Executive order entitled, "Consultation and Coordination with Indian Tribal Governments," being issued on this day.

(e) This order shall be effective 90 days after the date of this order.

WILLIAM J. CLINTON
THE WHITE HOUSE,
May 14, 1998.

Presidential Executive Order 13095

Suspension of Executive Order 13083

By the authority vested in me as President by the Constitution and the laws of the United States of America and in order to enable full and adequate consultation with State and local elected officials, their representative organizations, and other interested parties, it is hereby ordered that Executive Order **13083**, entitled ``Federalism," is suspended.

William J. Clinton
The White House,
August 5, 1998.

[Filed with the Office of the Federal Register, 8:45 a.m., August 6, 1998]

Unfunded Mandates Reform Act of 1995

SECTION 1. SHORT TITLE.

This Act may be cited as the 'Unfunded Mandates Reform Act of 1995'.

SECTION 2. PURPOSES.

The purposes of this Act are:

(1) to strengthen the partnership between the Federal Government and State, local, and tribal governments;

(2) to end the imposition, in the absence of full consideration by Congress, of Federal mandates on State, local, and tribal governments without adequate Federal funding, in a manner that may displace other essential State, local, and tribal governmental priorities;

(3) to assist Congress in its consideration of proposed legislation establishing or revising Federal programs containing Federal mandates affecting State, local, and tribal governments, and the private sector by:

   (A) providing for the development of information about the nature and size of mandates in proposed legislation; and

   (B) establishing a mechanism to bring such information to the attention of the Senate and the House of Representatives before the Senate and the House of Representatives vote on proposed legislation;

(4) to promote informed and deliberate decisions by Congress on the appropriateness of Federal mandates in any particular instance;

(5) to require that Congress consider whether to provide funding to assist State, local, and tribal governments in complying with Federal mandates, to require analyses of the impact of private sector mandates, and through the dissemination of that information provide informed and deliberate decisions by Congress and Federal agencies and retain competitive balance between the public and private sectors;

(6) to establish a point-of-order vote on the consideration in the Senate and House of Representatives of legislation containing significant Federal intergovernmental mandates without providing adequate funding to comply with such mandates;

(7) to assist Federal agencies in their consideration of proposed regulations affecting State, local, and tribal governments, by:

(A) requiring that Federal agencies develop a process to enable the elected and other officials of State, local, and tribal governments to provide input when Federal agencies are developing regulations; and

(B) requiring that Federal agencies prepare and consider estimates of the budgetary impact of regulations containing Federal mandates upon State, local, and tribal governments and the private sector before adopting such regulations, and ensuring that small governments are given special consideration in that process; and

(8) to begin consideration of the effect of previously imposed Federal mandates, including the impact on State, local, and tribal governments of Federal court interpretations of Federal statutes and regulations that impose Federal intergovernmental mandates.

"AND TO THE REPUBLIC FOR WHICH IT STANDS"

Common Sense (1776)
by Thomas Paine

(Excerpted)

2/7   Some writers have so confounded society with government . . .

SOME writers have so confounded society with government, as to leave little or no distinction between them; whereas they are not only different, but have different origins. Society is produced by our wants, and government by our wickedness; the former promotes our happiness Positively by uniting our affections, the latter negatively by restraining our vices. The one encourages intercourse, the other creates distinctions. The first is a patron, the last a punisher.

Society in every state is a blessing, but government even in its best state is but a necessary evil in its worst state an in tolerable one; for when we suffer, or are exposed to the same miseries by a government, which we might expect in a country without government, our calamities is heightened by reflecting that we furnish the means by which we suffer! Government, like dress, is the badge of lost innocence; the palaces of kings are built on the ruins of the bowers of paradise. For were the impulses of conscience clear, uniform, and irresistibly obeyed, man would need no other lawgiver; but that not being the case, he finds it necessary to surrender up a part of his property to furnish means for the protection of the rest; and this he is induced to do by the same prudence which in every other case advises him out of two evils to choose the least. Wherefore, security being the true design and end of government, it unanswerably follows that whatever form thereof appears most likely to ensure it to us, with the least expense and greatest benefit, is preferable to all others.

In order to gain a clear and just idea of the design and end of government, let us suppose a small number of persons settled in some sequestered part of the earth, unconnected with the rest, they will then represent the first peopling of any country, or of the world. In this state of natural liberty, society will be their first thought. A thousand motives will excite them thereto, the strength of one man is so unequal to his wants, and his mind so unfitted for perpetual solitude, that he is soon obliged to seek assistance and relief of another, who in his turn requires the same. Four or five united would be able to raise a tolerable dwelling in the midst of a wilderness, but one man might labor out the common period of life without accomplishing any thing; when he had felled his timber he could not remove it, nor erect it after it was removed; hunger in the mean time would urge him from his work, and every different want call him a different way. Disease, nay even misfortune would be death, for though neither might be mortal, yet either would disable him from living, and reduce him to a state in which he might rather be said to perish than to die.

Thus necessity, like a gravitating power, would soon form our newly arrived emigrants into society, the reciprocal blessings of which, would supersede, and render the obligations of law and government unnecessary while they remained perfectly just to each other; but as nothing but heaven is impregnable to vice, it will unavoidably happen, that in proportion as they surmount the first difficulties of emigration, which bound them together in a common cause, they will begin to relax in their duty and attachment to each other; and this remissness, will point out the necessity, of establishing some form of government to supply the defect of moral virtue.

Some convenient tree will afford them a State-House, under the branches of which, the whole colony may assemble to deliberate on public matters. It is more than probable that their first laws will have the title only of REGULATIONS, and be enforced by no other penalty than public disesteem. In this first parliament every man, by natural right will have a seat.

But as the colony increases, the public concerns will increase likewise, and the distance at which the members may be separated, will render it too inconvenient for all of them to meet on every occasion as at first, when their number was small, their habitations near, and the public concerns few and trifling. This will point out the convenience of their consenting to leave the legislative part to be managed by a select number chosen from the whole body, who are supposed to have the same concerns at stake which those have who appointed them, and who will act in the same manner as the whole body would act were they present. If the colony continue increasing, it will become necessary to augment the number of the representatives, and that the interest of every part of the colony may be attended to, it will be found best to divide the whole into convenient parts, each part sending its proper number; and that the elected might never form to themselves an interest separate from the electors, prudence will point out the propriety of having elections often; because as the elected might by that means return and mix again with the general body of the electors in a few months, their fidelity to the public will be secured by the prudent reflection of not making a rod for themselves. And as this frequent interchange will establish a common interest with every part of the community, they will mutually and naturally support each other, and on this (not on the unmeaning name of king) depends the strength of government, and the happiness of the governed.

Here then is the origin and rise of government; namely, a mode rendered necessary by the inability of moral virtue to govern the world; here too is the design and end of government, viz. freedom and security. And however our eyes may be dazzled with snow, or our ears deceived by sound; however prejudice may warp our wills, or interest darken our understanding, the simple voice of nature and of reason will say, it is right.

I draw my idea of the form of government from a principle in nature, which no art can overturn, viz. that the more simple any thing is, the less liable it is to be disordered, and the easier repaired when disordered; and with this maxim in view, I offer a few remarks on the so much boasted constitution of England. That it was noble for the dark and slavish times in which it was erected is granted. When the world was overrun with tyranny the least therefrom was a glorious rescue. But that it is imperfect, subject to convulsions, and incapable of producing what it seems to promise, is easily demonstrated.

Absolute governments (tho' the disgrace of human nature) have this advantage with them, that they are simple; if the people suffer, they know the head from which their suffering springs, know likewise the remedy, and are not bewildered by a variety of causes and cures. But the constitution of England is so exceedingly complex, that the nation may suffer for years together without being able to discover in which part the fault lies, some will say in one and some in another, and every political physician will advise a different medicine.

I know it is difficult to get over local or long standing prejudices, yet if we will suffer ourselves to examine the component parts of the English constitution, we shall find them to be the base remains of two ancient tyrannies, compounded with some new republican materials.

First. The remains of monarchical tyranny in the person of the king.

Secondly. The remains of aristocratical tyranny in the persons of the peers.

Thirdly. The new republican materials, in the persons of the commons, on whose virtue depends the freedom of England.

The two first, by being hereditary, are independent of the people; wherefore in a constitutional sense they contribute nothing towards the freedom of the state.

To say that the constitution of England is a union of three powers reciprocally checking each other, is farcical, either the words have no meaning, or they are flat contradictions.

To say that the commons is a check upon the king, presupposes two things.

First. That the king is not to be trusted without being looked after, or in other words, that a thirst for absolute power is the natural disease of monarchy.

Secondly. That the commons, by being appointed for that purpose, are either wiser or more worthy of confidence than the crown.

But as the same constitution which gives the commons a power to check the king by withholding the supplies, gives afterwards the king a power to check the commons, by empowering him to reject their other bills; it again supposes that the king is wiser than those whom it has already supposed to be wiser than him. A mere absurdity!

There is something exceedingly ridiculous in the composition of monarchy; it first excludes a man from the means of information, yet empowers him to act in cases where the highest judgment is required. The state of a king shuts him from the world, yet the business of a king requires him to know it thoroughly; wherefore the different parts, unnaturally opposing and destroying each other, prove the whole character to be absurd and useless.

Some writers have explained the English constitution thus; the king, say they, is one, the people another; the peers are an house in behalf of the king; the commons in behalf of the people; but this hath all the distinctions of an house divided against itself; and though the expressions be pleasantly arranged, yet when examined they appear idle and ambiguous; and it will always happen, that the nicest construction that words are capable of, when applied to the description of something which either cannot exist, or is too incomprehensible to be within the compass of description, will be words of sound only, and though they may amuse the ear, they cannot inform the mind, for this explanation includes a previous question, viz. how came the king by a Power which the people are afraid to trust, and always obliged to check? Such a power could not be the gift of a wise people, neither can any power, which needs checking, be from God; yet the provision, which the constitution makes, supposes such a power to exist.

But the provision is unequal to the task; the means either cannot or will not accomplish the end, and the whole affair is a felo de se; for as the greater weight will always carry up the less, and as all the wheels of a machine are put in motion by one, it only remains to know which power in the constitution has the most weight, for that will govern; and though the others, or a part of them, may clog, or, as the phrase is, check the rapidity of its motion, yet so long as they cannot stop it, their endeavors will be ineffectual; the first moving power will at last have its way, and what it wants in speed is supplied by time.

That the crown is this overbearing part in the English constitution needs not be mentioned, and that it derives its whole consequence merely from being the giver of places pensions is self-evident, wherefore, though we have and wise enough to shut and lock a door against absolute monarchy, we at the same time have been foolish enough to put the crown in possession of the key.

The prejudice of Englishmen, in favor of their own government by king, lords, and commons, arises as much or more from national pride than reason. Individuals are undoubtedly safer in England than in some other countries, but the will of the king is as much the law of the land in Britain as in France, with this difference, that instead of proceeding directly from his mouth, it is handed to the people under the most formidable shape of an act of parliament. For the fate of Charles the First, hath only made kings more subtle not more just.

Wherefore, laying aside all national pride and prejudice in favor of modes and forms, the plain truth is, that it is wholly owing to the constitution of the people, and not to the constitution of the government that the crown is not as oppressive in England as in Turkey.

An inquiry into the constitutional errors in the English form of government is at this time highly necessary; for as we are never in a proper condition of doing justice to others, while we continue under the influence of some leading partiality, so neither are we capable of doing it to ourselves while we remain fettered by any obstinate prejudice. And as a man, who is attached to a prostitute, is unfitted to choose or judge of a wife, so any prepossession in favor of a rotten constitution of government will disable us from discerning a good one.

Thoughts on Government
By John Adams

MY DEAR SIR,--If I was equal to the task of forming a plan for the government of a colony, I should be flattered with your request, and very happy to comply with it; because, as the divine science of politics is the science of social happiness, and the blessings of society depend entirely on the constitutions of government, which are generally institutions that last for many generations, there can be no employment more agreeable to a benevolent mind than a research after the best.

Pope flattered tyrants too much when he said,

> "For forms of government let fools contest,
> That which is best administered is best."

Nothing can be more fallacious than this. But poets read his tory to collect flowers, not fruits; they attend to fanciful images, not the effects of social institutions. Nothing is more certain, from the history of nations and nature of man, than that some forms of government are better fitted for being well administered than others.

We ought to consider what is the end of government, before we determine which is the best form. Upon this point all speculative politicians will agree, that the happiness of society is the end of government, as all divines and moral philosophers will agree that the happiness of the individual is the end of man. From this principle it will follow, that the form of government which communicates ease, comfort, security, or, in one word, happiness, to the greatest number of persons, and in the greatest degree, is the best.

All sober inquirers after truth, ancient and modern, pagan and Christian, have declared that the happiness of man, as well as his dignity, consists in virtue. Confucius, Zoroaster, Socrates, Mahomet, not to mention authorities really sacred, have agreed in this.

If there is a form of government, then, whose principle and foundation is virtue, will not every sober man acknowledge it better calculated to promote the general happiness than any other form?

Fear is the foundation of most governments; but it is so sordid and brutal a passion, and renders men in whose breasts it predominates so stupid and miserable, that Americans will not be likely to approve of any political institution which is founded on it.

Honor is truly sacred, but holds a lower rank in the scale of moral excellence than virtue. Indeed, the former is but a part of the latter, and consequently has not equal pretensions to support a frame of government productive of human happiness.

The foundation of every government is some principle or passion in the minds of the people. The noblest principles and most generous affections in our nature, then, have the fairest chance to support the noblest and most generous models of government.

A man must be indifferent to the sneers of modern English men, to mention in their company the names of Sidney, Harrington, Locke, Milton, Nedham, Neville, Burnet, and Hoadly. No small fortitude is necessary to confess that one has read them. The wretched condition of this country, however, for ten or fifteen years past, has frequently reminded me of their principles and reasonings. They will convince any candid mind, that there is no good government but what is republican. That the only valuable part of the British constitution is so; because the very definition of a republic is "an empire of laws, and not of men." That, as a republic is the best of governments, so that particular arrangement of the powers of society, or, in other words, that form of government which is best contrived to secure an impartial and exact execution of the laws, is the best of republics.

Of republics there is an inexhaustible variety, because the possible combinations of the powers of society are capable of innumerable variations.

As good government is an empire of laws, how shall your laws be made? In a large society, inhabiting an extensive country, it is impossible that the whole should assemble to make laws. The first necessary step, then, is to depute power from the many to a few of the most wise and good. But by what rules shall you choose your representatives? Agree upon the number and qualifications of persons who shall have the benefit of choosing, or annex this privilege to the inhabitants of a certain extent of ground.

The principal difficulty lies, and the greatest care should be employed, in constituting this representative assembly. It should be in miniature an exact portrait of the people at large. It should think, feel, reason, and act like them. That it may be the interest of this assembly to do strict justice at all times, it should be an equal representation, or, in other words, equal interests among the people should have equal interests in it. Great care should be taken to effect this, and to prevent unfair, partial, and corrupt elections. Such regulations, however, may be better made in times of greater tranquillity than the present; and they will spring up themselves naturally, when all the powers of government come to be in the hands of the people's friends. At present, it will be safest to proceed in all established modes, to which the people have been familiarized by habit.

A representation of the people in one assembly being obtained, a question arises, whether all the powers of government, legislative, executive, and judicial, shall be left in this body? I think a people cannot be long free, nor ever happy, whose government is in one assembly. My reasons for this opinion are as follow:--

1. A single assembly is liable to all the vices, follies, and frailties of an individual; subject to fits of humor, starts of passion, flights of enthusiasm, partialities, or prejudice, and consequently productive of hasty results and absurd judgments. And all these errors ought to be corrected and defects supplied by some controlling power.

2. A single assembly is apt to grow ambitious, and after a time will not hesitate to vote itself perpetual. This was one fault of the Long Parliament; but more remarkably of Holland, whose assembly first voted themselves from annual to septennial, then for life, and after a course of years, that all vacancies happening by death or otherwise, should be filled by themselves, without any application to constituents at all.

3. A representative assembly, although extremely well qualified, and absolutely necessary, as a branch of the legislative, is unfit to exercise the executive power, for want of two essential properties, secrecy and despatch.

4. A representative assembly is still less qualified for the judicial power, because it is too numerous, too slow, and too little skilled in the laws.

5. Because a single assembly, possessed of all the powers of government, would make arbitrary laws for their own interest, execute all laws arbitrarily for their own interest, and adjudge all controversies in their own favor.

But shall the whole power of legislation rest in one assembly? Most of the foregoing reasons apply equally to prove that the legislative power ought to be more complex; to which we may add, that if the legislative power is wholly in one assembly, and the executive in another, or in a single person, these two powers will oppose and encroach upon each other, until the contest shall end in war, and the whole power, legislative and executive, be usurped by the strongest.

The judicial power, in such case, could not mediate, or hold the balance between the two contending powers, because the legislative would undermine it. And this shows the necessity, too, of giving the executive power a negative upon the legislative, otherwise this will be continually encroaching upon that.

To avoid these dangers, let a distinct assembly be constituted, as a mediator between the two extreme branches of the legislature, that which represents the people, and that which is vested with the executive power.

Let the representative assembly then elect by ballot, from among themselves or their constituents, or both, a distinct assembly, which, for the sake of perspicuity, we will call a council. It may consist of any number you please, say twenty or thirty, and should have a free and independent exercise of its judgment, and consequently a negative voice in the legislature.

These two bodies, thus constituted, and made integral parts of the legislature, let them unite, and by joint ballot choose a governor, who, after being stripped of most of those badges of domination, called prerogatives, should have a free and independent exercise of his judgment, and be made also an integral part of the legislature. This, I know, is liable to objections; and, if you please, you may make him only president of the council, as in Connecticut. But as the governor is to be invested with the executive power, with consent of council, I think he ought to have a negative upon the legislative. If he is annually elective, as he ought to be, he will always have so much reverence and affection for the people, their representatives and counsellors, that, although you give him an independent exercise of his judgment, he will seldom use it in opposition to the two houses, except in cases the public utility of which would be conspicuous; and some such cases would happen.

In the present exigency of American affairs, when, by an act of Parliament, we are put out of the royal protection, and consequently discharged from our allegiance, and it has become necessary to assume government for our immediate security, the governor, lieutenant-governor, secretary, treasurer, commissary, attorney-general, should be chosen by joint ballot of both houses. And these and all other elections, especially of representatives and counsellors, should be annual, there not being in the whole circle of the sciences a maxim more infallible than this, "where annual elections end, there slavery begins."

These great men, in this respect, should be, once a year,

> "Like bubbles on the sea of matter borne,
> They rise, they break, and to that sea return."

This will teach them the great political virtues of humility, patience, and moderation, without which every man in power becomes a ravenous beast of prey.

This mode of constituting the great offices of state will answer very well for the present; but if by experiment it should be found inconvenient, the legislature may, at its leisure, devise other methods of creating them, by elections of the people at large, as in Connecticut, or it may enlarge the term for which they shall be chosen to seven years, or three years, or for life, or make any other alterations which the society shall find productive of its ease, its safety, its freedom, or, in one word, its happiness.

A rotation of all offices, as well as of representatives and counsellors, has many advocates, and is contended for with many plausible arguments. It would be attended, no doubt, with many advantages; and if the society has a sufficient number of suitable characters to supply the great number of vacancies which would be made by such a rotation, I can see no objection to it. These persons may be allowed to serve for three years, and then be excluded three years, or for any longer or shorter term.

Any seven or nine of the legislative council may be made a quorum, for doing business as a privy council, to advise the governor in the exercise of the executive branch of power, and in all acts of state.

The governor should have the command of the militia and of all your armies. The power of pardons should be with the governor and council.

Judges, justices, and all other officers, civil and military, should be nominated and appointed by the governor, with the advice and consent of council, unless you choose to have a government more popular; if you do, all officers, civil and military, may be chosen by joint ballot of both houses; or, in order to preserve the independence and importance of each house, by ballot of one house, concurred in by the other. Sheriffs should be chosen by the freeholders of counties; so should registers of deeds and clerks of counties.

All officers should have commissions, under the hand of the governor and seal of the colony.

The dignity and stability of government in all its branches, the morals of the people, and every blessing of society depend so much upon an upright and skillful administration of justice, that the judicial power ought to be distinct from both the legislative and executive, and independent upon both, that so it may be a check upon both, as both should be checks upon that. The judges, therefore, should be always men of learning and experience in the laws, of exemplary morals, great patience, calmness, coolness, and attention. Their minds should not be distracted with jarring interests; they should not be dependent upon any man, or body of men. To these ends, they should hold estates for life in their offices; or, in other words, their commissions should be during good behavior, and their salaries ascertained and established by law. For misbehavior, the grand inquest of the colony, the house of representatives, should impeach them before the governor and council, where they should have time and opportunity to make their defence; but, if convicted, should be removed from their offices, and subjected to such other punishment as shall be thought proper.

A militia law, requiring all men, or with very few exceptions besides cases of conscience, to be provided with arms and ammunition, to be trained at certain seasons; and requiring counties, towns, or other small districts, to be provided with public stocks of ammunition and entrenching utensils, and with some settled plans for transporting provisions after the militia, when marched to defend their country against sudden invasions; and requiring certain districts to be provided with field-pieces, companies of matrosses, and perhaps some regiments of light-horse, is always a wise institution, and, in the present circumstances of our country, indispensable.

Laws for the liberal education of youth, especially of the lower class of people, are so extremely wise and useful, that, to a humane and generous mind, no expense for this purpose would be thought extravagant.

The very mention of sumptuary laws will excite a smile. Whether our countrymen have wisdom and virtue enough to submit to them, I know not; but the happiness of the people might be greatly promoted by them, and a revenue saved sufficient to carry on this war forever. Frugality is a great revenue, besides curing us of vanities, levities, and fopperies, which are real antidotes to all great, manly, and warlike virtues.

But must not all commissions run in the name of a king? No. Why may they not as well run thus, "The colony of to A. B. greeting," and be tested by the governor?

Why may not writs, instead of running in the name of the king, run thus, "The colony of to the sheriff," &c., and be tested by the chief justice?

Why may not indictments conclude, "against the peace of the colony of and the dignity of the same?"

A constitution founded on these principles introduces know ledge among the people, and inspires them with a conscious dignity becoming freemen; a general emulation takes place, which causes good humor, sociability, good manners, and good morals to be general. That elevation of sentiment inspired by such a government, makes the common people brave and enterprising. That ambition which is inspired by it makes them sober, industrious, and frugal. You will find among them some elegance, perhaps, but more solidity; a little pleasure, but a great deal of business; some politeness, but more civility. If you compare such a country with the regions of domination, whether monarchical or aristocratical, you will fancy yourself in Arcadia or Elysium.

If the colonies should assume governments separately, they should be left entirely to their own choice of the forms; and if a continental constitution should be formed, it should be a congress, containing a fair and adequate representation of the colonies, and its authority should sacredly be confined to these cases, namely, war, trade, disputes between colony and colony, the post office, and the unappropriated lands of the crown, as they used to be called.

These colonies, under such forms of government, and in such a union, would be unconquerable by all the monarchies of Europe.

You and I, my dear friend, have been sent into life at a time when the greatest lawgivers of antiquity would have wished to live. How few of the human race have ever enjoyed an opportunity of making an election of government, more than of air, soil, or climate, for themselves or their children! When, before the present epocha, had three millions of people full power and a fair opportunity to form and establish the wisest and happiest government that human wisdom can contrive? I hope you will avail yourself and your country of that extensive learning and indefatigable industry which you possess, to assist her in the formation of the happiest governments and the best character of a great people. For myself, I must beg you to keep my name out of sight; for this feeble attempt, if it should be known to be mine, would oblige me to apply to myself those lines of the immortal John Milton, in one of his sonnets:--

> "I did but prompt the age to quit their clogs
> By the known rules of ancient liberty,
> When straight a barbarous noise environs me
> Of owls and cuckoos, asses, apes, and dogs."

The Declaration of Independence
July 4, 1776

The Unanimous Declaration of the thirteen united States of America.
When, in the course of human events, it becomes necessary for one people to dissolve the Political Bands which have connected them with another, and to assume among the Powers of the Earth, the separate and equal Station to which the Laws of Nature and of Nature's God entitle them, a decent Respect to the Opinions of Mankind requires that they should declare the causes which impel them to the Separation.

We hold these Truths to be self-evident, that all Men are created equal, that they are endowed by their Creator with certain unalienable Rights, that among these are Life, Liberty and the Pursuit of Happiness -- That to secure these Rights, Governments are instituted among Men, deriving their just Powers from the Consent of the Governed, that whenever any Form of Government becomes destructive to these Ends, it is the Right of the People to alter or to abolish it, and to institute new Government, laying its Foundation on such Principles and organizing its Powers in such Form, as to them shall seem most likely to effect their Safety and Happiness. Prudence, indeed, will dictate that Governments long established should not be changed for light and transient Causes; and accordingly all Experience hath shown that Mankind are more disposed to suffer, while Evils are sufferable, than to right themselves by abolishing the Forms to which they are accustomed. But when a long Train of Abuses and Usurpations, pursuing invariably the same Object, evinces a Design to reduce them under absolute Despotism, it is their Right, it is their Duty, to throw off such Government, and to provide new Guards for their future Security. Such has been the patient Sufferance of these Colonies; and such is now the Necessity which constrains them to alter their former Systems of Government. The History of the present King of Great- Britain is a History of repeated Injuries and Usurpations, all having in direct Object the Establishment of an absolute Tyranny over these States. To prove this, let Facts be submitted to a candid World.

HE has refused his Assent to Laws, the most wholesome and necessary for the public Good.

HE has forbidden his Governors to pass Laws of immediate and pressing Importance,

unless suspended in their Operation till his Assent should be obtained; and when so suspended, he has utterly neglected to attend to them.

HE has refused to pass other Laws for the Accommodation of large Districts of People, unless those People would relinquish the Right of Representation in the Legislature, a Right inestimable to them and formidable to Tyrants only.

HE has called together Legislative Bodies at Places unusual, uncomfortable, and distant from the Depository of their public Records, for the sole Purpose of fatiguing them into Compliance with his Measures.

HE has dissolved Representative Houses repeatedly, for opposing with manly Firmness his Invasions on the Rights of the People.

HE has refused for a long Time, after such Dissolutions, to cause others to be elected; whereby the Legislative Powers, incapable of Annihilation, have returned to the People at large for their exercise; the State remaining in the meantime exposed to all the Dangers of Invasion from without, and the Convulsions within.

HE has endeavored to prevent the Population of these States; for that Purpose obstructing the Laws for Naturalization of Foreigners; refusing to pass others to encourage their Migration hither, and raising the Conditions of new Appropriations of Lands.

HE has obstructed the Administration of Justice, by refusing his Assent to Laws for establishing Judiciary Powers.

HE has made Judges dependent on his Will alone, for the Tenure of their Offices, and the Amount and Payment of their Salaries.

HE has erected a Multitude of new Offices, and sent hither Swarms of Officers to harass our People, and eat out their Substance.

HE has kept among us, in Times of Peace, Standing Armies without the consent of our Legislature.

HE has affected to render the Military independent of and superior to Civil Power.

HE has combined with others to subject us to a Jurisdiction foreign to our Constitution, and unacknowledged by our Laws; giving his Assent to their Acts of pretended Legislation:

FOR quartering large Bodies of Armed Troops among us:

FOR protecting them, by mock Trial, from Punishment for any Murders which they should commit on the Inhabitants of these States:

FOR cutting off our Trade with all Parts of the World:

FOR imposing Taxes on us without our Consent:

FOR depriving us in many Cases, of the Benefits of Trial by Jury:

FOR transporting us beyond Seas to be tried for pretended Offences:

FOR abolishing the free System of English Laws in a neighboring Province, establishing therein an arbitrary Government, and enlarging its Boundaries so as to render it at once an Example and fit Instrument for introducing the same absolute Rule into these Colonies:

FOR taking away our Charters, abolishing our most valuable Laws, and altering fundamentally the Forms of our Governments:

FOR suspending our own Legislatures, and declaring themselves invested with Power to legislate for us in all Cases whatsoever.

HE has abdicated Government here, by declaring us out of his Protection and waging War against us.

HE has plundered our Seas, ravaged our Coasts, burned our Towns, and destroyed the Lives of our People.

HE is, at this Time, transporting large Armies of foreign Mercenaries to compleat the Works of Death, Desolation, and Tyranny, already begun with circumstances of Cruelty and Perfidy, scarcely paralleled in the most barbarous Ages, and totally unworthy the Head of a civilized Nation.

HE has constrained our fellow Citizens taken Captive on the high Seas to bear Arms against their Country, to become the Executioners of their Friends and Brethren, or to fall themselves by their Hands.

HE has excited domestic Insurrections amongst us, and has endeavored to bring on the Inhabitants of our frontiers, the merciless Indian Savages, whose known Rule of Warfare, is undistinguished Destruction of all Ages, Sexes and Conditions.

IN every stage of these Oppressions we have Petitioned for Redress in the most humble Terms: Our repeated Petitions have been answered only by repeated Injury. A Prince, whose Character is thus marked by every act which may define a Tyrant, is unfit to be the Ruler of a free People.

NOR have we been wanting in Attentions to our British Brethren. We have warned them from Time to Time of attempts by their Legislature to extend an unwarrantable Jurisdiction over us. We have reminded them of the Circumstances of our Emigration and Settlement here. We have appealed to their native Justice and Magnanimity, and we have conjured them by the Ties of our common Kindred to disavow these Usurpations, which, would inevitably interrupt our

Connections and Correspondence. They too have been deaf to the Voice of Justice and Consanguinity. We must, therefore, acquiesce in the Necessity, which denounces our Separation, and hold them, as we hold the rest of Mankind, Enemies in War, in Peace, Friends.

WE, therefore, the Representatives of the UNITED STATES of AMERICA, in General Congress, Assembled, appealing to the Supreme Judge of the World for the Rectitude of our Intentions, do, in the Name, and by the Authority of the good People of these Colonies, solemnly Publish and Declare, that these United Colonies are, and of Right ought to be, FREE AND INDEPENDENT STATES; that they are absolved from all Allegiance to the British Crown, and that all political Connection between them and the State of Great Britain, is and ought to be totally dissolved; and that as FREE AND INDEPENDENT STATES, they have full Power to levy War, conclude Peace, contract Alliances, establish Commerce, and to do all other Acts and Things which INDEPENDENT STATES may of right do. And for the support of this Declaration, with a firm Reliance on the Protection of Divine Providence, we mutually pledge to each other our Lives, our Fortunes, and our sacred Honor.

- NEW HAMPSHIRE: JOSIAH BARTLETT, WILLIAM WHIPPLE, MATTHEW THORNTON
- MASSACHUSETTS: JOHN HANCOCK, SAMUEL ADAMS, JOHN ADAMS, ROBERT TREAT PAINE, ELBRIDGE GERRY
- RHODE ISLAND: STEPHEN HOPKINS, WILLIAM ELLERY
- CONNECTICUT: ROGER SHERMAN, SAMUEL HUNTINGTON, WILLIAM WILLIAMS, OLIVER WOLCOTT
- NEW YORK: WILLIAM FLOYD, PHILIP LIVINGSTON, FRANCIS LEWIS, LEWIS MORRIS
- NEW JERSEY: RICHARD STOCKTON, JOHN WITHERSPOON, FRANCIS HOPKINSON, JOHN HART, ABRAHAM CLARK
- PENNSYLVANIA: ROBERT MORRIS, BENJAMIN RUSH, BENJAMIN FRANKLIN, JOHN MORTON, GEORGE CLYMER, JAMES SMITH, GEORGE TAYLOR, JAMES WILSON, GEORGE ROSS
- DELAWARE: CAESAR RODNEY, GEORGE READ, THOMAS MCKEAN
- MARYLAND: SAMUEL CHASE, WILLIAM PACA, THOMAS STONE, CHARLES CARROLL OF CARROLLTON
- VIRGINIA: GEORGE WYTHE, RICHARD HENRY LEE, THOMAS JEFFERSON, BENJAMIN HARRISON, THOMAS NELSON, JR., FRANCIS LIGHTFOOT LEE, CARTER BRAXTON
- NORTH CAROLINA: WILLIAM HOOPER, JOSEPH HEWES, JOHN PENN
- SOUTH CAROLINA: EDWARD RUTLEDGE, THOMAS HEYWARD, JR., THOMAS LYNCH, JR., ARTHUR MIDDLETON
- GEORGIA: BUTTON GWINNETT, LYMAN HALL, GEORGE WALTON.

Federalist No. 10

The Same Subject Continued
(The Union as a Safeguard Against Domestic Faction and Insurrection)
From the *New York Packet*.
Friday, November 23, 1787.

MADISON

To the People of the State of New York:

AMONG the numerous advantages promised by a well-constructed Union, none deserves to be more accurately developed than its tendency to break and control the violence of faction. The friend of popular governments never finds himself so much alarmed for their character and fate, as when he contemplates their propensity to this dangerous vice. He will not fail, therefore, to set a due value on any plan which, without violating the principles to which he is attached, provides a proper cure for it. The instability, injustice, and confusion introduced into the public councils, have, in truth, been the mortal diseases under which popular governments have everywhere perished; as they continue to be the favorite and fruitful topics from which the adversaries to liberty derive their most specious declamations. The valuable improvements made by the American constitutions on the popular models, both ancient and modern, cannot certainly be too much admired; but it would be an unwarrantable partiality, to contend that they have as effectually obviated the danger on this side, as was wished and expected. Complaints are everywhere heard from our most considerate and virtuous citizens, equally the friends of public and private faith, and of public and personal liberty, that our governments are too unstable, that the public good is disregarded in the conflicts of rival parties, and that measures are too often decided, not according to the rules of justice and the rights of the minor party, but by the superior force of an interested and overbearing majority. However anxiously we may wish that these complaints had no foundation, the evidence, of known facts will not permit us to deny that they are in some degree true. It will be found, indeed, on a candid review of our situation, that some of the distresses under which we labor have been erroneously charged on the operation of our governments; but it will be found, at the same time, that other causes will not alone account for many of our heaviest misfortunes; and, particularly, for that prevailing and increasing distrust of public engagements, and alarm for private rights, which are echoed from one end of the continent to the other. These must be chiefly, if not wholly, effects of the unsteadiness and injustice with which a factious spirit has tainted our public administrations.

By a faction, I understand a number of citizens, whether amounting to a majority or a minority of the whole, who are united and actuated by some common impulse of passion, or of interest, adversed to the rights of other citizens, or to the permanent and aggregate interests of the community.

There are two methods of curing the mischiefs of faction: the one, by removing its causes; the other, by controlling its effects.

There are again two methods of removing the causes of faction: the one, by destroying the liberty which is essential to its existence; the other, by giving to every citizen the same opinions, the same passions, and the same interests.

It could never be more truly said than of the first remedy, that it was worse than the disease. Liberty is to faction what air is to fire, an aliment without which it instantly expires. But it could not be less folly to abolish liberty, which is essential to political life, because it nourishes faction, than it would be to wish the annihilation of air, which is essential to animal life, because it imparts to fire its destructive agency.

The second expedient is as impracticable as the first would be unwise. As long as the reason of man continues fallible, and he is at liberty to exercise it, different opinions will be formed. As long as the connection subsists between his reason and his self-love, his opinions and his passions will have a reciprocal influence on each other; and the former will be objects to which the latter will attach themselves. The diversity in the faculties of men, from which the rights of property originate, is not less an insuperable obstacle to a uniformity of interests. The protection of these faculties is the first object of government. From the protection of different and unequal faculties of acquiring property, the possession of different degrees and kinds of property immediately results; and from the influence of these on the sentiments and views of the respective proprietors, ensues a division of the society into different interests and parties. The latent causes of faction are thus sown in the nature of man; and we see them everywhere brought into different degrees of activity, according to the different circumstances of civil society. A zeal for different opinions concerning religion, concerning government, and many other points, as well of speculation as of practice; an attachment to different leaders ambitiously contending for pre-eminence and power; or to persons of other descriptions whose fortunes have been interesting to the human passions, have, in turn, divided mankind into parties, inflamed them with mutual animosity, and rendered them much more disposed to vex and oppress each other than to co-operate for their common good. So strong is this propensity of mankind to fall into mutual animosities, that where no substantial occasion presents itself, the most frivolous and fanciful distinctions have been sufficient to kindle their unfriendly passions and excite their most violent conflicts. But the most common and durable source of factions has been the various and unequal distribution of property. Those who hold and those who are without property have ever formed distinct interests in society. Those who are creditors, and those who are debtors, fall under a like discrimination. A landed interest, a manufacturing interest, a mercantile interest, a moneyed interest, with many lesser interests, grow up of necessity in civilized nations, and divide them into different classes, actuated by different sentiments and views. The regulation of these various and interfering interests forms the principal task of modern legislation, and involves the spirit of party and faction in the necessary and ordinary operations of the government.

No man is allowed to be a judge in his own cause, because his interest would certainly bias his judgment, and, not improbably, corrupt his integrity. With equal, nay with greater reason, a body of men are unfit to be both judges and parties at the same time; yet what are many of the most important acts of legislation, but so many judicial determinations, not indeed concerning the rights of single persons, but concerning the rights of large bodies of citizens? And what are the different classes of legislators but advocates and parties to the causes which they determine? Is a law proposed concerning private debts? It is a question to which the creditors are parties on one side and the debtors on the other. Justice ought to hold the balance between them. Yet the parties are, and must be, themselves the judges; and the most numerous party, or, in other words, the most powerful faction must be expected to prevail. Shall domestic manufactures be encouraged, and in what degree, by restrictions on foreign manufactures? are questions which would be differently decided by the landed and the manufacturing classes, and probably by neither with a sole regard to justice and the public good. The apportionment of taxes on the various descriptions of property is an act which seems to require the most exact impartiality; yet there is, perhaps, no legislative act in which greater opportunity and temptation are given to a predominant party to trample on the rules of justice. Every shilling with which they overburden the inferior number, is a shilling saved to their own pockets.

It is in vain to say that enlightened statesmen will be able to adjust these clashing interests, and render them all subservient to the public good. Enlightened statesmen will not always be at the helm. Nor, in many cases, can such an adjustment be made at all without taking into view indirect and remote considerations, which will rarely prevail over the immediate interest which one party may find in disregarding the rights of another or the good of the whole. The inference to which we are brought is, that the CAUSES of faction cannot be removed, and that relief is only to be sought in the means of controlling its EFFECTS.

If a faction consists of less than a majority, relief is supplied by the republican principle, which enables the majority to defeat its sinister views by regular vote. It may clog the administration, it may convulse the society; but it will be unable to execute and mask its violence under the forms of the Constitution. When a majority is included in a faction, the form of popular government, on the other hand, enables it to sacrifice to its ruling passion or interest both the public good and the rights of other citizens. To secure the public good and private rights against the danger of such a faction, and at the same time to preserve the spirit and the form of popular government, is then the great object to which our inquiries are directed. Let me add that it is the great desideratum by which this form of government can be rescued from the opprobrium under which it has so long labored, and be recommended to the esteem and adoption of mankind.

By what means is this object attainable? Evidently by one of two only. Either the existence of the same passion or interest in a majority at the same time must be prevented, or the majority, having such coexistent passion or interest, must be rendered, by their number and local situation, unable to concert and carry into effect schemes of oppression. If the impulse and the opportunity be suffered to coincide, we well know that neither moral nor religious motives can be relied on as an adequate control. They are not found to be such on the injustice and violence of individuals, and lose their efficacy in proportion to the number combined together, that is, in proportion as their efficacy becomes needful.

From this view of the subject it may be concluded that a pure democracy, by which I mean a society consisting of a small number of citizens, who assemble and administer the government in person, can admit of no cure for the mischiefs of faction. A common passion or interest will, in almost every case, be felt by a majority of the whole; a communication and concert result from the form of government itself; and there is nothing to check the inducements to sacrifice the weaker party or an obnoxious individual. Hence it is that such democracies have ever been spectacles of turbulence and contention; have ever been found incompatible with personal security or the rights of property; and have in general been as short in their lives as they have been violent in their deaths. Theoretic politicians, who have patronized this species of government, have erroneously supposed that by reducing mankind to a perfect equality in their political rights, they would, at the same time, be perfectly equalized and assimilated in their possessions, their opinions, and their passions.

A republic, by which I mean a government in which the scheme of representation takes place, opens a different prospect, and promises the cure for which we are seeking. Let us examine the points in which it varies from pure democracy, and we shall comprehend both the nature of the cure and the efficacy which it must derive from the Union.

The two great points of difference between a democracy and a republic are: first, the delegation of the government, in the latter, to a small number of citizens elected by the rest; secondly, the greater number of citizens, and greater sphere of country, over which the latter may be extended.

The effect of the first difference is, on the one hand, to refine and enlarge the public views, by passing them through the medium of a chosen body of citizens, whose wisdom may best discern the true interest of their country, and whose patriotism and love of justice will be least likely to sacrifice it to temporary or partial considerations. Under such a regulation, it may well happen that the public voice, pronounced by the representatives of the people, will be more consonant to the public good than if pronounced by the people themselves, convened for the purpose. On the other hand, the effect may be inverted. Men of factious tempers, of local prejudices, or of sinister designs, may, by intrigue, by corruption, or by other means, first obtain the suffrages, and then betray the interests, of the people. The question resulting is, whether small or extensive republics are more favorable to the election of proper guardians of the public weal; and it is clearly decided in favor of the latter by two obvious considerations:

In the first place, it is to be remarked that, however small the republic may be, the representatives must be raised to a certain number, in order to guard against the cabals of a few; and that, however large it may be, they must be limited to a certain number, in order to guard against the confusion of a multitude. Hence, the number of representatives in the two cases not being in proportion to that of the two constituents, and being proportionally greater in the small republic, it follows that, if the proportion of fit characters be not less in the large than in the small republic, the former will present a greater option, and consequently a greater probability of a fit choice.

In the next place, as each representative will be chosen by a greater number of citizens in the large than in the small republic, it will be more difficult for unworthy candidates to practice with success the vicious arts by which elections are too often carried; and the suffrages of the people being more free, will be more likely to centre in men who possess the most attractive merit and the most diffusive and established characters.

It must be confessed that in this, as in most other cases, there is a mean, on both sides of which inconveniences will be found to lie. By enlarging too much the number of electors, you render the representatives too little acquainted with all their local circumstances and lesser interests; as by reducing it too much, you render him unduly attached to these, and too little fit to comprehend and pursue great and national objects. The federal Constitution forms a happy combination in this respect; the great and aggregate interests being referred to the national, the local and particular to the State legislatures.

The other point of difference is, the greater number of citizens and extent of territory which may be brought within the compass of republican than of democratic government; and it is this circumstance principally which renders factious combinations less to be dreaded in the former than in the latter. The smaller the society, the fewer probably will be the distinct parties and interests composing it; the fewer the distinct parties and interests, the more frequently will a majority be found of the same party; and the smaller the number of individuals composing a majority, and the smaller the compass within which they are placed, the more easily will they concert and execute their plans of oppression. Extend the sphere, and you take in a greater variety of parties and interests; you make it less probable that a majority of the whole will have a common motive to invade the rights of other citizens; or if such a common motive exists, it will be more difficult for all who feel it to discover their own strength, and to act in unison with each other. Besides other impediments, it may be remarked that, where there is a consciousness of unjust or dishonorable purposes, communication is always checked by distrust in proportion to the number whose concurrence is necessary.

Hence, it clearly appears, that the same advantage which a republic has over a democracy, in controlling the effects of faction, is enjoyed by a large over a small republic,--is enjoyed by the Union over the States composing it. Does the advantage consist in the substitution of representatives whose enlightened views and virtuous sentiments render them superior to local prejudices and schemes of injustice? It will not be denied that the representation of the Union will be most likely to possess these requisite endowments. Does it consist in the greater security afforded by a greater variety of parties, against the event of any one party being able to outnumber and oppress the rest? In an equal degree does the increased variety of parties comprised within the Union, increase this security. Does it, in fine, consist in the greater obstacles opposed to the concert and accomplishment of the secret wishes of an unjust and interested majority? Here, again, the extent of the Union gives it the most palpable advantage.

The influence of factious leaders may kindle a flame within their particular States, but will be unable to spread a general conflagration through the other States. A religious sect may degenerate into a political faction in a part of the Confederacy; but the variety of sects dispersed over the entire face of it must secure the national councils against any danger from that source. A rage for paper money, for an abolition of debts, for an equal division of property, or for any other improper or wicked project, will be less apt to pervade the whole body of the Union than a particular member of it; in the same proportion as such a malady is more likely to taint a particular county or district, than an entire State.

In the extent and proper structure of the Union, therefore, we behold a republican remedy for the diseases most incident to republican government. And according to the degree of pleasure and pride we feel in being republicans, ought to be our zeal in cherishing the spirit and supporting the character of Federalists.

PUBLIUS.

Federalist No. 39

The Conformity of the Plan to Republican Principles
For the *Independent Journal.*

MADISON

To the People of the State of New York:

The last paper having concluded the observations which were meant to introduce a candid survey of the plan of government reported by the convention, we now proceed to the execution of that part of our undertaking.

The first question that offers itself is, whether the general form and aspect of the government be strictly republican. It is evident that no other form would be reconcilable with the genius of the people of America; with the fundamental principles of the Revolution; or with that honorable determination which animates every votary of freedom, to rest all our political experiments on the capacity of mankind for self-government. If the plan of the convention, therefore, be found to depart from the republican character, its advocates must abandon it as no longer defensible.

What, then, are the distinctive characters of the republican form? Were an answer to this question to be sought, not by recurring to principles, but in the application of the term by political writers, to the constitution of different States, no satisfactory one would ever be found. Holland, in which no particle of the supreme authority is derived from the people, has passed almost universally under the denomination of a republic. The same title has been bestowed on Venice, where absolute power over the great body of the people is exercised, in the most absolute manner, by a small body of hereditary nobles. Poland, which is a mixture of aristocracy and of monarchy in their worst forms, has been dignified with the same appellation. The government of England, which has one republican branch only, combined with an hereditary aristocracy and monarchy, has, with equal impropriety, been frequently placed on the list of republics. These examples, which are nearly as dissimilar to each other as to a genuine republic, show the extreme inaccuracy with which the term has been used in political disquisitions.

If we resort for a criterion to the different principles on which different forms of government are established, we may define a republic to be, or at least may bestow that name on, a government which derives all its powers directly or indirectly from the great body of the people, and is administered by persons holding their offices during pleasure, for a limited period, or during good behavior. It is ESSENTIAL to such a government that it be derived from the great body of the society, not from an inconsiderable proportion, or a favored class of it; otherwise a handful of tyrannical nobles, exercising their oppressions by a delegation of their powers, might aspire to the rank of republicans, and claim for their government the honorable title of republic. It is SUFFICIENT for such a government that the persons administering it be appointed, either directly or indirectly, by the people; and that they hold their appointments by either of the tenures just specified; otherwise every government in the United States, as well as every other popular government that has been or can be well organized or well executed, would be degraded from the republican character. According to the constitution of every State in the Union, some or other of the officers of government are appointed indirectly only by the people. According to most of them, the chief magistrate himself is so appointed. And according to one, this mode of appointment is extended to one of the co-ordinate branches of the legislature. According to all the constitutions, also, the tenure of the highest offices is extended to a definite period, and in many instances, both within the legislative and executive departments, to a period of years. According to the provisions of most of the constitutions, again, as well as according to the most respectable and received opinions on the subject, the members of the judiciary department are to retain their offices by the firm tenure of good behavior.

On comparing the Constitution planned by the convention with the standard here fixed, we perceive at once that it is, in the most rigid sense, conformable to it. The House of Representatives, like that of one branch at least of all the State legislatures, is elected immediately by the great body of the people. The Senate, like the present Congress, and the Senate of Maryland, derives its appointment indirectly from the people. The President is indirectly derived from the choice of the people, according to the example in most of the States. Even the judges, with all other officers of the Union, will, as in the several States, be the choice, though a remote choice, of the people themselves, the duration of the appointments is equally conformable to the republican standard, and to the model of State constitutions The House of Representatives is periodically elective, as in all the States; and for the period of two years, as in the State of South Carolina. The Senate is elective, for the period of six years; which is but one year more than the period of the Senate of Maryland, and but two more than that of the Senates of New York and Virginia. The President is to continue in office for the period of four years; as in New York and Delaware, the chief magistrate is elected for three years, and in South Carolina for two years. In the other States the election is annual. In several of the States, however, no constitutional provision is made for the impeachment of the chief magistrate. And in Delaware and Virginia he is not impeachable till out of office. The President of the United States is impeachable at any time during his continuance in office. The tenure by which the judges are to hold their places, is, as it unquestionably ought to be, that of good behavior. The tenure of the ministerial offices generally, will be a subject of legal regulation, conformably to the reason of the case and the example of the State constitutions.

Could any further proof be required of the republican complexion of this system, the most decisive one might be found in its absolute prohibition of titles of nobility, both under the federal and the State governments; and in its express guaranty of the republican form to each of the latter. "But it was not sufficient," say the adversaries of the proposed Constitution, "for the convention to adhere to the republican form. They ought, with equal care, to have preserved the FEDERAL form, which regards the Union as a CONFEDERACY of sovereign states; instead of which, they have framed a NATIONAL government, which regards the Union as a CONSOLIDATION of the States." And it is asked by what authority this bold and radical innovation was undertaken? The handle which has been made of this objection requires that it should be examined with some precision.

Without inquiring into the accuracy of the distinction on which the objection is founded, it will be necessary to a just estimate of its force, first, to ascertain the real character of the government in question; secondly, to inquire how far the convention were authorized to propose such a government; and thirdly, how far the duty they owed to their country could supply any defect of regular authority.

First, in order to ascertain the real character of the government, it may be considered in relation to the foundation on which it is to be established; to the sources from which its ordinary powers are to be drawn; to the operation of those powers; to the extent of them; and to the authority by which future changes in the government are to be introduced.

On examining the first relation, it appears, on one hand, that the Constitution is to be founded on the assent and ratification of the people of America, given by deputies elected for the special purpose; but, on the other, that this assent and ratification is to be given by the people, not as individuals composing one entire nation, but as composing the distinct and independent States to which they respectively belong. It is to be the assent and ratification of the several States, derived from the supreme authority in each State, the authority of the people themselves. The act, therefore, establishing the Constitution, will not be a NATIONAL, but a FEDERAL act.

That it will be a federal and not a national act, as these terms are understood by the objectors; the act of the people, as forming so many independent States, not as forming one aggregate nation, is obvious from this single consideration, that it is to result neither from the decision of a MAJORITY of the people of the Union, nor from that of a MAJORITY of the States. It must result from the UNANIMOUS assent of the several States that are parties to it, differing no otherwise from their ordinary assent than in its being expressed, not by the legislative authority, but by that of the people themselves. Were the people regarded in this transaction as forming one nation, the will of the majority of the whole people of the United States would bind the minority, in the same manner as the majority in each State must bind the minority; and the will of the majority must be determined either by a comparison of the individual votes, or by considering the will of the majority of the States as evidence of the will of a majority of the people of the United States. Neither of these rules have been adopted. Each State, in ratifying the Constitution, is considered as a sovereign body, independent of all others, and only to be bound by its own voluntary act. In this relation, then, the new Constitution will, if established, be a FEDERAL, and not a NATIONAL constitution.

The next relation is, to the sources from which the ordinary powers of government are to be derived. The House of Representatives will derive its powers from the people of America; and the people will be represented in the same proportion, and on the same principle, as they are in the legislature of a particular State. So far the government is NATIONAL, not FEDERAL. The Senate, on the other hand, will derive its powers from the States, as political and coequal societies; and these will be represented on the principle of equality in the Senate, as they now are in the existing Congress. So far the government is FEDERAL, not NATIONAL. The executive power will be derived from a very compound source. The immediate election of the President is to be made by the States in their political characters. The votes allotted to them are in a compound ratio, which considers them partly as distinct and coequal societies, partly as unequal members of the same society. The eventual election, again, is to be made by that branch of the legislature which consists of the national representatives; but in this particular act they are to be thrown into the form of individual delegations, from so many distinct and coequal bodies politic. From this aspect of the government it appears to be of a mixed character, presenting at least as many FEDERAL as NATIONAL features.

The difference between a federal and national government, as it relates to the OPERATION OF THE GOVERNMENT, is supposed to consist in this, that in the former the powers operate on the political bodies composing the Confederacy, in their political capacities; in the latter, on the individual citizens composing the nation, in their individual capacities. On trying the

Constitution by this criterion, it falls under the NATIONAL, not the FEDERAL character; though perhaps not so completely as has been understood. In several cases, and particularly in the trial of controversies to which States may be parties, they must be viewed and proceeded against in their collective and political capacities only. So far the national countenance of the government on this side seems to be disfigured by a few federal features. But this blemish is perhaps unavoidable in any plan; and the operation of the government on the people, in their individual capacities, in its ordinary and most essential proceedings, may, on the whole, designate it, in this relation, a NATIONAL government.

But if the government be national with regard to the OPERATION of its powers, it changes its aspect again when we contemplate it in relation to the EXTENT of its powers. The idea of a national government involves in it, not only an authority over the individual citizens, but an indefinite supremacy over all persons and things, so far as they are objects of lawful government. Among a people consolidated into one nation, this supremacy is completely vested in the national legislature. Among communities united for particular purposes, it is vested partly in the general and partly in the municipal legislatures. In the former case, all local authorities are subordinate to the supreme; and may be controlled, directed, or abolished by it at pleasure. In the latter, the local or municipal authorities form distinct and independent portions of the supremacy, no more subject, within their respective spheres, to the general authority, than the general authority is subject to them, within its own sphere. In this relation, then, the proposed government cannot be deemed a NATIONAL one; since its jurisdiction extends to certain enumerated objects only, and leaves to the several States a residuary and inviolable sovereignty over all other objects. It is true that in controversies relating to the boundary between the two jurisdictions, the tribunal which is ultimately to decide, is to be established under the general government. But this does not change the principle of the case. The decision is to be impartially made, according to the rules of the Constitution; and all the usual and most effectual precautions are taken to secure this impartiality. Some such tribunal is clearly essential to prevent an appeal to the sword and a dissolution of the compact; and that it ought to be established under the general rather than under the local governments, or, to speak more properly, that it could be safely established under the first alone, is a position not likely to be combated.

If we try the Constitution by its last relation to the authority by which amendments are to be made, we find it neither wholly NATIONAL nor wholly FEDERAL. Were it wholly national, the supreme and ultimate authority would reside in the MAJORITY of the people of the Union; and this authority would be competent at all times, like that of a majority of every national society, to alter or abolish its established government. Were it wholly federal, on the other hand, the concurrence of each State in the Union would be essential to every alteration that would be binding on all. The mode provided by the plan of the convention is not founded on either of these principles. In requiring more than a majority, and principles. In requiring more than a majority, and particularly in computing the proportion by STATES, not by CITIZENS, it departs from the NATIONAL and advances towards the FEDERAL character; in rendering the concurrence of less than the whole number of States sufficient, it loses again the FEDERAL and partakes of the NATIONAL character.

The proposed Constitution, therefore, is, in strictness, neither a national nor a federal Constitution, but a composition of both. In its foundation it is federal, not national; in the sources from which the ordinary powers of the government are drawn, it is partly federal and partly national; in the operation of these powers, it is national, not federal; in the extent of them, again, it is federal, not national; and, finally, in the authoritative mode of introducing amendments, it is neither wholly federal nor wholly national.

PUBLIUS.

Federalist No. 47

The Particular Structure of the New Government and the Distribution
of Power Among Its Different Parts
From the *New York Packet*.
Friday, February 1, 1788.

MADISON

To the People of the State of New York:

Having reviewed the general form of the proposed government and the general mass of power allotted to it, I proceed to examine the particular structure of this government, and the distribution of this mass of power among its constituent parts.

One of the principal objections inculcated by the more respectable adversaries to the Constitution, is its supposed violation of the political maxim, that the legislative, executive, and judiciary departments ought to be separate and distinct. In the structure of the federal government, no regard, it is said, seems to have been paid to this essential precaution in favor of liberty. The several departments of power are distributed and blended in such a manner as at once to destroy all symmetry and beauty of form, and to expose some of the essential parts of the edifice to the danger of being crushed by the disproportionate weight of other parts.

No political truth is certainly of greater intrinsic value, or is stamped with the authority of more enlightened patrons of liberty, than that on which the objection is founded. The accumulation of all powers, legislative, executive, and judiciary, in the same hands, whether of one, a few, or many, and whether hereditary, self appointed, or elective, may justly be pronounced the very definition of tyranny. Were the federal Constitution, therefore, really chargeable with the accumulation of power, or with a mixture of powers, having a dangerous tendency to such an accumulation, no further arguments would be necessary to inspire a universal reprobation of the system. I persuade myself, however, that it will be made apparent to every one, that the charge cannot be supported, and that the maxim on which it relies has been totally misconceived and misapplied. In order to form correct ideas on this important subject, it will be proper to investigate the sense in which the preservation of liberty requires that the three great departments of power should be separate and distinct.

The oracle who is always consulted and cited on this subject is the celebrated Montesquieu. If he be not the author of this invaluable precept in the science of politics, he has the merit at least of displaying and recommending it most effectually to the attention of mankind. Let us endeavor, in the first place, to ascertain his meaning on this point.

The British Constitution was to Montesquieu what Homer has been to the didactic writers on epic poetry. As the latter have considered the work of the immortal bard as the perfect model from which the principles and rules of the epic art were to be drawn, and by which all similar works were to be judged, so this great political critic appears to have viewed the Constitution of England as the standard, or to use his own expression, as the mirror of political liberty; and to have delivered, in the form of elementary truths, the several characteristic principles of that particular system. That we may be sure, then, not to mistake his meaning in this case, let us recur to the source from which the maxim was drawn.

On the slightest view of the British Constitution, we must perceive that the legislative, executive, and judiciary departments are by no means totally separate and distinct from each other. The executive magistrate forms an integral part of the legislative authority. He alone has the prerogative of making treaties with foreign sovereigns, which, when made, have, under certain limitations, the force of legislative acts. All the members of the judiciary department are appointed by him, can be removed by him on the address of the two Houses of Parliament, and form, when he pleases to consult them, one of his constitutional councils. One branch of the legislative department forms also a great constitutional council to the executive chief, as, on another hand, it is the sole depositary of judicial power in cases of impeachment, and is invested with the supreme appellate jurisdiction in all other cases. The judges, again, are so far connected with the legislative department as often to attend and participate in its deliberations, though not admitted to a legislative vote.

From these facts, by which Montesquieu was guided, it may clearly be inferred that, in saying "There can be no liberty where the legislative and executive powers are united in the same person, or body of magistrates," or, "if the power of judging be not separated from the legislative and executive powers," he did not mean that these departments ought to have no PARTIAL AGENCY in, or no CONTROL over, the acts of each other. His meaning, as his own words import, and still more conclusively as illustrated by the example in his eye, can amount to no more than this, that where the WHOLE power of one department is exercised by the same hands which possess the WHOLE power of another department, the fundamental principles of a free constitution are subverted. This would have been the case in the constitution examined by him, if the king, who is the sole executive magistrate, had possessed also the complete legislative power, or the supreme administration of justice; or if the entire legislative body had possessed the supreme judiciary, or the supreme executive authority. This, however, is not among the vices of that constitution. The magistrate in whom the whole executive power resides cannot of himself make a law, though he can put a negative on every law; nor administer justice in person, though he has the appointment of those who do administer it. The judges can exercise no executive prerogative, though they are shoots from the executive stock; nor any legislative function, though they may be advised with by the legislative councils. The entire legislature can perform no judiciary act, though by the joint act of two of its branches the judges may be removed from their offices, and though one of its branches is possessed of the judicial power in the last resort. The entire legislature, again, can exercise no executive prerogative, though one of its branches constitutes the supreme executive magistracy, and another, on the impeachment of a third, can try and condemn all the subordinate officers in the executive department.

The reasons on which Montesquieu grounds his maxim are a further demonstration of his meaning. "When the legislative and executive powers are united in the same person or body," says he, "there can be no liberty, because apprehensions may arise lest THE SAME monarch or senate should ENACT tyrannical laws to EXECUTE them in a tyrannical manner. " Again: "Were the power of judging joined with the legislative, the life and liberty of the subject would be exposed to arbitrary control, for THE JUDGE would then be THE LEGISLATOR. Were it joined to the executive power, THE JUDGE might behave with all the violence of AN OPPRESSOR. " Some of these reasons are more fully explained in other passages; but briefly stated as they are here, they sufficiently establish the meaning which we have put on this celebrated maxim of this celebrated author.

If we look into the constitutions of the several States, we find that, notwithstanding the emphatical and, in some instances, the unqualified terms in which this axiom has been laid down, there is not a single instance in which the several departments of power have been kept absolutely separate and distinct. New Hampshire, whose constitution was the last formed, seems to have been fully aware of the impossibility and inexpediency of avoiding any mixture whatever of these departments, and has qualified the doctrine by declaring "that the legislative, executive, and judiciary powers ought to be kept as separate from, and independent of, each other AS THE NATURE OF A FREE GOVERNMENT WILL ADMIT; OR AS IS CONSISTENT WITH THAT CHAIN OF CONNECTION THAT BINDS THE WHOLE FABRIC OF THE CONSTITUTION IN ONE INDISSOLUBLE BOND OF UNITY AND AMITY. " Her constitution accordingly mixes these departments in several respects. The Senate, which is a branch of the legislative department, is also a judicial tribunal for the trial of impeachments. The President, who is the head of the executive department, is the presiding member also of the Senate; and, besides an equal vote in all cases, has a casting vote in case of a tie. The executive head is himself eventually elective every year by the legislative department, and his council is every year chosen by and from the members of the same department. Several of the officers of state are also appointed by the legislature. And the members of the judiciary department are appointed by the executive department.

The constitution of Massachusetts has observed a sufficient though less pointed caution, in expressing this fundamental article of liberty. It declares "that the legislative department shall never exercise the executive and judicial powers, or either of them; the executive shall never exercise the legislative and judicial powers, or either of them; the judicial shall never exercise the legislative and executive powers, or either of them. " This declaration corresponds precisely with the doctrine of Montesquieu, as it has been explained, and is not in a single point violated by the plan of the convention. It goes no farther than to prohibit any one of the entire departments from exercising the powers of another department. In the very Constitution to which it is prefixed, a partial mixture of powers has been admitted. The executive magistrate has a qualified negative on the legislative body, and the Senate, which is a part of the legislature, is a court of impeachment for members both of the executive and judiciary departments. The members of the judiciary department, again, are appointable by the executive department, and removable by the same authority on the address of the two legislative branches. Lastly, a number of the officers of government are annually appointed by the legislative department. As the appointment to offices, particularly executive offices, is in its nature an executive function, the compilers of the Constitution have, in this last point at least, violated the rule established by themselves.

I pass over the constitutions of Rhode Island and Connecticut, because they were formed prior to the Revolution, and even before the principle under examination had become an object of political attention.

The constitution of New York contains no declaration on this subject; but appears very clearly to have been framed with an eye to the danger of improperly blending the different departments. It gives, nevertheless, to the executive magistrate, a partial control over the legislative department; and, what is more, gives a like control to the judiciary department; and even blends the executive and judiciary departments in the exercise of this control. In its council of appointment members of the legislative are associated with the executive authority, in the appointment of officers, both executive and judiciary. And its court for the trial of impeachments and correction of errors is to consist of one branch of the legislature and the principal members of the judiciary department.

The constitution of New Jersey has blended the different powers of government more than any of the preceding. The governor, who is the executive magistrate, is appointed by the legislature; is chancellor and ordinary, or surrogate of the State; is a member of the Supreme Court of Appeals, and president, with a casting vote, of one of the legislative branches. The same legislative branch acts again as executive council of the governor, and with him constitutes the Court of Appeals. The members of the judiciary department are appointed by the legislative department and removable by one branch of it, on the impeachment of the other.

According to the constitution of Pennsylvania, the president, who is the head of the executive department, is annually elected by a vote in which the legislative department predominates. In conjunction with an executive council, he appoints the members of the judiciary department, and forms a court of impeachment for trial of all officers, judiciary as well as executive. The judges of the Supreme Court and justices of the peace seem also to be removable by the legislature; and the executive power of pardoning in certain cases, to be referred to the same department. The members of the executive council are made EX-OFFICIO justices of peace throughout the State.

In Delaware, the chief executive magistrate is annually elected by the legislative department. The speakers of the two legislative branches are vice-presidents in the executive department. The executive chief, with six others, appointed, three by each of the legislative branches constitutes the Supreme Court of Appeals; he is joined with the legislative department in the appointment of the other judges. Throughout the States, it appears that the members of the legislature may at the same time be justices of the peace; in this State, the members of one branch of it are EX-OFFICIO justices of the peace; as are also the members of the executive council. The principal officers of the executive department are appointed by the legislative; and one branch of the latter forms a court of impeachments. All officers may be removed on address of the legislature.

Maryland has adopted the maxim in the most unqualified terms; declaring that the legislative, executive, and judicial powers of government ought to be forever separate and distinct from each other. Her constitution, notwithstanding, makes the executive magistrate appointable by the legislative department; and the members of the judiciary by the executive department.

The language of Virginia is still more pointed on this subject. Her constitution declares, "that the legislative, executive, and judiciary departments shall be separate and distinct; so that neither exercise the powers properly belonging to the other; nor shall any person exercise the powers of more than one of them at the same time, except that the justices of county courts shall be eligible to either House of Assembly. " Yet we find not only this express exception, with respect to the members of the inferior courts, but that the chief magistrate, with his executive council, are appointable by the legislature; that two members of the latter are triennially displaced at the pleasure of the legislature; and that all the principal offices, both executive and judiciary, are filled by the same department. The executive prerogative of pardon, also, is in one case vested in the legislative department.

The constitution of North Carolina, which declares "that the legislative, executive, and supreme judicial powers of government ought to be forever separate and distinct from each other," refers, at the same time, to the legislative department, the appointment not only of the executive chief, but all the principal officers within both that and the judiciary department.

In South Carolina, the constitution makes the executive magistracy eligible by the legislative department. It gives to the latter, also, the appointment of the members of the judiciary department, including even justices of the peace and sheriffs; and the appointment of officers in the executive department, down to captains in the army and navy of the State.

In the constitution of Georgia, where it is declared "that the legislative, executive, and judiciary departments shall be separate and distinct, so that neither exercise the powers properly belonging to the other," we find that the executive department is to be filled by appointments of the legislature; and the executive prerogative of pardon to be finally exercised by the same authority. Even justices of the peace are to be appointed by the legislature.

In citing these cases, in which the legislative, executive, and judiciary departments have not been kept totally separate and distinct, I wish not to be regarded as an advocate for the particular organizations of the several State governments. I am fully aware that among the many excellent principles which they exemplify, they carry strong marks of the haste, and still stronger of the inexperience, under which they were framed. It is but too obvious that in some instances the fundamental principle under consideration has been violated by too great a mixture, and even an actual consolidation, of the different powers; and that in no instance has a competent provision been made for maintaining in practice the separation delineated on paper. What I have wished to evince is, that the charge brought against the proposed Constitution, of violating the sacred maxim of free government, is warranted neither by the real meaning annexed to that maxim by its author, nor by the sense in which it has hitherto been understood in America. This interesting subject will be resumed in the ensuing paper.

PUBLIUS

Federalist No. 48

These Departments Should Not Be So Far Separated as to Have No Constitutional Control Over Each Other
From the *New York Packet.*
Friday, February 1, 1788.

MADISON

To the People of the State of New York:

It was shown in the last paper that the political apothegm there examined does not require that the legislative, executive, and judiciary departments should be wholly unconnected with each other. I shall undertake, in the next place, to show that unless these departments be so far connected and blended as to give to each a constitutional control over the others, the degree of separation which the maxim requires, as essential to a free government, can never in practice be duly maintained.

It is agreed on all sides, that the powers properly belonging to one of the departments ought not to be directly and completely administered by either of the other departments. It is equally evident, that none of them ought to possess, directly or indirectly, an overruling influence over the others, in the administration of their respective powers. It will not be denied, that power is of an encroaching nature, and that it ought to be effectually restrained from passing the limits assigned to it. After discriminating, therefore, in theory, the several classes of power, as they may in their nature be legislative, executive, or judiciary, the next and most difficult task is to provide some practical security for each, against the invasion of the others. What this security ought to be, is the great problem to be solved.

Will it be sufficient to mark, with precision, the boundaries of these departments, in the constitution of the government, and to trust to these parchment barriers against the encroaching spirit of power? This is the security which appears to have been principally relied on by the compilers of most of the American constitutions. But experience assures us, that the efficacy of the provision has been greatly overrated; and that some more adequate defense is indispensably necessary for the more feeble, against the more powerful, members of the government. The legislative department is everywhere extending the sphere of its activity, and drawing all power into its impetuous vortex.

The founders of our republics have so much merit for the wisdom which they have displayed, that no task can be less pleasing than that of pointing out the errors into which they have fallen. A respect for truth, however, obliges us to remark, that they seem never for a moment to have turned their eyes from the danger to liberty from the overgrown and all-grasping prerogative of an hereditary magistrate, supported and fortified by an hereditary branch of the legislative authority. They seem never to have recollected the danger from legislative usurpations, which, by assembling all power in the same hands, must lead to the same tyranny as is threatened by executive usurpations.

In a government where numerous and extensive prerogatives are placed in the hands of an hereditary monarch, the executive department is very justly regarded as the source of danger, and watched with all the jealousy which a zeal for liberty ought to inspire. In a democracy, where a multitude of people exercise in person the legislative functions, and are continually exposed, by their incapacity for regular deliberation and concerted measures, to the ambitious intrigues of their executive magistrates, tyranny may well be apprehended, on some favorable emergency, to start up in the same quarter. But in a representative republic, where the executive magistracy is carefully limited; both in the extent and the duration of its power; and where the legislative power is exercised by an assembly, which is inspired, by a supposed influence over the people, with an intrepid confidence in its own strength; which is sufficiently numerous to feel all the passions which actuate a multitude, yet not so numerous as to be incapable of pursuing the objects of its passions, by means which reason prescribes; it is against the enterprising ambition of this department that the people ought to indulge all their jealousy and exhaust all their precautions.

The legislative department derives a superiority in our governments from other circumstances. Its constitutional powers being at once more extensive, and less susceptible of precise limits, it can, with the greater facility, mask, under complicated and indirect measures, the encroachments which it makes on the co-ordinate departments. It is not unfrequently a question of real nicety in legislative bodies, whether the operation of a particular measure will, or will not, extend beyond the legislative sphere. On the other side, the executive power being restrained within a narrower compass, and being more simple in its nature, and the judiciary being described by landmarks still less uncertain, projects of usurpation by either of these departments would immediately betray and defeat themselves. Nor is this all: as the legislative department alone has access to the pockets of the people, and has in some constitutions full discretion, and in all a prevailing influence, over the pecuniary rewards of those who fill the other departments, a dependence is thus created in the latter, which gives still greater facility to encroachments of the former.

I have appealed to our own experience for the truth of what I advance on this subject. Were it necessary to verify this experience by particular proofs, they might be multiplied without end. I might find a witness in every citizen who has shared in, or been attentive to, the course of public administrations. I might collect vouchers in abundance from the records and archives of every State in the Union. But as a more concise, and at the same time equally satisfactory, evidence, I will refer to the example of two States, attested by two unexceptionable authorities.

The first example is that of Virginia, a State which, as we have seen, has expressly declared in its constitution, that the three great departments ought not to be intermixed. The authority in support of it is Mr. Jefferson, who, besides his other advantages for remarking the operation of the government, was himself the chief magistrate of it. In order to convey fully the ideas with which his experience had impressed him on this subject, it will be necessary to quote a passage of some length from his very interesting "Notes on the State of Virginia," p. 195. "All the powers of government, legislative, executive, and judiciary, result to the legislative body. The concentrating these in the same hands, is precisely the definition of despotic government. It will be no alleviation, that these powers will be exercised by a plurality of hands, and not by a single one. One hundred and seventy-three despots would surely be as oppressive as one. Let those who doubt it, turn their eyes on the republic of Venice. As little will it avail us, that they are chosen by ourselves. An ELECTIVE DESPOTISM was not the government we fought for; but one which should not only be founded on free principles, but in which the powers of government should be so divided and balanced among several bodies of magistracy, as that no one could transcend their legal limits, without being effectually checked and restrained by the others. For this reason, that convention which passed the ordinance of government, laid its foundation on this basis, that the legislative, executive, and judiciary departments should be separate and distinct, so that no person should exercise the powers of more than one of them at the same time. BUT NO BARRIER WAS PROVIDED BETWEEN THESE SEVERAL POWERS. The judiciary and the executive members were left dependent on the legislative for their subsistence in office, and some of them for their continuance in it. If, therefore, the legislature assumes executive and judiciary powers, no opposition is likely to be made; nor, if made, can be effectual; because in that case they may put their proceedings into the form of acts of Assembly, which will render them obligatory on the other branches. They have accordingly, IN MANY instances, DECIDED RIGHTS which should have been left to JUDICIARY CONTROVERSY, and THE DIRECTION OF THE EXECUTIVE, DURING THE WHOLE TIME OF THEIR SESSION, IS BECOMING HABITUAL AND FAMILIAR. "

The other State which I shall take for an example is Pennsylvania; and the other authority, the Council of Censors, which assembled in the years 1783 and 1784. A part of the duty of this body, as marked out by the constitution, was "to inquire whether the constitution had been preserved inviolate in every part; and whether the legislative and executive branches of government had performed their duty as guardians of the people, or assumed to themselves, or exercised, other or greater powers than they are entitled to by the constitution. " In the execution of this trust, the council were necessarily led to a comparison of both the legislative and executive proceedings, with the constitutional powers of these departments; and from the facts enumerated, and to the truth of most of which both sides in the council subscribed, it appears that the constitution had been flagrantly violated by the legislature in a variety of important instances.

A great number of laws had been passed, violating, without any apparent necessity, the rule requiring that all bills of a public nature shall be previously printed for the consideration of the people; although this is one of the precautions chiefly relied on by the constitution against improper acts of legislature.

The constitutional trial by jury had been violated, and powers assumed which had not been delegated by the constitution.

Executive powers had been usurped.

The salaries of the judges, which the constitution expressly requires to be fixed, had been occasionally varied; and cases belonging to the judiciary department frequently drawn within legislative cognizance and determination.

Those who wish to see the several particulars falling under each of these heads, may consult the journals of the council, which are in print. Some of them, it will be found, may be imputable to peculiar circumstances connected with the war; but the greater part of them may be considered as the spontaneous shoots of an ill-constituted government.

It appears, also, that the executive department had not been innocent of frequent breaches of the constitution. There are three observations, however, which ought to be made on this head: FIRST, a great proportion of the instances were either immediately produced by the necessities of the war, or recommended by Congress or the commander-in-chief; SECONDLY, in most of the other instances, they conformed either to the declared or the known sentiments of the legislative department; THIRDLY, the executive department of Pennsylvania is distinguished from that of the other States by the number of members composing it. In this respect, it has as much affinity to a legislative assembly as to an executive council. And being at once exempt from the restraint of an individual responsibility for the acts of the body, and deriving confidence from mutual example and joint influence, unauthorized measures would, of course, be more freely hazarded, than where the executive department is administered by a single hand, or by a few hands.

The conclusion which I am warranted in drawing from these observations is, that a mere demarcation on parchment of the constitutional limits of the several departments, is not a sufficient guard against those encroachments which lead to a tyrannical concentration of all the powers of government in the same hands.

PUBLIUS

Federalist No. 49

Method of Guarding Against the Encroachments of Any One Department
of Government by Appealing to the People Through a Convention
From the *New York Packet*.
Tuesday, February 5, 1788.

HAMILTON OR MADISON

To the People of the State of New York:

The author of the "Notes on the State of Virginia," quoted in the last paper, has subjoined to that valuable work the draught of a constitution, which had been prepared in order to be laid before a convention, expected to be called in 1783, by the legislature, for the establishment of a constitution for that commonwealth. The plan, like every thing from the same pen, marks a turn of thinking, original, comprehensive, and accurate; and is the more worthy of attention as it equally displays a fervent attachment to republican government and an enlightened view of the dangerous propensities against which it ought to be guarded. One of the precautions which he proposes, and on which he appears ultimately to rely as a palladium to the weaker departments of power against the invasions of the stronger, is perhaps altogether his own, and as it immediately relates to the subject of our present inquiry, ought not to be overlooked.

His proposition is, "that whenever any two of the three branches of government shall concur in opinion, each by the voices of two thirds of their whole number, that a convention is necessary for altering the constitution, or CORRECTING BREACHES OF IT, a convention shall be called for the purpose. "

As the people are the only legitimate fountain of power, and it is from them that the constitutional charter, under which the several branches of government hold their power, is derived, it seems strictly consonant to the republican theory, to recur to the same original authority, not only whenever it may be necessary to enlarge, diminish, or new-model the powers of the government, but also whenever any one of the departments may commit encroachments on the chartered authorities of the others. The several departments being perfectly co-ordinate by the terms of their common commission, none of them, it is evident, can pretend to an exclusive or superior right of settling the boundaries between their respective powers; and how are the encroachments of the stronger to be prevented, or the wrongs of the weaker to be redressed, without an appeal to the people themselves, who, as the grantors of the commissions, can alone declare its true meaning, and enforce its observance?

There is certainly great force in this reasoning, and it must be allowed to prove that a constitutional road to the decision of the people ought to be marked out and kept open, for certain great and extraordinary occasions. But there appear to be insuperable objections against the proposed recurrence to the people, as a provision in all cases for keeping the several departments of power within their constitutional limits.

In the first place, the provision does not reach the case of a combination of two of the departments against the third. If the legislative authority, which possesses so many means of operating on the motives of the other departments, should be able to gain to its interest either of the others, or even one third of its members, the remaining department could derive no advantage from its remedial provision. I do not dwell, however, on this objection, because it may be thought to be rather against the modification of the principle, than against the principle itself.

In the next place, it may be considered as an objection inherent in the principle, that as every appeal to the people would carry an implication of some defect in the government, frequent appeals would, in a great measure, deprive the government of that veneration which time bestows on every thing, and without which perhaps the wisest and freest governments would not possess the requisite stability. If it be true that all governments rest on opinion, it is no less true that the strength of opinion in each individual, and its practical influence on his conduct, depend much on the number which he supposes to have entertained the same opinion. The reason of man, like man himself, is timid and cautious when left alone, and acquires firmness and confidence in proportion to the number with which it is associated. When the examples which fortify opinion are ANCIENT as well as NUMEROUS, they are known to have a double effect. In a nation of philosophers, this consideration ought to be disregarded. A reverence for the laws would be sufficiently inculcated by the voice of an enlightened reason. But a nation of philosophers is as little to be expected as the philosophical race of kings wished for by Plato. And in every other nation, the most rational government will not find it a superfluous advantage to have the prejudices of the community on its side.

The danger of disturbing the public tranquillity by interesting too strongly the public passions, is a still more serious objection against a frequent reference of constitutional questions to the decision of the whole society. Notwithstanding the success which has attended the revisions of our established forms of government, and which does so much honor to the virtue and intelligence of the people of America, it must be confessed that the experiments are of too ticklish a nature to be unnecessarily multiplied. We are to recollect that all the existing constitutions were formed in the midst of a danger which repressed the passions most unfriendly to order and concord; of an enthusiastic confidence of the people in their patriotic leaders, which stifled the ordinary diversity of opinions on great national questions; of a universal ardor for new and opposite forms, produced by a universal resentment and indignation against the ancient government; and whilst no spirit of party connected with the changes to be made, or the abuses to be reformed, could mingle its leaven in the operation. The future situations in which we must expect to be usually placed, do not present any equivalent security against the danger which is apprehended.

But the greatest objection of all is, that the decisions which would probably result from such appeals would not answer the purpose of maintaining the constitutional equilibrium of the government. We have seen that the tendency of republican governments is to an aggrandizement of the legislative at the expense of the other departments. The appeals to the people, therefore, would usually be made by the executive and judiciary departments. But whether made by one side or the other, would each side enjoy equal advantages on the trial? Let us view their different situations. The members of the executive and judiciary departments are few in number, and can be personally known to a small part only of the people. The latter, by the mode of their appointment, as well as by the nature and permanency of it, are too far removed from the people to share much in their prepossessions. The former are generally the objects of jealousy, and their administration is always liable to be discolored and rendered unpopular. The members of the legislative department, on the other hand, are numberous. They are distributed and dwell among the people at large. Their connections of blood, of friendship, and of acquaintance embrace a great proportion of the most influential part of the society. The nature of their public trust implies a personal influence among the people, and that they are more immediately the confidential guardians of the rights and liberties of the people. With these advantages, it can hardly be supposed that the adverse party would have an equal chance for a favorable issue.

But the legislative party would not only be able to plead their cause most successfully with the people. They would probably be constituted themselves the judges. The same influence which had gained them an election into the legislature, would gain them a seat in the convention. If this should not be the case with all, it would probably be the case with many, and pretty certainly with those leading characters, on whom every thing depends in such bodies. The convention, in short, would be composed chiefly of men who had been, who actually were, or who expected to be, members of the department whose conduct was arraigned. They would consequently be parties to the very question to be decided by them.

It might, however, sometimes happen, that appeals would be made under circumstances less adverse to the executive and judiciary departments. The usurpations of the legislature might be so flagrant and so sudden, as to admit of no specious coloring. A strong party among themselves might take side with the other branches. The executive power might be in the hands of a peculiar favorite of the people. In such a posture of things, the public decision might be less swayed by prepossessions in favor of the legislative party. But still it could never be expected to turn on the true merits of the question. It would inevitably be connected with the spirit of pre-existing parties, or of parties springing out of the question itself. It would be connected with persons of distinguished character and extensive influence in the community. It would be pronounced by the very men who had been agents in, or opponents of, the measures to which the decision would relate. The PASSIONS, therefore, not the REASON, of the public would sit in judgment. But it is the reason, alone, of the public, that ought to control and regulate the government. The passions ought to be controlled and regulated by the government.

We found in the last paper, that mere declarations in the written constitution are not sufficient to restrain the several departments within their legal rights. It appears in this, that occasional appeals to the people would be neither a proper nor an effectual provision for that purpose. How far the provisions of a different nature contained in the plan above quoted might be adequate, I do not examine. Some of them are unquestionably founded on sound political principles, and all of them are framed with singular ingenuity and precision.

PUBLIUS

Federalist No. 50

Periodical Appeals to the People Considered
From the *New York Packet.*
Tuesday, February 5, 1788.

HAMILTON OR MADISON

To the People of the State of New York:

It may be contended, perhaps, that instead of OCCASIONAL appeals to the people, which are liable to the objections urged against them, PERIODICAL appeals are the proper and adequate means of PREVENTING AND CORRECTING INFRACTIONS OF THE CONSTITUTION.

It will be attended to, that in the examination of these expedients, I confine myself to their aptitude for ENFORCING the Constitution, by keeping the several departments of power within their due bounds, without particularly considering them as provisions for ALTERING the Constitution itself. In the first view, appeals to the people at fixed periods appear to be nearly as ineligible as appeals on particular occasions as they emerge. If the periods be separated by short intervals, the measures to be reviewed and rectified will have been of recent date, and will be connected with all the circumstances which tend to vitiate and pervert the result of occasional revisions. If the periods be distant from each other, the same remark will be applicable to all recent measures; and in proportion as the remoteness of the others may favor a dispassionate review of them, this advantage is inseparable from inconveniences which seem to counterbalance it. In the first place, a distant prospect of public censure would be a very feeble restraint on power from those excesses to which it might be urged by the force of present motives. Is it to be imagined that a legislative assembly, consisting of a hundred or two hundred members, eagerly bent on some favorite object, and breaking through the restraints of the Constitution in pursuit of it, would be arrested in their career, by considerations drawn from a censorial revision of their conduct at the future distance of ten, fifteen, or twenty years? In the next place, the abuses would often have completed their mischievous effects before the remedial provision would be applied. And in the last place, where this might not be the case, they would be of long standing, would have taken deep root, and would not easily be extirpated.

The scheme of revising the constitution, in order to correct recent breaches of it, as well as for other purposes, has been actually tried in one of the States. One of the objects of the Council of Censors which met in Pennsylvania in 1783 and 1784, was, as we have seen, to inquire, "whether the constitution had been violated, and whether the legislative and executive departments had encroached upon each other. " This important and novel experiment in politics merits, in several points of view, very particular attention. In some of them it may, perhaps, as a single experiment, made under circumstances somewhat peculiar, be thought to be not absolutely conclusive. But as applied to the case under consideration, it involves some facts, which I venture to remark, as a complete and satisfactory illustration of the reasoning which I have employed.

First. It appears, from the names of the gentlemen who composed the council, that some, at least, of its most active members had also been active and leading characters in the parties which pre-existed in the State.

Secondly. It appears that the same active and leading members of the council had been active and influential members of the legislative and executive branches, within the period to be reviewed; and even patrons or opponents of the very measures to be thus brought to the test of the constitution. Two of the members had been vice-presidents of the State, and several other members of the executive council, within the seven preceding years. One of them had been speaker, and a number of others distinguished members, of the legislative assembly within the same period.

Thirdly. Every page of their proceedings witnesses the effect of all these circumstances on the temper of their deliberations. Throughout the continuance of the council, it was split into two fixed and violent parties. The fact is acknowledged and lamented by themselves. Had this not been the case, the face of their proceedings exhibits a proof equally satisfactory. In all questions, however unimportant in themselves, or unconnected with each other, the same names stand invariably contrasted on the opposite columns. Every unbiased observer may infer, without danger of mistake, and at the same time without meaning to reflect on either party, or any individuals of either party, that, unfortunately, PASSION, not REASON, must have presided over their decisions. When men exercise their reason coolly and freely on a variety of distinct questions, they inevitably fall into different opinions on some of them. When they are governed by a common passion, their opinions, if they are so to be called, will be the same.

Fourthly. It is at least problematical, whether the decisions of this body do not, in several instances, misconstrue the limits prescribed for the legislative and executive departments, instead of reducing and limiting them within their constitutional places.

Fifthly. I have never understood that the decisions of the council on constitutional questions, whether rightly or erroneously formed, have had any effect in varying the practice founded on legislative constructions. It even appears, if I mistake not, that in one instance the contemporary legislature denied the constructions of the council, and actually prevailed in the contest.

This censorial body, therefore, proves at the same time, by its researches, the existence of the disease, and by its example, the inefficacy of the remedy.

This conclusion cannot be invalidated by alleging that the State in which the experiment was made was at that crisis, and had been for a long time before, violently heated and distracted by the rage of party. Is it to be presumed, that at any future septennial epoch the same State will be free from parties? Is it to be presumed that any other State, at the same or any other given period, will be exempt from them? Such an event ought to be neither presumed nor desired; because an extinction of parties necessarily implies either a universal alarm for the public safety, or an absolute extinction of liberty.

Were the precaution taken of excluding from the assemblies elected by the people, to revise the preceding administration of the government, all persons who should have been concerned with the government within the given period, the difficulties would not be obviated. The important task would probably devolve on men, who, with inferior capacities, would in other respects be little better qualified. Although they might not have been personally concerned in the administration, and therefore not immediately agents in the measures to be examined, they would probably have been involved in the parties connected with these measures, and have been elected under their auspices.

PUBLIUS.

Federalist No. 51

The Structure of the Government Must Furnish the Proper Checks and Balances
Between the Different Departments
From the *New York Packet.*
Friday, February 8, 1788.

HAMILTON OR MADISON

To the People of the State of New York:

To what expedient, then, shall we finally resort, for maintaining in practice the necessary partition of power among the several departments, as laid down in the Constitution? The only answer that can be given is, that as all these exterior provisions are found to be inadequate, the defect must be supplied, by so contriving the interior structure of the government as that its several constituent parts may, by their mutual relations, be the means of keeping each other in their proper places. Without presuming to undertake a full development of this important idea, I will hazard a few general observations, which may perhaps place it in a clearer light, and enable us to form a more correct judgment of the principles and structure of the government planned by the convention.

In order to lay a due foundation for that separate and distinct exercise of the different powers of government, which to a certain extent is admitted on all hands to be essential to the preservation of liberty, it is evident that each department should have a will of its own; and consequently should be so constituted that the members of each should have as little agency as possible in the appointment of the members of the others. Were this principle rigorously adhered to, it would require that all the appointments for the supreme executive, legislative, and judiciary magistracies should be drawn from the same fountain of authority, the people, through channels having no communication whatever with one another. Perhaps such a plan of constructing the several departments would be less difficult in practice than it may in contemplation appear. Some difficulties, however, and some additional expense would attend the execution of it. Some deviations, therefore, from the principle must be admitted. In the constitution of the judiciary department in particular, it might be inexpedient to insist rigorously on the principle: first, because peculiar qualifications being essential in the members, the primary consideration ought to be to select that mode of choice which best secures these qualifications; secondly, because the permanent tenure by which the appointments are held in that department, must soon destroy all sense of dependence on the authority conferring them.

It is equally evident, that the members of each department should be as little dependent as possible on those of the others, for the emoluments annexed to their offices. Were the executive magistrate, or the judges, not independent of the legislature in this particular, their independence in every other would be merely nominal.

But the great security against a gradual concentration of the several powers in the same department, consists in giving to those who administer each department the necessary constitutional means and personal motives to resist encroachments of the others. The provision for defense must in this, as in all other cases, be made commensurate to the danger of attack. Ambition must be made to counteract ambition. The interest of the man must be connected with the constitutional rights of the place. It may be a reflection on human nature, that such devices should be necessary to control the abuses of government. But what is government itself, but the greatest of all reflections on human nature? If men were angels, no government would be necessary. If angels were to govern men, neither external nor internal controls on government would be necessary. In framing a government which is to be administered by men over men, the great difficulty lies in this: you must first enable the government to control the governed; and in the next place oblige it to control itself. A dependence on the people is, no doubt, the primary control on the government; but experience has taught mankind the necessity of auxiliary precautions.

This policy of supplying, by opposite and rival interests, the defect of better motives, might be traced through the whole system of human affairs, private as well as public. We see it particularly displayed in all the subordinate distributions of power, where the constant aim is to divide and arrange the several offices in such a manner as that each may be a check on the other that the private interest of every individual may be a sentinel over the public rights. These inventions of prudence cannot be less requisite in the distribution of the supreme powers of the State.

But it is not possible to give to each department an equal power of self-defense. In republican government, the legislative authority necessarily predominates. The remedy for this inconveniency is to divide the legislature into different branches; and to render them, by different modes of election and different principles of action, as little connected with each other as the nature of their common functions and their common dependence on the society will admit. It may even be necessary to guard against dangerous encroachments by still further precautions. As the weight of the legislative authority requires that it should be thus divided, the weakness of the executive may require, on the other hand, that it should be fortified. An absolute negative on the legislature appears, at first view, to be the natural defense with which the executive magistrate should be armed. But perhaps it would be neither altogether safe nor alone sufficient. On ordinary occasions it might not be exerted with the requisite firmness, and on extraordinary occasions it might be perfidiously abused. May not this defect of an absolute negative be supplied by some qualified connection between this weaker department and the weaker branch of the stronger department, by which the latter may be led to support the constitutional rights of the former, without being too much detached from the rights of its own department?

If the principles on which these observations are founded be just, as I persuade myself they are, and they be applied as a criterion to the several State constitutions, and to the federal Constitution it will be found that if the latter does not perfectly correspond with them, the former are infinitely less able to bear such a test.

There are, moreover, two considerations particularly applicable to the federal system of America, which place that system in a very interesting point of view.

First. In a single republic, all the power surrendered by the people is submitted to the administration of a single government; and the usurpations are guarded against by a division of the government into distinct and separate departments. In the compound republic of America, the power surrendered by the people is first divided between two distinct governments, and then the portion allotted to each subdivided among distinct and separate departments. Hence a double security arises to the rights of the people. The different governments will control each other, at the same time that each will be controlled by itself.

Second. It is of great importance in a republic not only to guard the society against the oppression of its rulers, but to guard one part of the society against the injustice of the other part. Different interests necessarily exist in different classes of citizens. If a majority be united by a common interest, the rights of the minority will be insecure. There are but two methods of providing against this evil: the one by creating a will in the community independent of the majority that is, of the society itself; the other, by comprehending in the society so many separate descriptions of citizens as will render an unjust combination of a majority of the whole very improbable, if not impracticable. The first method prevails in all governments possessing an hereditary or self-appointed authority. This, at best, is but a precarious security; because a power independent of the society may as well espouse the unjust views of the major, as the rightful interests of the minor party, and may possibly be turned against both parties. The second method will be exemplified in the federal republic of the United States. Whilst all authority in it will be derived from and dependent on the society, the society itself will be broken into so many parts, interests, and classes of citizens, that the rights of individuals, or of the minority, will be in little danger from interested combinations of the majority. In a free government the security for civil rights must be the same as that for religious rights. It consists in the one case in the multiplicity of interests, and in the other in the multiplicity of sects. The degree of security in both cases will depend on the number of interests and sects; and this may be presumed to depend on the extent of country and number of people comprehended under the same government. This view of the subject must particularly recommend a proper federal system to all the sincere and considerate friends of republican government, since it shows that in exact proportion as the territory of the Union may be formed into more circumscribed Confederacies, or States oppressive combinations of a majority will be facilitated: the best security, under the republican forms, for the rights of every class of citizens, will be diminished: and consequently the stability and independence of some member of the government, the only other security, must be proportionately increased. Justice is the end of government. It is the end of civil society. It ever has been and ever will be pursued until it be obtained, or until liberty be lost in the pursuit. In a society under the forms of which the stronger faction can readily unite and oppress the weaker, anarchy may as truly be said to reign as in a state of nature, where the weaker individual is not secured against the violence of the stronger; and as, in the latter state, even the stronger individuals are prompted, by the uncertainty of their condition, to submit to a government which may protect the weak as well as themselves; so, in the former state, will the more powerful factions or parties be gradually induced, by a like motive, to wish for a government which will protect all parties, the weaker as well as the more powerful. It can be little doubted that if the State of Rhode Island was separated from the Confederacy and left to itself, the insecurity of rights under the popular form of government within such narrow limits would be displayed by such reiterated oppressions of factious majorities that some power altogether independent of the people would soon be called for by the voice of the very factions whose misrule had proved the necessity of it. In the extended republic of the United States, and among the great variety of interests, parties, and sects which it embraces, a coalition of a majority of the whole society could seldom take place on any other principles than those of justice and the general good; whilst there being thus less danger to a minor from the will of a major party, there must be less pretext, also, to provide for the security of the former, by introducing into the government a will not dependent on the latter, or, in other words, a will independent of the society itself. It is no less certain than it is important, notwithstanding the contrary opinions which have been entertained, that the larger the society, provided it lie within a practical sphere, the more duly capable it will be of self-government. And happily for the REPUBLICAN CAUSE, the practicable sphere may be carried to a very great extent, by a judicious modification and mixture of the FEDERAL PRINCIPLE.

PUBLIUS.

Federalist Paper No. 68

The Mode of Electing the President
From the *New York Packet*.
Friday, March 14, 1788

HAMILTON

To the People of the State of New York:

The mode of appointment of the Chief Magistrate of the United States is almost the only part of the system, of any consequence, which has escaped without severe censure, or which has received the slightest mark of approbation from its opponents. The most plausible of these, who has appeared in print, has even deigned to admit that the election of the President is pretty well guarded. (1) I venture somewhat further, and hesitate not to affirm, that if the manner of it be not perfect, it is at least excellent. It unites in an eminent degree all the advantages, the union of which was to be wished for.

It was desirable that the sense of the people should operate in the choice of the person to whom so important a trust was to be confided. This end will be answered by committing the right of making it, not to any pre-established body, but to men chosen by the people for the special purpose, and at the particular conjuncture.

It was equally desirable, that the immediate election should be made by men most capable of analyzing the qualities adapted to the station, and acting under circumstances favorable to deliberation, and to a judicious combination of all the reasons and inducements which were proper to govern their choice. A small number of persons, selected by their fellow-citizens from the general mass, will be most likely to possess the information and discernment requisite to such complicated investigations.

It was also peculiarly desirable to afford as little opportunity as possible to tumult and disorder. This evil was not least to be dreaded in the election of a magistrate, who was to have so important an agency in the administration of the government as the President of the United States. But the precautions which have been so happily concerted in the system under consideration, promise an effectual security against this mischief. The choice of SEVERAL, to form an intermediate body of electors, will be much less apt to convulse the community with any extraordinary or violent movements, than the choice of ONE who was himself to be the final object of the public wishes. And as the electors, chosen in each State, are to assemble and vote in the State in which they are chosen, this detached and divided situation will expose them much less to heats and ferments, which might be communicated from them to the people, than if they were all to be convened at one time, in one place.

Nothing was more to be desired than that every practicable obstacle should be opposed to cabal, intrigue, and corruption. These most deadly adversaries of republican government might naturally have been expected to make their approaches from more than one quarter, but chiefly from the desire in foreign powers to gain an improper ascendant in our councils. How could they better gratify this, than by raising a creature of their own to the chief magistracy of the Union? But the convention have guarded against all danger of this sort, with the most provident and judicious attention. They have not made the appointment of the President to depend on any preexisting bodies of men, who might be tampered with beforehand to prostitute their votes; but they have referred it in the first instance to an immediate act of the people of America, to be exerted in the choice of persons for the temporary and sole purpose of making the appointment. And they have excluded from eligibility to this trust, all those who from situation might be suspected of too great devotion to the President in office. No senator, representative, or other person holding a place of trust or profit under the United States, can be of the numbers of the electors. Thus without corrupting the body of the people, the immediate agents in the election will at least enter upon the task free from any sinister bias. Their transient existence, and their detached situation, already taken notice of, afford a satisfactory prospect of their continuing so, to the conclusion of it. The business of corruption, when it is to embrace so considerable a number of men, requires time as well as means. Nor would it be found easy suddenly to embark them, dispersed as they would be over thirteen States, in any combinations founded upon motives, which though they could not properly be denominated corrupt, might yet be of a nature to mislead them from their duty.

Another and no less important desideratum was, that the Executive should be independent for his continuance in office on all but the people themselves. He might otherwise be tempted to sacrifice his duty to his complaisance for those whose favor was necessary to the duration of his official consequence. This advantage will also be secured, by making his re-election to depend on a special body of representatives, deputed by the society for the single purpose of making the important choice.

All these advantages will happily combine in the plan devised by the convention; which is, that the people of each State shall choose a number of persons as electors, equal to the number of senators and representatives of such State in the national government, who shall assemble within the State, and vote for some fit person as President. Their votes, thus given, are to be transmitted to the seat of the national government, and the person who may happen to have a majority of the whole number of votes will be the President. But as a majority of the votes might not always happen to centre in one man, and as it might be unsafe to permit less than a majority to be conclusive, it is provided that, in such a contingency, the House of Representatives shall select out of the candidates who shall have the five highest number of votes, the man who in their opinion may be best qualified for the office.

The process of election affords a moral certainty, that the office of President will never fall to the lot of any man who is not in an eminent degree endowed with the requisite qualifications. Talents for low intrigue, and the little arts of popularity, may alone suffice to elevate a man to the first honors in a single State; but it will require other talents, and a different kind of merit, to establish him in the esteem and confidence of the whole Union, or of so considerable a portion of it as would be necessary to make him a successful candidate for the distinguished office of President of the United States. It will not be too strong to say, that there will be a constant probability of seeing the station filled by characters pre-eminent for ability and virtue. And this will be thought no inconsiderable recommendation of the Constitution, by those who are able to estimate the share which the executive in every government must necessarily have in its good or ill administration. Though we cannot acquiesce in the political heresy of the poet who says: For forms of government let fools contest That which is best administered is best," yet we may safely pronounce, that the true test of a good government is its aptitude and tendency to produce a good administration.

The Vice-President is to be chosen in the same manner with the President; with this difference, that the Senate is to do, in respect to the former, what is to be done by the House of Representatives, in respect to the latter.

The appointment of an extraordinary person, as Vice-President, has been objected to as superfluous, if not mischievous. It has been alleged, that it would have been preferable to have authorized the Senate to elect out of their own body an officer answering that description. But two considerations seem to justify the ideas of the convention in this respect. One is, that to secure at all times the possibility of a definite resolution of the body, it is necessary that the President should have only a casting vote. And to take the senator of any State from his seat as senator, to place him in that of President of the Senate, would be to exchange, in regard to the State from which he came, a constant for a contingent vote. The other consideration is, that as the Vice-President may occasionally become a substitute for the President, in the supreme executive magistracy, all the reasons which recommend the mode of election prescribed for the one, apply with great if not with equal force to the manner of appointing the other. It is remarkable that in this, as in most other instances, the objection which is made would lie against the constitution of this State. We have a Lieutenant-Governor, chosen by the people at large, who presides in the

Senate, and is the constitutional substitute for the Governor, in casualties similar to those which would authorize the Vice-President to exercise the authorities and discharge the duties of the President.

PUBLIUS.

Marbury v. Madison

5 U.S. 137 (1803)

Syllabus

The clerks of the Department of State of the United States may be called upon to give evidence of transactions in the Department which are not of a confidential character.

The Secretary of State cannot be called upon as a witness to state transactions of a confidential nature which may have occurred in his Department. But he may be called upon to give testimony of circumstances which were not of that character.

Clerks in the Department of State were directed to be sworn, subject to objections to questions upon confidential matters.

Some point of time must be taken when the power of the Executive over an officer, not removable at his will, must cease. That point of time must be when the constitutional power of appointment has been exercised. And the power has been exercised when the last act required from the person possessing the power has been performed. This last act is the signature of the commission.

If the act of livery be necessary to give validity to the commission of an officer, it has been delivered when executed, and given to the Secretary of State for the purpose of being sealed, recorded, and transmitted to the party.

In cases of commissions to public officers, the law orders the Secretary of State to record them. When, therefore, they are signed and sealed, the order for their being recorded is given, and, whether inserted inserted into the book or not, they are recorded.

When the heads of the departments of the Government are the political or confidential officers of the Executive, merely to execute the will of the President, or rather to act in cases in which the Executive possesses a constitutional or legal discretion, nothing can be more perfectly clear than that their acts are only politically examinable. But where a specific duty is assigned by law, and individual rights depend upon the performance of that duty, it seems equally clear that the individual who considers himself injured has a right to resort to the laws of his country for a remedy.

The President of the United States, by signing the commission, appointed Mr. Marbury a justice of the peace for the County of Washington, in the District of Columbia, and the seal of the United States, affixed thereto by the Secretary of State, is conclusive testimony of the verity of the signature, and of the completion of the appointment; and the appointment conferred on him a legal right to the office for the space of five years. Having this legal right to the office, he has a consequent right to the commission, a refusal to deliver which is a plain violation of that right for which the laws of the country afford him a remedy.

To render a mandamus a proper remedy, the officer to whom it is directed must be one to whom, on legal principles, such writ must be directed, and the person applying for it must be without any other specific remedy.

Where a commission to a public officer has been made out, signed, and sealed, and is withheld from the person entitled to it, an action of detinue for the commission against the Secretary of State who refuses to deliver it is not the proper remedy, as the judgment in detinue is for the thing itself, or its value. The value of a public office, not to be sold, is incapable of being ascertained. It is a plain case for a mandamus, either to deliver the commission or a copy of it from the record.

To enable the Court to issue a mandamus to compel the delivery of the commission of a public office by the Secretary of State, it must be shown that it is an exercise of appellate jurisdiction, or that it be necessary to enable them to exercise appellate jurisdiction.

It is the essential criterion of appellate jurisdiction that it revises and corrects the proceedings in a cause already instituted, and does not create the cause.

The authority given to the Supreme Court by the act establishing the judicial system of the United States to issue writs of mandamus to public officers appears not to be warranted by the Constitution.

It is emphatically the duty of the Judicial Department to say what the law is. Those who apply the rule to particular cases must, of necessity, expound and interpret the rule. If two laws conflict with each other, the Court must decide on the operation of each.

If courts are to regard the Constitution, and the Constitution is superior to any ordinary act of the legislature, the Constitution, and not such ordinary act, must govern the case to which they both apply.

At the December Term, 1801, William Marbury, Dennis Ramsay, Robert Townsend Hooe, and William Harper, by their counsel, [p*138] severally moved the court for a rule to James Madison, Secretary of State of the United States, to show cause why a mandamus should not issue commanding him to cause to be delivered to them respectively their several commissions as justices of the peace in the District of Columbia. This motion was supported by affidavits of the following facts: that notice of this motion had been given to Mr. Madison; that Mr. Adams, the late President of the United States, nominated the applicants to the Senate for their advice and consent to be appointed justices of the peace of the District of Columbia; that the Senate advised and consented to the appointments; that commissions in due form were signed by the said President appointing them justices, &c., and that the seal of the United States was in due form affixed to the said commissions by the Secretary of State; that the applicants have requested Mr. Madison to deliver them their said commissions, who has not complied with that request; and that their said commissions are withheld from them; that the applicants have made application to Mr. Madison as Secretary of State of the United States at his office, for information whether the commissions were signed and sealed as aforesaid; that explicit and satisfactory information has not been given in answer to that inquiry, either by the Secretary of State or any officer in the Department of State; that application has been made to the secretary of the Senate for a certificate of the nomination of the applicants, and of the advice and consent of the Senate, who has declined giving such a certificate; whereupon a rule was made to show cause on the fourth day of this term. This rule having been duly served, [p*139]

Mr. Jacob Wagner and Mr. Daniel Brent, who had been summoned to attend the court, and were required to give evidence, objected to be sworn, alleging that they were clerks in the Department of State, and not bound to disclose any facts relating to the business or transactions of the office.

The court ordered the witnesses to be sworn, and their answers taken in writing, but informed them that, when the questions were asked, they might state their objections to answering each particular question, if they had any.

Virginia Plan
(1787) Transcript

State of the resolutions submitted to the consideration of the House by the honorable Mr. Randolph, as altered, amended, and agreed to, in a Committee of the whole House.

1. Resolved, that it is the opinion of this Committee that a national government ought to be established consisting of a Supreme Legislative, Judiciary, and Executive.

2. Resolved, that the national Legislature ought to consist of Two Branches.

3. Resolved, that the members of the first branch of the national Legislature ought to be elected by the People of the several States for the term of Three years. to receive fixed stipends, by which they may be compensated for the devotion of their time to public service to be paid out of the National Treasury. to be ineligible to any Office established by a particular State or under the authority of the United-States (except those peculiarly belonging to the functions of the first branch) during the term of service, and under the national government for the space of one year after it's expiration.

4. Resolved, that the members of the second Branch of the national Legislature ought to be chosen by the individual Legislatures. to be of the age of thirty years at least. to hold their offices for a term sufficient to ensure their independency, namely seven years. to receive fixed stipends, by which they may be compensated for the devotion of their time to public service — to be paid out of the National Treasury to be ineligible to any office established by a particular State, or under the authority of the United States (except those peculiarly belonging to the functions of the second branch) during the term of service, and under the national government, for the space of one year after it's expiration.

5. Resolved, that each branch ought to possess the right of originating acts.

6. Resolved, that the national Legislature ought to be empowered to enjoy the legislative rights vested in Congress by the confederation — and moreover to legislate in all cases to which the separate States are incompetent: or in which the harmony of the United States may be interrupted by the exercise of individual legislation. to negative all laws passed by the several States contravening, in the opinion of the national Legislature, the articles of union, or any treaties subsisting under the authority of the union.

7. Resolved, that the right of suffrage in the first branch of the national Legislature ought not to be according to the rule established in the articles of confederation: but according to some equitable ratio of representation — namely, in proportion to the whole number of white and other free citizens and inhabitants of every age, sex, and condition including those bound to servitude for a term of years, and three fifths of all other persons not comprehended in the foregoing description, except Indians, not paying taxes in each State.

8. Resolved, that the right of suffrage in the second branch of the national Legislature ought to be according to the rule established for the first.

9. Resolved, that a national Executive be instituted to consist of a single person. to be chosen by the National Legislature. for the term of seven years. with power to carry into execution the national Laws, to appoint to Offices in cases not otherwise provided for to be ineligible a second time, and to be removable on impeachment and conviction of mal practice or neglect of duty. to receive a fixed stipend, by which he may be compensated for the devotion of his time to public service to be paid out of the national Treasury.

10. Resolved, that the national executive shall have a right to negative any legislative act: which shall not be afterwards passed unless by two third parts of each branch of the national Legislature.

11. Resolved, that a national Judiciary be established to consist of One Supreme Tribunal. The Judges of which to be appointed by the second Branch of the National Legislature. to hold their offices during good behaviour to receive, punctually, at stated times, a fixed compensation for their services: in which no encrease or diminution shall be made so as to affect the persons actually in office at the time of such encrease or diminution.

12. Resolved, that the national Legislature be empowered to appoint inferior Tribunals.

13. Resolved, that the jurisdiction of the national Judiciary shall extend to cases which respect the collection of the national revenue: impeachments of any national officers: and questions which involve the national peace and harmony.

14. Resolved, that provision ought to be made for the admission of States, lawfully arising within the limits of the United States, whether from a voluntary junction of government and territory, or otherwise, with the consent of a number of voices in the national Legislature less than the whole.

15. Resolved, that provision ought to be made for the continuance of Congress and their authorities until a given day after the reform of the articles of Union shall be adopted; and for the completion of all their engagements.

16. Resolved, that a republican constitution, and its existing laws, ought to be guaranteed to each State by the United States.

17. Resolved, that provision ought to be made for the amendment of the articles of Union, whensoever it shall seem necessary.

18. Resolved, that the Legislative, Executive, and Judiciary powers within the several States ought to be bound by oath to support the articles of Union.

19. Resolved, that the amendments which shall be offered to the confederation by the Convention, ought at a proper time or times, after the approbation of Congress to be submitted to an assembly or assemblies of representatives, recommended by the several Legislatures, to be expressly chosen by the People to consider and decide thereon.

Received this sheet from the President of the United States, with the journals of the general

Convention, March 19th, 1796.
Timothy Pickering
Secy of State

State of the Resolutions submitted by Mr. Randolph to the Consideration of the House, as altered, amended and agreed to in a committee of the whole House.

Received from the President of the United States, March 19, 1796. by
Timothy Pickering
Secy of State

New Jersey Plan
15 June 1787

Farrand 1:242--45

1. Resolved, that the articles of Confederation ought to be so revised, corrected & enlarged, as to render the federal [Volume 1, Page 253] Constitution adequate to the exigences of Government, & the preservation of the Union.1

2. Resolved, that in addition to the powers vested in the U. States in Congress, by the present existing articles of Confederation, they be authorized to pass acts for raising a revenue, by levying a duty or duties on all goods or merchandizes of foreign growth or manufacture, imported into any part of the U. States, by Stamps on paper, vellum or parchment, and by a postage on all letters or packages passing through the general post-Office, to be applied to such federal purposes as they shall deem proper & expedient; to make rules & regulations for the collection thereof; and the same from time to time, to alter & amend in such manner as they shall think proper: to pass Acts for the regulation of trade & commerce as well with foreign nations as with each other: provided that all punishments, fines, forfeitures & penalties to be incurred for contravening such acts rules and regulations shall be adjudged by the Common law Judiciarys of the State in which any offence contrary to the true intent & meaning of such Acts rules & regulations shall have been committed or perpetrated, with liberty of commencing in the first instance all suits & prosecutions for that purpose in the superior Common law Judiciary in such State, subject nevertheless, for the correction of all errors, both in law & fact in rendering judgment, to an appeal to the Judiciary of the U. States

3. Resolved, that whenever requisitions shall be necessary, instead of the rule for making requisitions mentioned in the articles of Confederation, the United States in Congs. be authorized to make such requisitions in proportion to the whole number of white & other free citizens & inhabitants of every age sex and condition including those bound to servitude for a term of years & three fifths of all other persons not comprehended in the foregoing description, except Indians not paying taxes; that if such requisitions be not complied with, in the time specified therein, to direct the collection thereof in the non complying States & for that purpose to devise and pass acts directing & authorizing the same; provided that none of the powers hereby vested in the U. States in Congs. shall be exercised without the consent of at least States, and in that proportion if the number of Confederated States should hereafter be increased or diminished.

4. Resolved, that the United States in Congress be authorized to elect a federal Executive to consist of persons, to continue in office for the term of years, to receive punctually at stated times a fixed compensation for their services, in which no increase or diminution shall be made so as to affect the persons composing the Executive at the time of such increase or diminution, to be paid out of the federal treasury; to be incapable of holding any other office or appointment during their time of service and for years thereafter; to be ineligible a second time, & removeable by Congs. on application by a majority of the Executives of the several States; that the Executives besides their general authority to execute the federal acts ought to appoint all federal officers not otherwise provided for, & to direct all military operations; provided that none of the persons composing the federal Executive shall on any occasion take command of any troops, so as personally to conduct any enterprise as General, or in other capacity.

5. Resolved, that a federal Judiciary be established to consist of a supreme Tribunal the Judges of which to be appointed by the Executive, & to hold their offices during good behaviour, to receive punctually at stated times a fixed compensation for their services in which no increase or diminution shall be made, so as to affect the persons actually in office at the time of such increase or diminution; that the Judiciary so established shall have authority to hear & determine in the first instance on all impeachments of federal officers, & by way of appeal in the dernier resort in all cases touching the rights of Ambassadors, in all cases of captures from an enemy, in all cases of piracies & felonies on the high seas, in all cases in which foreigners may be interested, in the construction of any treaty or treaties, or which may arise on any of the Acts for regulation of trade, or the collection of the federal Revenue: that none of the Judiciary shall during the time they remain in Office be capable of receiving or holding any other office or appointment during their time of service, or for thereafter.

6. Resolved, that all Acts of the United States in Congress made by virtue & in pursuance of the powers hereby & by the articles of confederation vested in them, and all Treaties made & ratified under the authority of the United States shall be the supreme law of the respective States so far forth as those Acts or Treaties shall relate to the said States or their Citizens, and that the Judiciary of the several States shall be bound thereby in their decisions, any thing in the respective laws of the Individual States to the contrary notwithstanding; and that if any State, or any body of men in any State shall oppose or prevent ye carrying into execution such acts or treaties, the federal Executive shall be authorized to call forth ye power of the Confederated States, or so much thereof as may be necessary to enforce and compel an obedience to such Acts, or an Observance of such Treaties.

7. Resolved, that provision be made for the admission of new States into the Union.

8. Resolved, the rule for naturalization ought to be the same in every State

9. Resolved, that a Citizen of one State committing an offence [Volume 1, Page 254] in another State of the Union, shall be deemed guilty of the same offence as if it had been committed by a Citizen of the State in which the Offence was committed.

The Debates in the Federal Convention
of 1787 reported by James Madison

Monday May 31 [FN1], 1787

William Pierce from Georgia took his seat.

In Committee of the whole on Mr. Randolph's propositions.

The 3d. Resolution "that the national Legislature ought to consist of two branches" was agreed to without debate or dissent, except that of Pennsylvania, given probably from complaisance to Docr. Franklin who was understood to be partial to a single House of Legislation.

Resol: 4. [FN2] first clause "that the members of the first branch of the National Legislature ought to be elected by the people of the several States" being taken up,

Mr. SHERMAN opposed the election by the people, insisting that it ought to be by the State Legislatures. The people he said, immediately should have as little to do as may be about the Government. They want information and are constantly liable to be misled.

Mr. GERRY. The evils we experience flow from the excess of democracy. The people do not want virtue, but are the dupes of pretended patriots. In Massts. it had been fully confirmed by experience that they are daily misled into the most baneful measures and opinions by the false reports circulated by designing men, and which no one on the spot can refute. One principal evil arises from the want of due provision for those employed in the administration of Government. It would seem to be a maxim of democracy to starve the public servants. He mentioned the popular clamour in Massts. for the reduction of salaries and the attack made on that of the Govr. though secured by the spirit of the Constitution itself. He had he said been too republican heretofore: he was still however republican, but had been taught by experience the danger of the levilling spirit.

Mr. MASON argued strongly for an election of the larger branch by the people. It was to be the grand depository of the democratic principle of the Govtt. It was, so to speak, to be our House of Commons-It ought to know & sympathise with every part of the community; and ought therefore to be taken not only from different parts of the whole republic, but also from different districts of the larger members of it, which had in several instances particularly in Virga., different interests and views arising from difference of produce, of habits &c &c. He admitted that we had been too democratic but was afraid we sd. incautiously run into the opposite extreme. We ought to attend to the rights of every class of the people. He had often wondered at the indifference of the superior classes of society to this dictate of humanity & policy; considering that however affluent their circumstances, or elevated their situations, might be, the course of a few years, not only might but certainly would, distribute their posterity throughout the lowest classes of

Society. Every selfish motive therefore, every family attachment, ought to recommend such a system of policy as would provide no less carefully for the rights and happiness of the lowest than of the highest orders of Citizens.

Mr. WILSON contended strenuously for drawing the most numerous branch of the Legislature immediately from the people. He was for raising the federal pyramid to a considerable altitude, and for that reason wished to give it as broad a basis as possible. No government could long subsist without the confidence of the people. In a republican Government this confidence was peculiarly essential. He also thought it wrong to increase the weight of the State Legislatures by making them the electors of the national Legislature. All interference between the general and local Governments. should be obviated as much as possible. On examination it would be found that the opposition of States to federal measures had proceeded much more from the officers of the States, than from the people at large.

Mr. MADISON considered the popular election of one branch of the National Legislature as essential to every plan of free Government. He observed that in some of the States one branch of the Legislature was composed of men already removed from the people by an intervening body of electors. That if the first branch of the general legislature should be elected by the State Legislatures, the second branch elected by the first-the Executive by the second together with the first; and other appointments again made for subordinate purposes by the Executive, the people would be lost sight of altogether; and the necessary sympathy between them and their rulers and officers, too little felt. He was an advocate for the policy of refining the popular appointments by successive filtrations, but though it might be pushed too far. He wished the expedient to be resorted to only in the appointment of the second branch of the Legislature, and in the Executive & judiciary branches of the Government. He thought too that the great fabric to be raised would be more stable and durable, if it should rest on the solid foundation of the people themselves, than if it should stand merely on the pillars of the Legislatures.

Mr. GERRY did not like the election by the people. The maxims taken from the British constitution were often fallacious when applied to our situation which was extremely different. Experience he said had shewn that the State legislatures drawn immediately from the people did not always possess their confidence. He had no objection however to an election by the people if it were so qualified that men of honor & character might not be unwilling to be joined in the appointments. He seemed to think the people might nominate a certain number out of which the State legislatures should be bound to choose.

Mr. BUTLER thought an election by the people an impracticable mode.

On the question for an election of the first branch of the national Legislature by the people.

Massts. ay. Connect. divd. N. York ay. N. Jersey no. Pena. ay. Delawe. divd. Va. ay. N. C. ay. S. C. no. Georga. ay.

The remaining Clauses of Resolution 4th. [FN3] relating to the qualifications of members of the National Legislature, [FN3] being pospd. nem. con., as entering too much into detail for general propositions:

The Committee proceeded to Resolution 5. [FN4] "that the second, [or senatorial] branch of the National Legislature ought to be chosen by the first branch out of persons nominated by the State Legislatures."

Mr. SPAIGHT contended that the 2d. branch ought to be chosen by the State Legislatures and moved an amendment to that effect. Mr. BUTLER apprehended that the taking so many powers out of the hands of the States as was proposed, tended to destroy all that balance and security of interests among the States which it was necessary to preserve; and called on Mr. Randolph the mover of the propositions, to explain the extent of his ideas, and particularly the number of members he meant to assign to this second branch.

Mr. RAND observed that he had at the time of offering his propositions stated his ideas as far as the nature of general propositions required; that details made no part of the plan, and could not perhaps with propriety have been introduced. If he was to give an opinion as to the number of the second branch, he should say that it ought to be much smaller than that of the first; so small as to be exempt from the passionate proceedings to which numberous assemblies are liable. He observed that the general object was to provide a cure for the evils under which the U. S. laboured; that in tracing these evils to their origin every man had found it in the turbulence and follies of democracy: that some check therefore was to be sought for agst. this tendency of our Governments: and that a good Senate seemed most likely to answer the purpose.

Mr. KING reminded the Committee that the choice of the second branch as proposed (by Mr. Spaight) viz. by the State Legislatures would be impracticable, unless it was to be very numerous, or the idea of proportion among the States was to be disregarded. According to this idea, there must be 80 or 100 members to entitle Delaware to the choice of one of them. -Mr. SPAIGHT withdrew his motion.

Mr. WILSON opposed both a nomination by the State Legislatures, and an election by the first branch of the national Legislature, because the second branch of the latter, ought to be independent of both. He thought both branches of the National Legislature ought to be chosen by the people, but was not prepared with a specific proposition. He suggested the mode of chusing the Senate of N. York to wit of uniting several election districts, for one branch, in chusing members for the other branch, as a good model.

Mr. MADISON observed that such a mode would destroy the influence of the smaller States associated with larger ones in the same district; as the latter would chuse from within themselves, altho' better men might be found in the former. The election of Senators in Virga. where large & small counties were often formed into one district for the purpose, had illustrated this consequence Local partiality, would often prefer a resident within the County or State, to a candidate of superior merit residing out of it. Less merit also in a resident would be more known throughout his own State.

Mr. SHERMAN favored an election of one member by each of the State Legislatures.

Mr. PINKNEY moved to strike out the "nomination by the State Legislatures." On this question.

[FN5] Massts. no. Cont. no. N. Y. no. N. J. no. Pena. no. Del divd. Va. no. N. C. no. S. C. no. Georg no. [FN6]

On the whole question for electing by the first branch out of nominations by the State Legislatures, Mass. ay. Cont. no. N. Y. no. N. Jersey. no. Pena. no. Del. no. Virga. ay. N. C. no. S. C. ay. Ga. no. [FN7]

So the clause was disagreed to & a chasm left in this part of the plan.

[FN8] The sixth Resolution stating the cases in which the national Legislature ought to legislate was next taken into discussion: On the question whether each branch shd. originate laws, there was an unanimous affirmative without debate. On the question for transferring all the Legislative powers of the existing Congs. to this Assembly, there was also a silent affirmative nem. con.

On the proposition for giving "Legislative power in all cases to which the State Legislatures were individually incompetent."

Mr. PINKNEY & Mr. RUTLEDGE objected to the vagueness of the term incompetent, and said they could not well decide how to vote until they should see an exact enumeration of the powers comprehended by this definition.

Mr. BUTLER repeated his fears that we were running into an extreme in taking away the powers of the States, and called on Mr. Randolph for the extent of his meaning.

Mr. RANDOLPH disclaimed any intention to give indefinite powers to the national Legislature, declaring that he was entirely opposed to such an inroad on the State jurisdictions, and that he did not think any considerations whatever could ever change his determination. His opinion was fixed on this point.

Mr. MADISON said that he had brought with him into the Convention a strong bias in favor of an enumeration and definition of the powers necessary to be exercised by the national Legislature; but had also brought doubts concerning its practicability. His wishes remained unaltered; but his doubts had become stronger. What his opinion might ultimately be he could not yet tell. But he should shrink from nothing which should be found essential to such a form of Govt. as would provide for the safety, liberty and happiness of the community. This being the end of all our deliberations, all the necessary means for attaining it must, however reluctantly, be submitted to.

On the question for giving powers, in cases to which the States are not competent, Massts. ay. Cont. divd. [Sharman no Elseworth ay] N. Y. ay. N. J. ay. Pa. ay. Del. ay. Va. ay. N. C. ay. S. Carolina ay. Georga. ay. [FN9]

The other clauses [FN10] giving powers necessary to preserve harmony among the States to negative all State laws contravening in the opinion of the Nat. Leg. the articles of union, down to the last clause, (the words "or any treaties subsisting under the authority of the Union," being added after the words "contravening &c. the articles of the Union," on motion of Dr. FRANKLIN) were agreed to with. debate or dissent. The last clause of Resolution 6. [FN11] authorizing an exertion of the force of the whole agst. a delinquent State came next into consideration.

Mr. MADISON observed that the more he reflected on the use of force, the more he doubted the practicability, the justice and the efficacy of it when applied to people collectively and not individually. -A union of the States containing such an ingredient seemed to provide for its own destruction. The use of force agst. a State, would look more like a declaration of war, than an infliction of punishment, and would probably be considered by the party attacked as a dissolution of all previous compacts by which it might be bound. He hoped that such a system would be framed as might render this recourse [FN12] unnecessary, and moved that the clause be postponed. This motion was agreed to nem. con.

The Committee then rose & the House

Adjourned

FN1 The year "1787" is here inserted in the transcript.

FN2 The transcript changes "Resol: 4." to "The fourth Resolution."

FN3 In the transcript the words "Resolution 4th" are changed to "the fourth Resolution" and the phrase "the qualifications of members of the National Legislature" is italicized."

FN4 In the transcript the words "Resolution 5," are changed to "the fifth Resolution" and the words of the resolution are italicized.

FN5 This question [FN6] omitted in the printed Journal, & the votes applied to the succeeding one, instead of the votes as here stated [this note to be in the bottom margin]. [FN6]

FN6 In the transcript the vote reads: "*Massachusetts, Connecticut, New York, New Jersey, Pennsylvania, Virginia, North Carolina, South Carolina, Georgia, no-9; Delaware divided"; and Madison's direction concerning the footnote is omitted. The word "is" is inserted after the word "question."

FN7 In the transcript the vote reads: "Massachusetts, Virginia, South Carolina, aye-3; Connecticut, New York, New Jersey, Pennsylvania, Delaware, North Carolina, Georgia, no-7."

FN8 In this paragraph the transcript italicizes the following phrases: "the cases in which the national Legislature ought to legislate," "whether each branch shd. originate laws," "for transferring all the Legislative powers of the existing Cong. to this Assembly"; and the phrase "a silent affirmative nem. con." is changed to "an unanimous affirmative, without debate."

FN9 In the transcript the vote reads: "Massachusetts, New York, New Jersey, Pennsylvania, Delaware, Virginia, North Carolina, South Carolina, Georgia, aye- 9; Connecticut divided (Sherman, no. Ellsworth, aye)."

FN10 The phrase, "giving powers necessary to preserve harmony among the States to negative all State laws contravening in the opinion of the Nat. Leg. the articles of union" is italicized in the transcript.

FN11 The words "the sixth Resolution" are substituted in the transcript for "resolution 6" and the phrase "authorizing and exertion of the force of the whole ags.t a delinquent State" is italicized.

FN12 The word "resource" is substituted in the transcript for "recourse."

"The Era of Big Government is Over"
President Clinton's Radio Address

January 27, 1996

Good morning. Before I speak about the challenges we face today, I'd like to take just a moment to remember together a tragedy that 10 years ago tore at our nation's heart.

On January the 28, 1986, the seven courageous Americans of the Space Shuttle Challenger -- parents and scientists, pilots, and our first teacher in space -- gave their souls back to God.

Like the generations of American explorers, their sacrifice was made not in the name of personal gain, but in the pursuit of knowledge that would lead to the common good.

A decade has passed since that terrible day. The families of the Challenger crew have slowly and bravely rebuilt their lives.

The students Christa McAuliffe taught have now grown into adulthood. Countless shuttle missions have ventured beyond Earth's borders and returned safely to the home we all share.

A decade has passed, but their bravery, their commitment, their patriotism remain constant -- as fixed as the North Star.

We will forever honor their memory and forever remember the name of their ship -- Challenger. For America was built on challenges, not promises.

Earlier this week, I had the privilege of delivering the State of the Union address and discussing the challenges we face today, only five years from a new century.

As I said, the state of our union is strong. We are entering an age of possibility in which more Americans from all walks of life will have more chances to build the future of their dreams than ever before.

But we also face stiff challenges. Challenges we must meet and meet together if we are to preserve the American dream for all Americans, maintain America's leadership for peace and freedom, and continue to come together around our basic values.

These are the seven challenges I set forth Tuesday night -- to strengthen our families, to renew our schools and expand educational opportunity, to help every American who's willing to work for it achieve economic security, to take our streets back from crime, to protect our environment, to reinvent our government so that it serves better and costs less, and to keep America the leading force for peace and freedom throughout the world.

We will meet these challenges, not through big government. The era of big government is over, but we can't go back to a time when our citizens were just left to fend for themselves.

We will meet them by going forward as one America, by working together in our communities, our schools, our churches and synagogues, our workplaces across the entire spectrum of our civic life.

As we move forward with tomorrow's challenges, we also must take care of yesterday's unfinished business. First, we must balance the budget. In the 12 years before I took office the deficit skyrocketed and our national debt quadrupled.

I came to Washington determined to act, and we did. In the first three years of our administration -- thanks to the Deficit Reduction Act of 1993 -- we cut the deficit nearly in half. In fact, our budget would be in balance today were it not for the interest payments we have to make on the debt that accumulated in the 12 years before I took office.

Now it's time to finish the job. As you know, for some time, I've been working with Republicans and Democrats in Congress to forge a balanced budget that protects our values. Though significant differences remain between our two plans, Republicans and I have enough cuts in common to balance the budget in seven years and to provide a modest tax cut without devastating Medicare, Medicaid, education, and the environment and without raising taxes on working families.

So, again, last Tuesday, I asked Congress to join with me to make the cuts we agree on. Let's give the American people the balanced budget they deserve with a modest tax cut and the lower interest rates and brighter hope for the future it will bring.

My door is open. Let's get back to work.

There have been some hopeful signs this week that we can work together. Last night, the Senate ratified the START II treaty, which, when Russia ratifies it, will enable us to make continued dramatic reductions of our nuclear arsenal and remove further the nuclear cloud from our children's future.

And last night, Congress passed legislation to keep the government's operations open until March. It's a good step, but only a first step.

And while we are balancing the budget, there's another piece of business Congress must take care of right now. Like each of us, our nation is only as good as its word. For 220 years, the government of the United States has honored its obligation and kept its word. Through the Civil War, two World Wars, and the Depression, America has paid its bills and kept its word. When we borrow money, we promise to pay it back and we pay it back -- no matter what.

Our strong economy is built on the bedrock of this commitment. The world's economy relies on the full faith and credit of the United States, and it's one thing that enables us to keep all of our interest rates down, so that we can afford to borrow and grow and live.

From time to time, to keep its word, Congress has had to pass debt ceiling legislation so the government can meet its obligations. Congress has always done this when necessary. But this Congress, especially some in the House of Representatives, are trying to use the debt ceiling as a way to get its way in the budget negotiations.

Since November, Congress has failed to act on the debt ceiling. To prevent our nation from going into default, the Treasury secretary, Robert Rubin, has been forced to take extraordinary actions, and so far he has been successful. But our options are running out.

What could happen if the United States government failed to meet its obligations? Our unbroken record of keeping our word could end, with taxpayers bearing the cost for years to come, because interest rates would go up on United States obligations.

And interest rates could also go up for businesses, consumers, and homeowners, many of whom have interest rates that vary according to the government's interest rates.

And for tens of millions of Americans, the unthinkable could happen. The Social Security checks they count on would not be able to be mailed out.

My fellow Americans, we are a great country. We have never, never broken our word or defaulted on our obligations in our entire 220-year history. We've never failed to pay Social Security for senior citizens who've earned it.

So Congress should act responsibly and stop playing politics with America's good name. Let our government pay its bills. In order to avoid endangering the March 1 Social Security checks, Congress should pass a straightforward, long-term debt limit immediately.

We have worked hard, after years of wasteful spending, to restore confidence in the way our government does America's business. Americans are just beginning to believe again. This is no time to turn back.

I urge every member of Congress to reflect upon the gravity of this matter and to remember what the American people want from us is something quite simple -- to put partisanship aside, get the job done, and work together for the common good. That is what we must do today and what we must do on the question of the debt limit.

Thanks for listening.

Chapter 4
"One Nation Under God"

Maryland Act for Church Liberties

Be it enacted by the Lord Proprietarie of this Province by and with the Advice and approbation of the freemen of the same that Holy Church within this Province shall have all her rights liberties and immunities safe whole and inviolable in all things. This act to continue till the end of the next Generall Assembly and then with the Consent of the Lord Proprietarie to be perpetuall.

Pennsylvania Act for Freedom of Conscience
December 7, 1682

Wheras the glory of almighty God and the good of mankind is the reason and end of government and, therefore, government in itself is a venerable ordinance of God. And forasmuch as it is principally desired and intended by the Proprietary and Governor and the freemen of the province of Pennsylvania and territories thereunto belonging to make and establish such laws as shall best preserve true Christian and civil liberties in opposition to all unchristian, licentious, and unjust practices, whereby God may have his due, Caesar his due, and the people their due, from tyranny and oppression on the one side an insolence and licentiousness on the other, so that the best and firmest foundation may be laid for the present and future happiness of both the Governor and people of the province and territories aforesaid and their posterity.

Be it, therefore, enacted by William Penn, Proprietary and Governor, by and with the advice and consent of the deputies of the freemen of this province and counties aforesaid in assembly met and by the authority of the same, that these following chapters and paragraphs shall be the laws of Pennsylvania and the territories thereof.

Chapter 1. Almighty God, being only Lord of conscience, father of lights and spirits and the author as well as object of all divine knowledge, faith, and worship, who can only enlighten the mind and persuade and convince the understandings of people. In due reverence to his sovereignty over the souls of mankind;
Be it enacted, by the authority aforesaid, that no person now or at any time hereafter living in this province, who shall confess and acknowledge one almighty God to be the creator, upholder, and ruler of the world, an who professes him or herself obliged in conscience to live peaceably and quietly under the civil government, shall in any case be molested or prejudiced for his or her conscientious persuasion or practice. Nor shall he or she at any time be compelled to frequent or maintain any religious worship, place, or ministry whatever contrary to his or her mind, but shall b freely and fully enjoy his, or her, Christian liberty in that respect, without any interruption or reflection. And if any person shall abuse or deride any other for his or her different persuasion and practice in matters of religion, such a person shall be looked upon as a disturber of the peace and be punished accordingly.

But to the end that looseness, irreligion, and atheism may not creep in under pretense of conscience in this province, be it further enacted, by the authority aforesaid, that, according to the example of the primitive Christians and for the ease of the creation, every first day of the week, called the Lord's day, people shall abstain from their usual and common toil and labor that, whether masters, parents, children, or servants, they may the better dispose themselves to read the scriptures of truth at home or frequent such meetings of religious worship abroad as may best suit their respective persuasion.

Chapter II. And be it further enacted by, etc., that all officers an persons commissioned and employed in the service of the government in this province and all members and deputies elected to serve in the Assembly thereof and all that have a right to elect such deputies shall be such as profess and declare they believe in Jesus Christ to be the son of God, the savior of the world, and that are not convicted of ill-fame or unsober and dishonest conversation and that are of twenty-one years of age at least.

Chapter III. And be it further enacted, etc., that whosover shall swear in their common conversation by the name of God or Christ or Jesus, being legally convicted thereof, shall pay, for every such offense, five shillings or suffer five days imprisonment in the house of correction at hard labor to the behoof of public and be fed with bread and water only during that time.

Chapter V. And be it further enacted, etc., for the better prevention of corrupt communication, that whosoever shall speak loosely and profanely of almighty God, Christ Jesus, the Holy Spirit, or the scriptures of truth, and is legally convicted thereof, shall pay, for every such offense, five shillings or suffer five days imprisonment in the house of correction at hard labor to the behoof of the public and be fed with bread and water only during that time.

Chapter VI. And be it further enacted, etc., that whosoever shall, in their conversation, at any time curse himself or any other and is legally convicted thereof shall pay for every such offense five shillings or suffer five days imprisonment as aforesaid.

George Washington
The First Thanksgiving Proclamation
October 3, 1789

" Whereas it is the duty of all nations to acknowledge the Providence of Almighty God, to obey His will, to be grateful for His benefits, and humbly to implore His protection and favor, and whereas both Houses of Congress have by their joint committee requested me to commend to the people of United States a day of public thanksgiving and prayer to be observed by acknowledging with grateful hearts the many signal favors of Almighty God, especially by affording them an opportunity peaceably to establish a form of government for their safety and happiness, now therefore I do recommend and assign Thursday the 26th day of November next, to be devoted to the service of that great and glorious Being, Who is the beneficent Author of all the good that was, that is, or will be."

Give Me Liberty or Give Me Death!
By Patrick Henry
March 23, 1775

No man thinks more highly than I do of the patriotism, as well as abilities, of the very worthy gentlemen who have just addressed the house. But different men often see the same subject in different lights; and, therefore, I hope it will not be thought disrespectful to those gentlemen if, entertaining as I do opinions of a character very opposite to theirs, I shall speak forth my sentiments freely and without reserve. This is no time for ceremony. The question before the house is one of awful moment to this country. For my own part, I consider it as nothing less than a question of freedom or slavery; and in proportion to the magnitude of the subject ought to be the freedom of the debate. It is only in this way that we can hope to arrive at the truth, and fulfill the great responsibility which we hold to God and our country. Should I keep back my opinions at such a time, through fear of giving offense, I should consider myself as guilty of treason towards my country, and of an act of disloyalty toward the Majesty of Heaven, which I revere above all earthly kings.

Mr. President, it is natural to man to indulge in the illusions of hope. We are apt to shut our eyes against a painful truth, and listen to the song of that siren till she transforms us into beasts. Is this the part of wise men, engaged in a great and arduous struggle for liberty? Are we disposed to be of the numbers of those who, having eyes, see not, and, having ears, hear not, the things which so nearly concern their temporal salvation? For my part, whatever anguish of spirit it may cost, I am willing to know the whole truth, to know the worst, and to provide for it.

I have but one lamp by which my feet are guided, and that is the lamp of experience. I know of no way of judging of the future but by the past. And judging by the past, I wish to know what there has been in the conduct of the British ministry for the last ten years to justify those hopes with which gentlemen have been pleased to solace themselves and the House. Is it that insidious smile with which our petition has been lately received?

Trust it not, sir; it will prove a snare to your feet. Suffer not yourselves to be betrayed with a kiss. Ask yourselves how this gracious reception of our petition comports with those warlike preparations which cover our waters and darken our land. Are fleets and armies necessary to a work of love and reconciliation? Have we shown ourselves so unwilling to be reconciled that force must be called in to win back our love? Let us not deceive ourselves, sir. These are the implements of war and subjugation; the last arguments to which kings resort. I ask gentlemen, sir, what means this martial array, if its purpose be not to force us to submission? Can gentlemen assign any other possible motive for it? Has Great Britain any enemy, in this quarter of the world, to call for all this accumulation of navies and armies? No, sir, she has none. They are meant for us: they can be meant for no other. They are sent over to bind and rivet upon us those chains which the British ministry have been so long forging. And what have we to oppose to them? Shall we try argument? Sir, we have been trying that for the last ten years. Have we anything new to offer upon the subject? Nothing. We have held the subject up in every light of which it is capable; but it has been all in vain. Shall we resort to entreaty and humble supplication? What terms shall we find which have not been already exhausted? Let us not, I beseech you, sir, deceive ourselves. Sir, we have done everything that could be done to avert the storm which is now coming on. We have petitioned; we have remonstrated; we have supplicated; we have prostrated ourselves before the throne, and have implored its interposition to arrest the tyrannical hands of the ministry and Parliament. Our petitions have been slighted; our remonstrances have produced additional violence and insult; our supplications have been disregarded; and we have been spurned, with contempt, from the foot of the throne! In vain, after these things, may we indulge the fond hope of peace and reconciliation.

There is no longer any room for hope. If we wish to be free--if we mean to preserve inviolate those inestimable privileges for which we have been so long contending--if we mean not basely to abandon the noble struggle in which we have been so long engaged, and which we have pledged ourselves never to abandon until the glorious object of our contest shall be obtained--we must fight! I repeat it, sir, we must fight! An appeal to arms and to the God of hosts is all that is left us! They tell us, sir, that we are weak; unable to cope with so formidable an adversary. But when shall we be stronger? Will it be the next week, or the next year? Will it be when we are totally disarmed, and when a British guard shall be stationed in every house? Shall we gather strength but irresolution and inaction? Shall we acquire the means of effectual resistance by lying supinely on our backs and hugging the delusive phantom of hope, until our enemies shall have bound us hand and foot? Sir, we are not weak if we make a proper use of those means which the God of nature hath placed in our power. The millions of people, armed in the holy cause of liberty, and in such a country as that which we possess, are invincible by any force which our enemy can send against us. Besides, sir, we shall not fight our battles alone. There is a just God who presides over the destinies of nations, and who will raise up friends to fight our battles for us. The battle, sir, is not to the strong alone; it is to the vigilant, the active, the brave. Besides, sir, we have no election. If we were base enough to desire it, it is now too late to retire from the contest. There is no retreat but in submission and slavery! Our chains are forged! Their clanking may be heard on the plains of Boston! The war is inevitable--and let it come! I repeat it, sir, let it come.

It is in vain, sir, to extentuate the matter. Gentlemen may cry, Peace, Peace--but there is no peace. The war is actually begun! The next gale that sweeps from the north will bring to our ears the clash of resounding arms! Our brethren are already in the field! Why stand we here idle? What is it that gentlemen wish? What would they have? Is life so dear, or peace so sweet, as to be purchased at the price of chains and slavery? Forbid it, Almighty God! I know not what course others may take; but as for me, give me liberty or give me death!

Letters Between the Danbury Baptists and Thomas Jefferson

The address of the Danbury Baptist Association in the State of Connecticut, assembled October 7, 1801.
To Thomas Jefferson, Esq., President of the United States of America

Sir,

Among the many millions in America and Europe who rejoice in your election to office, we embrace the first opportunity which we have enjoyed in our collective capacity, since your inauguration, to express our great satisfaction in your appointment to the Chief Magistracy in the United States. And though the mode of expression may be less courtly and pompous than what many others clothe their addresses with, we beg you, sir, to believe, that none is more sincere.

Our sentiments are uniformly on the side of religious liberty: that Religion is at all times and places a matter between God and individuals, that no man ought to suffer in name, person, or effects on account of his religious opinions, [and] that the legitimate power of civil government extends no further than to punish the man who works ill to his neighbor. But sir, our constitution of government is not specific. Our ancient charter, together with the laws made coincident therewith, were adapted as the basis of our government at the time of our revolution. And such has been our laws and usages, and such still are, [so] that Religion is considered as the first object of Legislation, and therefore what religious privileges we enjoy (as a minor part of the State) we enjoy as favors granted, and not as inalienable rights. And these favors we receive at the expense of such degrading acknowledgments, as are inconsistent with the rights of freemen. It is not to be wondered at therefore, if those who seek after power and gain, under the pretense of government and Religion, should reproach their fellow men, [or] should reproach their Chief Magistrate, as an enemy of religion, law, and good order, because he will not, dares not, assume the prerogative of Jehovah and make laws to govern the Kingdom of Christ.

Sir, we are sensible that the President of the United States is not the National Legislator and also sensible that the national government cannot destroy the laws of each State, but our hopes are strong that the sentiment of our beloved President, which have had such genial effect already, like the radiant beams of the sun, will shine and prevail through all these States--and all the world--until hierarchy and tyranny be destroyed from the earth. Sir, when we reflect on your past services, and see a glow of philanthropy and goodwill shining forth in a course of more than thirty years, we have reason to believe that America's God has raised you up to fill the Chair of State out of that goodwill which he bears to the millions which you preside over. May God strengthen you for the arduous task which providence and the voice of the people have called you--to sustain and support you and your Administration against all the predetermined opposition of those who wish to rise to wealth and importance on the poverty and subjection of the people.

And may the Lord preserve you safe from every evil and bring you at last to his Heavenly Kingdom through Jesus Christ our Glorious Mediator.

Signed in behalf of the Association,

Neh,h Dodge }
Eph'm Robbins } The Committee
Stephen S. Nelson }

*A cite for this letter could read: Letter of Oct. 7, 1801 from Danbury (CT) Baptist Assoc. to Thomas Jefferson,
Thomas Jefferson Papers, Manuscript Division,
Library of Congress, Wash. D.C.

Jefferson's Reply

Messrs. Nehemiah Dodge, Ephraim Robbins, and Stephen s. Nelson
A Committee of the Danbury Baptist Association, in the State of Connecticut.

Washington, January 1, 1802

Gentlemen,

The affectionate sentiment of esteem and approbation which you are so good as to express towards me, on behalf of the Danbury Baptist Association, give me the highest satisfaction. My duties dictate a faithful and zealous pursuit of the interests of my constituents, and in proportion as they are persuaded of my fidelity to those duties, the discharge of them becomes more and more pleasing.

Believing with you that religion is a matter which lies solely between man and his God, that he owes account to none other for his faith or his worship, that the legislative powers of government reach actions only, and not opinions, I contemplate with sovereign reverence that act of the whole American people which declared that their legislature would "make no law respecting an establishment of religion, or prohibiting the free exercise thereof," thus building a wall of separation between Church and State. Adhering to this expression of the supreme will of the nation in behalf of the rights of conscience, I shall see with sincere satisfaction the progress of those sentiments which tend to restore to man all his natural rights, convinced he has no natural right in opposition to his social duties.

I reciprocate your kind prayers for the protection and blessing of the common Father and Creator of man, and tender you for yourselves and your religious association, assurances of my high respect and esteem.

Thomas Jefferson, Jan. 1, 1802

* A cite for this letter could read: Thomas Jefferson, *The Writings of Thomas Jefferson*, Albert E. Bergh, ed. (Washington, D. C.: The Thomas Jefferson Memorial Association of the United States, 1904), Vol. XVI, pp. 281-282.

Everson v. Board of Education
of the Township of Ewing
330 U.S. 1 (1947)

Syllabus

✠ Pursuant to a New Jersey statute authorizing district boards of education to make rules and contracts for the transportation of children to and from schools other than private schools operated for profit, a board of education by resolution authorized the reimbursement of parents for fares paid for the transportation by public carrier of children attending public and Catholic schools. The Catholic schools operated under the superintendency of a Catholic priest and, in addition to secular education, gave religious instruction in the Catholic Faith. A district taxpayer challenged the validity under the Federal Constitution of the statute and resolution so far as they authorized reimbursement to parents for the transportation of children attending sectarian schools. No question was raised as to whether the exclusion of private schools operated for profit denied equal protection of the laws; nor did the record show that there were any children in the district who attended, or would have attended but for the cost of transportation, any but public or Catholic schools.

✠ *Held:*

1. The expenditure of tax raised funds thus authorized was for a public purpose, and did not violate the due process clause of the Fourteenth Amendment. Pp. 5-8 .

2. The statute and resolution did not violate the provision of the First Amendment (made applicable to the states by the Fourteenth Amendment) prohibiting any "law respecting an establishment of religion." Pp. 8-18 .

133 N.J.L. 350, 44 A.2d 333, affirmed. [p*2]

Opinions

In a suit by a taxpayer, the New Jersey Supreme Court held that the state legislature was without power under the state constitution to authorize reimbursement to parents of bus fares paid for transporting their children to schools other than public schools. 132 N.J.L. 98, 39 A.2d 75. The New Jersey Court of Errors and Appeals reversed, holding that neither the statute nor a resolution passed pursuant to it violated the state constitution or the provisions of the Federal Constitution in issue. 133 N.J.L. 350, 44 A.2d 333. On appeal of the federal questions to this Court, *AFFIRMED,* p. 18 . [p*3]

BLACK, J., Opinion of the Court

MR. JUSTICE BLACK delivered the opinion of the Court.

A New Jersey statute authorizes its local school districts to make rules and contracts for the transportation of children to and from schools. [n1] The appellee, a township board of education, acting pursuant to this statute, authorized reimbursement to parents of money expended by them for the bus transportation of their children on regular busses operated by the public transportation system. Part of this money was for the payment of transportation of some children in the community to Catholic parochial schools. These church schools give their students, in addition to secular education, regular religious instruction conforming to the religious tenets and modes of worship of the Catholic Faith. The superintendent of these schools is a Catholic priest.

The appellant, in his capacity as a district taxpayer, filed suit in a state court challenging the right of the Board to reimburse parents of parochial school students. He [p*4] contended that the statute and the resolution passed pursuant to it violated both the State and the Federal Constitutions. That court held that the legislature was without power to authorize such payment under the state constitution. 132 N.J.L. 98, 39 A.2d 75. The New Jersey Court of Errors and Appeals reversed, holding that neither the statute nor the resolution passed pursuant to it was in conflict with the State constitution or the provisions of the Federal Constitution in issue. 133 N.J.L. 350, 44 A.2d 333. The case is here on appeal under 28 U.S.C. § 344(a).

Since there has been no attack on the statute on the ground that a part of its language excludes children attending private schools operated for profit from enjoying State payment for their transportation, we need not consider this exclusionary language; it has no relevancy to any constitutional question here presented. [n2] Furthermore, if the exclusion clause had been properly challenged, we do not know whether New Jersey's highest court would construe its statutes as precluding payment of the school [p*5] transportation of any group of pupils, even those of a private school run for profit. [n3] Consequently, we put to one side the question as to the validity of the statute against the claim that it does not authorize payment for the transportation generally of school children in New Jersey.

The only contention here is that the state statute and the resolution, insofar as they authorized reimbursement to parents of children attending parochial schools, violate the Federal Constitution in these two respects, which to some extent overlap. *First.* They authorize the State to take by taxation the private property of some and bestow it upon others to be used for their own private purposes. This, it is alleged, violates the due process clause of the Fourteenth Amendment. *Second.* The statute and the resolution forced inhabitants to pay taxes to help support and maintain schools which are dedicated to, and which regularly teach, the Catholic Faith. This is alleged to be a use of state power to support church schools contrary to the prohibition of the First Amendment which the Fourteenth Amendment made applicable to the states.

First. The due process argument that the state law taxes some people to help others carry out their private [p*6] purposes is framed in two phases. The first phase is that a state cannot tax A to reimburse B for the cost of transporting his children to church schools. This is said to violate the due process clause because the children are sent to these church schools to satisfy the personal desires of their parents, rather than the public's interest in the general education of all children. This argument, if valid, would apply equally to prohibit state payment for the transportation of children to any nonpublic school, whether operated by a church or any other non-government individual or group. But the New Jersey legislature has decided that a public purpose will be served by using tax raised funds to pay the bus fares of all school children, including those who attend parochial schools. The New Jersey Court of Errors and Appeals has reached the same conclusion. The fact that a state law, passed to satisfy a public need, coincides with the personal desires of the individuals most directly affected is certainly an inadequate reason for us to say that a legislature has erroneously appraised the public need.

It is true that this Court has, in rare instances, struck down state statutes on the ground that the purpose for which tax raised funds were to be expended was not a public one. *Loan Association v. Topeka,* 20 Wall. 655; *Parkersburg v. Brown,* 106 U.S. 487; *Thompson v. Consolidated Gas Utilities Corp.,* 300 U.S. 55. But the Court has also pointed out that this far-reaching authority must be exercised with the most extreme caution. *Green v. Frazier,* 253 U.S. 233, 240. Otherwise, a state's power to legislate for the public welfare might be seriously curtailed, a power which is a primary reason for the existence of states. Changing local conditions create new local problems which may lead a state's people and its local authorities to believe that laws authorizing new types of public services are necessary to promote the general wellbeing [p*7] of the people. The Fourteenth Amendment did not strip the states of their power to meet problems previously left for individual solution. *Davidson v. New Orleans,* 96 U.S. 97, 103-104; *Barbier v. Connolly,* 113 U.S. 27, 31-32; *Fallbrook Irrigation District v. Bradley,* 164 U.S. 112, 157-158.

It is much too late to argue that legislation intended to facilitate the opportunity of children to get a secular education serves no public purpose. *Cochran v. Louisiana State Board of Education,* 281 U.S. 370; Holmes, J., in *Interstate Ry. v. Massachusetts,* 207 U.S. 79, 87. *See* opinion of Cooley, J., in *Stuart v. School District No. 1 of Kalamazoo,* 30 Mich. 69 (1874). The same thing is no less true of legislation to reimburse needy parents, or all parents, for payment of the fares of their children so that they can ride in public busses to and from schools, rather than run the risk of traffic and other hazards incident to walking or "hitchhiking." *See Barbier v. Connolly, supra,* at 31. *See also cases* collected 63 A.L.R. 413; 118 A.L.R. 806. Nor does it follow that a law has a private, rather than a public, purpose because it provides that tax-raised funds will be paid to reimburse individuals on account of money spent by them in a way which furthers a public program. *See Carmichael v. Southern Coal & Coke Co.,* 301 U.S. 495, 518. Subsidies and loans to individuals such as farmers and home owners, and to privately owned transportation systems, as well as many other kinds of businesses, have been commonplace practices in our state and national history.

Insofar as the second phase of the due process argument may differ from the first, it is by suggesting that taxation for transportation of children to church schools constitutes support of a religion by the State. But if the law is invalid for this reason, it is because it violates the First Amendment's prohibition against the establishment of religion [p*8] by law. This is the exact question raised by appellant's second contention, to consideration of which we now turn.

Second. The New Jersey statute is challenged as a "law respecting an establishment of religion." The First Amendment, as made applicable to the states by the Fourteenth, *Murdock v.*

Pennsylvania, 319 U.S. 105, commands that a state "shall make no law respecting an establishment of religion, or prohibiting the free exercise thereof. . . ." These words of the First Amendment reflected in the minds of early Americans a vivid mental picture of conditions and practices which they fervently wished to stamp out in order to preserve liberty for themselves and for their posterity. Doubtless their goal has not been entirely reached; but so far has the Nation moved toward it that the expression "law respecting an establishment of religion" probably does not so vividly remind present-day Americans of the evils, fears, and political problems that caused that expression to be written into our Bill of Rights. Whether this New Jersey law is one respecting an "establishment of religion" requires an understanding of the meaning of that language, particularly with respect to the imposition of taxes. Once again,[n4] therefore, it is not inappropriate briefly to review the background and environment of the period in which that constitutional language was fashioned and adopted.

Engel v. Vitale (1962)

82 Supreme Court Reporter, p. 1261-1277

370 U.S. 421

STEVEN I. ENGEL ET AL., PETITIONERS, V. WILLIAM J. VITALE, JR., ET AL.

Argued April 3, 1962.

Decided June 25,1962

Syllabus

MR. JUSTICE BLACK delivered the opinion of the Court.

The respondent Board of Education of Union Free School District No. 9, New Hyde Park, New York, acting in its official capacity under state law, directed the School District's principal to cause the following prayer to be said aloud by each class in the presence of a teacher at the beginning of each school day:

"Almighty God, we acknowledge our dependence upon Thee, and we beg Thy blessings upon us, our parents, our teachers and our Country."

This daily procedure was adopted on the recommendation of the State Board of Regents, a governmental agency created by the State Constitution to which the New York Legislature has granted broad supervisory, executive, and legislative powers over the State's public school system. These state officials composed the prayer which they recommended and published as a part of their "Statement on Moral and Spiritual Training in the Schools," saying: "We believe that this Statement will be subscribed to by all men and women of good will, and we call upon all of them to aid in giving life to our program."

[1] Shortly after the practice of reciting the Regent's prayer was adopted by the School District, the parents of ten pupils brought this action in a New York State Court insisting that use of this official prayer in the public schools was contrary to the beliefs, religions, or religious practices of both themselves and their children. Among other things, these parents challenged the constitutionality of both the state law authorizing the School District to direct the use of prayer in public schools and the School District's regulation ordering the recitation of this particular prayer on the ground that these actions of official governmental agencies violate that part of the First Amendment of the Federal Constitution which commands that "Congress shall make no law respecting an establishment of religion"—a command which was "made applicable to the State of New York by the Fourteenth Amendment of the said Constitution." The New York Court of Appeals, over the dissents of Judges Dye and Fuld, sustained an order of the lower state courts which had upheld the power of New York to use the Regent's prayer as a part of the daily procedures of its public schools so long as the schools did not compel any pupil to join in the prayer over his or his parents' objection. We granted certiorari to review this important decision involving rights protected by the First and Fourteenth Amendments.

[2] We think by using its public school system to encourage recitation of the Regents' prayer, the State of New York has adopted a practice wholly inconsistent with the Establishment Clause. There can, of course, be no doubt that New York's program of daily classroom invocation of God's blessings as prescribed in the Regents' prayer is a religious activity. It is a solemn avowal of divine faith and supplication for the blessings of the Almighty. The nature of such prayer has always been religious, none of the respondents has denied this and the trial court expressly so found:

"The religious nature of prayer was recognized by Jefferson and has been concurred in by theological writers, the United States Supreme Court and state courts and administrative officials, including New York's Commissioner of Education. A committee of the New York Legislature has agreed.

"The Board of Regents as amicus curiae, the respondents and intervenors all concede the religious nature of prayer, but seek to distinguish this prayer because it is based on our spiritual heritage. * * *"

[3] The petitioners contend among other things that the state laws requiring or permitting use of the Regents' prayer must be struck down as a violation of the Establishment Clause because that prayer was composed by governmental officials as a part of a governmental program to further religious beliefs. For this reason, petitioners argue, the State's use of the Regents' prayer in its public school system breaches the constitutional wall of separation between Church and State. We agree with that contention since we think that the constitutional prohibition against laws respecting an establishment of religion must at least mean that in this country it is no part of the business of government to compose official prayers for any group of the American people to recite as a part of a religious program carried on by government.

194

It is a matter of history that this very practice of establishing governmentally composed prayers for religious services was one of the reasons which caused many of our early colonists to leave England and seek religious freedom in America. The Book of Common Prayer, which was created under governmental direction and which was approved by Acts of Parliament in 1548 and 1549, set out in minute detail the accepted form and content of prayer and other religious ceremonies to be used in the established, tax- supported Church of England. The controversies over the Book and what should be its content repeatedly threatened to disrupt the peace of that country as the accepted forms of prayer in the established church changed with the views of the particular ruler that happened to be in control at the time. Powerful groups representing some of the varying religious views of the people struggled among themselves to impress their particular views upon the Government and obtain amendments of the Book more suitable to their respective notions of how religious services should be conducted in order that the official religious establishment would advance their particular religious beliefs. Other groups, lacking the necessary political power to influence the Government on the matter, decided to leave England and its established church and seek freedom in America from England's governmentally ordained and supported religion.

It is an unfortunate fact of history that when some of the very groups which had most strenuously opposed the established Church of England found themselves sufficiently in control of colonial governments in this country to write their own prayers into law, they passed laws making their own religion the official religion of their respective colonies. Indeed, as late as the time of the Revolutionary War, there were established churches in at least eight of the thirteen former colonies and established religions in at least four of the other five. But the successful Revolution against English political domination was shortly followed by intense opposition to the practice of establishing religion by law. This opposition crystallized rapidly into an effective political force in Virginia where the minority religious groups such as Presbyterians, Lutherans, Quakers and Baptists had gained such strength that the adherents to the established Episcopal Church were actually a minority themselves. In 1785-1786, those opposed to the established Church, led by James Madison and Thomas Jefferson, who, though themselves not members of any of these dissenting religious groups, opposed all religious establishments by law on grounds of principle, obtained the enactment of the famous "Virginia Bill for Religious Liberty" by which all religious groups were placed on an equal footing so far as the State was concerned. Similar though less far-reaching legislation was being considered and passed in other States.

[4, 5] By the time of the adoption of the Constitution, our history shows that there was a widespread awareness among many Americans of the dangers of a union of Church and State. These people knew, some of them from bitter personal experience, that one of the greatest dangers to the freedom of the individual to worship in his own way lay in the Government's placing its official stamp of approval upon one particular kind of prayer or one particular form of religious services. They knew the anguish, hardship and bitter strife that could come when zealous religious groups struggled with one another to obtain the Government's stamp of approval from each King, Queen, or Protector that come to temporary power. The Constitution was intended to avert a part of this danger by leaving the government of this country in the hands of the people rather than in the hands of any monarch. But this safeguard was not enough. Our Founders were nor more willing to let the content of their prayers and their privilege of praying whenever they pleased be influenced by the ballot box than they were to let these vital matters of personal conscience depend upon the succession of monarchs. The First Amendment was added

to the Constitution to stand as a guarantee that neither the power nor the prestige of the Federal Government would be used to control, support or influence the kinds of prayer the American people can say—that the people's religions must not be subjected to the pressures of government for change each time a new political administration is elected to office. Under that Amendment's prohibition against governmental establishment of religion, as reinforced by the provisions of the Fourteenth Amendment, government in this country, be it state or federal, is without power to prescribe by law any particular form of prayer which is to be used as an official prayer in carrying on any program of governmentally sponsored religious activity.

[6-12] There can be no doubt that New York's state prayer program officially establishes the religious beliefs embodied in the Regents' prayer. The respondents' argument to the contrary, which is largely based upon the contention that the Regents' prayer is "non- denominational" and the fact that the program, as modified and approved by state courts, does not require all pupils to recite the prayer but permits those who wish to do so to remain silent or be excused from the room, ignores the essential nature of the program's constitutional defects. Neither the fact that the prayer may be denominationally neutral nor the fact that its observance on the part of the students is voluntary can serve to free it from the limitations of the Establishment Clause, as it might from the Free Exercise Clause, of the First Amendment, both of which are operative against the States by virtue of the Fourteenth Amendment. Although these two clauses may in certain instances overlap, they forbid two quite different kinds of governmental encroachment upon religious freedom. The Establishment Clause, unlike the Free Exercise Clause, does not depend upon any showing of direct governmental compulsion and is violated by the enactment of laws which establish an official religion whether those laws operate directly to coerce non-observing individuals or not. This is not to say, of course, that laws officially prescribing a particular form of religious worship do not involve coercion of such individuals. When the power, prestige and financial support of government is placed behind a particular religious belief, the indirect coercive pressure upon religious minorities to conform to the prevailing officially approved religion is plain. But the purposes underlying the Establishment Clause go much further than that. Its first and most immediate purpose rested on the belief that a union of government and religion tends to destroy government and to degrade religion. The history of governmentally established religion, both in England and in this country, showed that whenever government had allied itself with one particular form of religion, the inevitable result had been that it had incurred the hatred, disrespect and even contempt of those who held contrary beliefs. That same history showed that many people had lost their respect for any religion that had relied upon the support of government to spread its faith. The Establishment Clause thus stands as an expression of principle on the part of the Founders of our Constitution that religion is too personal, too sacred, too holy, to permit its "unhallowed perversion" by a civil magistrate. Another purpose of the Establishment Clause rested upon an awareness of the historical fact that governmentally established religions and religious persecutions go hand in hand. The Founders knew that only a few years after the Book of Common Prayer became the only accepted form or religious services in the established Church of England, an Act of Uniformity was passed to compel all Englishmen to attend those services and to make it a criminal offense to conduct or attend religious gatherings of any other kind—a law which was consistently flouted by dissenting religious groups in England and which contributed to widespread persecutions of people like John Bunyan who persisted in holding "unlawful [religious' meetings * * * to the great disturbance and distraction of the good subjects of this kingdom * * *." And they knew that similar persecutions had received the sanction of law in several of the colonies in this country

soon after the establishment of official religions in those colonies. It was in large part to get completely away from this sort of systematic religious persecution that the Founders brought into being our Nation, our Constitution, and our Bill or Rights with its prohibition against any governmental establishment of religion. The New York laws officially prescribing the Regents' prayer are inconsistent both with the purposes of the Establishment Clause and with the Establishment itself.

It has been argued that to apply the Constitution in such a way as to prohibit state laws respecting an establishment of religious services in public schools is to indicate a hostility toward religion or toward prayer. Nothing, of course, could be more wrong. The history of man is inseparable from the history of religion. And perhaps it is to too much to say that since the beginning of that history many people have devoutly believed that "More things are wrought by prayer than this world dreams of." It was doubtless largely due to men who believed this that there grew up a sentiment that caused men to leave the cross-currents of officially established state religions and religious persecution in Europe and come to this country filled with the hope that they could find a place in which they could pray when they pleased to the God of their faith in the language the chose. And there were men of this same faith in the power of prayer who led the fight for adoption of our Constitution and also for our Bill of Rights with the very guarantees of religious freedom that forbid the sort of governmental activity which New York has attempted here. These men know that the First Amendment, which tried to put an end to governmental control of religion and of prayer, was not written to destroy either. They knew rather that it was written to quiet well-justified fears which nearly all of them felt arising out of an awareness that governments of the past had shackled men's tongues to make them speak only the religious thoughts that government wanted them to speak and to pray only to the God that government wanted them to pray to. It is neither sacrilegious nor antireligious to say that each separate government in this country should stay out of the business of writing or sanctioning official prayers and leave that purely religious function to the people themselves and to those the people choose to look to for religious guidance.

[13] It is true that New York's establishment of its Reagent's prayer as an officially approved religious doctrine of that State does not amount to a total establishment of one particular religious sect to the exclusion of all other—that, indeed, the governmental endorsement of that prayer seems relatively insignificant when compared to the governmental encroachments upon religion which were commonplace 200 years ago. To these who may subscribe to the view that because the Reagent's official prayer is so brief and general there can be no danger to religious freedom in its governmental establishment, however, it may be appropriate to say in the words of James Madison, the author of the First Amendment:

"[I]t is proper to take alarm at the first experiment on our liberties. * * * Who does not see that the same authority which can establish Christianity, in exclusion of all other Religions, may establish with the same ease any particular sect of Christians, in exclusion of all other Sects? That the same authority which can force a citizen to contribute three pence only of his property for the support of any one establishment, may force him to conform to any other establishment in all cases whatsoever?"

197

The judgment of the Court of Appeals of New York is reversed and the cause remanded for further proceedings not inconsistent with this opinion.

REVERSED AND REMANDED.

Mr. Justice Frankfurter took no part in the decision of this case.

Mr. Justice White took no part in the consideration or decision of this case.

Mr. Justice Douglas, concurring.

It is customary in deciding a constitutional question to treat it in its narrowest form. Yet at times the setting of the question gives it a form and content which no abstract treatment could give. The point for decision is whether the Government can constitutionally finance a religious exercise. Our system at the federal and state levels is presently honeycombed with such financing. Nevertheless, I think it is an unconstitutional undertaking whatever form it takes.

First, a word as to what this case does not involve.

Plainly, our Bill of Rights would not permit a State or the Federal Government to adopt an official prayer and penalize anyone who would not utter it. This, however, is not that case, for there is no element of compulsion or coercion in New York's regulation requiring that public schools be opened each day with the following prayer:

"Almighty God, we acknowledge our dependence upon Thee, and we beg Thy blessings upon us, our parents, our teachers and our Country."

The prayer is said upon the commencement of the school day, immediately following the pledge of allegiance to the flag. The prayer is said aloud in the presence of a teacher, who either leads the recitation or selects a student to do so. No student, however, is compelled to take part. The respondents have adopted a regulation which provides that "Neither teachers nor any school authority shall comment on participation or nonparticipation * * * nor suggest or request that any posture or language be used or dress be worn or be not used or not worn." Provision is also made for excusing children, upon written request of a parent or guardian, from the saying of the prayer or from the room in which the prayer is said. A letter implementing and explaining this regulation has been sent to each taxpayer and parent in the school district. As I read this regulation, a child is free to stand or not stand, to recite or not recite, without fear of reprisal or even comment by the teacher or any other school official.

In short, the only one who need utter the prayer is the teacher; and no teacher is complaining of it. Students can stand mute or even leave the classroom, if they desire.

McCollum, etc. v. Board of Education, 333 U.S. 203, 68 S.Ct. 461, 92 L.Ed. 649, does not decide this case. It involved the use of public school facilities for religious education of students. Students either had to attend religious instruction or "go to some other place in the school building for pursuit of their secular studies. * * * Reports of their presence or absence were to be made to their secular teachers." Id., at 209, 68 S.Ct., at 464. The influence of the teaching staff was therefore brought to bear on the student body, to support the instilling of religious principles. In the present case, school facilities are used to say the prayer and the teaching staff is employed to lead the pupils in it. There is, however, no effort at indoctrination and no attempt at exposition. Prayers of course may be so long and of such a character as to amount to an attempt at the religious instruction that was denied the public schools by the McCollum case. But New York's prayer is of a character that does not involve any element of proselytizing as in the McCollum case.

The question presented by this case is therefore an extremely narrow one. It is whether New York oversteps the bounds when it finances a religious exercise.

What New York does on the opening of its public schools is what we do when we open court. Our Crier has from the beginning announced the convening of the Court and then added "God save the United States and this Honorable Court." That utterance is a supplication, a prayer in which we, the judges, are free to join, but which we need not recite any more than the students need recite the New York prayer.

What New York does on the opening of its public schools is what each House of Congress does at the opening of each day's business. Reverend Frederick B. Harris is Chaplain of the Senate; Reverend Bernard Braskamp is Chaplain of the House. Guest chaplains of various denominations also officiate.

In New York the teacher who leads in prayer is on the public payroll; and the time she takes seems minuscule as compared with the salaries appropriated by state legislatures and Congress for chaplains to conduct prayers in the legislative halls. Only a bare fraction of the teacher's time is given to reciting this short 22-word prayer, about the same amount of time that our Crier spends announcing the opening of our sessions and offering a prayer for this Court. Yet for me the principle is the same, no matter how briefly the prayer is said, for in each of the instances given the person praying is a public official on the public payroll, performing a religious exercise in a governmental institution. It is said that the element of coercion is inherent in the giving of this prayer. If that is true here, it is also true of the prayer with which this Court is convened, and of those that open the Congress. Few adults, let alone children, would leave our courtroom or the Senate or the House while those prayers are being given. Every such audience is in a sense a "captive" audience.

At the same time I cannot say that to authorize this prayer is to establish a religion in the strictly historic meaning of those words? A religion is not established in the usual sense merely be letting those who choose to do so say the prayer that the public school teacher leads. Yet once government finances a religious exercise it insert a divisive influence into our communities. The New York Court said that the prayer given does not conform to all of the tenets of the Jewish, Unitarian, and Ethical Culture groups. One of the petitioners is an agnostic.

"We are a religious people whose institutions presuppose a Supreme Being." Zorach v. Clauson, 343 U.S. 306, 313, 72 S.Ct. 679, 684, 96 L.Ed. 954. Under our Bill of Rights free play is given for making religion an active force in our lives. But "if a religious leaven is to be worked into the affairs of our people, it is to be done by individuals and groups, not by the Government." McGowan v. Maryland, 366 U.S. 420, 563, 81 S.Ct. 1101, 1219, 6 L.Ed.2d 393 (dissenting opinion). By reason of the First Amendment government is commanded "to have no interest in theology or ritual" (id., at 564, 81 S.Ct., at 1219), for on those matters "government must be neutral." Ibid. The First Amendment leaves the Government in a position not of hostility to religion but of neutrality. The philosophy is that the atheist or agnostic—the non- believer—is entitled to go his own way. The philosophy is that if government interferes in matters spiritual, it will be a divisive force. The First Amendment teaches that a government neutral in the field of religion better serves all religious interests.

My problem today would be uncomplicated but for Everson v. Board of Education, 330 U.S. 1, 17, 67 S.Ct. 504, 512, 91 L.Ed. 711, which allowed taxpayers' money to be used to pay "the bus fares of parochial school pupils as a part of a general program under which" the fares of pupils attending public and other schools were also paid. The Everson case seems in retrospect to be out of line with the First Amendment. Its result is appealing, as it allows aid to be given to needy children. Yet by the same token, public funds could be used to satisfy other needs of children in parochial schools—lunches, books, and tuition being obvious examples. Mr. Justice Rutledge stated in dissent what I think is durable First Amendment philosophy:

"The reasons underlying the Amendment's policy have not vanished with time or diminished in force. Now as when it was adopted the price of religious freedom is double. It is that the church and religion shall live both within and upon that freedom. There cannot be freedom of religion, safeguarded by the state, and intervention by the church or its agencies in the state's domain or dependency on its largesse. Madison's Remonstrance, Par. 6, 8. The great condition of religious liberty is that it be maintained free from sustenance, as also from other interferences, by the state. For when it comes to rest upon that secular foundation it vanishes with the resting. Id., Par. 7, 8. Public money devoted to payment of religious costs, educational or other, brings the quest for more. It brings too the struggle of sect against sect for the larger share or for any. Here one by numbers alone will benefit most, there another. That is precisely the history of societies which have had an established religion and dissident groups. Id., Par. 8, 11. It is the very thing Jefferson and Madison experienced and sought to guard against, whether in its blunt or in its more screened forms. Ibid. The end of such strife cannot be other than to destroy the cherished liberty. The dominating group will achieve the dominate benefit; or all will embroil the state in their dissensions. Id., Par. 11." Id., pp. 53-54, 67 S.Ct. pp. 529-530.

What New York does with this prayer is a break with that tradition. I therefore join the Court in reversing the judgment below.

Mr. Justice Stewart, dissenting.

A local school board in New York has provided that those pupils who wish to do so may join in a brief prayer at the beginning of each school day, acknowledging their dependence upon God and asking His blessing upon them and upon their parents, their teachers, and their country. The Court today decides that in permitting this brief non-denominational prayer the school board has violated the Constitutional of the United States. I think this decision is wrong.

The Court does not hold, nor could it, that New York has interfered with the free exercise of anybody's religion. For the state courts have made clear that those who object to reciting the prayer must be entirely free of any compulsion to do so, including any "embarrassments and pressures." Cf. West Virginia State Board of Education v. Barnette, 319 U.S. 624, 63 S.Ct. 1178, 87 L.Ed. 1628. But the Court says that in permitting school children to say this simple prayer, the New York authorities have established "an official religion."

With all respect, I think the Court has misapplied a great constitutional principle. I cannot see how an "official religion" is established by letting those who want to say a prayer say it. On the contrary, I think that to deny the wish of these school children to join in reciting this prayer is to deny them the opportunity of sharing in the spiritual heritage of our Nation.

The Court's historical review of the quarrels over the Book of Common Prayer in England throws no light for me on the issue before us in this case. England had then and has now an established church. Equally unenlightening, I think, is the history of the early establishment and later rejection of an official church in our own States. For we deal here not with the establishment of a state church, which would, of course, be constitutionally impermissible, but with whether school children who want to begin their day by joining in prayer must be prohibited from doing so. Moreover, I think that the Court's task, in this as in all areas of constitutional adjudication, is not responsibly aided by the uncritical invocation of metaphors like the "wall of separation," a phrase nowhere to be found in the Constitution. What is relevant to the issue here is not the history of an established church is sixteenth century England or in eighteenth century America, but the history of the religious traditions of our people, reflected in countless practices of the institutions and officials of our government.

At the opening of each day's Session of this Court we stand, while one of our officials invokes the protection of God. Since the days of John Marshall our Crier has said, "God save the United States and this Honorable Court." Both the Senate and the House of Representatives open their daily Sessions with prayer. Each of our Presidents, from George Washington to John F. Kennedy, has upon assuming his Office asked the protection and help of God.

The Court today says that the state and federal governments are without constitutional power to prescribe any particular form of words to be recited by any group of the American people on any subject touching religion. One of the stanzas of "The Star-Spangled Banner," made our National Anthem by Act of Congress in 1931, contains these verses:
"Blest with victory and peace, may the heav'n rescued land

Praise the Pow'r that hath made and preserved us a nation!

Then conquer we must, when our cause it is just,

And this be our motto 'In God is our Trust.'"

In 1954 Congress added a phrase to the Pledge of Allegiance to the Flag so that it now contains the words "one Nation under God, indivisible, with liberty and justice for all." In 1952 Congress enacted legislation calling upon the President each year to proclaim a National Day of Prayer. Since 1865 the words "In God we Trust" have been impressed on our coins.

Countless similar examples could be listed, but there is no need to belabor the obvious. It was all summed up by this Court just ten years ago in a single sentence: "We are a religious people whose institution presuppose a Supreme Being." Zorach v. Clauson, 343 U.S. 306, 313, 72 S.Ct. 679, 684 96 L.Ed. 954.

I do not believe that this Court, or the Congress, or the President has by the actions and practices I have mentioned established an "official religion" in violation of the Constitution. And I do not believe the State of New York has done so in this case. What each has done has been to recognize and to follow the deeply entrenched and highly cherished spiritual traditions of our Nation—traditions which come down to us from those who almost two hundred years ago avowed their "firm Reliance on the Protection of divine Providence" when they proclaimed the freedom and independence of this brave new world.

I dissent.

Abington School Dist. v. Schempp

U.S. Supreme Court

374 U.S. 203 (1963)

374 U.S. 203

SCHOOL DISTRICT OF ABINGTON TOWNSHIP, PENNSYLVANIA,

ET AL. v. SCHEMPP ET AL. APPEAL FROM THE UNITED STATES DISTRICT COURT

FOR THE EASTERN DISTRICT OF PENNSYLVANIA. No. 142.

Argued February 27-28, 1963.

Decided June 17, 1963.

Syllabus

[Footnote *] Together with No. 119, Murray et al. v. Curlett et al., Constituting the Board of School Commissioners of Baltimore City, on certiorari to the Court of Appeals of Maryland, argued February 27, 1963.

✠ Because of the prohibition of the First Amendment against the enactment by Congress of any law "respecting an establishment of religion," which is made applicable to the States by the Fourteenth Amendment, no state law or school board may require that passages from the Bible be read or that the Lord's Prayer be recited in the public schools of a State at the beginning of each school day - even if individual students may be excused from attending or participating in such exercises upon written request of their parents. Pp. 205-227.

201 F. Supp. 815, affirmed.

228 Md. 239, 179 A. 2d 698, reversed.

MR. JUSTICE CLARK delivered the opinion of the Court.

✠ Once again we are called upon to consider the scope of the provision of the First Amendment to the United States Constitution which declares that "Congress shall make no law respecting an establishment of religion, or prohibiting the free exercise thereof . . . ." These companion cases present the issues in the context of state action requiring that schools begin each day with readings from the Bible. While raising the basic questions under slightly different factual situations, the cases permit of joint treatment. In light of the history of the First Amendment and of our cases interpreting and applying its requirements, we hold that the practices at issue and the laws requiring them are unconstitutional under the Establishment Clause, as applied to the States through the Fourteenth Amendment.

I.

The Facts in Each Case: No. 142. The Commonwealth of Pennsylvania by law, 24 Pa. Stat. 15-1516, as amended, Pub. Law 1928 (Supp. 1960) Dec. 17, 1959, requires that "At least ten verses from the Holy Bible shall be read, without comment, at the opening of each public school on each school day. Any child shall be excused from such Bible reading, or attending such Bible reading, upon the written request of his parent or guardian." The Schempp family, husband and wife and two of their three children, brought suit to enjoin enforcement of the statute, contending that their rights under the Fourteenth Amendment to the Constitution of the United States are, have been, and will continue to be violated unless this statute be declared unconstitutional as violative of these provisions of the First Amendment. They sought to enjoin the appellant school district, wherein the Schempp children attend school, and its officers and the [374 U.S. 203, 206] Superintendent of Public Instruction of the Commonwealth from continuing to conduct such readings and recitation of the Lord's Prayer in the public schools of the district pursuant to the statute. A three-judge statutory District Court for the Eastern District of Pennsylvania held that the statute is violative of the Establishment Clause of the First Amendment as applied to the States by the Due Process Clause of the Fourteenth Amendment and directed that appropriate injunctive relief issue. 201 F. Supp. 815. 1 On appeal by the District, its officials and the Superintendent, under 28 U.S.C. 1253, we noted probable jurisdiction. 371 U.S. 807 .

The appellees Edward Lewis Schempp, his wife Sidney, and their children, Roger and Donna, are of the Unitarian faith and are members of the Unitarian church in Germantown, Philadelphia, Pennsylvania, where they, as well as another son, Ellory, regularly attend religious services. The latter was originally a party but having graduated from the school system pendente lite was voluntarily dismissed from the action. The other children attend the Abington Senior High School, which is a public school operated by appellant district.

On each school day at the Abington Senior High School between 8:15 and 8:30 a. m., while the pupils are attending their home rooms or advisory sections, opening exercises [374 U.S. 203, 207] are conducted pursuant to the statute. The exercises are broadcast into each room in the school building through an intercommunications system and are conducted under the supervision of a teacher by students attending the school's radio and television workshop. Selected students from this course gather each morning in the school's workshop studio for the exercises, which include readings by one of the students of 10 verses of the Holy Bible, broadcast to each room in the building. This is followed by the recitation of the Lord's Prayer, likewise over the intercommunications system, but also by the students in the various classrooms, who are asked to stand and join in repeating the prayer in unison. The exercises are closed with the flag salute and such pertinent announcements as are of interest to the students. Participation in the opening exercises, as directed by the statute, is voluntary. The student reading the verses from the Bible may select the passages and read from any version he chooses, although the only copies furnished by the school are the King James version, copies of which were circulated to each teacher by the school district. During the period in which the exercises have been conducted the King James, the Douay and the Revised Standard versions of the Bible have been used, as well as the Jewish Holy Scriptures. There are no prefatory statements, no questions asked or solicited, no comments or explanations made and no interpretations given at or during the exercises. The students and parents are advised that the student may absent himself from the classroom or, should he elect to remain, not participate in the exercises.

It appears from the record that in schools not having an intercommunications system the Bible reading and the recitation of the Lord's Prayer were conducted by the [374 U.S. 203, 208] home-room teacher, 2 who chose the text of the verses and read them herself or had students read them in rotation or by volunteers. This was followed by a standing recitation of the Lord's Prayer, together with the Pledge of Allegiance to the Flag by the class in unison and a closing announcement of routine school items of interest.

At the first trial Edward Schempp and the children testified as to specific religious doctrines purveyed by a literal reading of the Bible "which were contrary to the religious beliefs which they held and to their familial teaching." 177 F. Supp. 398, 400. The children testified that all of the doctrines to which they referred were read to them at various times as part of the exercises. Edward Schempp testified at the second trial that he had considered having Roger and Donna excused from attendance at the exercises but decided against it for several reasons, including his belief that the children's relationships with their teachers and classmates would be adversely affected. 3 [374 U.S. 203, 209]

II.

It is true that religion has been closely identified with our history and government. As we said in Engel v. Vitale, 370 U.S. 421, 434 (1962), "The history of man is inseparable from the history of religion. And . . . since [374 U.S. 203, 213] the beginning of that history many people have devoutly believed that 'More things are wrought by prayer than this world dreams of.'" In Zorach v. Clauson, 343 U.S. 306, 313 (1952), we gave specific recognition to the proposition that "[w]e are a religious people whose institutions presuppose a Supreme Being." The fact that the Founding Fathers believed devotedly that there was a God and that the unalienable rights of man were rooted in Him is clearly evidenced in their writings, from the Mayflower Compact to the

Constitution itself. This background is evidenced today in our public life through the continuance in our oaths of office from the Presidency to the Alderman of the final supplication, "So help me God." Likewise each House of the Congress provides through its Chaplain an opening prayer, and the sessions of this Court are declared open by the crier in a short ceremony, the final phrase of which invokes the grace of God. Again, there are such manifestations in our military forces, where those of our citizens who are under the restrictions of military service wish to engage in voluntary worship. Indeed, only last year an official survey of the country indicated that 64% of our people have church membership, Bureau of the Census, U.S. Department of Commerce, Statistical Abstract of the United States (83d ed. 1962), 48, while less than 3% profess no religion whatever. Id., at p. 46. It can be truly said, therefore, that today, as in the beginning, our national life reflects a religious people who, in the words of Madison, are "earnestly praying duty bound, that the Supreme Lawgiver of the Universe . . . guide them into every measure which may be worthy of his [blessing . . . .]" Memorial and Remonstrance Against Religious Assessments, quoted in Everson v. Board of Education, 330 U.S. 1, 71 -72 (1947) (Appendix to dissenting opinion of Rutledge, J.). [374 U.S. 203, 214]

This is not to say, however, that religion has been so identified with our history and government that religious freedom is not likewise as strongly imbedded in our public and private life. Nothing but the most telling of personal experiences in religious persecution suffered by our forebears, see Everson v. Board of Education, supra, at 8-11, could have planted our belief in liberty of religious opinion any more deeply in our heritage. It is true that this liberty frequently was not realized by the colonists, but this is readily accountable by their close ties to the Mother Country. 5 However, the views of Madison and Jefferson, preceded by Roger Williams, 6 came to be incorporated not only in the Federal Constitution but likewise in those of most of our States. This freedom to worship was indispensable in a country whose people came from the four quarters of the earth and brought with them a diversity of religious opinion. Today authorities list 83 separate religious bodies, each with membership exceeding 50,000, existing among our people, as well as innumerable smaller groups. Bureau of the Census. op. cit., supra, at 46-47.

III.

Almost a hundred years ago in Minor v. Board of Education of Cincinnati, 7 Judge Alphonso Taft, father [374 U.S. 203, 215] of the revered Chief Justice, in an unpublished opinion stated the ideal of our people as to religious freedom as one of

> absolute equality before the law, of all religious opinions and sects. . . .

> The government is neutral, and, while protecting all, it prefers none, and it disparages none.

Before examining this "neutral" position in which the Establishment and Free Exercise Clauses of the First Amendment place our Government it is well that we discuss the reach of the Amendment under the cases of this Court.

First, this Court has decisively settled that the First Amendment's mandate that "Congress shall make no law respecting an establishment of religion, or prohibiting the free exercise thereof" has been made wholly applicable to the States by the Fourteenth Amendment. Twenty-three years ago in Cantwell v. Connecticut, 310 U.S. 296, 303 (1940), this Court, through Mr. Justice Roberts, said:

> The fundamental concept of liberty embodied in that [Fourteenth] Amendment embraces the liberties guaranteed by the First Amendment. The First Amendment declares that Congress shall make no law respecting an establishment of religion or prohibiting the free exercise thereof. The Fourteenth Amendment [374 U.S. 203, 216] has rendered the legislatures of the states as incompetent as Congress to enact such laws. . . . 8

In a series of cases since Cantwell the Court has repeatedly reaffirmed that doctrine, and we do so now. Murdock v. Pennsylvania, 319 U.S. 105, 108 (1943); Everson v. Board of Education, supra; Illinois ex rel. McCollum v. Board of Education, 333 U.S. 203, 210 -211 (1948); Zorach v. Clauson, supra; McGowan v. Maryland, 366 U.S. 420 (1961); Torcaso v. Watkins, 367 U.S. 488 (1961); and Engel v. Vitale, supra.

Second, this Court has rejected unequivocally the contention that the Establishment Clause forbids only governmental preference of one religion over another. Almost 20 years ago in Everson, supra, at 15, the Court said that "[n]either a state nor the Federal Government can set up a church. Neither can pass laws which aid one religion, aid all religions, or prefer one religion over another." And Mr. Justice Jackson, dissenting, agreed:

> There is no answer to the proposition . . . that the effect of the religious freedom Amendment to our Constitution was to take every form of propagation of religion out of the realm of things which could directly or indirectly be made public business and thereby be supported in whole or in part at taxpayers' expense. . . . This freedom was first in the Bill of Rights because it was first in the forefathers' minds; it was set forth in absolute terms, and its strength is its rigidity. Id., at 26. [374 U.S. 203, 217]

Further, Mr. Justice Rutledge, joined by Justices Frankfurter, Jackson and Burton, declared:

> The [First] Amendment's purpose was not to strike merely at the official establishment of a single sect, creed or religion, outlawing only a formal relation such as had prevailed in England and some of the colonies. Necessarily it was to uproot all such relationships. But the object was broader than separating church and state in this narrow sense. It was to create a complete and permanent separation of the spheres of religious activity and civil authority by comprehensively forbidding every form of public aid or support for religion. Id., at 31-32.

The same conclusion has been firmly maintained ever since that time, see Illinois ex rel. McCollum, supra, at pp. 210-211; McGowan v. Maryland, supra, at 442-443; Torcaso v. Watkins, supra, at 492-493, 495, and we reaffirm it now.

While none of the parties to either of these cases has questioned these basic conclusions of the Court, both of which have been long established, recognized and consistently reaffirmed, others continue to question their history, logic and efficacy. Such contentions, in the light of the consistent interpretation in cases of this Court, seem entirely untenable and of value only as academic exercises.

IV.

The interrelationship of the Establishment and the Free Exercise Clauses was first touched upon by Mr. Justice Roberts for the Court in Cantwell v. Connecticut, supra, at 303-304, where it was said that their "inhibition of legislation" had

> a double aspect. On the one hand, it forestalls compulsion by law of the acceptance of any creed or the practice of any form of worship. Freedom of [374 U.S. 203, 218] conscience and freedom to adhere to such religious organization or form of worship as the individual may choose cannot be restricted by law. On the other hand, it safeguards the free exercise of the chosen form of religion. Thus the Amendment embraces two concepts, - freedom to believe and freedom to act. The first is absolute but, in the nature of things, the second cannot be.

A half dozen years later in Everson v. Board of Education, supra, at 14-15, this Court, through MR. JUSTICE BLACK, stated that the "scope of the First Amendment . . . was designed forever to suppress" the establishment of religion or the prohibition of the free exercise thereof. In short, the Court held that the Amendment "requires the state to be a neutral in its relations with groups of religious believers and non-believers; it does not require the state to be their adversary. State power is no more to be used so as to handicap religions than it is to favor them." Id., at 18. And Mr. Justice Jackson, in dissent, declared that public schools are organized

> on the premise that secular education can be isolated from all religious teaching so that the school can inculcate all needed temporal knowledge and also maintain a strict and lofty neutrality as to religion. The assumption is that after the individual has been instructed in worldly wisdom he will be better fitted to choose his religion. Id., at 23-24.

Moreover, all of the four dissenters, speaking through Mr. Justice Rutledge, agreed that

> Our constitutional policy . . . does not deny the value or the necessity for religious training, teaching or observance. Rather it secures their free exercise. But to that end it does deny that the state can undertake or sustain them in any form or degree. For this [374 U.S. 203, 219] reason the sphere of religious activity, as distinguished from the secular intellectual liberties, has been given the twofold protection and, as the state cannot forbid, neither can it perform or aid in performing the religious function. The dual prohibition makes that function altogether private. Id., at 52.

Only one year later the Court was asked to reconsider and repudiate the doctrine of these cases in McCollum v. Board of Education. It was argued that "historically the First Amendment was intended to forbid only government preference of one religion over another . . . . In addition they ask that we distinguish or overrule our holding in the Everson case that the Fourteenth

Amendment made the `establishment of religion' clause of the First Amendment applicable as a prohibition against the States." 333 U.S., at 211 . The Court, with Mr. Justice Reed alone dissenting, was unable to "accept either of these contentions." Ibid. Mr. Justice Frankfurter, joined by Justices Jackson, Rutledge and Burton, wrote a very comprehensive and scholarly concurrence in which he said that "[s]eparation is a requirement to abstain from fusing functions of Government and of religious sects, not merely to treat them all equally." Id., at 227. Continuing, he stated that:

> the Constitution . . . prohibited the Government common to all from becoming embroiled, however innocently, in the destructive religious conflicts of which the history of even this country records some dark pages. Id., at 228.

In 1952 in Zorach v. Clauson, supra, MR. JUSTICE DOUGLAS for the Court reiterated:

> There cannot be the slightest doubt that the First Amendment reflects the philosophy that Church and State should be separated. And so far as interference with the `free exercise' of religion and an [374 U.S. 203, 220] `establishment' of religion are concerned, the separation must be complete and unequivocal. The First Amendment within the scope of its coverage permits no exception; the prohibition is absolute. The First Amendment, however, does not say that in every and all respects there shall be a separation of Church and State. Rather, it studiously defines the manner, the specific ways, in which there shall be no concert or union or dependency one on the other. That is the common sense of the matter. 343 U.S., at 312 .

And then in 1961 in McGowan v. Maryland and in Torcaso v. Watkins each of these cases was discussed and approved. CHIEF JUSTICE WARREN in McGowan, for a unanimous Court on this point, said:

> But, the First Amendment, in its final form, did not simply bar a congressional enactment establishing a church; it forbade all laws respecting an establishment of religion. Thus, this Court has given the Amendment a "road interpretation . . . in the light of its history and the evils it was designed forever to suppress. . . ."66 U.S., at 441 -442.

And MR. JUSTICE BLACK for the Court in Torcaso, without dissent but with Justices Frankfurter and HARLAN concurring in the result, used this language:

> We repeat and again reaffirm that neither a State nor the Federal Government can constitutionally force a person `to profess a belief or disbelief in any religion.' Neither can constitutionally pass laws or impose requirements which aid all religions as against non-believers, and neither can aid those religions based on a belief in the existence of God as against those religions founded on different beliefs. 367 U.S., at 495 .

Finally, in Engel v. Vitale, only last year, these principles were so universally recognized that the Court, without [374 U.S. 203, 221] the citation of a single case and over the sole dissent of MR.

JUSTICE STEWART, reaffirmed them. The Court found the 22-word prayer used in "New York's program of daily classroom invocation of God's blessings as prescribed in the Regents' prayer . . . [to be] a religious activity." 370 U.S., at 424 . It held that "it is no part of the business of government to compose official prayers for any group of the American people to recite as a part of a religious program carried on by government." Id., at 425. In discussing the reach of the Establishment and Free Exercise Clauses of the First Amendment the Court said:

> Although these two clauses may in certain instances overlap, they forbid two quite different kinds of governmental encroachment upon religious freedom. The Establishment Clause, unlike the Free Exercise Clause, does not depend upon any showing of direct governmental compulsion and is violated by the enactment of laws which establish an official religion whether those laws operate directly to coerce non-observing individuals or not. This is not to say, of course, that laws officially prescribing a particular form of religious worship do not involve coercion of such individuals. When the power, prestige and financial support of government is placed behind a particular religious belief, the indirect coercive pressure upon religious minorities to conform to the prevailing officially approved religion is plain. Id., at 430-431.

And in further elaboration the Court found that the "first and most immediate purpose [of the Establishment Clause] rested on the belief that a union of government and religion tends to destroy government and to degrade religion." Id., at 431. When government, the Court said, allies itself with one particular form of religion, the [374 U.S. 203, 222] inevitable result is that it incurs "the hatred, disrespect and even contempt of those who held contrary beliefs." Ibid.

V.

The wholesome "neutrality" of which this Court's cases speak thus stems from a recognition of the teachings of history that powerful sects or groups might bring about a fusion of governmental and religious functions or a concert or dependency of one upon the other to the end that official support of the State or Federal Government would be placed behind the tenets of one or of all orthodoxies. This the Establishment Clause prohibits. And a further reason for neutrality is found in the Free Exercise Clause, which recognizes the value of religious training, teaching and observance and, more particularly, the right of every person to freely choose his own course with reference thereto, free of any compulsion from the state. This the Free Exercise Clause guarantees. Thus, as we have seen, the two clauses may overlap. As we have indicated, the Establishment Clause has been directly considered by this Court eight times in the past score of years and, with only one Justice dissenting on the point, it has consistently held that the clause withdrew all legislative power respecting religious belief or the expression thereof. The test may be stated as follows: what are the purpose and the primary effect of the enactment? If either is the advancement or inhibition of religion then the enactment exceeds the scope of legislative power as circumscribed by the Constitution. That is to say that to withstand the strictures of the Establishment Clause there must be a secular legislative purpose and a primary effect that neither advances nor inhibits religion. Everson v. Board of Education, supra; McGowan v. Maryland, supra, at 442. The Free Exercise Clause, likewise considered many times here, withdraws from legislative power, state and federal, the exertion of any restraint on the free exercise [374 U.S. 203, 223] of religion. Its purpose is to secure religious liberty in the individual by prohibiting any invasions thereof by civil authority. Hence it is necessary in a free exercise case for one to show the coercive effect of the enactment as it operates against him in the practice of his religion. The distinction between the two clauses is apparent - a violation of the Free Exercise Clause is predicated on coercion while the Establishment Clause violation need not be so attended.

Applying the Establishment Clause principles to the cases at bar we find that the States are requiring the selection and reading at the opening of the school day of verses from the Holy Bible and the recitation of the Lord's Prayer by the students in unison. These exercises are prescribed as part of the curricular activities of students who are required by law to attend school. They are held in the school buildings under the supervision and with the participation of teachers employed in those schools. None of these factors, other than compulsory school attendance, was present in the program upheld in Zorach v. Clauson. The trial court in No. 142 has found that such an opening exercise is a religious ceremony and was intended by the State to be so. We agree with the trial court's finding as to the religious character of the exercises. Given that finding, the exercises and the law requiring them are in violation of the Establishment Clause.

There is no such specific finding as to the religious character of the exercises in No. 119, and the State contends (as does the State in No. 142) that the program is an effort to extend its benefits to all public school children without regard to their religious belief. Included within its secular purposes, it says, are the promotion of moral values, the contradiction to the materialistic trends of our times, the perpetuation of our institutions and the teaching of literature. The case came up [374 U.S. 203, 224] on demurrer, of course, to a petition which alleged that the uniform practice under the rule had been to read from the King James version of the Bible and that the exercise was sectarian. The short answer, therefore, is that the religious character of the exercise was admitted by the State. But even if its purpose is not strictly religious, it is sought to be accomplished through readings, without comment, from the Bible. Surely the place of the Bible as an instrument of religion cannot be gainsaid, and the State's recognition of the pervading religious character of the ceremony is evident from the rule's specific permission of the alternative use of the Catholic Douay version as well as the recent amendment permitting nonattendance at the exercises. None of these factors is consistent with the contention that the Bible is here used either as an instrument for nonreligious moral inspiration or as a reference for the teaching of secular subjects.

The conclusion follows that in both cases the laws require religious exercises and such exercises are being conducted in direct violation of the rights of the appellees and petitioners. 9 Nor are these required exercises mitigated by the fact that individual students may absent [374 U.S. 203, 225] themselves upon parental request, for that fact furnishes no defense to a claim of unconstitutionality under the Establishment Clause. See Engel v. Vitale, supra, at 430. Further, it is no defense to urge that the religious practices here may be relatively minor encroachments on the First Amendment. The breach of neutrality that is today a trickling stream may all too soon become a raging torrent and, in the words of Madison, "it is proper to take alarm at the first experiment on our liberties." Memorial and Remonstrance Against Religious Assessments, quoted in Everson, supra, at 65.

It is insisted that unless these religious exercises are permitted a "religion of secularism" is established in the schools. We agree of course that the State may not establish a "religion of secularism" in the sense of affirmatively opposing or showing hostility to religion, thus "preferring those who believe in no religion over those who do believe." Zorach v. Clauson, supra, at 314. We do not agree, however, that this decision in any sense has that effect. In addition, it might well be said that one's education is not complete without a study of comparative religion or the history of religion and its relationship to the advancement of civilization. It certainly may be said that the Bible is worthy of study for its literary and historic qualities. Nothing we have said here indicates that such study of the Bible or of religion, when presented objectively as part of a secular program of education, may not be effected consistently with the First Amendment. But the exercises here do not fall into those categories. They are religious exercises, required by the States in violation of the command of the First Amendment that the Government maintain strict neutrality, neither aiding nor opposing religion.

Finally, we cannot accept that the concept of neutrality, which does not permit a State to require a religious exercise even with the consent of the majority of those [374 U.S. 203, 226] affected, collides with the majority's right to free exercise of religion. 10 While the Free Exercise Clause clearly prohibits the use of state action to deny the rights of free exercise to anyone, it has never meant that a majority could use the machinery of the State to practice its beliefs. Such a contention was effectively answered by Mr. Justice Jackson for the Court in West Virginia Board of Education v. Barnette, 319 U.S. 624, 638 (1943):

> The very purpose of a Bill of Rights was to withdraw certain subjects from the vicissitudes of political controversy, to place them beyond the reach of majorities and officials and to establish them as legal principles to be applied by the courts. One's right to . . . freedom of worship . . . and other fundamental rights may not be submitted to vote; they depend on the outcome of no elections.

The place of religion in our society is an exalted one, achieved through a long tradition of reliance on the home, the church and the inviolable citadel of the individual heart and mind. We have come to recognize through bitter experience that it is not within the power of government to invade that citadel, whether its purpose or effect be to aid or oppose, to advance or retard. In the relationship between man and religion, the State is firmly committed to a position of neutrality. Though the application of that rule requires interpretation of a delicate sort, the rule itself is clearly and concisely stated in the words of the First Amendment. Applying that rule to the facts of these cases, we affirm the judgment in No. 142. [374 U.S. 203, 227] In No. 119, the judgment is reversed and the cause remanded to the Maryland Court of Appeals for further proceedings consistent with this opinion.

IT IS SO ORDERED.

Lemon v. Kurtzman
403 U.S. 602
(1971)

Syllabus

✠ Rhode Island's 1969 Salary Supplement Act provides for a 15% salary supplement to be paid to teachers in nonpublic schools at which the average per-pupil expenditure on secular education is below the average in public schools. Eligible teachers must teach only courses offered in the public schools, using only materials used in the public schools, and must agree not to teach courses in religion. A three-judge court found that about 25% of the State's elementary students attended nonpublic schools, about 95% of whom attended Roman Catholic affiliated schools, and that to date about 250 teachers at Roman Catholic schools are the sole beneficiaries under the Act. The court found that the parochial school system was "an integral part of the religious mission of the Catholic Church," and held that the Act fostered "excessive entanglement" between government and religion, thus violating the Establishment Clause. Pennsylvania's Nonpublic Elementary and Secondary Education Act, passed in 1968, authorizes the state Superintendent of Public Instruction to "purchase" certain "secular educational services" from nonpublic schools, directly reimbursing those schools solely for teachers' salaries, textbooks, and instructional materials. Reimbursement is restricted to courses in specific secular subjects, the textbooks and materials must be approved by the Superintendent, and no payment is to be made for any course containing "any subject matter expressing religious teaching, or the morals or forms of worship of any sect." Contracts were made with schools that have more than 20% of all the students in the State, most of which were affiliated with the Roman Catholic Church. The complaint challenging the constitutionality of [p*603] the Act alleged that the church-affiliated schools are controlled by religious organizations, have the purpose of propagating and promoting a particular religious faith, and conduct their operations to fulfill that purpose. A three-judge court granted the State's motion to dismiss the complaint for failure to state a claim for relief, finding no violation of the Establishment or Free Exercise Clause.

✠ *Held:* Both statutes are unconstitutional under the Religion Clauses of the First Amendment, as the cumulative impact of the entire relationship arising under the statutes involves excessive entanglement between government and religion. Pp. 611-625 .

(a) The entanglement in the Rhode Island program arises because of the religious activity and purpose of the church-affiliated schools, especially with respect to children of impressionable age in the primary grades, and the dangers that a teacher under religious control and discipline poses to the separation of religious from purely secular aspects of elementary education in such schools. These factors require continuing state surveillance to ensure that the statutory restrictions are obeyed and the First Amendment otherwise respected. Furthermore, under the Act, the government must inspect school records to determine what part of the expenditures is attributable to secular education, as opposed to religious activity, in the event a nonpublic school's expenditures per pupil exceed the comparable figures for public schools. Pp. 615-620 .

(b) The entanglement in the Pennsylvania program also arises from the restrictions and surveillance necessary to ensure that teachers play a strictly non-ideological role and the state supervision of nonpublic school accounting procedures required to establish the cost of secular, as distinguished from religious, education. In addition, the Pennsylvania statute has the further defect of providing continuing financial aid directly to the church-related schools. Historically, governmental control and surveillance measures tend to follow cash grant programs, and here the government's post-audit power to inspect the financial records of church-related schools creates an intimate and continuing relationship between church and state. Pp. 620-622 .

(c) Political division along religious lines was one of the evils at which the First Amendment aimed, and in these programs, where successive and probably permanent annual appropriations that benefit relatively few religious groups are involved, political [p*604] fragmentation and divisiveness on religious lines are likely to be intensified. Pp. 622-624 .

(d) Unlike the tax exemption for places of religious worship, upheld in *Walz v. Tax Commission,* 397 U.S. 664 , which was based on a practice of 200 years, these innovative programs have self-perpetuating and self-expanding propensities which provide a warning signal against entanglement between government and religion. Pp. 624-625.

No. 89, 310 F.Supp. 35, reversed and remanded; Nos. 569 and 570, 316 F.Supp. 112, affirmed.

Opinions

BURGER, C.J., delivered the opinion of the Court, in which BLACK, DOUGLAS, HARLAN, STEWART, MARSHALL (as to Nos. 569 and 570), and BLACKMUN, JJ., joined. DOUGLAS, J., filed a concurring opinion, *post,* p. 625 , in which BLACK, J., joined, and in which MARSHALL, J. (as to Nos. 569 and 570), joined, filing a separate statement, *post,* p. 642 . BRENNAN, J., filed a concurring opinion, *post,* p. 642 . WHITE, J., filed an opinion concurring in the judgment in No. 89 and dissenting in Nos. 569 and 570, *post,* p. 661 . MARSHALL, J., took no part in the consideration or decision of No. 89. [p*606]

BURGER, C.J., Opinion of the Court

MR. CHIEF JUSTICE BURGER delivered the opinion of the Court.

These two appeals raise questions as to Pennsylvania and Rhode Island statutes providing state aid to church-related elementary and secondary schools. Both statutes are challenged as violative of the Establishment and Free Exercise Clauses of the First Amendment and the Due Process Clause of the Fourteenth Amendment.

Pennsylvania has adopted a statutory program that provides financial support to nonpublic elementary and [p*607] secondary schools by way of reimbursement for the cost of teachers' salaries, textbooks, and instructional materials in specified secular subjects. Rhode Island has adopted a statute under which the State pays directly to teachers in nonpublic elementary schools a supplement of 15% of their annual salary. Under each statute, state aid has been given to church-related educational institutions. We hold that both statutes are unconstitutional.

The Rhode Island Salary Supplement Act [n1] was enacted in 1969. It rests on the legislative finding that the quality of education available in nonpublic elementary schools has been jeopardized by the rapidly rising salaries needed to attract competent and dedicated teachers. The Act authorizes state officials to supplement the salaries of teachers of secular subjects in nonpublic elementary schools by paying directly to a teacher an amount not in excess of 15% of his current annual salary. As supplemented, however, a nonpublic school teacher's salary cannot exceed the maximum paid to teachers in the State's public schools, and the recipient must be certified by the state board of education in substantially the same manner as public school teachers.

In order to be eligible for the Rhode Island salary supplement, the recipient must teach in a nonpublic school at which the average per-pupil expenditure on secular education is less than the average in the State's public schools during a specified period. Appellant State Commissioner of Education also requires eligible schools to submit financial data. If this information indicates a per-pupil expenditure in excess of the statutory limitation, [p*608] the records of the school in question must be examined in order to assess how much of the expenditure is attributable to secular education and how much to religious activity. [n2]

The Act also requires that teachers eligible for salary supplements must teach only those subjects that are offered in the State's public schools. They must use "only teaching materials which are used in the public schools." Finally, any teacher applying for a salary supplement must first agree in writing "not to teach a course in religion for so long as or during such time as he or she receives any salary supplements" under the Act.

Lynch v. Donnelly
465 U.S. 668
(1984)

Syllabus

✚ The city of Pawtucket, R.I., annually erects a Christmas display in a park owned by a nonprofit organization and located in the heart of the city's shopping district. The display includes, in addition to such objects as a Santa Claus house, a Christmas tree, and a banner that reads "SEASONS GREETINGS," a creche or Nativity scene, which has been part of this annual display for 40 years or more. Respondents brought an action in Federal District Court, challenging the inclusion of the creche in the display on the ground that it violated the Establishment Clause of the First Amendment, as made applicable to the states by the Fourteenth Amendment. The District Court upheld the challenge and permanently enjoined the city from including the creche in the display. The Court of Appeals affirmed.

♣ *Held:* Notwithstanding the religious significance of the creche, Pawtucket has not violated the Establishment Clause. Pp. 672-687.

(a) The concept of a "wall" of separation between church and state is a useful metaphor, but is not an accurate description of the practical aspects of the relationship that in fact exists. The Constitution does not require complete separation of church and state; it affirmatively mandates accommodation, not merely tolerance, of all religions, and forbids hostility toward any. Anything less would require the "callous indifference," *Zorach v. Clauson,* 343 U.S. 306 , 314 , that was never intended by the Establishment Clause. Pp. 672-673.

(b) This Court's interpretation of the Establishment Clause comports with the contemporaneous understanding of the Framers' intent. That neither the draftsmen of the Constitution, who were Members of the First Congress, nor the First Congress itself saw any establishment problem in employing Chaplains to offer daily prayers in the Congress is a striking example of the accommodation of religious beliefs intended by the Framers. Pp. 673-674.

(c) Our history is pervaded by official acknowledgment of the role of religion in American life, and equally pervasive is evidence of accommodation of all faiths and all forms of religious expression and hostility toward none. Pp. 674-678. [p*669]

(d) Rather than taking an absolutist approach in applying the Establishment Clause and mechanically invalidating all governmental conduct or statutes that confer benefits or give special recognition to religion in general or to one faith, this Court has scrutinized challenged conduct or legislation to determine whether, in reality, it establishes a religion or religious faith or tends to do so. In the line-drawing process called for in each case, it has often been found useful to inquire whether the challenged law or conduct has a secular purpose, whether its principal or primary effect is to advance or inhibit religion, and whether it creates an excessive entanglement of government with religion. But this Court has been unwilling to be confined to any single test or criterion in this sensitive area. Pp. 678-679.

(e) Here, the focus of the inquiry must be on the creche in the context of the Christmas season. Focus exclusively on the religious component of any activity would inevitably lead to its invalidation under the Establishment Clause. Pp. 679-680.

(f) Based on the record in this case, the city has a secular purpose for including the creche in its Christmas display, and has not impermissibly advanced religion or created an excessive entanglement between religion and government. The display is sponsored by the city to celebrate the Holiday recognized by Congress and national tradition and to depict the origins of that Holiday; these are legitimate secular purposes. Whatever benefit to one faith or religion or to all religions inclusion of the creche in the display effects, is indirect, remote, and incidental, and is no more an advancement or endorsement of religion than the congressional and executive recognition of the origins of Christmas, or the exhibition of religious paintings in governmentally supported museums. This Court is unable to discern a greater aid to religion from the inclusion of the creche than from the substantial benefits previously held not violative of the Establishment Clause. As to administrative entanglement, there is no evidence of contact with church authorities concerning the content or design of the exhibition prior to or since the city's purchase of the creche. No expenditures for maintenance of the creche have been necessary, and, since the city owns the creche, now valued at $200, the tangible material it contributes is *de minimis*. Political divisiveness alone cannot serve to invalidate otherwise permissible conduct, and, in any event, apart from the instant litigation, there is no evidence of political friction or divisiveness over the creche in the 40-year history of the city's Christmas celebration. Pp. 680-685.

(g) It would be ironic if the inclusion of the creche in the display, as part of a celebration of an event acknowledged in the Western World for 20 centuries, and in this country by the people, the Executive Branch, [p*670] Congress, and the courts for 2 centuries, would so "taint" the exhibition as to render it violative of the Establishment Clause. To forbid the use of this one passive symbol while hymns and carols are sung and played in public places including schools, and while Congress and state legislatures open public sessions with prayers, would be an overreaction contrary to this Nation's history and this Court's holdings. Pp. 685-686.

691 F.2d 1029, reversed.

BURGER, C.J., delivered the opinion of the Court, in which WHITE, POWELL, REHNQUIST, and O'CONNOR, JJ., joined. O'CONNOR, J., filed a concurring opinion, *post,* p. 687 . BRENNAN, J., filed a dissenting opinion, in which MARSHALL, BLACKMUN, and STEVENS, JJ., joined, *post,* p. 694. BLACKMUN, J., filed a dissenting opinion, in which STEVENS, J., joined, *post,* p. 726.

Opinions

BURGER, C.J., Opinion of the Court

CHIEF JUSTICE BURGER delivered the opinion of the Court.

✠ We granted certiorari to decide whether the Establishment Clause of the First Amendment prohibits a municipality [p*671] from including a creche, or Nativity scene, in its annual Christmas display.

✠ Each year, in cooperation with the downtown retail merchants' association, the city of Pawtucket, R.I., erects a Christmas display as part of its observance of the Christmas holiday season. The display is situated in a park owned by a nonprofit organization and located in the heart of the shopping district. The display is essentially like those to be found in hundreds of towns or cities across the Nation -- often on public grounds -- during the Christmas season. The Pawtucket display comprises many of the figures and decorations traditionally associated with Christmas, including, among other things, a Santa Claus house, reindeer pulling Santa's sleigh, candy-striped poles, a Christmas tree, carolers, cutout figures representing such characters as a clown, an elephant, and a teddy bear, hundreds of colored lights, a large banner that reads "SEASONS GREETINGS," and the creche at issue here. All components of this display are owned by the city.

✠ The creche, which has been included in the display for 40 or more years, consists of the traditional figures, including the Infant Jesus, Mary and Joseph, angels, shepherds, kings, and animals, all ranging in height from 5" to 5'. In 1973, when the present creche was acquired, it cost the city $1,365; it now is valued at $200. The erection and dismantling of the creche costs the city about $20 per year; nominal expenses are incurred in lighting the creche. No money has been expended on its maintenance for the past 10 years.

Lee et al. *v.* Weisman, Personally and as Next Friend of Weisman

CERTIORARI TO THE UNITED STATES COURT OF APPEALS FOR THE FIRST CIRCUIT

No. 90-1014.

Argued November 6, 1991

Decided June 24, 1992

Syllabus

✤ Principals of public middle and high schools in Providence, Rhode Island, are permitted to invite members of the clergy to give invocations and benedictions at their schools' graduation ceremonies. Petitioner Lee, a middle school principal, invited a rabbi to offer such prayers at the graduation ceremony for Deborah Weisman's class, gave the Rabbi a pamphlet containing guidelines for the composition of public prayers at civic ceremonies, and advised him that the prayers should be nonsectarian. Shortly before the ceremony, the District Court denied the motion of respondent Weisman, Deborah's father, for a temporary restraining order to prohibit school officials from including the prayers in the ceremony. Deborah and her family attended the ceremony, and the prayers were recited. Subsequently, Weisman sought a permanent injunction barring Lee and other petitioners, various Providence public school officials, from inviting clergy to deliver invocations and benedictions at future graduations. It appears likely that such prayers will be conducted at Deborah's high school graduation. The District Court enjoined petitioners from continuing the practice at issue on the ground that it violated the Establishment Clause of the First Amendment. The Court of Appeals affirmed.

✤ *Held:* Including clergy who offer prayers as part of an official public school graduation ceremony is forbidden by the Establishment Clause. Pp. 7-19.

(a) This Court need not revisit the questions of the definition and scope of the principles governing the extent of permitted accommodation by the State for its citizens' religious beliefs and practices, for the controlling precedents as they relate to prayer and religious exercise in primary and secondary public schools compel the holding here. Thus, the Court will not reconsider its decision in *Lemon* v. *Kurtzman,* 40z3 U.S. 602. The principle that government may accommodate the free exercise of religion does not supersede the fundamental limitations imposed by the Establishment Clause, which guarantees at a minimum that a government may not coerce anyone to support or participate in religion or its exercise, or otherwise act in a way which "establishes a [state] religion or religious faith, or tends to do so." *Lynch* v. *Donnelly,* 465 U.S. 668, 678. Pp. 7-8.

(b) State officials here direct the performance of a formal religious exercise at secondary schools' promotional and graduation ceremonies. Lee's decision that prayers should be given and his selection of the religious participant are choices attributable to the State. Moreover, through the pamphlet and his advice that the prayers be nonsectarian, he directed and controlled the prayers' content. That the directions may have been given in a good faith attempt to make the prayers acceptable to most persons does not resolve the dilemma caused by the school's involvement, since the government may not establish an official or civic religion as a means of avoiding the establishment of a religion with more specific creeds. Pp. 8-11.

(c) The Establishment Clause was inspired by the lesson that in the hands of government what might begin as a tolerant expression of religious views may end in a policy to indoctrinate and coerce. Prayer exercises in elementary and secondary schools carry a particular risk of indirect coercion. *Engel* v. *Vitale,* 370 U.S. 421; *Abington School District* v. *Schempp,* 374 U.S. 203. The school district's supervision and control of a high school graduation ceremony places subtle and indirect public and peer pressure on attending students to stand as a group or maintain respectful silence during the invocation and benediction. A reasonable dissenter of high school age could believe that standing or remaining silent signified her own participation in, or approval of, the group exercise, rather than her respect for it. And the State may not place the student dissenter in the dilemma of participating or protesting. Since adolescents are often susceptible to peer pressure, especially in matters of social convention, the State may no more use social pressure to enforce orthodoxy than it may use direct means. The embarrassment and intrusion of the religious exercise cannot be refuted by arguing that the prayers are of a *de minimis* character, since that is an affront to the Rabbi and those for whom the prayers have meaning, and since any intrusion was both real and a violation of the objectors' rights. Pp. 11-15.

(d) Petitioners' argument that the option of not attending the ceremony excuses any inducement or coercion in the ceremony itself is rejected. In this society, high school graduation is one of life's most significant occasions, and a student is not free to absent herself from the exercise in any real sense of the term "voluntary." Also not dispositive is the contention that prayers are an essential part of these ceremonies because for many persons the occasion would lack meaning without the recognition that human achievements cannot be understood apart from their spiritual essence. This position fails to acknowledge that what for many was a spiritual imperative was for the Weismans religious conformance compelled by the State. It also gives insufficient recognition to the real conflict of conscience faced by a student who would have to choose whether to miss graduation or conform to the state sponsored practice, in an environment where the risk of compulsion is especially high. Pp. 15-17.

(e) Inherent differences between the public school system and a session of a state legislature distinguish this case from *Marsh* v. *Chambers,* 463 U.S. 783, which condoned a prayer exercise.

The atmosphere at a state legislature's opening, where adults are free to enter and leave with little comment and for any number of reasons, cannot compare with the constraining potential of the one school event most important for the student to attend. Pp. 17-18.

908 F. 2d 1090, AFFIRMED.

KENNEDY, J., delivered the opinion of the Court, in which BLACKMUN, STEVENS, O'CONNOR, and SOUTER, JJ., joined. BLACKMUN, J., and SOUTER, J., filed concurring opinions, in which Stevens and O'Connor, JJ., joined. Scalia, J., filed a dissenting opinion, in which REHNQUIST, C. J., and WHITE
and THOMAS, JJ., joined.

Chapter 5
"Indivisible"

The Missouri Compromise
1820-21

An Act to authorize the people of the Missouri territory to form a constitution and state government, and for the admission of such state into the Union on an equal footing with the original states, and to prohibit slavery in certain territories.

Be it enacted . . ., That the inhabitants of that portion of the Missouri territory included within the boundaries hereinafter designated, be, and they are hereby, authorized to form for themselves a Constitution and state government, and to assume such name as they shall deem proper; and the said state, when formed, shall be admitted into the Union, upon an equal footing with the original states, in all respects whatsoever.

Section 2. And be it further enacted, That the said state shall consist of all the territory included within the following boundaries, to wit: Beginning in the middle of the Mississippi river? on the parallel of thirty-six degrees of north latitude; thence west, along that parallel of latitude, to the St. Francois river; thence up, and following the course of that river, in the middle of the main channel thereof, to the parallel of latitude of thirty-six degrees and thirty minutes; thence west, along the same, to a point where the said parallel is intersected by a meridian line passing through the middle of the mouth of the Kansas river, where the same empties into the Missouri river, thence, from the point aforesaid north, along the said meridian line, to the intersection of the parallel of latitude which passes through the rapids of the river Des Moines, making the said line to correspond with the Indian boundary line; thence east, from the point of intersection last aforesaid, along the said parallel of latitude, to the middle of the channel of the main fork of the said river Des Moines; thence down and along the middle of the main channel of the said river Des Moines, to the mouth of the same, where it empties into the Mississippi river; thence, due east, to the middle of the main channel of the Mississippi river; thence down and following the course of the Mississippi river, in the middle of the main channel thereof, to the place of beginning: . . .

* * * * * * * *

Section 8. And be it further enacted, That in all that territory ceded by France to the United States, under the name of Louisiana, which lies north of thirty-six degrees and thirty minutes north latitude, not included within the limits of the state, contemplated by this act, slavery and involuntary servitude, otherwise than in the punishment of crimes, whereof the parties shall have been duly convicted, shall be, and is hereby, forever prohibited: Provided always, That any person escaping into the same, from whom labour or service is lawfully claimed, in any state or territory of the United States, such fugitive may be lawfully reclaimed and conveyed to the person claiming his or her labour or service as aforesaid.

Resolution For The Admission Of Missouri
March 2, 1821

Resolution providing for the admission of the State of Missouri into the Union, on a certain condition.

Resolved . . ., That Missouri shall be admitted into this union on an equal footing with the original states, in all respects whatever, upon the fundamental condition, that the fourth clause of the twenty-sixth section of the third article of the constitution submitted on the part of said state to Congress, shall never be construed to authorize the passage of any law, and that no law shall be passed in conformity thereto, by which any citizen, of either of the states in this Union, shall be excluded from the enjoyment of any of the privileges and immunities to which such citizen is entitled under the constitution of the United States: Provided, That the legislature of the said state, by a solemn public act, shall declare the assent of the said state to the said fundamental condition, and shall transmit to the President of the United States, on or before the fourth Monday in November next, an authentic copy of the said act; upon the receipt whereof, the President, by proclamation, shall announce the fact; whereupon, and without any further proceeding on the part of Congress, the admission of the said state into this Union shall be considered as complete.

Slavery Is Despotism
By
Harriet Beecher Stowe (1854)

It is always important, in discussing a thing, to keep before our minds exactly what it is. The only means of understanding precisely what a civil institution is, are an examination of the laws which regulate it. In different ages and nations, very different things have been called by the name of slavery. Patriarchal servitude was one thing, Hebrew servitude was another, Greek and Roman servitude still a third; and these institutions differed very much from each other. What, then, is American slavery, as we have seen it exhibited by law, and by the decision of Courts?

Let us begin by stating what it is not:--

1. It is not apprenticeship.
2. It is not guardianship.
3. It is in no sense a system for the education of a weaker race by a stronger.
4. The happiness of the governed is in no sense its object.
5. The temporal improvement or the eternal well-being of the governed is in no sense its object.

The object of it has been distinctly stated in one sentence by Judge Ruffin--"The end is the profit of the master, his security, and the public safety."

Slavery, then, is absolute despotism, of the most unmitigated form.

It would, however, be doing injustice to the absolutism of any civilised country to liken American slavery to it. The absolute governments of Europe none of them pretend to be founded on a property right of the governor to the persons and entire capabilities of the governed.

This is a form of despotism which exists only in some of the most savage countries of the world; as, for example, in Dahomey.

The European absolutism or despotism, now, does, to some extent, recognise the happiness and welfare of the governed as the foundation of government; and the ruler is considered as invested with power for the benefit of the people; and his right to rule is supposed to be in somewhat predicated upon the idea that he better understands how to promote the good of the people than they themselves do. No government in the civilised world now presents the pure despotic idea, as it existed in the old days of the Persian and Assyrian rule.

The arguments which defend slavery must be substantially the same as those which defend despotism of any other kind; and the objections which are to be urged against it are precisely those which can be urged against despotism of any other kind. The customs and practices to which it gives rise are precisely those to which despotisms in all ages have given rise.

Is the slave suspected of a crime? His master has the power to examine him by torture (see State v. Castleman). His master has, in fact, in most cases, the power of life and death, owing to the exclusion of the slave's evidence. He has the power of banishing the slave, at any time, and without giving an account to anybody, to an exile as dreadful as that of Siberia, and to labours as severe as those of the galleys. He has also unlimited power over the character of his slave. He can accuse him of any crime, yet withhold from him all right of trial or investigation, and sell him into captivity, with his name blackened by an unexamined imputation.

These are all abuses for which despotic governments are blamed. They are powers which good men who are despotic rulers are beginning to disuse; but, under the flag of every slaveholding State, and under the flag of the whole United States in the District of Columbia, they are committed indiscriminately to men of any character.

But the worst kind of despotism has been said to be that which extends alike over the body and over the soul; which can bind the liberty of the conscience, and deprive a man of all right of choice in respect to the manner in which he shall learn the will of God, and worship him. In other days, kings on their thrones, and cottagers by their fire-sides, alike trembled before a despotism which declared itself able to bind and to loose, to open and to shut the kingdom of heaven.

Yet this power to control the conscience, to control the religious privileges, and all the opportunities which man has of acquaintanceship with his Maker, and of learning to do his will, is, under the flag of every slave State, and under the flag of the United States, placed in the hands of any men of any character who can afford to pay for it.

It is a most awful and most solemn truth that the greatest republic in the world does sustain under her national flag the worst system of despotism which can possibly exist.

With regard to one point to which we have adverted--the power of the master to deprive the slave of a legal trial while accusing him of crime--a very striking instance has occurred in the District of Columbia, within a year or two. The particulars of the case, as stated at the time, in several papers, were briefly these: A gentleman in Washington, our national capital--an elder in the Presbyterian church--held a female slave, who had, for some years, supported a good character in a Baptist church of that city. He accused her of an attempt to poison his family, and immediately placed her in the hands of a slave-dealer, who took her over and imprisoned her in the slave-pen at Alexandria, to await the departure of a coffle. The poor girl had a mother, who felt as any mother would naturally feel.

When apprised of the situation of her daughter she flew to the pen, and, with tears, besought an interview with her only child; but she was cruelly repulsed, and told to be gone! She then tried to see the elder, but failed. She had the promise of money sufficient to purchase her daughter, but the owner would listen to no terms of compromise.

In her distress, the mother repaired to a lawyer in the city, and begged him to give form to her petition in writing. She stated to him what she wished to have said, and he arranged it for her in such a form as she herself might have presented it in, had not the benefits of education been denied her. The following is the letter:--

Washington, July 25, 1851.

SIR,--I address you as a rich Christian freeman and father, while I am myself but a poor slave-mother. I come to plead with you for an only child whom I love, who is a professor of the Christian religion with yourself, and a member of a Christian church; and who, by your act of ownership, now pines in her imprisonment in a loathsome man-warehouse, where she is held for sale. I come to plead with you for the exercise of that blessed law, "Whatsoever ye would that men should do unto you, do ye even so to them."

With great labour, I have found friends who are willing to aid me in the purchase of my child, to save us from a cruel separation. You, as a father, can judge of my feelings when I was told that you had decreed her banishment to distant as well as to hopeless bondage!

For nearly six years my child has done for you the hard labour of a slave; from the age of sixteen to twenty-two she has done the hard work of your chamber, kitchen, cellar, and stables. By night and by day, your will and your commands have been her highest law; and all this has been unrequited toil. If in all this time her scanty allowance of tea and coffee has been sweetened, it has been at the cost of her slave-mother, and not at yours.

You are an office-bearer in the church, and a man of prayer. As such, and as the absolute owner of my child, I ask candidly whether she has enjoyed such mild and gentle treatment, and amiable example, as she ought to have had, to encourage her in her monotonous bondage? Has she received at your hands, in faithful religious instruction in the Word of God, a full and fair compensation for all her toil? It is not to me alone that you must answer these questions. You acknowledge the high authority of His laws who preached a deliverance to the captive, and who commands you to give to your servant "that which is just and equal." Oh, I entreat you, withhold not, at this trying hour, from my child that which will cut off her last hope, and which may endanger your own soul!

It has been said that you charge my daughter with crime. Can this be really so? Can it be that you would set aside the obligations of honour and good citizenship --that you would dare to sell the guilty one away for money, rather than bring her to trial, which you know she is ready to meet? What would you say, if you were accused of guilt and refused a trial? Is not her fair name as precious to her, in the church to which she belongs, as yours can be to you?

Suppose, now, for a moment, that your daughter, whom you love, instead of mine, was in these hot days incarcerated in a negro-pen, subject to my control, fed on the coarsest food, committed to the entire will of a brute, denied the privilege commonly allowed even to the murderer--that of seeing the face of his friends? Oh, then you would FEEL!--feel soon, then, for a poor slave-mother and her child, and do for us as you shall wish you had done when we shall meet before the Great Judge, and when it shall be your greatest joy to say, "I did let the oppressed free!"

ELLEN BROWN. Mr.--

The girl, however, was sent off to the Southern market.

The writer has received these incidents from the gentleman who wrote the letter. Whether the course pursued by the master was strictly legal is a point upon which we are not entirely certain; that it was a course in which the law did not in fact interfere, is quite plain, and it is also very apparent that it was a course against which public sentiment did not remonstrate. The man who exercised this power was a professedly religious man, enjoying a position of importance in a Christian church; and it does not appear, from any movements in the Christian community about him, that they did not consider his course a justifiable one.

Yet is not this kind of power the very one at which we are so shocked when we see it exercised by foreign despots?

Do we not read with shuddering that in Russia, or in Austria, a man accused of crime is seized upon, separated from his friends, allowed no opportunities of trial or of self-defence, but hurried off to Siberia, or some other dreaded exile?

Why is despotism any worse in the governor of a State than in a private individual?

There is a great controversy now going on in the world between the despotic and the republican principle. All the common arguments used in support of slavery are arguments that apply with equal strength to despotic government, and there are some arguments in favour of despotic governments that do not apply to individual slavery. There are arguments, and quite plausible ones, in favour of despotic government. Nobody can deny that it possesses a certain kind of efficiency, compactness, and promptness of movement, which cannot, from the nature of things, belong to a republic. Despotism has established and sustained much more efficient systems of police than ever a republic did. The late King of Prussia, by the possession of absolute despotic power, was enabled to carry out a much more efficient system of popular education than we ever have succeeded in carrying out in America. He districted his kingdom in the most thorough manner, and obliged every parent, whether he would or not, to have his children thoroughly educated.

If we reply to all this, as we do, that the possession of absolute power in a man qualified to use it right is undoubtedly calculated for the good of the state, but that there are so few men that know how to use it, that this form of government is not, on the whole, a safe one, then we have stated an argument that goes to over-throw slavery as much as it does a despotic government; for certainly the chances are much greater of finding one man, in the course of fifty years, who is capable of wisely using this power, than of finding thousands of men every day in our streets, who can be trusted with such power. It is a painful and most serious fact, that America trusts to the hands of the most brutal men of her country, equally with the best, that despotic power which she thinks an unsafe thing even in the hands of the enlightened, educated, and cultivated Emperor of the Russias.

With all our republican prejudices, we cannot deny that Nicholas is a man of talent, with a mind liberalised by education; we have been informed, also, that he is a man of serious and religious character; he certainly, acting as he does in the eye of all the world, must have great restraint upon him from public opinion, and a high sense of character. But who is the man to whom American laws intrust powers more absolute than those of Nicholas of Russia, or Ferdinand of Naples? He may have been a pirate on the high seas; he may be a drunkard; he may, like Souther, have been convicted of a brutality at which humanity turns pale; but, for all that, American slave-law will none the less trust him with this irresponsible power,--power over the body, and power over the soul.

On which side, then, stands the American nation, in the great controversy which is now going on between self-government and despotism? On which side does America stand, in the great controversy for liberty of conscience?

Do foreign governments exclude their population from the reading of the Bible? The slave of America is excluded by the most effectual means possible. Do we say, "Ah! but we read the Bible to our slaves, and present the gospel orally?" This is precisely what religious despotism in Italy says. Do we say that we have no objection to our slaves reading the Bible, if they will stop there; but that with this there will come in a flood of general intelligence, which will upset the existing state of things? This is precisely what is said in Italy.

Do we say we should be willing that the slave should read his Bible, but that he, in his ignorance, will draw false and erroneous conclusions from it, and for that reason we prefer to impart its truths to him orally? This, also, is precisely what the religious despotism of Europe says.

Do we say in our vainglory that despotic government dreads the coming in of anything calculated to elevate and educate the people? And is there not the same dread through all the despotic slave governments of America?

On which side, then, does the American nation stand, in the great, last QUESTION of the age?

Kansas-Nebraska Act 1856

Section 14. That the Constitution and all the laws of the United States which are not locally inapplicable shall have the same force and effect within the said Territory of Nebraska (or Kansas, the language being the same in reference to both,) as elsewhere within the United States, except the 8th section of the act, preparatory to the admission of Missouri into the Union, approved March sixth, eighteen hundred and twenty, which, being inconsistent with the principles of non-intervention by Congress with slavery in the States and Territories, as recognized by the legislation of eighteen hundred and fifty, commonly called the compromise measures, is hereby declared inoperative and void; it being the true intent and meaning of this act not to legislate slavery into any Territory or State, nor to exclude it therefrom, but to leave the people thereof perfectly free to form and regulate their domestic institutions in their own way, subject only to the Constitution of the United States. Provided, That nothing herein contained shall be construed to revive or put in force any law or regulation which may have existed prior to the Act of 6th March, 1820, either protecting, establishing, prohibiting, or abolishing slavery.

Speech before the Republican State Convention

"House Divided"
by Abraham Lincoln
Springfield, June 16, 1858

Mr. President, and Gentlemen of the Convention:

If we could first know where we are, and whither we are tending, we could better judge what to do, and how to do it. We are now far into the fifth year, since a policy was initiated with the avowed object, and confident promise, of putting an end to slavery agitation. Under the operation of that policy, that agitation has not only not ceased, but has constantly augmented. In my opinion, it will not cease, until a crisis shall have been reached and passed. "A house divided against itself cannot stand." I believe this government cannot endure permanently half slave and half free. I do not expect the Union to be dissolved‹I do not expect the house to fall‹but I do expect it will cease to be divided. It will become all one thing, or all the other. Either the opponents of slavery will arrest the further spread of it, and place it where the public mind shall rest in the belief that it is in the course of ultimate extinction; or its advocates will push it forward, till it shall become alike lawful in all the States, old as well as new‹North as well as South.

Have we no tendency to the latter condition?

Let any one who doubts, carefully contemplate that now almost complete legal combination‹piece of machinery, so to speak‹compounded of the Nebraska doctrine, and the Dred Scott decision. Let him consider not only what work the machinery is adapted to do, and how well adapted; but also, let him study the history of its construction, and trace, if he can, or rather fail, if he can, to trace the evidences of design, and concert of action, among its chief architects, from the beginning.

The new year of 1854 found slavery excluded from more than half the States by State Constitutions, and from most of the national territory by Congressional prohibition. Four days later, commenced the struggle which ended in repealing that Congressional prohibition. This opened all the national territory to slavery, and was the first point gained.

But, so far, Congress only had acted; and an indorsement by the people, real or apparent, was indispensable, to save the point already gained, and give chance for more.

This necessity had not been overlooked; but had been provided for, as well as might be, in the notable argument of "squatter sovereignty," otherwise called "sacred right of self-government," which latter phrase, though expressive of the only rightful basis of any government, was so perverted in this attempted use of it as to amount to just this: That if any one man choose to enslave another, no third man shall be allowed to object. That argument was incorporated into the Nebraska bill itself, in the language which follows: "It being the true intent and meaning of this act not to legislate slavery into any Territory or State, nor to exclude it therefrom; but to leave the people thereof perfectly free to form and regulate their domestic institutions in their own way, subject only to the Constitution of the United States." Then opened the roar of loose declamation in favor of "Squatter Sovereignty," and "sacred right of self-government." "But," said opposition members, "let us amend the bill so as to expressly declare that the people of the Territory may exclude slavery." "Not we," said the friends of the measure; and down they voted the amendment.

While the Nebraska bill was passing through Congress, a law case involving the question of a negro's freedom, by reason of his owner having voluntarily taken him first into a free State and then into a Territory covered by the Congressional prohibition, and held him as a slave for a long time in each, was passing through the U. S. Circuit Court for the District of Missouri; and both Nebraska bill and law suit were brought to a decision in the same month of May, 1854. The negro's name was "Dred Scott," which name now designates the decision finally made in the case. Before the then next Presidential election, the law case came to, and was argued in, the Supreme Court of the United States; but the decision of it was deferred until after the election. Still, before the election, Senator Trumbull, on the floor of the Senate, requested the leading advocate of the Nebraska bill to state his opinion whether the people of a Territory can constitutionally exclude slavery from their limits; and the latter answers: "That is a question for the Supreme Court."

The election came. Mr. Buchanan was elected, and the indorsement, such as it was, secured. That was the second point gained. The indorsement, however, fell short of a clear popular majority by nearly four hundred thousand votes, and so, perhaps, was not overwhelmingly reliable and satisfactory. The outgoing President, in his last annual message, as impressively as possible echoed back upon the people the weight and authority of the indorsement. The Supreme Court met again; did not announce their decision, but ordered a re-argument. The Presidential inauguration came, and still no decision of the court; but the incoming President in his inaugural address, fervently exhorted the people to abide by the forthcoming decision, whatever it might be. Then, in a few days, came the decision.

The reputed author of the Nebraska bill finds an early occasion to make a speech at this capital indorsing the Dred Scott decision, and vehemently denouncing all opposition to it. The new President, too, seizes the early occasion of the Silliman letter to indorse and strongly construe that decision, and to express his astonishment that any different view had ever been entertained!

At length a squabble springs up between the President and the author of the Nebraska bill, on the mere question of fact, whether the Lecompton Constitution was or was not, in any just sense, made by the people of Kansas; and in that quarrel the latter declares that all he wants is a fair vote for the people, and that he cares not whether slavery be voted down or voted up. I do not understand his declaration that he cares not whether slavery be voted down or voted up, to be intended by him other than as an apt definition of the policy he would impress upon the public mind‹the principle for which he declares he has suffered so much, and is ready to suffer to the end. And well may he cling to that principle. If he has any parental feeling, well may he cling to it. That principle is the only shred left of his original Nebraska doctrine. Under the Dred Scott decision "squatter sovereignty" squatted out of existence, tumbled down like temporary scaffolding‹like the mould at the foundry served through one blast and fell back into loose sand‹helped to carry an election, and then was kicked to the winds. His late joint struggle with the Republicans, against the Lecompton Constitution, involves nothing of the original Nebraska doctrine. That struggle was made on a point‹the right of a people to make their own constitution‹upon which he and the Republicans have never differed.

The several points of the Dred Scott decision, in connection with Senator Douglas's "care not" policy, constitute the piece of machinery, in its present state of advancement. This was the third point gained. The working points of that machinery are:

First, That no negro slave, imported as such from Africa, and no descendant of such slave, can ever be a citizen of any State, in the sense of that term as used in the Constitution of the United States. This point is made in order to deprive the negro, in every possible event, of the benefit of that provision of the United States Constitution, which declares that "The citizens of each State shall be entitled to all privileges and immunities of citizens in the several States."

Secondly, That "subject to the Constitution of the United States," neither Congress nor a Territorial Legislature can exclude slavery from any United States territory. This point is made in order that individual men may fill up the Territories with slaves, without danger of losing them as property, and thus to enhance the chances of permanency to the institution through all the future.

Thirdly, That whether the holding a negro in actual slavery in a free State, makes him free, as against the holder, the United States courts will not decide, but will leave to be decided by the courts of any slave State the negro may be forced into by the master. This point is made, not to be pressed immediately; but, if acquiesced in for awhile, and apparently indorsed by the people at an election, then to sustain the logical conclusion that what Dred Scott's master might lawfully do with Dred Scott, in the free State of Illinois, every other master may lawfully do with any other one, or one thousand slaves, in Illinois, or in any other free State.

Auxiliary to all this, and working hand in hand with it, the Nebraska doctrine, or what is left of it, is to educate and mould public opinion, at least Northern public opinion, not to care whether slavery is voted down or voted up. This shows exactly where we now are; and partially, also, whither we are tending.

It will throw additional light on the latter, to go back, and run the mind over the string of historical facts already stated. Several things will now appear less dark and mysterious than they did when they were transpiring. The people were to be left "perfectly free," "subject only to the Constitution." What the Constitution had to do with it, outsiders could not then see. Plainly enough now, it was an exactly fitted niche, for the Dred Scott decision to afterward come in, and declare the perfect freedom of the people to be just no freedom at all. Why was the amendment, expressly declaring the right of the people, voted down? Plainly enough now: the adoption of it would have spoiled the niche for the Dred Scott decision. Why was the court decision held up? Why even a Senator's individual opinion withheld, till after the Presidential election? Plainly enough now: the speaking out then would have damaged the perfectly free argument upon which the election was to be carried. Why the outgoing President's felicitation on the indorsement? Why the delay of a reargument? Why the incoming President's advance exhortation in favor of the decision? These things look like the cautious patting and petting of a spirited horse, preparatory to mounting him, when it is dreaded that he may give the rider a fall. And why the hasty after indorsement of the decision by the President and others?

We cannot absolutely know that all these exact adaptations are the result of pre-concert. But when we see a lot of framed timbers, different portions of which we know have been gotten out at different times and places and by different workmen‹Stephen, Franklin, Roger and James, for instance‹and when we see these timbers joined together, and see they exactly make the frame of a house or a mill, all the tenons and mortices exactly fitting, and all the lengths and proportions of the different pieces exactly adapted to their respective places, and not a piece too many or too few‹not omitting even scaffolding‹or, if a single piece be lacking, we see the place in the frame exactly fitted and prepared yet to bring such a piece in‹in such a case, we find it impossible not to believe that Stephen and Franklin and Roger and James all understood one another from the beginning, and all worked upon a common plan or draft drawn up before the first blow was struck.

It should not be overlooked that, by the Nebraska bill, the people of a State as well as Territory, were to be left "perfectly free," "subject only to the Constitution." Why mention a State? They were legislating for Territories, and not for or about States. Certainly the people of a State are and ought to be subject to the Constitution of the United States; but why is mention of this lugged into this merely Territorial law? Why are the people of a Territory and the people of a State therein lumped together, and their relation to the Constitution therein treated as being precisely the same?

While the opinion of the court, by Chief Justice Taney, in the Dred Scott case, and the separate opinions of all the concurring Judges, expressly declare that the Constitution of the United States neither permits Congress nor a Territorial Legislature to exclude slavery from any United States

Territory, they all omit to declare whether or not the same Constitution permits a State, or the people of a State, to exclude it. Possibly, this is a mere omission; but who can be quite sure, if McLean or Curtis had sought to get into the opinion a declaration of unlimited power in the people of a State to exclude slavery from their limits, just as Chase and Mace sought to get such declaration, in behalf of the people of a Territory, into the Nebraska bill; I ask, who can be quite sure that it would not have been voted down in the one case as it had been in the other? The nearest approach to the point of declaring the power of a State over slavery, is made by Judge Nelson. He approaches it more than once, using the precise idea, and almost the language, too, of the Nebraska act. On one occasion, his exact language is, "except in cases where the power is restrained by the Constitution of the United States, the law of the State is supreme over the subject of slavery within its jurisdiction."

In what cases the power of the States is so restrained by the United States Constitution, is left an open question, precisely as the same question, as to the restraint on the power of the Territories, was left open in the Nebraska act. Put this and that together, and we have another nice little niche, which we may, ere long, see filled with another Supreme Court decision, declaring that the Constitution of the United States does not permit a State to exclude slavery from its limits. And this may especially be expected if the doctrine of "care not whether slavery be voted down or voted up," shall gain upon the public mind sufficiently to give promise that such a decision can be maintained when made.

Such a decision is all that slavery now lacks of being alike lawful in all the States. Welcome, or unwelcome, such decision is probably coming, and will soon be upon us, unless the power of the present political dynasty shall be met and overthrown. We shall lie down pleasantly dreaming that the people of Missouri are on the verge of making their State free, and we shall awake to the reality instead, that the Supreme Court has made Illinois a slave State. To meet and overthrow the power of that dynasty, is the work now before all those who would prevent that consummation. That is what we have to do. How can we best do it?

There are those who denounce us openly to their own friends, and yet whisper us softly, that Senator Douglas is the aptest instrument there is with which to effect that object. They do not tell us, nor has he told us, that he wishes any such object to be effected. They wish us to infer all, from the fact that he now has a little quarrel with the present head of the dynasty; and that he has regularly voted with us on a single point, upon which he and we have never differed.

They remind us that he is a great man, and that the largest of us are very small ones. Let this be granted. But "a living dog is better than a dead lion." Judge Douglas, if not a dead lion, for this work, is at least a caged and toothless one. How can he oppose the advances of slavery? He don't care anything about it. His avowed mission is impressing the "public heart" to care nothing about it.

A leading Douglas democratic newspaper thinks Douglas's superior talent will be needed to resist the revival of the African slave trade. Does Douglas believe an effort to revive that trade is approaching? He has not said so. Does he really think so? But if it is, how can he resist it? For years he has labored to prove it a sacred right of white men to take negro slaves into the new Territories. Can he possibly show that it is less a sacred right to buy them where they can be bought cheapest? And unquestionably they can be bought cheaper in Africa than in Virginia. He

231

has done all in his power to reduce the whole question of slavery to one of a mere right of property; and as such, how can he oppose the foreign slave trade‹how can he refuse that trade in that "property" shall be "perfectly free"‹unless he does it as a protection to the home production? And as the home producers will probably not ask the protection, he will be wholly without a ground of opposition.

Senator Douglas holds, we know, that a man may rightfully be wiser to-day than he was yesterday‹that he may rightfully change when he finds himself wrong. But can we, for that reason, run ahead, and infer that he will make any particular change, of which he, himself, has given no intimation? Can we safely base our action upon any such vague inference? Now, as ever, I wish not to misrepresent Judge Douglas's position, question his motives, or do aught that can be personally offensive to him. Whenever, if ever, he and we can come together on principle so that our cause may have assistance from his great ability, I hope to have interposed no adventitious obstacle. But clearly, he is not now with us‹he does not pretend to be‹he does not promise ever to be.

Our cause, then, must be intrusted to, and conducted by, its own undoubted friends‹those whose hands are free, whose hearts are in the work‹who do care for the result. Two years ago the Republicans of the nation mustered over thirteen hundred thousand strong. We did this under the single impulse of resistance to a common danger, with every external circumstance against us. Of strange, discordant, and even hostile elements, we gathered from the four winds, and formed and fought the battle through, under the constant hot fire of a disciplined, proud and pampered enemy. Did we brave all then, to falter now?‹now, when that same enemy is wavering, dissevered and belligerent? The result is not doubtful. We shall not fail‹if we stand firm, we shall not fail. Wise counsels may accelerate, or mistakes delay it, but, sooner or later, the victory is sure to come

Abraham Lincoln's The Gettysburg Address

Four score and seven years ago our fathers brought forth on this continent a new nation, conceived in liberty and dedicated to the proposition that all men are created equal. Now we are engaged in a great civil war, testing whether that nation or any nation so conceived and so dedicated can long endure. We are met on a great battlefield of that war. We have come to dedicate a portion of that field as a final resting-place for those who here gave their lives that that nation might live. It is altogether fitting and proper that we should do this. But in a larger sense, we cannot dedicate, we cannot consecrate, we cannot hallow this ground. The brave men, living and dead who struggled here have consecrated it far above our poor power to add or detract. The world will little note nor long remember what we say here, but it can never forget what they did here. It is for us the living rather to be dedicated here to the unfinished work which they who fought here have thus far so nobly advanced. It is rather for us to be here dedicated to the great task remaining before us --that from these honored dead we take increased devotion to that cause for which they gave the last full measure of devotion-- that we here highly resolve that these dead shall not have died in vain, that this nation under God shall have a new birth of freedom, and that government of the people, by the people, for the people shall not perish from the earth.

The Emancipation Proclamation

A Proclamation by the President of the United States of America:

Whereas on the 22nd day of September, A.D. 1862, a proclamation was issued by the President of the United States, containing, among other things, the following, to wit:

"That on the 1st day of January, A.D. 1863, all persons held as slaves within any State or designated part of a State the people whereof shall then be in rebellion against the United States shall be then, thenceforward, and forever free; and the executive government of the United States, including the military and naval authority thereof, will recognize and maintain the freedom of such persons and will do no act or acts to repress such persons, or any of them, in any efforts they may make for their actual freedom.

"That the executive will on the 1st day of January aforesaid, by proclamation, designate the States and parts of States, if any, in which the people thereof, respectively, shall then be in rebellion against the United States; and the fact that any State or the people thereof shall on that day be in good faith represented in the Congress of the United States by members chosen thereto at elections wherein a majority of the qualified voters of such States shall have participated shall, in the absence of strong countervailing testimony, be deemed conclusive evidence that such State and the people thereof are not then in rebellion against the United States."

Now, therefore, I, Abraham Lincoln, President of the United States, by virtue of the power in me vested as Commander-In-Chief of the Army and Navy of the United States in time of actual armed rebellion against the authority and government of the United States, and as a fit and necessary war measure for suppressing said rebellion, do, on this 1st day of January, A.D. 1863, and in accordance with my purpose so to do, publicly proclaimed for the full period of one hundred days from the first day above mentioned, order and designate as the States and parts of States wherein the people thereof, respectively, are this day in rebellion against the United States the following, to wit:

Arkansas, Texas, Louisiana (except the parishes of St. Bernard, Palquemines, Jefferson, St. John, St. Charles, St. James, Ascension, Assumption, Terrebone, Lafourche, St. Mary, St. Martin, and Orleans, including the city of New Orleans), Mississippi, Alabama, Florida, Georgia, South Carolina, North Carolina, and Virginia (except the forty-eight counties designated as West Virginia, and also the counties of Berkeley, Accomac, Morthhampton, Elizabeth City, York, Princess Anne, and Norfolk, including the cities of Norfolk and Portsmouth), and which excepted parts are for the present left precisely as if this proclamation were not issued.

And by virtue of the power and for the purpose aforesaid, I do order and declare that all persons held as slaves within said designated States and parts of States are, and henceforward shall be, free; and that the Executive Government of the United States, including the military and naval authorities thereof, will recognize and maintain the freedom of said persons.

And I hereby enjoin upon the people so declared to be free to abstain from all violence, unless in necessary self-defence; and I recommend to them that, in all case when allowed, they labor faithfully for reasonable wages.

And I further declare and make known that such persons of suitable condition will be received into the armed service of the United States to garrison forts, positions, stations, and other places, and to man vessels of all sorts in said service.

And upon this act, sincerely believed to be an act of justice, warranted by the Constitution upon military necessity, I invoke the considerate judgment of mankind and the gracious favor of Almighty God.

On Women's Right to Vote

Friends and fellow citizens:

I stand before you tonight under indictment for the alleged crime of having voted at the last presidential election, without having a lawful right to vote. It shall be my work this evening to prove to you that in thus voting, I not only committed no crime, but, instead, simply exercised my citizen's rights, guaranteed to me and all United States citizens by the National Constitution, beyond the power of any state to deny.

The preamble of the Federal Constitution says:

> "We, the people of the United States, in order to form a more perfect union, establish justice, insure domestic tranquillity, provide for the common defense, promote the general welfare, and secure the blessings of liberty to ourselves and our posterity, do ordain and establish this Constitution for the United States of America."

It was we, the people; not we, the white male citizens; nor yet we, the male citizens; but we, the whole people, who formed the Union. And we formed it, not to give the blessings of liberty, but to secure them; not to the half of ourselves and the half of our posterity, but to the whole people - women as well as men. And it is a downright mockery to talk to women of their enjoyment of the blessings of liberty while they are denied the use of the only means of securing them provided by this democratic-republican government - the ballot.

For any state to make sex a qualification that must ever result in the disfranchisement of one entire half of the people, is to pass a bill of attainder, or, an ex post facto law, and is therefore a violation of the supreme law of the land. By it the blessings of liberty are forever withheld from women and their female posterity.

To them this government has no just powers derived from the consent of the governed. To them this government is not a democracy. It is not a republic. It is an odious aristocracy; a hateful oligarchy of sex; the most hateful aristocracy ever established on the face of the globe; an oligarchy of wealth, where the rich govern the poor. An oligarchy of learning, where the educated govern the ignorant, or even an oligarchy of race, where the Saxon rules the African, might be endured; but this oligarchy of sex, which makes father, brothers, husband, sons, the oligarchs over the mother and sisters, the wife and daughters, of every household - which ordains all men sovereigns, all women subjects, carries dissension, discord, and rebellion into every home of the nation.

Webster, Worcester, and Bouvier all define a citizen to be a person in the United States, entitled to vote and hold office.

The only question left to be settled now is: Are women persons? And I hardly believe any of our opponents will have the hardihood to say they are not. Being persons, then, women are citizens; and no state has a right to make any law, or to enforce any old law, that shall abridge their privileges or immunities. Hence, every discrimination against women in the constitutions and laws of the several states is today null and void, precisely as is every one against Negroes.

Susan B. Anthony - 1873

First Inaugural Address
Franklin D. Roosevelt
March 4, 1933

I am certain that my fellow Americans expect that on my induction into the Presidency I will address them with a candor and a decision which the present situation of our Nation impels. This is preeminently the time to speak the truth, the whole truth, frankly and boldly. Nor need we shrink from honestly facing conditions in our country today. This great Nation will endure as it has endured, will revive and will prosper. So, first of all, let me assert my firm belief that the only thing we have to fear is fear itself‹nameless, unreasoning, unjustified terror which paralyzes needed efforts to convert retreat into advance. In every dark hour of our national life a leadership of frankness and vigor has met with that understanding and support of the people themselves which is essential to victory. I am convinced that you will again give that support to leadership in these critical days.

In such a spirit on my part and on yours we face our common difficulties. They concern, thank God, only material things. Values have shrunken to fantastic levels; taxes have risen; our ability to pay has fallen; government of all kinds is faced by serious curtailment of income; the means of exchange are frozen in the currents of trade; the withered leaves of industrial enterprise lie on every side; farmers find no markets for their produce; the savings of many years in thousands of families are gone.

More important, a host of unemployed citizens face the grim problem of existence, and an equally great number toil with little return. Only a foolish optimist can deny the dark realities of the moment.

Yet our distress comes from no failure of substance. We are stricken by no plague of locusts. Compared with the perils which our forefathers conquered because they believed and were not afraid, we have still much to be thankful for. Nature still offers her bounty and human efforts have multiplied it. Plenty is at our doorstep, but a generous use of it languishes in the very sight of the supply. Primarily this is because the rulers of the exchange of mankind's goods have failed, through their own stubbornness and their own incompetence, have admitted their failure, and abdicated. Practices of the unscrupulous money changers stand indicted in the court of public opinion, rejected by the hearts and minds of men.

True they have tried, but their efforts have been cast in the pattern of an outworn tradition. Faced by failure of credit they have proposed only the lending of more money. Stripped of the lure of profit by which to induce our people to follow their false leadership, they have resorted to exhortations, pleading tearfully for restored confidence. They know only the rules of a generation of self-seekers. They have no vision, and when there is no vision the people perish.

The money changers have fled from their high seats in the temple of our civilization. We may now restore that temple to the ancient truths. The measure of the restoration lies in the extent to which we apply social values more noble than mere monetary profit.

Happiness lies not in the mere possession of money; it lies in the joy of achievement, in the thrill of creative effort. The joy and moral stimulation of work no longer must be forgotten in the mad chase of evanescent profits. These dark days will be worth all they cost us if they teach us that our true destiny is not to be ministered unto but to minister to ourselves and to our fellow men.

Recognition of the falsity of material wealth as the standard of success goes hand in hand with the abandonment of the false belief that public office and high political position are to be valued only by the standards of pride of place and personal profit; and there must be an end to a conduct in banking and in business which too often has given to a sacred trust the likeness of callous and selfish wrongdoing. Small wonder that confidence languishes, for it thrives only on honesty, on honor, on the sacredness of obligations, on faithful protection, on unselfish performance; without them it cannot live.

Restoration calls, however, not for changes in ethics alone. This Nation asks for action, and action now.

Our greatest primary task is to put people to work. This is no unsolvable problem if we face it wisely and courageously. It can be accomplished in part by direct recruiting by the Government itself, treating the task as we would treat the emergency of a war, but at the same time, through this employment, accomplishing greatly needed projects to stimulate and reorganize the use of our natural resources.

Hand in hand with this we must frankly recognize the overbalance of population in our industrial centers and, by engaging on a national scale in a redistribution, endeavor to provide a better use of the land for those best fitted for the land. The task can be helped by definite efforts to raise the values of agricultural products and with this the power to purchase the output of our cities. It can be helped by preventing realistically the tragedy of the growing loss through foreclosure of our small homes and our farms. It can be helped by insistence that the Federal, State, and local governments act forthwith on the demand that their cost be drastically reduced. It can be helped by the unifying of relief activities which today are often scattered, uneconomical, and unequal. It can be helped by national planning for and supervision of all forms of transportation and of communications and other utilities which have a definitely public character. There are many ways in which it can be helped, but it can never be helped merely by talking about it. We must act and act quickly.

Finally, in our progress toward a resumption of work we require two safeguards against a return of the evils of the old order; there must be a strict supervision of all banking and credits and investments; there must be an end to speculation with other people's money, and there must be provision for an adequate but sound currency.

There are the lines of attack. I shall presently urge upon a new Congress in special session detailed measures for their fulfillment, and I shall seek the immediate assistance of the several States.

Through this program of action we address ourselves to putting our own national house in order and making income balance outgo. Our international trade relations, though vastly important, are in point of time and necessity secondary to the establishment of a sound national economy. I favor as a practical policy the putting of first things first. I shall spare no effort to restore world trade by international economic readjustment, but the emergency at home cannot wait on that accomplishment.

The basic thought that guides these specific means of national recovery is not narrowly nationalistic. It is the insistence, as a first consideration, upon the interdependence of the various elements in all parts of the United States' recognition of the old and permanently important manifestation of the American spirit of the pioneer. It is the way to recovery. It is the immediate way. It is the strongest assurance that the recovery will endure.

In the field of world policy I would dedicate this Nation to the policy of the good neighbor‹the neighbor who resolutely respects himself and, because he does so, respects the rights of others‹the neighbor who respects his obligations and respects the sanctity of his agreements in and with a world of neighbors.

If I read the temper of our people correctly, we now realize as we have never realized before our interdependence on each other; that we can not merely take but we must give as well; that if we are to go forward, we must move as a trained and loyal army willing to sacrifice for the good of a common discipline, because without such discipline no progress is made, no leadership becomes effective. We are, I know, ready and willing to submit our lives and property to such discipline, because it makes possible a leadership which aims at a larger good. This I propose to offer, pledging that the larger purposes will bind upon us all as a sacred obligation with a unity of duty hitherto evoked only in time of armed strife.

With this pledge taken, I assume unhesitatingly the leadership of this great army of our people dedicated to a disciplined attack upon our common problems.

Action in this image and to this end is feasible under the form of government which we have inherited from our ancestors. Our Constitution is so simple and practical that it is possible always to meet extraordinary needs by changes in emphasis and arrangement without loss of essential form. That is why our constitutional system has proved itself the most superbly enduring political mechanism the modern world has produced. It has met every stress of vast expansion of territory, of foreign wars, of bitter internal strife, of world relations.

It is to be hoped that the normal balance of executive and legislative authority may be wholly adequate to meet the unprecedented task before us. But it may be that an unprecedented demand and need for undelayed action may call for temporary departure from that normal balance of public procedure.

I am prepared under my constitutional duty to recommend the measures that a stricken nation in the midst of a stricken world may require. These measures, or such other measures as the Congress may build out of its experience and wisdom, I shall seek, within my constitutional authority, to bring to speedy adoption.

But in the event that the Congress shall fail to take one of these two courses, and in the event that the national emergency is still critical, I shall not evade the clear course of duty that will then confront me. I shall ask the Congress for the one remaining instrument to meet the crisis‹broad Executive power to wage a war against the emergency, as great as the power that would be given to me if we were in fact invaded by a foreign foe.

For the trust reposed in me I will return the courage and the devotion that befit the time. I can do no less.

We face the arduous days that lie before us in the warm courage of the national unity; with the clear consciousness of seeking old and precious moral values; with the clean satisfaction that comes from the stern performance of duty by old and young alike. We aim at the assurance of a rounded and permanent national life.

We do not distrust the future of essential democracy. The people of the United States have not failed. In their need they have registered a mandate that they want direct, vigorous action. They have asked for discipline and direction under leadership. They have made me the present instrument of their wishes. In the spirit of the gift I take it.

In this dedication of a Nation we humbly ask the blessing of God. May He protect each and every one of us. May He guide me in the days to come.

Roosevelt's Pearl Harbor Speech to Congress

Mr. Vice President, Mr. Speaker, members of the Senate and the House of Representatives:

Yesterday, December 7, 1941 - a date which will live in infamy - the United States of America was suddenly and deliberately attacked by naval and air forces of the Empire of Japan.

The United States was at peace with that nation, and, at the solicitation of Japan, was still in conversation with its government and its Emperor looking toward the maintenance of peace in the Pacific.

Indeed, one hour after Japanese air squadrons had commenced bombing in the American island of Oahu, the Japanese Ambassador to the United States and his colleague delivered to our Secretary of State a formal reply to a recent American message. And, while this reply stated that it seemed useless to continue the existing diplomatic negotiations, it contained no threat or hint of war or of armed attack.

It will be recorded that the distance of Hawaii from Japan makes it obvious that the attack was deliberately planned many days or even weeks ago. During the intervening time the Japanese Government has deliberately sought to deceive the United States by false statements and expressions of hope for continued peace.

The attack yesterday on the Hawaiian Islands has caused severe damage to American naval and military forces. I regret to tell you that very many American lives have been lost. In addition, American ships have been reported torpedoed on the high seas between San Francisco and Honolulu.

Yesterday the Japanese Government also launched an attack against Malaya.
Last night Japanese forces attacked Hong Kong.
Last night Japanese forces attacked Guam.
Last night Japanese forces attacked the Philippine Islands.
Last night the Japanese attacked Wake Island.
And this morning the Japanese attacked Midway Island.

Japan has therefore undertaken a surprise offensive extending throughout the Pacific area. The facts of yesterday and today speak for themselves. The people of the United States have already formed their opinions and well understand the implications to the very life and safety of our nation.

As Commander-in-Chief of the Army and Navy I have directed that all measures be taken for our defense, that always will our whole nation remember the character of the onslaught against us.

No matter how long it may take us to overcome this premeditated invasion, the American people, in their righteous might, will win through to absolute victory.

I believe that I interpret the will of the Congress and of the people when I assert that we will not only defend ourselves to the uttermost but will make it very certain that this form of treachery shall never again endanger us.

Hostilities exist. There is no blinking at the fact that our people, our territory and our interests are in grave danger.

With confidence in our armed forces, with the unbounding determination of our people, we will gain the inevitable triumph. So help us God.

I ask that the Congress declare that since the unprovoked and dastardly attack by Japan on Sunday, December 7, 1941, a state of war has existed between the United States and the Japanese Empire.

Franklin D. Roosevelt - December 8, 1941

Roosevelt's D-Day Prayer

My Fellow Americans:

Last night, when I spoke with you about the fall of Rome, I knew at that moment that troops of the United States and our Allies were crossing the Channel in another and greater operation. It has come to pass with success thus far.

And so, in this poignant hour, I ask you to join with me in prayer:

Almighty God: Our sons, pride of our nation, this day have set upon a mighty endeavor, a struggle to preserve our Republic, our religion, and our civilization, and to set free a suffering humanity.

Lead them straight and true; give strength to their arms, stoutness to their hearts, steadfastness in their faith.

They will need Thy blessings. Their road will be long and hard. For the enemy is strong. He may hurl back our forces. Success may not come with rushing speed, but we shall return again and again; and we know that by Thy grace, and by the righteousness of our cause, our sons will triumph.

They will be sore tried, by night and by day, without rest -- until the victory is won. The darkness will be rent by noise and flame. Men's souls will be shaken with the violences of war.

For these men are lately drawn from the ways of peace. They fight not for the lust of conquest. They fight to end conquest. They fight to liberate. They fight to let justice arise, and tolerance and goodwill among all Thy people. They yearn but for the end of battle, for their return to the haven of home.

Some will never return. Embrace these, Father, and receive them, Thy heroic servants, into Thy kingdom.

And for us at home -- fathers, mothers, children, wives, sisters, and brothers of brave men overseas, whose thoughts and prayers are ever with them -- help us, Almighty God, to rededicate ourselves in renewed faith in Thee in this hour of great sacrifice.

Many people have urged that I call the nation into a single day of special prayer. But because the road is long and the desire is great, I ask that our people devote themselves in a continuance of prayer. As we rise to each new day, and again when each day is spent, let words of prayer be on our lips, invoking Thy help to our efforts.

Give us strength, too -- strength in our daily tasks, to redouble the contributions we make in the physical and the material support of our armed forces.

And let our hearts be stout, to wait out the long travail, to bear sorrows that may come, to impart our courage unto our sons wheresoever they may be.

And, O Lord, give us faith. Give us faith in Thee; faith in our sons; faith in each other; faith in our united crusade. Let not the keeness of our spirit ever be dulled. Let not the impacts of temporary events, of temporal matters of but fleeting moment -- let not these deter us in our unconquerable purpose.

With Thy blessing, we shall prevail over the unholy forces of our enemy. Help us to conquer the apostles of greed and racial arrogances. Lead us to the saving of our country, and with our sister nations into a world unity that will spell a sure peace -- a peace invulnerable to the schemings of unworthy men. And a peace that will let all of men live in freedom, reaping the just rewards of their honest toil.

Thy will be done, Almighty God.

Amen.

Franklin D. Roosevelt - June 6, 1944

Brown v. Board of Education

May 17, 1954

BROWN ET AL. v. BOARD OF EDUCATION OF TOPEKA ET AL. APPEAL FROM THE

UNITED STATES DISTRICT COURT FOR THE DISTRICT OF KANSAS

Syllabus

Segregation of white and Negro children in the public schools of a State solely on the basis of race, pursuant to state laws permitting or requiring such segregation, denies to Negro children the equal protection of the laws guaranteed by the Fourteenth Amendment -- even though the physical facilities and other "tangible" factors of white and Negro schools may be equal.

- (a) The history of the Fourteenth Amendment is inconclusive as to its intended effect on public education.
- (b) The question presented in these cases must be determined not on the basis of conditions existing when the Fourteenth Amendment was adopted, but in the light of the full development of public education and its present place in American life throughout the Nation.
- (c) Where a State has undertaken to provide an opportunity for an education in its public schools, such an opportunity is a right which must be made available to all on equal terms.
- (d) Segregation of children in public schools solely on the basis of race deprives children of the minority group of equal educational opportunities, even though the physical facilities and other "tangible" factors may be equal.
- (e) The "separate but equal" doctrine adopted in *Plessy v. Ferguson*, has no place in the field of public education.
- (f) The cases are restored to the docket for further argument on specified questions relating to the forms of the decrees.

OPINION OF THE COURT
delivered by Mr. Chief Justice Warren

These cases come to us from the States of Kansas, South Carolina, Virginia, and Delaware. They are premised on different facts and different local conditions, but a common legal question justifies their consideration together in this consolidated opinion [347 U.S. 483, 487].

In each of the cases, minors of the Negro race, through their legal representatives, seek the aid of the courts in obtaining admission to the public schools of their community on a nonsegregated basis. In each instance, [347 U.S. 483, 488] they had been denied admission to schools attended by white children under laws requiring or permitting segregation according to race. This segregation was alleged to deprive the plaintiffs of the equal protection of the laws under the Fourteenth Amendment. In each of the cases other than the Delaware case, a three-judge federal district court denied relief to the plaintiffs on the so-called "separate but equal" doctrine announced by this Court in Plessy v. Ferguson. Under that doctrine, equality of treatment is accorded when the races are provided substantially equal facilities, even though these facilities be separate. In the Delaware case, the Supreme Court of Delaware adhered to that doctrine, but ordered that the plaintiffs be admitted to the white schools because of their superiority to the Negro schools.

The plaintiffs contend that segregated public schools are not "equal" and cannot be made "equal," and that hence they are deprived of the equal protection of the laws. Because of the obvious importance of the question presented, the Court took jurisdiction. Argument was heard in the 1952 Term, and reargument was heard this Term on certain questions propounded by the Court [347 U.S. 483, 489].

Reargument was largely devoted to the circumstances surrounding the adoption of the Fourteenth Amendment in 1868. It covered exhaustively consideration of the Amendment in Congress, ratification by the states, then existing practices in racial segregation, and the views of proponents and opponents of the Amendment. This discussion and our own investigation convince us that, although these sources cast some light, it is not enough to resolve the problem with which we are faced. At best, they are inconclusive. The most avid proponents of the post-War Amendments undoubtedly intended them to remove all legal distinctions among "all persons born or naturalized in the United States." Their opponents, just as certainly, were antagonistic to both the letter and the spirit of the Amendments and wished them to have the most limited effect. What others in Congress and the state legislatures had in mind cannot be determined with any degree of certainty.

An additional reason for the inconclusive nature of the Amendment's history, with respect to segregated schools, is the status of public education at that time. In the South, the movement toward free common schools, supported [347 U.S. 483, 490] by general taxation, had not yet taken hold. Education of white children was largely in the hands of private groups. Education of Negroes was almost nonexistent, and practically all of the race were illiterate. In fact, any education of Negroes was forbidden by law in some states. Today, in contrast, many Negroes have achieved outstanding success in the arts and sciences as well as in the business and professional world. It is true that public school education at the time of the Amendment had advanced further in the North, but the effect of the Amendment on Northern States was generally ignored in the congressional debates. Even in the North, the conditions of public education did not approximate those existing today. The curriculum was usually rudimentary; ungraded schools were common in rural areas; the school term was but three months a year in many states; and compulsory school attendance was virtually unknown. As a consequence, it is not surprising that there should be so little in the history of the Fourteenth Amendment relating to its intended effect on public education.

In the first cases in this Court construing the Fourteenth Amendment, decided shortly after its adoption, the Court interpreted it as proscribing all state-imposed discriminations against the

Negro race. The doctrine of [347 U.S. 483, 491] "separate but equal" did not make its appearance in this Court until 1896 in the case of Plessy v. Ferguson, supra, involving not education but transportation. American courts have since labored with the doctrine for over half a century. In this Court, there have been six cases involving the "separate but equal" doctrine in the field of public education. In Cumming v. County Board of Education, and Gong Lum v. Rice, the validity of the doctrine itself was not challenged. In more recent cases, all on the graduate school [347 U.S. 483, 492] level, inequality was found in that specific benefits enjoyed by white students were denied to Negro students of the same educational qualifications. Missouri ex rel. Gaines v. Canada, Sipuel v. Oklahoma, Sweatt v. Painter, McLaurin v. Oklahoma State Regents. In none of these cases was it necessary to re-examine the doctrine to grant relief to the Negro plaintiff. And in Sweatt v. Painter, supra, the Court expressly reserved decision on the question whether Plessy v. Ferguson should be held inapplicable to public education.

In the instant cases, that question is directly presented. Here, unlike Sweatt v. Painter, there are findings below that the Negro and white schools involved have been equalized, or are being equalized, with respect to buildings, curricula, qualifications and salaries of teachers, and other "tangible" factors. Our decision, therefore, cannot turn on merely a comparison of these tangible factors in the Negro and white schools involved in each of the cases. We must look instead to the effect of segregation itself on public education.

In approaching this problem, we cannot turn the clock back to 1868 when the Amendment was adopted, or even to 1896 when Plessy v. Ferguson was written. We must consider public education in the light of its full development and its present place in American life throughout [347 U.S. 483, 493] the Nation. Only in this way can it be determined if segregation in public schools deprives these plaintiffs of the equal protection of the laws.

Today, education is perhaps the most important function of state and local governments. Compulsory school attendance laws and the great expenditures for education both demonstrate our recognition of the importance of education to our democratic society. It is required in the performance of our most basic public responsibilities, even service in the armed forces. It is the very foundation of good citizenship. Today it is a principal instrument in awakening the child to cultural values, in preparing him for later professional training, and in helping him to adjust normally to his environment. In these days, it is doubtful that any child may reasonably be expected to succeed in life if he is denied the opportunity of an education. Such an opportunity, where the state has undertaken to provide it, is a right which must be made available to all on equal terms.

We come then to the question presented: Does segregation of children in public schools solely on the basis of race, even though the physical facilities and other "tangible" factors may be equal, deprive the children of the minority group of equal educational opportunities? We believe that it does.

In Sweatt v. Painter, supra, in finding that a segregated law school for Negroes could not provide them equal educational opportunities, this Court relied in large part on "those qualities which are incapable of objective measurement but which make for greatness in a law school." In McLaurin v. Oklahoma State Regents, supra, the Court, in requiring that a Negro admitted to a white graduate school be treated like all other students, again resorted to intangible considerations: ". . .

his ability to study, to engage in discussions and exchange views with other students, and, in general, to learn his profession." [347 U.S. 483, 494] Such considerations apply with added force to children in grade and high schools. To separate them from others of similar age and qualifications solely because of their race generates a feeling of inferiority as to their status in the community that may affect their hearts and minds in a way unlikely ever to be undone. The effect of this separation on their educational opportunities was well stated by a finding in the Kansas case by a court which nevertheless felt compelled to rule against the Negro plaintiffs:

"Segregation of white and colored children in public schools has a detrimental effect upon the colored children. The impact is greater when it has the sanction of the law; for the policy of separating the races is usually interpreted as denoting the inferiority of the negro group. A sense of inferiority affects the motivation of a child to learn. Segregation with the sanction of law, therefore, has a tendency to [retard] the educational and mental development of negro children and to deprive them of some of the benefits they would receive in a racial[ly] integrated school system."

Whatever may have been the extent of psychological knowledge at the time of Plessy v. Ferguson, this finding is amply supported by modern authority. Any language [347 U.S. 483, 495] in Plessy v. Ferguson contrary to this finding is rejected.

We conclude that in the field of public education the doctrine of "separate but equal" has no place. Separate educational facilities are inherently unequal. Therefore, we hold that the plaintiffs and others similarly situated for whom the actions have been brought are, by reason of the segregation complained of, deprived of the equal protection of the laws guaranteed by the Fourteenth Amendment. This disposition makes unnecessary any discussion whether such segregation also violates the Due Process Clause of the Fourteenth Amendment.

Because these are class actions, because of the wide applicability of this decision, and because of the great variety of local conditions, the formulation of decrees in these cases presents problems of considerable complexity. On reargument, the consideration of appropriate relief was necessarily subordinated to the primary question - the constitutionality of segregation in public education. We have now announced that such segregation is a denial of the equal protection of the laws. In order that we may have the full assistance of the parties in formulating decrees, the cases will be restored to the docket, and the parties are requested to present further argument on Questions 4 and 5 previously propounded by the Court for the reargument this Term. The Attorney General [347 U.S. 483, 496] of the United States is again invited to participate. The Attorneys General of the states requiring or permitting segregation in public education will also be permitted to appear as amici curiae upon request to do so by September 15, 1954, and submission of briefs by October 1, 1954.

IT IS SO ORDERED

President Kennedy's Inaugural Address
1961

Vice President Johnson, Mr. Speaker, Mr. Chief Justice, President Eisenhower, Vice President Nixon, President Truman, reverend clergy, fellow citizens, we observe today not a victory of party, but a celebration of freedom -- symbolizing an end, as well as a beginning -- signifying renewal, as well as change. For I have sworn before you and Almighty God the same solemn oath our forebears prescribed nearly a century and three quarters ago.

The world is very different now. For man holds in his mortal hands the power to abolish all forms of human poverty and all forms of human life. And yet the same revolutionary beliefs for which our forebears fought are still at issue around the globe -- the belief that the rights of man come not from the generosity of the state, but from the hand of God.

We dare not forget today that we are the heirs of that first revolution. Let the word go forth from this time and place, to friend and foe alike, that the torch has been passed to a new generation of Americans, born in this century, tempered by war, disciplined by a hard and bitter peace, proud of our ancient heritage and unwilling to witness or permit the slow undoing of those human rights to which this Nation has always been committed, and to which we are committed today at home and around the world.

Let every nation know, whether it wishes us well or ill, that we shall pay any price, bear any burden, meet any hardship, support any friend, oppose any foe, to assure the survival and the success of liberty.

This much we pledge and more.

To those old allies whose cultural and spiritual origins we share, we pledge the loyalty of faithful friends. United, there is little we cannot do in a host of cooperative ventures. Divided, there is little we can do -- for we dare not meet a powerful challenge at odds and split asunder.

To those new States whom we welcome to the ranks of the free, we pledge our word that one form of colonial control shall not have passed away merely to be replaced by a far more iron tyranny. We shall not always expect to find them supporting our view. But we shall always hope to find them strongly supporting their own freedom -- and to remember that, in the past, those who foolishly sought power by riding the back of the tiger ended up inside.

To those peoples in the huts and villages across the globe struggling to break the bonds of mass misery, we pledge our best efforts to help them help themselves, for whatever period is required, not because the Communists may be doing it, not because we seek their votes, but because it is right. If a free society cannot help the many who are poor, it cannot save the few who are rich.

To our sister republics south of our border, we offer a special pledge -- to convert our good words into good deeds in a new alliance for progress -- to assist free men and free governments in casting off the chains of poverty. But this peaceful revolution of hope cannot become the prey of hostile powers. Let all our neighbors know that we shall join with them to oppose aggression or subversion anywhere in the Americas. And let every other power know that this Hemisphere intends to remain the master of its own house.

To that world assembly of sovereign states, the United Nations, our last best hope in an age where the instruments of war have far outpaced the instruments of peace, we renew our pledge of support -- to prevent it from becoming merely a forum for invective -- to strengthen its shield of the new and the weak and to enlarge the area in which its writ may run.

Finally, to those nations who would make themselves our adversary, we offer not a pledge but a request -- that both sides begin anew the quest for peace, before the dark powers of destruction unleashed by science engulf all humanity in planned or accidental self-destruction.

We dare not tempt them with weakness. For only when our arms are sufficient beyond doubt can we be certain beyond doubt that they will never be employed.

But neither can two great and powerful groups of nations take comfort from our present course -- both sides overburdened by the cost of modern weapons, both rightly alarmed by the steady spread of the deadly atom, yet both racing to alter that uncertain balance of terror that stays the hand of mankind's final war.

So let us begin anew, remembering on both sides that civility is not a sign of weakness, and sincerity is always subject to proof. Let us never negotiate out of fear. But let us never fear to negotiate.

Let both sides explore what problems unite us instead of belaboring those problems which divide us.

Let both sides, for the first time, formulate serious and precise proposals for the inspection and control of arms and bring the absolute power to destroy other nations under the absolute control of all nations.

Let both sides seek to invoke the wonders of science instead of its terrors. Together let us explore the stars, conquer the deserts, eradicate disease, tap the ocean depths, and encourage the arts and commerce.

Let both sides unite to heed in all corners of the earth the command of Isaiah -- to "undo the heavy burdens...and let the oppressed go free."

And if a beachhead of cooperation may push back the jungle of suspicion, let both sides join in creating a new endeavor, not a new balance of power, but a new world of law, where the strong are just and the weak secure and the peace preserved.

All this will not be finished in the first 100 days. Nor will it be finished in the first 1,000 days, nor in the life of this administration, nor even perhaps in our lifetime on this planet. But let us begin.

In your hands, my fellow citizens, more than mine, will rest the final success or failure of our course. Since this country was founded, each generation of Americans has been summoned to give testimony to its national loyalty. The graves of young Americans who answered the call to service surround the globe.

Now the trumpet summons us again -- not as a call to bear arms, though arms we need -- not as a call to battle, though embattled we are -- but a call to bear the burden of a long twilight struggle, year in and year out, "rejoicing in hope, patient in tribulation" -- a struggle against the common enemies of man: tyranny, poverty, disease, and war itself.

Can we forge against these enemies a grand and global alliance, North and South, East and West, that can assure a more fruitful life for all mankind? Will you join in that historic effort?

In the long history of the world, only a few generations have been granted the role of defending freedom in its hour of maximum danger. I do not shrink from this responsibility -- I welcome it. I do not believe that any of us would exchange places with any other people or any other generation. The energy, the faith, the devotion which we bring to this endeavor will light our country and all who serve it -- and the glow from that fire can truly light the world.

And so, my fellow Americans: ask not what your country can do for you -- ask what you can do for your country.

My fellow citizens of the world: ask not what America will do for you, but what together we can do for the freedom of man.

Finally, whether you are citizens of America or citizens of the world, ask of us here the same high standards of strength and sacrifice which we ask of you. With a good conscience our only sure reward, with history the final judge of our deeds, let us go forth to lead the land we love, asking His blessing and His help, but knowing that here on earth God's work must truly be our own.

John F. Kennedy - January 20, 1961

Kennedy's Speech on the Cuban Missile Crisis

Good evening my fellow citizens:

This Government, as promised, has maintained the closest surveillance of the Soviet Military buildup on the island of Cuba. Within the past week, unmistakable evidence has established the fact that a series of offensive missile sites is now in preparation on that imprisoned island. The purpose of these bases can be none other than to provide a nuclear strike capability against the Western Hemisphere.

Upon receiving the first preliminary hard information of this nature last Tuesday morning at 9 a.m., I directed that our surveillance be stepped up. And having now confirmed and completed our evaluation of the evidence and our decision on a course of action, this Government feels obliged to report this new crisis to you in fullest detail.

The characteristics of these new missile sites indicate two distinct types of installations. Several of them include medium range ballistic missiles capable of carrying a nuclear warhead for a distance of more than 1,000 nautical miles. Each of these missiles, in short, is capable of striking Washington, D.C., the Panama Canal, Cape Canaveral, Mexico City, or any other city in the southeastern part of the United States, in Central America, or in the Caribbean area.

Additional sites not yet completed appear to be designed for intermediate range ballistic missiles--capable of traveling more than twice as far--and thus capable of striking most of the major cities in the Western Hemisphere, ranging as far north as Hudson Bay, Canada, and as far south as Lima, Peru. In addition, jet bombers, capable of carrying nuclear weapons, are now being uncrated and assembled in Cuba, while the necessary air bases are being prepared.

This urgent transformation of Cuba into an important strategic base--by the presence of these large, long range, and clearly offensive weapons of sudden mass destruction--constitutes an explicit threat to the peace and security of all the Americas, in flagrant and deliberate defiance of the Rio Pact of 1947, the traditions of this Nation and hemisphere, the joint resolution of the 87th Congress, the Charter of the United Nations, and my own public warnings to the Soviets on September 4 and 13. This action also contradicts the repeated assurances of Soviet spokesmen, both publicly and privately delivered, that the arms buildup in Cuba would retain its original defensive character, and that the Soviet Union had no need or desire to station strategic missiles on the territory of any other nation.

The size of this undertaking makes clear that it has been planned for some months. Yet only last month, after I had made clear the distinction between any introduction of ground-to-ground missiles and the existence of defensive antiaircraft missiles, the Soviet Government publicly stated on September 11, and I quote, "the armaments and military equipment sent to Cuba are designed exclusively for defensive purposes," that, and I quote the Soviet Government, "there is no need for the Soviet Government to shift its weapons . . . for a retaliatory blow to any other country, for instance Cuba," and that, and I quote their government, "the Soviet Union has so powerful rockets to carry these nuclear warheads that there is no need to search for sites for them beyond the boundaries of the Soviet Union." That statement was false.

Only last Thursday, as evidence of this rapid offensive buildup was already in my hand, Soviet Foreign Minister Gromyko told me in my office that he was instructed to make it clear once again, as he said his government had already done, that Soviet assistance to Cuba, and I quote, "pursued solely the purpose of contributing to the the defense capabilities of Cuba," that, and I quote him, "training by Soviet specialists of Cuban nationals in handling defensive armaments was by no means offensive, and if it were otherwise," Mr. Gromyko went on, "the Soviet

Government would never become involved in rendering such assistance." That statement also was false.

Neither the United States of America nor the world community of nations can tolerate deliberate deception and offensive threats on the part of any nation, large or small. We no longer live in a world where only the actual firing of weapons represents a sufficient challenge to a nation's security to constitute maximum peril. Nuclear weapons are so destructive and ballistic missiles are so swift, that any substantially increased possibility of their use or any sudden change in their deployment may well be regarded as a definite threat to peace.

For many years both the Soviet Union and the United States, recognizing this fact, have deployed strategic nuclear weapons with great care, never upsetting the precarious status quo which insured that these weapons would not be used in the absence of some vital challenge. Our own strategic missiles have never been transferred to the territory of any other nation under a cloak of secrecy and deception; and our history--unlike that of the Soviets since the end of World War II--demonstrates that we have no desire to dominate or conquer any other nation or impose our system upon its people. Nevertheless, American citizens have become adjusted to living daily on the Bull's-eye of Soviet missiles located inside the U.S.S.R. or in submarines.

In that sense, missiles in Cuba add to an already clear and present danger--although it should be noted the nations of Latin America have never previously been subjected to a potential nuclear threat.

But this secret, swift, and extraordinary buildup of Communist missiles--in an area well known to have a special and historical relationship to the United States and the nations of the Western Hemisphere, in violation of Soviet assurances, and in defiance of American and hemispheric policy--this sudden, clandestine decision to station strategic weapons for the first time outside of Soviet soil--is a deliberately provocative and unjustified change in the status quo which cannot be accepted by this country, if our courage and our commitments are ever to be trusted again by either friend or foe.

The 1930's taught us a clear lesson: aggressive conduct, if allowed to go unchecked and unchallenged ultimately leads to war. This nation is opposed to war. We are also true to our word. Our unswerving objective, therefore, must be to prevent the use of these missiles against this or any other country, and to secure their withdrawal or elimination from the Western Hemisphere.

Our policy has been one of patience and restraint, as befits a peaceful and powerful nation, which leads a worldwide alliance. We have been determined not to be diverted from our central concerns by mere irritants and fanatics. But now further action is required--and it is under way; and these actions may only be the beginning. We will not prematurely or unnecessarily risk the costs of worldwide nuclear war in which even the fruits of victory would be ashes in our mouth-- but neither will we shrink from that risk at any time it must be faced.

Acting, therefore, in the defense of our own security and of the entire Western Hemisphere, and under the authority entrusted to me by the Constitution as endorsed by the resolution of the Congress, I have directed that the following initial steps be taken immediately:

First: To halt this offensive buildup, a strict quarantine on all offensive military equipment under shipment to Cuba is being initiated. All ships of any kind bound for Cuba from whatever nation or port will, if found to contain cargoes of offensive weapons, be turned back. This quarantine will be extended, if needed, to other types of cargo and carriers. We are not at this time, however, denying the necessities of life as the Soviets attempted to do in their Berlin blockade of 1948.

Second: I have directed the continued and increased close surveillance of Cuba and its military buildup. The foreign ministers of the OAS, in their communique of October 6, rejected secrecy in such matters in this hemisphere. Should these offensive military preparations continue, thus increasing the threat to the hemisphere, further action will be justified. I have directed the Armed Forces to prepare for any eventualities; and I trust that in the interest of both the Cuban people and the Soviet technicians at the sites, the hazards to all concerned in continuing this threat will be recognized.

Third: It shall be the policy of this Nation to regard any nuclear missile launched from Cuba against any nation in the Western Hemisphere as an attack by the Soviet Union on the United States, requiring a full retaliatory response upon the Soviet Union.

Fourth: As a necessary military precaution, I have reinforced our base at Guantanamo, evacuated today the dependents of our personnel there, and ordered additional military units to be on a standby alert basis.

Fifth: We are calling tonight for an immediate meeting of the Organ of Consultation under the Organization of American States, to consider this threat to hemispheric security and to invoke articles 6 and 8 of the Rio Treaty in support of all necessary action. The United Nations Charter allows for regional security arrangements--and the nations of this hemisphere decided long ago against the military presence of outside powers. Our other allies around the world have also been alerted.

Sixth: Under the Charter of the United Nations, we are asking tonight that an emergency meeting of the Security Council be convoked without delay to take action against this latest Soviet threat to world peace. Our resolution will call for the prompt dismantling and withdrawal of all offensive weapons in Cuba, under the supervision of U.N. observers, before the quarantine can be lifted.

Seventh and finally: I call upon Chairman Khrushchev to halt and eliminate this clandestine, reckless and provocative threat to world peace and to stable relations between our two nations. I call upon him further to abandon this course of world domination, and to join in an historic effort to end the perilous arms race and to transform the history of man. He has an opportunity now to move the world back from the abyss of destruction--by returning to his government's own words that it had no need to station missiles outside its own territory, and withdrawing these weapons from Cuba--by refraining from any action which will widen or deepen the present crisis--and then by participating in a search for peaceful and permanent solutions.

This Nation is prepared to present its case against the Soviet threat to peace, and our own proposals for a peaceful world, at any time and in any forum--in the OAS, in the United Nations, or in any other meeting that could be useful--without limiting our freedom of action. We have in the past made strenuous efforts to limit the spread of nuclear weapons. We have proposed the elimination of all arms and military bases in a fair and effective disarmament treaty. We are prepared to discuss new proposals for the removal of tensions on both sides--including the possibility of a genuinely independent Cuba, free to determine its own destiny. We have no wish to war with the Soviet Union--for we are a peaceful people who desire to live in peace with all other peoples.

But it is difficult to settle or even discuss these problems in an atmosphere of intimidation. That is why this latest Soviet threat--or any other threat which is made independently or in response to our actions this week--must and will be met with determination. Any hostile move anywhere in the world against the safety and freedom of peoples to whom we are committed--including in particular the brave people of West Berlin--will be met by whatever action is needed.

Finally, I want to say a few words to the captive people of Cuba, to whom this speech is being directly carried by special radio facilities. I speak to you as a friend, as one who knows of your deep attachment to your fatherland, as one who shares your aspirations for liberty and justice for all. And I have watched and the American people have watched with deep sorrow how your nationalist revolution was betrayed-- and how your fatherland fell under foreign domination. Now your leaders are no longer Cuban leaders inspired by Cuban ideals. They are puppets and agents of an international conspiracy which has turned Cuba against your friends and neighbors in the Americas--and turned it into the first Latin American country to become a target for nuclear war--the first Latin American country to have these weapons on its soil.

These new weapons are not in your interest. They contribute nothing to your peace and well-being. They can only undermine it. But this country has no wish to cause you to suffer or to impose any system upon you. We know that your lives and land are being used as pawns by those who deny your freedom.

Many times in the past, the Cuban people have risen to throw out tyrants who destroyed their liberty. And I have no doubt that most Cubans today look forward to the time when they will be truly free--free from foreign domination, free to choose their own leaders, free to select their own system, free to own their own land, free to speak and write and worship without fear or degradation. And then shall Cuba be welcomed back to the society of free nations and to the associations of this hemisphere.

My fellow citizens: let no one doubt that this is a difficult and dangerous effort on which we have set out. No one can see precisely what course it will take or what costs or casualties will be incurred. Many months of sacrifice and self-discipline lie ahead--months in which our patience and our will will be tested--months in which many threats and denunciations will keep us aware of our dangers. But the greatest danger of all would be to do nothing.

The path we have chosen for the present is full of hazards, as all paths are--but it is the one most consistent with our character and courage as a nation and our commitments around the world. The cost of freedom is always high--and Americans have always paid it. And one path we shall never choose, and that is the path of surrender or submission.

Our goal is not the victory of might, but the vindication of right- -not peace at the expense of freedom, but both peace and freedom, here in this hemisphere, and, we hope, around the world. God willing, that goal will be achieved.

Thank you and good night.

President John F. Kennedy - October 22, 1962

Martin L. King - "I Have A Dream"
August 28, 1963

I am happy to join with you today in what will go down in history as the greatest demonstration for freedom in the history of our nation.

Five score years ago, a great American, in whose symbolic shadow we stand signed the Emancipation Proclamation. This momentous decree came as a great beacon light of hope to millions of Negro slaves who had been seared in the flames of withering injustice. It came as a joyous daybreak to end the long night of captivity. But one hundred years later, we must face the tragic fact that the Negro is still not free.

One hundred years later, the life of the Negro is still sadly crippled by the manacles of segregation and the chains of discrimination. One hundred years later, the Negro lives on a lonely island of poverty in the midst of a vast ocean of material prosperity. One hundred years later, the Negro is still languishing in the corners of American society and finds himself an exile in his own land.

So we have come here today to dramatize an appalling condition. In a sense we have come to our nation's capital to cash a check. When the architects of our republic wrote the magnificent words of the Constitution and the Declaration of Independence, they were signing a promissory note to which every American was to fall heir.

This note was a promise that all men would be guaranteed the inalienable rights of life, liberty, and the pursuit of happiness. It is obvious today that America has defaulted on this promissory note insofar as her citizens of color are concerned. Instead of honoring this sacred obligation, America has given the Negro people a bad check which has come back marked "insufficient funds." But we refuse to believe that the bank of justice is bankrupt. We refuse to believe that there are insufficient funds in the great vaults of opportunity of this nation.

So we have come to cash this check -- a check that will give us upon demand the riches of freedom and the security of justice. We have also come to this hallowed spot to remind America of the fierce urgency of now. This is no time to engage in the luxury of cooling off or to take the tranquilizing drug of gradualism. Now is the time to rise from the dark and desolate valley of segregation to the sunlit path of racial justice. Now is the time to open the doors of opportunity to all of God's children. Now is the time to lift our nation from the quicksands of racial injustice to the solid rock of brotherhood.

It would be fatal for the nation to overlook the urgency of the moment and to underestimate the determination of the Negro. This sweltering summer of the Negro's legitimate discontent will not pass until there is an invigorating autumn of freedom and equality. Nineteen sixty-three is not an end, but a beginning. Those who hope that the Negro needed to blow off steam and will now be content will have a rude awakening if the nation returns to business as usual. There will be neither rest nor tranquility in America until the Negro is granted his citizenship rights.

The whirlwinds of revolt will continue to shake the foundations of our nation until the bright day of justice emerges. But there is something that I must say to my people who stand on the warm threshold which leads into the palace of justice. In the process of gaining our rightful place we must not be guilty of wrongful deeds. Let us not seek to satisfy our thirst for freedom by drinking from the cup of bitterness and hatred.

We must forever conduct our struggle on the high plane of dignity and discipline. we must not allow our creative protest to degenerate into physical violence. Again and again we must rise to the majestic heights of meeting physical force with soul force.

The marvelous new militancy which has engulfed the Negro community must not lead us to distrust of all white people, for many of our white brothers, as evidenced by their presence here today, have come to realize that their destiny is tied up with our destiny and their freedom is inextricably bound to our freedom.

We cannot walk alone. And as we walk, we must make the pledge that we shall march ahead. We cannot turn back. There are those who are asking the devotees of civil rights, "When will you be satisfied?" we can never be satisfied as long as our bodies, heavy with the fatigue of travel, cannot gain lodging in the motels of the highways and the hotels of the cities. We cannot be satisfied as long as the Negro's basic mobility is from a smaller ghetto to a larger one. We can never be satisfied as long as a Negro in Mississippi cannot vote and a Negro in New York believes he has nothing for which to vote. No, no, we are not satisfied, and we will not be satisfied until justice rolls down like waters and righteousness like a mighty stream.

I am not unmindful that some of you have come here out of great trials and tribulations. Some of you have come fresh from narrow cells. Some of you have come from areas where your quest for freedom left you battered by the storms of persecution and staggered by the winds of police brutality. You have been the veterans of creative suffering. Continue to work with the faith that unearned suffering is redemptive.

Go back to Mississippi, go back to Alabama, go back to Georgia, go back to Louisiana, go back to the slums and ghettos of our northern cities, knowing that somehow this situation can and will be changed. Let us not wallow in the valley of despair. I say to you today, my friends, that in spite of the difficulties and frustrations of the moment, I still have a dream. It is a dream deeply rooted in the American dream.

I have a dream that one day this nation will rise up and live out the true meaning of its creed: "We hold these truths to be self-evident: that all men are created equal." I have a dream that one day on the red hills of Georgia the sons of former slaves and the sons of former slave owners will be able to sit down together at a table of brotherhood. I have a dream that one day even the state of Mississippi, a desert state, sweltering with the heat of injustice and oppression, will be transformed into an oasis of freedom and justice. I have a dream that my four children will one day live in a nation where they will not be judged by the color of their skin but by the content of their character. I have a dream today.

I have a dream that one day the state of Alabama, whose governor's lips are presently dripping with the words of interposition and nullification, will be transformed into a situation where little black boys and black girls will be able to join hands with little white boys and white girls and walk together as sisters and brothers. I have a dream today. I have a dream that one day every valley shall be exalted, every hill and mountain shall be made low, the rough places will be made plain, and the crooked places will be made straight, and the glory of the Lord shall be revealed, and all flesh shall see it together. This is our hope. This is the faith with which I return to the South. With this faith we will be able to hew out of the mountain of despair a stone of hope. With this faith we will be able to transform the jangling discords of our nation into a beautiful symphony of brotherhood. With this faith we will be able to work together, to pray together, to struggle together, to go to jail together, to stand up for freedom together, knowing that we will be free one day.

This will be the day when all of God's children will be able to sing with a new meaning, "My country, 'tis of thee, sweet land of liberty, of thee I sing. Land where my fathers died, land of the pilgrim's pride, from every mountainside, let freedom ring." And if America is to be a great nation, this must become true. So let freedom ring from the prodigious hilltops of New Hampshire. Let freedom ring from the mighty mountains of New York. Let freedom ring from the heightening Alleghenies of Pennsylvania! Let freedom ring from the snowcapped Rockies of Colorado! Let freedom ring from the curvaceous peaks of California! But not only that; let freedom ring from Stone Mountain of Georgia! Let freedom ring from Lookout Mountain of Tennessee! Let freedom ring from every hill and every molehill of Mississippi. From every mountainside, let freedom ring.

When we let freedom ring, when we let it ring from every village and every hamlet, from every state and every city, we will be able to speed up that day when all of God's children, black men and white men, Jews and Gentiles, Protestants and Catholics, will be able to join hands and sing in the words of the old Negro spiritual, "Free at last! free at last! thank God Almighty, we are free at last!"

Robert Kennedy on Martin Luther King's Assassination

Ladies and Gentlemen

I'm only going to talk to you just for a minute or so this evening. Because...

I have some very sad news for all of you, and I think sad news for all of our fellow citizens, and people who love peace all over the world, and that is that Martin Luther King was shot and was killed tonight in Memphis, Tennessee.

Martin Luther King dedicated his life to love and to justice between fellow human beings. He died in the cause of that effort. In this difficult day, in this difficult time for the United States, it's perhaps well to ask what kind of a nation we are and what direction we want to move in.

For those of you who are black - considering the evidence evidently is that there were white people who were responsible - you can be filled with bitterness, and with hatred, and a desire for revenge.

We can move in that direction as a country, in greater polarization - black people amongst blacks, and white amongst whites, filled with hatred toward one another. Or we can make an effort, as Martin Luther King did, to understand and to comprehend, and replace that violence, that stain of bloodshed that has spread across our land, with an effort to understand, compassion and love.

For those of you who are black and are tempted to be filled with hatred and mistrust of the injustice of such an act, against all white people, I would only say that I can also feel in my own heart the same kind of feeling. I had a member of my family killed, but he was killed by a white man.

But we have to make an effort in the United States, we have to make an effort to understand, to get beyond these rather difficult times.

My favorite poet was Aeschylus. He once wrote: "Even in our sleep, pain which cannot forget falls drop by drop upon the heart, until, in our own despair, against our will, comes wisdom through the awful grace of God."

What we need in the United States is not division; what we need in the United States is not hatred; what we need in the United States is not violence and lawlessness, but is love and wisdom, and compassion toward one another, and a feeling of justice toward those who still suffer within our country, whether they be white or whether they be black.

(Interrupted by applause)

So I ask you tonight to return home, to say a prayer for the family of Martin Luther King, yeah that's true, but more importantly to say a prayer for our own country, which all of us love - a prayer for understanding and that compassion of which I spoke. We can do well in this country. We will have difficult times. We've had difficult times in the past. And we will have difficult times in the future. It is not the end of violence; it is not the end of lawlessness; and it's not the end of disorder.

But the vast majority of white people and the vast majority of black people in this country want to live together, want to improve the quality of our life, and want justice for all human beings that abide in our land.

(Interrupted by applause)

Let us dedicate ourselves to what the Greeks wrote so many years ago: to tame the savageness of man and make gentle the life of this world.

Let us dedicate ourselves to that, and say a prayer for our country and for our people. Thank you very much. (Applause)

Robert F. Kennedy - April 4, 1968

President Johnson Will Not
Seek Re-election Speech

Good evening, my fellow Americans:

Tonight I want to speak to you of peace in Vietnam and Southeast Asia.

No other question so preoccupies our people. No other dream so absorbs the 250 million human beings who live in that part of the world. No other goal motivates American policy in Southeast Asia.

For years, representatives of our Government and others have traveled the world--seeking to find a basis for peace talks.

Since last September, they have carried the offer that I made public at San Antonio. That offer was this:

That the United States would stop its bombardment of North Vietnam when that would lead promptly to productive discussions--and that we would assume that North Vietnam would not take military advantage of our restraint.

Hanoi denounced this offer, both privately and publicly. Even while the search for peace was going on, North Vietnam rushed their preparations for a savage assault on the people, the government, and the allies of South Vietnam.

Their attack--during the Tet holidays--failed to achieve its principal objectives.

It did not collapse the elected government of South Vietnam or shatter its army--as the Communists had hoped.

It did not produce a "general uprising" among the people of the cities as they had predicted.

The Communists were unable to maintain control of any of the more than 30 cities that they attacked. And they took very heavy casualties.

But they did compel the South Vietnamese and their allies to move certain forces from the countryside into the cities.

They caused widespread disruption and suffering. Their attacks, and the battles that followed, made refugees of half a million human beings.

The Communists may renew their attack any day.

They are, it appears, trying to make 1968 the year of decision in South Vietnam--the year that brings, if not final victory or defeat, at least a turning point in the struggle.

This much is clear: If they do mount another round of heavy attacks, they will not succeed in destroying the fighting power of South Vietnam and its allies.

But tragically, this is also clear: Many men--on both sides of the struggle--will be lost. A nation that has already suffered 20 years of warfare will suffer once again. Armies on both sides will take new casualties. And the war will go on.

There is no need for this to be so.

There is no need to delay the talks that could bring an end to this long and this bloody war.

Tonight, I renew the offer I made last August--to stop the bombardment of North Vietnam. We ask that talks begin promptly, that they be serious talks on the substance of peace. We assume that during those talks Hanoi will not take advantage of our restraint.

We are prepared to move immediately toward peace through negotiations.

So, tonight, in the hope that this action will lead to early talks, I am taking the first step to deescalate the conflict. We are reducing--substantially reducing--the present level of hostilities.

And we are doing so unilaterally, and at once.

Tonight, I have ordered our aircraft and our naval vessels to make no attacks on North Vietnam, except in the area north of the demilitarized zone where the continuing enemy buildup directly threatens allied forward positions and where the movements of their troops and supplies are clearly related to that threat.

The area in which we are stopping our attacks includes almost 90 percent of North Vietnam's population, and most of its territory. Thus there will be no attacks around the principal populated areas, or in the food-producing areas of North Vietnam.

Even this very limited bombing of the North could come to an early end--if our restraint is matched by restraint in Hanoi. But I cannot in good conscience stop all bombing so long as to do so would immediately and directly endanger the lives of our men and our allies. Whether a complete bombing halt becomes possible in the future will be determined by events.

Our purpose in this action is to bring about a reduction in the level of violence that now exists.

It is to save the lives of brave men--and to save the lives of innocent women and children. It is to permit the contending forces to move closer to a political settlement.

And tonight, I call upon the United Kingdom and I call upon the Soviet Union--as cochairmen of the Geneva Conferences, and as permanent members of the United Nations Security Council--to do all they can to move from the unilateral act of de-escalation that I have just announced toward genuine peace in Southeast Asia.

Now, as in the past, the United States is ready to send its representatives to any forum, at any time, to discuss the means of bringing this ugly war to an end.

I am designating one of our most distinguished Americans, Ambassador Averell Harriman, as my personal representative for such talks. In addition, I have asked Ambassador Llewellyn Thompson, who returned from Moscow for consultation, to be available to join Ambassador Harriman at Geneva or any other suitable place--just as soon as Hanoi agrees to a conference.

I call upon President Ho Chi Minh to respond positively, and favorably, to this new step toward peace.

But if peace does not come now through negotiations, it will come when Hanoi understands that our common resolve is unshakable, and our common strength is invincible.

Tonight, we and the other allied nations are contributing 600,000 fighting men to assist 700,000 South Vietnamese troops in defending their little country.

Our presence there has always rested on this basic belief: The main burden of preserving their freedom must be carried out by them--by the South Vietnamese themselves.

We and our allies can only help to provide a shield behind which the people of South Vietnam can survive and can grow and develop. On their efforts--on their determination and resourcefulness--the outcome will ultimately depend.

That small, beleaguered nation has suffered terrible punishment for more than 20 years.

I pay tribute once again tonight to the great courage and endurance of its people. South Vietnam supports armed forces tonight of almost 700,000 men--and I call your attention to the fact that this is the equivalent of more than 10 million in our own population. Its people maintain their firm determination to be free of domination by the North.

There has been substantial progress, I think, in building a durable government during these last 3 years. The South Vietnam of 1965 could not have survived the enemy's Tet offensive of 1968. The elected government of South Vietnam survived that attack--and is rapidly repairing the devastation that it wrought.

The South Vietnamese know that further efforts are going to be required:

- to expand their own armed forces,
- to move back into the countryside as quickly as possible,
- to increase their taxes,
- to select the very best men that they have for civil and military responsibility,
- to achieve a new unity within their constitutional government, and
- to include in the national effort all those groups who wish to preserve South Vietnam's control over its own destiny.

Last week President Thieu ordered the mobilization of 135,000 additional South Vietnamese. He plans to reach--as soon as possible--a total military strength of more than 800,000 men.

To achieve this, the Government of South Vietnam started the drafting of 19-year-olds on March 1st. On May 1st, the Government will begin the drafting of 18-year-olds.

Last month, 10,000 men volunteered for military service--that was two and a half times the number of volunteers during the same month last year. Since the middle of January, more than 48,000 South Vietnamese have joined the armed forces--and nearly half of them volunteered to do so.

All men in the South Vietnamese armed forces have had their tours of duty extended for the duration of the war, and reserves are now being called up for immediate active duty.

President Thieu told his people last week:

"We must make greater efforts and accept more sacrifices because, as I have said many times, this is our country. The existence of our nation is at stake, and this is mainly a Vietnamese responsibility."

He warned his people that a major national effort is required to root out corruption and incompetence at all levels of government.

We applaud this evidence of determination on the part of South Vietnam. Our first priority will be to support their effort.

We shall accelerate the re-equipment of South Vietnam's armed forces--in order to meet the enemy's increased firepower. This will enable them progressively to undertake a larger share of combat operations against the Communist invaders.

On many occasions I have told the American people that we would send to Vietnam those forces that are required to accomplish our mission there. So, with that as our guide, we have previously authorized a force level of approximately 525,000.

Some weeks ago--to help meet the enemy's new offensive--we sent to Vietnam about 11,000 additional Marine and airborne troops. They were deployed by air in 48 hours, on an emergency basis. But the artillery, tank, aircraft, medical, and other units that were needed to work with and to support these infantry troops in combat could not then accompany them by air on that short notice.

In order that these forces may reach maximum combat effectiveness, the Joint Chiefs of Staff have recommended to me that we should prepare to send--during the next 5 months--support troops totaling approximately 13,500 men.

A portion of these men will be made available from our active forces. The balance will come from reserve component units which will be called up for service.

The actions that we have taken since the beginning of the year:

- to re-equip the South Vietnamese forces,
- to meet our responsibilities in Korea, as well as our responsibilities in Vietnam,
- to meet price increases and the cost of activating and deploying reserve forces,
- to replace helicopters and provide the other military supplies we need, all of these actions are going to require additional expenditures.

The tentative estimate of those additional expenditures is $2.5 billion in this fiscal year, and $2.6 billion in the next fiscal year.

These projected increases in expenditures for our national security will bring into sharper focus the Nation's need for immediate action: action to protect the prosperity of the American people and to protect the strength and the stability of our American dollar.

On many occasions I have pointed out that, without a tax bill or decreased expenditures, next year's deficit would again be around $20 billion. I have emphasized the need to set strict priorities in our spending. I have stressed that failure to act and to act promptly and decisively would raise very strong doubts throughout the world about America's willingness to keep its financial house in order.

Yet Congress has not acted. And tonight we face the sharpest financial threat in the postwar era-- a threat to the dollar's role as the keystone of international trade and finance in the world.

Last week, at the monetary conference in Stockholm, the major industrial countries decided to take a big step toward creating a new international monetary asset that will strengthen the international monetary system. I am very proud of the very able work done by Secretary Fowler and Chairman Martin of the Federal Reserve Board.

But to make this system work the United States just must bring its balance of payments to--or very close to--equilibrium. We must have a responsible fiscal policy in this country. The passage of a tax bill now, together with expenditure control that the Congress may desire and dictate, is absolutely necessary to protect this Nation's security, to continue our prosperity, and to meet the needs of our people.

What is at stake is 7 years of unparalleled prosperity. In those 7 years, the real income of the average American, after taxes, rose by almost 30 percent--a gain as large as that of the entire preceding 19 years.

So the steps that we must take to convince the world are exactly the steps we must take to sustain our own economic strength here at home. In the past 8 months, prices and interest rates have risen because of our inaction.

We must, therefore, now do everything we can to move from debate to action--from talking to voting. There is, I believe--I hope there is--in both Houses of the Congress--a growing sense of urgency that this situation just must be acted upon and must be corrected.

My budget in January was, we thought, a tight one. It fully reflected our evaluation of most of the demanding needs of this Nation.

But in these budgetary matters, the President does not decide alone. The Congress has the power and the duty to determine appropriations and taxes.

The Congress is now considering our proposals and they are considering reductions in the budget that we submitted.

As part of a program of fiscal restraint that includes the tax surcharge, I shall approve appropriate reductions in the January budget when and if Congress so decides that that should be done.

One thing is unmistakably clear, however: Our deficit just must be reduced. Failure to act could bring on conditions that would strike hardest at those people that all of us are trying so hard to help.

These times call for prudence in this land of plenty. I believe that we have the character to provide it, and tonight I plead with the Congress and with the people to act promptly to serve the national interest, and thereby serve all of our people.

Now let me give you my estimate of the chances for peace:

- the peace that will one day stop the bloodshed in South Vietnam,
- that will permit all the Vietnamese people to rebuild and develop their land,
- that will permit us to turn more fully to our own tasks here at home.

I cannot promise that the initiative that I have announced tonight will be completely successful in achieving peace any more than the 30 others that we have undertaken and agreed to in recent years.

But it is our fervent hope that North Vietnam, after years of fighting that have left the issue unresolved, will now cease its efforts to achieve a military victory and will join with us in moving toward the peace table.

And there may come a time when South Vietnamese--on both sides--are able to work out a way to settle their own differences by free political choice rather than by war.

As Hanoi considers its course, it should be in no doubt of our intentions. It must not miscalculate the pressures within our democracy in this election year.

We have no intention of widening this war.

But the United States will never accept a fake solution to this long and arduous struggle and call it peace.

No one can foretell the precise terms of an eventual settlement.

Our objective in South Vietnam has never been the annihilation of the enemy. It has been to bring about a recognition in Hanoi that its objective--taking over the South by force--could not be achieved.

We think that peace can be based on the Geneva Accords of 1954--under political conditions that permit the South Vietnamese--all the South Vietnamese--to chart their course free of any outside domination or interference, from us or from anyone else.

So tonight I reaffirm the pledge that we made at Manila--that we are prepared to withdraw our forces from South Vietnam as the other side withdraws its forces to the north, stops the infiltration, and the level of violence thus subsides.

Our goal of peace and self-determination in Vietnam is directly related to the future of all of Southeast Asia--where much has happened to inspire confidence during the past 10 years. We have done all that we knew how to do to contribute and to help build that confidence.

A number of its nations have shown what can be accomplished under conditions of security. Since 1966, Indonesia, the fifth largest nation in all the world, with a population of more than 100 million people, has had a government that is dedicated to peace with its neighbors and improved conditions for its own people. Political and economic cooperation between nations has grown rapidly.

I think every American can take a great deal of pride in the role that we have played in bringing this about in Southeast Asia. We can rightly judge--as responsible Southeast Asians themselves do--that the progress of the past 3 years would have been far less likely--if not completely impossible--if America's sons and others had not made their stand in Vietnam.

At Johns Hopkins University, about 3 years ago, I announced that the United States would take part in the great work of developing Southeast Asia, including the Mekong Valley, for all the people of that region. Our determination to help build a better land--a better land for men on both sides of the present conflict--has not diminished in the least. Indeed, the ravages of war, I think, have made it more urgent than ever.

So, I repeat on behalf of the United States again tonight what I said at Johns Hopkins--that North Vietnam could take its place in this common effort just as soon as peace comes.

Over time, a wider framework of peace and security in Southeast Asia may become possible. The new cooperation of the nations of the area could be a foundation-stone. Certainly friendship with the nations of such a Southeast Asia is what the United States seeks--and that is all that the United States seeks.

One day, my fellow citizens, there will be peace in Southeast Asia.

It will come because the people of Southeast Asia want it--those whose armies are at war tonight, and those who, though threatened, have thus far been spared.

Peace will come because Asians were willing to work for it--and to sacrifice for it--and to die by the thousands for it.

But let it never be forgotten: Peace will come also because America sent her sons to help secure it.

It has not been easy--far from it. During the past 4½ years, it has been my fate and my responsibility to be Commander in Chief. I have lived---daily and nightly--with the cost of this war. I know the pain that it has inflicted. I know, perhaps better than anyone, the misgivings that it has aroused.

Throughout this entire, long period, I have been sustained by a single principle: that what we are doing now, in Vietnam, is vital not only to the security of Southeast Asia, but it is vital to the security of every American.

Surely we have treaties which we must respect. Surely we have commitments that we are going to keep. Resolutions of the Congress testify to the need to resist aggression in the world and in Southeast Asia.

But the heart of our involvement in South Vietnam--under three different presidents, three separate administrations--has always been America's own security.

And the larger purpose of our involvement has always been to help the nations of Southeast Asia become independent and stand alone, self-sustaining, as members of a great world community-- at peace with themselves, and at peace with all others.

With such an Asia, our country--and the world--will be far more secure than it is tonight.

I believe that a peaceful Asia is far nearer to reality because of what America has done in Vietnam. I believe that the men who endure the dangers of battle--fighting there for us tonight-- are helping the entire world avoid far greater conflicts, far wider wars, far more destruction, than this one.

The peace that will bring them home someday will come. Tonight I have offered the first in what I hope will be a series of mutual moves toward peace.

I pray that it will not be rejected by the leaders of North Vietnam. I pray that they will accept it as a means by which the sacrifices of their own people may be ended. And I ask your help and your support, my fellow citizens, for this effort to reach across the battlefield toward an early peace.

Finally, my fellow Americans, let me say this:

Of those to whom much is given, much is asked. I cannot say and no man could say that no more will be asked of us.

Yet, I believe that now, no less than when the decade began, this generation of Americans is willing to "pay any price, bear any burden, meet any hardship, support any friend, oppose any foe to assure the survival and the success of liberty."

Since those words were spoken by John F. Kennedy, the people of America have kept that compact with mankind's noblest cause.

And we shall continue to keep it.

Yet, I believe that we must always be mindful of this one thing, whatever the trials and the tests ahead. The ultimate strength of our country and our cause will lie not in powerful weapons or infinite resources or boundless wealth, but will lie in the unity of our people.

This I believe very deeply.

Throughout my entire public career I have followed the personal philosophy that I am a free man, an American, a public servant, and a member of my party, in that order always and only.

For 37 years in the service of our Nation, first as a Congressman, as a Senator, and as Vice President, and now as your President, I have put the unity of the people first. I have put it ahead of any divisive partisanship.

And in these times as in times before, it is true that a house divided against itself by the spirit of faction, of party, of region, of religion, of race, is a house that cannot stand.

There is division in the American house now. There is divisiveness among us all tonight. And holding the trust that is mine, as President of all the people, I cannot disregard the peril to the progress of the American people and the hope and the prospect of peace for all peoples.

So, I would ask all Americans, whatever their personal interests or concern, to guard against divisiveness and all its ugly consequences.

Fifty-two months and 10 days ago, in a moment of tragedy and trauma, the duties of this office fell upon me. I asked then for your help and God's, that we might continue America on its course, binding up our wounds, healing our history, moving forward in new unity, to clear the American agenda and to keep the American commitment for all of our people.

United we have kept that commitment. United we have enlarged that commitment.

Through all time to come, I think America will be a stronger nation, a more just society, and a land of greater opportunity and fulfillment because of what we have all done together in these years of unparalleled achievement.

Our reward will come in the life of freedom, peace, and hope that our children will enjoy through ages ahead.

What we won when all of our people united just must not now be lost in suspicion, distrust, selfishness, and politics among any of our people.

Believing this as I do, I have concluded that I should not permit the Presidency to become involved in the partisan divisions that are developing in this political year.

With America's sons in the fields far away, with America's future under challenge right here at home, with our hopes and the world's hopes for peace in the balance every day, I do not believe that I should devote an hour or a day of my time to any personal partisan causes or to any duties other than the awesome duties of this office--the Presidency of your country.

Accordingly, I shall not seek, and I will not accept, the nomination of my party for another term as your President.

But let men everywhere know, however, that a strong, a confident, and a vigilant America stands ready tonight to seek an honorable peace--and stands ready tonight to defend an honored cause--whatever the price, whatever the burden, whatever the sacrifice that duty may require.

Thank you for listening.

Good night and God bless all of you.

President Lyndon B. Johnson - March 31, 1968

Roe v. Wade, 410 U.S. 113 (1973) (USSC+)

No. 70-18

SUPREME COURT OF THE UNITED STATES

410 U.S. 113

December 13, 1971Reargued October 11, 1972

January 22, 1973

APPEAL FROM THE UNITED STATES DISTRICT COURT FOR THE NORTHERN
DISTRICT OF TEXAS

Syllabus

✚ A pregnant single woman (Roe) brought a class action challenging the constitutionality of the Texas criminal abortion laws, which proscribe procuring or attempting an abortion except on medical advice for the purpose of saving the mother's life. A licensed physician (Hallford), who had two state abortion prosecutions pending against him, was permitted to intervene. A childless married couple (the Does), the wife not being pregnant, separately attacked the laws, basing alleged injury on the future possibilities of contraceptive failure, pregnancy, unpreparedness for parenthood, and impairment of the wife's health. A three-judge District Court, which consolidated the actions, held that Roe and Hallford, and members of their classes, had standing to sue and presented justiciable controversies. Ruling that declaratory, though not injunctive, relief was warranted, the court declared the abortion statutes void as vague and overbroadly infringing those plaintiffs' Ninth and Fourteenth Amendment rights. The court ruled the Does' complaint not justiciable. Appellants directly appealed to this Court on the injunctive rulings, and appellee cross-appealed from the District Court's grant of declaratory relief to Roe and Hallford.

✚ *Held:*

1.   While 28 U.S.C. § 1253 authorizes no direct appeal to this Court from the grant or denial of declaratory relief alone, review is not foreclosed when the case is properly before the Court on appeal from specific denial of injunctive relief and the arguments as to both injunctive and declaratory relief are necessarily identical. P. 123 .

2.   Roe has standing to sue; the Does and Hallford do not. Pp. 123-129 .

(a) Contrary to appellee's contention, the natural termination of Roe's pregnancy did not moot her suit. Litigation involving pregnancy, which is "capable of repetition, yet evading review," is an exception to the usual federal rule that an actual controversy [p*114] must exist at review stages, and not simply when the action is initiated. Pp. 124-125 .

(b) The District Court correctly refused injunctive, but erred in granting declaratory, relief to Hallford, who alleged no federally protected right not assertable as a defense against the good faith state prosecutions pending against him. *Samuels v. Mackell,* 401 U.S. 66. Pp. 125-127 .

(c) The Does' complaint, based as it is on contingencies, any one or more of which may not occur, is too speculative to present an actual case or controversy. Pp. 127-129 .

3. State criminal abortion laws, like those involved here, that except from criminality only a life-saving procedure on the mother's behalf without regard to the stage of her pregnancy and other interests involved violate the Due Process Clause of the Fourteenth Amendment, which protects against state action the right to privacy, including a woman's qualified right to terminate her pregnancy. Though the State cannot override that right, it has legitimate interests in protecting both the pregnant woman's health and the potentiality of human life, each of which interests grows and reaches a "compelling" point at various stages of the woman's approach to term. Pp. 147-164 .

(a) For the stage prior to approximately the end of the first trimester, the abortion decision and its effectuation must be left to the medical judgment of the pregnant woman's attending physician. Pp. 163 , 164 .

(b) For the stage subsequent to approximately the end of the first trimester, the State, in promoting its interest in the health of the mother, may, if it chooses, regulate the abortion procedure in ways that are reasonably related to maternal health. Pp. 163 , 164 .

(c) For the stage subsequent to viability the State, in promoting its interest in the potentiality of human life, may, if it chooses, regulate, and even proscribe, abortion except where necessary, in appropriate medical judgment, for the preservation of the life or health of the mother. Pp. 163-164 ; 164-165 .

4. The State may define the term "physician" to mean only a physician currently licensed by the State, and may proscribe any abortion by a person who is not a physician as so defined. P. 165 .

5. It is unnecessary to decide the injunctive relief issue, since the Texas authorities will doubtless fully recognize the Court's ruling [p*115] that the Texas criminal abortion statutes are unconstitutional. P. 166 .

314 F.Supp. 1217, affirmed in part and reversed in part.

Opinions

BLACKMUN, J., delivered the opinion of the Court, in which BURGER, C.J., and DOUGLAS, BRENNAN, STEWART, MARSHALL, and POWELL, JJ., joined. BURGER, C.J., *post,* p. 207, DOUGLAS, J., *post,* p. 209 , and STEWART, J., *post,* p. 167 , filed concurring opinions. WHITE,

J., filed a dissenting opinion, in which REHNQUIST, J., joined, *post,* p. 221 . REHNQUIST, J., filed a dissenting opinion, *post,* p. 171 . [p*116]

BLACKMUN, J., Opinion of the Court

MR. JUSTICE BLACKMUN delivered the opinion of the Court.

Planned Parenthood v. Casey

505 U.S. 833 (1992)

At issue are five provisions of the Pennsylvania Abortion Control Act of 1982: § 3205, which requires that a woman seeking an abortion give her informed consent prior to the procedure, and specifies that she be provided with certain information at least 24 hours before the abortion is performed; § 3206, which mandates the informed consent of one parent for a minor to obtain an abortion, but provides a judicial bypass procedure; § 3209, which commands that, unless certain exceptions apply, a married woman seeking an abortion must sign a statement indicating that she has notified her husband; § 3203, which defines a "medical emergency" that will excuse compliance with the foregoing requirements; and §§ 3207(b), 3214(a), and 3214(f), which impose certain reporting requirements on facilities providing abortion services. The District Court held all the provisions unconstitutional, and permanently enjoined their enforcement. The Court of Appeals affirmed in part and reversed in part, striking down the husband notification provision but upholding the others.

Held: The judgment in No. 91-902 is affirmed; the judgment in No. 91-744 is affirmed in part and reversed in part, and the case is remanded.

JUSTICE O'CONNOR, JUSTICE KENNEDY, and **JUSTICE SOUTER** delivered the opinion of the Court, concluding that:

Consideration of the fundamental constitutional question resolved by Roe v. Wade, principles of institutional integrity, and the rule of stare decisis require that Roe's essential holding be retained and reaffirmed as to each of its three parts:

(1) a recognition of a woman's right to choose to have an abortion before fetal viability and to obtain it without undue interference from the State, whose pre-viability interests are not strong enough to support an abortion prohibition or the imposition of substantial obstacles to the woman's effective right to elect the procedure;

(2) a confirmation of the State's power to restrict abortions after viability, if the law contains exceptions for pregnancies endangering a woman's life or health; and

(3) the principle that the State has legitimate interests from the outset of the pregnancy in protecting the health of the woman and the life of the fetus that may become a child.

(a) A reexamination of the principles that define the woman's rights and the State's authority regarding abortions is required by the doubt this Court's subsequent decisions have cast upon the meaning and reach of Roe's central holding, by the fact that The Chief Justice would overrule Roe, and by the necessity that state and federal courts and legislatures have adequate guidance on the subject.

(b) Roe determined that a woman's decision to terminate her pregnancy is a "liberty" protected against state interference by the substantive component of the Due Process Clause of the Fourteenth Amendment.

(c) Application of the doctrine of stare decisis confirms that Roe's essential holding should be reaffirmed.

(d) Although Roe has engendered opposition, it has in no sense proven unworkable, representing as it does a simple limitation beyond which a state law is unenforceable.

(e) The Roe rule's limitation on state power could not be repudiated without serious inequity to people who, for two decades of economic and social developments, have organized intimate relationships and made choices that define their views of themselves and their places in society, in reliance on the availability of abortion in the event that contraception should fail. The ability of women to participate equally in the economic and social life of the Nation has been facilitated by their ability to control their reproductive lives.

(f) No evolution of legal principle has left Roe's central rule a doctrinal anachronism discounted by society. If Roe is placed among the cases exemplified by Griswold, supra, it is clearly in no jeopardy, since subsequent constitutional developments have neither disturbed, nor do they threaten to diminish, the liberty recognized in such cases.

(g) No change in Roe's factual underpinning has left its central holding obsolete, and none supports an argument for its overruling. Although subsequent maternal health care advances allow for later abortions safe to the pregnant woman, and post-Roe neonatal care developments have advanced viability to a point somewhat earlier, these facts go only to the scheme of time limits on the realization of competing interests.

(h) A comparison between Roe and Lochner v. New York, 198 U.S. 45, and Plessy v. Ferguson, 163 U.S. 537—confirms the result reached here. Those lines were overruled—by, respectively, West Coast Hotel Co. v. Parrish, 300 U.S. 379, and Brown v. Board of Education, 347 U.S. 483—on the basis of facts, or an understanding of facts, changed from those which furnished the claimed justifications for the earlier constitutional resolutions. The overruling decisions were comprehensible to the Nation, and defensible, as the Court's responses to changed circumstances.

(i) Overruling Roe's central holding would not only reach an unjustifiable result under stare decisis principles, but would seriously weaken the Court's capacity to exercise the judicial power and to function as the Supreme Court of a Nation dedicated to the rule of law.

JUSTICE O'CONNOR, JUSTICE KENNEDY, and **JUSTICE SOUTER** concluded in Part IV that an examination of Roe v. Wade, and subsequent cases, reveals a number of guiding principles that should control the assessment of the Pennsylvania statute:

(a) To protect the central right recognized by Roe while at the same time accommodating the State's profound interest in potential life, the undue burden standard should be employed.

(b) Roe's rigid trimester framework is rejected. To promote the State's interest in potential life throughout pregnancy, the State may take measures to ensure that the woman's choice is informed. Measures designed to advance this interest should not be invalidated if their purpose is to persuade the woman to choose childbirth over abortion.

(c) As with any medical procedure, the State may enact regulations to further the health or safety of a woman seeking an abortion, but may not impose unnecessary health regulations that present a substantial obstacle to a woman seeking an abortion.

(d) Adoption of the undue burden standard does not disturb Roe's holding that, regardless of whether exceptions are made for particular circumstances, a State may not prohibit any woman from making the ultimate decision to terminate her pregnancy before viability.

(e) Roe's holding that, subsequent to viability, the State, in promoting its interest in the potentiality of human life, may, if it chooses, regulate, and even proscribe, abortion except where it is necessary, in appropriate medical judgment, for the preservation of the life or health of the mother is also reaffirmed.

JUSTICE O'CONNOR, JUSTICE KENNEDY, and **JUSTICE SOUTER** delivered the opinion of the Court with respect to Parts V-A and V-C, concluding that:

1. As construed by the Court of Appeals, § 3203's medical emergency definition is intended to assure that compliance with the State's abortion regulations would not in any way pose a significant threat to a woman's life or health, and thus does not violate the essential holding of Roe.

2. Section 3209's husband notification provision constitutes an undue burden, and is therefore invalid. A significant number of women will likely be prevented from obtaining an abortion just as surely as if Pennsylvania had outlawed the procedure entirely. Section 3209 embodies a view of marriage consonant with the common law status of married women, but repugnant to this

Court's present understanding of marriage and of the nature of the rights secured by the Constitution.

JUSTICE O'CONNOR, JUSTICE KENNEDY, and **JUSTICE SOUTER,** joined by **JUSTICE STEVENS,** concluded in Part V-E that all of the statute's recordkeeping and reporting requirements, except that relating to spousal notice, are constitutional. The reporting provision relating to the reasons a married woman has not notified her husband that she intends to have an abortion must be invalidated, because it places an undue burden on a woman's choice.

JUSTICE O'CONNOR, JUSTICE KENNEDY, and **JUSTICE SOUTER** concluded in Parts V-B and V-D that:

1. Section 3205's informed consent provision is not an undue burden on a woman's constitutional right to decide to terminate a pregnancy. Requiring that the woman be informed of the availability of information relating to the consequences to the fetus does not interfere with a constitutional right of privacy between a pregnant woman and her physician, since the doctor-patient relation is derivative of the woman's position, and does not underlie or override the abortion right. There is no evidence here that requiring a doctor to give the required information would amount to a substantial obstacle to a woman seeking abortion. Although § 3205's 24-hour waiting period may make some abortions more expensive and less convenient, it cannot be said that it is invalid on the present record and in the context of this facial challenge.
2. Section 3206's one-parent consent requirement and judicial bypass procedure are constitutional.

JUSTICE BLACKMUN, concurring in part and dissenting in part, concluded that application of the strict scrutiny standard of review required by this Court's abortion precedents results in the invalidation of all the challenged provisions in the Pennsylvania statute, including the reporting requirements, and therefore concurred in the judgment that the requirement that a pregnant woman report her reasons for failing to provide spousal notice is unconstitutional.

President Nixon's Resignation Speech

Good evening. This is the 37th time I have spoken to you from this office, where so many decisions have been made that shaped the history of this Nation. Each time I have done so to discuss with you some matter that I believe affected the national interest.

In all the decisions I have made in my public life, I have always tried to do what was best for the Nation. Throughout the long and difficult period of Watergate, I have felt it was my duty to persevere, to make every possible effort to complete the term of office to which you elected me.

In the past few days, however, it has become evident to me that I no longer have a strong enough political base in the Congress to justify continuing that effort. As long as there was such a base, I felt strongly that it was necessary to see the constitutional process through to its conclusion, that to do otherwise would be unfaithful to the spirit of that deliberately difficult process and a dangerously destabilizing precedent for the future.

But with the disappearance of that base, I now believe that the constitutional purpose has been served, and there is no longer a need for the process to be prolonged.

I would have preferred to carry through to the finish whatever the personal agony it would have involved, and my family unanimously urged me to do so. But the interest of the Nation must always come before any personal considerations.

From the discussions I have had with Congressional and other leaders, I have concluded that because of the Watergate matter I might not have the support of the Congress that I would consider necessary to back the very difficult decisions and carry out the duties of this office in the way the interests of the Nation would require.

I have never been a quitter. To leave office before my term is completed is abhorrent to every instinct in my body. But as President, I must put the interest of America first.

America needs a full-time President and a full-time Congress, particularly at this time with problems we face at home and abroad.

To continue to fight through the months ahead for my personal vindication would almost totally absorb the time and attention of both the President and the Congress in a period when our entire focus should be on the great issues of peace abroad and prosperity without inflation at home.

Therefore, I shall resign the Presidency effective at noon tomorrow. Vice President Ford will be sworn in as President at that hour in this office.

As I recall the high hopes for America with which we began this second term, I feel a great sadness that I will not be here in this office working on your behalf to achieve those hopes in the next 2 1/2 years. But in turning over direction of the Government to Vice President Ford, I know, as I told the Nation when I nominated him for that office 10 months ago, that the leadership of America will be in good hands.

In passing this office to the Vice President, I also do so with the profound sense of the weight of responsibility that will fall on his shoulders tomorrow and, therefore, of the understanding, the patience, the cooperation he will need from all Americans.

As he assumes that responsibility, he will deserve the help and the support of all of us. As we look to the future, the first essential is to begin healing the wounds of this Nation, to put the bitterness and divisions of the recent past behind us, and to rediscover those shared ideals that lie at the heart of our strength and unity as a great and as a free people.

By taking this action, I hope that I will have hastened the start of that process of healing which is so desperately needed in America.

I regret deeply any injuries that may have been done in the course of the events that led to this decision. I would say only that if some of my judgments were wrong, and some were wrong, they were made in what I believed at the time to be the best interest of the Nation.

To those who have stood with me during these past difficult months, to my family, my friends, to many others who joined in supporting my cause because they believed it was right, I will be eternally grateful for your support.

And to those who have not felt able to give me your support, let me say I leave with no bitterness toward those who have opposed me, because all of us, in the final analysis, have been concerned with the good of the country, however our judgments might differ.

So, let us all now join together in affirming that common commitment and in helping our new President succeed for the benefit of all Americans.

I shall leave this office with regret at not completing my term, but with gratitude for the privilege of serving as your President for the past 5 1/2 years. These years have been a momentous time in the history of our Nation and the world. They have been a time of achievement in which we can all be proud, achievements that represent the shared efforts of the Administration, the Congress, and the people.

But the challenges ahead are equally great, and they, too, will require the support and the efforts of the Congress and the people working in cooperation with the new Administration.

We have ended America's longest war, but in the work of securing a lasting peace in the world, the goals ahead are even more far-reaching and more difficult. We must complete a structure of peace so that it will be said of this generation, our generation of Americans, by the people of all nations, not only that we ended one war but that we prevented future wars.

We have unlocked the doors that for a quarter of a century stood between the United States and the People's Republic of China.

We must now ensure that the one quarter of the world's people who live in the People's Republic of China will be and remain not our enemies but our friends.

In the Middle East, 100 million people in the Arab countries, many of whom have considered us their enemy for nearly 20 years, now look on us as their friends. We must continue to build on that friendship so that peace can settle at last over the Middle East and so that the cradle of civilization will not become its grave.

Together with the Soviet Union we have made the crucial breakthroughs that have begun the process of limiting nuclear arms. But we must set as our goal not just limiting but reducing and finally destroying these terrible weapons so that they cannot destroy civilization and so that the threat of nuclear war will no longer hang over the world and the people.

We have opened the new relation with the Soviet Union. We must continue to develop and expand that new relationship so that the two strongest nations of the world will live together in cooperation rather than confrontation.

Around the world, in Asia, in Africa, in Latin America, in the Middle East, there are millions of people who live in terrible poverty, even starvation. We must keep as our goal turning away from production for war and expanding production for peace so that people everywhere on this earth can at last look forward in their children's time, if not in our own time, to having the necessities for a decent life.

Here in America, we are fortunate that most of our people have not only the blessings of liberty but also the means to live full and good and, by the world's standards, even abundant lives. We must press on, however, toward a goal of not only more and better jobs but of full opportunity for every American and of what we are striving so hard right now to achieve, prosperity without inflation.

For more than a quarter of a century in public life I have shared in the turbulent history of this era. I have fought for what I believed in. I have tried to the best of my ability to discharge those duties and meet those responsibilities that were entrusted to me.

Sometimes I have succeeded and sometimes I have failed, but always I have taken heart from what Theodore Roosevelt once said about the man in the arena, "whose face is marred by dust and sweat and blood, who strives valiantly, who errs and comes short again and again because there is not effort without error and shortcoming, but who does actually strive to do the deed, who knows the great enthusiasms, the great devotions, who spends himself in a worthy cause, who at the best knows in the end the triumphs of high achievements and who at the worst, if he fails, at least fails while daring greatly."

I pledge to you tonight that as long as I have a breath of life in my body, I shall continue in that spirit. I shall continue to work for the great causes to which I have been dedicated throughout my years as a Congressman, a Senator, a Vice President, and President, the cause of peace not just for America but among all nations, prosperity, justice, and opportunity for all of our people.

There is one cause above all to which I have been devoted and to which I shall always be devoted for as long as I live.

When I first took the oath of office as President 5 1/2 years ago, I made this sacred commitment, to "consecrate my office, my energies, and all the wisdom I can summon to the cause of peace among nations."

I have done my very best in all the days since to be true to that pledge. As a result of these efforts, I am confident that the world is a safer place today, not only for the people of America but for the people of all nations, and that all of our children have a better chance than before of living in peace rather than dying in war.

This, more than anything, is what I hoped to achieve when I sought the Presidency. This, more than anything, is what I hope will be my legacy to you, to our country, as I leave the Presidency.

To have served in this office is to have felt a very personal sense of kinship with each and every American. In leaving it, I do so with this prayer: May God's grace be with you in all the days ahead.

President Richard Nixon - August 8, 1974

President Ford's Speech Pardoning President Richard Nixon

Ladies and gentlemen:

I have come to a decision which I felt I should tell you and all of my fellow American citizens, as soon as I was certain in my own mind and in my own conscience that it is the right thing to do.

I have learned already in this office that the difficult decisions always come to this desk. I must admit that many of them do not look at all the same as the hypothetical questions that I have answered freely and perhaps too fast on previous occasions.

My customary policy is to try and get all the facts and to consider the opinions of my countrymen and to take counsel with my most valued friends. But these seldom agree, and in the end, the decision is mine. To procrastinate, to agonize, and to wait for a more favorable turn of events that may never come or more compelling external pressures that may as well be wrong as right, is itself a decision of sorts and a weak and potentially dangerous course for a President to follow.

I have promised to uphold the Constitution, to do what is right as God gives me to see the right, and to do the very best that I can for America.

I have asked your help and your prayers, not only when I became President but many times since. The Constitution is the supreme law of our land and it governs our actions as citizens. Only the laws of God, which govern our consciences, are superior to it.

As we are a nation under God, so I am sworn to uphold our laws with the help of God. And I have sought such guidance and searched my own conscience with special diligence to determine the right thing for me to do with respect to my predecessor in this place, Richard Nixon, and his loyal wife and family.

Theirs is an American tragedy in which we all have played a part. It could go on and on and on, or someone must write the end to it. I have concluded that only I can do that, and if I can, I must.

There are no historic or legal precedents to which I can turn in this matter, none that precisely fit the circumstances of a private citizen who has resigned the Presidency of the United States. But it is common knowledge that serious allegations and accusations hang like a sword over our former President's head, threatening his health as he tries to reshape his life, a great part of which was spent in the service of this country and by the mandate of its people.

After years of bitter controversy and divisive national debate, I have been advised, and I am compelled to conclude that many months and perhaps more years will have to pass before Richard Nixon could obtain a fair trial by jury in any jurisdiction of the United States under governing decisions of the Supreme Court.

I deeply believe in equal justice for all Americans, whatever their station or former station. The law, whether human or divine, is no respecter of persons; but the law is a respecter of reality.

The facts, as I see them, are that a former President of the United States, instead of enjoying equal treatment with any other citizen accused of violating the law, would be cruelly and excessively penalized either in preserving the presumption of his innocence or in obtaining a speedy determination of his guilt in order to repay a legal debt to society.

During this long period of delay and potential litigation, ugly passions would again be aroused. And our people would again be polarized in their opinions. And the credibility of our free institutions of government would again be challenged at home and abroad.

In the end, the courts might well hold that Richard Nixon had been denied due process, and the verdict of history would even be more inconclusive with respect to those charges arising out of the period of his Presidency, of which I am presently aware.

But it is not the ultimate fate of Richard Nixon that most concerns me, though surely it deeply troubles every decent and every compassionate person. My concern is the immediate future of this great country.

In this, I dare not depend upon my personal sympathy as a longtime friend of the former President, nor my professional judgment as a lawyer, and I do not.

As President, my primary concern must always be the greatest good of all the people of the United States whose servant I am. As a man, my first consideration is to be true to my own convictions and my own conscience.

My conscience tells me clearly and certainly that I cannot prolong the bad dreams that continue to reopen a chapter that is closed. My conscience tells me that only I, as President, have the constitutional power to firmly shut and seal this book. My conscience tells me it is my duty, not merely to proclaim domestic tranquility but to use every means that I have to insure it. I do believe that the buck stops here, that I cannot rely upon public opinion polls to tell me what is right. I do believe that right makes might and that if I am wrong, ten angels swearing I was right would make no difference. I do believe, with all my heart and mind and spirit, that I, not as President but as a humble servant of God, will receive justice without mercy if I fail to show mercy.

Finally, I feel that Richard Nixon and his loved ones have suffered enough and will continue to suffer, no matter what I do, no matter what we, as a great and good nation, can do together to make his goal of peace come true.

Now, therefore, I, Gerald R. Ford, President of the United States, pursuant to the pardon power conferred upon me by Article II, Section 2, of the Constitution, have granted and by these presents do grant a full, free, and absolute pardon unto Richard Nixon for all offenses against the United States which he, Richard Nixon, has committed or may have committed or taken part in during the period from July (January) 20, 1969, through August 9, 1974.

In witness whereof, I have hereunto set my hand this eighth day of September, in the year of our Lord nineteen hundred and seventy-four, and of the Independence of the United States of America the one hundred and ninety-ninth.

Gerald R. Ford - September 8, 1974

President Reagan's "Tear Down This Wall" Speech

Remarks at the Brandenburg Gate
West Berlin, Germany
June 12, 1987

(This speech was delivered to the people of West Berlin, yet it was also audible on the East side of the Berlin wall.)

Thank you very much.

Chancellor Kohl, Governing Mayor Diepgen, ladies and gentlemen: Twenty-four years ago, President John F. Kennedy visited Berlin, speaking to the people of this city and the world at the City Hall. Well, since then two other presidents have come, each in his turn, to Berlin. And today I, myself, make my second visit to your city.

We come to Berlin, we American presidents, because it's our duty to speak, in this place, of freedom. But I must confess, we're drawn here by other things as well: by the feeling of history in this city, more than 500 years older than our own nation; by the beauty of the Grunewald and the Tiergarten; most of all, by your courage and determination. Perhaps the composer Paul Lincke understood something about American presidents. You see, like so many presidents before me, I come here today because wherever I go, whatever I do: Ich hab noch einen Koffer in Berlin. [I still have a suitcase in Berlin.]

Our gathering today is being broadcast throughout Western Europe and North America. I understand that it is being seen and heard as well in the East. To those listening throughout Eastern Europe, a special word: Although I cannot be with you, I address my remarks to you just as surely as to those standing here before me. For I join you, as I join your fellow countrymen in the West, in this firm, this unalterable belief: Es gibt nur ein Berlin. [There is only one Berlin.]

Behind me stands a wall that encircles the free sectors of this city, part of a vast system of barriers that divides the entire continent of Europe. From the Baltic, south, those barriers cut across Germany in a gash of barbed wire, concrete, dog runs, and guard towers. Farther south, there may be no visible, no obvious wall. But there remain armed guards and checkpoints all the same--still a restriction on the right to travel, still an instrument to impose upon ordinary men and women the will of a totalitarian state. Yet it is here in Berlin where the wall emerges most clearly; here, cutting across your city, where the news photo and the television screen have imprinted this brutal division of a continent upon the mind of the world. Standing before the Brandenburg Gate, every man is a German, separated from his fellow men. Every man is a Berliner, forced to look upon a scar.

President von Weizsacker has said, "The German question is open as long as the Brandenburg Gate is closed." Today I say: As long as the gate is closed, as long as this scar of a wall is permitted to stand, it is not the German question alone that remains open, but the question of freedom for all mankind. Yet I do not come here to lament. For I find in Berlin a message of hope, even in the shadow of this wall, a message of triumph.

In this season of spring in 1945, the people of Berlin emerged from their air-raid shelters to find devastation. Thousands of miles away, the people of the United States reached out to help. And in 1947 Secretary of State--as you've been told--George Marshall announced the creation of what would become known as the Marshall Plan. Speaking precisely 40 years ago this month, he said: "Our policy is directed not against any country or doctrine, but against hunger, poverty, desperation, and chaos."

In the Reichstag a few moments ago, I saw a display commemorating this 40th anniversary of the Marshall Plan. I was struck by the sign on a burnt-out, gutted structure that was being rebuilt. I understand that Berliners of my own generation can remember seeing signs like it dotted throughout the western sectors of the city. The sign read simply: "The Marshall Plan is helping here to strengthen the free world." A strong, free world in the West, that dream became real. Japan rose from ruin to become an economic giant. Italy, France, Belgium--virtually every nation in Western Europe saw political and economic rebirth; the European Community was founded.

In West Germany and here in Berlin, there took place an economic miracle, the Wirtschaftswunder. Adenauer, Erhard, Reuter, and other leaders understood the practical importance of liberty--that just as truth can flourish only when the journalist is given freedom of speech, so prosperity can come about only when the farmer and businessman enjoy economic freedom. The German leaders reduced tariffs, expanded free trade, lowered taxes. From 1950 to 1960 alone, the standard of living in West Germany and Berlin doubled.

Where four decades ago there was rubble, today in West Berlin there is the greatest industrial output of any city in Germany--busy office blocks, fine homes and apartments, proud avenues, and the spreading lawns of parkland. Where a city's culture seemed to have been destroyed, today there are two great universities, orchestras and an opera, countless theaters, and museums. Where there was want, today there's abundance--food, clothing, automobiles--the wonderful goods of the Ku'damm. From devastation, from utter ruin, you Berliners have, in freedom, rebuilt a city that once again ranks as one of the greatest on earth. The Soviets may have had other plans. But my friends, there were a few things the Soviets didn't count on--Berliner Herz, Berliner Humor, ja, und Berliner Schnauze. [Berliner heart, Berliner humor, yes, and a Berliner Schnauze.]

In the 1950s, Khrushchev predicted: "We will bury you." But in the West today, we see a free world that has achieved a level of prosperity and well-being unprecedented in all human history. In the Communist world, we see failure, technological backwardness, declining standards of health, even want of the most basic kind--too little food. Even today, the Soviet Union still cannot feed itself. After these four decades, then, there stands before the entire world one great and inescapable conclusion: Freedom leads to prosperity. Freedom replaces the ancient hatreds among the nations with comity and peace. Freedom is the victor.

And now the Soviets themselves may, in a limited way, be coming to understand the importance of freedom. We hear much from Moscow about a new policy of reform and openness. Some political prisoners have been released. Certain foreign news broadcasts are no longer being jammed. Some economic enterprises have been permitted to operate with greater freedom from state control.

Are these the beginnings of profound changes in the Soviet state? Or are they token gestures, intended to raise false hopes in the West, or to strengthen the Soviet system without changing it? We welcome change and openness; for we believe that freedom and security go together, that the advance of human liberty can only strengthen the cause of world peace. There is one sign the Soviets can make that would be unmistakable, that would advance dramatically the cause of freedom and peace.

General Secretary Gorbachev, if you seek peace, if you seek prosperity for the Soviet Union and Eastern Europe, if you seek liberalization: Come here to this gate! Mr. Gorbachev, open this gate! Mr. Gorbachev, tear down this wall!

I understand the fear of war and the pain of division that afflict this continent-- and I pledge to you my country's efforts to help overcome these burdens. To be sure, we in the West must resist Soviet expansion. So we must maintain defenses of unassailable strength. Yet we seek peace; so we must strive to reduce arms on both sides.

Beginning 10 years ago, the Soviets challenged the Western alliance with a grave new threat, hundreds of new and more deadly SS-20 nuclear missiles, capable of striking every capital in Europe. The Western alliance responded by committing itself to a counter-deployment unless the Soviets agreed to negotiate a better solution; namely, the elimination of such weapons on both sides. For many months, the Soviets refused to bargain in earnestness. As the alliance, in turn, prepared to go forward with its counter-deployment, there were difficult days--days of protests like those during my 1982 visit to this city--and the Soviets later walked away from the table.

But through it all, the alliance held firm. And I invite those who protested then-- I invite those who protest today--to mark this fact: Because we remained strong, the Soviets came back to the table. And because we remained strong, today we have within reach the possibility, not merely of limiting the growth of arms, but of eliminating, for the first time, an entire class of nuclear weapons from the face of the earth.

As I speak, NATO ministers are meeting in Iceland to review the progress of our proposals for eliminating these weapons. At the talks in Geneva, we have also proposed deep cuts in strategic offensive weapons. And the Western allies have likewise made far-reaching proposals to reduce the danger of conventional war and to place a total ban on chemical weapons.

While we pursue these arms reductions, I pledge to you that we will maintain the capacity to deter Soviet aggression at any level at which it might occur. And in cooperation with many of our allies, the United States is pursuing the Strategic Defense Initiative--research to base deterrence not on the threat of offensive retaliation, but on defenses that truly defend; on systems, in short, that will not target populations, but shield them. By these means we seek to increase the safety of Europe and all the world. But we must remember a crucial fact: East and West do not mistrust each other because we are armed; we are armed because we mistrust each other. And our differences are not about weapons but about liberty. When President Kennedy spoke at the City Hall those 24 years ago, freedom was encircled, Berlin was under siege. And today, despite all the pressures upon this city, Berlin stands secure in its liberty. And freedom itself is transforming the globe.

In the Philippines, in South and Central America, democracy has been given a rebirth. Throughout the Pacific, free markets are working miracle after miracle of economic growth. In the industrialized nations, a technological revolution is taking place--a revolution marked by rapid, dramatic advances in computers and telecommunications.

In Europe, only one nation and those it controls refuse to join the community of freedom. Yet in this age of redoubled economic growth, of information and innovation, the Soviet Union faces a choice: It must make fundamental changes, or it will become obsolete.

Today thus represents a moment of hope. We in the West stand ready to cooperate with the East to promote true openness, to break down barriers that separate people, to create a safe, freer world. And surely there is no better place than Berlin, the meeting place of East and West, to make a start. Free people of Berlin: Today, as in the past, the United States stands for the strict observance and full implementation of all parts of the Four Power Agreement of 1971. Let us use this occasion, the 750th anniversary of this city, to usher in a new era, to seek a still fuller, richer life for the Berlin of the future. Together, let us maintain and develop the ties between the Federal Republic and the Western sectors of Berlin, which is permitted by the 1971 agreement.

And I invite Mr. Gorbachev: Let us work to bring the Eastern and Western parts of the city closer together, so that all the inhabitants of all Berlin can enjoy the benefits that come with life in one of the great cities of the world.

To open Berlin still further to all Europe, East and West, let us expand the vital air access to this city, finding ways of making commercial air service to Berlin more convenient, more comfortable, and more economical. We look to the day when West Berlin can become one of the chief aviation hubs in all central Europe.

With our French and British partners, the United States is prepared to help bring international meetings to Berlin. It would be only fitting for Berlin to serve as the site of United Nations meetings, or world conferences on human rights and arms control or other issues that call for international cooperation.

There is no better way to establish hope for the future than to enlighten young minds, and we would be honored to sponsor summer youth exchanges, cultural events, and other programs for young Berliners from the East. Our French and British friends, I'm certain, will do the same. And it's my hope that an authority can be found in East Berlin to sponsor visits from young people of the Western sectors.

One final proposal, one close to my heart: Sport represents a source of enjoyment and ennoblement, and you may have noted that the Republic of Korea--South Korea--has offered to permit certain events of the 1988 Olympics to take place in the North. International sports competitions of all kinds could take place in both parts of this city. And what better way to demonstrate to the world the openness of this city than to offer in some future year to hold the Olympic games here in Berlin, East and West? In these four decades, as I have said, you Berliners have built a great city. You've done so in spite of threats--the Soviet attempts to impose the East-mark, the blockade. Today the city thrives in spite of the challenges implicit in the very presence of this wall. What keeps you here? Certainly there's a great deal to be said for your fortitude, for your defiant courage. But I believe there's something deeper, something that involves Berlin's whole look and feel and way of life--not mere sentiment. No one could live long in Berlin without being completely disabused of illusions. Something instead, that has seen the difficulties of life in Berlin but chose to accept them, that continues to build this good and proud city in contrast to a surrounding totalitarian presence that refuses to release human energies or aspirations. Something that speaks with a powerful voice of affirmation, that says yes to this city, yes to the future, yes to freedom. In a word, I would submit that what keeps you in Berlin is love--love both profound and abiding.

Perhaps this gets to the root of the matter, to the most fundamental distinction of all between East and West. The totalitarian world produces backwardness because it does such violence to the spirit, thwarting the human impulse to create, to enjoy, to worship. The totalitarian world finds even symbols of love and of worship an affront. Years ago, before the East Germans began rebuilding their churches, they erected a secular structure: the television tower at Alexander Platz. Virtually ever since, the authorities have been working to correct what they view as the tower's one major flaw, treating the glass sphere at the top with paints and chemicals of every kind. Yet even today when the sun strikes that sphere--that sphere that towers over all Berlin--the light makes the sign of the cross. There in Berlin, like the city itself, symbols of love, symbols of worship, cannot be suppressed.

As I looked out a moment ago from the Reichstag, that embodiment of German unity, I noticed words crudely spray-painted upon the wall, perhaps by a young Berliner: "This wall will fall. Beliefs become reality." Yes, across Europe, this wall will fall. For it cannot withstand faith; it cannot withstand truth. The wall cannot withstand freedom.

And I would like, before I close, to say one word. I have read, and I have been questioned since I've been here about certain demonstrations against my coming. And I would like to say just one thing, and to those who demonstrate so. I wonder if they have ever asked themselves that if they should have the kind of government they apparently seek, no one would ever be able to do what they're doing again.

Thank you and God bless you all.

President Clinton's "I Am Profoundly Sorry" Speech

Good afternoon.

As anyone close to me knows, for months I have been grappling with how best to reconcile myself to the American people, to acknowledge my own wrongdoing and still to maintain my focus on the work of the presidency.

Others are presenting my defense on the facts, the law and the Constitution. Nothing I can say now can add to that.

What I want the American people to know, what I want the Congress to know is that I am profoundly sorry for all I have done wrong in words and deeds.

I never should have misled the country, the Congress, my friends or my family. Quite simply, I gave in to my shame. I have been condemned by my accusers with harsh words.

And while it's hard to hear yourself called deceitful and manipulative, I remember Ben Franklin's admonition that our critics are our friends, for they do show us our faults.

Mere words cannot fully express the profound remorse I feel for what our country is going through and for what members of both parties in Congress are now forced to deal with. These past months have been a torturous process of coming to terms with what I did. I understand that accountability demands consequences, and I'm prepared to accept them.

Painful as the condemnation of the Congress would be, it would pale in comparison to the consequences of the pain I have caused my family. There is no greater agony.

Like anyone who honestly faces the shame of wrongful conduct, I would give anything to go back and undo what I did.

But one of the painful truths I have to live with is the reality that that is simply not possible. An old and dear friend of mine recently sent me the wisdom of a poet who wrote, "The moving finger writes and having writ, moves on. Nor all your piety nor wit shall lure it back to cancel half a line. Nor all your tears wash out a word of it."

So nothing, not piety, nor tears, nor wit, nor torment can alter what I have done. I must make my peace with that.

I must also be at peace with the fact that the public consequences of my actions are in the hands of the American people and their representatives in the Congress.

Should they determine that my errors of word and deed require their rebuke and censure, I am ready to accept that.

Meanwhile, I will continue to do all I can to reclaim the trust of the American people and to serve them well.

We must all return to the work, the vital work, of strengthening our nation for the new century. Our country has wonderful opportunities and daunting challenges ahead. I intend to seize those opportunities and meet those challenges with all the energy and ability and strength God has given me.

That is simply all I can do -- the work of the American people.

Thank you very much.

President Bill Clinton - December 11, 1998

George W. Bush et al., Petitioners, v. Albert Gore, Jr., et al. (2000)

On writ of certiorari to the Florida Supreme Court

I. On December 8, 2000, the Supreme Court of Florida ordered that the Circuit Court of Leon County tabulate by hand 9,000 ballots in Miami-Dade County. It also ordered the inclusion in the certified vote totals of 215 votes identified in Palm Beach County and 168 votes identified in Miami-Dade County for Vice President Albert Gore, Jr., and Senator Joseph Lieberman, Democratic Candidates for President and Vice President. The Supreme Court noted that petitioner Governor George W. Bush asserted that the net gain for Vice President Gore in Palm Beach County was 176 votes and directed the Circuit Court to resolve that dispute on remand. (So. 2d, at (slip op., at 4, n. 6). The court further held that relief would require manual recounts in all Florida counties where so-called "undervotes" had not been subject to manual tabulation. The court ordered all manual recounts to begin at once. Governor Bush and Richard Cheney, Republican Candidates for the Presidency and Vice Presidency, filed an emergency application for a stay of this mandate. On December 9, we granted the application, treated the application as a petition for a writ of certiorari, and granted certiorari.

The proceedings leading to the present controversy are discussed in some detail in our opinion in Bush v. Palm Beach County Canvassing Board. On November 26, the Florida Elections Canvassing Commission certified the results of the election and declared Governor Bush the winner of Florida's 25 electoral votes. On November 27, Vice President Gore, pursuant to Florida's contest provisions, filed a complaint in Leon County Circuit Court contesting the certification. The Circuit Court denied relief, stating that Vice President Gore failed to meet his burden of proof. He appealed to the First District Court of Appeal, which certified the matter to the Florida Supreme Court. Accepting jurisdiction, the Florida Supreme Court affirmed in part and reversed in part. Gore v. Harris (2000). The (Florida) Supreme Court held that Vice President Gore had satisfied his burden of proof under §102.168(3)© with respect to his challenge to Miami-Dade County's failure to tabulate, by manual count, 9,000 ballots on which the machines had failed to detect a vote for President ("under-votes").

The petition presents the following questions: whether the Florida Supreme Court established new standards for resolving Presidential election contests, thereby violating Art. II, §1, cl. 2, of the United States Constitution and failing to comply with 3 U. S. C. §5, and whether the use of standardless manual recounts violates the Equal Protection and Due Process Clauses. With respect to the equal protection question, we find a violation of the Equal Protection Clause.

II.   A. This case has shown that punch card balloting machines can produce an unfortunate number of ballots which are not punched in a clean, complete way by the voter. After the current counting, it is likely legislative bodies nationwide will examine ways to improve the mechanisms and machinery for voting.

B. The individual citizen has no federal constitutional right to vote for electors for the President of the United States unless and until the state legislature chooses a statewide election as the means to implement its power to appoint members of the Electoral College. See U. S. Constitution, Art. II, §1.

Having once granted the right to vote on equal terms, the State may not, by later arbitrary and disparate treatment, value one person's vote over that of another. The question before us is whether the recount procedures the Florida Supreme Court has adopted are consistent with its obligation to avoid arbitrary and disparate treatment of the members of its electorate.

Much of the controversy seems to revolve around ballot cards designed to be perforated by a stylus but which, either through error or deliberate omission, have not been perforated with sufficient precision for a machine to count them. In some cases a piece of the card—a chad—is hanging, say by two corners. In other cases there is no separation at all, just an indentation.

The Florida Supreme Court has ordered that the intent of the voter be discerned from such ballots. The problem inheres in the absence of specific standards to ensure its equal application. The formulation of uniform rules to determine intent based on these recurring circumstances is practicable and, we conclude, necessary. The search for intent can be confined by specific rules designed to ensure uniform treatment.

The want of those rules here has led to unequal evaluation of ballots in various respects. As seems to have been acknowledged at oral argument, the standards for accepting or rejecting contested ballots might vary not only from county to county but (also) indeed within a single county from one recount team to another.

The record provides some examples. A monitor in Miami-Dade County testified at trial that he observed that three members of the county canvassing board applied different standards in defining a legal vote. And testimony at trial also revealed that at least one county changed its evaluative standards during the counting process. This is not a process with sufficient guarantees of equal treatment. . . .

The State Supreme Court ratified this uneven treatment. It mandated that the recount totals from two counties, Miami-Dade and Palm Beach, be included in the certified total. The court also appeared to hold sub silentio that the recount totals from Broward County, which were not completed until after the original November 14 certification by the Secretary of State, were to be considered part of the new certified vote totals even though the county certification was not contested by Vice President Gore. Yet each of the counties used varying standards to determine what was a legal vote. Broward County used a more forgiving standard than Palm Beach County, and uncovered almost three times as many new votes, a result markedly disproportionate to the difference in population between the counties.

The recount process, in its features here described, is inconsistent with the minimum procedures necessary to protect the fundamental right of each voter in the special instance of a statewide recount under the authority of a single state judicial officer. When a court orders a statewide remedy, there must be at least some assurance that the rudimentary requirements of equal treatment and fundamental fairness are satisfied.

Given the Court's assessment that the recount process underway was probably being conducted in an unconstitutional manner, the Court stayed the order directing the recount so it could hear this case and render an expedited decision.
Upon due consideration of the difficulties identified to this point, it is obvious that the recount cannot be conducted in compliance with the requirements of equal protection and due process without substantial additional work. It would require not only the adoption (after opportunity for argument) of adequate statewide standards for determining what is a legal vote, and practicable procedures to implement them, but also orderly judicial review of any disputed matters that might arise.

The Supreme Court of Florida has said that (3 U. S. C. §5) requires that any controversy or contest that is designed to lead to a conclusive selection of electors be completed by December 12. Because it is evident that any recount seeking to meet the December 12 date will be unconstitutional for the reasons we have discussed, we reverse the judgment of the Supreme Court of Florida ordering a recount to proceed.

Seven Justices of the Court agree that there are constitutional problems with the recount ordered by the Florida Supreme Court that demand a remedy.

The judgment of the Supreme Court of Florida is reversed, and the case is remanded for further proceedings not inconsistent with this opinion. It is so ordered.

JUSTICE STEVENS, with whom **JUSTICE GINSBURG** and **JUSTICE BREYER** join, dissenting.

The Constitution assigns to the States the primary responsibility for determining the manner of selecting the Presidential electors. See Art. II, §1, cl. 2. When questions arise about the meaning of state laws, including election laws, it is our settled practice to accept the opinions of the highest courts of the States as providing the final answers.

What must underlie petitioners' entire federal assault on the Florida election procedures is an unstated lack of confidence in the impartiality and capacity of the state judges who would make the critical decisions if the vote count were to proceed. Otherwise, their position is wholly without merit. The endorsement of that position by the majority of this Court can only lend credence to the most cynical appraisal of the work of judges throughout the land. It is confidence in the men and women who administer the judicial system that is the true backbone of the rule of law. Time will one day heal the wound to that confidence that will be inflicted by today's decision. One thing, however, is certain. Although we may never know with complete certainty the identity of the winner of this year's Presidential election, the identity of the loser is perfectly clear. It is the Nation's confidence in the judge as an impartial guardian of the rule of law.

Al Gore's Concession Speech in 2000

Good evening.

Just moments ago, I spoke with George W. Bush and congratulated him on becoming the 43rd President of the United States, and I promised him that I wouldn't call him back this time. I offered to meet with him as soon as possible so that we can start to heal the divisions of the campaign and the contest through which we just passed.

Almost a century and a half ago, Senator Stephen Douglas told Abraham Lincoln, who had just defeated him for the presidency, "Partisan feeling must yield to patriotism. I'm with you, Mr. President, and God bless you." Well, in that same spirit, I say to President-elect Bush that what remains of partisan rancor must now be put aside, and may God bless his stewardship of this country. Neither he nor I anticipated this long and difficult road. Certainly neither of us wanted it to happen. Yet it came, and now it has ended, resolved, as it must be resolved, through the honored institutions of our democracy.

Over the library of one of our great law schools is inscribed the motto, "Not under man but under God and law." That's the ruling principle of American freedom, the source of our democratic liberties. I've tried to make it my guide throughout this contest as it has guided America's deliberations of all the complex issues of the past five weeks. Now the U.S. Supreme Court has spoken. Let there be no doubt, while I strongly disagree with the court's decision, I accept it. I accept the finality of this outcome which will be ratified next Monday in the Electoral College. And tonight, for the sake of our unity of the people and the strength of our democracy, I offer my concession.

I also accept my responsibility, which I will discharge unconditionally, to honor the new President elect and do everything possible to help him bring Americans together in fulfillment of the great vision that our Declaration of Independence defines and that our Constitution affirms and defends.

Let me say how grateful I am to all those who supported me and supported the cause for which we have fought. Tipper and I feel a deep gratitude to Joe and Hadassah Lieberman who brought passion and high purpose to our partnership and opened new doors, not just for our campaign but for our country.

This has been an extraordinary election. But in one of God's unforeseen paths, this belatedly broken impasse can point us all to a new common ground, for its very closeness can serve to remind us that we are one people with a shared history and a shared destiny. Indeed, that history gives us many examples of contests as hotly debated, as fiercely fought, with their own challenges to the popular will.

Other disputes have dragged on for weeks before reaching resolution. And each time, both the victor and the vanquished have accepted the result peacefully and in the spirit of reconciliation.

So let it be with us.

I know that many of my supporters are disappointed. I am too. But our disappointment must be overcome by our love of country.

And I say to our fellow members of the world community, let no one see this contest as a sign of American weakness. The strength of American democracy is shown most clearly through the difficulties it can overcome.

Some have expressed concern that the unusual nature of this election might hamper the next President in the conduct of his office. I do not believe it need be so. President-elect Bush inherits a nation whose citizens will be ready to assist him in the conduct of his large responsibilities.

I personally will be at his disposal, and I call on all Americans -- I particularly urge all who stood with us to unite behind our next President. This is America. Just as we fight hard when the stakes are high, we close ranks and come together when the contest is done. And while there will be time enough to debate our continuing differences, now is the time to recognize that that which unites us is greater than that which divides us. While we yet hold and do not yield our opposing beliefs, there is a higher duty than the one we owe to political party. This is America and we put country before party. We will stand together behind our new President.

As for what I'll do next, I don't know the answer to that one yet. Like many of you, I'm looking forward to spending the holidays with family and old friends. I know I'll spend time in Tennessee and mend some fences, literally and figuratively.

Some have asked whether I have any regrets and I do have one regret: that I didn't get the chance to stay and fight for the American people over the next four years, especially for those who need burdens lifted and barriers removed, especially for those who feel their voices have not been heard. I heard you and I will not forget. I've seen America in this campaign and I like what I see. It's worth fighting for and that's a fight I'll never stop.

As for the battle that ends tonight, I do believe as my father once said, that no matter how hard the loss, defeat might serve as well as victory to shape the soul and let the glory out. So for me this campaign ends as it began: with the love of Tipper and our family; with faith in God and in the country I have been so proud to serve, from Vietnam to the vice presidency; and with gratitude to our truly tireless campaign staff and volunteers, including all those who worked so hard in Florida for the last 36 days.

Now the political struggle is over and we turn again to the unending struggle for the common good of all Americans and for those multitudes around the world who look to us for leadership in the cause of freedom. In the words of our great hymn, "America, America": "Let us crown thy good with brotherhood, from sea to shining sea."

And now, my friends, in a phrase I once addressed to others, it's time for me to go.

Thank you and good night, and God bless America.

Al Gore - December 13, 2000

President Bush to Congress in Aftermath of September 11, 2001

Mr. Speaker, Mr. President Pro Tempore, members of Congress, and fellow Americans:

In the normal course of events, presidents come to this chamber to report on the state of the Union. Tonight, no such report is needed. It has already been delivered by the American people.

We have seen it in the courage of passengers who rushed terrorists to save others on the ground. Passengers like an exceptional man named Todd Beamer. And would you please help me welcome his wife Lisa Beamer here tonight?

We have seen the state of our Union in the endurance of rescuers working past exhaustion. We've seen the unfurling of flags, the lighting of candles, the giving of blood, the saying of prayers in English, Hebrew and Arabic. We have seen the decency of a loving and giving people who have made the grief of strangers their own.

My fellow citizens, for the last nine days, the entire world has seen for itself the state of union, and it is strong.

Tonight, we are a country awakened to danger and called to defend freedom. Our grief has turned to anger and anger to resolution. Whether we bring our enemies to justice or bring justice to our enemies, justice will be done.

I thank the Congress for its leadership at such an important time. All of America was touched on the evening of the tragedy to see Republicans and Democrats joined together on the steps of this Capitol singing "God Bless America." And you did more than sing. You acted, by delivering $40 billion to rebuild our communities and meet the needs of our military. Speaker Hastert, Minority Leader Gephardt, Majority Leader Daschle and Senator Lott, I thank you for your friendship, for your leadership and for your service to our country.

And on behalf of the American people, I thank the world for its outpouring of support. America will never forget the sounds of our national anthem playing at Buckingham Palace, on the streets of Paris and at Berlin's Brandenburg Gate. We will not forget South Korean children gathering to pray outside our embassy in Seoul, or the prayers of sympathy offered at a mosque in Cairo. We will not forget moments of silence and days of mourning in Australia and Africa and Latin America. Nor will we forget the citizens of 80 other nations who died with our own. Dozens of Pakistanis, more than 130 Israelis, more than 250 citizens of India, men and women from El Salvador, Iran, Mexico and Japan, and hundreds of British citizens.

America has no truer friend than Great Britain. Once again, we are joined together in a great cause. I'm so honored the British prime minister has crossed an ocean to show his unity with America. Thank you for coming, friend.

On September the 11th, enemies of freedom committed an act of war against our country. Americans have known wars, but for the past 136 years they have been wars on foreign soil, except for one Sunday in 1941. Americans have known the casualties of war, but not at the center of a great city on a peaceful morning. Americans have known surprise attacks, but never before on thousands of civilians. All of this was brought upon us in a single day, and night fell on a different world, a world where freedom itself is under attack.

Americans have many questions tonight. Americans are asking, "Who attacked our country?" The evidence we have gathered all points to a collection of loosely affiliated terrorist organizations known as al-Qaida. They are some of the murderers indicted for bombing American embassies in Tanzania and Kenya and responsible for bombing the USS Cole.

Al-Qaida is to terror what the Mafia is to crime. But its goal is not making money. Its goal is remaking the world and imposing its radical beliefs on people everywhere. The terrorists practice a fringe form of Islamic extremism that has been rejected by Muslim scholars and the vast majority of Muslim clerics; a fringe movement that perverts the peaceful teachings of Islam.

The terrorists' directive commands them to kill Christians and Jews, to kill all Americans and make no distinctions among military and civilians, including women and children. This group and its leader, a person named Osama bin Laden, are linked to many other organizations in different countries, including the Egyptian Islamic Jihad, the Islamic Movement of Uzbekistan.

There are thousands of these terrorists in more than 60 countries. They are recruited from their own nations and neighborhoods and brought to camps in places like Afghanistan, where they are trained in the tactics of terror. They are sent back to their homes or sent to hide in countries around the world to plot evil and destruction.

The leadership of al-Qaida has great influence in Afghanistan and supports the Taliban regime in controlling most of that country. In Afghanistan we see al-Qaida's vision for the world. Afghanistan's people have been brutalized, many are starving and many have fled.

Women are not allowed to attend school. You can be jailed for owning a television. Religion can be practiced only as their leaders dictate. A man can be jailed in Afghanistan if his beard is not long enough.

The United States respects the people of Afghanistan -- after all, we are currently its largest source of humanitarian aid -- but we condemn the Taliban regime. It is not only repressing its own people, it is threatening people everywhere by sponsoring and sheltering and supplying terrorists. By aiding and abetting murder, the Taliban regime is committing murder. And tonight the United States of America makes the following demands on the Taliban:

- Deliver to United States authorities all of the leaders of al-Qaida who hide in your land.
- Release all foreign nationals, including American citizens you have unjustly imprisoned. Protect foreign journalists, diplomats and aid workers in your country. Close immediately and permanently every terrorist training camp in Afghanistan. And hand over every terrorist and every person and their support structure to appropriate authorities.
- Give the United States full access to terrorist training camps, so we can make sure they are no longer operating.
- These demands are not open to negotiation or discussion. The Taliban must act and act immediately. They will hand over the terrorists, or they will share in their fate.

I also want to speak tonight directly to Muslims throughout the world. We respect your faith. It's practiced freely by many millions of Americans and by millions more in countries that America counts as friends. Its teachings are good and peaceful, and those who commit evil in the name of Allah blaspheme the name of Allah. The terrorists are traitors to their own faith, trying, in effect, to hijack Islam itself.

The enemy of America is not our many Muslim friends. It is not our many Arab friends. Our enemy is a radical network of terrorists and every government that supports them. Our war on terror begins with al-Qaida, but it does not end there. It will not end until every terrorist group of global reach has been found, stopped and defeated.

Americans are asking, "Why do they hate us?"

They hate what they see right here in this chamber: a democratically elected government. Their leaders are self-appointed. They hate our freedoms: our freedom of religion, our freedom of speech, our freedom to vote and assemble and disagree with each other.

They want to overthrow existing governments in many Muslim countries such as Egypt, Saudi Arabia and Jordan. They want to drive Israel out of the Middle East. They want to drive Christians and Jews out of vast regions of Asia and Africa.

These terrorists kill not merely to end lives, but to disrupt and end a way of life. With every atrocity, they hope that America grows fearful, retreating from the world and forsaking our friends. They stand against us because we stand in their way.

We're not deceived by their pretenses to piety.

We have seen their kind before. They're the heirs of all the murderous ideologies of the 20th century. By sacrificing human life to serve their radical visions, by abandoning every value except the will to power, they follow in the path of fascism, Nazism and totalitarianism. And they will follow that path all the way to where it ends in history's unmarked grave of discarded lies.

Americans are asking, "How will we fight and win this war?" We will direct every resource at our command -- every means of diplomacy, every tool of intelligence, every instrument of law enforcement, every financial influence and every necessary weapon of war -- to the destruction and to the defeat of the global terror network.

Now this war will not be like the war against Iraq a decade ago, with a decisive liberation of territory and a swift conclusion. It will not look like the air war above Kosovo two years ago, where no ground troops were used and not a single American was lost in combat.

Our response involves far more than instant retaliation and isolated strikes. Americans should not expect one battle, but a lengthy campaign unlike any other we have ever seen. It may include dramatic strikes visible on TV and covert operations secret even in success.

We will starve terrorists of funding, turn them one against another, drive them from place to place until there is no refuge or no rest. And we will pursue nations that provide aid or safe haven to terrorism. Every nation in every region now has a decision to make: Either you are with us, or you are with the terrorists.

From this day forward, any nation that continues to harbor or support terrorism will be regarded by the United States as a hostile regime. Our nation has been put on notice, we're not immune from attack. We will take defensive measures against terrorism to protect Americans.

Today, dozens of federal departments and agencies, as well as state and local governments, have responsibilities affecting homeland security. These efforts must be coordinated at the highest level. So tonight, I announce the creation of a Cabinet-level position reporting directly to me, the Office of Homeland Security. And tonight, I also announce a distinguished American to lead this effort, to strengthen American security: a military veteran, an effective governor, a true patriot, a trusted friend, Pennsylvania's Tom Ridge. He will lead, oversee and coordinate a comprehensive national strategy to safeguard our country against terrorism and respond to any attacks that may come.

These measures are essential. The only way to defeat terrorism as a threat to our way of life is to stop it, eliminate it and destroy it where it grows. Many will be involved in this effort, from FBI agents, to intelligence operatives, to the reservists we have called to active duty. All deserve our thanks, and all have our prayers.

And tonight a few miles from the damaged Pentagon, I have a message for our military: Be ready. I have called the armed forces to alert, and there is a reason. The hour is coming when America will act, and you will make us proud.

This is not, however, just America's fight. And what is at stake is not just America's freedom. This is the world's fight. This is civilization's fight. This is the fight of all who believe in progress and pluralism, tolerance and freedom. We ask every nation to join us.

We will ask and we will need the help of police forces, intelligence services and banking systems around the world. The United States is grateful that many nations and many international organizations have already responded with sympathy and with support -- nations from Latin America, to Asia, to Africa, to Europe, to the Islamic world.

Perhaps the NATO charter reflects best the attitude of the world: An attack on one is an attack on all. The civilized world is rallying to America's side. They understand that if this terror goes unpunished, their own cities, their own citizens may be next. Terror unanswered cannot only bring down buildings, it can threaten the stability of legitimate governments. And you know what? We're not going to allow it.

Americans are asking, "What is expected of us?"

- I ask you to live your lives and hug your children.
- I know many citizens have fears tonight, and I ask you to be calm and resolute, even in the face of a continuing threat.
- I ask you to uphold the values of America and remember why so many have come here.
- We're in a fight for our principles, and our first responsibility is to live by them. No one should be singled out for unfair treatment or unkind words because of their ethnic background or religious faith.
- I ask you to continue to support the victims of this tragedy with your contributions. Those who want to give can go to a central source of information, libertyunites.org, to find the names of groups providing direct help in New York, Pennsylvania and Virginia.
- The thousands of FBI agents who are now at work in this investigation may need your cooperation, and I ask you to give it. I ask for your patience with the delays and inconveniences that may accompany tighter security and for your patience in what will be a long struggle.
- I ask your continued participation and confidence in the American economy. Terrorists attacked a symbol of American prosperity; they did not touch its source.

America is successful because of the hard work and creativity and enterprise of our people. These were the true strengths of our economy before September 11, and they are our strengths today.

And finally, please continue praying for the victims of terror and their families, for those in uniform and for our great country. Prayer has comforted us in sorrow and will help strengthen us for the journey ahead.

Tonight I thank my fellow Americans for what you have already done and for what you will do.

And ladies and gentlemen of the Congress, I thank you, their representatives, for what you have already done and for what we will do together.

Tonight we face new and sudden national challenges. We will come together to improve air safety, to dramatically expand the number of air marshals on domestic flights and take new measures to prevent hijacking. We will come together to promote stability and keep our airlines flying with direct assistance during this emergency. We will come together to give law enforcement the additional tools it needs to track down terror here at home. We will come together to strengthen our intelligence capabilities to know the plans of terrorists before they act and to find them before they strike. We will come together to take active steps that strengthen America's economy and put our people back to work.

Tonight, we welcome two leaders who embody the extraordinary spirit of all New Yorkers, Gov. George Pataki and Mayor Rudolf Giuliani. As a symbol of America's resolve, my administration will work with Congress and these two leaders to show the world that we will rebuild New York City.

After all that has just passed, all the lives taken, and all the possibilities and hopes that died with them, it is natural to wonder if America's future is one of fear. Some speak of an age of terror. I know there are struggles ahead and dangers to face. But this country will define our times, not be defined by them. As long as the United States of America is determined and strong, this will not be an age of terror. This will be an age of liberty here and across the world.

Great harm has been done to us. We have suffered great loss. And in our grief and anger, we have found our mission and our moment. Freedom and fear are at war. The advance of human freedom, the great achievement of our time and the great hope of every time, now depends on us.

Our nation, this generation, will lift the dark threat of violence from our people and our future. We will rally the world to this cause by our efforts, by our courage. We will not tire, we will not falter, and we will not fail.

It is my hope that in the months and years ahead life will return almost to normal. We'll go back to our lives and routines, and that is good. Even grief recedes with time and grace.

But our resolve must not pass. Each of us will remember what happened that day and to whom it happened. We will remember the moment the news came, where we were and what we were doing.

Some will remember an image of a fire or story of rescue. Some will carry memories of a face and a voice gone forever.

And I will carry this. It is the police shield of a man named George Howard, who died at the World Trade Center trying to save others. It was given to me by his mom, Arlene, as a proud memorial to her son. It is my reminder of lives that ended and a task that does not end.

I will not forget the wound to our country and those who inflicted it. I will not yield, I will not rest, I will not relent in waging this struggle for freedom and security for the American people. The course of this conflict is not known, yet its outcome is certain. Freedom and fear, justice and cruelty, have always been at war, and we know that God is not neutral between them.

Fellow citizens, we'll meet violence with patient justice, assured of the rightness of our cause and confident of the victories to come.

In all that lies before us, may God grant us wisdom, and may He watch over the United States of America.

Thank you.

George W. Bush - September 20, 2001

Chapter 6
"With Liberty and Justice for All

Little Speech on Liberty
By John Winthrop
1645

I suppose something may be expected from me, upon this charge that is befallen me which moves me to speak now to you; yet I intend not to intermeddle in the proceedings of the court or with any of the persons concerned therein. Only I bless God that I see an issue of this troublesome business. I also acknowledge the justice of the court, and, for mine own part, I am well satisfied, I was publicly charged, and I am publicly and legally acquitted, which is all I did expect or desire. And though this be sufficient for my justification before men, yet not so before the God, who hath seen so much amiss in my dispensations (and even in this affair) as calls me to be humble. For to be publicly and criminally charged in this court is matter of humiliation (and I desire to make a right use of it), notwithstanding I be thus acquitted. If her father had spit in her face (saith the Lord concerning Miriam), should she not have been ashamed seven days? Shame had lien upon her, whatever the occasion had been. I am unwilling to stay you from your urgent affairs, yet give me leave (upon this special occasion) to speak a little more to this assembly. It may be of some good use, to inform and rectify the judgments of some of the people, and may prevent such distempers as have arisen amongst us. The great questions that have troubled the country are about the authority of the magistrates and the liberty of the people. It is yourselves who have called us to this office, and, being called by you, we have our authority from God, in way of an ordinance, such as hath the image of God eminently stamped upon it, the contempt and violation whereof hath been vindicated with examples of divine vengeance. I entreat you to consider that, when you choose magistrates, you take them from among yourselves, men subject to like passions as you are. Therefore, when you see infirmities in us, you should reflect upon your own, and that would make you bear the more with us, and not be severe censurers of the failings of your magistrates, when you have continual experience of the like infirmities in yourselves and others. We account him a good servant who breaks not his covenant. The covenant between you and us is the oath you have taken of us, which is to this purpose: that we shall govern you and judge your causes by the rules of God's laws and our own, according to our best skill. When you agree with a workman to build you a ship or house, etc., he undertakes as well for his skill as for his faithfulness, for it is his profession, and you pay him for both. But when you call one to be a magistrate, he doth not profess nor undertake to have sufficient skill for that office, nor can you furnish him with gifts, etc., therefore you must run the hazard of his skill and ability. But if he fail in faithfulness, which by his oath he is bound unto, that he must answer for. If it fall out that the case be clear to common apprehension, and the rule clear also, if he transgress here, the error is not in the skill, but in the evil of the will: it must be required of him. But if the case be doubtful, or the rule doubtful, to men of such understanding and parts as your magistrates are, if your magistrates should err here, yourselves must bear it.

For the other point concerning liberty, I observe a great mistake in the country about that. There is a twofold liberty, natural (I mean as our nature is now corrupt) and civil or federal. The first is common to man with beasts and other creatures. By this, man, as he stands in relation to man simply, hath liberty to do what he lists; it is a liberty to evil as well as to good. This liberty is incompatible and inconsistent with authority, and cannot endure the least restraint of the most just authority. The exercise and maintaining of this liberty makes men grow more evil, and in time to be worse than brute beasts: omnes sumus licentia deteriores. This is that great enemy of truth and peace, that wild beast, which all of the ordinances of God are bent against, to restrain and subdue it. The other kind of liberty I call civil or federal; it may also be termed moral, in reference to the covenant between God and man, in the moral law, and the politic covenants and constitutions amongst men themselves. This liberty is the proper end and object of authority and cannot subsist without it; and it is a liberty to that only which is good, just, and honest. This liberty you are to stand for, with the hazard (not only of your goods, but) of your lives, if need be. Whatsoever crosseth this is not authority but a distemper thereof. This liberty is maintained and exercised in a way of subjection to authority; it is of the same kind of liberty wherewith Christ hath made us free. The women's own choice makes such a man her husband; yet, being so chosen, he is her lord, and she is to be subject to him, yet in a way of liberty, not of bondage; and a true wife accounts her subjection her honor and freedom and would not think her condition safe and free but in her subjection to her husband's authority. Such is the liberty of the church under the authority of Christ, her king and husband; his yoke is so easy and sweet to her as a bride's ornaments; and if through forwardness or wantonness, etc., she shake it off, at any time, she is at no rest in her spirit, until she take it up again; and whether her lord smiles upon her and embraceth her in his arms, or whether he frowns, or rebukes, or smites her, she apprehends the sweetness of his love in all, and is refreshed, supported, and instructed by every such dispensation of his authority over her. On the other side, ye know who they are that complain of this yoke and say, Let us break their bands, etc.; we will not have this man to rule over us. Even so, brethren, it will be between you and your magistrates. If you want to stand for your natural corrupt liberties, and will do what is good in your own eyes, you will not endure the least weight of authority, but will murmur, and oppose, and be always striving to shake off that yoke; but if you will be satisfied to enjoy such civil and lawful liberties, such as Christ allows you, then will you quietly and cheerfully submit unto that authority which is set over you, in all the administrations of it, for your good. Wherein, if we fail at any time, we hope we shall be willing (by God's assistance) to hearken to good advice from any of you, or in any other way of God; so shall your liberties be preserved in upholding the honor and power of authority amongst you.

An Act Respecting Alien Enemies

Section 1. Be it enacted by the Senate and House of Representatives of the United States of America in Congress assembled, That whenever there shall be a declared war between the United States and any foreign nation or government, or any invasion or predatory incursion shall be perpetrated, attempted, or threatened against the territory of the United States, by any foreign nation or government, and the President of the United States shall make public proclamation of the event, all natives, citizens, denizens, or subjects of the hostile nation or government, being males of the age of fourteen years and upwards, who shall be within the United States, and not actually naturalized, shall be liable to be apprehended, restrained, secured and removed, as alien enemies. And the President of the United States shall be, and he is hereby authorized, in any event, as aforesaid, by his proclamation thereof, or other public act, to direct the conduct to be observed, on the part of the United States, towards the aliens who shall become liable, as aforesaid; the manner and degree of the restraint to which they shall be subject, and in what cases, and upon what security their residence shall be permitted, and to provide for the removal of those, who, not being permitted to reside within the United States, shall refuse or neglect to depart therefrom; and to establish any other regulations which shall be found necessary in the premises and for the public safety: Provided, that aliens resident within the United States, who shall become liable as enemies, in the manner aforesaid, and who shall not be chargeable with actual hostility, or other crime against the public safety, shall be allowed, for the recovery, disposal, and removal of their goods and effects, and for their departure, the full time which is, or shall be stipulated by any treaty, where any shall have been between the United States, and the hostile nation or government, of which they shall be natives, citizens, denizens or subjects: and where no such treaty shall have existed, the President of the United States may ascertain and declare such reasonable time as may be consistent with the public safety, and according to the dictates of humanity and national hospitality.

Section 2. And be it further enacted, That after any proclamation shall be made as aforesaid, it shall be the duty of the several courts of the United States, and of each state, having criminal jurisdiction, and of the several judges and justices of the courts of the United States, and they shall be, and are hereby respectively, authorized upon complaint, against any alien or alien enemies, as aforesaid, who shall be resident and at large within such jurisdiction or district, to the danger of the public peace or safety, and contrary to the tenor or intent of such proclamation, or other regulations which the President of the United States shall and may establish in the premises, to cause such alien or aliens to be duly apprehended and convened before such court, judge or justice; and after a full examination and hearing on such complaint. and sufficient cause therefore appearing, shall and may order such alien or aliens to be removed out of the territory of the United States, or to give sureties of their good behaviour, or to be otherwise restrained, conformably to the proclamation or regulations which shall and may be established as aforesaid, and may imprison, or otherwise secure such alien or aliens, until the order which shall and may be made, as aforesaid, shall be performed.

SEC. 3. And be it further enacted, That it shall be the duty of the marshal of the district in which any alien enemy shall be apprehended, who by the President of the United States, or by order of any court, judge or justice, as aforesaid, shall be required to depart, and to be removed, as aforesaid, to provide therefore, and to execute such order, by himself or his deputy, or other discreet person or persons to be employed by him, by causing a removal of such alien out of the territory of the United States; and for such removal the marshal shall have the warrant of the President of the United States, or of the court, judge or justice ordering the same, as the case may be.

APPROVED, July 6, 1798.

An Act in Addition to the Act, Entitled "An Act for the Punishment of Certain Crimes Against the United States."

Section 1. Be it enacted by the Senate and House of Representatives of the United States of America, in Congress assembled, That if any persons shall unlawfully combine or conspire together, with intent to oppose any measure or measures of the government of the United States, which are or shall be directed by proper authority, or to impede the operation of any law of the United States, or to intimidate or prevent any person holding a place or office in or under the government of the United States, from undertaking, performing or executing his trust or duty, and if any person or persons, with intent as aforesaid, shall counsel, advise or attempt to procure any insurrection, riot, unlawful assembly, or combination, whether such conspiracy, threatening, counsel, advice, or attempt shall have the proposed effect or not, he or they shall be deemed guilty of a high misdemeanor, and on conviction, before any court of the United States having jurisdiction thereof, shall be punished by a fine not exceeding five thousand dollars, and by imprisonment during a term not less than six months nor exceeding five years; and further, at the discretion of the court may be ho]den to find sureties for his good behaviour in such sum, and for such time, as the said court may direct.

Section 2. And be it farther enacted, That if any person shall write, print, utter or publish, or shall cause or procure to be written, printed, uttered or published, or shall knowingly and willingly assist or aid in writing, printing, uttering or publishing any false, scandalous and malicious writing or writings against the government of the United States, or either house of the Congress of the United States, or the President of the United States, with intent to defame the said government, or either house of the said Congress, or the said President, or to bring them, or either of them, into contempt or disrepute; or to excite against them, or either or any of them, the hatred of the good people of the United States, or to stir up sedition within the United States, or to excite any unlawful combinations therein, for opposing or resisting any law of the United States, or any act of the President of the United States, done in pursuance of any such law, or of the powers in him vested by the constitution of the United States, or to resist, oppose, or defeat any such law or act, or to aid, encourage or abet any hostile designs of any foreign nation against United States, their people or government, then such person, being thereof convicted before any court of the United States having jurisdiction thereof, shall be punished by a fine not exceeding two thousand dollars, and by imprisonment not exceeding two years.

Section 3. And be it further enacted and declared, That if any person shall be prosecuted under this act, for the writing or publishing any libel aforesaid, it shall be lawful for the defendant, upon the trial of the cause, to give in evidence in his defence, the truth of the matter contained in Republication charged as a libel. And the jury who shall try the cause, shall have a right to determine the law and the fact, under the direction of the court, as in other cases.

Section 4*. And be it further enacted,* That this act shall continue and be in force until the third day of March, one thousand eight hundred and one, and no longer: Provided, that the expiration of the act shall not prevent or defeat a prosecution and punishment of any offence against the law, during the time it shall be in force.

APPROVED, July 14, 1798.

The Kentucky and Virginia Resolutions
17988

The Kentucky Resolutions

1. *Resolved,* that the several states composing the United States of America are not united on the principle of unlimited submission to their general government; but that, by compact, under the style and title of a Constitution for the United States, and of amendments thereto, they constituted a general government for special purposes, delegated to that government certain definite powers, reserving, each state to itself, the residuary mass of right to their own self-government. And that whensoever the general government assumes undelegated powers, its acts are unauthoritative, void, and of no force; that to this compact each state acceded as a state and is an integral party; that this government, created by this compact, was not made the exclusive or final judge of the extent of the powers delegated to itself, since that would have made its discretion, and not the Constitution, the measure of its powers; but that, as in all other cases of compact among parties having no common judge, each party has an equal right to judge for itself, as well of infractions as of the mode and measure of redress.

2. *Resolved,* that the Constitution of the United States having delegated to Congress a power to punish treason, counterfeiting the securities and current coin of the United States, piracies and felonies committed on the high seas, and offenses against the laws of nations, and no other crimes whatever; and it being true, as a general principle, and one of the amendments to the Constitution having also declared "that the powers not delegated to the United States by the Constitution, nor prohibited by it to the states, are reserved to the states respectively, or to the people"; therefore, also, the same act of Congress, passed on the 14th day of July, 1798, and entitled "An Act in Addition to the Act Entitled 'An Act for the Punishment of Certain Crimes Against the United States,'" as also the act passed by them on the 27th day of June, 1799, entitled "An Act to Punish Frauds Committed on the Bank of the United States" (and all other their acts which assume to create, define, or punish crimes other than those enumerated in the Constitution), are altogether void and of no force; and that the power to create, define, and punish, such other crimes is reserved, and of right appertains, solely and exclusively, to the respective states, each within its own territory.

3. *Resolved,* that it is true, as a general principle, and is also expressly declared by one of the amendments to the Constitution, that "the powers not delegated to the United States by the Constitution, nor prohibited by it to the states, are reserved to the states respectively, or to the people;" and that no power over the freedom of religion, freedom of speech, or freedom of the press, being delegated to the United States by the Constitution, nor prohibited by it to the states, all lawful powers respecting the same did of right remain, and were reserved to the states, or to the people; that thus was manifested their determination to retain to themselves the right of judging how far the licentiousness of speech, and of the press, may be abridged without lessening their useful freedom, and how far those abuses, which cannot be separated from their use, should be tolerated rather than the use be destroyed. And thus also they guarded against all abridgment, by the United States, of the freedom of religious principles and exercises, and retained to themselves the right of protecting the same, as this, stated by a law passed on the general demand of its citizens, had already protected them from all human restraint or interference; and that, in addition to this general principle and express declaration, another and more special provision has been made by one of the amendments to the Constitution, which expressly declares that "Congress shall make no laws respecting an establishment of religion, or prohibiting the free exercise thereof, or abridging the freedom of speech, or of the press," thereby guarding, in the same sentence, and under the same words, the freedom of religion, of speech, and of the press, insomuch that whatever violates either throws down the sanctuary which covers the others; and that libels, falsehood, and defamation, equally with heresy and false religion, are withheld from the cognizance of federal tribunals. That, therefore, the act of the Congress of the United States, passed on the 14th of July, 1798, entitled "An Act in Addition to the Act Entitled 'An Act for the Punishment of Certain Crimes Against the United States,'" which does abridge the freedom of the press, is not law, but is altogether void and of no force.

4. *Resolved,* that alien friends are under the Jurisdiction and protection of the laws of the state wherein they are; that no power over them has been delegated to the United States, nor prohibited to the individual states, distinct from their power over citizens; and it being true, as a general principle, and one of the amendments to the Constitution having also declared, that "the powers not delegated to the United States by the Constitution, nor prohibited to the states, are reserved to the states, respectively, or to the people," the act of the Congress of the United States, passed the 22nd day of June, 1798, entitled "An Act Concerning Aliens," which assumes power over alien friends not delegated by the Constitution, is not law, but is altogether void and of no force.

5. *Resolved,* that, in addition to the general principle, as well as the express declaration, that powers not delegated are reserved, another and more special provision inserted in the Constitution from abundant caution has declared, "that the migration or importation of such persons as any of the states now existing shall think proper to admit shall not be prohibited by the Congress prior to the year 1808." That this commonwealth does admit the migration of alien friends described as the subject of the said act concerning aliens; that a provision against prohibiting their migration is a provision against all acts equivalent thereto, or it would be nugatory; that to remove them, when migrated, is equivalent to a prohibition of their migration, and is, therefore, contrary to the said provision of the Constitution, and void.

6. *Resolved,* that the imprisonment of a person under the protection of the laws of this commonwealth, on his failure to obey the simple order of the president to depart out of the United States, as is undertaken by the said act, entitled, "An Act Concerning Aliens," is contrary to the Constitution, one amendment in which has provided, that "no person shall be deprived of liberty without due process of law;" and that another having provided, "that, in all criminal

prosecutions, the accused shall enjoy the right of a public trial by an impartial jury, to be informed as to the nature and cause of the accusation, to be confronted with the witnesses against him, to have compulsory process for obtaining witnesses in his favor, and to have assistance of counsel for his defense," the same act undertaking to authorize the president to remove a person out of the United States who is under the protection of the law, on his own suspicion, without jury, without public trial, without confrontation of the witnesses against him, without having witnesses in his favor, with, out defense, without counsel, contrary to these provisions also of the Constitution, is therefore not law, but utterly void and of no force.

That transferring the power of judging any person who is under the protection of the laws from the courts to the President of the United States, as is undertaken by the same act concerning aliens, is against the article of the Constitution which provides, that "the judicial power of the United States shall be vested in the courts, the judges of which shall hold their office during good behavior," and that the said act is void for that reason also. And it is further to be noted that this transfer of judiciary power is to that magistrate of the general government who already possesses all the executive, and a qualified negative in all the legislative powers.

7. Resolved, that the construction applied by the general government (as is evident by. sundry of their proceedings) to those parts of the Constitution of the United States which delegate to Congress power to lay and collect taxes, duties, imposts, excises; to pay the debts, and provide for the common defense and general welfare of the United States, and to make all laws which shall be necessary and proper for carrying into execution the powers vested by the Constitution in the government of the United States, or any department thereof, goes to the destruction of all the limits prescribed to their power by the Constitution; that words meant by that instrument to be subsidiary only to the execution of the limited powers, ought not to be so construed as themselves to give unlimited powers, nor a part so to be taken as to destroy the whole residue of the instrument; that the proceedings of the general government, under color of those articles, will be a fit and necessary subject for revisal and correction at a time of greater tranquillity, while those specified in the preceding resolutions call for immediate redress.

8. Resolved, that the preceding resolutions be transmitted to the senators and representatives in Congress from this commonwealth, who are enjoined to present the same to their respective houses and to use their best endeavors to procure, at the next session of Congress, a repeal of the aforesaid unconstitutional and obnoxious acts.

9. Resolved, lastly, that the governor of this commonwealth be, and is, authorized and requested to communicate the preceding resolutions to the legislatures of the several states, to assure them that this commonwealth considers union for special national purposes, and particularly for those specified in their late federal compact, to be friendly to the peace, happiness, and prosperity, of all the states: that, faithful to that compact, according to the plain intent and meaning in which it was understood and acceded to by the several parties, it Is sincerely anxious for its preservation.

That it does also believe, that, to take from the states all the powers of self-government and transfer them to a general and consolidated government, without regard to the special government, and reservations solemnly agreed to in that compact, is not for the peace, happiness, or prosperity of these states; and that, therefore, this commonwealth is determined, as it doubts not its co-states are, to submit to undelegated and consequently unlimited powers in no man, or body of men, on earth; that, if the acts before specified should stand, these conclusions would flow from them.

That the general government may place any act they think proper on the list of crimes, and punish it themselves, whether enumerated or not enumerated by the Constitution as cognizable by them; that they may transfer its cognizance to the President, or any other person, who may himself be the accuser, counsel, judge, and jury, whose suspicions may be the evidence, his order the sentence, his officer the executioner, and his breast the sole record of the transaction; that a very numerous and valuable description of the inhabitants of these states, being, by this precedent, reduced, as outlaws, to absolute dominion of one man, and the barriers of the Constitution thus swept from us all, no rampart now remains against the passions and the power of a majority of Congress, to protect from a like exportation, or other grievous punishment, the minority of the same body, the legislatures, judges, governors, and counselors of the states, nor their other peaceable inhabitants, who may venture to reclaim the constitutional rights and liberties of the states and people, or who, for other causes, good or bad, may be obnoxious to the view, or marked by the suspicions, of the President, or be thought dangerous to his or their elections, or other interests, public or personal.

That the friendless alien has been selected as the safest subject of a first experiment; but the citizen will soon follow, or rather has already followed; for already has a Sedition Act marked him as a prey. That these and successive acts of the same character, unless arrested on the threshold, may tend to drive these states into revolution and blood, and will furnish new calumnies against republican governments, and new pretexts for those who wish it to be believed that man cannot be governed but by a rod of iron; that it would be a dangerous delusion were a confidence in the men of our choice to silence our fears for the safety of our rights; that confidence is everywhere the parent of despotism; free government is founded in jealousy, and not in confidence; it is jealousy, and not confidence, which prescribes limited constitutions to bind down those whom we are obliged to trust with power; that our Constitution has accordingly fixed the limits to which, and no farther, our confidence may go; and let the honest advocate of confidence read the Alien and Sedition Acts, and say if the Constitution has not been wise in fixing limits to the government it created, and whether we should be wise in destroying those limits. Let him say what the government is, if it be not a tyranny, which the men of our choice have conferred on the President, and the President of our choice has assented to and accepted, over the friendly strangers to whom the mild spirit of our country and its laws had pledged hospitality and protection; that the men of our choice have more respected the bare suspicions of the President than the solid rights of innocence, the claims of Justification, the sacred force of truth, and the forms and substance of law and justice.

In questions of power, then, let no more be said of confidence in man, but bind him down from mischief by the chains of the Constitution. That this commonwealth does therefore call on its co-states for an expression of their sentiments on the acts concerning aliens, and for the punishment of certain crimes herein before specified, plainly declaring whether these acts are or are not authorized by the federal compact. And it doubts not that their sense will be so announced as to prove their attachment to limited government, whether general or particular, and that the rights and liberties of their co-states will be exposed to no dangers by remaining embarked on a common bottom with their own; but they will concur with this commonwealth in considering the said acts as so palpably against the Constitution as to amount to an undisguised declaration, that the compact is not meant to be the measure of the powers of the general government, but that it will proceed in the exercise over these states of all powers whatsoever. That they will view this as seizing the rights of the states, and consolidating them in the hands of the general government with a power assumed to bind the states, not merely in cases made federal but in all cases whatsoever, by laws made, no, with their consent but by others against their consent. That this would be to surrender the form of government we have chosen, and live under one deriving its power from its own will, and not from our authority; and that the co-states, recurring to their natural rights not made federal, will concur in declaring these void and of no force, and will each unite with this commonwealth in requesting their repeal at the next session of Congress.

The Virginia Resolutions

*R*esolved, that the General Assembly of Virginia does unequivocally express a firm resolution to maintain and defend the Constitution of the United States, and the constitution of this state against every aggression, either foreign or domestic; and that they will support the government of the United States in all measures warranted by the former.

That this Assembly most solemnly declares a warm attachment to the union of the states, to maintain which it pledges its powers; and that, for this end, it is their duty to watch over and oppose every infraction of those principles which constitute the only basis of that union, because a faithful observance of them can alone secure its existence and the public happiness.

That this Assembly does explicitly and peremptorily declare that it views the powers of the federal government as resulting from the compact to which the states are parties, as limited by the plain sense and intention of the instrument constituting that compact, as no further valid than they are authorized by the grants enumerated in that compact; and that, in case of a deliberate, palpable, and dangerous exercise of other powers, not granted by the said compact, the states who are parties thereto, have the right, and are in duty bound to interpose for arresting the progress of the evil, and for maintaining, within their respective limits, the authorities, rights, and liberties, appertaining to them.

That the General Assembly does also express its deep regret that a spirit has, in sundry instances, been manifested by the federal government to enlarge its powers by forced constructions of the constitutional charter which defines them; and that indications have appeared of a design to expound certain general phrases (which, having been copied from the very limited grant of powers in the former Articles of Confederation, were the less liable to be misconstrued) so as to destroy the meaning and effect of the particular enumeration which necessarily explains and limits the general phrases, and so as to consolidate the states, by degrees, into one sovereignty, the obvious tendency and inevitable result of which would be to transform the present republican system of the United States into an absolute or, at best, a mixed monarchy.

That the General Assembly does particularly protest against the palpable and alarming infractions of the Constitution in the two late cases of the Alien and Sedition Acts, passed at the last session of Congress; the first of which exercises a power nowhere delegated to the federal government, and which, by uniting legislative and judicial powers to those of executive, subverts the general principles of free government, as well as the particular organization and positive provisions of the federal Constitution; and the other of which acts exercises, in like manner, a power not delegated by the Constitution, but, on the contrary, expressly and positively forbidden by one of the amendments thereto, a power which, more than any other, ought to produce universal alarm, because it is leveled against the right of freely examining public characters and measures, and of free communication among the people thereon, which has ever been justly deemed the only effectual guardian of every other right.

That this state having, by its Convention, which ratified the federal Constitution, expressly declared that, among other essential rights, "the liberty of conscience and the press cannot be canceled, abridged, restrained, or modified, by any authority of the United States," and from its extreme anxiety to guard these rights from every possible attack of sophistry and ambition, having, with other states, recommended an amendment for that purpose, which amendment was, in due time, annexed to the Constitution, it would mark a reproachful inconsistency and criminal degeneracy if an indifference were now shown to the most palpable violation of one of the rights thus declared and secured, and to the establishment of a precedent which may be fatal to the other.

That the good people of this commonwealth, having ever felt, and continuing to feel, the most sincere affection for their brethren of the other states; the truest anxiety for establishing and perpetuating the union of all; and the most scrupulous fidelity to that Constitution, which is the pledge of mutual friendship and the instrument of mutual happiness; the General Assembly does solemnly appeal to the like dispositions in the other states, in confidence that they will concur with this commonwealth in declaring, as it does hereby declare, that the acts aforesaid are unconstitutional; and that the necessary and proper measures will be taken by each for cooperating with this state, in maintaining unimpaired the authorities, rights, and liberties, reserved to the states respectively, or to the people.

That the governor be desired to transmit a copy of the foregoing resolutions to the executive authority of each of the other states, with a request that the same may be communicated to the legislature thereof and that a copy be furnished to each of the senators and representatives representing this state in the Congress of the United States.

Ex Parte Merryman

Circuit Court, D. Maryland.

April Term, 1861.

Syllabus

Citation: 17 F. Cas. 144, No. 9487   **Concepts:** Writ of Habeas Corpus/(Cir. Ct., D. Maryland, 1861) Executive Power v. Civilian Due Process

Facts

John Merryman favored the South in the Civil War. A month after the war began in 1861, he was arrested and jailed for burning railroad bridges. His arrest was based on a vague suspicion of treason. There was no warrant issued, nor were there any witnesses nor proof of any illegal action. Merryman wrote to Chief Justice Roger Taney, asking for a writ of habeas corpus so that his case would be tried in a civilian court. Chief Justice Taney issued the writ. However, the military commander in charge of Merryman's trial ignored the writ, citing President Lincoln's suspension of habeas corpus in certain parts of the country.

Issue

Whether the President of the United States has the power to suspend a writ of habeas corpus without the consent of Congress; and whether Merryman was deprived of life, liberty, or property without due process.

Opinion

Chief Justice Taney, who was holding circuit court (which Supreme Court justices did then), challenged President Lincoln's suspension of the writ of habeas corpus. The Chief Justice believed that the President drew too much power to himself without the consent of Congress. He criticized the President for improperly substituting military authority for civilian authority and emphatically warned that the people of the United States were "no longer living under a government of laws, but ... at the will and pleasure of the army officer in whose military district they happen to be found."

[Eventually, Merryman was handed over to civilian authorities, and Congress gave the President the power, which he had previously drawn to himself, to suspend the privilege of habeas corpus at his discretion during wartime].

U.S. Espionage Act, 15 June 1917

Reproduced below is a portion of the text of the Espionage Act passed by the U.S. Congress on 15 June, some two months following America's <u>declaration of war</u> with Germany.

Be it enacted by the Senate and House of Representatives of the United States of America in Congress assembled

Title I

ESPIONAGE

That:

Section 1.

(a) whoever, for the purpose of obtaining information respecting the national defence with intent or reason to believe that the information to be obtained is to be used to the injury of the United States, or to the advantage of any foreign nation, goes upon, enters, flies over, or otherwise obtains information, concerning any vessel, aircraft, work of defence, navy yard, naval station, submarine base, coaling station, fort, battery, torpedo station, dockyard, canal, railroad, arsenal, camp, factory, mine, telegraph, telephone, wireless, or signal station, building, office, or other place connected with the national defence, owned or constructed, or in progress of construction by the United States or under the control or the United States, or of any of its officers or agents, or within the exclusive jurisdiction of the United States, or any place in which any vessel, aircraft, arms, munitions, or other materials or instruments for use in time of war are being made, prepared, repaired. or stored, under any contract or agreement with the United States, or with any person on behalf of the United States, or otherwise on behalf of the United States, or any prohibited place within the meaning of section six of this title; or

(b) whoever for the purpose aforesaid, and with like intent or reason to believe, copies, takes, makes, or obtains, or attempts, or induces or aids another to copy, take, make, or obtain, any sketch, photograph, photographic negative, blue print, plan, map, model, instrument, appliance, document, writing or note of anything connected with the national defence; or

(c) whoever, for the purpose aforesaid, receives or obtains or agrees or attempts or induces or aids another to receive or obtain from any other person, or from any source whatever, any document, writing, code book, signal book, sketch, photograph, photographic negative, blue print, plan, map, model, instrument, appliance, or note, of anything connected with the national defence, knowing or having reason to believe, at the time he receives or obtains, or agrees or attempts or induces or aids another to receive or obtain it, that it has been or will be obtained, taken, made or disposed of by any person contrary to the provisions of this title; or

(d) whoever, lawfully or unlawfully having possession of, access to, control over, or being entrusted with any document, writing, code book, signal book, sketch, photograph, photographic negative, blue print, plan, map, model, instrument, appliance, or note relating to the national defence, wilfully communicates or transmits or attempts to communicate or transmit the same and fails to deliver it on demand to the officer or employee of the United States entitled to receive it; or

(e) whoever, being entrusted with or having lawful possession or control of any document, writing, code book, signal book, sketch, photograph, photographic negative, blue print, plan, map, model, note, or information, relating to the national defence, through gross negligence permits the same to be removed from its proper place of custody or delivered to anyone in violation of his trust, or to be list, stolen, abstracted, or destroyed, shall be punished by a fine of not more than $10,000, or by imprisonment for not more than two years, or both.

Section 2: Whoever, with intent or reason to believe that it is to be used to the injury or the United States or to the advantage of a foreign nation, communicated, delivers, or transmits, or attempts to, or aids, or induces another to, communicate, deliver or transmit, to any foreign government, or to any faction or party or military or naval force within a foreign country, whether recognized or unrecognized by the United States, or to any representative, officer, agent, employee, subject, or citizen thereof, either directly or indirectly and document, writing, code book, signal book, sketch, photograph, photographic negative, blue print, plan, map, model, note, instrument, appliance, or information relating to the national defence, shall be punished by imprisonment for not more than twenty years: Provided, That whoever shall violate the provisions of subsection:

(a) of this section in time of war shall be punished by death or by imprisonment for not more than thirty years; and

(b) whoever, in time of war, with intent that the same shall be communicated to the enemy, shall collect, record, publish or communicate, or attempt to elicit any information with respect to the movement, numbers, description, condition, or disposition of any of the armed forces, ships, aircraft, or war materials of the United States, or with respect to the plans or conduct, or supposed plans or conduct of any naval of military operations, or with respect to any works or measures undertaken for or connected with, or intended for the fortification of any place, or any other information relating to the public defence, which might be useful to the enemy, shall be punished by death or by imprisonment for not more than thirty years.

Section 3: Whoever, when the United States is at war, shall wilfully make or convey false reports or false statements with intent to interfere with the operation or success of the military or naval forces of the United States or to promote the success of its enemies and whoever when the United States is at war, shall wilfully cause or attempt to cause insubordination, disloyalty, mutiny, refusal of duty, in the military or naval forces of the United States, or shall wilfully obstruct the recruiting or enlistment service of the United States, to the injury of the service or of the United States, shall be punished by a fine of not more than $10,000 or imprisonment for not more than twenty years, or both.

Section 4: If two or more persons conspire to violate the provisions of section two or three of this title, and one or more of such persons does any act to effect the object of the conspiracy, each of the parties to such conspiracy shall be punished as in said sections provided in the case of the doing of the act the accomplishment of which is the object of such conspiracy. Except as above provided conspiracies to commit offences under this title shall be punished as provided by section thirty-seven of the Act to codify, revise, and amend the penal laws of the United States approved March fourth, nineteen hundred and nine.

Section 5: Whoever harbours or conceals any person who he knows, or has reasonable grounds to believe or suspect, has committed, or is about to commit, an offence under this title shall be punished by a fine of not more than $10,000 or by imprisonment for not more than two years, or both.

Section 6: The President in time of war or in case of national emergency may by proclamation designate any place other than those set forth in subsection:

(a) of section one hereof in which anything for the use of the Army or Navy is being prepared or constructed or stored as a prohibited place for the purpose of this title: Provided, That he shall determine that information with respect thereto would be prejudicial to the national defence.

Section 7: Nothing contained in this title shall be deemed to limit the jurisdiction of the general courts-martial, military commissions, or naval courts-martial under sections thirteen hundred and forty-two, thirteen hundred and forty-three, and sixteen hundred and twenty-four of the Revised Statutes as amended.

Section 8: The provisions of this title shall extend to all Territories, possessions, and places subject to the jurisdiction of the United States whether or not contiguous thereto, and offences under this title, when committed upon the high seas or elsewhere within the admiralty and maritime jurisdiction of the United States and outside the territorial limits thereof shall be punishable hereunder.

Section 9: The Act entitles "An Act to prevent the disclosure of national defence secrets," approved March third, nineteen hundred and eleven, is hereby repealed.

U.S. Espionage Act, 16 May 1918
(Amended 1917 Act)

Be it enacted, That section three of the Act... approved June 15, 1917, be... amended so as to read as follows:

Section 3. Whoever, when the United States is at war, shall wilfully make or convey false reports or false statements with intent to interfere with the operation or success of the military or naval forces of the United States, or to promote the success of its enemies, or shall wilfully make or convey false reports, or false statements, or say or do anything except by way of bona fide and not disloyal advice to an investor... with intent to obstruct the sale by the United States of bonds... or the making of loans by or to the United States, or whoever, when the United States is at war, shall wilfully cause . . . or incite . . . insubordination, disloyalty, mutiny, or refusal of duty, in the military or naval forces of the United States, or shall wilfully obstruct . . . the recruiting or enlistment service of the United States, and whoever, when the United States is at war, shall wilfully utter, print, write, or publish any disloyal, profane, scurrilous, or abusive language about the form of government of the United States, or the Constitution of the United States, or the military or naval forces of the United States, or the flag . . . or the uniform of the Army or Navy of the United States, or any language intended to bring the form of government... or the Constitution . . . or the military or naval forces . . . or the flag . . . of the United States into contempt, scorn, contumely, or disrepute... or shall wilfully display the flag of any foreign enemy, or shall wilfully . . . urge, incite, or advocate any curtailment of production in this country of any thing or things . . . necessary or essential to the prosecution of the war . . . and whoever shall wilfully advocate, teach, defend, or suggest the doing of any of the acts or things in this section enumerated and whoever shall by word or act support or favour the cause of any country with which the United States is at war or by word or act oppose the cause of the United States therein, shall be punished by a fine of not more than $10,000 or imprisonment for not more than twenty years, or both.

The Smith Act of 1940
54 Stat. 670, 671, title I, §§2-3 (June 28, 1940)

Section 2. (a) It shall be unlawful for any person--

(1) to knowingly or willfully advocate, abet, advise, or teach the duty, necessity, desirability, or propriety of overthrowing or destroying any government in the United States by force or violence, or by the assassination of any officer of any such government;

(2) with the intent to cause the overthrow or destruction of any government in the United States, to print, publish, edit, issue, circulate, sell, distribute, or publicly display any written or printed matter advocating, advising, or teaching the duty, necessity, desirability, or propriety of overthrowing or destroying any government in the United States by force or violence;

(3) to organize or help to organize any society, group, or assembly of persons who teach, advocate, or encourage the overthrow or destruction of any government in the United States by force or violence; or to be or become a member of, or affiliate with, any such society, group, or assembly of persons, knowing the purposes thereof.

(b) For the purposes of this section, the term "government in the United States" means the Government of the United States, the government of any State, Territory, or possession of the United States, the government of the District of Columbia, or the government of any political subdivision of any of them.

Section 3. It shall be unlawful for any person to attempt to commit, or to conspire to commit, any of the acts prohibited by the provisions of this title.

Section 2385. Advocating overthrow of Government

Whoever knowingly or willfully advocates, abets, advises, or teaches the duty, necessity, desirability, or propriety of overthrowing or destroying the government of the United States or the government of any State, Territory, District or Possession thereof, or the government of any political subdivision therein, by force or violence, or by the assassination of any officer of any such government; or

Whoever, with intent to cause the overthrow or destruction of any such government, prints, publishes, edits, issues, circulates, sells, distributes, or publicly displays any written or printed matter advocating, advising, or teaching the duty, necessity, desirability, or propriety of overthrowing or destroying any government in the United States by force or violence, or attempts to do so; or

Whoever organizes or helps or attempts to organize any society, group, or assembly of persons who teach, advocate, or encourage the overthrow or destruction of any such government by force or violence; or becomes or is a member of, or affiliates with, any such society, group, or assembly of persons, knowing the purposes thereof--

Shall be fined under this title or imprisoned not more than twenty years, or both, and shall be ineligible for employment by the United States or any department or agency thereof, for the five years next following his conviction.

If two or more persons conspire to commit any offense named in this section, each shall be fined under this title or imprisoned not more than twenty years, or both, and shall be ineligible for employment by the United States or any department or agency thereof, for the five years next following his conviction.

As used in this section, the terms "organizes" and "organize", with respect to any society, group, or assembly of persons, include the recruiting of new members, the forming of new units, and the regrouping or expansion of existing clubs, classes, and other units of such society, group, or assembly of persons.

The McCarran Internal Security Act of 1950
(Excerpt and Summary)

Section 1.

(a) This title may be cited as the "Subversive Activities Control Act of 1950."

(b) Nothing in this Act shall be construed to authorize, require, or establish military or civilian censorship or in any way to limit or infringe upon freedom of the press or of speech as guaranteed by the Constitution of the United States and no regulation shall be promulgated hereunder having that effect.

Necessity for Legislation

Section 2. As a result of evidence adduced before various committees of the Senate and House of Representatives, the Congress hereby finds that . . .

6) The Communist action organizations so established and utilized in various countries, acting under such control, direction, and discipline, endeavor to carry out the objectives of the world Communist movement by bringing about the overthrow of existing governments by any available means, including force if necessary, and setting up Communist totalitarian dictatorships which will be subservient to the most powerful existing Communist totalitarian dictatorship. Although such organizations usually designate themselves as political parties, they are in fact constituent elements of the world-wide Communist movement and promote the objectives of such movement by conspiratorial and coercive tactics, instead of through the democratic processes of a free elective system or through the freedom-preserving means employed by a political party which operates as an agency by which people govern themselves.

(7) In carrying on the activities referred to in paragraph (6), such Communist organizations in various countries are organized on a secret, conspiratorial basis and operate to a substantial extent through organizations, commonly known as "Communist fronts," which in most instances are created and maintained, or used, in such manner as to conceal the facts as to their true character and purposes and their membership. One result of this method of operation is that such affiliated organizations are able to obtain financial and other support from persons who would not extend such support if they knew the true purposes of, and the actual nature of the control and influence exerted upon, such "Communist fronts."

(8) Due to the nature and scope of the world Communist movement, with the existence of affiliated constituent elements working toward common objectives in various countries of the world, travel of Communist members, representatives, and agents from country to country facilitates communication and is a prerequisite for the carrying on of activities to further the purposes of the Communist movement.

(9) In the United States those individuals who knowingly and willfully participate in the world Communist movement, when they so participate, in effect repudiate their allegiance to the United States, and in effect transfer their allegiance to the foreign country in which is vested the direction and control of the world Communist movement.

(10) In pursuance of communism's stated objectives, the most powerful existing Communist dictatorship has, by the methods referred to above, already caused the establishment in numerous foreign countries of Communist totalitarian dictatorships, and threatens to establish similar dictatorships in still other countries.

(11) The agents of communism have devised clever and ruthless espionage and sabotage tactics which are carried out in many instances in form or manner successfully evasive of existing law.

(12) The Communist network in the United States is inspired and controlled in large part by foreign agents who are sent into the United States ostensibly as attaches of foreign legations, affiliates of international organizations, members of trading commissions, and in similar capacities, but who use their diplomatic or semi-diplomatic status as a shield behind which to engage in activities prejudicial to the public security.

(13) There are, under our present immigration laws, numerous aliens who have been found to be deportable, many of whom are in the subversive, criminal, or immoral classes who are free to roam the country at will without supervision or control.

(14) One device for infiltration by Communists is by procuring naturalization for disloyal aliens who use their citizenship as a badge for admission into the fabric of our society.

(15) The Communist movement in the United States is an organization numbering thousands of adherents, rigidly and ruthlessly disciplined. Awaiting and seeking to advance a moment when the United States may be so far extended by foreign engagements, so far divided in counsel, or so far in industrial or financial straits, that overthrow of the Government of the United States by force and violence may seem possible of achievement, it seeks converts far and wide by an extensive system of schooling and indoctrination. Such preparations by Communist organizations in other countries have aided in supplanting existing governments. The Communist organization in the United States, pursuing its stated objectives, the recent successes of Communist methods in other countries, and the nature and control of the world Communist movement itself, present a clear and present danger to the security of the United States and to the existence of free American institutions, and make it necessary that Congress, in order to provide for the common defense, to preserve the sovereignty of the United States as an independent nation, and to guarantee to each State a republican form of government, enact appropriate legislation recognizing the existence of such world-wide conspiracy and designed to prevent it from accomplishing its purpose in the United States.

Section 3. For the purposes of this title . . .

(3) The term "Communist-action organization" means--(a) any organization in the United States (other than a diplomatic representative or mission of a foreign government accredited as such by the Department of State) which (i) is substantially directed, dominated, or controlled by the foreign government or foreign organization controlling the world Communist movement referred to in section 2 of this title, and (ii) operates primarily to advance the objectives of such world Communist movement as referred to in section 2 of this title; and (b) any section, branch, fraction, or cell of any organization defined in subparagraph (a) of this paragraph which has not complied with the registration requirements of this title.

(4) The term Communist-front organization means any organization in the United States (other than a Communist-action organization as defined in paragraph (3) of this section) which (A) is substantially directed, dominated, or controlled by a Communist-action organization, and (B) is primarily operated for the purpose of giving aid and support to a Communist-action organization, a Communist foreign government, or the world Communist movement referred to in section 2 of this title. [*4A below and subsequent provisions dealing with "Communist-infiltrated organizations" were added by the Communist Control Act of 1954. 68 Stat. 775.*]

(4A) The term "Communist-infiltrated organization" means any organization in the United States (other than a Communist-action organization or a Communist-front organization) which (A) is substantially directed, dominated, or controlled by an individual or individuals who are, or who within three years have been actively engaged in, giving aid or support to a Communist-action organization, a Communist foreign government, or the world Communist movement referred to in section 2 of this title, and (B) is serving, or within three years has served, as a means for (i) the giving of aid or support to any such organization, government, or movement, or (ii) the impairment of the military strength of the United States or its industrial capacity to furnish logistical or other material support required by its Armed Forces: Provided, however, That any labor organization which is an affiliate in good standing of a national federation or other labor organization whose policies and activities have been directed to opposing Communist organizations, any Communist foreign government, or the world Communist movement, shall be presumed prima facie not to be a "Communist-infiltrated organization." (5) The term "Communist means organization any Communist-action organization, Communist-front organization, or Communist-infiltrated organization. . . .

(14) The term "world communism" means a revolutionary movement, the purpose of which is to establish eventually a Communist totalitarian dictatorship in any or all of the countries of the world through the medium of an internationally coordinated Communist movement.

(15) The terms "totalitarian dictatorship" and "totalitarianism" mean and refer to systems of government not representative in fact, characterized by (A) the existence of a single political party, organized on a dictatorial basis, with so close an identity between such party and its policies and the governmental policies of the country in which it exists, that the party and the government constitute an indistinguishable unit, and (B) the forcible suppression of opposition to such party. . . .

Certain Prohibited Acts

Section 4.

(a) It shall be unlawful for any person knowingly to combine, conspire, or agree with any other person to perform any act which would substantially contribute to the establishment within the United States of a totalitarian dictatorship, as defined in paragraph (15) of section 3 of this title, the direction and control of which is to be vested in, or exercised by or under the domination or control of, any foreign government, foreign organization, or foreign individual: Provided, however, That this subsection shall not apply to the proposal of a constitutional amendment. . . .

(d) Any person who violates any provision of this section shall, upon conviction thereof, be punished by a fine of not more than $10,000 or imprisonment for not more than ten years, or by both such fine and such imprisonment, and shall, moreover, be thereafter ineligible to hold any office, or place of honor, profit, or trust created by the Constitution or laws of the United States....

(f) Neither the holding of office nor membership in any Communist organization by any person shall constitute per se a violation of subsection (a) or subsection (c) of this section or of any other criminal statute. The fact of the registration of any person under section 7 or section 8 of this title as an officer or member of any Communist organization shall not be received in evidence against such person in any prosecution for any alleged violation of subsection (a) or subsection (c) of this section or for any alleged violation of any other criminal statute.

[*Section 5 provides, inter alia, that it is unlawful for a member of a registered "Communist organization" to hold any nonelective office or employment under the United States or any office or employment with any labor organization, or represent any employer in a proceeding under the National Labor Relations Act; or for any member of a registered "Communist-action" organization to engage in any employment in any defense facility.*

Section 6 provides that it is unlawful for a member of a registered "Communist organization" to apply for or use a passport; or for a government official to issue a passport to any individual knowing or having reason to believe that he is a member of a registered "Communist-action" organization.]

Registration and Annual Reports of Communist Organizations

Section 7. [*Subsections (a) to (c) provide that a Communist organization shall register with the Attorney General within 30 days after (1) enactment of the Act, (2) the date it becomes a Communist organization, or (3) the date a Board order requiring registration becomes final.*]

(d) The registration made under subsection (a) or (b) shall be accompanied by a registration statement, to be prepared and filed in such manner and form as the Attorney General shall by regulations prescribe, containing the following information:

(1) The name of the organization and the address of its principal office.

(2) The name and last-known address of each individual who is at the time of filing such registration statement, and of each individual who was at any time during the period of twelve full calendar months next preceding the filing of such statement, an officer of the organization, with the designation or title of the office so held, and with a brief statement of the duties and functions of such individual as such officer.

(3) An accounting, in such form and detail as the Attorney General shall by regulations prescribe, of all moneys received and expended (including the sources from which received and the purposes for which expended) by the organization during the period of twelve full calendar months next preceding the filing of such statement.

(4) In the case of a Communist-action organization, the name and last-known address of each individual who was a member of the organization at any time during the period of twelve full calendar months preceding the filing of such statement.

(5) In the case of any officer or member whose name is required to be shown in such statement, and who uses or has used or who is or has been known by more than one name, each name which such officer or member uses or has used or by which he is known or has been known.

(6) A listing, in such form and detail as the Attorney General shall by regulation prescribe, of all printing presses and machines including but not limited to rotary presses, flatbed cylinder presses, platen presses, lithographs, offsets, photo-offsets, mimeograph machines, multigraph machines, multilith machines, duplicating machines, ditto machines, linotype machines, intertype machines, monotype machines, and all other types of printing presses, typesetting machines or any mechanical devices used or intended to be used, or capable of being used to produce or publish printed matter or material, which are in the possession, custody, ownership, or control of the Communist-action or Communist-front organization or its officers, members, affiliates, associates, group, or groups in which the Communist-action or Communist-front organization, its officers or members have an interest.

[*Subsection (e) provides that each organization registered shall thereafter file with the Attorney General an annual report containing the same information as is required by subsection (d).*]

(f)   (1) It shall be the duty of each organization registered under this section to keep, in such manner and form as the Attorney General shall by regulations prescribe, accurate records and accounts of moneys received and expended (including the sources from which received and purposes for which expended) by such organization.
(2) It shall be the duty of each Communist-action organization registered under this section to keep, in such manner and form as the Attorney General shall by regulations prescribe, accurate records of the names and addresses of the members of such organization and of persons who actively participate in the activities of such organization. . . .

(h) In the case of failure on the part of any organization to register or to file any registration statement or annual report as required by this section, it shall be the duty of the executive officer (or individual performing the ordinary and usual duties of an executive officer) and of the secretary (or individual performing the ordinary and usual duties of a secretary) of such organization, and of such officer or officers of such organization as the Attorney General shall by

regulations prescribe, to register for such organization, to file such registration statement, or to file such annual report, as the case may be.

Registration of Members of Communist-Action Organizations

Section 8.

(a) Any individual who is or becomes a member of any organization concerning which (1) there is in effect a final order of the Board requiring such organization to register under section 7(a) of this title as a Communist-action organization, (2) more than thirty days have elapsed since such order has become final, and (3) such organization is not registered under section 7 of this title as a Communist-action organization, shall within sixty days after said order has become final or within thirty days after becoming a member of such organization, whichever is later, register with the Attorney General as a member of such organization.

(b) Each individual who is or becomes a member of any organization which he knows to be registered as a Communist-action organization under section 7(a) of this title, but to have failed to include his name upon the list of members thereof filed with the Attorney General, pursuant to the provisions of subsections (d) and (e) of section 7 of this title, shall, within sixty 155 days after he shall have obtained such knowledge, register with the Attorney General as a member of such organization....

[*Section 9 provides that the Attorney General shall make the data filed with him open for public inspection and shall submit annual reports on such data to the President and to the Congress*].

Use of the Mails and Instrumentalities of Interstate or Foreign Commerce

Section 10. It shall be unlawful for any organization which is registered under section 7, or for any organization with respect to which there is in effect a final order of the Board requiring it to register under section 7 or determining that it is a Communist-infiltrated organization, or for any person acting for or on behalf of any such organization--

> (1) to transmit or cause to be transmitted, through the United States mails or by any means or instrumentality of interstate or foreign commerce, any publication which is intended to be, or which it is reasonable to believe is intended to be, circulated or disseminated among two or more persons, unless such publication, and any envelope, wrapper, or other container in which it is mailed or otherwise circulated or transmitted, bears the following, printed in such manner as may be provided in regulations prescribed by the Attorney General, with the name of the organization appearing in lieu of the blank: "Disseminated by --, a Communist organization"; or

> (2) to broadcast or cause to be broadcast any matter over any radio or television station in the United States, unless such matter is preceded by the following statement, with the

name of the organization being stated in place of the blank: "The following program is sponsored by a Communist organization."

[Section 11 provides that no tax deduction shall be allowed for contributions to any registered organization and no such organization shall be entitled to tax exemption.

Section 12 establishes a Subversive Activities Control Board of five members with power to determine, upon application by the Attorney General or any organization, whether an organization is a "Communist-action," "Communist-front" or "Communist-infiltrated" organization; and, upon application by the Attorney General or any individual to determine whether such individual is a member of a registered "Communist-action" organization.

Section 13 sets up an administrative procedure under which the Board may, upon petition by the Attorney General order organizations to register as "Communist-action" or "Communist-front" organizations, or individuals to register as members of "Communist-action" organizations under Section 8; and a procedure to review orders of the Attorney General denying petitions to cancel registration. It goes on to provide.]

(e) In determining whether any organization is a "Communist-action organization," the Board shall take into consideration --

(1) the extent to which its policies are formulated and carried out and its activities performed, pursuant to directives or to effectuate the policies of the foreign government or foreign organization in which is vested, or under the domination or control of which is exercised, the direction and control of the world Communist movement referred to in section 2 of this title; and

(2) the extent to which its views and policies do not deviate from those of such foreign government or foreign organization; and

(3) the extent to which it receives financial or other aid, directly or indirectly, from or at the direction of such foreign government or foreign organization; and

(4) the extent to which it sends members or representatives to any foreign country for instruction or training in the principles, policies, strategy, or tactics of such world Communist movement; and

(5) the extent to which it reports to such foreign government or foreign organization or to its representatives; and

(6) the extent to which its principal leaders or a substantial number of its members are subject to or recognize the disciplinary power of such foreign government or foreign organization or its representatives; and

(7) the extent to which, for the purpose of concealing foreign direction, domination, or control, or of expediting or promoting its objectives, (i) it fails to disclose, or resists efforts to obtain information as to, its membership (by keeping membership lists in code,

by instructing members to refuse to acknowledge membership, or by any other method); (ii) its members refuse to acknowledge membership therein; (iii) it fails " to disclose, or resists efforts to obtain information as to, records other than membership lists; (iv) its meetings are secret; and (v) it otherwise operates on a secret basis; and (8) the extent to which its principal leaders or a substantial number of its members consider the allegiance they owe to the United States as subordinate to their obligations to such foreign government or foreign organization.

(f) In determining whether any organization is a "Communist-front organization," the Board shall take into consideration:

(1) the extent to which persons who are active in its management, direction, or supervision, whether or not holding office therein, are active in the management, direction, or supervision of, or as representatives of, any Communist-action organization, Communist foreign government, or the world Communist movement referred to in section 2; and

(2) the extent to which its support, financial or otherwise, is derived from any Communist-action organization, Communist foreign government, or the world Communist movement referred to in section 2; and

(3) the extent to which its funds, resources, or personnel are used to t further or promote the objectives of any Communist-action organization, Communist foreign government, or the world Communist movement referred to in section 2; and

(4) the extent to which the positions taken or advanced by it from time to time on matters of policy do not deviate from those of any Communist-action organization, Communist-foreign government, or the world Communist movement referred to in section 2....

[Section 13A establishes a similar procedure with respect to "Communist-infiltrated" organizations, establishes criteria for determining whether an organization is "Communist-infiltrated," and provides that a labor organization or employer so found shall be ineligible to exercise any "right or privilege or receive any other benefit" provided by the National Labor Relations Act.]

[Section 14 provides that any party aggrieved by an order of the Board may appeal to the Court of Appeals of the District of Columbia and, by certiorari, to the Supreme Court.]

Penalties

Section 15.

(a) If there is in effect with respect to any organization or individual a final order of the Board requiring registration under section 7 or section 8 of this title:

(1) such organization shall, upon conviction of failure to register, to file any registration statement or annual report, or to keep records as required by section 7, be punished for each such offense by a fine of not more than $10,000, and

(2) each individual having a duty under subsection (h) of section 7 to register or to file any registration statement or annual report on behalf of such organization, and each individual having a duty to register under section 8, shall, upon conviction of failure to so register or to file any such registration statement or annual report, be punished for each such offense by a fine of not more than $10,000, or imprisonment for not more than five years, or by both such fine and imprisonment. For the purposes of this subsection, each day of failure to register, whether on the part of the organization or any individual, shall constitute a separate offense.

(b) Any individual who, in a registration statement or annual report filed under section 7 or section 8, willfully makes any false statement or willfully omits to state any fact which is required to be stated, or which is necessary to make the statements made or information given not misleading, shall upon conviction thereof be punished for each such offense by a fine of not more than $10,000, or by imprisonment for not more than five years, or by both such fine and imprisonment. For the purposes of this subsection:

(1) each false statement willfully made, and each willful omission to state any fact which is required to be stated, or which is necessary to make the statements made or information given not misleading, shall constitute a separate offense; and

(2) each listing of the name or address of any one individual shall be deemed to be a separate statement.

(c) Any organization which violates any provision of section 10 of this title shall, upon conviction thereof, be punished for each such violation by a fine or not more than $10,000. Any individual who violates any provision of sections 5, 6, or 10 of this title shall, upon conviction thereof, be punished for each such violation by a fine of not more than $10,000 or by imprisonment for not more than five years, or by both such fine and imprisonment.

321

Title II--Emergency Detention

Short Title

Section 100. This title may be cited as the "Emergency Detention Act of 1950."

[Section 101 contains findings of fact similar to those made in Title I, with certain omissions and additions.]

Section 102.

(a) In the event of any one of the following:

> (1) Invasion of the territory of the United States or its possessions,

> (2) Declaration of war by Congress, or

> (3) Insurrection within the United States in aid of a foreign enemy, and if, upon the occurrence of one or more of the above, the President shall find that the proclamation of an emergency pursuant to this section is essential to the preservation, protection and defense of the Constitution, and to the common defense and safety of the territory and people of the United States, the President is authorized to make public proclamation of the existence of an "Internal Security Emergency.

(b) A state of "Internal Security Emergency" (hereinafter referred to as the "emergency") so declared shall continue in existence until terminated by proclamation of the President or by concurrent resolution of the Congress.

Section 103.

(a) Whenever there shall be in existence such an emergency, the President, acting through the Attorney General, is hereby authorized to apprehend and by order detain, pursuant to the provisions of this title, each person as to whom there is reasonable ground to believe that such person probably will engage in, or probably will conspire with others to engage in, acts of espionage or of sabotage.

(b) Any person detained hereunder (hereinafter referred to as "the detainee") shall be released from such emergency detention upon:

> (1) the termination of such emergency by proclamation of the President or by concurrent resolution of the Congress;

> (2) an order of release by the Attorney General;

> (3) a final order of release after hearing by the Board of Detention Review, hereinafter established;

(4) a final order of release by a United States court, after review of the action of the Board of Detention Review, or upon a writ of habeas corpus.

[Sections 104 to 111 provide the procedure for apprehension and detention. Any person apprehended has a right to a preliminary hearing before a hearing officer appointed by the President. "Such person may introduce evidence in his own behalf, and may cross-examine witnesses against him, except that the Attorney General or his representative shall not be required to furnish information the revelation of which would disclose the identity or evidence of Government agents or officers which he believes it would be dangerous to national safety and security to divulge." Thereafter the detainee may appeal to the Board of Detention Review, consisting of nine members appointed by the President, and from there to the Court of Appeals and, by certiorari, to the Supreme Court. Section 112 establishes criminal penalties for resisting or evading apprehension or advising or assisting others to do so.]

Schenck v. United States

Nos. 437, 438

SUPREME COURT OF THE UNITED STATES

249 U.S. 47

January 9, 10, 1919

March 3, 1919

Syllabus

✢ Evidence *held* sufficient to connect the defendants with the mailing of printed circulars in pursuance of a conspiracy to obstruct the recruiting and enlistment service, contrary to the Espionage Act of June 15, 1917. P 49 . [p*48]

Incriminating document seized under a search warrant directed against a Socialist headquarters, *held* admissible in evidence, consistently with the Fourth and Fifth Amendment, in a criminal prosecution against the general secretary of a Socialist party, who had charge of the office. P. 50

Words which, ordinarily and in many places, would be within the freedom of speech protected by the First Amendment may become subject to prohibition when of such a nature and used in such circumstances a to create a clear and present danger that they will bring about the substantive evils which Congress has a right to prevent. The character of every act depends upon the circumstances in which it is done. P. 51 .

A conspiracy to circulate among men called and accepted for military service under the Selective Service Act of May 18, 1917, a circular tending to influence them to obstruct the draft, with the intent to effect that result, and followed by the sending of such circulars, is within the power of Congress to punish, and is punishable under the Espionage Act, § 4, although unsuccessful. P. 52 .The word "recruiting," as used in the Espionage Act, § 3, means the gaining of fresh supplies of men for the military forces, as well by draft a otherwise. P. 52

The amendment of the Espionage Act by the Act of May 16, 1918, c. 75, 40 Stat. 553, did not affect the prosecution of offenses under the former. P. 53.

AFFIRMED

Opinions

The case is stated in the opinion.

HOLMES, J., Opinion of the Court

MR. JUSTICE HOLMES delivered the opinion of the court.

This is an indictment in three counts. The first charges a conspiracy to violate the Espionage Act of June 15, 1917, c. 30, § 3, 40 Stat. 217, 219, by causing and attempting [p*49] to cause insubordination, &c., in the military and naval forces of the United States, and to obstruct the recruiting and enlistment service of the United States, when the United States was at war with the German Empire, to-wit, that the defendants willfully conspired to have printed and circulated to men who had been called and accepted for military service under the Act of May 18, 1917, a document set forth and alleged to be calculated to cause such insubordination and obstruction. The count alleges overt acts in pursuance of the conspiracy, ending in the distribution of the document set forth. The second count alleges a conspiracy to commit an offence against the United States, to-wit, to use the mails for the transmission of matter declared to be nonmailable by Title XII, § 2 of the Act of June 15, 1917, to-wit, the above mentioned document, with an averment of the same overt acts. The third count charges an unlawful use of the mails for the transmission of the same matter and otherwise as above. The defendants were found guilty on all the counts. They set up the First Amendment to the Constitution forbidding Congress to make any law abridging the freedom of speech, or of the press, and bringing the case here on that ground have argued some other points also of which we must dispose.

It is argued that the evidence, if admissible, was not sufficient to prove that the defendant Schenck was concerned in sending the documents. According to the testimony, Schenck said he was general secretary of the Socialist party, and had charge of the Socialist headquarters from which the documents were sent. He identified a book found there as the minutes of the Executive Committee of the party. The book showed a resolution of August 13, 1917, that 15,000 leaflets should be printed on the other side of one of them in use, to be mailed to men who had passed exemption boards, and for distribution. Schenck personally attended to the printing. On [p*50] August 20, the general secretary's report said "Obtained new leaflets from printer and started work addressing envelopes" &c., and there was a resolve that Comrade Schenck be allowed $125 for sending leaflets through the mail. He said that he had about fifteen or sixteen thousand printed. There were files of the circular in question in the inner office which he said were printed on the other side of the one sided circular, and were there for distribution. Other copies were proved to have been sent through the mails to drafted men. Without going into confirmatory details that were proved, no reasonable man could doubt that the defendant Schenck was largely instrumental in sending the circulars about. As to the defendant Baer, there was evidence that she was a member of the Executive Board, and that the minutes of its transactions were hers. The argument as to the sufficiency of the evidence that the defendants conspired to send the documents only impairs the seriousness of the real defence.

It is objected that the documentary evidence was not admissible because obtained upon a search warrant, valid so far as appears. The contrary is established. *Adams v. New York,* 192 U.S. 585; *Weeks v. United States,* 232 U.S. 383, 395, 396. The search warrant did not issue against the defendant, but against the Socialist headquarters at 1326 Arch Street, and it would seem that the documents technically were not even in the defendants' possession. *See Johnson v. United States,* 228 U.S. 457. Notwithstanding some protest in argument, the notion that evidence even directly proceeding from the defendant in a criminal proceeding is excluded in all cases by the Fifth Amendment is plainly unsound. *Holt v. United States,* 218 U.S. 245, 252, 253.

The document in question, upon its first printed side, recited the first section of the Thirteenth Amendment, said that the idea embodied in it was violated by the Conscription Act, and that a conscript is little better than a [p*51] convict. In impassioned language, it intimated that conscription was despotism in its worst form, and a monstrous wrong against humanity in the interest of Wall Street's chosen few. It said "Do not submit to intimidation," but in form, at least, confined itself to peaceful measures such as a petition for the repeal of the act. The other and later printed side of the sheet was headed "Assert Your Rights." It stated reasons for alleging that anyone violated the Constitution when he refused to recognize "your right to assert your opposition to the draft," and went on

If you do not assert and support your rights, you are helping to deny or disparage rights which it is the solemn duty of all citizens and residents of the United States to retain.

It described the arguments on the other side as coming from cunning politicians and a mercenary capitalist press, and even silent consent to the conscription law as helping to support an infamous conspiracy. It denied the power to send our citizens away to foreign shores to shoot up the people of other lands, and added that words could not express the condemnation such cold-blooded ruthlessness deserves, &c., &c., winding up, "You must do your share to maintain, support and uphold the rights of the people of this country." Of course, the document would not have been sent unless it had been intended to have some effect, and we do not see what effect it could be expected to have upon persons subject to the draft except to influence them to obstruct the carrying of it out. The defendants do not deny that the jury might find against them on this point.

But it is said, suppose that that was the tendency of this circular, it is protected by the First Amendment to the Constitution. Two of the strongest expressions are said to be quoted respectively from well known public men. It well may be that the prohibition of laws abridging the freedom of speech is not confined to previous restraints, although to prevent them may have been the [p*52] main purpose, as intimated in *Patterson v. Colorado,* 205 U.S. 454, 462. We admit that, in many places and in ordinary times, the defendants, in saying all that was said in the circular, would have been within their constitutional rights. But the character of every act depends upon the circumstances in which it is done. *Aikens v. Wisconsin,* 195 U.S. 194, 205, 206. The most stringent protection of free speech would not protect a man in falsely shouting fire in a theatre and causing a panic. It does not even protect a man from an injunction against uttering words that may have all the effect of force. *Gompers v. Bucks Stove & Range Co.,* 221 U.S. 418, 439. The question in every case is whether the words used are used in such circumstances and are of such a nature as to create a clear and present danger that they will bring about the substantive evils that Congress has a right to prevent. It is a question of proximity and degree. When a nation is at war, many things that might be said in time of peace are such a hindrance to its effort that their utterance will not be endured so long as men fight, and that no Court could regard them as protected by any constitutional right. It seems to be admitted that, if an actual obstruction of the recruiting service were proved, liability for words that produced that effect might be enforced. The statute of 1917, in § 4, punishes conspiracies to obstruct, as well as actual obstruction. If the act (speaking, or circulating a paper), its tendency, and the intent with which it is done are the same, we perceive no ground for saying that success alone warrants making the act a crime. *Goldman v. United States,* 245 U.S. 474, 477. Indeed, that case might be said to dispose of the present contention if the precedent covers all *media concludendi.* But, as the right to free speech was not referred to specially, we have thought fit to add a few words.

Dennis v. United States, 341 U.S. 494 (1951)

SUPREME COURT OF THE UNITED STATES

341 U.S. 494

December 4, 1950

June 4, 1951

Syllabus

1. As construed and applied in this case, §§ 2(a)(1), 2(a)(3) and 3 of the Smith Act, 54 Stat. 671, making it a crime for any person knowingly or willfully to advocate the overthrow or destruction of the Government of the United States by force or violence, to organize or help to organize any group which does so, or to conspire to do so, do not violate the First Amendment or other

provisions of the Bill of Rights and do not violate the First or Fifth Amendments because of indefiniteness. Pp. 495-499, 517 .

2. Petitioners, leaders of the Communist Party in this country, were indicted in a federal district court under § 3 of the Smith Act for willfully and knowingly conspiring (1) to organize as the Communist Party a group of persons to teach and advocate the overthrow and destruction of the Government of the United States by force and violence, and (2) knowingly and willfully to advocate and teach the duty and necessity of overthrowing and destroying the Government of the United States by force and violence. The trial judge instructed the jury that they could not convict unless they found that petitioners intended to overthrow the Government "as speedily as circumstances would permit," but that, if they so found, then, as a matter of law, there was sufficient danger of a substantive evil that Congress has a right to prevent to justify application of the statute under the First Amendment. Petitioners were convicted, and the convictions were sustained by the Court of Appeals. This Court granted certiorari, limited to the questions: (1) Whether either § 2 or § 3 of the Smith Act, inherently or as construed and applied in the instant case, violates the First Amendment and other provisions of the Bill of Rights, and (2) whether either § 2 or § 3, inherently or as construed and applied in the instant case, violates the First and Fifth Amendments because of indefiniteness.

Held: The convictions are affirmed. Pp. 495-499; 511-512; 517; 183 F.2d 201, affirmed. [p*495]

Opinions

For the opinions of the Justices constituting the majority of the Court, *see:* Opinion of THE CHIEF JUSTICE, joined by MR. JUSTICE REED, MR. JUSTICE BURTON and MR. JUSTICE MINTON, p. 495 .

Opinion of MR. JUSTICE FRANKFURTER, p. 517 .

Opinion of MR. JUSTICE JACKSON, p. 561.

For the dissenting opinion of MR. JUSTICE BLACK, *see* p. 579.

For the dissenting opinion of MR. JUSTICE DOUGLAS, *see* p. 581.

The case is stated in the opinion of THE CHIEF JUSTICE, pp. 495-499 .

AFFIRMED, p. 517.

VINSON, C.J., Judgment of the Court

MR. CHIEF JUSTICE VINSON announced the judgment of the Court and an opinion in which MR. JUSTICE REED, MR. JUSTICE BURTON and MR. JUSTICE MINTON join.

♣ Petitioners were indicted in July, 1948, for violation of the conspiracy provisions of the Smith Act, 54 Stat. 671, 18 U.S.C. (1946 ed.) § 11, during the period of April, 1945, to July, 1948. The pretrial motion to quash the indictment on the grounds, *inter alia,* that the statute was unconstitutional was denied, *United States v. Foster,* 80 F.Supp. 479, and the case was set for trial on January 17, 1949. A verdict of guilty as to all the petitioners was returned by the jury on October 14, 1949. The Court of Appeals affirmed the convictions. 183 F.2d 201. We granted certiorari, 340 U.S. 863, limited to the following two questions: (1) Whether either § 2 or § 3 of the Smith [p*496] Act, inherently or as construed and applied in the instant case, violates the First Amendment and other provisions of the Bill of Rights; (2) whether either § 2 or § 3 of the Act, inherently or as construed and applied in the instant case, violates the First and Fifth Amendments because of indefiniteness.

Yates v. United States, 354 U.S. 298 (1957)

No. 6

SUPREME COURT OF THE UNITED STATES

354 U.S. 298

October 8-9, 1956

June 17, 1957

Syllabus

♣ The 14 petitioners, leaders of the Communist Party in California, were indicted in 1951 in a Federal District Court under § 3 of the Smith Act and 18 U.S.C. § 371 for conspiring (1) to advocate and teach the duty and necessity of overthrowing the Government of the United States by force and violence, and (2) to organize, as the Communist Party of the United States, a society of persons who so advocate and teach, all with the intent of causing the overthrow of the Government by force and violence as speedily as circumstances would permit. The indictment charged that the conspiracy originated in 1940 and continued down to the date of the indictment, and that, in carrying it out, petitioners and their coconspirators would (a) become members and officers of the Communist Party, with knowledge of its unlawful purposes, and assume leadership in carrying out its policies and activities, (b) cause to be organized units of the Party in California and elsewhere, (c) write and publish articles on such advocacy and teaching, (d) conduct schools for the indoctrination of Party members in such advocacy and teaching, and (e) recruit new Party members, particularly from among persons employed in the key industries of the Nation. It also alleged 23 overt acts in furtherance of the conspiracy. Petitioners were convicted after a jury trial, and their convictions were sustained by the Court of Appeals.

✤ *Held:* The convictions are reversed, and the cause is remanded to the District Court with directions to enter judgments of acquittal as to five of the petitioners and to grant a new trial as to the others. Pp. 300-338.

1. Since the Communist Party came into being in 1945, and the indictment was not returned until 1951, the three-year statute of limitations had run on the "organizing" charge, and required the withdrawal of that part of the indictment from the jury's consideration. Pp. 303-312. [p*299]

> (a) Applying the rule that criminal statutes are to be construed strictly, the word "organize," as used in the Smith Act, is construed as referring only to acts entering into the creation of a new organization, and not to acts thereafter performed in carrying on its activities, even though the latter may loosely be termed "organizational." Pp. 303-311.

> (b) The trial court's mistaken construction of the word "organize" was not harmless error; the circumstances are such as to call for application of the rule which requires a verdict to be set aside where it is supportable on one ground, but not another, and it is impossible to tell which ground the jury selected. Pp. 311-312.

2. The Smith Act does not prohibit advocacy and teaching of forcible overthrow of the Government as an abstract principle, divorced from any effort to instigate action to that end; the trial court's charge to the jury furnished wholly inadequate guidance on this central point in the case, and the conviction cannot be allowed to stand. *Dennis v. United States,* 341 U.S. 494 , distinguished. Pp. 312-327 .

3. The evidence against five of the petitioners is so clearly insufficient that their acquittal should be ordered, but that as to the others is such as not to justify closing the way to their retrial. Pp. 327-334 .

4. Determinations favorable to petitioner Schneiderman made by this Court in *Schneiderman v. United States,* 320 U.S. 118, a denaturalization proceeding in which he was the prevailing party, are not conclusive in this proceeding under the doctrine of collateral estoppel, and he is not entitled to a judgment of acquittal on that ground. *Federal Trade Commission v. Cement Institute,* 333 U.S. 683. Pp. 335-338 .

*225 F.2d 146, REVERSED AND REMANDED. [p*300]*

Opinions

HARLAN, J., Opinion of the Court

MR. JUSTICE HARLAN delivered the opinion of the Court.

✤ We brought these cases here to consider certain questions arising under the Smith Act which have not heretofore been passed upon by this Court, and otherwise to review the convictions of these petitioners for conspiracy to violate that Act. Among other things, the convictions are claimed to rest upon an application of the Smith Act which is hostile to the principles upon which its constitutionality was upheld in *Dennis v. United States,* 341 U.S. 494 .

These 14 petitioners stand convicted, after a jury trial in the United States District Court for the Southern District of California, upon a single count indictment charging them with conspiring (1) to advocate and teach the duty and necessity of overthrowing the Government of the United States by force and violence, and (2) to organize, as the Communist Party of the United States, a society of persons who so advocate and teach, all with the intent of causing the overthrow of the Government by force and violence as speedily as circumstances would permit. Act of June 28, 1940, § 2(a)(1) and (3), 54 [p*301] Stat. 670, 671, 18 U.S.C. §§ 371, 2385. [n1] The conspiracy is alleged to have originated in 1940 and continued down to the date of the indictment in 1951. The indictment charged that, in carrying out the conspiracy, the defendants [p*302] and their co-conspirators would (a) become members and officers of the Communist Party, with knowledge of its unlawful purposes, and assume leadership in carrying out its policies and activities; (b) cause to be organized units of the Party in California and elsewhere; (c) write and publish, in the "Daily Worker" and other Party organs, articles on the proscribed advocacy and teaching; (d) conduct schools for the indoctrination of Party members in such advocacy and teaching, and (e) recruit new Party members, particularly from among persons employed in the key industries of the nation. Twenty-three overt acts in furtherance of the conspiracy were alleged.

Upon conviction, each of the petitioners was sentenced to five years' imprisonment and a fine of $10,000. The [p*303] Court of Appeals affirmed. 225 F.2d 146. We granted certiorari for the reasons already indicated. 350 U.S. 860.

In the view we take of this case, it is necessary for us to consider only the following of petitioners' contentions: (1) that the term "organize," as used in the Smith Act, was erroneously construed by the two lower courts; (2) that the trial court's instructions to the jury erroneously excluded from the case the issue of "incitement to action"; (3) that the evidence was so insufficient as to require this Court to direct the acquittal of these petitioners, and (4) that petitioner Schneiderman's conviction was precluded by this Court's judgment in *Schneiderman v. United States,* 320 U.S. 118, under the doctrine of collateral estoppel. [n2] For reasons given hereafter, we conclude that these convictions must be reversed and the case remanded to the District Court with instructions to enter judgments of acquittal as to certain of the petitioners, and to grant a new trial as to the rest.

I. *The Term "Organize"*

One object of the conspiracy charged was to violate the third paragraph of 18 U.S.C. § 2385, which provides:

Whoever organizes or helps or attempts to organize any society, group, or assembly of persons who teach, advocate, or encourage the overthrow or destruction of any [government in the United States] by force or violence . . . [s]hall be fined not more than $10,000 or imprisoned not more than ten years, or both. [p*304]

Petitioners claim that "organize" means to "establish," "found," or "bring into existence," and that, in this sense, the Communist Party was organized by 1945 at the latest. On this basis, petitioners contend that this part of the indictment, returned in 1951, was barred by the three-year statute of limitations. The Government, on the other hand, says that "organize" connotes a continuing process which goes on throughout the life of an organization, and that, in the words of the trial court's instructions to the jury, the term includes such things as "the recruiting of new members and the forming of new units, and the regrouping or expansion of existing clubs, classes and other units of any society, party, group or other organization." The two courts below accepted the Government's position. We think, however, that petitioners' position must prevail, upon principles stated by Chief Justice Marshall more than a century ago in *United States v. Wiltberger*, 5 Wheat. 76, 95-96, as follows:

The rule that penal laws are to be construed strictly is perhaps not much less old than construction itself. It is founded on the tenderness of the law for the rights of individuals, and on the plain principle that the power of punishment is vested in the legislative, not in the judicial, department. It is the legislature, not the Court, which is to define a crime, and ordain its punishment. [p*305]

It is said that, notwithstanding this rule, the intention of the lawmaker must govern in the construction of penal as well as other statutes. This is true. But this is not a new independent rule which subverts the old. It is a modification of the ancient maxim, and amounts to this: that, though penal laws are to be construed strictly, they are not to be construed so strictly as to defeat the obvious intention of the legislature. The maxim is not to be so applied as to narrow the words of the statute to the exclusion of cases which those words, in their ordinary acceptation, or in that sense in which the legislature has obviously used them, would comprehend. The intention of the legislature is to be collected from the words they employ. Where there is no ambiguity in the words, there is no room for construction. The case must be a strong one indeed which would justify a Court in departing from the plain meaning of words, especially in a penal act, in search of an intention which the words themselves did not suggest. To determine that a case is within the intention of a statute, its language must authorize us to say so. It would be dangerous indeed to carry the principle that a case which is within the reason or mischief of a statute is within its provisions so far as to punish a crime not enumerated in the statute because it is of equal atrocity, or of kindred character, with those which are enumerated. If this principle has ever been recognized in expounding criminal law, it has been in cases of considerable irritation, which it would be unsafe to consider as precedents forming a general rule for other cases.

The statute does not define what is meant by "organize." Dictionary definitions are of little help, for, as those offered us sufficiently show, the term is susceptible [p*306] of both meanings attributed to it by the parties here. The fact that the Communist Party comprises various components and activities, in relation to which some of the petitioners bore the title of "Organizer," does not advance us towards a solution of the problem. The charge here is that petitioners conspired to organize the Communist Party, and, unless "organize" embraces the continuing concept contended for by the Government, the establishing of new units within the Party and similar activities, following the Party's initial formation in 1945, have no independent significance or vitality so far as the "organizing" charge is involved. Nor are we here concerned with the quality of petitioners' activities as such -- that is, whether particular activities may properly be categorized as "organizational." Rather, the issue is whether the term "organize," as used in this statute, is limited by temporal concepts. Stated most simply, the problem is to choose between two possible answers to the question: when was the Communist Party "organized"?

331

Petitioners contend that the only natural answer to the question is the formation date -- in this case, 1945. The Government would have us answer the question by saying that the Party today is still not completely "organized"; [p*307] that "organizing" is a continuing process that does not end until the entity is dissolved.

The legislative history of the Smith Act is no more revealing as to what Congress meant by "organize" than is the statute itself. The Government urges that "organize" should be given a broad meaning, since acceptance of the term in its narrow sense would require attributing to Congress the intent that this provision of the statute should not apply to the Communist Party as it then existed. The argument is that, since the Communist Party as it then existed had been born in 1919 and the Smith Act was not passed until 1940, the use of "organize" in its narrow sense would have meant that these provisions of the statute would never have reached the act of organizing the Communist Party, except for the fortuitous rebirth of the Party in 1945 -- an occurrence which, of course, could not have been foreseen in 1940. This, says the Government, could hardly have been the congressional purpose, since the Smith Act as a whole was particularly aimed at the Communist Party, and its "organizing" provisions were especially directed at the leaders of the movement.

We find this argument unpersuasive. While the legislative history of the Smith Act does show that concern about communism was a strong factor leading to this legislation, it also reveals that the statute, which was patterned on state anti-sedition laws directed not against Communists but against anarchists and syndicalists, was aimed equally at all groups falling within its scope. [p*308] More important, there is no evidence whatever to support the thesis that the organizing provision of the statute was written with particular reference to the Communist Party. Indeed, the congressional hearings indicate that it was the "advocating and teaching" provision of the Act, rather than the "organizing" provision, which was especially thought to reach Communist activities.

Nor do there appear to be any other reasons for ascribing to "organize" the Government's broad interpretation. While it is understandable that Congress should have wished to supplement the general provisions of the Smith Act by a special provision directed at the activities of those responsible for creating a new organization of the proscribed type, such as was the situation involved in the *Dennis* case, we find nothing which suggests that the "organizing" provision was intended to reach beyond this, that is, to embrace the activities of those concerned with carrying on the affairs of an already existing organization. Such activities were already amply covered by other provisions of the Act, such as the "membership" clause, and the basic prohibition of "advocacy" in conjunction with the conspiracy provision, and there is thus no need to stretch the "organizing" provision to fill any gaps in the statute. Moreover, it is difficult to find any considerations, comparable to those relating to persons responsible for creating a new organization, which would have led the Congress to single out for special treatment those persons occupying so-called organizational positions in an existing organization, especially when this same section of the statute proscribes membership in such an organization without drawing any distinction between those holding executive office and others. [p*309]

On the other hand, we also find unpersuasive petitioners' argument as to the intent of Congress. In support of the narrower meaning of "organize," they argue that the Smith Act was patterned after the California Criminal Syndicalism Act; that the California courts have consistently taken "organize" in that Act in its narrow sense; and that, under such cases as *Willis v. Eastern Trust & Banking Co.,* 169 U.S. 295, 304, 309, and *Joines v. Patterson,* 274 U.S. 544, 549, it should be presumed that Congress in adopting the wording of the California Act intended "organize" to have the same meaning as that given it by the California courts. As the hearings on the Smith Act show, however, its particular prototype was the New York Criminal Anarchy Act, not the California statute, and the "organizing" provisions of the New York Act have never been construed by any court. Moreover, to the extent that the language of the California statute, which itself was patterned on the earlier New York legislation, might be significant, we think that little weight can be given to these California decisions. The general rule that adoption of the wording of a statute from another legislative jurisdiction carries with it the previous judicial interpretations of the wording . . . is a presumption of legislative intention . . . which varies in strength with the similarity of the language, the established character of the decisions in the jurisdiction from which the language was adopted and the presence or lack of other indicia of intention.

Carolene Products Co. v. United States, 323 [p*310] U.S. 18, 26. Here, the three California cases relied on by petitioners were all decisions of lower courts, and, in the absence of anything in the legislative history indicating that they were called to its attention, we should not assume that Congress was aware of them.

We are thus left to determine for ourselves the meaning of this provision of the Smith Act, without any revealing guides as to the intent of Congress. In these circumstances, we should follow the familiar rule that criminal statutes are to be strictly construed, and give to "organize" its narrow meaning, that is, that the word refers only to acts entering into the creation of a new organization, and not to acts thereafter performed in carrying on its activities, even though such acts may loosely be termed "organizational." *See United States v. Wiltberger, supra; United States v. Lacher,* 134 U.S. 624, 628; *United States v. Gradwell,* 243 U.S. 476, 485; *Fasulo v. United States,* 272 U.S. 620, 628. Such indeed is the normal usage of the word "organize," and, until the decisions below in this case, the federal trial courts in which the question had arisen uniformly gave it that meaning. *See United States v. Flynn,* unreported (D.C.S.D.N.Y.), No. C. 137-37, *aff'd,* 216 F.2d 354, 358; *United States v. Mesarosh,* 116 F.Supp. 345, *aff'd,* 223 F.2d 449, 465 (dissenting opinion of Hastie, J.); *see also United States v. Dennis,* unreported (D.C.S.D.N.Y.), No. C. 128-87, *aff'd,* 183 F.2d 201, 341 U.S. 494. [p*311] We too think this statute should be read according to the natural and obvious import of the language, without resorting to subtle and forced construction for the purpose of either limiting or extending its operation.

United States v. Temple, 105 U.S. 97, 99.

The Government contends that, even if the trial court was mistaken in its construction of the statute, the error was harmless because the conspiracy charged embraced both "advocacy" of violent overthrow and "organizing" the Communist Party, and the jury was instructed that, in order to convict, it must find a conspiracy extending to both objectives. Hence, the argument is, the jury must, in any event, be taken to have found petitioners guilty of conspiring to advocate, and the convictions are supportable on that basis alone. We cannot accept this proposition for a number of reasons. The portions of the trial court's instructions relied on by the Government are not sufficiently clear or specific to warrant our drawing the inference that the jury understood it

333

must find an agreement extending to *both* "advocacy" and "organizing" in order to convict. Further, in order to convict, the jury was required, as the court charged, to find an overt act which was "knowingly done in furtherance of an object or purpose of the conspiracy charged in the indictment," and we have no way of knowing whether the overt act found by the jury was one which it believed to be in furtherance [p*312] of the "advocacy", rather than the "organizing" objective of the alleged conspiracy. The character of most of the overt acts alleged associates them as readily with "organizing" as with "advocacy." In these circumstances, we think the proper rule to be applied is that which requires a verdict to be set aside in cases where the verdict is supportable on one ground, but not on another, and it is impossible to tell which ground the jury selected. *Stromberg v. California,* 283 U.S. 359, 367-368; *Williams v. North Carolina,* 317 U.S. 287, 291-292; *Cramer v. United States,* 325 U.S. 1, 36, n. 45.

We conclude, therefore, that, since the Communist Party came into being in 1945, and the indictment was not returned until 1951, the three-year statute of limitations had run on the "organizing" charge, and required the withdrawal of that part of the indictment from the jury's consideration. *Samuel v. United States,* 169 F.2d 787, 798. *See also Haupt v. United States,* 330 U.S. 631, 641, n. 1; *Stromberg v. California, supra,* at 368.

Brandenburg v. Ohio, 395 U.S. 444 (1969)

SUPREME COURT OF THE UNITED STATES

395 U.S. 444

1969

Syllabus

✠ Appellant, a Ku Klux Klan leader, was convicted under the Ohio Criminal Syndicalism statute for advocat[ing] . . . the duty, necessity, or propriety of crime, sabotage, violence, or unlawful methods of terrorism as a means of accomplishing industrial or political reform and for voluntarily assembl[ing] with any society, group or assemblage of persons formed to teach or advocate the doctrines of criminal syndicalism.

Neither the indictment nor the trial judge's instructions refined the statute's definition of the crime in terms of mere advocacy not distinguished from incitement to imminent lawless action.

✠ *Held:* Since the statute, by its words and as applied, purports to punish mere advocacy and to forbid, on pain of criminal punishment, assembly with others merely to advocate the described type of action, it falls within the condemnation of the First and Fourteenth Amendments. Freedoms of speech and press do not permit a State to forbid advocacy of the use of force or of law violation except where such advocacy is directed to inciting or producing imminent lawless action and is likely to incite or produce such action. *Whitney v. California,* 274 U.S. 357 , overruled.

REVERSED.

Opinions

Per Curiam Opinion

PER CURIAM.

The appellant, a leader of a Ku Klux Klan group, was convicted under the Ohio Criminal Syndicalism statute for "advocat[ing] . . . the duty, necessity, or propriety [p*445] of crime, sabotage, violence, or unlawful methods of terrorism as a means of accomplishing industrial or political reform" and for voluntarily assembl[ing] with any society, group, or assemblage of persons formed to teach or advocate the doctrines of criminal syndicalism.

Ohio Rev.Code Ann. § 2923.13. He was fined $1,000 and sentenced to one to 10 years' imprisonment. The appellant challenged the constitutionality of the criminal syndicalism statute under the First and Fourteenth Amendments to the United States Constitution, but the intermediate appellate court of Ohio affirmed his conviction without opinion. The Supreme Court of Ohio dismissed his appeal *sua sponte* "for the reason that no substantial constitutional question exists herein." It did not file an opinion or explain its conclusions. Appeal was taken to this Court, and we noted probable jurisdiction. 393 U.S. 94 (196). We reverse.

The record shows that a man, identified at trial as the appellant, telephoned an announcer-reporter on the staff of a Cincinnati television station and invited him to come to a Ku Klux Klan "rally" to be held at a farm in Hamilton County. With the cooperation of the organizers, the reporter and a cameraman attended the meeting and filmed the events. Portions of the films were later broadcast on the local station and on a national network.

The prosecution's case rested on the films and on testimony identifying the appellant as the person who communicated with the reporter and who spoke at the rally. The State also introduced into evidence several articles appearing in the film, including a pistol, a rifle, a shotgun, ammunition, a Bible, and a red hood worn by the speaker in the films.

One film showed 12 hooded figures, some of whom carried firearms. They were gathered around a large wooden cross, which they burned. No one was present [p*446] other than the participants and the newsmen who made the film. Most of the words uttered during the scene were incomprehensible when the film was projected, but scattered phrases could be understood that were derogatory of Negroes and, in one instance, of Jews. [n1] Another scene on the same film showed the appellant, in Klan regalia, making a speech. The speech, in full, was as follows:

This is an organizers' meeting. We have had quite a few members here today which are -- we have hundreds, hundreds of members throughout the State of Ohio. I can quote from a newspaper clipping from the Columbus, Ohio, Dispatch, five weeks ago Sunday morning. The

Klan has more members in the State of Ohio than does any other organization. We're not a revengent organization, but if our President, our Congress, our Supreme Court, continues to suppress the white, Caucasian race, it's possible that there might have to be some revengeance taken.

We are marching on Congress July the Fourth, four hundred thousand strong. From there, we are dividing into two groups, one group to march on St. Augustine, Florida, the other group to march into Mississippi. Thank you. [p*447]

Patriot Act Summary

H.R.3162
Sponsor: Rep Sensenbrenner, F. James, Jr.(introduced 10/23/2001)
Related Bills: H.R.2975, S.1510
Latest Major Action: 10/26/2001 Became Public Law No: 107-56.
Title: To deter and punish terrorist acts in the United States and around the world, to enhance law enforcement investigatory tools, and for other purposes.

SUMMARY AS OF: 10/24/2001--Passed House, without amendment.

Uniting and Strengthening America by Providing Appropriate Tools Required to Intercept and Obstruct Terrorism (USA PATRIOT ACT) Act of 2001 - Title I: Enhancing Domestic Security Against Terrorism - Establishes in the U.S. Treasury the Counterterrorism Fund.

(Section 102) Expresses the sense of Congress that: (1) the civil rights and liberties of all Americans, including Arab Americans, must be protected, and that every effort must be taken to preserve their safety; (2) any acts of violence or discrimination against any Americans be condemned; and (3) the Nation is called upon to recognize the patriotism of fellow citizens from all ethnic, racial, and religious backgrounds.

(Section 103) Authorizes appropriations for the Federal Bureau of Investigation's (FBI) Technical Support Center.

(Section 104) Authorizes the Attorney General to request the Secretary of Defense to provide assistance in support of Department of Justice (DOJ) activities relating to the enforcement of Federal criminal code (code) provisions regarding the use of weapons of mass destruction during an emergency situation involving a weapon (currently, chemical weapon) of mass destruction.

(Section 105) Requires the Director of the U.S. Secret Service to take actions to develop a national network of electronic crime task forces throughout the United States to prevent, detect, and investigate various forms of electronic crimes, including potential terrorist attacks against critical infrastructure and financial payment systems.

(Section 106) Modifies provisions relating to presidential authority under the International Emergency Powers Act to: (1) authorize the President, when the United States is engaged in armed hostilities or has been attacked by a foreign country or foreign nationals, to confiscate any property subject to U.S. jurisdiction of a foreign person, organization, or country that he determines has planned, authorized, aided, or engaged in such hostilities or attacks(the rights to which shall vest in such agency or person as the President may designate); and (2) provide that, in any judicial review of a determination made under such provisions, if the determination was based on classified information such information may be submitted to the reviewing court ex parte and in camera.

Title II: Enhanced Surveillance Procedures - Amends the Federal criminal code to authorize the interception of wire, oral, and electronic communications for the production of evidence of: (1)specified chemical weapons or terrorism offenses; and (2) computer fraud and abuse.

(Section 203) Amends rule 6 of the Federal Rules of Criminal Procedure (FRCrP) to permit the sharing of grand jury information that involves foreign intelligence or counterintelligence with Federal law enforcement, intelligence, protective, immigration, national defense, or national security officials (such officials), subject to specified requirements.

Authorizes an investigative or law enforcement officer, or an attorney for the Government, who, by authorized means, has obtained knowledge of the contents of any wire, oral, or electronic communication or evidence derived therefrom to disclose such contents to such officials to the extent that such contents include foreign intelligence or counterintelligence.

Directs the Attorney General to establish procedures for the disclosure of information (pursuant to the code and the FRCrP) that identifies a United States person, as defined in the Foreign Intelligence Surveillance Act of 1978 (FISA).

Authorizes the disclosure of foreign intelligence or counterintelligence obtained as part of a criminal investigation to such officials.

(Section 204) Clarifies that nothing in code provisions regarding pen registers shall be deemed to affect the acquisition by the Government of specified foreign intelligence information, and that procedures under FISA shall be the exclusive means by which electronic surveillance and the interception of domestic wire and oral (current law) and electronic communications may be conducted.

(Section 205) Authorizes the Director of the FBI to expedite the employment of personnel as translators to support counter-terrorism investigations and operations without regard to applicable Federal personnel requirements. Requires: (1) the Director to establish such security requirements as necessary for such personnel; and (2) the Attorney General to report to the House and Senate Judiciary Committees regarding translators.

(Section 206) Grants roving surveillance authority under FISA after requiring a court order approving an electronic surveillance to direct any person to furnish necessary information, facilities, or technical assistance in circumstances where the Court finds that the actions of the surveillance target may have the effect of thwarting the identification of a specified person.

(Section 207) Increases the duration of FISA surveillance permitted for non-U.S. persons who are agents of a foreign power.

(Section 208) Increases (from seven to 11) the number of district court judges designated to hear applications for and grant orders approving electronic surveillance. Requires that no fewer than three reside within 20 miles of the District of Columbia.

(Section 209) Permits the seizure of voice-mail messages under a warrant.

(Section 210) Expands the scope of subpoenas for records of electronic communications to include the length and types of service utilized, temporarily assigned network addresses, and the means and source of payment (including any credit card or bank account number).

(Section 211) Amends the Communications Act of 1934 to permit specified disclosures to Government entities, except for records revealing cable subscriber selection of video programming from a cable operator.

(Section 212) Permits electronic communication and remote computing service providers to make emergency disclosures to a governmental entity of customer electronic communications to protect life and limb.

(Section 213) Authorizes Federal district courts to allow a delay of required notices of the execution of a warrant if immediate notice may have an adverse result and under other specified circumstances.

(Section 214) Prohibits use of a pen register or trap and trace devices in any investigation to protect against international terrorism or clandestine intelligence activities that is conducted solely on the basis of activities protected by the first amendment to the U.S. Constitution.

(Section 215) Authorizes the Director of the FBI (or designee) to apply for a court order requiring production of certain business records for foreign intelligence and international terrorism investigations. Requires the Attorney General to report to the House and Senate Intelligence and Judiciary Committees semi-annually.

(Section 216) Amends the code to: (1) require a trap and trace device to restrict recoding or decoding so as not to include the contents of a wire or electronic communication; (2) apply a court order for a pen register or trap and trace devices to any person or entity providing wire or electronic communication service in the United States whose assistance may facilitate execution of the order; (3) require specified records kept on any pen register or trap and trace device on a packet-switched data network of a provider of electronic communication service to the public; and (4) allow a trap and trace device to identify the source (but not the contents) of a wire or electronic communication.

(Section 217) Makes it lawful to intercept the wire or electronic communication of a computer trespasser in certain circumstances.

(Section 218) Amends FISA to require an application for an electronic surveillance order or search warrant to certify that a significant purpose (currently, the sole or main purpose) of the surveillance is to obtain foreign intelligence information.

(Section 219) Amends rule 41 of the FRCrP to permit Federal magistrate judges in any district in which terrorism-related activities may have occurred to issue search warrants for searches within or outside the district.

(Section 220) Provides for nationwide service of search warrants for electronic evidence.

(Section 221) Amends the Trade Sanctions Reform and Export Enhancement Act of 2000 to extend trade sanctions to the territory of Afghanistan controlled by the Taliban.

(Section 222) Specifies that: (1) nothing in this Act shall impose any additional technical obligation or requirement on a provider of a wire or electronic communication service or other person to furnish facilities or technical assistance; and (2) a provider of such service, and a landlord, custodian, or other person who furnishes such facilities or technical assistance, shall be reasonably compensated for such reasonable expenditures incurred in providing such facilities or assistance.

(Section 223) Amends the Federal criminal code to provide for administrative discipline of Federal officers or employees who violate prohibitions against unauthorized disclosures of information gathered under this Act. Provides for civil actions against the United States for damages by any person aggrieved by such violations.

(Section 224) Terminates this title on December 31, 2005, except with respect to any particular foreign intelligence investigation beginning before that date, or any particular offense or potential offense that began or occurred before it.

(Section 225) Amends the Foreign Intelligence Surveillance Act of 1978 to prohibit a cause of action in any court against a provider of a wire or electronic communication service, landlord, custodian, or any other person that furnishes any information, facilities, or technical assistance in accordance with a court order or request for emergency assistance under such Act (for example, with respect to a wiretap).

Title III: International Money Laundering Abatement and Anti-Terrorist Financing Act of 2001 - International Money Laundering Abatement and Anti-Terrorist Financing Act of 2001- Sunsets this Act after the first day of FY2005 if Congress enacts a specified joint resolution to that effect.

Subtitle A: International Counter Money Laundering and Related Measures - Amends Federal law governing monetary transactions to prescribe procedural guidelines under which the Secretary of the Treasury (the Secretary) may require domestic financial institutions and agencies to take specified measures if the Secretary finds that reasonable grounds exist for concluding that jurisdictions, financial institutions, types of accounts, or transactions operating outside or within the United States, are of primary money laundering concern. Includes mandatory disclosure of specified information relating to certain correspondent accounts.

(Section 312) Mandates establishment of due diligence mechanisms to detect and report money laundering transactions through private banking accounts and correspondent accounts.

(Section 313) Prohibits U.S. correspondent accounts with foreign shell banks.

(Section 314) Instructs the Secretary to adopt regulations to encourage further cooperation among financial institutions, their regulatory authorities, and law enforcement authorities, with the specific purpose of encouraging regulatory authorities and law enforcement authorities to share with financial institutions information regarding individuals, entities, and organizations engaged in or reasonably suspected (based on credible evidence) of engaging in terrorist acts or money laundering activities. Authorizes such regulations to create procedures for cooperation and information sharing on matters specifically related to the finances of terrorist groups as well as their relationships with international narcotics traffickers.

Requires the Secretary to distribute annually to financial institutions a detailed analysis identifying patterns of suspicious activity and other investigative insights derived from suspicious activity reports and investigations by Federal, State, and local law enforcement agencies.

(Section 315) Amends Federal criminal law to include foreign corruption offenses as money laundering crimes.

(Section 316) Establishes the right of property owners to contest confiscation of property under law relating to confiscation of assets of suspected terrorists.

(Section 317) Establishes Federal jurisdiction over: (1) foreign money launderers (including their assets held in the United States); and (2) money that is laundered through a foreign bank.

(Section 319) Authorizes the forfeiture of money laundering funds from interbank accounts. Requires a covered financial institution, upon request of the appropriate Federal banking agency, to make available within 120 hours all pertinent information related to anti-money laundering compliance by the institution or its customer. Grants the Secretary summons and subpoena powers over foreign banks that maintain a correspondent bank in the United States. Requires a covered financial institution to terminate within ten business days any correspondent relationship with a foreign bank after receipt of written notice that the foreign bank has failed to comply with certain judicial proceedings. Sets forth civil penalties for failure to terminate such relationship.

(Section 321) Subjects to record and report requirements for monetary instrument transactions: (1) any credit union; and (2) any futures commission merchant, commodity trading advisor, and commodity pool operator registered, or required to register, under the Commodity Exchange Act.

(Section 323) Authorizes Federal application for restraining orders to preserve the availability of property subject to a foreign forfeiture or confiscation judgment.

(Section 325) Authorizes the Secretary to issue regulations to ensure that concentration accounts of financial institutions are not used to prevent association of the identity of an individual customer with the movement of funds of which the customer is the direct or beneficial owner.

(Section 326) Directs the Secretary to issue regulations prescribing minimum standards for financial institutions regarding customer identity in connection with the opening of accounts.

Requires the Secretary to report to Congress on: (1) the most timely and effective way to require foreign nationals to provide domestic financial institutions and agencies with appropriate and accurate information; (2) whether to require foreign nationals to obtain an identification number (similar to a Social Security or tax identification number) before opening an account with a domestic financial institution; and (3) a system for domestic financial institutions and agencies to review Government agency information to verify the identities of such foreign nationals.

(Section 327) Amends the Bank Holding Company Act of 1956 and the Federal Deposit Insurance Act to require consideration of the effectiveness of a company or companies in combating money laundering during reviews of proposed bank shares acquisitions or mergers.

(Section 328) Directs the Secretary take reasonable steps to encourage foreign governments to require the inclusion of the name of the originator in wire transfer instructions sent to the United States and other countries, with the information to remain with the transfer from its origination until the point of disbursement. Requires annual progress reports to specified congressional committees.

(Section 329) Prescribes criminal penalties for Federal officials or employees who seek or accept bribes in connection with administration of this title.

(Section 330) Urges U.S. negotiations for international cooperation in investigations of money laundering, financial crimes, and the finances of terrorist groups, including record sharing by foreign banks with U.S. law enforcement officials and domestic financial institution supervisors.

Subtitle B: Bank Secrecy Act Amendments and Related Improvements - Amends Federal law known as the Bank Secrecy Act to revise requirements for civil liability immunity for voluntary financial institution disclosure of suspicious activities. Authorizes the inclusion of suspicions of illegal activity in written employment references.

(Section 352) Authorizes the Secretary to exempt from minimum standards for anti-money laundering programs any financial institution not subject to certain regulations governing financial recordkeeping and reporting of currency and foreign transactions.

(Section 353) Establishes civil penalties for violations of geographic targeting orders and structuring transactions to evade certain recordkeeping requirements. Lengthens the effective period of geographic targeting orders from 60 to 180 days.

(Section 355) Amends the Federal Deposit Insurance Act to permit written employment references to contain suspicions of involvement in illegal activity.

(Section 356) Instructs the Secretary to: (1) promulgate regulations requiring registered securities brokers and dealers, futures commission merchants, commodity trading advisors, and commodity pool operators, to file reports of suspicious financial transactions; (2) report to Congress on the role of the Internal Revenue Service in the administration of the Bank Secrecy Act; and (3) share monetary instruments transactions records upon request of a U.S. intelligence agency for use in the conduct of intelligence or counterintelligence activities, including analysis, to protect against international terrorism.

(Section 358) Amends the Right to Financial Privacy Act to permit the transfer of financial records to other agencies or departments upon certification that the records are relevant to intelligence or counterintelligence activities related to international terrorism.

Amends the Fair Credit Reporting Act to require a consumer reporting agency to furnish all information in a consumer's file to a government agency upon certification that the records are relevant to intelligence or counterintelligence activities related to international terrorism.

(Section 359) Subjects to mandatory records and reports on monetary instruments transactions any licensed sender of money or any other person who engages as a business in the transmission of funds, including through an informal value transfer banking system or network (e.g., hawala) of people facilitating the transfer of money domestically or internationally outside of the conventional financial institutions system.

(Section 360) Authorizes the Secretary to instruct the United States Executive Director of each international financial institution to use his or her voice and vote to: (1) support the use of funds for a country (and its institutions) which contributes to U.S. efforts against international terrorism; and (2) require an auditing of disbursements to ensure that no funds are paid to persons who commit or support terrorism.

(Section 361) Makes the existing Financial Crimes Enforcement Network a bureau in the Department of the Treasury.

(Section 362) Directs the Secretary to establish a highly secure network in the Network that allows financial institutions to file certain reports and receive alerts and other information regarding suspicious activities warranting immediate and enhanced scrutiny.

(Section 363) Increases to $1 million the maximum civil penalties (currently $10,000) and criminal fines (currently $250,000) for money laundering. Sets a minimum civil penalty and criminal fine of double the amount of the illegal transaction.

(Section 364) Amends the Federal Reserve Act to provide for uniform protection authority for Federal Reserve facilities, including law enforcement officers authorized to carry firearms and make warrantless arrests.

(Section 365) Amends Federal law to require reports relating to coins and currency of more than $10,000 received in a nonfinancial trade or business.

(Section 366) Directs the Secretary to study and report to Congress on: (1) the possible expansion of the currency transaction reporting requirements exemption system; and (2) methods for improving financial institution utilization of the system as a way of reducing the submission of currency transaction reports that have little or no value for law enforcement purposes.

Subtitle C: Currency Crimes - Establishes as a bulk cash smuggling felony the knowing concealment and attempted transport (or transfer) across U.S. borders of currency and monetary instruments in excess of $10,000, with intent to evade specified currency reporting requirements.

(Section 372) Changes from discretionary to mandatory a court's authority to order, as part of a criminal sentence, forfeiture of all property involved in certain currency reporting offenses. Leaves a court discretion to order civil forfeitures in money laundering cases.

(Section 373) Amends the Federal criminal code to revise the prohibition of unlicensed (currently, illegal) money transmitting businesses.

(Section 374) Increases the criminal penalties for counterfeiting domestic and foreign currency and obligations.

(Section 376) Amends the Federal criminal code to extend the prohibition against the laundering of money instruments to specified proceeds of terrorism.

(Section 377) Grants the United States extraterritorial jurisdiction where: (1) an offense committed outside the United States involves an access device issued, owned, managed, or controlled by a financial institution, account issuer, credit card system member, or other entity within U.S. jurisdiction; and (2) the person committing the offense transports, delivers, conveys, transfers to or through, or otherwise stores, secrets, or holds within U.S. jurisdiction any article used to assist in the commission of the offense or the proceeds of such offense or property derived from it.

Title IV: Protecting the Border -

Subtitle A: Protecting the Northern Border - Authorizes the Attorney General to waive certain Immigration and Naturalization Service (INS) personnel caps with respect to ensuring security needs on the Northern border.

(Section 402) Authorizes appropriations to: (1) triple the number of Border Patrol, Customs Service, and INS personnel (and support facilities) at points of entry and along the Northern border; and (2) INS and Customs for related border monitoring technology and equipment.

(Section 403) Amends the Immigration and Nationality Act to require the Attorney General and the Federal Bureau of Investigation (FBI) to provide the Department of State and INS with access to specified criminal history extracts in order to determine whether or not a visa or admissions applicant has a criminal history. Directs the FBI to provide periodic extract updates. Provides for confidentiality.

Directs the Attorney General and the Secretary of State to develop a technology standard to identify visa and admissions applicants, which shall be the basis for an electronic system of law enforcement and intelligence sharing system available to consular, law enforcement, intelligence, and Federal border inspection personnel.

(Section 404) Amends the Department of Justice Appropriations Act, 2001 to eliminate certain INS overtime restrictions.

(Section 405) Directs the Attorney General to report on the feasibility of enhancing the Integrated Automated Fingerprint Identification System and other identification systems to better identify foreign individuals in connection with U.S. or foreign criminal investigations before issuance of a visa to, or permitting such person's entry or exit from the United States. Authorizes appropriations.

Subtitle B: Enhanced Immigration Provisions - Amends the Immigration and Nationality Act to broaden the scope of aliens ineligible for admission or deportable due to terrorist activities to include an alien who: (1) is a representative of a political, social, or similar group whose political endorsement of terrorist acts undermines U.S. antiterrorist efforts; (2) has used a position of prominence to endorse terrorist activity, or to persuade others to support such activity in a way that undermines U.S. antiterrorist efforts (or the child or spouse of such an alien under specified circumstances); or (3) has been associated with a terrorist organization and intends to engage in threatening activities while in the United States.

(Section 411) Includes within the definition of "terrorist activity" the use of any weapon or dangerous device.

Redefines "engage in terrorist activity" to mean, in an individual capacity or as a member of an organization, to: (1) commit or to incite to commit, under circumstances indicating an intention to cause death or serious bodily injury, a terrorist activity; (2) prepare or plan a terrorist activity; (3) gather information on potential targets for terrorist activity; (4) solicit funds or other things of value for a terrorist activity or a terrorist organization (with an exception for lack of knowledge); (5) solicit any individual to engage in prohibited conduct or for terrorist organization membership (with an exception for lack of knowledge); or (6) commit an act that the actor knows, or reasonably should know, affords material support, including a safe house, transportation, communications, funds, transfer of funds or other material financial benefit, false documentation or identification, weapons (including chemical, biological, or radiological weapons), explosives, or training for the commission of a terrorist activity; to any individual who the actor knows or reasonably should know has committed or plans to commit a terrorist activity; or to a terrorist organization (with an exception for lack of knowledge).

Defines "terrorist organization" as a group: (1) designated under the Immigration and Nationality Act or by the Secretary of State; or (2) a group of two or more individuals, whether related or not, which engages in terrorist-related activities.

Provides for the retroactive application of amendments under this Act. Stipulates that an alien shall not be considered inadmissible or deportable because of a relationship to an organization that was not designated as a terrorist organization prior to enactment of this Act. States that the amendments under this section shall apply to all aliens in exclusion or deportation proceedings on or after the date of enactment of this Act.

Directs the Secretary of State to notify specified congressional leaders seven days prior to designating an organization as a terrorist organization. Provides for organization redesignation or revocation.

(Section 412) Provides for mandatory detention until removal from the United States (regardless of any relief from removal) of an alien certified by the Attorney General as a suspected terrorist or threat to national security. Requires release of such alien after seven days if removal proceedings have not commenced, or the alien has not been charged with a criminal offense. Authorizes detention for additional periods of up to six months of an alien not likely to be deported in the reasonably foreseeable future only if release will threaten U.S. national security or the safety of the community or any person. Limits judicial review to habeas corpus proceedings in the U.S. Supreme Court, the U.S. Court of Appeals for the District of Columbia, or any district court with jurisdiction to entertain a habeas corpus petition. Restricts to the U.S. Court of Appeals for the District of Columbia the right of appeal of any final order by a circuit or district judge.

(Section 413) Authorizes the Secretary of State, on a reciprocal basis, to share criminal- and terrorist-related visa lookout information with foreign governments.

(Section 414) Declares the sense of the Congress that the Attorney General should: (1) fully implement the integrated entry and exit data system for airports, seaports, and land border ports of entry with all deliberate speed; and (2) begin immediately establishing the Integrated Entry and Exit Data System Task Force. Authorizes appropriations.

Requires the Attorney General and the Secretary of State, in developing the integrated entry and exit data system, to focus on the use of biometric technology and the development of tamper-resistant documents readable at ports of entry.

(Section 415) Amends the Immigration and Naturalization Service Data Management Improvement Act of 2000 to include the Office of Homeland Security in the Integrated Entry and Exit Data System Task Force.

(Section 416) Directs the Attorney General to implement fully and expand the foreign student monitoring program to include other approved educational institutions like air flight, language training, or vocational schools.

(Section 417) Requires audits and reports on implementation of the mandate for machine readable passports.

(Section 418) Directs the Secretary of State to: (1) review how consular officers issue visas to determine if consular shopping is a problem; and (2) if it is a problem, take steps to address it, and report on them to Congress.

Subtitle C: Preservation of Immigration Benefits for Victims of Terrorism - Authorizes the Attorney General to provide permanent resident status through the special immigrant program to an alien (and spouse, child, or grandparent under specified circumstances) who was the beneficiary of a petition filed on or before September 11, 2001, to grant the alien permanent residence as an employer-sponsored immigrant or of an application for labor certification if the petition or application was rendered null because of the disability of the beneficiary or loss of employment due to physical damage to, or destruction of, the business of the petitioner or applicant as a direct result of the terrorist attacks on September 11, 2001 (September attacks), or because of the death of the petitioner or applicant as a direct result of such attacks.

(Section 422) States that an alien who was legally in a nonimmigrant status and was disabled as a direct result of the September attacks may remain in the United States until his or her normal status termination date or September, 11, 2002. Includes in such extension the spouse or child of such an alien or of an alien who was killed in such attacks. Authorizes employment during such period.

Extends specified immigration-related deadlines and other filing requirements for an alien (and spouse and child) who was directly prevented from meeting such requirements as a result of the September attacks respecting: (1) nonimmigrant status and status revision; (2) diversity immigrants; (3) immigrant visas; (4) parolees; and (5) voluntary departure.

(Section 423) Waives, under specified circumstances, the requirement that an alien spouse (and child) of a U.S. citizen must have been married for at least two years prior to such citizen's death in order to maintain immediate relative status if such citizen died as a direct result of the September attacks. Provides for: (1) continued family-sponsored immigrant eligibility for the spouse, child, or unmarried son or daughter of a permanent resident who died as a direct result of such attacks; and (2) continued eligibility for adjustment of status for the spouse and child of an employment-based immigrant who died similarly.

(Section 424) Amends the Immigration and Nationality Act to extend the visa categorization of "child" for aliens with petitions filed on or before September 11, 2001, for aliens whose 21st birthday is in September 2001 (90 days), or after September 2001 (45 days).

(Section 425) Authorizes the Attorney General to provide temporary administrative relief to an alien who, as of September, 10, 2001, was lawfully in the United States and was the spouse, parent, or child of an individual who died or was disabled as a direct result of the September attacks.

(Section 426) Directs the Attorney General to establish evidentiary guidelines for death, disability, and loss of employment or destruction of business in connection with the provisions of this subtitle.

(Section 427) Prohibits benefits to terrorists or their family members.

Title V: Removing Obstacles to Investigating Terrorism - Authorizes the Attorney General to pay rewards from available funds pursuant to public advertisements for assistance to DOJ to combat terrorism and defend the Nation against terrorist acts, in accordance with procedures and regulations established or issued by the Attorney General, subject to specified conditions, including a prohibition against any such reward of $250,000 or more from being made or offered without the personal approval of either the Attorney General or the President.

(Section 502) Amends the State Department Basic Authorities Act of 1956 to modify the Department of State rewards program to authorize rewards for information leading to: (1) the dismantling of a terrorist organization in whole or significant part; and (2) the identification or location of an individual who holds a key leadership position in a terrorist organization. Raises the limit on rewards if the Secretary State determines that a larger sum is necessary to combat terrorism or defend the Nation against terrorist acts.

(Section 503) Amends the DNA Analysis Backlog Elimination Act of 2000 to qualify a Federal terrorism offense for collection of DNA for identification.

(Section 504) Amends FISA to authorize consultation among Federal law enforcement officers regarding information acquired from an electronic surveillance or physical search in terrorism and related investigations or protective measures.

(Section 505) Allows the FBI to request telephone toll and transactional records, financial records, and consumer reports in any investigation to protect against international terrorism or clandestine intelligence activities only if the investigation is not conducted solely on the basis of activities protected by the first amendment to the U.S. Constitution.

(Section 506) Revises U.S. Secret Service jurisdiction with respect to fraud and related activity in connection with computers. Grants the FBI primary authority to investigate specified fraud and computer related activity for cases involving espionage, foreign counter-intelligence, information protected against unauthorized disclosure for reasons of national defense or foreign relations, or restricted data, except for offenses affecting Secret Service duties.

(Section 507) Amends the General Education Provisions Act and the National Education Statistics Act of 1994 to provide for disclosure of educational records to the Attorney General in a terrorism investigation or prosecution.

Title VI: Providing for Victims of Terrorism, Public Safety Officers, and Their Families - Subtitle A: Aid to Families of Public Safety Officers - Provides for expedited payments for: (1) public safety officers involved in the prevention, investigation, rescue, or recovery efforts related to a terrorist attack; and (2) heroic public safety officers. Increases Public Safety Officers Benefit Program payments.

Subtitle B: Amendments to the Victims of Crime Act of 1984 - Amends the Victims of Crime Act of 1984 to: (1) revise provisions regarding the allocation of funds for compensation and assistance, location of compensable crime, and the relationship of crime victim compensation to means-tested Federal benefit programs and to the September 11th victim compensation fund; and (2) establish an antiterrorism emergency reserve in the Victims of Crime Fund.

Title VII: Increased Information Sharing for Critical Infrastructure Protection - Amends the Omnibus Crime Control and Safe Streets Act of 1968 to extend Bureau of Justice Assistance regional information sharing system grants to systems that enhance the investigation and prosecution abilities of participating Federal, State, and local law enforcement agencies in addressing multi-jurisdictional terrorist conspiracies and activities. Authorizes appropriations.

Title VIII: Strengthening the Criminal Laws Against Terrorism - Amends the Federal criminal code to prohibit specific terrorist acts or otherwise destructive, disruptive, or violent acts against mass transportation vehicles, ferries, providers, employees, passengers, or operating systems.

(Section 802) Amends the Federal criminal code to: (1) revise the definition of "international terrorism" to include activities that appear to be intended to affect the conduct of government by mass destruction; and (2) define "domestic terrorism" as activities that occur primarily within U.S. jurisdiction, that involve criminal acts dangerous to human life, and that appear to be intended to intimidate or coerce a civilian population, to influence government policy by intimidation or coercion, or to affect government conduct by mass destruction, assassination, or kidnapping.

(Section 803) Prohibits harboring any person knowing or having reasonable grounds to believe that such person has committed or to be about to commit a terrorism offense.

(Section 804) Establishes Federal jurisdiction over crimes committed at U.S. facilities abroad.

(Section 805) Applies the prohibitions against providing material support for terrorism to offenses outside of the United States.

(Section 806) Subjects to civil forfeiture all assets, foreign or domestic, of terrorist organizations.

(Section 808) Expands: (1) the offenses over which the Attorney General shall have primary investigative jurisdiction under provisions governing acts of terrorism transcending national boundaries; and (2) the offenses included within the definition of the Federal crime of terrorism.

(Section 809) Provides that there shall be no statute of limitations for certain terrorism offenses if the commission of such an offense resulted in, or created a foreseeable risk of, death or serious bodily injury to another person.

(Section 810) Provides for alternative maximum penalties for specified terrorism crimes.

(Section 811) Makes: (1) the penalties for attempts and conspiracies the same as those for terrorism offenses; (2) the supervised release terms for offenses with terrorism predicates any term of years or life; and (3) specified terrorism crimes Racketeer Influenced and Corrupt Organizations statute predicates.

(Section 814) Revises prohibitions and penalties regarding fraud and related activity in connection with computers to include specified cyber-terrorism offenses.

(Section 816) Directs the Attorney General to establish regional computer forensic laboratories, and to support existing laboratories, to develop specified cyber-security capabilities.

(Section 817) Prescribes penalties for knowing possession in certain circumstances of biological agents, toxins, or delivery systems, especially by certain restricted persons.

Title IX: Improved Intelligence - Amends the National Security Act of 1947 to require the Director of Central Intelligence (DCI) to establish requirements and priorities for foreign intelligence collected under the Foreign Intelligence Surveillance Act of 1978 and to provide assistance to the Attorney General (AG) to ensure that information derived from electronic surveillance or physical searches is disseminated for efficient and effective foreign intelligence purposes. Requires the inclusion of international terrorist activities within the scope of foreign intelligence under such Act.

(Section 903) Expresses the sense of Congress that officers and employees of the intelligence community should establish and maintain intelligence relationships to acquire information on terrorists and terrorist organizations.

(Section 904) Authorizes deferral of the submission to Congress of certain reports on intelligence and intelligence-related matters until: (1) February 1, 2002; or (2) a date after February 1, 2002, if the official involved certifies that preparation and submission on February 1, 2002, will impede the work of officers or employees engaged in counterterrorism activities. Requires congressional notification of any such deferral.

(Section 905) Requires the AG or the head of any other Federal department or agency with law enforcement responsibilities to expeditiously disclose to the DCI any foreign intelligence acquired in the course of a criminal investigation.

(Section 906) Requires the AG, DCI, and Secretary of the Treasury to jointly report to Congress on the feasibility and desirability of reconfiguring the Foreign Asset Tracking Center and the Office of Foreign Assets Control to provide for the analysis and dissemination of foreign intelligence relating to the financial capabilities and resources of international terrorist organizations.

(Section 907) Requires the DCI to report to the appropriate congressional committees on the establishment and maintenance of the National Virtual Translation Center for timely and accurate translation of foreign intelligence for elements of the intelligence community.

(Section 908) Requires the AG to provide a program of training to Government officials regarding the identification and use of foreign intelligence.

Title X: Miscellaneous - Directs the Inspector General of the Department of Justice to designate one official to review allegations of abuse of civil rights, civil liberties, and racial and ethnic profiling by government employees and officials.

(Section 1002) Expresses the sense of Congress condemning acts of violence or discrimination against any American, including Sikh-Americans. Calls upon local and Federal law enforcement authorities to prosecute to the fullest extent of the law all those who commit crimes.

(Section 1004) Amends the Federal criminal code with respect to venue in money laundering cases to allow a prosecution for such an offense to be brought in: (1) any district in which the financial or monetary transaction is conducted; or (2) any district where a prosecution for the underlying specified unlawful activity could be brought, if the defendant participated in the transfer of the proceeds of the specified unlawful activity from that district to the district where the financial or monetary transaction is conducted.

States that: (1) a transfer of funds from one place to another, by wire or any other means, shall constitute a single, continuing transaction; and (2) any person who conducts any portion of the transaction may be charged in any district in which the transaction takes place.

Allows a prosecution for an attempt or conspiracy offense to be brought in the district where venue would lie for the completed offense, or in any other district where an act in furtherance of the attempt or conspiracy took place.

(Section 1005) First Responders Assistance Act - Directs the Attorney General to make grants to State and local governments to improve the ability of State and local law enforcement, fire department, and first responders to respond to and prevent acts of terrorism. Authorizes appropriations.

(Section 1006) Amends the Immigration and Nationality Act to make inadmissible into the United States any alien engaged in money laundering. Directs the Secretary of State to develop a money laundering watch list which: (1) identifies individuals worldwide who are known or suspected of money laundering; and (2) is readily accessible to, and shall be checked by, a consular or other Federal official before the issuance of a visa or admission to the United States.

(Section 1007) Authorizes FY 2002 appropriations for regional antidrug training in Turkey by the Drug Enforcement Administration for police, as well as increased precursor chemical control efforts in South and Central Asia.

(Section 1008) Directs the Attorney General to conduct a feasibility study and report to Congress on the use of a biometric identifier scanning system with access to the FBI integrated automated fingerprint identification system at overseas consular posts and points of entry to the United States.

(Section 1009) Directs the FBI to study and report to Congress on the feasibility of providing to airlines access via computer to the names of passengers who are suspected of terrorist activity by Federal officials. Authorizes appropriations.

(Section 1010) Authorizes the use of Department of Defense funds to contract with local and State governments, during the period of Operation Enduring Freedom, for the performance of security functions at U.S. military installations.

(Section 1011) Crimes Against Charitable Americans Act of 2001 - Amends the Telemarketing and Consumer Fraud and Abuse Prevention Act to cover fraudulent charitable solicitations. Requires any person engaged in telemarketing for the solicitation of charitable contributions, donations, or gifts to disclose promptly and clearly the purpose of the telephone call.

(Section 1012) Amends the Federal transportation code to prohibit States from licensing any individual to operate a motor vehicle transporting hazardous material unless the Secretary of Transportation determines that such individual does not pose a security risk warranting denial of the license. Requires background checks of such license applicants by the Attorney General upon State request.

(Section 1013) Expresses the sense of the Senate on substantial new U.S. investment in bio-terrorism preparedness and response.

(Section 1014) Directs the Office for State and Local Domestic Preparedness Support of the Office of Justice Programs to make grants to enhance State and local capability to prepare for and respond to terrorist acts. Authorizes appropriations for FY 2002 through 2007.

(Section 1015) Amends the Crime Identification Technology Act of 1998 to extend it through FY 2007 and provide for antiterrorism grants to States and localities. Authorizes appropriations.

(Section 1016) Critical Infrastructures Protection Act of 2001 - Declares it is U.S. policy: (1) that any physical or virtual disruption of the operation of the critical infrastructures of the United States be rare, brief, geographically limited in effect, manageable, and minimally detrimental to the economy, human and government services, and U.S. national security; (2) that actions necessary to achieve this policy be carried out in a public-private partnership involving corporate and non-governmental organizations; and (3) to have in place a comprehensive and effective program to ensure the continuity of essential Federal Government functions under all circumstances.

Establishes the National Infrastructure Simulation and Analysis Center to serve as a source of national competence to address critical infrastructure protection and continuity through support for activities related to counterterrorism, threat assessment, and risk mitigation.

Defines critical infrastructure as systems and assets, whether physical or virtual, so vital to the United States that their incapacity or destruction would have a debilitating impact on security, national economic security, national public health or safety, or any combination of those matters.

AUTHORIZES APPROPRIATIONS.

Bibliography

BOOKS

America I Love You.
William Mulvey Inc, New Canaan, Conn. 06840, 1986.
Potter, Peter.
ISBN 0-934791-00-7
323.65 AMERICA

An Album For Americans.
Triangle Publications, Inc ,New York 1983.
Appel, David H.
ISBN 0-517-54374-5
323.65 ALB

The Days We Celebrate.
Dodd Mead, New York, 1965
Robert H. Schauffler
394.26 vol. 3

The Flag Book of the United States
William Morrow & Company, Inc., New York 1970
Smith, Whitney.
Library of Congress Card Number:78-86879
929.92 SMITH, W

Flags of American History.
Hammond,Inc., Maplewood, New Jersey 1973.
Crouther, David D.
ISBN 0-8437-3965-7
929.90973 CRO

The Flags of the Confederacy: an illustrated history.
St. Lukes Press and Bradfoot Publishing.
Memphis, TN 1988
Cannon, Devereaux D.
ISBN 0-918518-62-8
929.9209

The Flags of the Union: an illustrated history.
Pelican Publishing Company, Inc.
1101 Monroe St., Gretna, Louisiana 70053, 1994
Cannon, Devereaux D.
ISBN 0-88289-953-8
929.9209

Flags of the U.S.A.
Thomas Y. Crowell Company, New York. 1964
Eggenberger, David
Library of Congress Card Number: 64-12115
ISBN 0-690-30491-9
929.9 EGG

The New Constellation
National Flag Foundation, Flag Plaza, Pittsburgh, PA 15219, 1977
Library of Congress Card Number: 76-57294

Old Glory : A History and Celebration
Crescent Books New York, 1992 ed.
Nancy Grant.
ISBN 0-517-06986-5
929.9 GRA

Our Flag
U.S. Government Printing Office, Washington, DC 20402
United States Congress, House Document 100-247

Saga of the American Flag.
Harbinger House, Tucson, Arizona 1990.
DeBarr, Candice M., Bonkowske, Jack A.
ISBN 0-943173-65-5
929.9209 DEB

So Proudly We Hail, The History of the United States Flag.
Smithsonian Institute Press 1981.
Wiliam R. Furlong and Byron McCandless.
ISBN 0-87474-448-2
929.92 FUR

The Star Spangled Banner.
Doubleday & Company, Inc., Garden City, New York 1973.
Illustrations by Peter Spier.
ISBN 0-385-07746-7
782.42 STA

Star-Spangled Banner : Our nation and its flag
National Geographic Society (U.S.). Book Division.Washington, D.C.1993.
Margaret Sedeen
ISBN 0870449443. 0870449451 (deluxe)
929.92 SED

The Stars and the Stripes; the American flag as art and as history
Knopf, New York,1973.
Boleslaw and Marie-Louise D'Otrange Mastai.
ISBN 0394472179.
929.9 MAS

Stars & Stripes Forever The History of our Flag
Brompton Books Corp., 15 Sherwood Place, Greenwich, CT 06830 1992
Adams, John Winthrop
ISBN 0-8317-6658-1
929.92 STARS

The World Almanac and Book of Facts 1995
Funk and Wagnalls, One International Boulevard, Suite 444, Mahwah, New Jersey
07495-0017
1994
Robert Famighetti, Editor
ISBN 0-88687-766-0

What You Should Know About The American Flag.
Maryland Historical Press, Lanham,MD.
Wiliiams,Jr.,Earl P.
ISBN 0-917882-25-3
929.92 Williams,E

Websites

http://news.uns.purdue.edu/UNS/html3month/020517.Christian.bio.html
Purdue University News

Wallbuilders.com
http://wallbuilders.com/resources/search/detail.php?ResourceID=82
The United States Flag Page
http://www.usflag.org/fold.flag.html
http://www.usflag.org/
http://www.usflag.org/skeltonspledge.html
http://www.usflag.org/flag.day.html

USA Flag Site
http://www.usa-flag-site.org/etiquette.shtml
http://www.usa-flag-site.org/history.shtml

Duane Streufert,
 oldglory@usflag.org.

The National Flag Day Foundation, Inc.
http://flagday.org

The White House Official Web Page
http://www.whitehouse.gov/news/releases/2001/06/print/20010607-1.html

The Avalon Project at Yale Law School
http://www.yale.edu/lawweb/avalon/debates/531.htm
http://www.yale.edu/lawweb/avalon/statutes/alien.htm
http://www.yale.edu/lawweb/avalon/statutes/sedact.htm

CNN Interactive
http://edition.cnn.com/US/9601/budget/01-27/clinton_radio/

Action America
http://frwebgate4.access.gpo.gov/cgi-
bin/waisgate.cgi?WAISdocID=58301026340+1+0+0&WAISaction=retrieve
http://frwebgate4.access.gpo.gov/cgi-
bin/waisgate.cgi?WAISdocID=58301026340+0+0+0&WAISaction=retrieve

Legal Information Institute/Cornell Law School
http://www.law.cornell.edu/
http://www2.law.cornell.edu/cgi-
bin/foliocgi.exe/historic/query=[group+249+u!2Es!2E+47!3A]!28[group+edited!3A]!7C[level+
+case+citation!3A]!29/doc/{@1}/hit_headings/words=4/hits_only?
http://www2.law.cornell.edu/cgi-
bin/foliocgi.exe/historic/query=[group+341+u!2Es!2E+494!3A]!28[group+edited!3A]!7C[level+
+case+citation!3A]!29/doc/{@1}/hit_headings/words=4/hits_only?
http://www2.law.cornell.edu/cgi-
bin/foliocgi.exe/historic/query=[group+491+u!2Es!2E+397!3A]!28[group+edited!3A]!7C[level+
+case+citation!3A]!29/doc/{@1}/hit_headings/words=4/hits_only?
http://www2.law.cornell.edu/cgi-
bin/foliocgi.exe/historic/query=[group+496+u!2Es!2E+310!3A]!28[group+edited!3A]!7C[level+
+case+citation!3A]!29/doc/{@1}/hit_headings/words=4/hits_only?
http://www2.law.cornell.edu/cgi-
bin/foliocgi.exe/historic/query=[group+465+u!2Es!2E+668!3A]!28[group+edited!3A]!7C[level+
+case+citation!3A]!29/doc/{@1}/hit_headings/words=4/hits_only?
http://www2.law.cornell.edu/cgi-
bin/foliocgi.exe/historic/query=[group+403+u!2Es!2E+602!3A]!28[group+edited!3A]!7C[level+
+case+citation!3A]!29/doc/{@1}/hit_headings/words=4/hits_only?

http://www2.law.cornell.edu/cgi-bin/foliocgi.exe/historic/query=[group+330+u!2Es!2E+1!3A]!28[group+edited!3A]!7C[level++case+citation!3A]!29/doc/{@1}/hit_headings/words=4/hits_only?

http://www2.law.cornell.edu/cgi-bin/foliocgi.exe/historic/query=[group+370+u!2Es!2E+421!3A]!28[group+edited!3A]!7C[level++case+citation!3A]!29/doc/{@1}/hit_headings/words=4/hits_only?

http://www2.law.cornell.edu/cgi-bin/foliocgi.exe/historic/query=[group+505+u!2Es!2E+833!3A]!28[group+edited!3A]!7C[level++case+citation!3A]!29/doc/{@1}/hit_headings/words=4/hits_only?

http://supct.law.cornell.edu/supct/search/display.html?terms=Bush%20v.%20Gore%202000&url=/supct/html/00-949.ZPC.html

The McCarran Internal Security Act of 1950
http://www.rosenbergtrial.org/docmcaran.html
http://www.rosenbergtrial.org/docsmith.html

Unfunded Mandates Reform Act of 1995
http://216.239.39.104/search?q=cache:XGDB6eFnrqQJ:www.sba.gov/ADVO/laws/unfund.pdf+Unfunded+Mandates+Reform+Act+of+1995&hl=en&ie=UTF-8

Crown Rights Book Company
http://www.crownrights.com/books/ex_parte_merryman.htm

The Federalist
The Conservative E-Journal of Record
http://www.federalist.com/histdocs/jeff1.htm
http://www.federalist.com/histdocs/roevwade.htm
http://www.federalist.com/histdocs/brownvboard.htm
http://www.federalist.com/histdocs/HaveDream.htm
http://www.federalist.com/histdocs/Emancipation.htm
http://www.federalist.com/histdocs/lincolnhouse.htm
http://www.federalist.com/histdocs/fundorders.htm
http://www.federalist.com/histdocs/contract.htm
http://www.federalist.com/histdocs/north_atlantic_treaty.asp
http://www.federalist.com/histdocs/charter_united_nations.asp

Reagan 2000
Federalism and the New Republicans
http://www.reagan2000.com/
http://www.federalist.com/histdocs/fundorders.htm
http://www.federalist.com/histdocs/liberty.htm
http://www.federalist.com/histdocs/tofp.htm
http://www.federalist.com/histdocs/gwthanksproc.html
http://www.federalist.com/histdocs/jeff1.htm
http://www.federalist.com/histdocs/stspban.htm
http://reagan2000.com/reaganeo.asp
http://www.federalist.com/histdocs/fdr1.htm

http://www.federalist.com/histdocs/kennedy.htm
http://www.federalist.com/histdocs/marburyvmadison.htm
http://www.federalist.com/histdocs/roevwade.htm
http://www.federalist.com/histdocs/brownvboard.htm

The History Place
Great Speeches Collection
http://www.historyplace.com/speeches/anthony.htm
http://www.historyplace.com/speeches/gw-bush-9-11.htm
http://www.historyplace.com/speeches/clinton-rose-garden.htm
http://www.historyplace.com/speeches/ford.htm
http://www.historyplace.com/speeches/gore-concedes.htm
http://www.historyplace.com/speeches/lbj-decision.htm
http://www.historyplace.com/speeches/jfk-inaug.htm
http://www.historyplace.com/speeches/jfk-cuban.htm
http://www.historyplace.com/speeches/rfk.htm
http://www.historyplace.com/speeches/nixon.htm
http://www.historyplace.com/speeches/fdr-infamy.htm
http://www.historyplace.com/speeches/fdr-first-inaug.htm
http://www.historyplace.com/speeches/henry.htm
http://www.historyplace.com/speeches/reagan-challenger.htm
http://www.historyplace.com/speeches/fdr-prayer.htm
http://www.historyplace.com/speeches/gettysburg.htm
http://www.historyplace.com/speeches/anthony.htm

University of Oklahoma College of Law
http://www.law.ou.edu/hist/
Steve's Flag Page
http://www.steve4u.com/Stevesflagpage.htm

The Internet Modern History Source Book
http://www.fordham.edu/halsall/mod/modsbook.html

FirstWorldWar.com
http://www.firstworldwar.com/source/espionageact.htm
http://www.firstworldwar.com/source/espionageact1918.htm

Acknowledgements

Readings in American Government: I Pledge Allegiance to the Flag is a collection of historical documents from the public domain selected and edited by ORU instructor Sonny Branham with the assistance of his student Jesus Adrian Cantu. The cover design is an adaptation of the United States Marine Corps War Memorial (Iwo Jima) in Washington, D.C. Printing and publishing was completed by the ORU Word Processing Center, with special thanks to Sandy Stephenson. Copyright 2003 in Tulsa, Oklahoma.

INTRODUCTION TO AMERICAN GOVERNMENT—101

DEPARTMENT OF HISTORY AND GOVERNMENT

AMERICAN GOVERNMENT NOTES

A Supplement to
"I Pledge Allegiance to the Flag"
Readings in American Government

1.   ☐ **INTRODUCTION: Lesson 1**

2.   ☐ "If men were angels, no government would be necessary. If angels were to govern men, neither external nor internal controls on government would be necessary. In framing a government which is to be administered by men over men, the great difficulty lies in this: you must first enable the government to control the governed; and in the next place, oblige it to control itself." **James Madison, Federalist No. 51**

3.   ☐ **Today, we will examine the definition, purpose, and biblical basis of civil government. Civil government is mandated by God.**

4.   ☐ **What is civil government?**

     # One of three institutions, besides the family and the church, established by God to bring order, authority, and freedom to their respective spheres of influence.

5.   ☐ **Purpose of civil government is biblical in origin:**

     # **Romans 13:1-7 & I Peter 2:13-14**
       — Uphold the law (Rom. 13:3)
       — Protect law-abiding citizens (v. 3)

6.   ☐ **Purpose of Government (cont.)**

       — Punish criminals (vv. 2, 4; I Pet. 2:14)
       — Provide domestic peace and foreign defense (v. 4)
       — Collect taxes (v. 7)

7.   ☐ **Likewise, citizens have responsibility toward government:**

     # **Romans 13:1-7 & I Pet 2:13-14 again:**
       — <u>Submit to or respect govt. authority</u> (Rom. 13:1, 2 Pet. 2:13)
       — <u>Obey civil law</u> (Rom. 13:3)
     # **I Tim. 2:1-4**
       — <u>Pray for our civil leaders</u>

8.   ☐ **Further, we see in:**

     # **Matt. 22:21**
       — Acknowledge the proper distinctions between civil and church authority
     # **Acts 5:28-29**
       — To obey God's law over man's law, especially when man's law directly opposes God's law

9. ☐ **Civil government is founded upon five principles of Judeo-Christianity:**

   \# <u>First</u>, delegated authority is the proper use of political power. (Genesis 1:26)
   \# <u>Second</u>, stewardship is the proper management of private and public property. (Genesis 1:28; Matthew 25:15)

10. ☐ **Principles (cont.)**

   \# <u>Third</u>, covenant relationship forms the basis of constitutional authority: (Genesis 12:1-3; 17:10)
   \# <u>Fourth</u>, leaders are to be servants, not self-serving. (Mark 10:42-45)

11. ☐ **Principles (concluded):**

   \# <u>Fifth</u>, the essence and foundation of law originates with God, but is imperfectly administered by man. (Exodus 20:3-17; Matthew 5:17)

12. ☐ **Summary:**

   1. We have examined the definition of civil government and its purpose.
   2. Next we discussed the Judeo-Christian principles of civil government.

13. ☐ *"It is the duty of all nations to acknowledge the Providence of Almighty God, to obey His will, to be grateful for His benefits, and humbly to implore His protection and favor."* **George Washington, Thanksgiving Proclamation of 1789**

Suggested Readings

History of the American Flag
Flag Etiquette
Flag Folding Ceremony
The Story of the Pledge of Allegiance
National Flag Day
The Star Spangled Banner
The Michael Christianson Story
Red Skelton's Commentary on the Pledge of Allegiance
President Bush's Declaration of "Patriot Day"

1. ☐ **CONSTITUTION: PART 1—Lesson 2**

2. ☐ *"Our Constitution was made for a moral and religious people. It is wholly inadequate for the government of any other."* John Adams, 1798

3. ☐ **Further, it was Noah Webster who wrote:** *"The religion which has introduced civil liberty, is the religion of Christ and His apostles, which enjoins humility, piety, and benevolence . . . This is genuine Christianity, and to this we owe our free constitutions of government."*

4. ☐ **Let us examine the definition, purposes, and characteristics of our U.S. Constitution, and in doing so we will be better able to clarify the divine influence of God, and the original intention of the Founding Fathers.**

5. ☐ **What were the motivations of the Founders?**

   \# Economic? political? or truly public oriented? Of course, the truth of the matter is that all three motives were readily apparent.

   But so was—as the quotes above represent—the Founders' religious value systems.

6. ☐ **A Constitution is:**

   \# A written agreement between the government and governed in order to:
   — establish the organs of government
   — restrict government authority
   — promote individual freedom
   — provide for civil justice

7. ☐ **A covenant is a Christian concept that "holds at least two parties accountable for their actions and therefore secures the blessings of a mutual relationship."**

   \# Examples of biblical covenants are:
   — Genesis 12:1-3, 17:10
   — Isaiah 55:3

8. ☐ **The purpose of a covenant therefore is twofold:**

   \# Accountability
   \# Secure blessings

9. ☐ **Notice then, that a covenant and a constitution are similar:**

   \# Both establish guidelines or parameters of action;
   \# Both provide benefits when the guidelines are kept.

5022\30504.014

10. ☐ **Does the U.S. Constitution, which is indeed an 'organic' document, display any religious or especially Judeo-Christian principles? The answer is yes. Let's examine these principles in the preamble of the constitution.**

11. ☐ **Biblical Principles of Preamble:**

   \#   To establish justice
   — Romans 13:4
   — I Peter 2:14
   — Difference between God's and man's justice
   \#   To insure domestic peace
   — I Timothy 2:1, 2

12. ☐ **Biblical Principles (cont.)**

   \#   Provide for common defense
   — Eccl. 3:8
   — Romans 13:4
   — I Peter 2:14
   \#   Promote the general welfare
   — Romans 13:4
   — God is the provider; government is the promoter

13. ☐ **Biblical Principles (cont.)**

   \#   Liberty—key to spiritual progress
   — II Corinthians 3:17
   — Lev. 25:10
   — Luke 4:18

14. ☐ **Biblical Principles (cont.)**

   \#   Life (a government that will not protect life will ultimately not protect any freedom)
   — Genesis 1:27
   — Psalm 139:13-16
   \#   Private Property
   — Eccl. 5:19

1.   ☐ **CONSTITUTION: PART II—Lesson 3**

2.   ☐ **The following four topic areas provide us with an overview of the organic nature of the U.S. Constitution. We will see the careful considerations of the Founders as they constructed this most valued civil document.**

3.   ☐ **First, republicanism is defined as: "rule by the law"**

       # Civil government, as well as the family and church (i.e. the three basic governing institutions in society), are to be established by God's rule and not man's.
       # Prov. 29:2

4.   ☐ **Republicanism (cont.)**

       # Democracy alone is simply rule by the majority, not rule by law. Democracy was not the principle sought after by the Founders.

5.   ☐ **Second, federalism is defined as the division of governmental powers between the national and state levels.**

       # The three types of governing systems are:
       — unitary
       — confederal
       — and federal

6.   ☐ **Federalism defined (cont.)**

       # Federalism, more so than the other two, upheld and preserved liberty.

7.   ☐ **Third is the separation of powers doctrine.**

       # James Madison wrote that: ***"The accumulation of all powers, legislative, executive, and judiciary, in the same hands whether of one, a few, or many . . . may justly be pronounced the very definition of tyranny."***

8.   ☐ **Separation of Powers (cont.)**

       # Executive, Legislative, and Judicial
       # Isaiah 33:22

9.

       # Even Montesquieu, the famous French philosopher wrote: ***"There can be no liberty where the legislative and executive powers are united in the same person . . . or if the power of judging be not separated from the legislative and executive power."***

10. ☐ **But it was not the Founders or other political philosophers who required that governing powers be separate. It was God.**

   Isa. 33:22: *"For the Lord is our judge, the Lord is our lawgiver, the Lord is our King; He will save us."*

11. ☐ **Fourth, is the concept of checks and balances.**

   \# They are a series of constitutionally instituted mechanisms which prevents overt control of power by one branch over the other.
   \# Executive: Art 2, sec. 2
   \# Legislative: Art. 1, sec. 8
   \# Judicial: Art. 3, sec. 1

12.

   \# **Some examples are:**
   — Legislative (Art. 1, sec.7, 8): passing laws, overriding vetoes, impeaching officials, advise and consent
   — Executive (Art. II, sec. 2): proposing laws, calling special sessions, pardoning criminals etc.
   — Judicial (Art. III, sec. 1): interpreting laws.

13. ☐ **We have examined four topic areas of the constitution:**

   1. the concept of republicanism
   2. federalism
   3. separation of powers
   4. and checks and balances

Suggested Readings

Mayflower Compact
Plymouth Oath
Dorchester Agreement
Fundamental Orders of Connecticut

1. ☐ **CONSTITUTION: PART III—Lesson 4**

2. ☐ **Fifth topic area is limited government powers:**

   \# First set of constitutional powers is delegated or enumerated powers.
   — Legislative: (Art. 1, sec. 8)
   — Executive: (Art. 2, sec. 2)
   — Judicial: (Art. 3, sec. 2)

3. ☐ **Limited government powers (cont.)**

   \# Second set of constitutional powers is implied powers.
   — Necessary and proper clause (Article 1, sec. 8, #18)
   — <u>McCulloch vs. Maryland</u> (1819) established broad congressional powers.

4. ☐ **Limited government powers (cont.)**

   ☐ **The third set of powers are the reserved powers found in Amendment X.**

   — "The powers are not delegated to the United States by the Constitution, nor prohibited by it to the states, are reserved to the states respectively, or to the people."

5. ☐ **Limited government powers (cont.)**

   ☐ Police powers of the state to protect "health, safety, welfare, morals, and provide for the education of the people."

   ☐ State laws and rules, such as compulsory education laws, mandatory drinking ages, seat belt laws, and others.

6. ☐ **Limited government powers (cont.)**

   \# The fourth set of powers are the <u>prohibited powers</u>.
   — National government (Art. 1, sec. 9), such as not prohibiting due process
   — State government (Art. 1, sec. 10), such as not entering into a treaty or alliance with another country or coining of money

7. ☐ **Sixth is the supremacy of national laws:**

   \# Constitution, national laws, and treaties are superior to state laws. (Article VI)
   \# Alexander Hamilton, in Federalist #33, wrote: ***"A law, by the very meaning of the term, includes supremacy."***

8. ☐ **Seventh, is the power of judicial review.**

   \# It is the power of the courts to declare acts of president and Congress or states unconstitutional.

9. ☐ **Judicial Review (cont.)**

Unique to U.S. government
<u>Marbury v. Madison</u> (1803) established the constitutional precedent for the reviewing of laws and executive acts in view of the constitutional requirements.

10. ☐ **Eighth is the civilian supremacy over the military.**

It is the basic concept which provides for domestic and foreign peace and political stability.

11. ☐ **Examples of civilian supremacy:**

— Only Congress can declare war. (Art. I, sec. 8, #11)
— Only Congress can appropriate money for the military. (Art. I, sec. 8, #12)
— The president is the commander in chief, not a general. (Art. II, sec. 2)

12. ☐ **Ninth is the changeability of Constitution:**

Out of some 7,000 proposals made over the last 206 years, only 27 have been ratified.
The preservation of the constitution's originality is the key to stability and longevity.

13. ☐ **Changeability (cont.)**

Article 5 stipulates the method of changing the Constitution.
— Proposal: by two-thirds vote of both houses of Congress or by two-thirds of state legislatures to call a constitutional convention.

14. ☐ **Changeability (cont.)**

— Ratification: by three-fourths vote of state legislatures or by state conventions held in three-fourths of all the states

Suggested Readings

Articles of Confederation
Constitution of the United States of America
Preamble to the United Nations Charter
Republican Contract With America

1. ☐ **FEDERALISM: PART 1—Lesson 5**

2. ☐ **Federalism is the key to the success of the U.S.'s political and governmental system:**

   1. Federalism balances the need for a unified central government with the preservation of state sovereignty.

   2. Further, federalism stresses the importance of state and individual freedom within the complex process of governing.

3. ☐ **Federalism is best defined as a political system where the national (i.e. federal) government and subnational (state, local) governments operate within separate spheres of constitutional and political power.**

4.
   1. For example, the federal or national government funds Medicare, the medical insurance program for the elderly, from general revenue funds. However, the 50 state governments have some authority as to whom, how, when, and where the funds will be distributed.

   2. Or, unlike other countries, police forces are under local control.

5. ☐ **What were the Founders' intentions and views of a 'federal republic?'**

   \# Thomas Jefferson said: *"the way to have good and safe government is not to trust it all to one, but to divide it among the many . . . "*

6.
   \# James Madison said: *"The powers delegated by the . . . Constitution to the federal government are few and defined. Those which are to remain in the State governments are numerous and indefinite."*

   \# But if no other nation before the U.S.'s founding had even experimented with a federation, where did the Founders get the idea? The Bible, of course.

7. ☐ **Dual federalism is essentially dual sovereignty:**

   \# The local church of the first century as established by one level of authority (the apostle, see Acts 15:2, 6);
   \# And governed by a second level of authority (pastors or elders, see I Tim. 3:1-5)

8. ☐ **Dual Federalism (cont.)**

   \# This dual authority was also apparent in the churches of New England. The principal reason for this dual authority was rooted in Puritan belief of the sin nature of man.

9. ☐ **Summary:**

    1. Federalism, as understood by the founding fathers, was distinctly dual in formation.
    2. Dual federalism is essentially dual sovereignty.

Suggested Reading

Federalist Papers #1, #9
Brutus – Anti-Federalist Paper Essay V
Jefferson's 1801 Inaugural Address
McCulloch v. Maryland (1819)
Reagan's 1981 Inauguration Speech
Reagan's order on Federalism
Clinton – The Era of Big Government is Over

1. ☐ **FEDERALISM: PART II—Lesson 6**

2. ☐ **Chronological View of Federalism**

    # Dual Federalism (1787-1933)
    # Layer cake metaphor
    # Evident in the area of commerce, which the Supreme Court defined in both interstate (which Congress could regulate) and intrastate commerce (which Congress could not regulate, at least not as easily)

3. ☐ **Cooperative Federalism (1930s-1960s)**

    # Fostered new era of federalism, with the national government interacting more with the state and even local governments in order to try and solve complex policy problems

4. ☐ **Cooperative Federalism (cont.)**

    # The best example is F.D.R.'s New Deal programs
    # Able to function only by incorporating a new form of economics: called Keynesianism

5. ☐ **Creative Federalism (1960s):**

    # President Johnson's "War on Poverty" programs
    # Interaction with state/local governments to "solve" social ills, such as poverty, crime, drugs

6. ☐ **Creative Federalism (cont.)**

    — One political journalist said this of the 1995 Republican version of federalism: *"... it is the fourth modern version ... of the simple notion that Washington ought to be doing less governing and the states ought to be doing more."*

7. ☐ **New Federalism (1970s-1990s):**

    # Richard Nixon's "New Federalism"
    — Revenue sharing (now eliminated)
    — Block grants and categorical grants are popular tools to help states and localities combat the same social problems battled by Johnson

8. ☐ **New Federalism (cont.)**

    # Ronald Reagan's "New, New Federalism"
    — Further devolution of political and fiscal power to states and localities
    — Same problems are still apparent.

9. ☐ **Summary:**

1. Federalism is the key to state and individual liberty.
2. The Founders conceived of a limited central government with few powers and state governments with more powers.
3. Finally, federalism has evolved full circle.

Suggested Readings

Thomas Paine's "Common Sense"
John Adams' "Thoughts on Government"
The Declaration of Independence
Federalist Papers # 10, #39, 47 thru 51, and #68
Marbury v. Madison (1803)
Virginia and New Jersey Plans
Madison - Debates at the Federal Convention

1. ☐ **POLITICAL CULTURE: PART I—Lesson 7**

2. ☐ **We turn now to a brief examination of political culture:**

   # <u>First</u>, we will define political culture.
   # <u>Second</u>, we will describe the basic components of any cultural system.

3. ☐ **What is political culture?**

   # Culture overall is any society's "personality," so to speak.
   # French culture is obviously quite different from South Africa's culture, which is also much different from Saudi Arabia's culture.

4. ☐ **Political culture is best defined as a "set of widely diverse beliefs and values about the nature of politics and governance within any particular country."**

5. ☐ **Basic components of political culture in any society:**

   # <u>First</u> is <u>identification</u> with country's political system.
   # <u>Second</u> is <u>trust</u> in governmental institutions.
   # <u>Third</u> is the level of <u>political efficacy</u>.
   # <u>Fourth</u> is the country's level of <u>political knowledge</u>.

6. ☐ **Distinct American cultural values:**

   # Liberty – Americans are preoccupied with their rights.
   # Equality – Americans believe everyone should have an equal vote and an equal chance to participate and succeed.
   # Democracy – Americans think government officials should be accountable to the people.
   # Civic Duty – Americans generally feel people ought to take community affairs seriously and help out when they can.
   # Individual Responsibility – Americans believe that, barring some disability, individuals are responsible for their own actions and well-being.

7. ☐ **Culture war in America: A culture war is about what kind of a country we ought to live in.**

   # Areas of conflict are drug use, school prayer, abortion, pornography, same-sex marriage; not about foreign policy, business regulation, or taxes

   # Orthodox conservatism
   — Tradition: Morality is more important than self-expression and is based on unchanging rules from God.

- \# Progressive liberalism
  - — Non-tradition: Personal freedom is more important than tradition, and the rules of morality vary with circumstances.
- \# Religious fundamentalism
  - — Rising in political influence: Fundamentalist Protestants and evangelical Christians, dismissed by orthodox view which dismisses them as "fanatical expressions of the Religious Right."
- \# Differs from other political disputes in that:
  - — money is not at stake.
  - — compromise is almost impossible.
  - — the conflict is more profound.

8.   ☐ **Summary**

There is a war in America: it is a spiritual war.
> Eph. 6:12: ***"For we wrestle not against flesh and blood, but against principalities, against powers, against the rulers of the darkness of this world, against spiritual wickedness in (heavenly places)."***

Suggested Reading

Providence Agreement
Maryland Act for Church Liberties
Pennsylvania's Freedom of Conscience Act
First Thanksgiving Proclamation
Washington's Thanksgiving Proclamation
Patrick Henry's "Give Me Liberty or Give Me Death"
Jefferson's Letter to Danbury Baptist Association

1.   ☐ **Political Culture: Part II—Lesson 8**

   Introduction to American Government

2.   ☐ **In <u>Democracy and America</u>, (vol. 2), Alexis de Tocqueville said: "...** *but there is no country in the world where the Christian religion retains a greater influence over the souls of men than in America...*"

3.   ☐ **Religious influence upon American political culture (from Ken Wald's <u>Religion and Politics</u>, 2nd ed., 1992)**

   #   <u>First</u>, the Puritan influence
   #   <u>Second</u>, the influence of covenant theology
   #   <u>Third</u>, Puritanism and democratic practice
   #   <u>Fourth</u>, a brief look at civil religion.

4.   ☐ **Puritan influence:**

   #   Puritan vision engulfed the colonies
   #   State constitutions reflected Puritan thought
   #   Bible was principal text in developing the political community
   #   Sense of unity was formed

5.   ☐ **Covenant theology:**

   #   Puritan's valued covenant relationship
   #   Political implications of covenant relationship: severing ties with England
   #   Was the Revolutionary War a true revolution? Or was it a biblical fulfillment of covenant theology?

6.   ☐ **Puritanism and democracy have three primary linkages:**

   #   Pluralism fostered by Puritanism
   — If biblical truths could be learned by individuals without interference of church hierarchy, then civic affairs could be applied without interference of central government.

7.   ☐ **Linkages (cont.)**

   #   Self-rule: the cornerstone of democratic-republicanism
   #   Church/state relations were expected; influence was strong

8. □ **Civil religion:**

    # Defined as a code or creed of religious values and beliefs communicated through the use of language and symbols

    # Purpose: to allow people of all faiths, Christian and non-Christian, to ***"harmonize their religious and political beliefs."*** (Wald).

9. □ **Civil religion (cont.)**

    # Produces loyalty and respect to a nation

    # Helps establish moral codes

10. □ **Summary**

    1. Religious influence in American political culture is strong.
    2. To what extent, however, should religious beliefs and values affect our political system?
    3. Richard Neuhaus argued that religion is the root of our political culture.

Suggested Reading

Supreme Court Interpretations of Separation of Church and State

    Everson v. Bd. of Education 1947
    Engle v. Vitale 1952
    Abbington v. Schempp
    Lemon v. Kurtzman 1971
    Lynch v. Donnelly 1984
    Lee v. Weisman (1992)

1. ☐ **PUBLIC OPINION—Lesson 9**

2. ☐ **Public opinion is the heartbeat of a nation:**

   \# In I Sam. 8:7 the Lord speaks to Samuel: *". . . Hearken unto the voice of the people in all that they say unto thee: for they have not rejected thee, but they have rejected me, that I should not reign over them."*

3. ☐ **Public Opinion (cont.)**

   \# In Joshua 24:24 public opinion spoke: *"And the people said unto Joshua, The Lord our God will we serve, and his voice will we obey."*
   \# Today, polls elicit the public's opinion on a variety of issues, everything from the popularity of the president to a myriad of policy issues.

4. ☐ **Public Opinion (cont.)**

   \# So, what exactly is public opinion? What are the characteristics of opinion? And how do we measure public opinion?

5. ☐ **What is public opinion? It is a collection of individual learned or acquired opinions.**

   \# Public opinion formed by external factors
   \# National media important in the influencing of public opinion

6. ☐ **Some characteristics of individual opinions:**

   \# <u>One</u>, opinions are temporary.
   \# <u>Two</u>, opinions are affected by political, social, and economic conditions.
   \# <u>Three</u>, opinions tend to be unreliable over the long term.

7. ☐ **Individual Opinions (cont.)**

   \# <u>Four</u>, elites' as opposed to non-elites' opinions are longer lasting and deeper rooted in ideology.
   \# And <u>five</u>, elites' opinions, as opposed to nonelites' opinions, tend to be anchored in ideology or some other value system and therefore are longer lasting.

8. ☐ **Origins of and development of public opinion:**

   1. Role of family
      — Party identification formed at an early age.
      — More politically active/participatory families pass on political values more so than non politically active families.

9. ☐ **Public Opinion (cont.)**

    2. Religion
      — Denominational impact seen
        ☐ Catholics—more liberal on economic issues; moderate to conservative on social issues, such as abortion

10. ☐ **Public Opinion (cont.)**

    ☐ Protestants
      <u>Mainline</u>—tend to be more liberal on both economic and social issues
      <u>Evangelical and charismatic</u>—tend to be conservative on both
    ☐ <u>Jews</u>—mostly liberal on both economic and social issues, recently joining with Bush administration for pro-Israel vote

11. ☐ **Public Opinion (cont.)**

    3. Education
      — Largely a liberalizing effect, especially at the college level
        ☐ 1970s—college students more liberal than peers in 1990s on issues such as abolishing the death penalty, legalizing abortion, and illegal drugs.
    4. Gender
      — The difference in political views of men and women, with men increasingly becoming more Republican since the mid 1960s.

12. ☐ **Public Opinion (cont.)**

    — More of a conservative trend during the Reagan and Bush terms
    — More and more people say God (90%) and the local church (55%) play an active role in their lives, including their political lives.

13. ☐ **Reasons for cleavages in public opinion:**

    # Social class: differences between European countries and U.S.
    — Social class differences exist within the U.S.
    — However, social class has less to do with formation of public opinion than in western European countries.

14. ☐ **Cleavages in Public Opinion (cont.)**

    # Race and ethnicity become quite distinctive
    — Black Americans more consistently liberals; more so than any other category within the Democratic party.
    — Caucasians, mainly white, have greater differences in opinions than do black Americans.

15. ☐ **Cleavages in Public Opinion (cont.)**

   \#   Geographical region
   — Southern states traditionally more conservative
   — Northern, especially northeastern states, more liberal
   — Midwest to plains, more moderate to conservative

16. ☐ **In conclusion, public opinion is essential because it:**

   \#   Assesses the ideas and values of the governed, without which a self-governing republic would be impossible;
   \#   Satisfies the need for communicating and influences the decisions of public officials.

17. ☐ **Summary (cont.)**

   Generates the ongoing support or rejection of rules, regulations, laws, etc., made and implemented by the government

   Suggested Reading

1. ☐ **IDEOLOGY: PART I—Lesson 10**

2. ☐ **Ideology and Americans** – A patterned set of beliefs about how government and other important institutions in fact operate and how they ought to operate, and in particular about what kinds of policies government ought to pursue.

3. ☐ **Ideology:**

   \# Definition: a coherent and consistent set of beliefs about who ought to rule, what principles rulers ought to obey, and what policy rulers ought to pursue.

4. ☐ **Four main types of ideology expressed in U.S.:**

   \# Liberalism
   \# Conservatism
   \# Populism
   \# Libertarianism

5. ☐ **Liberalism has two forms:**

   \# Classical (17th and 18th century)
   — Restricted central government powers
   — To promote individual and social freedom

6. ☐ **Liberalism (cont.)**

   \# Modern (beginning with Roosevelt's New Deal)
   — Use of broad and expansive central government powers to try and ensure:
      ☐ economic equality
      ☐ individual freedom
      ☐ social justice
      ☐ income redistribution

7. ☐ **Conservatism: belief in traditional use of institutions and power structures in order to preserve freedom, order, and justice.**

   \# Freedom: individual and societal
   \# Order: belief and practice of natural law and preservation of inalienable rights
   \# Justice: belief in common law and consistency in original interpretation

8.   ☐ **Summary:**

1. We have examined the two fundamental ideologies in America: liberalism and conservatism.
2. Both do not completely reveal all Americans' political beliefs.
3. Next time we will examine two other ideologies as well as conclude with a biblical insight.

1. ☐ **IDEOLOGY: PART II—Lesson 11**

2. ☐ **Let's examine two more ideological patterns of beliefs: populism and libertarianism**

3. ☐ **Populism: belief in the use of government to reduce economic inequality, but not regulate personal conduct**

   # Liberal on economic issues like taxes
   # Conservative on social and private conduct issues like abortion and same-sex marriage.

4. ☐ **Libertarianism: extreme limitation on government**

   # Conservative on economic issues like taxes
   # Liberal on social and private conduct issues like abortion and same-sex marriage.

5. ☐ **Economic intervention:**

   # Liberals favor redistribution of income and progressive taxation in order to attack social and economic inequality.
   # Conservatives, however, favor competitive individualism and lower taxes in order to stimulate economic growth, and thus lower inequality.

6. ☐ **Civil rights and liberties:**

   # Liberals favor national government intervention, especially through judicial and congressional policy making, in order to correct racial and other discrimination
   — Employ broad definition of due process and equal protection clauses of 14th Amendment

7. ☐ **Civil rights and liberties (cont.)**

   # Conservatives, on the other hand, favor strong state governments and less federal judicial intervention.
   — Conservatives believed in strengthening states' protection of individual liberty.

8. ☐ **Foreign policy:**

   # Liberals favored lower military spending, including during times of peace.
   # Conservatives, on the other hand, favored increased spending for a strong national defense and the war on terrorism.

9.   ☐ **Social policies and lifestyles:**

    \# Liberals: labeled as more tolerant of social and moral issues such as homosexuality, abortion, same-sex marriage and attitudes toward criminals and their "rights."
    \# Conservatives: favored traditional values and lifestyles; were labeled "pro-family."

10.   ☐ **Summary:**

    A.   Ideology is but the way man constructs his world, in this case, his political world.

        1.   Prov. 5:21 says: *"For the ways of man (are) before the eyes of the Lord, and he ponders all his goings."*
        2.   Prov. 19:21 reads: *"(There are) many devices in a man's heart; nevertheless the counsel of the Lord, that shall stand."*
        3.   And Prov. 21:30 says: *"(There is) no wisdom nor understanding nor counsel against the Lord."*

    B.   But it is God's word which is to be our source of wisdom and direction:

        1.   Prov. 1:7: *"The fear of the Lord (is) the beginning of knowledge: (but) fools despise wisdom and instruction."*
        2.   Joshua 1:8 says in part: *". . . for then thou shalt make thy way prosperous, and then thou shalt have good success."*
        3.   And Deut. 17:10 reads: *". . . and he shall read therein all the days of his life: that he may learn to fear the Lord his God, to keep all the words of the law and these statutes, to do them."*

Suggested Reading

1. ☐ **POLITICAL PARTICIPATION AND CITIZENSHIP—Lesson 12**

2. ☐ **Old Testament:**

   \# The people helping Nehemiah rebuild the wall (Neh. 4:6)

3. ☐ **New Testament: participatory acts which further the kingdom of God:**

   \# Submission to authority (Rom. 13:1, 2)
   \# Obedience of laws (Rom. 13:5)
   \# Paying taxes (Rom 13:7; Matt. 12:21)
   \# Praying for leadership (I Tim. 2:1-4)

4. ☐ **Voting is the basic form of participation:**

   \# Suffrage rights
   \# Voter turnout rates poor in U.S. compared with other constitutional democracies

5. ☐ **Other forms of Political Participation:**

   \# Campaign activities
   \# Community activities including church attendance
   \# Unconventional activities like protests

6. ☐ **Citizenship:**

   \# Biblical basis (Ephesians 2:12)
   — A person without Christ is alien to, not a citizen or 'townsman' of, the commonwealth, or (political) community.
   — Citizenship implies ownership, or at the very least, stewardship of community.

7. ☐ **Citizenship (cont.)**

   \# Paul used his Roman citizenship to implore the Romans to let him have an opportunity to speak to the Jews (Acts 21:39).
   \# Responsibility of citizenship status
   \# Privileges/rights of citizenship status

8. ☐ **Summary:**

   1. Participation in the political or civic process is both a responsibility and a privilege.
   2. Our citizenship, or political stewardship of our community, requires our participation.

Suggested Reading

1. **POLITICAL PARTIES—Lesson 13**

2. ☐ **The first session discusses the history and evolution of the American political party. The next session will address the characteristics, organization and operation of the modern political party.**

3. ☐ **History of the American political party system:**

   \# Pre-party period (1789-1796)
   \# First Party System (1796-1820)
   \# Period of no competition (1820-1828)
   \# Second party system (1828-1856)

4. ☐ **History (cont.)**

   \# Third party system (1856-present)
   — Republican dominance (1856-1932)
   — Democratic dominance (1932-1968)
   — Basic balance, with slight edge to Republicans (1968-1997)

5. ☐ **Founders' position was to control the divisive effects of party:**

   \# The underlying social basis for parties is political division.
   \# Madison and Federalist Paper No. 10
   \# Founders' intention was not for parties to control political power; political power was to be with the people.

6. ☐ **The Founders' fears came to pass:**

   \# Parties were a logical way to divide and compete for political power.
   \# Parties also became ideological bastions.

7. ☐ **Founders' fears (cont.)**

   \# The Democratic party became the party for the politically and economically weak lower social class, and thus, policies developed which were aimed at both those particular categories of people and solving particular associated problems.
   \# The Republican party then became known as the party of the rich and affluent.

8. ☐ **Summary:**

   1. Parties are based on the divisive characteristics of man.
   2. It was G. Washington who declared the "baneful effects" of parties.
   3. But it is political parties which help label, identify, and control political power in order to compete for the prize of elected political office.

Selected Reading

Anthony's "A Woman's Right to Vote"

1. ☐ **POLITICAL PARTIES: PART II—Lesson 14**

   A political party is a group that seeks to elect candidates to public office by supporting them with a label—party identification—by which they are known to the electorate.

2. ☐ **Characteristics of American parties**

   \# <u>First</u> is the factor of decentralization.
   \# <u>Second</u>, candidates are chosen through primaries, not by party leaders.
   \# <u>Third</u>, presidents and governors are elected separately from the legislative body, unlike in a parliamentary system.

3. ☐ **Characteristics (cont.)**

   \# <u>Fourth</u>, parties, as a political body, are less important to a citizen's political life than are, for example, interest groups.
   \# <u>Fifth</u>, parties are less important to the typical citizen's life than are other voluntary associations or groups.

4. ☐ **Functions of political parties:**

   \# To mobilize voters during election periods
   \# To provide political information about candidates and complex issues

5. ☐ **Functions (cont.)**

   \# To stimulate political participation
   \# To provide information about candidates and issues
   \# To encourage political participation
   \# Watchdog role

6. ☐ **Why does the U.S. have a two-party system?**

   \# <u>First</u>, because of history and tradition
   \# <u>Second</u>, because of social-economic differences that began with the Federalists and Antifederalists

7. ☐ **Two Party System (cont.)**

   \# And <u>third</u> is the legal reason
      — Winner-take-all plurality v. proportional system

8. ☐ **Third parties have made some differences in presidential electoral politics:**

    \# For example, the Free Soil Party (1848-1852) was fairly effective in raising the standard of awareness and consciousness of the vile practice of slavery.
    \# The Prohibition Party was partly responsible for helping to get alcohol banned.

9. ☐ **Third Parties (cont.)**

    \# The Bull Moose Progressive party (1912) used the charisma of Teddy Roosevelt to challenge the thinking of the Republican party.
    \# And today the grassroots Reform Party of Ross Perot is challenging the elitism of the two major parties.
    \# The candidacy of Ralph Nader for the Green Party in 2000 took votes from Democratic candidate Al Gore, possibly costing him the election.

10. ☐ **Finally, let's look at some specific demographic and policy differences between the two major parties.**

    \# Demographics – Northeast and West Coast tends to vote Democratic, with the Heartland and South voting Republican
    \# Issue differences –Democrats tend to attract liberal voters on issues like abortion, homosexuality, and same-sex marriage while Republicans attract conservative voters on family values issues.

11. ☐ **Summary:**

    1. The weakening position of the parties provides for some challenges for the future of American electoral politics, such as:
    2. Parties need to take more meaningful and contrasting positions on issues in order for people to determine a difference between the two major parties.
    3. Party membership has little if any meaning, and should probably be strengthened in order to encourage stronger group participation in electoral politics.
    4. Stronger parties may help toward the selection of better candidates, especially for president.

1.   ☐ **ELECTIONS AND CAMPAIGNS—Lesson 15**

2.   ☐ **This first of two lectures will cover the following:**

   \# The ingredients necessary to get elected into public office, especially the president
   \# The influence of primaries and caucuses
   \# The differences between primary and general elections

3.   ☐ **Several ingredients necessary to get nominated by party for president:**

   \# <u>Name recognition</u>—The candidate has to answer the question, "Who are you?"
   \# <u>Time investment</u>—How much time and effort is the candidate willing to invest in order to have a chance to win?
   \# <u>Money</u>—Money is the key!

4.   ☐ **Ingredients (cont)**

   \# <u>A sound organization</u>—A solid grassroots organization is necessary in order to win.
   \# <u>Strategy and theme</u>

5.   ☐ **Primaries V. General Elections:**

   \# A primary is the pre-nomination stage where registered voters go to designated polling place and vote for candidate of choice.
   \# Nearly 100% of both Dem. and Rep. delegates chosen by primaries.

6.   ☐ **Primary V. General (cont.)**

   \# A <u>caucus</u> is pre-nomination stage where registered voters go to designated place to discuss issues and vote on candidate of choice. Most notable is the Iowa Caucus

7.   ☐ **Types of Primaries – A primary election is used to select a party's candidates for an elective office.**

   \# Closed Primaries
   \# Open Primaries
   \# Blanket Primaries
   \# Runoff Primaries

8.   ☐ **General Election: Vote to actually put a person into elective office.**

   \# Once the Presidential candidate is officially nominated, the general election begins, lasting from about Labor Day until election eve—approx. 2 months.

9. ☐ **Differences between primary and general elections:**

  # Primary voters more ideological than general election voters
  # State organizations very important for primary elections
  # Direct mail campaigns more important in primary
  — Telemarketing major tool
    ☐ Television plays a major role with debates usually favoring the challenger

10. ☐ **Summary:**

  1. We have covered the nomination process and the primary differences between primaries and general elections.
  2. Let's look next at a major factor in national campaigns: money.

  Selected Readings

  Bush v. Gore (2000)
  Gore Concedes

1. | □ **CAMPAIGNS AND MONEY—Lesson 16**

2. | □ **How much money is spent on campaigns?**

The amount spent on elections for Congressional candidates in 2000 was over $1 billion

The campaign for president by Bush and Gore in 2000 was the most expensive on record.

3. | □ **Sources of Campaign Money:**

Presidential primaries: part private, part public

4. | □ **Money (cont.)**

— Political Action Committees (P.A.C.s) risen in popularity and importance since early 1970s
— P.A.C.s are effective tools of election fund raising because they are attached to powerful interest groups, corporations, labor unions.

5. | □ **Money (cont.)**

— Influence of P.A.C. money is substantial.
   □ Amount of dollars: 1992 elections: $160 million dollars given (mostly to Democrats and incumbents); 1996 elections: nearly $200 million dollars.

6. | □ **Money (cont.)**

   □ Influence: generally accepted that more dollars spent on incumbents get them elected, but not conclusive on direct connection between dollars spent and direction of public policy.

7. | □ **Money (cont.)**

Presidential general election: all public money
Congressional elections: all private money

8. | □ **How does American campaign spending compare with some European countries?**

The major difference is that many European countries have some type of free TV time, whereas that is not an option in the U.S.
Also, in Denmark, Italy, and Germany there is little or no limit on fund-raising or spending. That also is not true in the U.S.

9. □ **Campaign Finance Rules:**

Federal Election Campaign Act (amended 2002)
 — Individuals: $2,000/candidate/election
 — Political Action Committees: $10,000/candidate/election

10. □ **Finance Rules (cont)**

In <u>Buckely v. Valeo</u> (1976), the S.C. ruled that spending money was akin to free speech, and to limit spending would be akin to limiting speech--a constitutional no-no; but in 2003 the ruling was to be looked at again by the courts.
 — Candidate spending could be limited if the candidate took matching funds.

11. □ **Reform**

The Bipartisan Campaign Reform Act of 2002 banned soft money contributions to national parties from corporations and unions. The individual contribution was raised to $2,000, and independent expenditures by corporations, unions, and nonprofit organizations are sharply restricted.

Remember, the Word indicates that the "love of money is the root of all evil."
 — When money so strongly dictates who will win and lose political elections, money becomes god, and public service falls by the proverbial wayside.

12. □ **Summary:**

1. Campaigns are indeed important to the democratic process.
2. But at what cost?

1. □ **INTEREST GROUPS—Lesson 17**

2. □ **Interest groups are indeed a fixture in American politics:**

   \# Alexis de Toqueville noted that Americans: *". . . constantly form interest groups."*
   \# What is the nature of interest groups? What is the biblical basis for groups and their participation in society and politics? How are interest groups organized? And what are their principal functions?

3. □ **What is the nature of man in the nature of IGs?**

   \# Aristotle: *"Man is by nature a social animal."*
   \# James Madison: *"The latent causes of faction are sown into the nature of man."*

4. □ **The Biblical basis for groups:**

   \# First, groups are a channel for God's salvation.
   \# Second, the group is a go-between through which God can reach the individual.
   — Deut. 32:30: *". . . where one puts a thousand to flight, but two put ten thousand . . ."*

5. □ **Biblical Basis (cont.)**

   — Matt. 18:19-20: *"Where two or three are gathered together in my name . . . "*
   — I Cor. 12:12: *". . . as the body is one, and hath many members . . . "*

   \# Three, God continues to use the group, especially the local church, for both spiritual and social outreach.

6. □ **Factors that make-up an interest group:**

   \# Organization
   \# Leadership
   \# Shared Interest

7. □ **Primary purpose of interest groups is to influence or change public policy.**

8. □ **People join interest groups for a variety of reasons:**

   \# For social reasons: people desire the company and social interaction of others.
   \# For psychological reasons: people get a sense of accomplishment and efficacy from joining an interest group.

9. ☐ **Why do people join IGs? (cont.)**

   \# For political reasons: to make political gains
   \# For economical reasons: to make economic gains

10. ☐ **There are several effective functions of interest groups:**

   \# to gather and share information about variety of issues and candidates during elections
   \# to lobby congressmen on behalf of the particular interest

11. ☐ **Functions of IGs (cont.)**

   \# to funnel money into campaigns (via P.A.C.s)
   \# Public interests
   \# Governmental interests
   \# Single-issue interests

12. ☐ **Summary:**

   1. We have briefly covered interest groups as an influencing factor in social, economic, and political arenas.
   2. As the 21st century nears, the Church as a group must further the kingdom of God while influencing the kingdom of man.

1. ☐ **MEDIA AND THE POLITICAL PROCESS: PART I—Lesson 18**

2. ☐ **The American media plays a significant role in the development and influence of politics and governance.**

3. ☐ **History of American Media:**

 \# Newspapers
 \# 1770s—weeklies (Party Press)
 \# 1820s-1850s—Christian emphasis in news
 \# 1880s—competition is high (Popular Press)
 \# 1900-1940s—empires built
 \# 1960s—competition disappears

4. ☐ **Magazines:**

 \# Not a true news forum; editorial and features based
 \# Big Three: <u>Time</u>, <u>Newsweek,</u> and <u>U.S. News & World Report</u>
 \# Online magazines like <u>Salon</u>

5. ☐ **Radio:**

 \# First used in early 1920s
 \# Primary use is for talk shows and entertainment
 \# Rush Limbaugh and conservative hosts have political influence

6. ☐ **Television:**

 \# 1940s—birth of TV
 \# 1960s—medium explodes
 \# TV becomes major factor in the delivery and interpretation of political news.
 \# Proliferation of cable news outlets beginning with CNN

7. ☐ **The Internet – in 1998, 40 million people who are voters and political activists talked to each other**

8. ☐ **Political functions of media:**

 \# Interpreting the news
 — Gatekeeper role
 — Race horse journalism as Scorekeeper
 — Watchdog
 \# Influencing public opinion
 — Over 90% of Americans believe media influences their opinion.

9. ☐ **Political functions of media (cont.)**

> \# Agenda setting
> — TV has biggest impact.
> — Correlation between media coverage and what public sees as important

10. ☐ **Liberal bias is evident and prevalent:**

> \# Bias affects content and presentation
> \# Bias generated from and by newsmakers generally social, economic, and politically liberal views
> \# Identified by authors like Bernard Kalb and Ann Coulter in their books.
> \# Decline in trust of the media

11. **Constraints on a free press in the US:**

> \# The President and Congress
> \# Leaks
> \# An adversarial press?
> \# Sensationalism

11. ☐ **Summary:**

> 1. We have discussed the basic political functions of the national media: interpretation, influencing, and agenda setting.
> 2. We have also examined the inherent liberal bias present in the national media.
> 3. Next time we will discuss the influence of media 'power brokers'.

Selected Readings

Johnson Not to Seek Re-election Speech
Nixon's Resignation Speech
Ford's Pardon of Nixon Speech
Clinton's "I am Profoundly Sorry" Speech

1. | ☐ **MEDIA AND THE POLITICAL PROCESS: PART II—Lesson 19**

2. | ☐ **Newsmakers are political power brokers:**

   \# David Halberstam, <u>Powers That Be</u> (1979)
   1. National media influential in establishing political agenda
   2. Creating media empires
   3. Creating a business of news

3. | ☐ **Political Power Brokers (cont.)**

   \# Thomas Dye, <u>Who's Running America? The Clinton Years</u> (1995)
   1. Agenda setting function most powerful
   2. Straight reporting of news is a myth; news reporting is really news interpretation.

4. | ☐ **Political Power Brokers:**

   \# Bad news sells more than 3 to 1 over good news.
   \# Characteristics of the average media elite are quite liberal:
   — 68% believe government should reduce income inequalities
   — 80% favor affirmative action plans and programs
   — 90% favor elective abortion.
   — Only 47% believe adultery is wrong.

5. | ☐ **Summary:**

   1. TV's overall impact is large and growing, especially with advent of cable and other telecommunications technology.
   2. Straight news reporting is almost a bygone idea; news interpretation, which leads to news control, is most common.
   3. Remember, the Word is clear about our filling our mind with good things:
   Rom. 12:2: ***"And be not conformed to this world: but be ye transformed by the renewing of your mind . . ."***
   4. Philippians 4:8: ***"Finally, brethren, whatsoever things are true, whatsoever things are honest, whatsoever things are just, whatsoever things are pure, whatsoever things are lovely, whatsoever things are of good report; if there by any virtue, and if there be any praise, think on these things."***
   5. The Word is not telling us we are not to watch TV or listen to news, but we are to filter what we watch, read, and hear through our spiritual filter.

1.   ☐ **CONGRESS: PART I—Lesson 20**

2.   ☐ *"Congress on the floor is Congress on show. Congress in committee is Congress at work."* **Woodrow Wilson**

3.   ☐ **Biblical view of legislatures and legislative power:**

     # Isa. 33:22: *". . . the Lord is our lawgiver . . ."*
     # Jas. 4:12: *"There is one lawgiver, who is able to save and to destroy . . ."*
     # Heb. 8:10: *". . . I will put my laws into their mind, and write them in their hearts: and I will be to them a God, and they shall be to me a people."*

4.   ☐ **National assembly, or representatives of the Hebrew people, both in civil and ecclesiastical matters:**

     # Assembly of elders (also referred to as 'people') upheld the law as sacred (Ex. 19-7-8; 24:3).
     # Also ratified the king (I Sam 8:4-5; 11:15; 2 Sam. 5:3)

5.   ☐ **National assembly (cont.)**

     # Assisted in ceremonial functions, such as dedication of temple (I Kings 8:1)
     # Giving (I Kings 12:6-7 with Rehoboam) and receiving (Eze. 8, 14, 20 with Ezekiel prophesying to them) counsel

6.   ☐ **Uniqueness of Congress:**

     # Congress means: *"assembly of elected representatives empowered to make laws"*;
     # Whereas parliament means: *"an assembly of elected representatives who make laws and choose the prime minister."*

7.   ☐ **Let us examine some criticisms of Congress:**

     1. Congress is unrepresentative of the American people.
     2. Congress is mismanaged.

8.   ☐ **Criticisms of Congress (cont.)**

     3. Congress is wasteful of public resources.
     4. Congress is corrupt.
     5. Congress is unresponsive to public demands.

1. ☐ **CONGRESS: PART II—Lesson 21**

2. ☐ **What are Congress' powers?**

- \# Economic powers (Art. 1, sec. 8)
  - — Budgetary power shared with the President
- \# Commerce powers (Art 1, sec. 8)
  - — Regulate commerce
  - — Establish regulatory agencies, such EPA, FTC, and FCC

3. ☐ **Congress powers (cont.)**

- \# Impeachment power (Art. 1, sec. 3)
- \# Investigative power
- \# Foreign policy powers (Art. 1, sec. 2, 8)

4. ☐ **Congress powers (cont.)**

- \# Foreign policy powers (Art. 1, sec. 8)
  - — Declaration of war
  - — Confirmation of treaties
  - — Appropriation of money to armed services

5. ☐ **How is Congress Organized to use these powers?**

6. ☐ **Party structure in Senate:**

- \# Senate Majority Leader
- \# Majority Whip
- \# Minority Leader
- \# Minority Whip

7. ☐ **Party structure in House:**

- \# Speaker of the House
- \# Majority Leader
- \# Majority Whip
- \# Minority Leader
- \# Minority Whip

8. ☐ **Party voting in both chambers:**

   \# Party voting with weak, moderate, or strong majority
   \# Ideology plays role

9. ☐ **Committee Structure**

   \# What do committees do?
   \# Various types of committees:
   — Standing committees
   — Select committees
   — Joint committees

10. ☐ **A third area of congressional power is staffs and staffing agencies**

   \# Staff members, their role and importance
   \# Rapid growth and impact of staffs
   \# Offer specialized information as primary function
   \# Staffing agencies, such as CRS, GAO, OTA, and CBO

How a Bill becomes a Law:

Introduction, Committee, Debate, Vote, Signed or Vetoed

11. ☐ **Summary:**

   1. Congress is extremely political and complex
   2. The long and short outcomes: are the people satisfied with their representation?
   3. Is lawmaking being done for the betterment of the country?

1. ☐ **PRESIDENCY: PART I—Lesson 22**

2. ☐ **Biblical view of executive power :**

   # Isa. 33:22: *". . . the Lord (is) our king . . . "*
   # Prov. 29:4: *"The king by judgment establisheth the land . . . "*
   # I Peter 2:17: *". . . Honor the king."*
   # Matt. 22:21: *". . . Rend therefore unto Caesar the things which are Caesar's; and unto God the things that are God's."*

3. ☐ **Evolution of the Presidency:**

   # Founders' concerns: strong v. weak executive
   # Convention delegates feared return to monarch; thus the prime emphasis on the congressional branch

4. ☐ **Constitutional qualifications (Article 2):**

   # Natural born citizen; not naturalized citizen
   # 35 years
   # Resident of the U.S. for 14 years

5. ☐ **Unwritten qualifications (by tradition):**

   # Male
   # White
   # High social and economic status
   # Protestant faith
   # Usually some military experience
   # Some previous government experience
   # Generally a college education
   # Political connections a must

6. ☐ **God's qualifications (according to the Word):**

   # To speak righteously (Pr. 16:10)
   # To meditate on the Word daily (Deut. 17:18-20)
   # To abhor wickedness (Pr. 16:12)
   # To favor wisdom (Pr. 14:35)
   # To honor God (I Sam. 2:30)

7. ☐ **God's Qualifications (cont.)**

   # To be a servant with a servant's heart (Mk. 10:42-45)
   # To acknowledge personal faults and repent of them (Ps. 51)

To acknowledge the truly poor and needy and have compassion for them (Pr. 29:14)

8. ☐ **Constitutional changes to the Presidency:**

12th Amendment (1804)—revision of electoral college
20th Amendment (1933)—change of terms and emergency succession of president-elect
22nd Amendment (1951)—establishment of presidential terms
25th Amendment (1967)—how to handle the removal of President from office
   — Presidential Succession Act (1886; amended 1947)

9. ☐ **2000 Election Highlighted the Electoral College**

Bush vs. Gore decided by controversial Florida vote count
Each state gets electoral votes equal to number of its senators and representatives
Candidate who gets the most popular votes wins all the states' electoral votes
Electors cast their votes at the state capitals about six weeks after the election
If no candidate wins a majority the House of Representatives chooses a President.

10. ☐ **Summary:**

1. Founders had to balance strong executive with limited government powers.
2. Next time we will examine the presidential powers as well as discuss the role of executive power for the future.

1. ☐ **PRESIDENCY: PART II—Lesson 23**

2. ☐ **Presidential powers: Constitutional**

    # Constitutional powers found in Art. 2, sections 2, 3
    — Appointment power
    — Judicial powers (granting of reprieves and pardons)
    — Veto power
        ☐ <u>Kennedy v. Sampson</u> (1974)

3. ☐ **Presidential powers (cont.)**

    — State of Union address
    — Foreign policy powers (commander-in-chief)

4. ☐ **Presidential powers: Political/traditional**

    — Executive privilege
        ☐ <u>U.S. v. Nixon</u> (1974)
    — Executive order
    — Speeches
    — Budget preparation and presentation

5. ☐ **Characteristics of the modern presidency:**

    # Greater influence in foreign policy making
    # Expansion of domestic related powers, especially in budget making
    # Explosion of White House Office personnel

6. ☐ **Modern presidency characteristics (cont.)**

    # More influence from policy advisors
    # Expansion of public relations factor
    # Highly electoral oriented office

7. **Restraints on Presidential Power**

The Media
Congress' power of impeachment seen in Clinton presidency.

8. ☐ **Problems facing the modern presidency:**

    # Will face international hot spots, including:
    — China and North Korea
    — European alliance
    — Pacific Rim countries

    # African crises
      — coups and take-overs
      — refugee problems

9.   ☐ **Problems (cont.)**

    # Third world problems, such as hunger and starvation
    # Middle East situation
    # The War Against Terrorism

10.   **Summary:**

    1. We must return to Godly principles of leadership.
    2. Most importantly, we must pray for presidents (I Tim. 2:1-4).

Selected Readings

Roosevelt's Inauguration Speech
Kennedy's Inaugural Address 1961
Bush v. Gore (2000)
Gore Concedes

1. ☐ **BUREAUCRACY—Lesson 24**

2. ☐ **Biblical basis of public organizational principles:**

   \# Delegation of authority
   — Ex. 18:13-23: Jethro's admonition to Moses
   \# Authorization of rules
   — Ex. 20 (Ten Commandments)
   — Ps. 119 (importance of obeying God's laws)

3. ☐ **Biblical basis for bureaucracy (cont.)**

   \# Hierarchy
   — I Cor. 11:3 (Divine order detailed)
   \# The principal key of God's divine organizational principles is order.

4. ☐ **Distinctiveness of the American Bureaucracy:**

   \# Constitutional power for the bureaucracy is found in Article 2, section 3: *"... take care that the laws be faithfully executed. ..."*

   \# Public attitudes toward American bureaucracy
   — nearly 50% of people expect government to do more, but only 23% have confidence in government to do the right thing.

5. ☐ **Definition of Bureaucracy:**

   \# Literal meaning: rule by one who writes
   \# <u>Definition</u>: *an ordered pattern of rules, procedures, and people designed to carry out policy decisions*
   \# Called the Fourth Branch of Government

6. ☐ **Bureaucrats or civil servants:**

   \# Competitive service (66% of all appointed officials)
   — Pass examinations (by OPM)
   — Possess particular, professional skills

7. ☐ **Bureaucrats or civil servants (cont.)**

   \# Exempt service (33%)
   — Appointed on partisan basis (only about 3%)
   — Some, like Postal Service, FBI, CIA, and others are also exempt, but are governed by own personnel agencies.

8. ☐ **The Federal Bureaucracy Today:**

    \# 56% are male; 44% female
    \# 73% white; 27% nonwhite
    \# 33% work for Defense Department; 26% for Postal service; 41% in all other departments
    \# 88% work outside D.C. area
      — Major occupation within Beltway is combination of lawyer/lobbyist.

9. ☐ **Characteristics (cont.)**

    \# More "pro-government" than the public at-large
    \# Liberals prominent in social service agencies
    \# Conservatives over represented in military and defense agencies

10. ☐ **Explanations for the growth of government bureaucracy:**

    \# <u>First</u>, government bureaucracy increases because of increased demand for services.
    \# <u>Second</u>, government grows because of increased regulation.

11. ☐ **Growth of Government (cont.)**

    \# <u>Third</u>, government grows because of increased demand by public to solve economic and social problems.
    \# <u>Fourth</u>, government grows based upon increase in specialization of function and technological innovations.
    \# <u>Fifth</u>, the War Against Terrorism and the new Department of Homeland Security

12. ☐ **Summary:**

    1. The bureaucracy is a slow moving institution.
    2. Because of its neutrality, or supposed neutrality, it is to be nonideological; however, it is anything but.

Selected Readings

Reagan's 1981 Inauguration Speech
Reagan's order on Federalism
Clinton – The Era of Big Government is Over

1.   ☐ **JUDICIARY: PART I—Lesson 25**

2.   ☐ *"For God . ... laid down certain rules, whereby that free-will is regulated and restrained . . . These rules are the eternal laws of good and evil to which the Creator himself . . . has enabled human reason to discover."* **William Blackstone**

3.   ☐ **Biblical basis for law and judiciary:**

     # Law originates with God
       — The Ten Commandments (Controversy in Alabama with Roy Moore)

     # God is a righteous judge, and He expects His chosen ones to be likewise
       — Deut. 1:16: *"And I charged your judges . . . judge righteously . . ."*

       — Ps. 58:11: *"Verily (there is) a reward for the righteous: verily he is a God that judgeth in the earth."*

     # God's law is to secure justice and judgment, to maintain order, and insure against abuse of freedom.

4.   ☐ **Supreme Court and the Constitution:**

     # Constitutional basis for the judiciary is Article III
       — Section 1: power of interpretation
       — Section 2: jurisdiction
       — Section 3: definition of treason, and penalty

5.   ☐ **Constitutional power of the court is interpretation of law:**

     # Strict constructionism or judicial restraint
     # Judicial activism

6.   ☐ **Summary:**

   1. The biblical basis of law is clear and distinct.
   2. The Supreme Court's foundation is the Constitution.
   3. Interpretation of the Constitution is based upon two competing value systems; judicial restraint and activism.

1. ☐ **JUDICIARY: PART II—Lesson 26**

2. ☐ **Dual court system:**

   # Federal—Three tiered system
   # State and Local—different depending upon the state

3. ☐ **U.S. District Courts:**

   # Trial courts
   # Original jurisdiction only
   # Case load includes federal crimes, civil suits under federal law, even maritime cases

4. ☐ **Appellate courts:**

   # Appellate jurisdiction only
   # Hear appeals from federal district courts, regulatory commissions

5. ☐ **United States Supreme Court:**

   # Court of highest appeals
   # Both original and appellate jurisdiction
   # Chance of a case making it to the S.C.s docket to be heard: only 5%

6. ☐ **What is the role of the U.S. Supreme Court in the political process?**

   # Presidential appointment
   # Congressional confirmation
   # A litmus test

7. ☐ **Political powers of Supreme Court:**

   # Judicial Review
   # Overturning previous cases; not following *stare decisis*
   # Use of judicial remedies go beyond what "justice" calls for.

8. ☐ **Political powers of Supreme Court (cont.)**

   # Too little deference to congressional branch
   # Vague language in Constitution
   # Political values of justices and judges affect the objectivity of decisions.

9.   ☐ **Checks on Judicial Power**

     # No force to its rulings
     # Congress can alter the composition, use its confirmation power, impeach a Justice, or amend the Constitution.
     # Public opinion

10.   ☐ **Summary:**

    1. The Supreme Court is a highly political institution.
    2. Is the Supreme Court adequately checked and balanced?
    3. Is the current political role of the Supreme Court something envisioned by the Founders?

1. ☐ **INTRODUCTION TO PUBLIC POLICY—Lesson 27**

   Setting the Agenda – "He who decides what politics is about runs the country"- anonymous

2. ☐ **What is the legitimate reach of government into the private affairs of humans?**

   ☐ **One answer is that government is always necessary for aiding in the solutions of man's problems.**

3. ☐ **A second solution argues that expansive government is not always necessary, and that more responsibility and corresponding authority should and must go to the people.**

4. ☐ **But are these the only answers? No.**

   \# As we have determined, God is the origin of all that is Good, and that His ways are perfect, while man's ways are not.
   \# God's decisions are righteous and just, while man's are arbitrary and unjust.

5. ☐ **Answers (cont.)**

   \# Therefore, it is imperative to enlist God's principles into the making of decisions, especially those which are public in origin.

6. ☐ **Following is an overview of the public areas we will examine over the next few lessons:**

   \# First area is **civil liberties**: freedoms enjoyed by all and guaranteed by the Constitution, such as religion, speech, and press.

7.
   \# Second area is **civil rights**: rights guaranteed by political and legal statute and to particular groups, not all people, such as due process, equal protection of the laws, prohibition of discrimination, affirmative action, and abortion.

8.
   \# Third area is **social welfare policy**: specifically looking at the poor and needy.
   — Overview of past and contemporary policy positions

9.
   \# Fourth area is **economic policy**: a biblical view of economics.
   — Overview of economic theory and economic policy making

10.

　　# Fifth area is **American foreign policy** since W.W.II
　　　— Containment of Communism in cold-war environment
　　　— Post-society Communism

11.

　　# Sixth area is the War Against Terrorism, including engagement in the Middle East

12.　　☐ **How do each of these policy areas affect our lives and the direction that the U.S. will take for the 21st Century?**

The answer to this question lies in the evaluation and examination of laws, executive actions, and judicial rulings covering these policy areas.

1. ☐ **POLICY ISSUES: CIVIL LIBERTIES AND FREEDOM OF RELIGION—Lesson 28**

2. ☐ **Civil Liberties: basic freedoms all people enjoy which are protected by the Constitution.**

3. ☐ **Freedom of Religion**

   \# Establishment Clause: Original intent was that no religion (specifically a denomination) would be treated disproportionately over any other religion or denomination

4. ☐ **Establishment (cont.)**

   \# "Wall of Separation" controversy
   — Founders' meaning and intention
   — Contemporary meaning and intention
   — David Barton

5. ☐ **Selected establishment clause cases:**

   \# Everson v. Board of Education (1947)
   — Child benefit theory
   \# Engle v. Vitale (1962)
   — Outlawed school-sponsored voluntary and nondenominational prayer
   — Redefined religion

6. ☐ **Establishment clause cases (cont.)**

   \# Abington v. Schemmp (1963)
   — Outlawed Bible reading as part of school instruction
   \# Epperson v. Arkansas (1968)
   — Affirmed that prohibition of teaching evolution or requiring teaching creationism is unconstitutional

7. ☐ **Establishment clause cases (cont.)**

   \# Lee v. Weisman (1992)
   — Banned invocations and benedictions at public high school graduation ceremonies
   \# Newdow v. Congress (2002)
   — Called the phrase "under God" from the Pledge of Allegiance a violation of separation of church and state

8. | ☐ **Establishment clause cases (cont.)**

    6. <u>Lamb's Chapel v. Center Moriches Union Free School District</u> (1993)
    — Allowed the use of public school buildings for showing of religious videos

9. | ☐ **Freedom of Religion (cont.)**

    # Free Exercise Clause: means that a person cannot be compelled to do something against his religious beliefs
    — Less controversy here

10. | ☐ **Selected free exercise cases:**

    # <u>Wisconsin v. Yoder</u> (1972)
    — Old order Amish may keep their children out of public schools
    # <u>Sherbert v. Verner</u> (1963)
    — Government may not withhold unemployment payments

11. | ☐ **Free exercise cases (cont.)**

    # <u>Employment Division, Dept. of Human Resources of Oregon v. Smith</u> (1990)
    — Use of illegal hallucinogenic drug, such as drug peyote, is not permissible by one group (Native Americans) if the law applies to all.

12. | ☐ **Free exercise cases (cont.)**

    # <u>Church of the Lukumi Babalu Aye v. City of Hialeah</u> (1993)
    — State cannot ban animal sacrifices performed by religious groups.

13. | ☐ **Summary:**

    1. Court's rulings are ambiguous in areas, clear in other areas.
    2. Redefinition of religion is paramount to extreme government intrusion.
    3. People of Christian faith must unite in prayer and civic action.
    4. Court decisions seen as part of the culture war.

Selected Reading

Jefferson's Letter to Danbury Baptist Association
Everson v. Bd. of Education 1947
Engle v. Vitale 1952
Abbington v. Schempp
Lemon v. Kurtzman 1971
Lynch v. Donnelly 1984
Lee v. Weisman (1992)

1.   ☐ **POLICY ISSUES: CIVIL LIBERTIES AND FREEDOM OF SPEECH AND PRESS—Lesson 29**

2.   ☐ **Freedom of Speech:**

   \# Basic human freedom
   \# God ordained
   — Acts 19:8: *"And he went into the synagogue, and spake boldly for the space of three months, disputing and persuading the things concerning the kingdom of God."*
   \# Acts 26:1: *"Agrippa said unto Paul, Thou art permitted to speak for thyself. . . . "*

3.   ☐ **Five basic types of speech include:**

   \# Pure speech: verbal communication which is almost always protected
   \# Speech plus: verbal plus action (such as parade, protest, marches). Verbal generally protected; the plus may not be

4.   ☐ **Freedom of Speech (cont.)**

   \# Symbolic speech: nonverbal communication through use of symbols; may or may not be protected.
   — U.S. v. O'Brien (1968)
      ☐ Burning of draft cards is unconstitutional.

5.   ☐ **Freedom of Speech (cont.)**

   — Tinker v. DSM School District (1969)
      ☐ Wearing of black arm bands to symbolize dislike of Vietnam War is constitutional

6.   ☐ **Freedom of Speech (cont.)**

   \# Seditious speech: speech that incites resistance to or insurrection against lawful authority, such as government
   — Schenck v. U.S. (1919)
      ☐ Clear and present danger test developed

7.   ☐ **Freedom of Speech (cont.)**

   — Gitlow v. N.Y. (1925)
      ☐ Banning of subversive publication or speech is constitutional.
   — Texas v. Johnson (1998)
      ♦ Burning the American flag is constitutionally protected free speech

8.   ☐ **Freedom of Speech (cont.)**

    # Obscenity: Is never constitutionally protected speech
    # <u>Miller v. California</u> (1973)
      — Lustful appeal? If so, not protected.
      — Violate local community standard? If so, not protected.

9.   ☐ **Freedom of Speech (cont.)**

    — No serious literary, artistic, political, or scientific value? If not, not protected.

10.   ☐ **FREEDOM OF PRESS:**

    # God ordained also
      — Ex. 17:14: *"And the Lord said unto Moses, Write this (for) a memorial in a book, and rehearse it in the ears of Joshua . . . "*
      — Neh. 9:38: *"And because of all this we make a sure (covenant), and write (it) . . . . "*

11.   ☐ **Censorship and Prior Restraint:**

    # <u>Near v. Minnesota</u> (1931)
      — No prior restraint
    # <u>Hazlewood School District v. Kuhlmeier</u> (1988)
      — High school papers can be controlled as long as controls are academically related.

12.   ☐ **Libelous writing and statements:**

    # <u>N.Y. Times v. Sullivan</u> (1964)
      — Public official cannot recover for libelous writing unless there is actual malice.

13.   ☐ **Summary:**

    1. The Court has endeavored to maintain basic freedoms.
    2. Free speech and free press are basic rights. Keeping them in balance is difficult.

1. ☐ **CIVIL RIGHTS AND THE 14TH AMENDMENT—Lesson 30**

2. ☐ **God's word is clear against the use of discrimination generally or specifically:**

   # James 2:9: *"But if ye have respect to persons, ye commit sin, and are convinced of the law as transgressors."*
   # Acts 10:34-35: *"Of a truth I perceive that God is no respecter of persons; But in every nation he that feareth him, and worketh righteousness, is accepted with him."*
   # Romans 2:11: *"For there is no respect of persons with God."*

3. ☐ **We see that Jesus personally did not respect Jew nor Gentile alike:**

   # Zaccheus, the rich and despised publican, was to be Jesus' house guest.
   # In Matthew 8, Jesus marveled at the Roman officer's faith.
   # In Acts 10 the gift of salvation was given to the Gentile as well as the Jew.

4. ☐ **What does Jesus respect? Faith:**

   # Hebrews 10:6: *"But without faith (it is) impossible to please (him). . . ."*

5. ☐ **Amendment 14, section 1**

   # Citizenship for former slaves
   # Prohibition against states to "abridge privileges or immunities;"
   # Not to deny due process
   # Nor to deny any person equal protection of the law

6. ☐ **Due process:**

   # Conservative interpretation: specific process given to defendant with regard to particular crime committed
   # Liberal interpretation: general guarantee of procedural fairness, extending to any number of legal situations

7. ☐ **Equal Protection of Laws**

   # Definition is three-pronged
   — Legal equality to ensure equal voting rights
   — To apply the bill of rights to the states
   — Forbidding racial discrimination

8. ☐ **Summary:**

   1. It is clear from God's word that god is no respecter of persons
   2. The 14th Amendment's aim was to prevent discrimination

1. | ☐ **POLICY ISSUES: CIVIL RIGHTS AND MINORITY DISCRIMINATION—Lesson 31**

2. | ☐ **Racial discrimination is contrary to God's Genesis principle:**

   # *"Let us make man in our image, after our likeness . . . "* (Gen. 1:26)
   # To discriminate based upon skin color, religion, or gender is baseless.

3. | ☐ **But to discriminate based upon behavior, or lack thereof, for example, is not negatively discriminatory:**

   # 2 Thess. 3:10: *"For even when we were with you, this we commanded you, that if any would not work, neither should he eat."*

4. | ☐ **We will examine some areas of racial discrimination decided upon by the Supreme Court. You be the judge: did the Supreme Court decide according to God's standards?**

5. | ☐ **Racial discrimination and state action:**

   # S.C.'s track record is poor
     — Dred Scott v. Sanford (1857)
     — Civil Rights Cases (1883)
     — Plessy v. Ferguson (1896)
   # Civil Rights Act of 1875

6. | ☐ **One area rife with racial discrimination was education:**

   # Gaines v. Canada (1938)
   # Sweatt v. Painter (1950)
   # McLaurin v. OK. St. Regents (1950)
   # Brown v. Board of Education of Topeka, KS (1954)

7. | ☐ **Education (cont.)**

   # What was the answer?
   # One answer was court-ordered busing.
     — Swann v. Charlotte-Mecklenberg Board of Education (1971)

8. ☐ **Summary:**

The Supreme Court's track record was poor.
To correct it the Court must abandon its humanistic approach to judicial interpretation and employ the biblical method of interpretation found in 2 Tim. 2:15:

2 Tim. 2:15—*"Study to show thyself approved unto God, a workman that needeth not to be ashamed, rightly dividing the word of truth."*

Selected Readings

The Missouri Compromise
Harriet Beecher Stowe's "Slavery is Despotism"
Kansas-Nebraska Act
Lincoln's "House Divided" Speech
Lincoln's "Gettysburg Address"
Lincoln's "Emancipation Proclamation"
Brown v. Board of Education Supreme Court Case
Martin Luther King's "I Have A Dream" Speech
Robert Kennedy on MLK Assassination

1. | ☐ **POLICY ISSUES: CIVIL RIGHTS AND AFFIRMATIVE ACTION—Lesson 32**

2. | ☐ **Affirmation Action:**

    \# Affirmative action is a government policy designed to promote minority interests above the interests of the majority.

    \# According to its staunchest supporters affirmative action is necessary to reverse decades of discrimination.

3. | ☐ **Historical evolution of Affirmative Action:**

    \# Initiated by executive order of President Johnson, 1964

    \# 1960s through the 1970s saw public policy shift considerably toward implementation of affirmative action programs

4. | ☐ **Proponents of Affirmative Action:**

    \# Argument is that affirmative action aids in the reversing of past discrimination.

    \# Further, proponents contend that there is no reverse discrimination affect.

5. | ☐ **Opponents of Affirmative Action:**

    \# Contend that affirmative action has little if any effect on past discrimination

    \# Argue that lesser qualified candidates are hired and admitted into higher education

    \# Further, that reverse discrimination is prevalent

6. | ☐ **What has been the Supreme Court's position on affirmative action? Cases upholding affirmative action:**

    \# United Steelworkers of America v. Weber (1979)

    — Job training programs for minorities could be established.

7. | ☐ **Cases (cont.)**

    \# Fullilove v. Klutznick (1980)

    — Upheld 10% set aside for public works contracts for minority owned businesses

8. | ☐ **By 1980s and into early 1990s, Court began shifting to the right:**

    \# Firefighters Local Union No. 1784 v. Scotts (1984)

    — Seniority interests of white workers not to be sacrificed to preserve jobs for less senior minority workers

9. ☐ **What about reverse discrimination?**

    \# <u>Regents of the University of California v. Bakke</u> (1978)
       — Ruled against racial quotas, but upheld affirmative action programs aimed at promoting diverse student bodies

10. ☐ **Current issues with affirmative action:**

    \# California and the repeal of affirmative action in public jobs, and the University of California system (1996)

11. ☐ **Summary:**

    1. The preceding cases point to the uncertainty behind legal decision-making with regard to discrimination.
    2. Affirmative action distorts the idea of work ethic and fairness.
    3. Court decisions concerning affirmative action attempt to address and correct previous unfairness and discrimination toward minorities.

1. ☐ **POLICY ISSUES: CIVIL RIGHTS AND ABORTION—Lesson 33**

2. ☐ **There is no doubt about the clarity of God's word toward the preservation of life, life at any stage of development:**

   \# Psalm 139:13-14: *"For thou has possessed my reins: thou has covered me in my mother's womb . . . I am fearfully (and) wonderfully made . . . "*

3. ☐ **Biblical view of life (cont.)**

   \# John 10:10: *"The thief cometh not, but for to steal, and to kill, and to destroy: I am come that they might have life, and that they might have (it) more abundantly."*

4. ☐ **The states' right to rule versus the woman's right to "choose." This was the issue before the Supreme Court in January 1973.**

5. ☐ **Roe v. Wade (1973): The Court ruled unconstitutional state laws which forbid abortions.**

   \# Contentious issue, but Court has not given in to either of the two opposing sides: opponents want a constitutional amendment allowing states right to outlaw abortions, and proponents want more federal funding.

6. ☐ **In <u>Planned Parenthood v. Casey</u> (1992) the Court refused to overturn Roe. What the court said: "It is a constitutional liberty . . . to terminate . . . pregnancy. No state may prohibit a woman from terminating her pregnancy before fetus becomes viable."**

7. ☐ **<u>Viability</u>—that time when the fetus may live outside of the womb; however, the Court argued, may change with medical science**

8. ☐ **Further, the Court contended in Casey that states may place restrictions on right to an abortion, but the restriction must not place an <u>undue burden</u> on the exercise of a woman's rights.**

9. ☐ **<u>Undue burden</u>: legal restriction that has "purpose or effect" of placing "substantial obstacle in the path of a woman seeking an abortion before the fetus attains viability."**

10. ☐ **Other positions the Court has used to clarify its position since Roe:**

   \# Constitutional: a flexible definition of 'viability' and the informed, voluntary and written consent of woman (<u>Planned Parenthood of Central Missouri v. Danforth</u>, 1976)
   \# Constitutional: for city owned hospitals to refuse to do elective abortions (<u>Poelker v. Doe</u>, 1977)
   \# Constitutional: state requirement of 48-hour waiting period between notification of minor's parents and the procedure (<u>Hodgson v. Minnesota</u>, 1990)
   \# Congress banned partial birth abortions in 2003.

11. ☐ **Summary:**

   1. Abortion has taken over 40 million lives since the Roe decision
      — Economic ramifications
      — Moral and spiritual consequences are even more grave.
   2. When will the debate end?
   3. Abortion is a fundamental element in the culture war.
   4. A nation that does not protect the right of life will ultimately not protect any liberty.

Suggested Readings

Roe v. Wade Supreme Court Case
Planned Parenthood v. Casey Supreme Court Case

1. | ☐ **POLICY ISSUES: A BIBLICAL VIEW OF THE POOR AND NEEDY—Lesson 34**

2. | ☐ **We will ask and answer five basic questions concerning the spiritual dimension of the poor and the needy:**

   \# First, who are the poor?
   \# Second, what is God's attitude toward the poor?
   \# Third, what is to be the government's attitude toward the poor?
   \# Fourth, what is to be the Christian church's attitude toward the poor?
   \# Fifth, where has the government and the church failed in their godly responsibilities to the poor?

3. | ☐ **First, who is the poor?**

   \# First, is to be depressed in mind; to be destitute in feelings
   — Ps. 40:17 reads: *"But I am poor and needy (yet) the Lord thinks upon me; thou art my help and my deliverer. . . . "*

4. | ☐ **Poor (cont.)**

   — In Matthew 5:3 (Sermon on the mount), Jesus refers to the 'poor' as if crouching as a beggar, or cringing in spirit.
   \# The second dimension is material.
   — It is to be destitute, or lacking (Prov. 17:5; 19:1, 17, 22).

5. | ☐ **The second question is : What is God's attitude toward the poor? The answer is found in two attributes of God:**

   \# His compassion—
   — Ps. 69:33: *"The Lord hears the poor . . ."*
   — Ps. 107:41: *"God sets the poor on high, away from affliction. . . ."*
   \# His protection of the poor
   — Isa. 25:4: *"For thou has been a strength to the poor, a strength to the needy in his distress. . . ."*
   — In fact Amos 2:6 reveals God's anger toward a nation which despises the poor.

6. | ☐ **Third, what is to be the Christian's attitude toward the poor?**

   \# First, we are to give to the poor: Matt. 11:5; 19:21; 26:9
   \# Second, we are to remember the poor
   — Remember means to "keep it before our eyes"
   — Even stronger is the idea of feeling the pain and suffering of the poor
   \# Third, we are not to despise the poor—Jas. 2:6
   — God has chosen the poor, but you have despised them. (Jas. 2:5-6)
   — The definition of pure religion (Jas. 1:27) strongly infers the Church's responsibility includes societal caring for the poor.

7.   ☐ **Fourth, what is the government's attitude to be toward the poor?**

   \#   First, to rule righteously over, not to oppress—Eze. 18:5, 12; Prov. 29:14
   \#   And second, to not exalt the rich over the poor—Prov. 22:2; v. 16

8.   ☐ **Fifth, what are the failings of government and the Church?**

   \#   The church has failed miserably in its responsibility to the poor. The welfare state we now labor under is nothing short of an indictment on the complacency of the Church.
   \#   The government has taken advantage of the poor through harsh taxes, unfair interest rates, and the welfare state.

9.   ☐ **Summary:**

   1.   God is a compassionate God, and He is saddened by treatment of the poor and needy by both the government and the church.
   2.   What type of social welfare policy is fair?

1. ☐ **POLICY ISSUES: SOCIAL WELFARE POLICY—Lesson 35**

2. ☐ **Biblical View of Welfare:**

      # First, we know that God cares for the poor and needy.
      # N.T. examples
        — True widows are to be taken care of by the church (I Tim 5:3-16)
        — Poor should work (II Thess. 3:6-15)
        — Children are precious to the Lord (Matthew 19:14)
        — Aged and infirmed were healed (Matthew 14:14)

3. ☐ **Is there a culture of poverty?**

      # Has the U.S. government created a culture of dependency?
      # Is the welfare state the death knell of the underclass?
      # Does the needy have a negative attitude toward work, family, and even success?

4. ☐ **Culture of Poverty (cont.)**

      # Conservatives argue yes: behavior change is necessary
      # Liberals no: environment change

5. ☐ **How does public policy affect income?**

      # Government can manipulate income through taxation policies
        — Progressive (current income tax)
        — Flat (proposal)
        — Regressive (such as sales tax)

6. ☐ **Affects on Income (cont.)**

      # Government can use spending policies for:
        — Writing checks to the poor
        — Supporting the use of "In-kind" payments such as food stamps and low interest loans for college education

7. ☐ **U.S. Comparison with Other Countries:**

      # How does U.S. compare with other countries?
        — U.S. ranks fairly low in all institutionalized countries with regard to welfare payments.
        — U.S. pays out less relative to total revenue as part of GDP compared to other countries.

8. ☐ **What is the answer to poverty?**

   # Jesus Christ is the answer.
   # Who is to care for the poor?
     — The poor themselves
     — The government only
     — The private sector only
     — Combinations of the above

9. ☐ **God's compassion, according to Marvin Olasky, is for Christians to "suffer with the poor" to help them to escape poverty.**

10. ☐ **According to Michael Bauman, Prof. of Theology of Hillsdale College, men and government must approach the concept of poverty differently:**

   # First, put welfare program in hands of contributors, not government or recipients— encouraged through tax credits.

11. ☐ **Concept of poverty (cont.)**

   # Second, redefine "poverty" to reflect a stricter, narrower definition.
   # Third, "re-educate the poor and politicians that true biblical compassion for the poor is defined in terms of responsibility, not dollars spent.

12. ☐ **Concept of poverty (cont.)**

   # And fourth, quoting Bauman: **"Poverty cannot be eliminated, only reduced and managed."**
     — Necessary to support market-place incentives, not worn out welfare dependent means

13. ☐ **Summary:**

Social welfare policies of the past 40 plus years have failed because they have not addressed the spiritual root of the problem, and that is lacking the knowledge of, faith in, and compassion of Jesus Christ.

1. ☐ **POLICY ISSUES: A BIBLICAL VIEW OF ECONOMICS—Lesson 36**

2. ☐ **Economics is best defined as a "science of production, distribution, and consumption of goods and services."**

3. ☐ **A biblical definition then would be: "The application of biblical principles to the production, distribution, and consumption of goods and services."**

4. ☐ **What is the underlying basis for a biblical economy and thus biblical economic policy?**

5. ☐ **The following ideas are taken from Mark A. Beliles and Stephen K. McDowells, America's Providential History (1989)**

   \# Christian liberty is the foundation upon which a biblical economy is formed (2 Cor. 3:17). Freedom is attained not through the State, but in God himself through the person of Jesus Christ, and the power of the Holy Spirit.

6. ☐ **Upon this foundation then is what a biblical economy is formed. Its principal components are:**

   \# First, the use of individual talents, gifts, calling, or enterprise are important not only to the body of Christ, but to the production of a sound biblical economy.
   \# Second, the morality of free enterprise as opposed to the bondage of a planned economy, including the caring for the truly poor and needy.
   \# Third, the evolution and impact of Christian character, including industriousness or Protestant work ethic, is essential.
   \# Fourth is the use of a solid money system, such as the gold standard.
   \# Fifth is the protection of private property.
   \# Sixth and quite obviously is a self-governing rule.
   \# Seventh is a fair and unencumbered tax system.

7. ☐ **Steven Forbes wrote: *"It (capitalism) encourages individuals to freely devote their energies and impulses to peaceful pursuits, to the satisfaction of others' wants and needs, and to constructive action for the welfare of all."***

8. ☐ **Warren Brokes in The Economy in Mind (1982) wrote that economics is a metaphysical rather than a mathematical science: *"in which intangible spiritual values and attitudes are at least as important as physical assets and morals more fundamental than the money supply.***

9.   □ **Ken Ewert, a Regent University graduate, countered several charges by critics of capitalism that it is not a moral system.**

     # Selfishness: capitalism is self-directed but not selfish because many people benefit from it.
     # Materialism is not limited to capitalism, but also found in planned economics.

10.   □ **Critics of Capitalism (cont.)**

     # Impersonalism and Individualism—Capitalism is very much relational oriented, not individualistic.

11.   **Summary:**

     1. The biblical basis for economy is based upon factors which are internally based, not externally.
     2. Capitalism is a moral system because it is based upon individual liberty.
     3. Taxes are to be used by civil governments, not abused.

1.   ☐ **POLICY ISSUES: AMERICAN ECONOMIC POLICY—Lesson 37**

2.   ☐ **Four basic theories of economic policy:**

3.   ☐ <u>First,</u> is laissez-faire economics, which calls for an absence of government control (theoretically) in order to produce profits and is most closely related to a Judeo-Christian economy.

4.   ☐ <u>Second,</u> is Keynesian economics which maintains government should control aggregate demand, engage in deficit spending, and is the economic system which is least like a Judeo-Christian economy.

5.   ☐ <u>Third,</u> is monetary theory which calls for controlling the nation's money supply through a central banking system, such as the Federal Reserve System.

6.   ☐ And <u>fourth,</u> is supply-side economics, which is to stimulate the level of supply rather than demand, accomplished through tax cuts and investment.

7.   ☐ Now, let us briefly examine budget policy and taxation policy:

8.   ☐ **Budget:**

   \# Financial plan
   \# Political tool used by both parties
   \# Congress controlled up to 1921; then Budgeting Act of 1921 required president to prepare budget.

9.   ☐ **Preparing the Budget:**

   \# Done by OMB in conjunction with CBO
   \# Procedure
      — Committee (tax, authorization, and appropriation)
      — CBO

10.   ☐ **Preparing the Budget (cont.)**

   \# First, the reforms of the 1970s: Install budget committees over the old committees (hasn't really worked)
   \# Second, external constraints such as Gramm-Rudman (1985)

11.   ☐ **Preparing the Budget (cont.)**

   \# Line Item Veto and Balanced Budget Amendment of 1996

12. ☐ **Tax policies:**

   \# Progressive Taxation v. Flat Tax
   \# Fairness and morality of tax burdens under question
   \# "Across the board" tax cuts labeled by Democrats as favoring the rich.

13. ☐ **Spending policies:**

   \# Budget size
   — FY 1997 = $1.7 trillion
   \# Significant areas, by outlays:
   — 22.1% Soc. Sec.
   — 17.9% Defense
   — 15.3% net interest
   — 14.5% income security
   — 10.5% Medicare

14. ☐ **Spending policies (cont.)**

   \# Net interest on debt—generally increasing
   \# Payments for individuals never fell below 40% from 1940 to 1995.
   \# And defense spending has remained high, except through the Clinton administrations.
   \# Budget surpluses in the Clinton administrations turned to deficits under President Bush.

15. ☐ **Summary:**

   1. Conflicting theories—which work best?
   2. Use of taxes—when and how much?
   3. All are political as well as economic tools.

1. ☐ **POLICY ISSUES: AMERICAN FOREIGN POLICY—Lesson 38**

2. ☐ **Isolationist approach:**

   # Articulated by G. Washington in his Farewell Address of Sept. 1796 (i.e. U.S. to stay out of European wars)
   # Monroe Doctrine (Pres. James Monroe, 1820)—warned Europe to stay out of Latin America

3. ☐ **Isolationist approach (cont.)**

   # W.W.I ended America's isolationist position
   # End of W.W.II, America began a new role: world leader, at least for the free world.

4. ☐ **Containment—to isolate the former Soviet Union and stop its advances into other countries:**

   # George Kennan in 1947 coined the term.
   # Truman Doctrine—help other nations oppose Communist
   # U.S. invasion of Northern Korea—1950

5. ☐ **Responses came:**

   # 1948-1949 Berlin Blockage
   # 1949—Fall of China to Mao Zedong's communist forces

6. ☐ **Vietnam (1959-1975)**

   # R. Nixon brought a new term to the foreign policy table: Detente
   # Detente: cooperation in foreign policy strategy between U.S.S.R. and U.S.
      — With guarantees of slow down in arms build-up (i.e., SALT talks)
      — And mutual cooperation in other areas

7. ☐ **Between 1955-1981 defense spending was down (with slight exception during Vietnam War):**

   # Reagan increased defense spending during peace time
   # Within five years $1.5 trillion increase brought about record deficits
   # "Star Wars" also implemented

8. ☐ **Containment "officially" ended when in 1989 the Soviet Union fell.**

9. ☐ **With the attack on the United States on September 11, 2001 the War Against Terrorism began**

10. ☐ **Summary:**

1. We have examined a brief history of American foreign policy and found the U.S. to be highly involved in international affairs.
2. Is this biblical? How involved is one nation to be in the affairs of another, or of several nations? What is the U. S. role in the Middle East?
3. We will examine that question among others next time.

Selected Readings

Alien and Sedition Acts
Virginia and Kentucky Resolutions
Taney Ex Parte Merryman
Espionage Act of 1917
Amended as Espionage Act of 1918
Smith Act of 1940
International Security Act of 1950 (Korea)
Roosevelt's Pearl Harbor Speech
Roosevelt's D-Day Prayer
Kennedy on the Cuban Missile Crisis
Johnson Not to Seek Re-election Speech
Bush to Congress September 11, 2001

1. ☐ **AMERICAN FOREIGN POLICY: PART II—Lesson 39**

2. ☐ **The Politics of defense spending changes**

   # 1960—52% + fed. government outlays
   # 1996—20% of fed. government outlays
   # Rose dramatically with the War Against Terrorism and military action in Iraq

3. ☐ **Ideological differences abound:**

   # Conservatives
   — Fight cuts in defense spending
   — Fight for high level of military readiness
   # Liberals
   — Too many "guns," not enough "butter"
   — Social programs over defense

4. ☐ **What does reducing defense spending mean to military preparedness?**

   # Personnel size: 1.5 mil—reg forces; 900,000—reserve forces; 2.4 mil total
   # Weapons
   — Substantial decrease in nuclear weapons

5. ☐ **Reduce defense spending (cont.)**

   # Changes in defense policy
   ☐ 1988—Elimination of Intermediate Nuclear Forces (INF) 12,500 weapons with ranges of 300-3400 miles
   ☐ 1991—Strategic Arms Reduction Treaty (START)—to eliminate ALL nuclear weapons.

6. ☐ **Changes (cont.)**

   ☐ 1993 START II to cut nuclear weapons (total in the world) to less than 6500 by 2003

7. ☐ **What is a Christian role in foreign policy?**

8. ☐ **Must avoid a "politicization of faith," a social gospel so to speak:**

   # Don't privatize faith
   # Be a political and economic witness for Jesus Christ

9.   □ **M. Amstutz's three basic principles governing foreign policy:**

    # God's sovereignty and love
      — Isa. 40:15, 22-23—God's Omnipotence
      — Jn. 3:16—God loves the world
    # The Universality of sin
      — All problems are rooted in the nature of sin. (Romans 3:23)
      — To overcome these problems, sin must be overcome. It has in the work and person of Jesus Christ.
    # Justice—God's style!
      — Begins with "Shalom"—*"Humans dwelling at peace in all his relationships"*
      — Examples
        □ King David—Ps. 85:10 *(". . . righteousness and peace kiss . . .")*
        □ Isaiah—Isa. 58:6-7 ("loose the bands of wickedness . . . undo the heavy burdens . . . .")
        □ N.T. peace

10.   □ **Summary:**

    1. We have examined U.S. foreign policy in light of God's principles.
    2. Where are we then?
    3. The U.S.'s future role in the world depends in large part on its commitment to its people and to the distribution of the Gospel message. (I Tim. 2:1-4)

Selected Readings

Supreme Court Cases
    1. Schenck v. U.S.
    2. Dennis v. U.S. (1952)
    3. Yates v. U.S. (1957)
    4. Brandenburg v. Ohio (1969)
The Patriot Act

1. ☐ **AMERICAN GOVERNMENT IN PERSPECTIVE—Lesson 40**

2. ☐ **God is the ultimate judge of history:**

   \# Eccl. 3:14, 17: *"I know that whatsoever God does, it shall be forever. . . I said in mine heart, God shall judge the righteous and the wicked: for (there is) a time there for every purpose and for every work."*

3. ☐ **God's kingdom is perfect and everlasting:**

   \# Ps. 145:13: *"Thy kingdom is an everlasting kingdom, and thy dominion (endures) throughout all generations."*

4. ☐ **He is the ruler of all nations:**

   \# Ps. 22:28: *"For the kingdom is the Lord's: and he is the governor among the nations."*

5. ☐ **We are sojourners—but for a short time:**

   \# I John 5:4: *". . . we who are born of God overcome the world."*

6. ☐ **But even though we are not of this world, we have a responsibility to fulfill our spiritual responsibility:**

   \# II Corinthians 5:20: *"Now then we are ambassadors (diplomats) for Christ, as though God did beseech you by us . . ."*

7. ☐ **This responsibility carries over to the civic realm as well:**

   \# We have learned in Romans 13:1-7 and I Peter 2:13-17 what our civic duties are.
   \# We know that from Acts 5:28-29 we are to always obey God.
   \# We are responsible according to Proverbs 29:2 for the men and women we elect to public office.

8. ☐ **Responsibilities (cont.)**

   \# And we have learned that according to Deuteronomy 17:18-20 our public leaders are to uphold God's laws and statutes.

9. ☐ **What then is God's promise to our nation, to the wicked, and to the Church?**

10. ☐ **For the nation it is found in II Chronicles 7:14:** *"If my people which are called by my name, shall humble themselves and pray, and seek my face, and turn from their wicked ways, then will I hear from heaven, and will forgive their sin, and will heal their land."*

11. ☐ **For the wicked it is found in Proverbs 10:28, 29, and 30:** *"... But the expectation of the wicked shall perish ... but destruction to ... the workers of iniquity ... (and) ... the wicked shall not inhabit the earth."*

12. ☐ **And for the people of God it is found in Deuteronomy 28:13:** *"And the Lord shall make thee the head, and not the tail; and thou shalt be above only, and thou shalt not be beneath; if that thou hearken unto the commandments of the Lord thy God, to observe and to do ..."*